C000061064

1 MONTH OF
FREE
READING

at
www.ForgottenBooks.com

By purchasing this book you are eligible for one month membership to ForgottenBooks.com, giving you unlimited access to our entire collection of over 1,000,000 titles via our web site and mobile apps.

To claim your free month visit:
www.forgottenbooks.com/free114431

ISBN 978-1-5282-7724-2
PIBN 10114431

REPORT

OF

CASES ARGUED AND DETERMINED

IN THE

SUPREME COURT OF ALABAMA

DURING THE

NOVEMBER TERM, 1910-11

· BY

LAWRENCE H. LEE

Supreme Court Reporter

VOL. 173.

0

Montgomery, Ala.
BROWN PRINTING COMPANY.
1912

OFFICERS OF THE COURT

DURING THE TIME OF THESE DECISIONS.

JUDGES OF CIRCUIT COURTS DURING THE TIME THE CASES REPORTED IN THIS VOLUME WERE TRIED.

1st Circuit_____Hon. John T. Lackland_____Grove Hill.
2d Circuit_____Hon. A. E. Gamble_____Greenville.
3d Circuit_____Hon. M. Sollie _____Ozark.
4th Circuit_____Hon. B. M. Miller_____Camden.
5th Circuit_____Hon. S. L. Brewer_____Tuskegee.
6th Circuit_____Hon. Bernard Harwood_____Tuscaloosa.
7th Circuit_____Hon. Hugh D. Merrill_____Anniston.
8th Circuit_____Hon. D. W. Speake_____Decatur.
9th Circuit_____Hon. W. W. Haralson_____Fort Payne.
10th Circuit_____{ Hon. E. C. Crow_____Birmingham.
                       { Hon. John C. Pugh_____Birmingham.
11th Circuit_____Hon. C. B. Almon_____Sheffield.
12th Circuit_____Hon. H. A. Pearce_____Dothan.
13th Circuit_____Hon. Samuel B. Browne_____Mobile.
14th Circuit_____Hon. J. J. Curtis_____Double Springs.
15th Circuit_____Hon. W. W. Pearson_____Montgomery.
16th Circuit_____Hon. J. E. Blockwood_____Gadsden.

CHANCELLORS DURING THE TIME THE CASES REPORTED IN THIS VOLUME WERE HEARD.

Northern Chancery Division_____Hon. William H. Simpson,
                                                    Decatur.
Northeastern Chancery Division____Hon. W. W. Whiteside, Anniston.
Northwestern Chancery Division____Hon. Alfred H. Benners, B'ham.
Southeastern Chancery Division____Hon. L. D. Gardner, Troy.
Southwestern Chancery Division____Hon. Thomas H. Smith, Mobile.

SUPERNUMERARY JUDGE.

Hon. A. H. Alston_____Clayton.

JUDGES OF INFERIOR COURTS OF LAW AND EQUITY DURING THE TIME THE CASES REPORTED IN THIS VOLUME WERE TRIED.

Anniston City Court	HON. THOMAS W. COLEMAN, JR.—Anniston.
Bessemer City Court	HON. J. C. B. GWIN—Bessemer.
Birmingham City Court	HON. CHAS. A. SENN—Birmingham. HON. CHAS. W. FERGUSON—Birmingham. HON. C. C. NESMITH—Birmingham. HON. H. A. SHARPE—Birmingham.
Criminal Court of Jefferson County	HON. WM. E. FORT—Birmingham. HON. S. L. WEAVER—Birmingham.
Clarke County Court	HON. THOS. W. DAVIS—Grove Hill.
Gadsden City Court	HON. JOHN H. DISQUE—Gadsden. HON. JAS. A. BILBRO—Gadsden.
Hale County Court	HON. C. E. WALLER—Greensboro.
Clay County Court	HON. E. J. GARRISON—Ashland
Mobile City Court	HON. O. J. SEMMES—Mobile.
Montgomery City Court	HON. GASTON GUNTER—Montgomery. HON. ARMSTEAD BROWN—Montgomery.
Mobile Law and Equity Court	HON. SAFFOLD BERNEY—Mobile.
Morgan County Law and Equity Court	HON. THOMAS W. WERT—Decatur.
Madison County Law and Equity Court	HON. J. H. BALLENTINE—Huntsville.
Lee County Law and Equity Court	HON. LUM DUKE—Opelika.
Walker County Law and Equity Court	HON. T. L. SOWELL—Jasper.
Selma City Court	HON. J. W. MABRY—Selma.
Talladega City Court	HON. CECIL BROWNE—Talladega.
Tuscaloosa Co'ty Court	HON. H. B. FOSTER—Tuscaloosa.
Andalusia City Court	HON. A. L. RANKIN—Andalusia.

TABLE OF CASES REPORTED IN THIS VOLUME

MEMORANDA

OF

CASES DECIDED DURING THE PERIOD EMBRACED IN THIS VOLUME, WHICH ARE ORDERED NOT TO BE REPORTED IN FULL.

ALABAMA CASES CITED IN THIS VOLUME.

CASES

IN THE

SUPREME COURT OF ALABAMA

NOVEMBER-TERM 1910-1911

Forney *v.* City of Birmingham.

Specific Performance.

(Decided May 11, 1911. 55 South. 618.)

1. *Specific Performance; Persons Liable.*—A grantee of land with knowledge of an existing contract giving a third person an option to purchase, occupies the same position as to such third person as the grantor, and may be compelled to specifically perform just as the grantor could, had he not parted with the legal title.

2. *Same; Remedy at Law.*—The fact that the holder of an option contract for the purchase of land has a remedy against his vendor for breach of the contract because he has conveyed the property to another who had knowledge of the existence of the option, does not take away from the holder of the option his equitable remedy to compel specific performance of the contract.

3. *Same; Option Contract; Validity; Enforcement.*—The fact that the holder of an option contract for the purchase of real estate was an alderman of the city, which subsequently purchased the property from the original vendor with knowledge of the option contract, does not destroy the right of the holder of the option contract to compel specific performance, the holder not having acquired his rights through any transaction with the city.

APPEAL from Jefferson Chancery Court.

Heard before Hon. A. H. BENNERS.

Bill by J. C. Forney against the City of Birmingham for specific performance of a contract. From a decree overruling demurrers to the bill, defendant appeals. Affirmed.

The facts made by the bill are that Forney held options to purchase from the owner thereof certain de-

scribed lands; that the option was running in the name
of one M. V. Henry, or his assigns, who was in truth
and in fact acting for orator in the transaction; that
the options were in full force and effect on the day the
respondent corporation, becoming aware that the tract
of land could be secured for the purpose of the city and
desiring such tract of land, entered into negotiations
with the owner for the purchase of it, but that before
said negotiations were closed respondent had full, complete, and accurate notice of the right of complainant
under his said options; and that respondents contended
that, as orator was a member of the board of aldermen
of respondent, he had no rights in the premises which
respondent was bound to respect, and so, in defiance of
the rights of complainant, concluded negotiations for
the purchase, and purchased and became the owner of
the property. The offer is then made to comply with
the options and to pay what is due to complete the purchase, with a prayer for specific performance, together
with certain interrogatories. The demurrer is that
there is no equity in the bill.

R. H. THACH, for appellant. The respondent had a
perfect right to purchase the land without infringing
upon the rights of appellee, and if appellee has any redress, it is against his vendor for breach of contract.—
4 Mayfield, 839; 44 Am. Dig. 1750. There was no averment of any consideration paid for the option, or for
its extension, and this is necessary.—21 A. & E. Encyc.
of Law, 926. Being an alderman of the city, complain
ant could not be interestetd in any sale of the land to
the city, or receive any pecuniary benefit therefrom.—
Sec. 1194, Code 1907.

A. LATADY, for appelllee. Appellants had full knowledge of the existence of the option, and therefore occu-

pied the same position as the original vendor, and hence were liable to specifically perform.—*Ross v. Parks*, 93 Ala. 153; *Meyer Bros. v. Mitchell*, 75 Ala. 475; *Dickinson v. Amy*, 25 Ala. 427; *Davis v. Roberts*, 89 Ala. 402. There is absolutely no merit in the other positions taken by appellant.

DOWDELL, C. J.—The bill is in the nature of a bill for the specific performance of a contract. A general demurrer for want of equity was filed to the bill, and from the decree of the chancellor, overruling the demurrer, this appeal is prosecuted.

If the appellant's grantor had not parted with the legal title to the land, no one would question the right of the appellee, on the facts averred in the bill, to compel such grantor, in a bill for that purpose in a court of equity, to convey title to the appellee. The respondent, the appellant here, having purchased the land with full knowledge of the existing contract of its grantor and of the appellee's rights as alleged in the bill, can occupy no higher ground than its grantor. In equity it simply takes the place of its grantor in respect to the appellee's rights.—*Ross v. Parks*, 93 Ala. 153, 8 South. 368, 11 L. R. A. 148, 30 Am. St. Rep. 47; *Meyer Bros. v. Mitchell*, 75 Ala. 475; *Dickinson & Winn v. Any*, 25 Ala. 424.

The fact that the appellee may have a remedy at law against the appellant's grantor for a breach of contract does not take away appellee's equitable remedy to compel specific performance of the contract by such grantor's vendee.

The fact that the complainant is a member of the board of aldermen of the city of Birmingham cannot destroy or affect his property right in the alleged option contract. He acquired the property right through no transaction with the city. The averments of the bill negative any such suggestion.

We are of the opinion that the facts stated in the bill, and which are confessed on demurrer, give it equity. The decree of the chancellor, overruling the demurrer, will be affirmed.

Affirmed.

SIMPSON, MCCLELLAN, and SOMERVILLE, JJ., concur.

Davis, *et al. v.* Grant.

Bill to Establish Disputed Boundary.

(Decided April 6. 1911.   Rehearing denied April 27. 1911.
55 South. 210.)

Adverse Possession; Agreed Line; Occupancy.—Where coterminous owners of land agreed on a dividing line, and followed up the agreement by the joint construction of a division fence, and afterwards occupied to the fence, their possession was adverse, and having continued for twenty years, conferred title to the line.

APPEAL from Jefferson Chancery Court.

Heard before Hon. A. H. BENNERS.

Bill by Winston B. Grant against James H. Davis and another to establish a disputed boundary line. Decree for complainant, and respondents appeal. Affirmed.

GEO. HUDDLESTON, for appellant.   The allegations of the bill fall far short of what would have been necessary to have authorized a reformation of White's deed if the latter conveyed land north of the line.—*Turner v. Kelly,* 70 Ala. 85; *Dexter v. Orlander,* 95 Ala. 467. There has been no adverse possession as against respondent.—*Brown v. Cockrell,* 33 Ala. 38; *Walker v. Wy-*

man, 157 Ala. 478; *Taylor v. Fombey,* 116 Ala. 621. The evidence offered by respondent was of the highest class. —*Billingsley v. Bates,* 30 Ala. 376. There was a fatal variance in the pleadings and the proof.—*Helmetag v. Frank,* 61 Ala. 67; *Gilmer v. Wallace,* 75 Ala. 220; *Westbrook v. Hayes,* 137 Ala. 572.

SAM WILL JOHN, for appellee. The bill is filed under section 3052 sub.-div. 5, Code 1907. If two co-terminus proprietors agree upon a dividing line and follow up that agreement by a joint construction of a division fence, and afterwards occupy to the fence, the possession is adverse, and if continued for the requisite time will confer a complete title.—*Brown v. Cockerell,* 33 Ala. 44; *Lucas v. Daniels,* 34 Ala. 193; *Rountree v. Brantley,* 34 Ala. 552; *Farley v. Smith,* 39 Ala. 44; *Marston v. Rowe,* 39 Ala. 725; *Marston v. Rowe,* 43 Ala. 284; *Shorter v. Smith,* 56 Ala. 210; *Humes v. Berustein,* 72 Ala. 556; *Dothard v. Denson,* 72 Ala. 544; *Alexander v. Wheeler,* 69 Ala. 340; *Davis v. Caldwell,* 107 Ala. 529.

SIMPSON, J.—The bill in this case was filed by the appellee to establish a disputed boundary line, under section 3052, subd. 5, Code of 1907. Both complainant and respondents derive title through mesne conveyances from one A. G. Morris, who owned the entire tract of land previous to the year 1883. On the 1st day of January, 1883, said Morris and his wife conveyed to William P. White a portion of the land held by him, describing it as "that part of the southwest quarter of section (18) eighteen, township (18) eighteen, range (2) two west, described by metes and bounds as follows, viz: Commencing at the southwest corner of said section eighteen; thence north twenty chains; thence north

(65° 16′) sixty-five degrees and sixteen minutes east ten chains; thence south (70°) seventy degrees east eleven and 70/100 chains (11.70); thence south (3° 30′) three degrees and thirty minutes east eleven and 8/100 chains (11.08); thence south (27°) twenty-seven degrees east eight and 94/100 chains (8.94); thence south (87°) eighty-seven degrees west twenty-four (24) chains, to the southwest corner of said section eighteen, containing forty-five and 4/100 acres; situated in Jefferson county, Ala." This is the basis of the title of respondents; and the complainant's title is under subsequent conveyances, commencing January 22, 1887, describing the southern boundary of the lands conveyed as "the lands of William White."

The point of controversy is as to the true location of the northern line of the lands conveyed to White, there being a conflict in various surveys, made at different times, as to the true location of the southwest corner of said section 18; the surveys offered in evidence by the respondents placing said corner about 165 feet north of the point fixed by the surveys introduced by the complainant. The evidence shows that, at the time said Morris sold to White, he (Morris) had the lines run under his own supervision and direction; that the northern line was run in the direction shown, in order to convey to White an orchard in the apex of the angle constituting said northern line, which White had stipulated for; that this line was marked by monuments, and a fence run along it; that White went into possession according to the line thus run; that said line was never disputed "until right recently;" that the line was still marked, or partly marked, by a fence when the respondent Grant bought in 1907; that some of the old rails, marking the "angle line," are there still. In short, the evidence shows that the two coterminous proprietors

[Woodward v. The State.]

fixed and marked the boundary line, and they and successors occupied up to it, claiming the same as the boundary line, for more than 20 years, before the respondents set up any claim to a different boundary line. "If two coterminous proprietors agree upon a dividing line, and follow up that agreement by the joint construction of a dividing fence, and afterwards occupy up to that fence, the possession is certainly adverse, and, if continued for the period prescribed in the statute of limitations, will confer a complete title."—*Brown v. Cockerell*, 33 Ala. 44; *Walker v. Wyman*, 157 Ala. 478, 483-485, 47 South. 1011, and cases cited; 5 Am. & Eng. Ency. Law (2d Ed.) 859, and cases cited; 5 Cyc. 942, and cases cited.

So it is unnecessary to enter into an analysis of the various surveys, and determine which correctly located the southwest corner of section 18. The decree of the chancellor is affirmed.

Affirmed.

MCCLELLAN, MAYFIELD, and SAYRE, JJ., concur.

Woodward *v.* The State.

Bill to Abate Liquor Nuisance.

(Decided June 1, 1911. 55 South. 506.)

1. *Intoxicating Liquors; Injunction: Bill; Verification.*—Where a bill was filed by the solicitor under Acts 1909, p. 70, and set forth the solicitor had probable cause for believing, and did believe on information, that the defendant, etc., and the bill was verified by a citizen, who recited upon oath that he, the affiant, was informed and had probable cause for believing, and did believe, that the statements in the bill were true, the verification was insufficient under section 20 of said Act, as it was an affirmation merely of the affiant's belief that the solicitor believed that the facts stated existed.

2. *Same.*—Construing section 20 of the Fuller Bill, and Rule 15 Chancery Practice, it is held that where a bill filed by the solicitor to abate a liquor nuisance was verified by a citizen, it must appear

that the officer was unwilling to make affidavit, and the citizens authority for making the affidavit should be disclosed by the affidavit.

3. *Same; Injunction; Facts to be Stated.*—Where the solicitor filed a bill for injunction to abate a liquor nuisance, and alleged that he was informed, and had probable cause for believing, and did believe, that the defendant had in his possession, or operated a room or place of business wherein he kept for sale and sold prohibited liquors, that he had within the past twelve months offered and sold quantities of such liquors, and allowed some of it to be drunk on the premises creating and maintaining a common liquor nuisance in violation of law, and that the accused was not a druggist, and did not keep a drugstore at his place of business, and that his place of business was not exclusively used as a dwelling house, the bill averred no facts, and was therefore insufficient, and could not be supported by the rule that a bill will be given every reasonable intendment.

4. *Injunction; Motion to Discharge; Motion to Dissolve.*—A motion to dissolve an injunction lies only where there is a want of equity in the bill, or where there has been a full and complete denial of its equities by the answer; a motion to discharge lies for irregularities in the bill, or for irregularities in the order granting the injunction.

5. *Same; Waiver of Defect.*—Section 4526 Code 1907, authorizes a motion to discharge and to dissolve to be made and to be heard at the same time without prejudice, and hence a motion to dissolve is not a waiver of a right to move to discharge.

6. *Same; Discharge; Defect of Verification.*—The defect in verification of a bill is an irregularity, and it should be attacked by a motion to discharge the injunction, but the motion should not be granted until opportunity is given to supply the defective affidavit.

7. *Equity; Pleading; Bill; Construction.*—A bill will be sustained if the facts alleged, whether well or poorly pleaded, show a case for equitable relief, as a bill will be given every reasonable intendment, except adding facts not set forth therein.

8. *Same; Bill; Dismissal.*—Although section 3121, Code 1907, puts the respondent to a general demurrer, instead of motion to dismiss for want of equity, that right, in cases of injunction, is preserved by § 4526, Code 1907.

APPEAL from Morgan Law and Equity Court.

Heard before Hon. THOS. W. WERT.

Bill by the State of Alabama, by its solicitor, against M. E. Woodward, to abate a liquor nuisance. From decree overruling demurrer to bill and motion to dismiss, respondent appeals. Reversed and rendered.

The bill alleges that the solicitor of the Morgan law and equity court is informed and has probable cause for believing and does believe that M. E. Woodward, whose name is otherwise unknown to complainant, has in his possession or under his control or operates a room or

place of business at No. 418 Bank street, in the city of
Decatur, Ala., wherein he kept for sale, offered for sale,
or keeps for sale and sells, the prohibited liquors mentioned in the Fuller bill, and that he has on divers days
within the past 12 months kept said liquors for sale, offered them for sale, and sold quantities thereof, and allowed some of it to be drunk on the premises, and has
thus created and maintained the common nuisance or
liquor nuisance in violation of law; that the above-
named person is not a druggist, and did not keep a drug
store at the above-mentioned place; and that the room
where he operated was not in a building used exclusively for a ‘dwelling house. The place is then described, and it is alleged that to effectually abate said
described nuisance it is necessary to grant complainant
a writ of injunction to restrain the same, and to grant
a writ of seizure, etc. The affidavit attached is as follows: "Before me, T. W. Wert, judge, personally appeared Richard N. McCulloch, who, being by me first
duly sworn, did upon oath say that he was informed,
and has probable cause to believe, and does believe that
the statements contained in the foregoing bill are true."

WERT & LYNNE, and KYLE & HUTSON, for appellant.
An appeal lies.—Section 2839, Code 1907. A motion
to discharge and a motion to dissolve may be made and
considered together without prejudice to either motion.
—Section 4526, Code 1907. A motion to discharge is
proper where the officer granting it had no authority to
do so on the facts stated in the bill, or where it was irregularly issued.—*E. & W. R. R. Co. v. E. T. V. & G. R.
R. Co.*, 75 Ala. 278; *Jones v. Ewing.* 56 Ala. 350. The
verification was irregular and insufficient, and the bill
fails to state sufficient facts to authorize the issuance of
an injunction.—Authorities supra; 22 Cyc. 755 and

925; 10 Encyc. P. & P. 927; 9 Page 305. The bill must be properly sworn to.—*Thorington v. Gould,* 59 Ala. 461; *Bolling v. Tate,* 65 Ala. 417; *Jones v. Cowles,* 26 Ala. 612; *Lucas v. Oliver,* 34 Ala. 628; *Cameron v. Abbott,* 30 Ala. 416.

R. C. BRICKELL, Attorney General, and SAM'L BLACK-WELL, Solicitor, for appellee. No brief reached the Reporter.

ANDERSON, J.—The bill in this case was filed and the injunction was sought to abate a nuisance as defined by the Fuller liquor bill.—Acts Sp. Sess. 1909, p. 63. Section 20 provides that the bill or petition must state the facts upon which the application is based, and shall be verified by the affidavit of the officer or citizen filing the suit, either upon knowledge or information and belief, as the circumstances may warrant, and in case the bill is filed by any one of the officers named, and he be unwilling to make the affidavit, the verification may be made by any citizen or citizens in the same manner. The bill in the present case was filed by Solicitor Blackwell, who sets forth "that he is informed, and has probable cause for believing, and does believe, that the succeeding facts exist," etc. Blackwell does not make the affidavit, but one is made by one McCulloch, which does no more than affirm that affiant "is informed, and has cause to believe, and does believe that the statements contained in the foregoing bill are true." The bill does not aver an unequivocal existence of the facts complained of, but that Blackwell is informed and believes that they do exist, and the affidavit by McCulloch is nothing more than an affirmance that McCulloch believes that Blackwell was informed and believes the existence of the facts as set out in the bill. This is an extraordinary remedy, authorizing the seizure and destruction of

[Woodward v. The State.]

property, and the issuance of an injunction must rest
upon a sufficient and valid affidavit, and cannot be sustained upon such an affidavit as the one in question, as
it in no sense affirms the existence of the facts complained of upon the knowledge or information of the affiant, and is at best a mere affirmation that affiant believes that Blackwell believes that said facts exist. Citation of authority is needless to demonstrate the insufficiency of this affidavit, and, indeed, the learned trial
judge concedes in his opinion that the affidavit would
be insufficient, but for the recent cases of *Fitzpatrick v.
State,* 169 Ala. 1, 53 South. 1021, and *State v. Abraham,*
165 Ala. 201, 51 South. 788. The affidavit in the *Fitzpatrick Case* is unlike the one in question, and avers
that affiant has probable cause for believing and does
believe the succeeding facts therein set out. The objection to the affidavit did not go to affiant's belief or
knowledge, but the insufficiency of the facts detailed to
charge an offense, and to the constitutionality of the
law; so this case in no way supports the sufficiency of
the affidavit in the present case. The *Abraham Case,
supra,* does not, as reported, disclose the affidavit, or
that any point was made as to the sufficiency of same.

It seems to be settled by the decisions of this court,
as well as the English cases, that if the injunction has
been irregularly granted, or if the order for it is erroneous, the remedy is not by a motion to dissolve. Such
a motion, founded, as it can be only, on a want of equity
in the bill, or the full and complete denial of its equity
by the answer, is a waiver of the irregularity, if any has
occurred, in the grant of the writ. The irregularity is a
ground for a motion to discharge, not for an application
to dissolve the injunction. The one is directed against
the mode of granting or issuing the writ, and the other
against the case made by the bill, or the sufficiency of

the answer to overcome it. The irregularities are amendable, and may be cured whenever attention is called to them, and may exist when the bill abounds in equity and the answer admits it.—*Jones v. Ewing,* 56 Ala. 360; *East & West R. R. v. East Tenn., Va. & Ga. R. R.,* 75 Ala. 275.

It appears, however, that since the rendition of these decisions the statute (section 4526 of the Code of 1907) authorizes motions to dissolve and discharge to be made and heard at the same time without prejudice. Consequently a motion to dissolve is not a waiver of the right

A defective verification of the bill is a mere irregularity and the court should not discharge the injunction until opportunity is given to supply a sufficient affidavit.—*Calhoun v. Cozens,* 3 Ala. 498; *Jacoby v. Goetter,* 74 Ala. 427; *Forney v. Calhoun Co.,* 84 Ala. 215, 4 South. 153. It is true, these last cases dealt with a motion to dissolve, and failed to consider the distinction between it and a motion to discharge, as brought out in the cases of *Jones v. Ewing, supra,* and *East & West R. R. v. E. T., V. & G. R. R., supra;* but they do hold, and properly so, that a defective verification of the bill is no cause for dissolving or discharging an injunction, unless the complainant, upon being ruled thereto, fails to verify his bill by a sufficient affidavit.—*Jacoby v. Goetter, supra.* We therefore hold that the judge of the law and equity court erred in not holding the verification of the bill insufficient, with a conditional decree that the injunction be discharged, unless a sufficient affidavit be made within the time fixed by the decree.

Section 20 of the act requires the bill to be sworn to by the complaining officer therein named, but further provides that the verification may be made by any citizen in case the officer is unwilling to make same. McCulloch, therefore, had no authority to make the affidavit, except in the event that Blackwell was unwilling to do so, and McCulloch's authority should be disclosed in the affidavit. Rule 15 of Chancery practice (page 1532, vol. 2, of the Code of 1907) ; *Kinney v. Reeves,* 142 Ala. 604, 39 South. 29; *Guyton v. Terrell,* 132 Ala. 67, 31 South. 83. But, as this case must be finally disposed of upon the motion to dissolve, there is no need for a remandment, in order that the affidavit may be amended or the injunction be discharged in case of failure to make said amendment.

While Section 3121 of the Code of 1907 abandons the motion to dismiss a bill for want of equity and puts the respondent to a general demurrer, yet the right to move to dissolve an injunction for want of equity in the bill is still preserved by section 4526, and which was made in the present case. The present bill avers no facts whatever, and falls far short of the requirements as to equity pleading (*Seals v. Robinson,* 75 Ala. 363), and is, therefore, wanting in equity. It is true that, in passing upon the equity of a bill, its equity will be sustained, if the facts, whether well or poorly pleaded, make out a case for equitable relief, and all defects as to manner or form of pleading will be considered as made; but this presumption does not extend to the addition of facts not set forth. The present bill avers no facts, and all intendments may be resolved in favor of the manner or form of pleading, and it would still be wanting in equity.

The law and equity court erred in not sustaining the motion to dissolve the injunction for want of equity in the bill, and the decree is reversed, and one is here rendered sustaining the motion and dissolving the injunction.

Reversed and rendered.

DOWDELL, C. J., and SAYRE and SOMERVILLE, JJ., concur.

Nelson, *et al. v.* Hammonds.

Specific Performance.

(Decided April 13, 1911. 55 South. 301.)

1. *Specific Performance; Bill; Sufficiency.*—Where the bill alleges a contract for the sale and purchase of land, payment of part of the purchase price by the complainant and his taking possession and that respondent is attempting to or has contracted to sell 80 acres of said land to another, and that such other has entered and cut timber to plaintiff's damage; that complainant has offered to pay defendant the balance due, which defendant had refused to accept, that the purchaser of the 80 acres had notice of complainant's equity, and praying for specific performance, and an accounting for timber cut, and general relief, as well as for injunction to restrain defendant from disposing of said 80 acres, it was not demurrable for want of equity, even if the agreement alleged was not reduced to writing, since the bill alleges a sufficient compliance with the statute of fraud by alleging part payment and the putting of complainant in possession, and any unnecessary allegation as to the subordinate relief sought could not have the effect to nullify the equity of the bill.

2. *Injunction; Dissolution.*—Section 4535 Code 1907, abrogated the former rule and now the court may consider the affidavit of the parties as well as the sworn bill and the answer on the motion to dissolve the injunction.

3. *Same; Affidavit.*—The reduction of plaintiff's testimony to writing after his oral examination before the chancellor on a motion to dissolve the injunction was not an affidavit within the meaning of section 4535 Code 1907, and should not be substituted for the affidavit required unless waived by the opposite party.

4. *Appeal and Error, Findings; Injunction.*—Conclusions for or against dissolving an injunction made on a motion for dissolution must, under the statutes, be treated on appeal as any other finding of fact at equity.

5. *Same; Record; Conclusiveness.*—An assertion in brief of counsel cannot be taken to supplement or contradict the record.

6. *Same; Findings; Conclusiveness.*—Where motion was made to dissolve an injunction and the complainant and his son were improperly permitted to testify orally and have their testimony reduced to writing, although irregular, this court will review the findings upon such testimony, the affidavits and sworn bill and answer, and the findings will not be annulled unless so insufficiently supported that a verdict thereon will be set aside, and this notwithstanding the chancellor's findings of the facts should have no weight upon a review thereof.

APPEAL from Limestone Chancery Court.

Heard before Hon. W. H. SIMPSON.

Bill by Daniel Hammonds against J. B. Nelson and another to specifically perform a contract for the sale of lands and for other relief. From a decree overruling demurrers to the bill and refusing to dissolve a temporary injunction, respondents appeal. Affirmed.

The bill alleges an agreement to purchase and a contract to sell certain lands described in the bill, the payment of a part of the purchase money, and the going into possession of the land. The bill further alleges that Nelson is attempting to sell, or has contracted to sell, to Frank Turner and Will Staten, 80 acres of said land, which is also described. It is then alleged from information and belief that the purchasers of the 80 acres have entered thereon and cut timber therefrom to the damage of orator in a large sum. The bill then offers to do equity, and further alleges that complainant has requested and offered to pay Nelson the balance due on said land, but that he declined and refused to permit him to do so. It is further alleged on information and belief that the purchasers had notice of the equity of the complainant at the time of their purchase. Attached to the bill are interrogatories propounded to each defendant, seeking to elicit testimony relative to the facts set up in the bill, and the prayer is for specific performance of the contract, and an accounting for timber cut, and for such other, further, and general relief as orator may be entitled to. Injunction is also sought against the respondents, restraining them from interfering with or disposing of the 80 acres pending the disposition of this cause. The other matters sufficiently appear from the opinion.

JAMES E. HORTON, JR., for appellant.—An answer that is a full, unequivocal and positive denial of every fact upon which the equity of the bill for an injunction

rests, entitles the defendant to a dissolution of the tem-
porary injunction issued.—*Harrison v. Maury*, 140 Ala.
523; *Webster v. DeBardelaben*, 147 Ala. 280; *Weeks v.
Bynum*, 158 Ala. 231; *Long v. Shepherd*, 159 Ala. 595;
Turner v. Stevens, 106 Ala. 546; *E. & W. R. R. Co. v. E.
T. V. & G. R. R. Co.*, 75 Ala. 275; *Barnard v. Davis*, 54
Ala. 555; *Hays v. Aldrichs*, 115 Ala. 239; *L. & N. Railroad Co. v. Philyau*, 94 Ala. 463; 2 High on Injunctions,
Sec. 1505. A man who stands by and encourages or
acquiesces in the sale of land which is his own, as the
property of another, will be restrained from disputing
the title of the purchaser, or even compelled to perfect
it by conveying the estate to such purchaser.—Herman
on Estoppel and Res Judicata, Sections 935, 943 and
961; *Fields v. Killion*, 129 Ala. 373; *Tobias v. Josiah
Morris & Co.*, 126 Ala. 535; *Bain v. Wells*, 107 Ala. 562;
Forman v. Weil Brothers, 98 Ala. 495; *Hendricks v.
Kelly*, 64 Ala. 388; 16 Cyc. pp. 749 and 761; *Chancellor
v. Law*, 148 Ala. 511. Upon the hearing of motions to
dissolve an injunction, the court may consider the sworn
bill and answer, whether the answer contains denials
of the allegations of the bill or independent defensive
matter, *and also such affidavits as any party may introduce.*—Section 4535 of the Code of 1907. Affidavits are
only proper to be considered at hearing or motion to
dissolve injunction in actions of waste or in the nature
of waste.—*Harrison v. Maury*, 140 Ala. 543. On appeal
from a final judgment or decree of the chancellor no
weight shall be given to the decision of the chancellor
upon the facts, the appellate court must hear the evidence and render such judgment as they think just.—
H. B. Claflin v. Muskogee Co., 127 Ala. 376; *Shaws v.
Folmar & Son*, 133 Ala. 599; Code of Alabama of 1907,
Sec. 5955, subdivision 1.

[Nelson, et al. v. Hammonds.]

W. R. WALKER, for appellee. Contracts for conveyance of land may be specifically enforced.—Pom. Spfc.
Perf. Contr. Secs. 9-10; *Derrick v. Monette,* 73 Ala. 75;
Kirby v. Fike, 27 Ala. 383; *Westbrook v. Hayes,* 37 Ala.
383; *Westbrook v. Hayes,* 37 Ala. 572; 1 Pom. Eq. Jur.
Sec. 221; 4 Pom. Eq. Jur. Sec. 1402. A party must not
be turned out of court when the proofs fix his right of
recovery, but lessens its measure from what is averred
in the pleadings.—*Bogan v. Daughdrill,* 57 Ala. 312,
316. The motion to dissolve an injunction cannot operate as a demurrer but is similar to the motion to dismiss a bill for want of equity.—*E. & W. R. v. E. T. V. &
G. R. Co.,* 75 Ala. 275; *Nathan v. Tompkins,* 82 Ala.
437; *Ex parte Campbell,* 130 Ala. 196. A complainant
may have partial relief when he proves only a part of
his claim unless the failure to prove it all makes a material variance.—*Shelby v. Tardy,* 84 Ala. 337; *Moses v.
McClain,* 83 Ala. 370; 4 Pom. Eq. Jur. Secs. 1405-7. On
a motion to dissolve an injunction the answer can only
be considered in so far as it is responsive to the bill, except in so far as changed by section 4535 of the Code.—
M. & M. Ry. Co. v. Ala. Mid. Ry. Co., 123 Ala. 145; *Hart
v. Clark,* 54 Ala. 490; *Jackson v. Jackson,* 34 Ala. 343;
Rogers v. Bradford, 29 Ala. 474; *Moore v. Barkley,* 25
Ala. 739; *Mable Mine Co. v. Pearson, C. & I. Co.,* 121
Ala. 567; *Rembert v. Brown,* 17 Ala. 667; Second High
Injunction (3rd Ed.) Secs. 1470-72, 1481-1513. The
rule that on appeal from the chancery court no weight
shall be given to the decision of the chancellor upon the
facts, is only applicable on appeal where the Supreme
Court has before it all the legal evidence and data which
was before the trial court and where witnesses are examined *ore tenus,* the decision of the chancellor stands
upon the same footing as the verdict of the jury and
will not be disturbed unless it is plainly erroneous.—

Nelson v. Larmer, 95 Ala. 300; *Woodrow v. Hawving,* 105 Ala. 40; *Rowland's Case,* 147 Ala. 149-151; *Miller's Case,* 150 Ala. 95; *Denman v. Payne,* 152 Ala. 342-344; *York's Case,* 154 Ala. 60; *Pollard v. A., F., L. & M. Co.,* 139 Ala. 183; *Jones v. White,* 112 Ala. 449, 450. On motion to dissolve injunctions the court has a discretion as to its dissolution and balances the conveniences in exercising that discretion.—*E. & W. R. Co. v. E., T. V. & G. R. Co.,* 75 Ala. 275; *C. & W. Ry. Co. v. Witherow,* 82 Ala. 190; *Davis v. Sowell & Co.,* 77 Ala. 262; *Chambers v. Ala. Iron Co.,* 67 Ala. 353; *Weems v. Weems,* 73 Ala. 462; *Turner v. Stephens,* 106 Ala. 546, 548. On motions to dissolve injunctions for want of equity in the bill all amendable defects shall be regarded *pro hac vice* as cured by amendment.—*E. & W. R. Co. v. E. T. V. & G. R. Co.; Ex parte Campbell,* 130 Ala. 196, 201. Upon a bill filed to prevent the threatened breach of contract same may be enjoined where the injury or damages cannot be adequately compensated by an action at law. —*Fullington v. Kyle Lumber Co.,* 139 Ala. 242; *Clay v. Powell,* 85 Ala. 538. "It is not an unbending rule that an injunction should be dissolved even when the equity of the bill is denied. The court may, notwithstanding such denial, retain it when it finds in the facts disclosed a good reason for doing so."—*Miller v. Bates,* 35 Ala. 580; *Rembert & Hale v. Brown,* 17 Ala. 667; *Planters, etc. v. Laucheimer,* 102 Ala. 454; *Scholze v. Steiner,* 100 Ala. 148; *Barnard v. Davis,* 54 Ala. 565; *Henry v. Watson,* 109 Ala. 235; *Jackson v. Jackson,* 91 Ala. 292; *Satterfield v. John,* 53 Ala. 127; *Bibb v. Shackelford,* 38 Ala. 611; *Harrison v. Yerby,* 87 Ala. 185; *Nichaus v. Cook,* 134 Ala. 228, 229.

McCLELLAN, J.—The demurrer, taking the objection that the bill is without equity, was properly overruled. The broad equitable foundation of the bill is specific performance of a contract to convey land. If it be assumed that the agreement for the averred sale and purchase was not reduced to writing, since it is not expressly alleged that it was reduced to writing, the exception provided in the fifth subdivision of the statute of frauds (Code 1907, § 4289; Code 1896, § 2152) is averred to have been complied with by the payment of the purchase money, and by putting the complainant (purchaser) into possession. If other subordinate phases of the relief sought by the bill are (we assume, without affirming) vain, that fact cannot neutralize the broader equity asserted in the bill.

The other question presented for review is that the chancellor erred in overruling the joint and several motion of respondents to dissolve the temporary injunction, issued in accordance with the prayer of the bill.—Code, § 2839; sections 4526, 4535.

Code, § 4535, provides: "Upon the hearing of motion to dissolve an injunction. the court may consider the sworn bill and answer, whether the answer contains denials of the allegations of the bill or independent defensive matter, and also such affidavits as any party may introduce." Previous to this statute on motion to dissolve injunction affidavits were receivable, in certain exceptional cases, in refutation of the denials of an unequivocal, full, specific, sworn answer.—*Barnard v. Davis*, 54 Ala. 565; *Harrison v. Maury*, 140 Ala. 523, 37 South. 361, among others. One of these exceptions was where waste was a probability if restraint of the adversary was not enforced. The cited statute entirely changes this rule by rendering serviceable upon the issue of dissolution vel non in all cases evidence consisting of the bill, the answer, whether it carries denials of the bill's averments of fact or not, and "affidavit" in-

troduced by any party. The feature of the earlier rule
in respect of the largely conclusive character of the sufficient denials of the sworn answer cannot consist with
the practice established by the statute quoted. It is
hence abrogated; and with the overthrow of the rule of
practice in that particular must, of course, go any influence otherwise to have been accorded decisions illus-
trating the now abrogated rule of practice. The full
consequence of the change, as wrought by the statute, is
not now attempted to be described.

It will suffice to say at this time that conclusions for
or against dissolution of injunctions will and must under the statute be treated here on review as any other
finding of fact at equity upon a defined issue. This interpretation of the quoted statute accords with that provided in the feature of the system where the hearing is
to determine the issuance vel non of an injunction.—
Code, §§ 4528, 4529.

In the cause at bar, the complainant and his son were
orally examined before the chancellor in opposition to
the dissolution sought; and their testimony was reduced
to writing and appears in the transcript. This was irregular, since the statute (Code, § 4535) stipulates that
affidavits may be submitted by the parties. Strictly
speaking, such examinations of the complainant and his
son, as this transcript describes, though reduced to
writing, as shown, did not constitute these statements
affidavits.—*Watts v. Womack*, 44 Ala. 605; *Wright v.
Smith*, 66 Ala. 545; *Savage x. Atkins*, 124 Ala. 378, 27
South. 514. However, it does not appear from the transcript that any objection was made to this manner
(oral examination) of availing of the evidence of complainant and of his son. Indeed, it affirmatively appears that these two persons were cross-examined.

In brief, the solicitor for appellants asserts that objection was made to this oral examination, but this as-

sertion cannot, of course, avail to supplement, if not re-
fute, the record. Without waiver by the party opposed,
oral examination should not be substituted for the affidavits contemplated by Code, § 4535.

In this state of the record we feel bound to review the
propriety of the chancellor's conclusion as that may be
affected by the consideration of the several affidavits,
offered by the movants for dissolution, and by the testimony, taken ore tenus, of complainant and of his son,
as well as by the bill and sworn answers.

To this status of the evidence before the chancellor,
solicitor for appellee invokes the application of the rule,
reannounced in *Denman v. Payne*, 152 Ala. 342, 44
South. 635, among others cited in brief, that the finding
will be treated as would be the finding of a jury upon
evidence delivered ore tenus and that the conclusion of
fact will not be disturbed unless the testimony so illy
supports it as that a verdict might under similar circumstances, be annulled. We see no escape from the
application of the rule indicated to the conclusion here
brought up for review. Nor does its application im-
pinge upon the rule of the statute, viz., that the chancellor's findings upon fact shall have no influence upon
the review thereof. The absence here of the same bases
of conclusion distinguishes the operation of each rule.

Whether the facts alleged in the bill, upon which its
equity must depend, were true was the subject of sharp
conflict between the affidavits and the sworn answers,
on the one hand, and, on the other, the testimony of
complainant and his son. A conclusion for or against
the dissolution sought was invited by one or the other
phase of the evidence. We are hence not assured by
any means that the chancellor's finding was erroneous.

Affirmed.

SIMPSON, ANDERSON, and MAYFIELD, JJ., concur.

Clisby *v.* Clisby.

Petition to Compel Payment of Alimony.

(Decided April 4, 1911. Rehearing April 27th, 1911.
55 South. 208.)

Husband and Wife; Maintenance; Action Reviewed.—Where
the petitioner, the wife, filed a petition for separate maintenance
and had a decree awarding her a certain amount monthly as alimony, and she thereafter filed a bill in the city court for divorce and
alimony, the order of the chancellor, denying without prejudice her
petition filed, pending the divorce suit, setting up that the husband
was five months in arrears in the payments of such allowance, and
seeking an order to compel the payment, will not be disturbed on
appeal; especially where from all that appears on the record, temporary alimony covering a part of such five months may have been
allowed in the divorce suit filed in the city court, it being inequitable for petitioner to receive alimony from both sources at the same
time.

APPEAL from Jefferson Chancery Court.

Heard before Hon. A. H. BENNERS.

Petition by Daisy I. Clisby against A. A. Clisby, her
husband, to require the payment of alimony already
decreed and alleged to be in arrears. From a decree
denying the petition, petitioner appeals. Affirmed.

See also 160 Ala. 575, 49 South. 446, 135 Am. St. Rep.
110.

B. B. BOONE and S. D. WEAKLY, for appellant. The
decretal order of reference in the divorce case in the
city court did not settle or adjudge any rights, and was
not a final decree.—*Vice v. Littlejohn,* 109 Ala. 294;
Thompson v. Maddox, 105 Ala. 326. The decree rendered here was a decree from which an appeal will lie.
—*Thornton v. H. H. & B. R. R. Co.,* 94 Ala. 353; *Webb
v. Webb,* 140 Ala. 262. The defendant was entitled to
the relief prayed in her petition.—*Murry v. Murry,* 84

Ala. 363. The appellants also filed motion for mandamus in connection with the appeal.

SAM WILL JOHN, for appellee. This cause should be
affirmed on the authority of *Clisby v. Clisby*, 160 Ala.
574; *Brady v. Brady*, 144 Ala. 419; *Jones v. Jones*, 131
Ala. 447; s. c. 95 Ala. 451.

MAYFIELD. J.—Appellant filed her petition in the
chancery court of Jefferson county to compel the payment, by appellee, of a continuing allowance for alimony, in accordance with a decree theretofore rendered
in that court on March 11, 1908. This decree awarded
petitioner $100 per month as alimony. The petition
alleged that appellee was five months in arrears in the
payment of such allowance, and sought an order of the
court to compel the payment by appropriate process
and orders. The chancellor denied the petition, and
appellant prosecutes an appeal to this court from that
order, and seeks, as an alternative, an order of mandamus from this court to the chancellor directing him to
proceed to compel the payments of such decree as theretofore rendered in that court.

The decree for alimony was rendered on a bill filed by
appellant, for alimony only, on February 2, 1907. On
February 26, 1908, the chancellor made an order allowing complainant $100 per month as alimony pendente
lite to begin from November 6, 1907; and on the hearing
on March 11, 1908, the chancellor made this allowance
a continuing order of $100 per month, but disallowed
any counsel fees to complainant. The original bill had
been amended by alleging that complainant had two
children, the result of the marriage, to support and care
for, and set up an agreement of separation by which appellee promised to pay her $100 per month for the sup-

port of herself and children. From that decree of continuing alimony of March 23, 1908, and which disallowed counsel fees to complainant, she appealed to this court; and the decree of the chancery court was affirmed in part (in so far as it allowed $100 per month as continuing alimony), and reversed in part, so as to require the payment of $400 as counsel fees, and to allow $100 to complainant from the time respondent had failed to pay $100 per month in accordance with the agreement. On the remandment of the cause to the chancery court, a decree in accordance with the decision of this court was by agreement entered on June 29, 1909. Since that date the respondent had paid to the complainant $1,500 as attorney's fees and allowance; and this petition is to enforce the payment of the balance due thereunder.

Appellee answered the petition of appellant, setting up the fact that since the rendition of the decrees and orders in the chancery court heretofore mentioned the petitioner had filed a separate and distinct bill against the petitioner for divorce in another court, to-wit, the city court of Birmingham; that she allowed that bill to be dismissed for want of prosecution, and then filed another, in the same court, against appellee, for both divorce and alimony; that he had answered this bill, and the testimony had been taken, and on July 28, 1909, a decree was there rendered granting complainant the relief prayed, and ordering a reference to ascertain the proper amount to be awarded complainant as alimony; that the reference had been taken, and the clerk and register of that court had reported back to the court his findings and recommended the amounts to be so allowed complainant. The respondent made copies of all these subsequent proceedings in the city court of Birmingham exhibits to his answer to the petition. These

exhibits show that the city court has granted an interlocutory decree for complainant, and awarded her permanent alimony in connection therewith, and that evidence for these purposes has been taken by both parties,
showing the property owned by each and the financial
and social condition of each. The financial condition
of the parties is now made to appear to be different
from that alleged by complainant in her various bills
and petitions against respondent for divorce and alimony.

It may be that this change of status or condition of
the parties induced the chancellor to deny appellant's
petition to compel the payment of the continuing alimony in accordance with the former orders and decrees of the chancery court in her suit for alimony
alone; or it may be that the chancellor decided that
complainant had abandoned or relinquished her claim
for alimony by filing her subsequent bill for divorce
and alimony in another court and proceeding to hearing as to both. The chancellor has prepared no opinion, and consequently we are not informed upon what
ground he denied complainant's petition. It was said
by this court on the former appeal as to the bill for alimony without a divorce: "The object and purpose of
such a bill as this is not to sever the ties of matrimony,
but to provide for the wife during the separation. The
parties still remain husband and wife, with the rights
and disabilities of husband and wife continuing, and,
as said by Stone, C. J., time may bring better counsels
and reunite the family, and courts must deal with the
proceeding with this possibility in view. Courts in this
proceeding cannot take property from one and give it
to the other. The only duty which the court can enforce is maintenance, and for this purpose can only
deal with the incomes of the parties, having no power

to compel either to labor for the other, nor should the
court divest either of the corpus of his estate."—160
Ala. 575, 49 South. 446, 135 Am. St. Rep. 110. "The
allowance in a case like this ought not to be a fixed or
permanent amount. It should always be left open, that
it may be increased or diminished as the circumstances
or necessities may change."—160 Ala. 576, 49 South.
447, 135 Am. St. Rep. 110. The status of the parties as
it existed when the above was said no longer exists.

The complainant having filed her bill for divorce and
permanent alimony in another court, and an interlocutory decree having been entered declaring her entitled
to all the relief prayed, and directing a reference to ascertain the proper amount for such allowance, and the
reference having been held and the findings reported to
the court, nothing remains to be done but to enter up
the final decree therefor. It would be inequitable to enforce the decrees of both courts for this alimony which
is certainly in part for the same purpose. The first, of
course, should not be continued after the second becomes operative. We are not prepared to say that the
chancellor was in error in denying the petition to compel the payment of the amounts as prayed therein. The
complainant certainly should not be allowed to prosecute and enforce two suits in different courts, even in
part for the same purpose. The complainant, of course,
did not necessarily relinquish her claim or right for all
alimony by filing her bill for divorce. She could have
filed her bill for divorce without claiming, but she
ought not to be allowed to continue to enforce the decree in the chancery court for continuing alimony
alone, and at the same time to obtain a divorce and a
decree for permanent alimony. The two decrees are
necessarily in part for the same object and purpose,

[Clisby v. Clisby.]

and would therefore be a double allowance and inequitable.

The decree of the chancellor appealed from denying the petition was without prejudice to the rights of the parties; and will in no way prevent complete justice from being done both parties in the further progress of this unfortunate litigation in the chancery or city court.

The decree or order of the chancellor was proper, and the writ of mandamus prayed will be denied.

Affirmed.

SIMPSON, McCLELLAN, and SAYRE, JJ., concur.

On Rehearing.

SIMPSON, J.—We place our concurrence in the result on the ground that, for all that appears upon the record, it may be that, in the case in the city court, temporary alimony has already been allowed, covering a part of the time for which alimony is claimed under the former allowance. It would be manifestly inequitable for the party to receive alimony from both sources at the same time, and therefore it is proper to leave the matter in the hands of the chancellor to allow or refuse the alimony prayed for, as the exigencies of the case may demand, after the city court has acted. We do not place our concurrence on the fact that the two cases are pending at the same time, or on any decree of divorce, which the record does not show has yet been granted.

Barker, *et al. v.* Mobile Electric Co.,

Bill to Declare an Easement in, and to Enjoin the Obstruction of an Alley.

(Decided April 18, 1911. Rehearing denied May 5, 1911.
55 South. 364.)

1. *Boundaries; Monuments; Courses and Distances.*—Where by giving monuments a controlling influence, absurd consequences would ensue, and where it is obvious that courses and distances furnish the most certain guide to the location and quantity of the land, courses and distances must be followed, and the rule that in the description of the boundaries of land conveyed, monuments, whether natural or artificial, dominate courses and distances, does not apply.

2. *Same; Evidence.*—Evidence examined and held to show that the alley was located on the lands of another who held exclusive possession thereof as his own, and that the adjacent owner had no rights therein.

3. *Same; Distances; Courses.*—A deed conveying a lot on the side of an alley, describing the lot by depth so as to take in a part of the alley, but further describing it as extending to a point on the alley, and thence along the boundary line of the alley, does not convey any part of the alley.

4. *Easement; Injunction; Right of Complainant.*—One seeking an injunction to protect a right of way over an alley must establish his right thereto, and cannot rely on the weakness of the title of the adversary party.

5. *Same; Establishment; Rights Acquired.*—Where a way established as of legal right divides the property of two owners, the presumption is that each has contributed the land for the way in equal parts, and a conveyance of an abutting ownership carries a fee to the center of the way; where the way has been laid out entirely on the land on one side of the property line, a subsequent grant by the owner must be deemed to convey the fee in the whole way.

6. *Same; Right of Way; Adverse User.*—Where one has no title to the soil in a way which he uses as common with the owner, his user is presumptively permissive, and so remains until knowledge of the claim as of right is brought home to the owner, and to establish an easement by adverse user, the user must have been adverse and continuous for a period of time which will pass title to the land by adverse possession.

7. *Same; Evidence.*—The fact that a tenant of one claiming an easement in a right of way by adverse user had complained that on one occasion, that poles had been piled on the right of way obstructing it, and that the agent of the owner removed the same, was not evidence of an assertion of right to use the way sufficient to ripen into title by adverse user.

[Barker, et al. v. Mobile Electric Co.]

8. *Evidence; Ancient Documents.*—A copy of the map of the city, prepared about fifty years ago by one employed by the city to lay out a map thereof, is an ancient document, and when coming from the proper custody is competent to show boundary lines of property owners.

9. *Estoppel; By Deed; Person Estopped.*—Recitals in a deed as to the boundaries of the land thereby conveyed are not binding on strangers to the deed.

10. *Same.*—Where the owner of the entire frontage on a street conveyed a certain amount of frontage to a grantee, and subsequently conveyed to a third person a further frontage, the first grantee and those claiming under him, were not estopped, by the subsequent deed, from relying on the boundaries described in the earlier deed, especially where the deed to the third person described the land conveyed as bounded by the land of the grantee.

11. *Deeds; Property Conveyed; Description.*—Where the evidence showed that the entire length of the square was 242 feet, that complainants held under deed describing their lot as 82 feet deep from the street on which it fronted, and bounded on the rear by the land claimed by defendant under deeds describing the depth of his lot as 157 feet from the opposite street, complainants did not show title to an alley way which lay 82 feet from the street on which his lot fronted.

12. *Adverse Possession; Effect; Evidence of Title.*—Actual possession of land for about fifty years under color of title extending proximately to the boundary line of the land of an adjacent owner, and exclusive user of an alley over the land for over thirty years is of itself evidence of title to the alley.

13. *Principal and Agent; Acts of Agent; Effect as to Principal.*—The mere fact that an agent of one claiming to be the sole owner of a right of way had joined in a petition to the board of public works of a city, requesting that one-half of the cost of paving the street in front of the way should be taxed against the owner, did not estop the owner from insisting on his exclusive ownership of the way, especially where the agent was unacquainted with the status of the title at the time, and the adjacent owner claiming an interest in the way, did not suffer any change of condition by reason of said petition.

14. *Landlord and Tenant; Estoppel of Tenant.*—The fact that one owning the soil of an alley and the exclusive right to use the same accepted a lease from the adjacent owner describing the alley as a joint alley used by the parties jointly, did not estop him from asserting his superior right and title.

APPEAL from Mobile Chancery Court.

Heard before Hon. THOS. H. SMITH.

Bill by Prelate D. Barker and another against the Mobile Electric Company to declare an easement in an alley, and to enjoin its obstructions. From a decree for respondents, complainants appeal. Affirmed.

[Barker. et al. v. Mobile Electric Co.]

GAILARD & MAHORNER, and GREGORY L. and H. T. SMITH, for appellant. In construing descriptions of boundaries, monuments, whether natural or artificial, dominate courses and distances.—*Crampton v. Prince*, 83 Ala. 250; *Pearson v. Heard*, 135 Ala. 348. The legal presumption is that the owner on an alley owns the soil to the center thereof and this presumption places the burden on complainant of proving that such is not the fact.—*Haberman v. Baker*, 37 N. Y. 251; 14 Cyc. 1181. The court erred in admitting the map made by the city engineer, as this was not even prima facie evidence.— 56 Ala. 327; 63 Ala. 284. The burden was on the respondent to show that the use of the way was by license, and not adverse.—*Wanger v. Hipple*, 13 Atl. 81; *McKenzie v. Elliott*, 24 N. E. 966; 12 A. & E. Encyc. of Law, 1200; 10 Ib. 299; *Jesse French Piano Co. v. Forbes*, 129 Ala. 477; *Sharpe v. Marcus*, 137 Ala. 149. The evidence shows that an agreement was entered into by complainant and respondent fixing the center of the alley as the dividing line between their property.—4 A. & E. Encyc. of Law, 860-865; 5 Cyc. 930, 936; *Magee v. Doe*, 22 Ala. 718. Such an agreement is not within the statute of frauds.—*Shaw v. State*, 125 Ala. 80; 26 N. J. L. 61; 35 Pa. St. 409; 4 Wheaton, 513, 14 South. 805; 24 Ill. 367; 17 S. W. 1047. This agreement estops the parties from later denying that such is the true boundary.—105 N. W. 367; 106 N. W. 862; 78 N. E. 649; 13 S. W. 30; 16 S. W. 877; 5 Cyc. 930, 936.

L. H. & E. W. FAITH, for appellee. The designation of the south boundary line of appellant's lot excludes any presumption that the fee to any part of the soil of the alley was covered by deed, or that the alley was claimed as an easement appurtenant to the lot so conveyed.—*Tus. Land Co. v. B'ham Realty Co.*, 161 Ala. 542. Monuments must give way to courses and distances in defining boundaries when to let the former control would lead to absurdities.—*Jackson v. Moore,* 6 Cow. 717; *Miller v. Cullom,* 4 Ala. 56. No way of necessity is shown.—*Trump v. McDonald,* 120 Ala. 200. No prescription is shown.—*Jesse French Piano Co. v. Forbes,* 129 Ala. 477; s. c. 135 Ala. 277. The joint use of the alley by the claimant with the owner is not an adverse user.—*Gaynor v. Bauer,* 144 Ala. 455; *Stewart v. White,* 128 Ala. 208; *Steele v. Sullivan,* 70 Ala. 589. Under these authorities the user will be referable to a license from the owner, and will be regarded as permissive, hence no right of easement by adverse user is made out.—*Jones v. Barker,* 50 South. 890. The fact that some of the deeds in appellant's chain of title say that the grantee shall have the right to use the alley in common did not prevent the soil of the alley from vesting in the purchaser originally, and his grantees.—*Gould v. Eastern Ry. Co.,* 7 N. E. 543. Appellants can take nothing because of the agent's offer to pay part of the paving taxes, or because of the lease taken by them.— *Blankinship v. Blackwell,* 124 Ala. 355; *Shroeder v. Packer,* 129 U. S. 689. Title and interest in land does not pass by estoppel.—*Hicks v. Swift Creek Mill Co.,* 133 Ala. 418; *Sullivan v. Conway,* 81 Ala. 152. The map was an ancient document, and admissible as such.

SAYRE, J.—Complainants seek an injunction for the protection of an alleged right of way over and through an alley at one time in use between their property and that of the defendant. By its cross-bill the defendant claims to own the soil of the alley in fee, unincumbered by any servitude, and would have the court make a quietus of complainants' claim of right. For many years the alley in question opened into Royal street, between St. Anthony and St. Louis streets, in

the city of Mobile. The square from which it issued
had a front on the west side of Royal street of 242 feet,
some inches more or less. The north line of this alley
is 82 feet and 10 inches south from the south line of St.
Anthony street, and its south line is approximately 140
feet north from the north line of St. Louis street. The
alley is, or was during its use as such, 19 feet wide.
Probably from a time prior to 1848—certainly from
1859, at the latest—and until 1892, this alley was precisely defined at its Royal street end by substantial
buildings on either side which stood flush with the line
of Royal street. The property to the rear on either
hand was acquired from different sources, and the evidence as to that part of the alley differs somewhat from
that which relates to the rights of the parties in respect
to the part next to Royal street. We think on the
whole that it lends weight to the defendant's case; but
the mass of evidence is so great that we have avoided a
detailed statement of the titles of the parties to the
property attingent upon the alley towards the rear.
The easement claimed is of value and consequence only
as it may afford an approach to Royal street. From
1840 to about 1869 one McDermott owned and occupied the premises to the north now owned by complainants. English—there were two Englishes, father and
son, who owned the property in succession, but for convenience we refer to them as English—under whom defendant claims, owned the property to the south on
Royal street from 1835 to 1859, and that to the rear until 1868. The alley was defined by the erection of buildings on either side during the ownership of these parties. In 1892 the buildings on the property now
claimed by complainants were condemned and destroyed by the municipal authorities. The English
property having been acquired in the meantime by the

Electric Light Company of Mobile, defendant's immediate predecessor in title, that company took also, in
1895, a lease of complainants' property from its then
owner, so that, from that time until shortly before this
bill was filed, the property on both sides of the alley
was in one possession. Complainants state their case
substantially as follows: That the soil of the alley at
the time it was opened was owned by McDermott or
jointly by McDermott and English; that McDermott
and English each claimed the ownership of the alley or
a part thereof, and opened it in mutual recognition of
their respective rights to its use; or that, wholly apart
from their alleged ownership of the soil, they have acquired an easement of passage by prescription. The
case here stated concedes throughout defendant's right
to the use of the alley. The evidence for complainants
has been directed to the proof of two propositions: (1)
That they own a part, if not the whole, of the soil of the
alley; and (2) that for more than 20 years they were
in the open, notorious, continuous, and adverse user of
the easement claimed.

1.   The early records bearing upon the title in question are imperfect, and the measurements recited in the
conveyances shown are manifestly inaccurate. We consider the case on the evidence at hand. Complainants
are in undisputed possession of a lot measuring 82 feet
on Royal street south from St. Anthony. Except for
their use of the alley in common with those under whom
the defendant claims, to which we will refer later, neither the complainants nor their predecessors in title are shown to have ever had a possession extending
south of the line 82 feet south from St. Anthony street.
From 1816 to 1835 the various deeds which appear in
their chain of title described their lot as fronting 72
feet on Royal street and bounded on the south by lands

of Thomas P. Norris and Louis Baudin. In a deed
from George J. S. Walker to John Byrnes, dated February 9, 1835, the lot is described as fronting 82 feet
on Royal street and bounded on the south by the property of English. A number of later conveyances, including that to McDermott in the year 1840, follow the
description of the deed from Walker to Byrnes. In
1884 a deed described the lot as bounded on the south
by an alley. In 1886 the City Railroad Company conveyed the lot at the corner of St. Anthony and Royal
streets, fronting 85 feet on Royal, to Hannah Lazo. Its
southern boundary is not described otherwise. Hannah
Lazo, under the name of Canizas, conveyed to Tolbert
by the same description in 1890. And so Tolbert to
Jordan in the same year; Jordan to A. M. Blair in
1898; and A. M. Blair to F. G. Blair in 1903. The first
effort to convey in terms a mere easement in the alley
appears in a deed from F. G. Blair to A. M. Blair, dated
March 26, 1904, in which the lot is described as fronting
84 feet on Royal street and bounded on the south by an
alley. "This conveyance includes all grantor's interest
in said alley." In 1904, April 4th, Blair and wife conveyed to complainants 85 feet, more or less, on Royal
street, and "their right to use said alley, and whatever
interest they may have therein." Having shown this
much, complainants, in order to give to those descriptions in their early muniments of title which bound
their lot on the south by the lands of Thomas P. Norris and Louis Baudin, and those which bound it by the
property of English, a meaning which would extend
their ownership beyond the point 82 feet south of St.
Anthony street, undertake to show, in part at least, the
right and title of defendant. They show by the recitals
of deeds offered in evidence that in 1814 a Madame
Baudin died seised and possessed of a lot on the corner

of St. Louis and Royal streets described as fronting 127 feet on Royal. The title to this lot passed in separate parcels and through several persons, heirs of Madame Baudin, into one Judson in 1815. In 1827 Judson sold first the 50 feet on the corner of St. Louis to Thomas P. Norris, and, a few days later, to Thomas P. Norris and Jonathan Hunt 77 feet on Royal, described as bounded on the south by the lands of Thomas P. Norris and on the north by the lands of the grantor. This Judson appeared also among the predecessors in title of the complainants. In 1816, one Kennedy, who subsequently got a patent from the United States, had conveyed to Judson the lot on the corner of St. Anthony and Royal streets, fronting 72 feet on Royal, and bounded on the south by a lot then owned by the grantee. In 1828 Judson conveyed the lot to Victor Gannard, describing it as fronting 72 feet on Royal street and bounded on the south by lands belonging to Thomas P. Norris. In 1831 English acquired the 50 feet next to St. Louis street from Norris, and in 1835 he got a deed from Hunt and Norris of a lot fronting 77 feet on Royal street and described in part as bounded "on the north by lands belonging now or late to Lewis Judson, on the south by lands belonging to Thomas M. English." From these conveyances complainants hold that we must infer, not only that Judson owned in his day the entire front on Royal street between St. Anthony and St. Louis, but that the deeds by which he disposed of designated frontages aggregating 199 feet on Royal street, 127 to Norris and Hunt, 72 to Gannard, must by reason of the further descriptions referring to the ownership of adjacent property, be held to have disposed of the entire frontage of 240 feet; and not only so, but that the effect of these conveyances was to fix the line between the two properties at a point 127 feet from St.

Louis street, thus allowing complainants' title to far overlay the soil of the alley in question.

This, on the principle that, in the description of the boundaries of land conveyed, monuments, whether natural objects or artificial marks, are allowed to dominate courses and distances.—*Crampton v. Prince,* 83 Ala. 250, 3 South. 519, 3 Am. St. Rep. 718. But, as was said in *Miller v. Cullum,* 4 Ala. 576: "This rule is not without its exceptions. These are to be ascertained by a reference to the reason or principle of the rule itself. —Ratione cessante, ipsa lex cessat. Thus, where, by giving to monuments a controlling influence, absurd consequences would ensue, or where it is obvious that courses and distances furnish the most certain guides to the locations and quantity of the land, the latter should be followed." "What is most material and most certain in a description shall prevail over that which is less material and less certain."—*Jackson v. Moore,* 6 Cow. (N. Y.) 711. It has been shown that, if the deeds under which McDermott and English claimed be taken as conveying only such property as they describe by frontage in foot-measure, they fail to account for about 40 feet of the square, and that in this twilight zone lies the alley in question. Defendant has undertaken to account for this part of the square by introducing a quitclaim from one Vecque of a lot on the west side of Royal street, between St. Louis and St. Anthony, "fronting on Royal street one hundred feet or thereabouts, be the same more or less," and bounded on the north by property formerly belonging to George J. S. Walker, and on the south by the property of English then occupied by him as a dwelling. This quitclaim was executed in 1836, and contained a recital that English was then in possession. It has been noted also that the Walker lot, when he came to make title, was described as having a

front of 82 feet instead of 72 feet as theretofore. If
the lot on the corner of St. Louis had then taken the
form which it kept for many years in later times—that
is, was inclosed and occupied as a residence lot showing
a well-defined front of 53 feet on Royal street—this
quitclaim would suffice to extend the possession of English far enough to account with close approximation
for the entire square, with the result that in subsequent
conveyances, under which complainants hold and claim
title, the call for a boundary on the south by the property of English might be held to coincide with the call
for a front of 82 feet, thus leaving complainants with
no evidence of title beyond that line.

But there is no evidence of actual possession of any
part of the defendant's property at that time, nor can
the recitals of the quitclaim bind the complainants or
their predecessors who were strangers to it.

Now complainants' contention is that Judson's deed
to Norris and Hunt, being first in point of time, fixed
defendant's line at 127 feet from St. Louis street on the
theory of *Crampton v. Prince, supra.* But the deed to
Gannard was executed after the deed to Norris and
Hunt, so that neither the latter, nor their successors in
interest, are to be estopped by it. It derogated nothing
from any right, title, interest, or possession they may
have had at the time or acquired subsequently. Moreover, Judson's deed to Gannard did not describe the 72-
foot lot as bounded on the south by property which the
grantor had before that conveyed to Norris; but the lot
is described as bounded on the south by lands then belonging to Norris. It is apparent therefore that the
meaning of this description, and the true location of
the line to which the grantor referred, depended upon
matters of fact. Non constat, the land proximately
south of complainants' 72-foot line did at that date be-

long to Norris. One call of Gannard's deed was for a
line 72 feet south of St. Anthony street. If complainants would show that the dominant call for a boundary
by property of another ownership established a different
line—a fact not to be presumed because it involves the
deed in conflict and ambiguity—the burden was on
them to show that fact. And they are in the same pre-
dicament in regard to a number of later conveyances
under which they claim and in which their lot is described as fronting 82 feet on Royal street and bounded
on the south by the property of English.

As for the lots in the rear, complainants' fronting on
St. Anthony street and defendant's on St. Louis, and
which are separated by this same alley, complainants
hold under deeds as early as 1840 describing their lot
as running south from St. Anthony street 82 feet, and
bounded on the south by the land of English. Defendant, on the other side, claims under deeds dated as early
as 1834 describing its property as running north 175
feet from St. Louis street. So, then, if the case were to
be determined on the muniments of title antedating the
time when the evidence shows anything in respect to
actual possession, it would seem proper to hold that
complainants have failed to sustain the burden of proof
which they assumed when they alleged their ownership
of the soil of the alley.

Consideration of the title deeds of later date and of
the evidence touching the origin and use of the alley
lead to a like conclusion. As we have already said, complainants have not shown at any time any possession
south of their lot as now defined, except such possession
as went with the use of the alley as a passageway.

On the other hand, defendant has shown, in those under whom it claims, actual possession since 1850, or
thereabouts, under a color of title extending approxi-

mately to the south line of complainants' said lot, and
an exclusive user of the alley from that time down to
1866. This possession was of itself evidence of title.—
L. & N. R. R. Co. v. Philyaw, 88 Ala. 264, 6 South. 837.

Official records show that about 1848 one Troost was
employed by the city of Mobile to lay out a map of the
city. A copy of so much of this map as shows the block
containing the property in controversy was introduced
in evidence. This map was hearsay, but it was an ancient document and came from a proper custody. It
was competent to show boundary lines of private ownership.—1 Greenl. Ev. (16th Ed.) § 140a; *Taylor v.
Fomby*, 116 Ala. 621, 22 South. 910, 67. Am. St. Rep.
149; *Boardman v. Reed,* 6 Pet. 328, 8 L. Ed. 415; Jones
on Ev. § 308.

This map shows the McDermott lot as fronting 82
feet and 10 inches on Royal street next to St. Anthony
and as improved by a brick building of 1½ stories. It
shows the English property as fronting 159 feet and 1
inch on Royal street and as improved by two frame
dwellings. It shows the rear part of the last-named
property as divided into four lots of 28 feet, 6 inches,
each, fronting on St. Louis street and improved by
brick dwellings. It shows no alley opening on Royal
street, though the property lines indicate that an alley
had been laid off on the rear of the English lots which
fronted on St. Louis street. From other sources we
learn that, from 1852, at the latest the McDermott lot
was used as a slave mart and was improved in a way
which that use would probably suggest. A number of
buildings were distributed about over the rear of the
lot. The entire property to the rear of the building on
Royal street was inclosed by a 15-foot brick wall. Complainants brought testimony which tended to show that

there were openings in the south wall as early as 1862, but as to that the testimony was in conflict, and we are satisfied that there were no such openings prior to 1866, about which time the property was converted into a tenement for free negroes. In the meantime—about 1850, probably even earlier—the passageway had been opened along the entire north margin of the English lots and was in use by those who occupied that property. When the McDermott property began to be used as a tenement, openings were made through the south wall for the convenience of its tenants, who thereafter used the alley without interference until 1892, when the buildings were destroyed. For these reasons we conclude, as did the chancellor, that the alley was laid off by English upon land claimed and held in possession as his own.

The first claim, on the part of those to whom the complainants have succeeded, that the lots north of the alley had a greater frontage than 72 feet in the direction of Royal street, is to be found in the deed of the master in chancery to McDermott in 1884. This deed is of the rear lot, and calls for a depth of 85.2 feet; but another and dominant description is that it extends to a point on an alley "and thence eastwardly along the north boundary line of said alley." That and several subsequent deeds giving 85 feet as the south and north dimension of the lot, to the extent they overlaid property belonging to defendant and in its possession, were mere pieces of waste paper.

In 1859 the administrator of the elder English sold, under the orders of the probate court, to John D. Ragland property described as follows: "That lot or parcel of land situate on the west side of Royal street between St. Louis and St. Anthony street in the city of Mobile, commencing at a point at the northwest corner of the brick inclosure of the former family residence of said decedent (shown by other conveyances and by oral evidence to be a point 53 feet from the corner of Royal and St. Louis streets) and running thence northwardly along the line of Royal street ninety-four feet and one-half to a point in an alleyway, extending thence westwardly in a line parallel with said brick inclosure seventy-six feet, and having the same width in rear as in front, bounded on the south by said inclosure, on the east by Royal street, on the west by other property of said decedent, and on the north by an alleyway." This lot has come down to defendant with this same description. In 1868 the English heirs disposed of the narrow lots to the rear of the Royal street property by deeds which described those lots as extending to the south line of the alley, and conveyed also "the use in common of an alley-way of 19 feet 3 inches in width, which leads from Royal street to the rear of the premises." Defendant holds those lots also under successive deeds containing like descriptions.

Complainants contend that the descriptions of the deed to Ragland must be taken as a recognition of their ownership to the center of the alley, seeming to attach importance to the expression "in an alley." It would seem to be enough to say that the complainants are not parties to the English deeds and take nothing by them. They are in a position which demands that they make good their claim on its own merits, rather than on the weakness of the adverse claim. The argument is otherwise faulty, in that it begs the question. It assumes the right claimed in order to give the desired operation to the deeds. It is not claimed that in 1859 McDermott had acquired an easement by adverse user. As we think we have shown, he had no title to the soil. The only interest in the alley, or its maintenance as such, was

posesssed by the grantor estate and its grantees. Although "it is not admissible to prove that the parties
intended something different from that which the written language expresses, or which may be the legal inference and conclusion to be drawn from it, yet it is always competent to give in evidence existing circumstances, such as the actual condition and situation of
the land, buildings, passages, * * * in order to
give a definite meaning to the language used in the
deed, and to show the sense in which particular words
were probably used by the parties, especially in matters
of description."—*Salisbury v. Andrews,* 19 Pick.
(Mass.) 250; *Jacobs v. Roach,* 161 Ala. 201, 49 South.
576. On these considerations we feel sure that the descriptions in the deed must be construed as the creation
or reservation—the mere phraseology is immaterial—
of a right of way appurtenant to the St. Louis street
property retained by the estate of English as well as
that conveyed to Ragland.

Where a way, established as of legal right, divides
the properties of two owners, the presumption is that
each has contributed the land for the way in equal
parts, and a conveyance of an abutting ownership carries a fee to the center of the way. But where, as in the
present case, the way has been laid out entirely upon
the land on one side of the property line, a subsequent
grant by the owner must be deemed to comprehend the
fee in the whole way, upon the same principle that carries the fee to the center in other cases. It results that
the several conveyances, by which defendant acquired
title to all the lots for the benefit of which the easement
was reserved or created in the beginning, vested also in
it the land covered by the easement.—*Haberman v.
Baker,* 128 N. Y. 253, 28 N. E. 370, 13 L. R. A. 611;
Gould v. Eastern Railroad, 142 Mass. 85, 7 N. E. 543;

Matter of Robbins, 34 Minn. 99, 24 N. W. 356, 57 Am. Rep. 40.

2. Much of what has been already said bears upon the question raised by complainants' claim of an easement by adverse user. There was no user of any character by the predecessors of complainants prior to 1866, nor subsequent to 1892. From 1892 to 1895 the premises were vacant. From 1895 to until shortly before bill filed the premises on both sides were in the possession of defendant. "The time for acquiring an easement by prescription does not run while the dominant and servient estates are in the occupation of the same person." —Jones on Easements, § 166. So, then, complainants' right must have been acquired, if at all, in the period from 1866 to 1892. The title to the soil was with defendant. The user was common. Complainants' user was therefore presumptively permissive; and so remained until it was brought home to defendant or its predecessors that it was claimed as a right and without regard to their wishes. It must then have been continuous—that is, without such interruptions as would indicate an abandonment—for at least a period which would pass title to land by adverse possession.—*Jesse French Co. v. Forbes,* 129 Ala. 471, 29 South. 683, 87 Am. St. Rep. 71; *Trump v. McDonnell,* 120 Ala. 200, 24 South. 353. But in the view we take of the testimony there is but one circumstance which indicates an assertion of right. On one occasion a tenant on complainants' lot complained that some poles, which had been piled in the alley, were obstructing the way. Thereupon the agent for the then owner went to Rubira, president of the Electric Company then the owner of defendant's lot, "in person and told him that he must move them, and he did so." This could not have been before 1885; it may have been as late as 1890. Rubira

had nothing to do with the alley or the lots abutting on
it until his company got its deed from Ragland's heirs
in 1885. The facts here shown are insufficient to establish a right of way by adverse user.

Our conclusion is that the chancellor's decree ought
to be affirmed.

Affirmed.

SIMPSON, ANDERSON, and SOMERVILLE, JJ., concur.

On Rehearing.

SAYRE, J.—On the original submission, appellants
called attention to the fact that Theo. K. Jackson, defendant's agent, had in 1906 joined in a petition to the
board of public works requesting that one-half of the
cost of paving Royal street in front of the alley be
taxed against the defendant, and that in a lease taken
by defendant from complainants in 1907 the complainants' property was described as "the property owned by
them at the southwest corner of Royal and St. Anthony
street, and about 83 feet on Royal street, to a joint alley used by the parties of the first and second part
jointly." These facts were referred to in appellants'
brief as going to support their contention that appellee
and its predecessors had knowledge of appellants' alleged adverse user of the alley under claim of right and
had acquiesced in that use and claim. There was no
suggestion that the facts referred to constituted a sufficient ground for decreeing a title by estoppel in the
complainants. It then seemed, and now seems, that in
view of the previous relations of the parties to this alleyway, which relations were stated in the opinion, the
date of these transactions, their detachment from appellants' previous assertion of right by appellee's intervening possession, was enough to show that they were in-

sufficient either alone or in combination with the other facts to show a continuous hostile user covering the statutory period of limitation. We think they are insufficient to pass title by estoppel. So far as the act of Jackson in joining in the petition is concerned, it was deprived of all significance adverse to appellee by the undisputed explanation of it, which was that Jackson was unacquainted with the status of the title at the time, he having then just recently gone into the appellee's employment, and its title deeds being in Chicago for investigation preparatory to a loan the appellee was then negotiating; that he signed the petition on Barker's request accompanied by a statement that the alley was a joint alley; and that he gave Barker clearly to understand that he (Jackson) knew nothing whatever of the facts stated in the petition or referred to in Barker's request, and at the same time asked for further information on the subject of the title to the alley. The record fails to show that appellee ever paid any part of the tax or otherwise suffered any change of condition for the worse by reason of this petition.

As for the recital of the lease, it is not even now insisted upon as an estoppel, though it is woven into an argument looking to the establishment of an estoppel. It is still specifically referred to as a mere admission, and that it is an admission of a kind may be conceded. Its effect in that aspect has been considered. That it cannot operate to convey title by estoppel seems plain. At best it could operate only as a conveyance of appellants' right to the use of the alleyway during the term of the lease. But appellee was not taking a conveyance of a right to use the alley. That right was and is undisputed. The recital that the alley was a joint alley was wholly unnecessary to the lease and did not operate as an estoppel against the grantee to assert its own superior right and title.—*Osborne v. Endicott*, 6 Cal. 149, 65 Am. Dec. 498; *Wilcoxon v. Osborn*, 77 Mo. 621; *Cooper v. Watson*, 73 Ala. 252.

In other respects the application is a restatement of propositions which have been heretofore considered. We are satisfied with the conclusion then reached.

Application denied.

Winkles *v.* Powell.

Sale for Partition.

(Decided May 18, 1911. 55 South. 536.)

1. *Judgment; Res Adjudicata; When Available.*—Unless pleaded, a former adjudication is not available.

2. *Divorce; Special Legislation; Granting Divorce.*—A special act granting a divorce was unconstitutional under section 23, Article 4, Constitution 1871.

3. *Same; Grounds; Abandonment.*—The refusal of the wife to accompany the husband to the domicile selected by him is an abandonment, and if continued for the statutory period is grounds for divorce.

4. *Life Estate; Character of Possession; Life Tenant.*—The possession of the widow as a life tenant of lands belonging to her husband is not adverse to the heirs of the husband.

5. *Husband and Wife; Domicile; Husband's Right to Select.*—If the wife's health or safety is not imperiled thereby the husband has the right to select and designate the family domicile.

6. *Homestead; Right of Wife.*—The wife has no estate in the husband's homestead, he having the legal title. Her only right is that of joint occupancy with him, and the right to veto his alienation of it under the statute.

7. *Same; Abandonment; Right of Husband.*—Under Section 4190 Code 1907, a husband may be entitled without his wife's consent to abandon the homestead, but he cannot, by abandoning both the homestead and the family, deprive them of their right to hold the homestead so long as they use it as such.

8. *Same; Ratification by Wife.*—Where the husband conveyed the homestead by deed without the wife joining therein, or consenting thereto, a subsequent approval of the deed by the wife did not validate the deed.

9. *Partition; Apportionment of Costs; Discretion.*—The apportionment of the costs among the several heirs in a partition proceed-

ing rests in the sound discretion of the chancellor, and will not be disturbed on appeal.

(McClellan, J. dissenting.)

APPEAL from Marshall Chancery Court.

Heard before Hon. W. H. SIMPSON.

Bill for partition by Annie Winkles against James Powell and others. From a decree granting partition and allowing petitioner a one-sixth interest, she appeals. Affirmed.

E. O. McCORD, for appellant. The ejectment suit settled the interest of the parties in the land and became res adjudicata as to the matter. The vital question in this cause is, where was the homestead of Powell when he executed the deed to a one-half interest in the lands in controversy? Homestead is defined to be the home place—the place of the home.—*Lyon v. Harden,* 129 Ala. 645; *McGuire v. VanPelt,* 55 Ala. 35. Having abandoned the place and taken up his abode elsewhere, these lands ceased to be the homestead.—*Striplin & Co. v. Cooper & Son,* 80 Ala. 256; *Land v. Boykin,* 122 Ala. 627; *Blackman v. Moore H. H. Co.,* 106 Ala. 458; *Sides v. Schharff,* 93 Ala. 106; *Boyd v. Shulman,* 59 Ala. 566. The husband has the right to fix, choose and designate the domicile or place of abode.—*Talmage v. Talmage,* 66 Ala. 199; 58 Ala. 451. The court erred in its apportionment of the cost.

STREET & ISBELL, for appellee. The act divorcing Powell from his first wife and legalizing his second marriage was void as being clearly unconstitutional.—*Jones v. Jones,* 95 Ala. 443. The desertion of his family did not operate as an abandonment of the homestead by them.—15 A. & E. Ency. Law, 658; 21 Cyc. 597; *Palmer v. Sawyer,* 103 N. W. 1088; *Weatherington v. Smith,* 13

L. R. A. N. S. 430; *Bremseth v. Olsen*, 13 L. R. A. N. S. 170; *Frazier v. Lyas*, 35 Am. Rep. 466; *Lynn v. Sentel*, 75 Am. St. Rep. 110; *Moore v. Dunning*, 81 Am. Dec. 301; Code, Sec. 4190, 1907. The land was therefore a homestead at the time of the attempted conveyance.— Sec. 4161, Code 1907. Res adjudicata to be available must be pleaded.—*Hooper v. Strahm*, 71 Ala. 75; *Winter v. Merrick*, 69 Ala. 86. Where a title asserted depends upon an estoppel, it must be pleaded in equity. —*Hall v. Henderson*, 126 Ala. 490; *Jones v. Peebles*, 130 Ala. 269.

SOMERVILLE, J.—The original bill is for the sale of 80 acres of land for distribution among the tenants in common, and is filed by complainant against her brothers and sisters, or their representatives in blood. The bill alleges that complainant owns an undivided seven-twelfths interest in the land, and that respondents own the remaining undivided five-twelfths. The respondents filed their answer and cross-bill, denying that complainant owned more than a one-sixth interest in the land, and setting forth the following facts with respect to the title thereof. The land in question was owned by one Lewis R. Powell in 1885, and was then occupied as a homestead by himself and wife, Sarah A. Powell, and their daughter, Annie E. Winkles, the complainant. In that year—1885—said Powell charged his said wife with adultery, and abandoned her and their home, to which he never returned, and took up his abode elsewhere. In May, 1885, he filed a bill for divorce on the ground of adultery, and in November, 1885, a decree was rendered divorcing him from his said wife. In February, 1887, on appeal to the Supreme Court, this decree was reversed, and the bill of complaint dismissed. In the meantime, in January, 1886,

Powell had married one Fannie Windsor, and, after the adverse decree of the Supreme Court, he procured the passage in February, 1889, of a legislative bill divorcing him from his wife, Sarah, validating his marriage with Fannie Windsor, and legitimating the issue thereof. After this Powell and his new wife, the said Fannie, removed to Winston county, where he purchased 130 acres of land, which they resided on until his death in November, 1897, raising a family in the meanwhile. In May, 1891, said Powell and Fannie Windsor, as his alleged wife, executed a deed to certain parties conveying to them an undivided half interest in the lands described in the bill. In November, 1904, said grantees conveyed to Annie Winkles, the complainant, all their interest in said lands; and previously, in January, 1899, the said Sarah Powell executed a deed conveying said lands to complainant, after which, as before, the said Sarah and complainant continued to occupy the lands jointly until the former's death, which occurred in February, 1906. The lands in suit were never worth in excess of $2,000; and the parties to this suit are all of the heirs of said Lewis Powell, representing six original shares. The foregoing facts are embodied in an agreed statement of facts upon which the cause was tried. In this agreed statement is a recital that the respondents sued the complainant in ejectment for these same lands in September, 1906, and in October, 1907, recovered a judgment against her for a five-twelfths undivided interest, of which they were placed in possession.

The chancellor, disregarding the conveyances under which complainant claims, apportioned the ownership of the land in accordance with the original heirship of the parties, allowing complainant a one-sixth interest only; and he taxed her with one-half the costs of suit.

4—173

His decree in both of these particulars is assigned as erroneous.

1. The fact that in an ejectment suit these respondents recovered of complainant only a five-twelfths interest in these lands, even if every essential of an estoppel by judgment appeared (which is not the case), can avail the complainant nothing here, since she has nowhere pleaded it. This rule is inflexible.—*Clark v. Johnson,* 155 Ala. 648, 47 South. 82; *Jones v. Peebles,* 130 Ala. 269, 30 South. 564; *Hall v. Henderson,* 126 Ala. 490, 28 South. 531, 61 L. R. A. 621, 85 Am. St. Rep. 53. Properly pleaded and proved, the result would, it seems, have been otherwise.—*Coleman v. Stewart,* 170 Ala. 255, 53 South. 1020.

2. The legislative divorce granted to Lewis Powell, being violative of section 23 of article 4 of the Constitution of 1875, was an absolute nullity, and Sarah Powell continued to be his lawful wife as long as he lived, his attempted marriage with another woman notwithstanding.—*Jones v. Jones,* 95 Ala. 443, 11 South. 11, 18 L. R. A. 93. Nor would it make any difference if it were acquiesced in and treated as valid by the lawful wife.

3. As surviving widow of Lewis Powell, Sarah Powell owned but a life estate in these lands, and her deed to complainant conveyed no more than that. There is nothing in the record to show that the widow ever claimed the lands adversely to her husband; and, if she had, her possession could not have become adverse since it was at all times rightful and lawful, and neither her husband nor his heirs could have disturbed it.

4. It only remains to consider whether, under the conditions shown, Lewis Powell could make a valid deed to these lands without the voluntary signature and assent of his lawful wife, Sarah. Undoubtedly, the law authorizes the husband to choose and fix the domi-

cile of himself and wife and children; and, when he exercises this power, the wife's refusal to accompany him
and share with him the home of his selection is tantamount to an abandonment of him by her, and, if continued for the statutory period, becomes a ground of
divorce against her. Of course, this power has its limitations and cannot be so exercised as to imperil the
health or safety of the wife.

The wife has no estate in the homestead when the legal title is in the husband, and the only rights she has
with respect thereto are the common-law right of occupancy jointly with the husband, and the statutory right
of veto against its alienation, so long as it remains the
family homestead.—*Witherington v. Mason*, 86 Ala.
349, 5 South. 679, 11 Am. St. Rep. 41.

It results from these principles that the husband may
without the wife's consent abandon the homestead, and
by so doing deprive it of the privileges and free it from
the restraints attached to it by law. It is clear, therefore, that had Powell simply abandoned his home in
Marshall county, and acquired a home in Winston
county, which he invited his wife to share, her refusal
to do so, and her continued occupancy of the former
home, would not have preserved the homestead character of such former home, and he could have alienated it
without her signature or assent, subject, of course, to
her inchoate right of dower. But the record shows that
he permanently abandoned both his home and his family; and so far was he from desiring the further presence of his wife that in less than a year he took another
woman and installed her in the new home which he acquired. In accordance with the spirit and purpose of
our homestead laws, we are of the opinion that the husband could not thus abandon the homestead occupied by
himself and his wife; and, while she continued to oc-

cupy it as her home, and was excluded from his presence and his home elsewhere, thereby empower himself to convey it away without her lawfully expressed consent. And the principle of this view has been approved by the courts of many states.—21 Cyc. 597; 95 Am. St. Rep. 936, note.

5. By section 2537, Code 1886, brought forward as section 4190, Code 1907, it is provided that when, among other things, the husband absconds or abandons his family, the wife shall be entitled to interpose any and all claims of homestead or other exemption which the husband could have interposed, conditioned on her intention to continue a resident of the state. While this statute does not in terms forbid alienation of the homestead by the husband without the wife's consent during the period of his abandonment, it does plainly show a legislative intent to preserve the character and immunities of the homestead in favor of the dependent members of the family, in despite of its attempted abandonment by the husband. Such solicitude would be barren of the good results intended if the husband could nevertheless declare the homestead abandoned, and by his deed alone authorize any stranger to enter and expel his helpless family. Its policy and effect are therefore strongly confirmatory of our conclusion above announced.

It is strongly urged by counsel for appellant that in denying the power of the husband to alienate in this case we are not protecting the wife at all, but are in fact actually thwarting her wishes with respect to the disposition and beneficial enjoyment of this property, which she wished to go to her daughter, the complainant, as shown by the deed she made to her. But this is wholly apart from the question, which is solely upon the validity of her husband's deed to strangers. If that deed was void when made—and we hold that it was—it could not be afterwards validated by the tacit or expressed approval of the wife not evidenced as the statute requires. Nor, indeed, would the result be different if the husband's grantees had reconveyed to the wife instead of to her daughter, the complainant.

6. The apportionment of costs, especially in a case like this, rests in the sound discretion of the chancellor, and will not be reviewed on appeal.—*Kitchell v. Jackson,* 71 Ala. 556.

There being no error in the record, the decree of the chancery court is affirmed.

Affirmed.

DOWDELL, C. J., and SIMPSON, ANDERSON, MAYFIELD, and SAYRE, JJ., concur. McCLELLAN, J., dissents.

SIMPSON, J., holds that section 4190 of the Code is decisive of the question.

McCLELLAN, J. (dissenting).—By express provision of the Constitution, ownership and actual occupancy (with a single quasi exception, to be noted) are twin prerequisites—the one no more important than the other—to the establishment and retention of an homestead, with its attendant rights of exemption in this state.—Const. 1875, art. 10, §§ 2, 3; Const. 1901, §§ 205, 206; *McConnaughy v. Baxter,* 55 Ala. 379; *Turner v. Turner,* 107 Ala. 465, 18 South. 210, 54 Am. St. Rep. 110; *Murphy v. Hunt,* 75 Ala. 438; *Barber v. Williams,* 74 Ala. 331; *Boyle v. Shulman,* 59 Ala. 567, among others. The quasi exception mentioned is with respect to temporary absence from the homestead or the leasing of the same.—*Turner v. Turner, supra.* Its statutory creation is confirmatory of the existence of the prerequisite of actual occupation. In *Boyle v. Shulman, supra,* it was said, Brickell, C. J., writing: "Actual occupation as a dwelling place as a home is the characteristic which distinguishes it (homestead) from other real estate. * * * A man can no more have two homes than he can have two domiciles at the same time." In *Woodstock Iron Co. v. Richardson,* 94 Ala. 629, 10 South. 144, following *Boyle v. Shulman,* it was said: "It is legally impossible to have two homesteads at the same time." In *Barber v. Williams,* it was said: "Occupancy as a home, as a dwelling place, is the fact which impresses upon land the character of a homestead, drawing it within the influence of constitutional and statutory provisions, exempting it from liability for the payment of debts, or from subjection to administration, or intercepting the descent to the heir." As is obvious from Const. §§ 205, 206, statute and decision, the wife has no legal power with respect to the selection or establishment of an homestead by the husband in his lands. The fixing of that status—that impression of the homestead characteristic—upon his lands is unrestrictedly and unqualifiedly reposed in the husband. He may abandon an homestead once established. Indeed, he during his life may, if he chooses, so order his habitation as to have no homestead whatever in this state. "Neither the Constitution nor the statute confers on the wife any right or estate in the homestead during his life, *but a mere power to prevent its alienation.*" (Italics supplied.)—*Witherington v. Mason,* 86 Ala. 345, 349, 5 South. 679, 681, 11 Am. St. Rep. 41.

The statute (Code, § 4190) referred to in the majority opinion only has reference to the claim of exemptions against the demands of creditors. It does not assume to confer on the wife or minor children the right to fix the homestead character on lands of the husband or father; for, under our system, only the owner may do that. Indeed, the statute clearly presupposes that

the exempt character of the property that may be
claimed as exempt by the wife or minor children has
been previously impressed upon it by the owner, the
husband or father. This appears from the terms of the
statute wherein it is provided that the wife or minor
children shall, upon the contingencies enumerated with
respect to the husband or father, "be entitled to interpose any and all claims of homestead or other exemption which the *husband or father could have interposed.*" (Italics supplied.)

If the statute should be read as conferring upon the
wife or minor children the right to prevent the husband
or father from abandoning an homestead once established, or, to qualify, correlatively, the owner's right to
select his homestead, it would offend the Constitution
by attempting to unwarrantably impose conditions on
the benefit and exercise of a constitutional right.—
Coolsey's Const. Lim. p. 99; *Marks v. Wilson,* 115 Ala.
561, 563, 22 South. 134. However, the statute makes no
such attempt. It merely confers under the circumstances enumerated upon the wife or minor children the
claim power, as against the creditors of the husband or
father, the absent or disabled husband or father could
have exercised were he present and not disabled. It
makes no effort to affect the establishment of the homestead, nor to trench upon the rules with respect to its
alienation. In the writer's opinion the statute is not in
any way a factor in the matter presented for review.

As appears from the statement of facts in the majority opinion, Powell ceased, in 1885, to occupy the Marshall county place as an homestead, charged his wife
with infidelity, and took up his abode elsewhere. This
departure from its occupancy denuded that area in
Marshall county of the characteristic of an homestead.
He could not have claimed it as exempt against the

claims of a creditor. He bought 130 acres of land in Winston county, Ala., and resided on it until his death, there raising a family by one not his wife. If homestead he had, it was this place in Winston county. He could not have two homesteads at the same time. He could not, under Constitution, statute, and decision, have an homestead in an area which he did not in the accepted legal sense actually occupy. As against a judgment creditor's execution, surely he could not have claimed the Marshall county place as exempt, for he did not occupy it in any sense.

However outrageous and unjustifiable may have been Powell's abandonment and treatment of his wife Sarah and their daughter, that fact cannot in my opinion have any bearing or influence upon the inquiry, Was the Marshall county place the homestead of Powell when he undertook to convey it? If the deprivation of his right to select and establish another homestead, or to abandon one already established is a penalty for such wrongs, it is clear that the wife is given a far greater power with respect to the homestead than has been heretofore supposed to exist. In the Constitution she is given during the life of the husband only "a mere power to prevent its (homestead's) alienation."—*Witherington v. Mason, supra.* But if an homestead, once established, cannot be abandoned as Powell undertook to do here, then, as the writer views it, the power of the wife is greater than the Constitution's grant of the right of selection to the owner; its language being, "Every homestead * * * to be selected by the owner * * *" It seems to me that the result attained on this appeal is the pronouncement of the forfeiture of Powell's constitutional right to select his homestead upon the wholly unrelated ground of his dereliction in duty to his wife Sarah and their daughter. However reprehensible may have been his conduct in so doing, and however prone all good men are to frown upon wrong and to discountenance immorality, the writer cannot find therein any justification for the negation in any degree of Powell's unqualified constitutional right to select his homestead, which necessarily imports the right to abandon one already selected.

So, holding these views, I cannot concur.

Wilkins v. Hardaway.

Specific Performance.

(Decided May 11, 1911. Re-hearing Denied June 27, 1911. 55 South. 817).

1. *Vendor and Purchaser; Contract; Option; Effect.*—An option to purchase land is unilateral and only becomes effective and binding upon the purchaser exercising the right of option.

2. *Frauds, Statute of; Contracts for Sale of Land; Description.*—Where the option to purchase definitely described the lands, except as to its western boundary, and that was to be determined by a line run on a level with the crest of the contemplated dam across a river, which dam was to be erected by the purchaser who could fix the crest of the dam in advance of its actual construction, and the purchaser within the period of the option, fixed the crest of the proposed dam, and located the western boundary line by survey, and ascertained the number of acres included within the boundary so fixed, the exercise of the option and a designation of the land rendered the contract valid under the statute of frauds.

APPEAL from Chambers Chancery Court.

Heard before Hon. W. W. WHITESIDE.

Bill by B. H. Hardaway against J. C. Wilkins to enforce the specific performance of a contract. Decree for complainant and respondent appeals. Affirmed.

STROTHER, HINDS AND FULLER, for appellant. The terms of the contract are not sufficient to meet the requirements of the statute of fraud, and the demurrers to the bill should have been sustained.—*Ala. Min. Land Co. v. Jackson,* 121 Ala. 172; *Alba v. Strong,* 94 Ala. 163; *Kopp v. Reiter,* 37 A. St. Rep. 156; *Raub v. Smith,* 1 Am. St. Rep. 619; *Wardell v. Williams,* 4 Am. St. Rep. 814. Under these conditions the contract cannot be enforced.—*Westbrook v. Hayes,* 137 Ala. 572; *Farmer v. Sellers,* 137 Ala. 112; 4 Pom. Eq. sec. 1405. The ala-gata and probata must correspond.—*Alston v. Marshall,* 112 Ala. 641; *Carter v. Thompson,* 41 Ala. ·375. The contract was not sufficiently definite in description. —*Pait v. Gerst,* 149 Ala. 287, and authorities there cited.

E. M. OLIVER, for appellee. The description was suf-ficiently definite, and the option was properly exercised to render the agreement valid.—20 Cyc. 271; 26 A. & E. Enc. of Law, 36; *Fleishman v. Wood,* 135 Cal. 256. The cases cited by appellant state correct principles of law but are without application to the case at bar.

DOWDELL, C. J.—The contract, a specific perfor-mance of which is sought by the bill, in its inception was what is known as an "option contract," and hence uni-lateral, and only became an agreement of contract and sale, binding on the parties as such, upon the exercise of the right of option.

In the option contract the land in question was defin-itely described, except as to its western boundary, and this boundary was to be determined by a line run on a level with the crest of a contemplated dam across the Tallapoosa river, to be erected by the owner of the right of the option, who, by the terms of the contract, had the right to fix and determine the height and crest of the dam in advance of its actual construction.

Within the period of the option the crest of the pro-posed dam was fixed and determined, which furnished

the data for a determinate survey and location of the
western boundary line according to the contract. A
survey was then made, locating and defining the said
western boundary line of said land, and ascertaining
the number of acres included within the boundaries so
fixed and described. All of which having been done,
the complainant, appellee here, within the time, claimed
and exercised his right of option. Then the option contract became an agreement and contract of sale of the
land between the parties. There was no indefiniteness
and uncertainty in description at this time. That
which was uncertain had been rendered certain, pursuant to the terms of the option agreement, before the
same ripened into a contract of sale.

The case of *Alabama Mineral Land Co. v. Jackson*,
121 Ala. 172, 25 South. 709, 77 Am. St. Rep. 46, relied
on by appellant, is without application to the case at
bar. The facts in the two cases are different. In that
case there was no exercise of right of option, and therefore no designation of the lands. The cases of *Howison
v. Bartlett*, 141 Ala. 593, 37 South. 590, and *Alabama
Mineral Land Co. v. Long*, 158 Ala. 301, 48 South. 363,
are more in point, and we think in principle support
our view that the statute of frauds is no defense
against the present bill. In those cases, as here, there
was an exercise of the option and a designation of the
lands.

As to the certainty and definiteness in description of
the land, we refer to what was said on a former appeal
in this case.—159 Ala. 565, 48 South. 678.

The record fully sustains the chancellor in his conclusion on the facts. No error appearing, the decree of
the chancellor is affirmed.

Affirmed.

SIMPSON, McCLELLAN, and MAYFIELD, JJ., concur.

Rankin *v.* Dean, *et al.*

Bill to Enjoin an Action of Ejectment and to Quiet Title.

(Decided April 13, 1911. 55 South. 217).

1. *Quieting Title; Right of Action; Cloud on Title.*—Where the bill was not only to enjoin an action of ejectment, but also to require entry of satisfaction for payment of purchase money for the property in question, and to declare invalid a conveyance made during complainant's possession under a conditional deed, and to remove the conveyance as a cloud upon title, the test as to whether there is an adequate remedy at law is whether the holder of the property, in an action of ejectment brought by the adverse party founded on his deed, would be required to offer evidence to defeat a recovery. If such proof would be necessary, the cloud exists.

2. *Same; Right of Action; Remedy at Law.*—Purchasers of land holding under a conditional deed, which they cannot set up in a court of law till the payment of the purchase money, have no adequate remedy at law which would defeat a bill to enjoin an action of ejectment brought against them by a subsequent grantee of their vendor, and to declare invalid such subsequent conveyance and to remove it as a cloud on the title.

APPEAL from St. Clair Chancery Court.

Heard before Hon. W. W. WHITESIDE.

Bill by Mary Dean and others against D. P. Rankin, Sr., to enjoin an action of ejectment, and to remove the cloud from title. From a decree for complainants, respondent appeals. Affirmed.

JAMES EMBREY, for appellant. The legal rights of these parties were settled on former appeal.—*Rankin v. Dean,* 157 Ala. 490. On this authority the case should be reversed and remanded. The tender was not available or sufficient because not accompanied by the money. —*T. & D. Engine Co. v. Hall,* 89 Ala. 630; *Bingham v. Vandegrift,* 93 Ala. 286. Rankin did not estop himself by accepting partial payments on the debt mentioned.—

Edmonson v. Montague, 14 Ala. 370; 1 Brickell's Dig. 796; *Miller v. Hampton,* 37 Ala. 342.

GIBSON & DAVIS, for appellee. Dean's right was merely equitable, and not cognizable in a court of law. —*Rankin v. Dean,* 157 Ala. 490. The instrument on which complainant relied is no more than a bond for title and was not cognizable in a court of law.—*Chapman v. Glassell,* 13 Ala. 50; *Lomb v. Pioneer S. & L. Co.,* 106 Ala. 599. Hence complainant did not have an adequate remedy at law.—*McPherson v. Walters,* 16 Ala. 717. The doctrine of laches cannot apply for the reason that during all this time complainants have been in the actual open, and notorious possession of the land. —*Ogletree v. Rainer,* 152 Ala. 467; *Torrent F. E. Co. v. City of Mobile,* 101 Ala. 564; *Harold v. Weaver,* 72 Ala. 373; 32 Cyc. 1345.

SIMPSON, J.—The bill in this case was filed by the appellees to enjoin an action of ejectment and for other purposes hereafter to be specifically mentioned. Said ejectment suit was before this court at a previous term, from which it will be seen that the complainants claim under a deed to their ancestor, made in 1873, which this court held to be a conditional deed, the title not to be absolutely vested in the grantee until the purchase money named therein should be paid, and that, until the payment of the purchase money, the purchaser, being in possession, held only an equitable title, which could not be set up in a court of law, and the vendor held the legal title as trustee for the benefit of the vendee.—*Rankin v. Dean et al.,* 157 Ala. 490, 47 South. 1015.

The bill alleges that John R. Dean, the grantee, went into possession of the premises conveyed immediately

on the execution of the conveyance, occupied them to
the time of his death, and that complainants have remained in possession of the same ever since; that various payments had been made on same, at different
times specified, leaving unpaid only $8, with accrued
interest, which has been tendered to the duly authorized agent of the grantor, but he declined to accept the
same until he could find the purchase-money note, or
obtain proper power of attorney to satisfy said indebtedness; that complainants have ever been ready to pay
the same, and are now ready and willing to pay whatever is due on said note; also that on December 16, 1873,
the grantor executed some kind of conveyance to respondent of said land, the particular description of
which is unknown to complainants. It recites the proceedings in ejectment, that respondent is the transferee
of said indebtedness, and that respondent had notice of
the provisions of said original conveyance prior to and
at the time of the making of said second conveyance.
The bill prays for an order of reference to ascertain
what amount is due on said purchase, and offers to pay
whatever may be found due; also prays for the injunction, that respondent be required to accept the amount
found due, and to satisfy the said debt, also that said
alleged title of respondent be declared void, and complainants be vested with a clear, unclouded title to said
lands, in so far as any claims of respondent may affect
the same, and for general relief.

Respondent moved to dismiss, demurred, and answered the bill, admitting the conveyance and possession (though denying that it has been adverse), denied
that the payments amount to as much as claimed, denied the tender, admitted the conveyance to him, but
alleged that complainants could have ascertained the
nature of said conveyance by an examination of the

records, and claimed that said conveyance is paramount to the title of complainants.

The amendment to the bill brings the money into court, particularizes the times and amounts of payment, and claims that the respondent, after receiving the payments, delivering up one of the notes, etc., is estopped from proceeding in ejectment. It will be noticed that the bill seeks, not only to enjoin the action of ejectment, but also to require the entry of satisfaction by the payment of purchase money, and to declare invalid the conveyance made during complainants' possession under the conditional deed, and remove the same as a cloud on the title, so that there is no adequate remedy at law.

The test is: "Would the owner of the property, in an action of ejectment brought by the adverse party, founded upon the deed, be required to offer evidence to defeat a recovery? If such proof would be necessary the cloud would exist."—*Rea, pro ami, v. Longstreet & Sedgwick*, 54 Ala. 291, 294; *Eufaula National Bank v. Pruett, et al.*, 128 Ala. 470, 473, 30 South. 731.

The remedy at law in this case is not adequate, and the chancellor properly held that the complainants are entitled to relief. The decree of the court is affirmed.

Affirmed.

McCLELLAN, MAYFIELD, and SAYRE, JJ., concur.

Singo, *et al. v.* Brainard.

Bill to Set Aside a Sale and Declare a Trust.

(Decided May 17, 1911. Re-hearing denied June 8, 1911.
55 South. 603.)

1. *Attorney and Client; Duties and Liabilities to Client.*—So long as the relation of attorney and client exists, the attorney is a trustee for his client in and about the cause or the subject thereof, and any trade that he makes or benefit that he may derive resulting from the litigation, or a sale of the subject thereof, will inure to the benefit of the client.

2. *Appeal and Error; Objections Below; Parties.*—If not taken advantage of by plea, demurrer or answer, an objection that a bill is defective because of want of proper parties, is waived, but if the cause cannot be properly disposed of on its merits, without the presence of the absent parties, the objection may be made at the hearing, or on error, or may be taken by the court ex mero motu. However, the question of a person, not made a party, being a necessary party cannot be considered on appeal from a decree sustaining demurrers to the bill, where want of proper parties is not one of the grounds of demurrer.

3. *Equity; Bill; Amendment.*—Under section 2837 Code 1907, a decree sustaining or overruling a demurrer to a bill for want of equity is an interlocutory decree, and where the supreme court renders a decree reversing a decree overruling such a demurrer, and remanding the cause, this was an interlocutory decree, and could not become final until the bill was formally dismissed by the trial court, and hence the provisions of section 3126 Code 1907, are applicable. The rule that in passing on a general demurrer to a bill amendable defects should be considered as made relates only to facts set out defectively, and not to facts not set out in the bill.

APPEAL from Montgomery City Court.
Heard before Hon. WM. H. THOMAS.

Bill by Will Singo and others against Mark D. Brainard to set aside a sale and declare a trust. From a decree sustaining demurrer to the amended bill, complainants appeal. Reversed, rendered and remanded.

WARREN S. REESE, for appellant. A general demurrer should never be sustained unless complainant is without right to equitable relief.—*Seals v. Robinson,*

75 Ala. 363. Under the facts stated in the bill the relation is properly set out, the undue influence fully alleged and a proper case made for relief by the client against the acts of the attorney.—*Johnson v. Johnson,* 5 Ala. 90; *Noble v. Moses,* 81 Ala. 530, and cases therein cited. Jury Fritz is not a necessary party, as they were all tenants in common and one might file a bill for all.—*Le Croix v. Malone,* 47 South. 2027; *Dorlan v. Westovitch,* 140 Ala. 294; *Harden v. Collins,* 138 Ala. 400; *Hinds v. Trentham,* 27 Ala. 359.

GOODWYN & MCINTYRE, J. WINTER THORINGTON, and A. A. EVANS, for appellee. On all the issues involved in this case the court has decided adversely to the complainants.—*Singo v. Fritz,* 51 South. 867; *Singo v. McGhee,* 49 South. 290; *Brainard v. Singo,* 51 South. 522. The bill shows on its face that Jury Fritz should have been made a party complainant.—*Perkins v. Brierfield I. & C. Co.,* 77 Ala. 403; *Mobile L. I. Co. v. Goss,* 129 Ala. 214. Where there is a general decree sustaining demurrers it will be referred to the causes which will support the decree, and not to others which will render it erroneous.—*Kenny v. Reeves,* 139 Ala. 386; *McDonald v. Pearson,* 114 Ala. 630. The supreme court rendered a decree sustaining the general demurrer to the bill for want of equity. —51 South. 522. This had the effect of a final decree dismissing the bill.—*Seals v. Robinson,* 75 Ala. 363; *Pate v. Hinson,* 104 Ala. 599; *Turner v. City of Mobile,* 135 Ala. 73; *Eddins v. Murphy,* 142 Ala. 617; *Brown v. Mie,* 119 Ala. 10. It therefore follows that if the court was in error in its ruling on the demurrers it was error without injury as the bill stood as if formally dismissed.

ANDERSON, J.—This case on former appeal is reported in 164 Ala. 353, 51 South. 522. It was there held that the bill was without equity, and the demurrer for want of equity was sustained, but there was no formal decree of this court dismissing the bill; the cause being remanded to the lower court.

As we understand the amendment to the bill, it does not attack the decree of the probate court for fraud; for, while it sets up fraudulent acts and omissions on the part of respondent, Brainard, in and about the defense and prosecution of the probate proceeding, it does not charge the beneficiaries, under said decree, or the parties to the cause, with such conduct as would vacate the decree for fraud. It does aver, however, that the respondent Brainard, while still the attorney and trustee for the complainants, purchased the subject of the litigation (the land) for a sum greatly less than its value, and that said purchase should inure to the benefit of his clients, these complainants.

It can be safely stated as a sound and salutary legal principle that, so long as the relationship of client and attorney exists, the attorney is a trustee for his client in and about the cause or the subject thereof, and any trade that he makes or benefits he may derive, resulting from the litigation or a sale of the subject of the litigation, will inure to the benefit of the client, the cestui que trust. This is a rule so wholesome and just that citation of authority is needless, and it would be difficult to find an authority holding to the contrary. The amended bill avers that Brainard was the attorney of the complainants up to and at the time of the purchase of the land by Parker, and that Parker was in fact acting for and in behalf of Brainard.

It has been suggested in brief of counsel that Jury Fritz, who was interested in the estate of Singo, but

who did not employ Brainard, should have been made
a party to this cause. Whether she is or is not a necessary party, either as complainant or respondent, we
need not determine, as this question is not properly
presented for our consideration. "The general rule is
that, if a bill is defective for the want of proper parties,
advantage should be taken of the defect, by plea, demurrer, or answer, and, if not taken the objection is
waived. The rule is subject to the exception that if the
cause cannot be properly disposed of, on the merits,
without the presence of the absent parties, the objection
may be made at the hearing, or on error, or it may be
taken by the court ex mero motu."—*Prout v. Hoge*, 57
Ala. 28; 3 Mayfield's Digest, p. 258, §§ 1503, 1504. We
are not considering this case upon the merits, but upon
an appeal from an interlocutory decree, rendered on
May 21st, sustaining the respondent's demurrers, of
date May 20, 1910, to the amended bill. The demurrers so considered and sustained contain no ground for
want of proper parties.

It is next insisted that the error of the city court in
sustaining the demurrer to the amended bill can be
tolled upon the theory that the amendment was not
properly allowed, that the previous decree of this court
in sustaining the demurrer for want of equity operated
ipso facto as a dismissal of the bill, and that it could not
be amended after remandment. It is needless for us to
enter into the discussion of a distinction between a motion to dismiss for the want of equity and a general demurrer for want of equity, or to imagine all that was
in the legislative mind when making the change in the
statute as it appears—section 3121 of the Code of 1907.
For a discussion of this subject, we refer to chapter 15,
Sims' Chancery Practice, which is not only interesting
and instructive, but can be read with profit by the

bench and bar. It is sufficient to say that, whether they are or are not similar methods of testing the equity of the bill, the sustaining of the demurrer without more does not operate as a final decree dismissing the bill.—*Rose v. Gibson,* 71 Ala. 35; *Lide v. Park,* 132 Ala. 222, 31 South. 360; *McCrory v. Guyton,* 154 Ala. 355, 45 South. 658. A decree sustaining a demurrer, but not dismissing the bill, is but an interlocutory decree covered by section 2838 of the Code of 1907, and is not a final decree, as is contemplated by section 2837. Whether or not the mere sustaining of a motion to dismiss for want of equity without a further order or decree dismissing the bill would be a final decree we need not determine, as there could be drawn a very decided distinction between a decree sustaining a motion to dismiss a bill and one sustaining a demurrer. The former seeks affirmatively to strike or get rid of the bill; while the latter merely questions the sufficiency of same, leaving it for the court to determine whether or not the decree sustaining same should be followed up with an order of dismissal. It is questionable, however, whether or not the mere sustaining of a motion to dismiss a bill for want of equity, not followed up with a decree actually dismissing the bill, would be a final decree, as section 2838 of the Code of 1907 (section 427 of the Code of 1896) makes such a decree an interlocutory one, and not a final decree, as mentioned in the preceding section. If, therefore, the lawmakers considered it a final decree, it would have been covered by section 426, and there was no need to put it in section 427, Code of 1896. True, if the decree went beyond merely sustaining the motion and dismissed the bill, it would become a final decree and governed by section 426 of the Code of 1896, but if the motion was merely sustained, and not followed up with an order of dismissal, it would doubtless be an interlocutory decree, as mentioned in section 427. At any rate, the decree of this court sustaining the demurrer was merely interlocutory, and could not become a final decree until the bill was formally dismissed by the city court. Section 3126 of the Code of 1907 provides that: "Amendments to bills *must* be allowed at any time before final decree, by striking out or adding new parties, or to meet any state of evidence which will authorize relief," etc. The decree in this case not being final, the amendment to the bill was properly allowed.

It has been suggested that to permit amendments, after sustaining a demurrer settling the equities of a bill, will tend to prolong and protract litigation. As to this apprehension, we are not concerned, as it is our duty to construe and not legislate. Moreover, the courts will no doubt wisely guard against abuses of the statute of amendments, and the case will no doubt be rare when a complainant will inject into the original bill new facts, by way of amendment, which do not exist and which cannot be proven, simply to give his bill equity, and occasional delays are far preferable to a denial of equity and justice.

The more recent decisions of our court (*Turner v. City of Mobile*, 135 Ala. 73, 33 South. 132, and many others) invoked the rule of always dismissing the bill after sustaining a motion to dismiss for want of equity, thus cutting off all opportunity for the operation of section 3126, as to the amendment of said bill, and it is evident that the Code committee, with this line of decisions in mind, desired to relax to some extent this rigorous method, by substituting a general demurrer and giving the courts some latitude to permit the operation of section 3126, even in cases where the general demurrer had been sustained for want of equity, and espe-

cially is this true in view of the fact that the same Code
(section 3095) made a very sweeping change as to the
rule against multifariousness.　In time past, however,
upon sustaining of a general demurrer to the whole bill,
the case was out of court, and ;no subsequent proceedings could be taken thereon.　The rigor of this rule has
been relaxed in many jurisdictions by liberal statutory
provisions relative to amendments.—Fletchers Equity
Pl. & Pr. § 229, and cases cited in note 149; Beachs
Modern Equity Pr. § 279, and note 4.　Our statute (section 3126) gives the right to amend any time before final
decree, and it is evident, as above noted, that the Code
committee had some object in view in substituting the
general demurrer for the motion to dismiss, and that
they intended to give the courts some latitude to retain
the bill, even after sustaining the general demurrer, in
order to give the statute as to amendments some field
for operation in such cases, and which it could not have
after a motion to dismiss was sustained, under that line
of decisions holding that the proper practice was to dismiss the bill upon sustaining said motion.

As to when the sustaining of a general demurrer for
want of equity should or should not be followed up
with a final decree dismissing the bill of complaint, we
need not decide until the exact question is presented;
but it is safe to say that, in view of the change made
in the statute, from a motion to dismiss to a demurrer
for want of equity, and the further fact that section
3126 and chancery rules 41 and 42 (32 South. iv) contemplate a liberal policy as to the amendment of bills,
the complainant should be given an opportunity to
amend his bill before dismissing same.　It is true that
in passing upon the general demurrer, as formerly upon
a motion to dismiss for want of equity, amendable defects should be considered as made, but this presump-

[Singo, et al. v. Brainard.]

tion does not relate to facts not set out in the bill, and merely means that, upon the facts set out, there is or is not equity in the bill, whether well or improperly pleaded; and if the facts establish a case for equitable relief, though not properly pleaded, the general demurrer will be overruled upon the presumption that all defects as to form of pleading are amended. On the other hand, if the complainant omits material facts from his bill, he should be permitted to add them by way of amendment, if they will inject equity into his said bill. It stands to reason, that a complainant will put his best foot forward and will set out all of his material averments in his original bill, whether properly pleaded or not, and, if they make out a case for equitable relief, a demurrer for want of equity should not be sustained and the authorization of amendments for the addition of new facts, after the equity of the bill has been tested, so as to give it equity, will no doubt tend to encourage perjury and the manufacture of essential facts in some instances, as well as protract the controversy; but, be this as it may, it was the legislative intention to give the statute and rules authorizing amendments some field of operation, even in cases where a demurrer for want of equity is sustained, by giving a complainant an opportunity to give his bill equity by way of amendment, before the same is finally dismissed.

The city court erred in sustaining the demurrers to the amended bill, and the decree must be reversed, and one is here rendered overruling same, and the cause is remanded.

Reversed, rendered, and remanded.

DOWDELL, C. J., and SAYRE and SOMERVILLE, JJ., concur.

Turner *v.* Durr, *et al.*

Injunction and Damages.

(Decided April 13, 1911. 55 South. 230.)

1. *Equity; Demurrer; Amendment to; Right to File.*—After a demurrer is overruled, and the time for an appeal from such decree has passed, the defendant cannot file a so-called amended demurrer, which raises no other objection than those determined by the former demurrer.

2. *Same; Effect.*—A decree overruling a demurrer to a bill, though interlocutory, tests and determines the sufficiency of the bill as to the grounds of demurrer interposed.

APPEAL from Shelby Chancery Court.

Heard before Hon. W. W. WHITESIDE.

Bill by John W. Durr, executor, against J. B. Turner to enjoin the cutting of timber from land, and for damages therefor. From a decree upon a so-called amended demurrer respondent appeals. Reversed, rendered and remanded at appellant's costs.

BURGIN, JENKINS AND BROWN, for appellant. The court erred in overruling the demurrers to the bill for want of equity.—*Keller v. Bullington,* 14 South. 466; High on Injunctions, sections 698-700. Counsel discussed the effect of joining with the prayer for injunction a prayer for damages under the penalty statute for cutting down or destroying trees, but in view of the opinion it is not deemed necessary to here set them out.

J. M. CHILTON, and STEINER, CRUM & WEIL, for appellee. This court is without jurisdiction to hear and determine this appeal as it was taken more than thirty days after the rendition of the decree on demurrer, and the decree on the alleged amended demurrer was a mere nullity and will not support an appeal.—Section 2838, Code 1907; *Dennis v. Currier*, 142 Ala. 637; *Blackburn v. H. M. Co.*, 135 Ala. 598; *Lide v. Park*, 132 Ala. 222. Counsel also discuss the merits of the controversy, but in view of the opinion it is not deemed necessary to here set it out.

MAYFIELD, J.—On the 20th day of August, 1910, the chancellor overruled the demurrer to the bill, and on the 20th day of September, 1910, respondent attempted to take an appeal from the decree by executing an appeal bond. This attempt was not efficacious for the reason that it came one day too late, the statute requiring appeals from such interlocutory orders or decrees to be taken within 30 days. After this attempted appeal, the chancellor entered another order or interlocutory decree, on the 15th day of September, this order reciting that, since the demurrer was overruled on the 20th day of August, 1910, the bill had not been amended, and that another demurrer had been filed, which raised only one question, the same raised on a former demurrer, and that it should be overruled. He then decrees the demurrer thus filed on the 16th day of September, 1910, to be the same he had theretofore overruled, and taxed the respondent with the costs.

The complainants objected to the filing of the demurrer of the 16th of September—the amended demurrer, so called—upon the ground that it had not been amended since the decree overruling the demurrer, and that the demurrer proposed to be filed raised no other objections than those which were determined and decided by the decree of August 20, 1910. The chancellor should have sustained complainants objection to the filing of this last demurrer, and declined to again pass upon the sufficiency of the bill which was undertaken to be tested by the demurrer. The chancellor seems to have been of this opinion; but being satisfied of the correctness of the former decree, and, thinking that the result would be the same if he entered a decree again overruling the demurrer, as it would be, should he decline to hear it, he rendered a decree to the same effect as the former. But this was error prejudicial to complainants, for two reasons: First, the decree in effect allowed the respondent 30 days additional time in which to appeal; second, it delayed the complainants in the prosecution of their suit, without sufficient cause. If such a course should be pursued by the respondent, he could prevent a final decree by perpetually refiling his demurrer on the day before the expiration of the time in which he is allowed to take an appeal. Such a practice should not be encouraged.

While a decree on demurrer is interlocutory, and not final, yet a decree overruling a demurrer to the bill does test and determine the sufficiency of the bill as tested by the demurrer. A party is not allowed to demur by piecemeal. He may assign any number of grounds of demurrer, but there can be only one demurrer to a bill or other pleading. A party will not be allowed to assign one or more grounds of demurrer, and, upon the overruling of that demurrer, assign other grounds of demurrer, or demur again, and thus continue to prevent a submission and hearing on final decree. We do not decide that it would be beyond the discretion of the chancellor to set aside a former decree on demurrer and allow another, with additional grounds, to be filed; yet we can see no good to be accomplished in the chancellor's allowing the filing of another demurrer, which raises no other questions of law than those raised by the first demurrer, and rendering decree thereupon, though the effect of both decrees may be the same. Of

[Turner v. Durr, et al.]

course, if the bill has been amended after the first decree, and the amendment has changed in the least the material allegations of the original bill, then the respondent will be allowed to demur to the amended bill, and to assign the same or other grounds of demurrer; but he has no such right, after his demurrer is overruled, unless the bill has been amended.

The effect of the action of the chancellor in this case, as it appears, was to give the respondent the right to appeal from the decree on demurrer, which he had lost by failing to take the appeal within the time prescribed by the statute. In this condition of the record, we cannot pass upon the sufficiency of the bill. It results that the second decree of the chancellor on the demurrer—the only decree that could be appealed from when this appeal was taken—was improper, and it must be reversed. The chancellor should have declined to allow the demurrer to be filed and the resubmission on demurrer, and should have required the respondent to answer within a reasonable time to be fixed by the chancellor.

A decree will be here rendered, requiring the respondent to answer the bill within 30 days, and ordering, adjudging, and decreeing that, upon respondent's failure to so answer, a decree pro confesso may be taken against him in the chancery court. The appellee being guilty of no fault, the appellant will be taxed with all the costs of this appeal.

Reversed, rendered, and remanded.

SIMPSON, MCCLELLAN, and SOMERVILLE, JJ., concur.

Sloss-Sheffield Steel & Iron Co., v. McLaughlin.

Bill to Abate a Nuisance.

(Decided June 1, 1911. 55 South. 522.)

1. *Nuisances; Public; Special Injury.*—Where the value of property abutting on a street is lessened by the dumping of slag in the street, whereby the owner of the property is compelled to take a more round about way in travelling from his property to the business section of the city, such property owner sustains a special damage, and may file bill to abate the nuisance; and in determining the question the court will not compare the injury to the complainant by the maintenance of the nuisance with the inconvenience and expense accruing to the respondent in having to remove the slag elsewhere.

2. *Same; Abatement; Adequate Remedy at Law.*—One suffering special damages on account of the maintenance of a public nuisance is not deprived of his right to have the same abated by bill because he has a right of action at law for damages resulting from the maintenance of such nuisance.

APPEAL from Jefferson Chancery Court.

Heard before Hon. A. H. BENNERS.

Bill by Mrs. Mary McLaughlin against the Sloss-Sheffield Steel & Iron Company to abate a nuisance occasioned by the piling of slag in a street. Decree for complainant, and respondent appeals.

TILLMAN, BRADLEY & MORROW, for appellant. The first question to be considered is whether a general averment of mere circuity of route to reach complainant's property is sufficient to give the bill equity for injunctive relief, whether the circuity be great or small, or whether it be a slight or considerable inconvenience. We insist that such an averment is insufficient.—*Sloss-Sheffield Steel & Iron Co. v. Johnson*, 147 Ala. 384; *Keller v. Atchison R. R. Co.*, 28 Kan. 624; *Dantler v. I. U. S. R. R. Co.*, 34 L. R. A. 769; see also 59 Am. St. Rep.

795, 40 Am Rep. 598, 57 L. R. A. 282; 7 Cush. 254; 23
L. R. A. 392; 14 L. R. A. 822; 16 L. R. A. 591; *Albes v.
So. R. R. Co.*, 51 South. 327; *Jackson v. B. M. & F. Co.*,
154 Ala. 464; *Hall v. A. G. & A. R. R. Co.*, 48 South.
365. Counsel insist that the decisions relied on and
cited as upholding the principles laid down in *Sloss-
Sheffield Steel & Iron Co. v. Johnson supra* are not
applicable to the case made by the averments of the bill
then under consideration and they cite and discuss the
cases therein cited and ask a reconsideration of said
case. They further insist that the averment that the
obstruction consisted of a large pile of slag, shows a
permanent obstruction in the street, thus affording to
the complainant an adequate remedy at law in one suit.
—*Dennis v. M. & M. R. R. Co.* 137 Ala. 567; *Bowling
v. Crook*, 104 Ala. 130.

TOMLINSON & McCULLOUGH, for appellee. The
owner of private property abutting on a street is entitled to have a public nuisance abated as one suffering
special damages therefrom, who is compelled to take a
circuitous or roundabout way along other streets in
traveling between his property and the markets and
intercourse with the outside world by reason of the
stopping up of the abutting streets by dumping slag
therein.—*Sloss-Sheffield Steel & Iron Co. v. Johnson*,
147 Ala., page 384. A right to maintain a public nuisance cannot be acquired by prescription and a private
person is not estopped at any time to maintain a bill in
chancery to have said public nuisance abated.—*Richards v. Dougherty*, 133 Ala. 569; *Whaley v. Wilison*,
112 Ala. 627; *Mayor and Aldermen of Birmingham v.
Land*, 137 Ala. 538.

SAYRE, J.—Appellee filed her bill to abate a nuisance, a slag pile, deposited by the appellant so as to

cover and obstruct all passing along two adjacent and parallel public streets leading from complainant's property, which fronts on both streets, to the business center of the city of Birmingham. The facts alleged are in every substantial particular the same as in the case of *Sloss-Sheffield Co. v. Johnson,* 147 Ala. 384, 41 South. 907, 8 L. R. A. (N. S.) 226, 119 Am. St. Rep. 89. Showing her damage, to quote the bill, "complainant alleges that by reason of the obstruction of said portions of said avenues, and by reason of the more circuitous route therefrom necessary to be taken to approach her property, the value of her property is greatly impaired and injured, and she suffers thereby a special and particular damage beyond that suffered by the public in general by the obstruction of said portions of said avenues." An identical averment was contained in the bill in the *Johnson Case.* Counsel for appellant, criticising the decision in that case, and asking some recession therefrom, seem to treat it as placing the equity of the bill upon the mere fact that the obstruction there complained of drove complainant to a circuitous way, seeming to overlook the averment that the circuity of way was such as to greatly impair the value of complainant's property; but this last-mentioned averment was of material consequence, as going to show that complainant had suffered injury peculiar to herself, that is, injury in kind and degree different from that suffered by the public (*Walls v. Smith,* 167 Ala. 138, 52 South. 320), and it is entirely clear that such was the hypothesis of the court's conclusion that the bill contained equity. In this view of the case the question hardly requires further discussion. The mere circuity of travel caused by the obstruction is an inconvenience suffered in common by the complainant and all others having occasion to approach her property along these streets. But if the value of complainant's property has been diminished, that is an injury different in kind and degree from any suffered by the general public. True, it is to be gathered from the bill that the obstruction requires complainant to go only one block out of the way in passing between her property and the main parts of the city, and it may be that these blocks are of no very great length, for their length is not shown; but the averment is that this situation results in a depreciation of the value of her property. In the practical solution of questions of this kind, everything depends upon how far the obstruction may be away from complainant's property, what may be on the other side, and, in short, upon the relations developed by use between complainant's property and the trans-obstruction country. If complainant's property has been injured and its value diminished, as she alleges, she is entitled to the law's protection against the invasion of her rights, and the quantum of interest involved on her side will not, in favor of a wrongdoer, be weighed in scales too gross, nor can we afford to let her go without remedy because the detriment to her property involved in the maintenance of the obstruction may be small in comparison with the inconvenience and expense that will come to defendant if it shall be required to deposit its slag at another place where it lawfully may.

Appellant also insists that complainant appears to have an adequate remedy at law and that she ought to be relegated to the law forum. The same argument, rested upon the same authorities now cited, was made in *Johnson's Case. supra.* Appellant quotes this language from the case of *Dennis v. M. & M. Ry. Co.*, 137 Ala. 649, 35 South. 30, 97 Am. St. Rep. 69: "For an injury to real property of a permanent character, without other special damage, the depreciation of the market value of the land furnishes the measure of damages, and such damages are, in a case proper in other respects, recoverable in a single action at law." In that case the complainant's real grievance was, not merely that the street had been obstructed, but that it had been vacated. There is a difference between obstruction and vacation. The one has no authority of law; the other has. The one is a nuisance; the other is not. In the *Dennis Case* the court argued that if it should be assumed that the city council, under whose authority the defendant there acted, was without power to authorize the erection of the warehouse on the part of the street, yet the obstruction was permanent, the defendant able to answer, and complainant had an adequate remedy at law. Just why that structure, if it had no authority of law, should have been considered permanent, does not appear. Whatever may have been the reasons for that conclusion, in the case at bar the alleged obstruction put by defendant in the streets need not be permanent. It is without authority of law. It is in fact and in law abatable. No doubt, if the complainant had recovered a judgment against the defendant for damages on account of the nuisance alleged, and had laid her damages at the whole injury to her property, past and prospective, she would be estopped to deny the adequacy of her legal remedy; for it would seem clear that if a person has suffered injury from a nuisance, which he has elected to treat as permanent by suing for and recovering damages which it will cause in the future, he ought not to be permitted to recover in successive suits damages by piece-meal for which he has had compensation in solido, or to have other relief which must proceed upon the theory that complainant has not been fully compensated for the wrong and injury done.—*Sloss-*

[Harris, et al. v. Cosby, et al.]

Sheffield Co. v. Mitchell, 161 Ala. 278, 49 South. 851.
Still the plaintiff in such a case has not had a full, adequate, and complete remedy; for he is entitled to have,
not only the value of his property as it was, but to have
the unimpaired and undisturbed use of it and of the
street in connection with it. If, then, the owner refuses
to treat as permanent a nuisance which is in law and in
fact abatable, he can have no adequate redress at law;
for he would be put to repeated suits, and his compensation could not be measured and ascertained with any
degree of precision. We see, therefore, no occasion for
a withdrawal of anything said in the *Johnson Case.*

Appellant suggests some other considerations, but
they are not based upon averments to be found in the
bill, and cannot be brought into the case on this appeal.
The chancellor's decree overruling the demurrer was
correct.

A ffirmed.

DOWDELL, C. J., and ANDERSON and SOMERVILLE, JJ.,
concur.

Harris, *et al. v.* Cosby, *et al.*

Bill to Determine the Right to Certain Church Property.

(Decided Feb. 2, 1911. Re-hearing denied Apr. 27, 1911.
55 South. 231.)

1. *Religious Societies; Presbyterian Church; General Assembly;
Authority; Constitution.*—Under the constitution of the Cumberland Presbyterian Church, with the consent of the majority of the
Presbyteries, the General Assembly of said church could abolish itself and create another supreme judicial legislative body, and hence
had constitutional power to carry out a desire to unite the Cumberland Presbyterian Church with the Presbyterian Church of the

[Harris. et al. v. Cosby, et al.]

United States of America, and to so modify the church creed and government as to make such union possible.

2. *Same; Church Government; Right of Majority.*—Where property is held by a religious congregation which, by virtue of its organization, is strictly independent of other ecclesiastical associations, and. so far as church government is concerned, owes no fealty to higher authority, and its principles of government is that the majority rule, then the majority of the members are entitled to control the property

3. *Same; Church; Courts; Decisions; Conclusiveness.*—Where an eccle-iastical body or congregation holding property is but a subordinate member of some general church organization in which there are superior ecclesiastical tribunals with a general and ultimate power of control in some supreme judiciary over the whole membership. the determination of questions of ecclesiastical rule, discipline or faith, by the highest of such judiciatories, will be regarded as binding on the civil courts.

4. *Same; Church Adjudicatories; Jurisdiction; Union with Other Churches.*—Under the constitution of the Cumberland Presbyterian Church the general assembly, with the consent of the Presbyteries, had full power to conduct proceedings for union with the Presbyterian Church of America, such general assembly being the highest judicatory in that church, and it also had power to determine that the proceedings to carry out the desired union had been legally and constitutionally conducted. and that the union had been effectuated, notwithstanding the constitution of the church. since it must be regarded as a grant rather than a limitation of power.

5. *Same; Civil Rights; Doctrine.*—Where a civil right depends upon an ecclesiastical matter. its determination is for the civil. and not for the ecclesiastical courts though the civil court try only the civil rights, taking the ecclesiastical decisions out of which the right arises as it finds it.

6. *Charities; Religious Doctrine; Judicial Determination.*—Where property is devoted to the teaching of some specific form of religious doctrine by the express terms of the deed or will, the courts. as in all cases. of special trust, will take jurisdiction to see that the property is not diverted from the special purpose for which it has been conveyed.

APPEAL from Birmingham City Court.

Heard before Hon. H. A. SHARPE.

Bill by P. H. Harris and others as trustees and members of the First Cumberland Presbyterian Church of Birmingham against W. M. Cosby and others to determine the right to possession to certain church property. Decree for respondents, and complainants appeal. Affirmed.

[Harris, et al. v. Cosby, et al.]

NATHAN L. MILLER, H. C. SELHEIMER, CARMICHEL & WYNN, W. C. CALDWELL and W. V. LAMB, for appellant. There was *no power* in the General Assembly acting alone, nor in the General Assembly with the aid of an affirmative answer from a majority of the Presbyteries to the question submitted to the Presbyteries, to effectuate the union attempted to be consummated between the Presbyterian Church in the United States of America and the Cumberland Presbyterian Church, and the action taken therein is contrary to the constitution, without authority *ultra vires* and void.—*Broyles v. Roberts*, 222 Mo. 613, 121 S. W. 805; *Landrith v. Hudgins*, 120 S. W. 783; *Clark et al. v. Brown*, 108 S. W. 421; *General Assembly of the Free Church of Scotland v. Lord Overton et al.;* 20 The Times Law Reports, 730; *Medical and Surgical Society v. Weatherly*, 76 Ala. 567; *Sullivan v. L. & N. R. R. Co.*, 138 Ala. 650, 662; 2 Page on Contracts, Secs. 1123, 1130; *Robins v. Clark*, 127 U. S. 622; *L. & N. R. R. Co. v. Shepard*, 126 Ala. 416, 422; *Bullock Co. v. Coleman*, 136 Ala. 610, 615. Webster's Int. Dictionary, "Limited" and "By" Standard Dictionary, "Limited" and "By." 5 Words & Phrases, pp. 4167, 4164; 25 Cyc. 960; 6 Cyc. 262; *First Cumberland Pres. Ch. v. Keith;* 2 Page on Contracts, Sec. 1126, pp. 1751, 1752; *Gadsden & A. N. Railway Company v. G. L. & Imp. Company*, 128 Ala. 510; *The Phaa. W. & B. R. R. Co. v. Trimble, et al.*, 77 U. S. 367; *Abercrombie & W. v. Vandiver*, 126 Ala. 513, 534; *Cincinnati v. Coke Company*, 41 N. E. 234. There is no power conferred upon the General Assembly and Presbyteries to form a new Christian denomination out of the Cumberland Presbyterian Church and another denomination of Christians or in such manner to form another body of any character or to merge the Cumberland Presbyterian Church into another denomination. The proceedings had by which the alleged union was sought to be effectuated did not constitute an amendment to the Constitution of the Cumberland Presbyterian Church.—*Broyles v. Roberts,* 121 S. W. 805; *Clark v. Brown,* 108 S. W. 421; *Collier v. Frierson,* 24 Ala. 100; *State of Miss. ex rel. v. Powell,* 48 L. R. A. 652; 8 Cyc. 719; *Ex parte Cowart,* 98 Ala. 94, 99, 100. Such power as was vested in the General Assembly and Presbyteries to amend the Constitution was not exercised in the mode and manner prescribed by the Constitution, as regards any of the proceedings had relating to the alleged union, and considered as an amendment said proceedings are void and of no effect.—Authorities, supra; *Landrith v. Hudgings,* 120 S. W. 783. The joint report on union and reunion made to and adopted by the respective General Assemblies contemplated that only a part of the plan of union should be submitted to the Presbyteries for their approval or disapproval, or acted upon by them.—Authorities supra. The alleged "Reunion and Union" if any such has been consummated, *is a merger* of the Cumberland Presbyterian Church into the then already existing *Presbyterian Church in the United States of America,* and not an union with another organization creating a new ecclesiastical organization or denomination having its origin in such union.—*Broyles v. Roberts,* 121 S. W. 805; *Clark v. Brown,* 108 S. W. 421; *Landrith v. Hudgins,* 120 S. W. 783; *First Cum. Pres. Chrch v. Keith,* opinion by Bullock Chancellor. "Civil Courts are presumed to know all the law touching property rights, and if questions of ecclesiastical law connected with property rights come before them, they are compelled to decide them. They have no power to abdicate their own jurisdiction and transfer it to other tribunals." The decrees and judgments of ecclesiastical courts are not final and conclusive upon the Civil

courts, in the determination by the civil courts, of property rights.—*Broyles v. Roberts*, 121 S. W. 805; *Hous-
ton v. Howe*, 162 Ala. 500, 503; *State ex rel. McNeil v.
Bibb Street Church*, 84 Ala. 23; *Christian Church v.
Sommers*, 149 Ala. 145, 18, 19; *Brundage v. Deardorff*,
55 Fed. 839; *Hundley v. Collins*, 131 Ala. 234; *R. R.
Coms. of Ala. v. Central of Ga. R. R. Co.*, 170 Fed. 225,
237; *Clarke v. Brown*, 108 S. W. 421; *Landrith v. Hudgins*, 120 S. W. 783; *First Cumberland Pres. Church v.
Keith*, opinion by Bullock, Chancellor. *The title to
Church property of a divided congregation* is in that
part of it which adheres to the original organization and
is acting in harmony with its own laws and the ecclesiastical customs, usages and principles which were
accepted among them before the dispute arose.—*McAuley's Appeal*, 77 Pa. 397; *Broyles v. Roberts*, 121 S. W.
805, 813. The property in question is charged with a
specific trust and devoted to the maintenance of the
Cumberland Presbyterian Church as such church
existed in September, 1872, and the present application
of it to the maintenance of a Presbyterian Church of
the United States of America, is a diversion of said
trust.—*Landrith v. Hudgins*, 120 S. W. 783. A party
holding property in trust and diverting it from the use
charged upon it may be directed to deliver same to complainants and pay damages for detention.—*Elec. L. Co.
v. Rust*, 131 Ala. 484, 491, 492.

JOHN M. GAUT, SAM'L D. WEAKLEY, and JOE C.
HALE, for appellee. The union has been upheld by the
Supreme Court of Georgia, Kentucky, Texas, California, Illinois, Indiana and Arkansas.—*Ramsey v. Hicks*,
91 N. E. 344; *First Presbyterian Church v. First Cumberland Church*, 91 N. E. 761; *Sanders v. Baggerly*, 131
S. W. 48; *Watson v. Jones*, 13 Wall. 679; *Hundley v.

Collins, 131 Ala. 234. Under these authorities it is contended that the union was properly brought about and that the decree of the lower court should be in all things affirmed.

SIMPSON, J.—This is a bill in equity filed by the appellants as trustees and members of the First Cumberland Presbyterian Church of Birmingham against the appellees, who are claimed by the bill to have abandoned the Cumberland Presbyterian Church, and become members of the Presbyterian Church, U. S. A.

The matter involved is certain property in Birmingham, Ala., which originally belonged to the Cumberland Presbyterian Church, and is claimed by the respondents as representatives of the Presbyterian Church, U. S. A. by virtue of a union effected by that church with the Cumberland Presbyterian Church, while the complainants claim that said union was never legally consummated, and that they, representing the Cumberland Presbyterian Church, are entitled to the property, and that the respondents should be enjoined, etc. So the question to be decided is whether or not the Cumberland Presbyterian Church has been united with the Presbyterian Church, U. S. A., under the name of the latter.

The Presbyterian Church, U. S. A., is a denomination of Christians holding as their doctrinal system the Confession of Faith, Catechisms, and form of government which were formulated by that famous assembly of learned men of the time called by the English Parliament to meet in Westminster Abbey, in London, in 1643, hence called the Westminster Assembly, which labored for 5½ years, and, besides the doctrinal standards, claimed to be based directly on the Holy Scriptures, also presented a form of government. republican

[Harris, et al. v. Cosby, et al.]

in form, as distinguished from monarchial or hierarchical, on the one hand, and from the strictly democratic, or congregational form, on the other, in which the people of each congregation vote directly on all matters pertaining to the church. Under this system the people vote on nothing save the matters pertaining to the congregation, the election of the pastor, and of church officers and trustees. The Session, composed of the pastor and ruling elders, is the ruling body of the church. The Session elects delegates to the Presbytery and Synod; each pastor being ex officio a member of each. The Presbytery elects delegates, called "commissioners," to the General Assembly. These are called "Judicatories," but they possess not only judicial, but legislative, powers, and the General Assembly is the supreme judicatory of last resort. We will allude more in detail to its powers later on, for the form of government of the Cumberland Presbyterian Church is the same as that of the Presbyterian Church, U. S. A.

In the year 1810, there being differences of opinion among the members of said church in regard to the interpretation of certain of the standards of faith in their confession, three ministers withdrew from said church, and organized an independent Presbytery called the "Cumberland Presbytery." They claimed that a proper interpretation of certain articles in said Confession of Faith amounted to fatalism, while the Presbyterian Church, U. S. A., claimed that such was not their meaning. They also claimed that a certain other article indicated that some infants are lost eternally, while the other contended that it meant nothing of the kind, and that it was only an explanation of how infants are saved. The Cumberlands also thought that the requirements for the education of the ministry were too strict. Thus it will be seen that one party simply interpreted

their standards one way and the other another, and the
lay mind, in contemplating the long contention over,
and final adjustment of these abstruse theological questions, is reminded of the fabled battle between the two
knights as to whether the shield was brass or copper,
who, when they saw both sides, found it brass on one
side and copper on the other. However, on the 4th day
of February, 1810, the Cumberland Presbytery was organized by three ministers who state that they are regularly ordained ministers of the Presbyterian Church,
that they have waited four years for a redress of their
grievances, and a restoration of their rights. They
then proceed to define the qualifications of candidates
for the ministry thereafter, to wit, "that they shall be
required to receive and adopt the Confession and Discipline of the Presbyterian Church, except the idea of fatality, which seems to be taught under the mysterious
doctrine of predestination. It is to be understood,
however, that such as can clearly receive the Confession without an exception shall not be required to make
any." They then provide for the qualifications of the
ministry (educationally). The Presbytery subsequently adopted "a circular letter," addressed "to the Societies and Brethren of the Presbyterian Church," etc.,
stating their differences, and stating that "the exception or condition in which they were indulged was only
designed to meet some conscientious scruples, in points
not fundamental or essential, particularly the idea of
fatality, that seemed to some of them to be there taught,
under the high and mysterious doctrine of predestination." They also state in said circular "that we have it
in view as a Presbytery to continue or make another
proposition to the Synod of Kentucky or some other
Synod for a reunion. If we can obtain it without violating our natural and scriptural rights, it will meet
the most ardent wish of our hearts."

[Harris, et al. v. Cosby, et al.]

Afterwards a Synod was formed, followed by others, and a General Assembly. The Confession of Faith was revised, and in reporting it to the General Assembly in 1882 the committee state: "We have not changed a single doctrine fundamental to your scheme of theology, or any of its correlates," and that no material changes were made in the government of the church "except such as were found necessary to present more clearly the practice and usage of the church courts and such as were deemed proper to develop more certainly our work and resources," and that "in the constitution, which takes the place of what is now termed 'form of government,' are included only those fundamental principles, which, with the Rules of Discipline, are not to be changed without the approval of the Presbyteries," while the General Assembly alone is allowed to make changes in general regulations, not fundamental in character, "Directory of Worship and Rules of Order."

The General Assembly in adopting this report provides "that those who have heretofore received and adopted the Confession of Faith approved by the General Assembly in 1829, and who prefer to adhere to the doctrinal statements contained therein, are at liberty to do so." This matter was submitted to the Presbyteries for their vote on the same. In 1811 committees were appointed by the Cumberland Presbytery to confer with similar committees of the Presbyteries of Muhlenburg and West Tennessee (Presbyterian) on the subject of reunion, and in 1812 the Cumberland Presbytery unanimously adopted resolutions referring to the failure of said committees to agree, in one of which it is resolved "that this Presbytery have always been, and expect always to be, ready and willing for union with the general Presbyterian Church, on gospel principles."

Without entering into a tedious detail, the records of the Cumberland Presbyterian Church show that committees were appointed at different times to confer with similar committees of the Presbyterian Church, U. S., the Presbyterian Church, U. S. A., and the Evangelical Lutheran Church, in all of which their general agreement in doctrine and government was emphasized, and their differences were stated to be not fundamental, and the union was stated to be desirable.

This history shows that it has been one of the cardinal principles of the Cumberland Presbyterian Church since the organization of the first Presbytery that a union with the original church and other members of the Presbyterian family was desirable and would be effected, whenever, by mutual concession in the statement of their creeds, the Cumberland Church could go into the union without a sacrifice of principle. This history shows another fact important to the decision of this case, to wit, that the entire government of the church is committed to the church courts so called, which have both judicial and legislative power and authority, and that the individual members of the congregations are not called upon to vote, save to elect their elders; that the elders compose the Church Sessions, which elect members to the Presbyteries, and the Presbyteries elect members (called commissioners) to the General Assembly; and that the action of the General Assembly, confirmed by the vote of the majority of the Presbyteries, is the supreme law of the church. It will be noted that the first Presbytery was organized by three ministers alone, that subsequently the Synods and General Assembly were organized by the Presbyteries, and the Confession of Faith and constitution were adopted by the General Assembly, and its action confirmed by the Presbyteries, and there is no intimation that the people ever voted on any of these matters.

[Harris. et al. v. Cosby, et al.]

We will not unduly lengthen this opinion by discussing the successive steps by which the union was consummated. The Supreme Courts of Arkansas and California have summarized them very clearly, and shown that, although a short form of ballot was used, yet the entire plan of union was fairly and properly submitted to the Presbyteries.—*Sanders v. Baggerly* (Ark.) 131 S. W. 58, cols. 1, 2; *Permanent Com. of Missions (C. P. Ch.) v. Pacific Synod (Pres. Ch., U. S. A.)* 157 Cal. 105, 106 Pac. 395, 401.

According to the constitution of the Cumberland Presbyterian Church, the jurisdiction and powers of the various church courts are defined, and by it the General Assembly is the supreme judicial, and also the supreme legislative body. In its legislative capacity it is limited only by section 60 of said constitution, which provides that "upon the recommendation of the General Assembly, at a stated meeting, by a two-thirds vote of the members thereof voting thereon, the Confession of Faith, Catechism, Constitution, and Rules of Discipline, may be amended or changed, when a majority of the Presbyteries, upon the same being transmitted for their action, shall approve thereof," and then provides that other changes may be made by the General Assembly alone. Section 40 provides that "the General Assembly is the highest court of this church, and represents in one body all the particular churches thereof, * * * and constitutes the bond of union, peace, correspondence, and mutual confidence among all its churches and courts." If the General Assembly, with the concurrence of the Presbyteries, could adopt the Confession of Faith and the constitution, it would seem to necessarily follow that they could amend or change it. It cannot be doubted that, under this constitution, the General Assembly, with the concurrence of the

Presbyteries, could abolish the General Assembly and create another supreme judicial and legislative body, and certainly could carry out the expressed desire of the church from its inception to reunite it with the church from which it so reluctantly separated by the satisfactory adjustment of differences which it has repeatedly said were not fundamental.

The entire history of the Presbyterian family of churches is a history of divisions, separations, and reunions always effected by the action of the representative bodies, and not by the body of the people directly. In fact, it seems to be admitted, and it is true, that all church as well as other organizations have the inherent power to unite with other similar organizations; the only question being whether that power resides in official authorities, or in the people, by majority or by the consent of every individual. We think we have shown that the supreme power is by the constitution of this church lodged in the General Assembly with a concurrence of the Presbyteries. But, as the church has created a supreme judicial tribunal, it is important to decide whether it has passed on this matter and what is its binding force on the decision of this court. If the General Assembly with the concurrence of a majority of the Presbyteries had the power to change the constitution and effect the union, it necessarily follows that, unless there is some constitutional restriction, they must determine the terms of the union, and whether there has come about such an agreement in doctrine as to justify the union. But to the point as to whether the General Assembly in its judicial capacity has passed upon the legality of the union. It is insisted that it is incongruous for the same body to decide judicially that its legislative acts are constitutional. It may be that, when the Constitution of the United States was (as

claimed) modeled on the form of government of the
Presbyterian Church, it was a wise provision which differentiated the two by separating entirely the executive, judicial, and legislative branches of the government; yet the fact remains that, according to the constitution of this church, they are not so separated, but, on
the contrary, the judicial and legislative departments
are united in one body. That being the case, it follows
that the supreme judicial body must pass upon the constitutionality of its own acts in connection with that of
the Presbyteries required to concur with it. Did it do
this?

In its legislative capacity it passed the resolutions
adopting the report of the committee, which, in connection with a similar committee of the Presbyterian
Church, U. S. A., had formulated the plan for a union
of the two churches, and sent the matter down to the
Presbyteries for their action on the same. The reports
from the Presbyteries came in. The committee appointed for that purpose, by a majority report, reported
that a majority of the Presbyteries had voted in favor
of the plan of union, and presented a resolution "that
this General Assembly does hereby find and declare that
a constitutional majority of the Presbyteries of the
Cumberland Presbyterian Church have voted approval
of the reunion and union of said churches upon the basis set forth in said joint report, and does find and declare that said reunion and union has been constitutionally agreed to by the Cumberland Presbyterian
Church, and that said basis of union has, for the purposes of the union, been constitutionally adopted."

There was a minority report, stating, among other
things, "(1) that there is no power given the General
Assembly, by the constitution of the Cumberland Presbyterian Church, to negotiate, enter into, or confirm

such union as is proposed, and was submitted by the Moderator and Clerk of our Assembly; (2) that such action is contrary to, and in violation of, the provision and spirit of the constitution of the Cumberland Presbyterian Church, and such action is without authority and void." It will thus be seen that the legality and constitutionality of the adoption of the plan of union was distinctly presented to this supreme judicature, and it adopted the majority report, thus deciding the question in favor of the regularity and constitutionality of the adoption of the plan of union. In the case of *Watson v. Jones,* 13 Wall. 679, 20 L. Ed. 666, there having been a schism in the church, it was a question as to which of two sets of officers represented the Walnut Street Church.

The court classifies the questions which have come before the courts in regard to rights of property held by ecclesiastical bodies into three, to wit, first, when the property, by the express terms of the deed or will, is devoted to the teaching of some specific form of religious doctrine; second, when the property is held by a religious congregation which, by the virtue of its organization, is strictly independent of other ecclesiastical associations, and, so far as church government is concerned, owes no fealty or obligation to any higher authority; and, third, where the religious congregation or ecclesiastical body holding the property is but a subordinate member of some general church organization, in which there are superior ecclesiastical tribunals with a general and ultimate power of control more or less complete, in some supreme judiciary over the whole membership of that general organization.

The court recognizes that in the first class the court will, as in all special trusts, see that the property is not diverted from the special purpose for which it has been conveyed.

[Harris, et al. v. Cosby, et al.]

In the second class, if the principle of government be that the majority rules, then the majority of the members have the right to control the property.

In the third class (which applies to the case now under consideration), to wit, "property acquired in any of the usual modes for the general use of a religious congregation which is itself a part of a large and general organization of some religious denomination, with which it is more or less intimately connected by religious views and ecclesiastical government," the court is "bound to look at the fact that the local congregation is itself but a member of a much larger and more important religious organization, and is under its government and control, and is bound by its orders and judgments," and, after referring to the Presbyterian system of the church session, the Presbytery, the Synod, and the General Assembly, over all, the court says: "In this class of cases we think the rule of action which should govern the civil courts, founded on a broad and sound view of the relations of church and state under our system of laws, and supported by a preponderating weight of judicial authority, is that, whenever the question of discipline or of faith or ecclesiastical rule, custom, or law has been decided by the highest of these church judicatories to which the matter has been carried, the legal tribunals must accept such decisions as final, and as binding on them, in their application to the case before them." It is conceded by the court that the doctrine of the English courts is otherwise, but in this country, where there is no union of church and state, where the laws know no heresy, and churches are not voluntary religious organizations, with the same right that other voluntary associations have to adopt their own form of government, "and to create tribunals for the decision of controverted questions," "all who

unite themselves to such a body do so with an implied
consent to this government, and are bound to submit
to it."

Quoting from the case of *Harmon v. Dreher,* Speer's
Eq. (S. C.) 87, reaffirmed in the *Johns Island Church
Case,* 2 Rich. Eq. (S. C.) 215, the court says: "When
a civil right depends upon an ecclesiastical matter, it is
the civil court, and not the ecclesiastical court, which
is to decide.   But the civil tribunal tries the civil right,
and no more, taking the ecclesiastical decisions out of
which the civil right arises as it finds them." We hold
this to be a clear statement of sound law, but we do not
accept the intimation in the following portion of the
opinion (though it is not directly said) that the matters
of ecclesiastical law are so metaphysical and abstruse
that the civil court will not inquire into the jurisdiction of the ecclesiastical court. Upon principle its decisions must stand upon the basis of any other court
or tribunal having the right and power to pass upon
any matter; and, however difficult it may be, the civil
court must ascertain whether or not it had jurisdiction,
and according to the decisions of our own courts, when
it is charged with the ascertainment of the jurisdictional facts, its ascertainment is final.

This is in accordance with the decisions of the Su-
preme Court of the United States and of our own court.
—*Rose v. Himely,* 4 Cranch, 241, 269, 2 L. Ed. 608;
Wilcox v. Jackson, 13 Pet. 498, 511, 10 L. Ed. 264;
Hickey's Lessee v. Stewart, 3 How. 750, 762, 11 L. Ed.
814; *Elliott v. Piersol,* 1 Pet. 328, 340, 7 L. Ed. 164;
Thompson v. Whitman, 18 Wall. 457, 466, 21 L. Ed.
897; *In re Sawyer,* 124 U. S. 200, 220, 8 Sup. Ct. 482, 31
L. Ed. 402; *Ex parte Terry,* 128 U. S. 289, 305, 9 Sup.
Ct. 77, 32 L. Ed. 405; *Kingsbury v. Yniestra,* 59 Ala.
320; *Hunt & Condry v. Mayfield,* 2 Stew. 124; *Kohn,
Leiberman & Co. v. Haas,* 95 Ala. 478, 12 South. 577.

From what has been said and quoted in regard to the constitution of the Cumberland Presbyterian Church, even though it be admitted that said constitution is a grant of power, like the Constitution of the United States, and not a limitation of power, as our state Constitutions are, according to the great leading decision of *Dorman v. State,* 34 Ala. 216, we hold that this jurisdiction is distinctly conferred by the constitution of the Cumberland Presbyterian Church, and consequently the decision of that high tribunal must control the decision of this court, to the effect that the union of the two churches has been legally and constitutionally effected.

It is insisted by the appellants that "the first and great principle of the duties of a society—nation, state or church—towards itself, as a society distinguished from its government, is self-preservation." It is true that Vattel states the general principle that a nation in carrying out its obligation to promote the general welfare "is obliged to perform the duty of self-preservation," but the learned author goes on to remark that "it is therefore not absolute, but conditional; that is to say, it supposes a human act, to wit, the social compact, and as compacts may be dissolved by the common consent of the parties—if the individuals that compose the nation should unanimously agree to break the link that binds them, it will be lawful for them to do so, and thus destroy the state or the nation."—Law of Nations, c. 2, § 16.

Other quotations are made from various writers, to the effect that a state or nation which existed before the adoption of its constitution remains a state or nation through successive changes in its constitution. Among others Wheaton is quoted, as saying that "such a body or society, when once organized as a state, by an established government, must remain so until it is destroyed. This may be done by disintegration of its parts, by its absorption into and identification with some other state or nation, or by the absolute and total dissolution of the ties which bind the society together. We know of no other way in which it can cease to be a state."

Even as to a state, if it has the power by the vote of its people to break the link that binds the people together, to disintegrate its parts and to be absorbed into, or identified with some other state, it follows that, if the only bond of union is a written constitution which prescribes how it may be changed, then, when that constitution is changed in the manner prescribed, the powers that made that constitution have consented to that change, whether it be merely to place it under a different legislative body, to identify it with some other organization, or to disintegrate its parts. In fact, the substance of all these utterances is that only the power which creates can destroy. Judge Cooley, also, is quoted as saying that "a written constitution is in every instance a limitation upon the powers of government in the hands of its agents; for there never was a written republican constitution which delegated to functionaries all the latent powers which lie dormant in every nation, and are boundless in extent and incapable of definition."—Cooley, Const. Lim. (7th Ed.) p. 69. This expression is preceded by the statement that the constitution is not the beginning of a community, nor the origin of private rights, that it presupposes organized society, law, order, etc. Evidently the learned author is not referring to changes in government, or to the substitution of one supreme authority for another, but to personal freedom, political freedom, etc., which he holds to be inalienable.

It is true, also, as stated by Judge Cooley, that a mere legislative body cannot delegate its authority, but that has no application to the abolition of one legislative body and the setting up of another by a change in the constitution. Motley, in his great History of the Rise of the Dutch Republic, says: "The signers of the declaration of independence acted in the name and by the authority of the Netherland people. The estates were in the constitutional representatives of that people," and, the king's sovereignty having been forfeited, "inquiring what had become of the sovereignty, they found it not in the mass of the people, but in the representative body, which actually personated the people."—Volume 3, p. 515. Such changes and unions of states are not unknown in the history of governments. Scotland was an independent kingdom, and yet, by the action of her Parliament, and without any vote of the people, she ceased to be an independent kingdom and became a part of the kingdom of Great Britain, her Parliaments ceased to meet, and she is simply represented in the British Parliament as England is. The same is true of Ireland. It matters not that the Scottish King James VI became King James I of England. Scotland maintained an independent kingdom, afterwards had its own king (James VII), and the union was effected in the reign of Queen Anne by concurrent acts of the Scottish Parliament and that of England. It is true that this was not a republic, but it was the act of a representative body, uniting Scotland with England, under the British crown, which, according to the theory contended for, could not be done without the consent of every citizen. Texas was an independent republic, yet it surrendered its independence, and became one of the family of states under the Constitution of the United States. The treaties and negotiations for annexation were carried on by the Texas Congress and governmental officials with those of the United States, and while, as under their Constitution the Congress did not have the power to change their Constitution, the matter was referred, for ratification, to a convention, which was to change the Constitution so as to harmonize it with the new relations about to be assumed, yet that convention was a representative body, and, if the powers conferred upon it had been originally conferred on Congress, it cannot be doubted that it could have completed the annexation without a reference to the convention. This illustration at least shows that it is not correct to say that a republic cannot efface itself and enter into a union with another power without the consent of every individual in it. The quotation from the case of *McCulloch v. State of Maryland*, 4 Wheat. 404, 4 L. Ed. 579, to the effect that "the powers delegated to state sovereignties were to be exercised by themselves, and that while they were competent to enter into the confederacy, by mere legislative action, yet when the 'more perfect union' came to be formed it was referred to the conventions called for that purpose," was merely the basis of an argument that the people who had conferred the powers of sovereignty on their state Legislatures could withdraw a portion of that sovereignty and confer it on the United States government. So in this case the Assembly, with the concurrence of the Presbyteries which had adopted the Constitution, could change it, so as to place at the head of the sovereign power another General Assembly, thus effecting the union. But it is not necessary to pursue this point further. While it is true that the government of this church is republican in form, yet it is not a state or nation, but merely a voluntary religious association, or, in other words, a voluntary corporation. Its constitution was adopted in the same way that this plan of union was adopted, and all members who have come into it entered it subject to the fundamental law of its organization. The change made in its constitution did not disintegrate its churches or its Presbyteries, but simply substituted for its General Assembly the General Assembly of the re-united church, and, as shown, this was within the powers conferred, and was accomplished in the way provided by its constitution, and the only way, according to its constitution, by which the church, as a body, could act. It is not only not unusual, but it is in accordance with the law and practice of corporations generally, for, as a general rule, so far from being indestructible, the charters of corporations and statutes for their organization provide how they may be dissolved, and how united with other corporations, and, whenever the course prescribed is pursued, the union is accomplished or the corporation dissolved and ceases to exist.

The decree of the court is affirmed.

Affirmed.

DOWDELL, C. J., and MAYFIELD, and SAYRE, JJ., concur. MCCLELLAN, J., not sitting.

Southern States Fire & Casualty Ins. Co. *v.* Whatley.

Bill to Cancel Contract and Notes.

(Decided May 18, 1911. 55 South. 620.)

1. *Cancellation of Instrument; Equity Jurisdiction; Legal Remedy* —A court of equity has jurisdiction to cancel a fraudulent contract at the instance of the injured party, notwithstanding he may sue at law upon the covenants of warrant therein, or for deceit.

2. *Parties; Transferee of Notes.*—Where the bill to rescind a contract for the purchase of stock and for the surrender and cancellation of the notes given therefor, on the grounds of fraud inducing the purchase, avers that on discovery of the fraud, and before the certificates of stock was received, complainant offered to rescind the contract and the respondent declined, and also refused to deliver him his notes, and that the notes were discounted and the proceeds placed to the credit of the defendant, the bill shows equity and can be maintained, whether the holder be a bona fide holder or not, and whether the bank discounting the note be joined as a party respondent or not.

3. *Equity; Remedy at Law; Adequacy.*—The test of equity jurisdiction, where there is a concurrent remedy at law is whether the remedy is adequate and will not subject the party to vexatious litigation.

4. *Same; Demurrer; Sufficiency.*—Where the bill has equity independent of the defect set up in the demurrer, a demurrer addressed to the whole bill should be overruled.

APPEAL from Birmingham Chancery Court.

Heard before Hon. A. H. BENNERS.

Bill by R. L. Whatley against the Southern States Fire & Casualty Company. From a decree overruling a demurrer to the bill respondent appeals. Affirmed.

The case made by the bill is that an agent of the respondent approached the complainant for the purpose of selling him stock in the respondent company and in order to induce complainant to purchase he represented first that the certificate which was issued to him would show on its face that the stock was $25 per share; second that the respondent had already declared a dividend of 25 per cent. upon its stock which would be divided between them, and that if the complainant bought stock then he would participate in a division of the dividend; and, third, that Adam Glass, a prominent citizen and business man of Mobile, had already purchased stock in said corporation in the amount of $1,250; that, relying on these representations, he was induced to and did purchase 55 shares of stock, for which he executed his two promissory notes, for the sum of $520 and $910, respectively, and that the said

[Southern States Fire & Casualty Ins. Co. v. Whatley.]

notes were discounted by said Cozart to the Bank of
Wilmer, and that the amount was placed to the credit
of the Southern States Fire & Casualty Insurance Company. It is alleged that the representations were
untrue when made, and are still untrue, and that they
were fraudulently made for the purpose of inducing
the purchase, and that as soon as complainants discovered the falsity of said representation, and before he
received his certificates of stock he offered to rescind
said contract, and the respondents declined and failed,
and also refused to deliver him his notes or a sum of
money equal thereto. It is then alleged that the stock
was forwarded the Bank of Wilmer, but that complainant refused to receive it, and so notified the bank, with
the request that they notify respondent. The demurrers raise the point that there is not equity in the bill,
nor offer by the complainant to do equity; plain, adequate, and complete remedy at law; and because the bill
shows on its face that said notes are not in possession
or under the control of defendant, but have passed into
the hands of the purchaser for value, and that this court
is therefore without the power or jurisdiction to decree
the cancellation of or to return them.

LAMKIN & WATTS, for appellant. Having failed to
make the holder of the notes a party, and the only relief
that could be granted being the rescision of the contract
and a money judgment for the value of the notes, the
case cannot be maintained.—*Sadler's Case*, 2 Stew. 520.
Fraud itself is never a ground of equity jurisdiction.—
Knotts v. Tarver, 8 Ala. 743; *Smith v. Cockrell*, 66 Ala.
77; *Merritt v. Ehrman*, 116 Ala. 278; *Ins. Co. v. Kemp-
ber*, 73 Ala. 225. The appellee has a plain, complete
and adequate remedy at law.—*Barnett v. Warren*, 82
Ala. 557; *Landford v. Lee*, 119 Ala. 248; *Hudson v.*

Scott, 125 Ala.. 172; 27 Cyc. 851. It follows therefore that the court erred in overruling the demurrers to the bill.

GORDON & EDDINGTON, and PAUL A. SAVAGE, for appellee. The bill alleges a legal fraud and hence contains equity.—Section 4298, Code 1907. The remedy at law is not plain and adequate as used to deny jurisdiction to equity.—*Foster v. Kennedy*, 38 Ala. 359; *Moncrief v. Wilkinson*, 93 Ala. 373. When a material fact is misrepresented and the other party relies and acts upon it, a court of equity will rescind the contract.—*Lester v. Mahon*, 25 Ala. 445; *Merritt v. Ehrman*, 116 Ala. 279; *Perry v. Boyd*. 126 Ala. 168. The allegation of misrepresentation and fraud were sufficient.—*Duy v. Higdon*, 162 Ala. 528; *Harrison v. Ala. Mid. Railway*, 144 Ala. 257.

ANDERSON, J.—The bill seeks to avoid the contract cf subscription to stock and the cancellation of notes executed for the purchase of same, and sets up that complainant was fraudulently induced to subscribe for said stock and execute said notes, by the false and fraudulent misrepresentation of material facts. A court of equity will entertain jurisdiction to cancel a fraudulent contract, at the instance of the injured party, notwithstanding he may sue at law upon the covenants of warranty or for deceit.—*Perry v. Boyd*, 126 Ala. 162, 28 South. 711, 85 Am. St. Rep. 17; *Cullum v. Bank*, 4 Ala. 21, 37 Am. Dec. 725; *Baptiste v. Peters*, 51 Ala. 158. The test is, not that he has a remedy at law, but whether or not the remedy will be adequate and complete, or that he will not be subjected to vexatious litigation at a distance of time.—*Merritt v. Ehrman*, 116 Ala. 278, 22 South. 51b.

The bill avers that the notes are held by the Bank of
Wilmer. Therefore the matters set up in the bill would
be no defense to the notes, if the bank is a bona fide
holder of same. The result is, if the complainant does
not pay them. he is subject to a suit in the future by the
bank, and would then have to seek his redress against
the respondent insurance company. On the other hand,
if the bank is not a bona fide holder of the notes, the
complainant will be put to the trouble and expense of
defending a suit on same. Although he may succeed,
yet success on his part in a litigation with the bank
would not necessarily cancel the contract of subscription; the respondent company not being a party. Moreover, the bill seeks in the alternative to make the respondent indemnify the complainant in case the notes cannot be delivered up and canceled. It is therefore apparent that the bill contains equity. The relief would no
doubt be more perfect and complete by making the
bank, the holder of the notes, a party to this cause, in
order that the chancery court could require the respondent, in case the complainant is entitled to relief, to
reimburse the bank and procure the notes, and deliver
or surrender them to this complainant or to the court
for cancellation; or if the bank is not a bona fide holder
of the notes, it, being the custodian of same, should be
made a party to the bill, in order that the court may
cancel same in the event the complainant is entitled to
cancel his subscription to the stock. This omission of
parties however is not essential to the equity of the bill,
and the chancery court did not err in overruling the
ground of demurrer proceeding upon that theory.

In so far as the bill seeks a cancellation of the notes,
it was subject to grounds 4 and 6 of the demurrer, had
they been directed at the bill in so far as it sought a
restoration or cancellation of the notes, instead of as a

whole. The bill has equity independent of the surrender or cancellation of the notes, as it seeks to cancel the issue of the stock and the alternative relief of reimbursing the complainant, in case the respondent cannot restore the notes now held by the bank. If a bill has equity independent of the point or defect set up in the demurrer, but the said demurrer is addressed to the whole bill, it should be overruled.—*Nelson v. Wadsworth,* 11 Ala. 603, 55 South. 120; *MacMahon v. MacMahon,* 170 Ala. 338, 54 South. 165; *Beall v. Lehman, Durr & Co.,* 110 Ala. 446, 18 South. 230.

The decree of the chancery court is affirmed.

Affirmed.

DOWDELL, C. J., and SAYRE and SOMERVILLE, JJ., concur.

Martin *v.* Martin, *et al.*

Bill to Remove an Estate from the Probate to the Chancery Court and for Other Purposes.

(Decided May 11, 1911. Rehearing denied June 8, 1911.
55 South. 632.)

1. *Divorce; Equity; Jurisdiction.*—The power to grant a divorce a vinculo is not within the general jurisdiction of courts of equity; their jurisdiction to grant divorces is purely statutory and although a court of general jurisdiction, yet when exercising a special authority in derogation of the common law, it is quoad hoc an inferior or limited court.

2. *Same: Decree; Jurisdictional Facts; Residence of Parties.*—Section 3802 Code 1907, established bona fide residence in this State for one year next before the filing of the bill as a jurisdictional prerequisite to a valid decree of divorce against a respondent who is a non-resident;. and this must be shown by the record in order for the decree to withstand a collateral attack.

3. *Same.*—The allegations of the bill for divorce stated and examined and held insufficient as jurisdictional averment of residence within the provisions of section 3802 Code 1907 to protect the de.

cree entered thereon against collateral attack, and declaring the decree void.

4. *Same; Jurisdiction; Residence; Pleading.*—It is not necessary that a pleading in an action for divorce adopt the exact terms of the statute as to the jurisdictional fact of residence; it is sufficient if the averments convey the same idea in equivalent terms.

5. *Courts; Jurisdiction; Shown by Record.*—The existence of jurisdictional facts in respect to judicial acts of courts exercising special and limited jurisdiction is not to be inferred from the mere exercise of that jurisdiction but must affirmatively appear from the record.

6. *Judgment; Collateral Attack; Presumption.*—On collateral attack of a judgment or decree there is no presumption of the existence of jurisdictional facts, but every reasonable intendent will be made in favor of the validity. thereof, as a matter of construction only; and where the pleading is reasonably susceptible of a construction presenting the essential jurisdictional facts, without supplying omitted essential averments, that construction will be adopted, but pleading must be understood as it is reasonable to infer that the party who made it and the judge who acted upon it understood it, and not as they were bound to understand it.

7. *Same; Laches.*—Where it appears from the face of the record that a judgment or decree is wholly void, delay or inaction by the party whose rights will·be affected thereby, will not invest the judgment or decree with any force as against a collateral attack, it being a nullity under all circumstances.

8. *Executors and Administrators; Action; Parties; Sureties on Bond.*—Where the bill is against the administrator to remove the administration of the estate from the probate to the chancery court the sureties on the administrator's bond are not proper parties.

APPEAL from Anniston City Court.

Heard before Hon. THOS. W. COLEMAN.

Bill by Gussie Martin against Ance Martin, as administrator of the estate of M. J. Martin, deceased, and others, for the removal of the estate from the probate to the chancery court, and for other purposes. From a decree for respondents, complainant appeals. Reversed in part, affirmed in part, and remanded.

The case made by the bill is substantially as follows: The complainant is alleged to be the widow of one M. J. Martin, who died intestate on the 6th day of February, 1910, at which time he was an inhabitant of Calhoun county. He left surviving him several children, and the complainant in the bill, claiming to be his widow,

and he died possessed of real and personal property in
this state, and his estate is in the course of administration in the probate court of Calhoun county. It is further alleged that on June 16, 1906, an original bill was
filed in the Cleburne county court by M. J. Martin, praying for a divorce from the complainant on certain statutory grounds, and that on the 9th day of August, 1906,
a final decree was entered in said cause, divorcing said
M. J. Martin, from said Gussie Martin. It is alleged
that at the time of the filing of said bill in Cleburne
county the said M. J. Martin, as well as the said Gussie
Martin, were both residents of Pope county, Ga., and
not residents of Cleburne county, Ala., and that the
complainant had not resided in the state of Alabama for
one year next before the filing of the bill, and it is
alleged that for that reason the Cleburne county court
acquired no jurisdiction to render the decree of divorce,
and hence it is void. The administrator of the estate of
M. J. Martin, the heirs at law, and the sureties on the
administrator's bond are made parties defendant, and
it is prayed that Gussie Martin be allowed dower rights
and a distributive share out of the estate of said M. J.
Martin. The demurrers of the administrator raise the
points decided in the opinion. Hanson and Studdard,
sureties on the bond of the administrator, interposed
demurrers because of improper joinders of parties
defendant. The other facts sufficiently appear from the
opinion.

BLACKWELL & AGEE, for appellant. By sustaining
the demurrer the learned chancellor held that the
divorce proceedings were regular and not subject to collateral attack. In this he was in error. The courts of
equity have no general jurisdiction to grant divorces a
vinculo.—9 A. & E. Encyc. Law, 746; Bishop Marriage

& Divorce, sec. 90. The jurisdiction is purely statutory.
—1 Pom. pp. 98, 112, 117. Hence, the statutes must be
strictly construed.—*Sayre v. Elyton Land Co.*, 73 Ala.
85; Sims Chan. Prac. sec. 382. They are therefore
courts of limited and inferior jurisdiction when granting a statutory divorce.—*Wells v. Am. Mort. Co.*, 123
Ala. 421; *Goodwater W. Co. v. Street*, 137 Ala. 621; *The
State v. M. & G. R. R. Co.*, 108 Ala. 31. The bill must
therefore show all jurisdictional facts, and under the
statute (sec. 3802, Code 1907) the fact of residence of
one year before the filing of the bill was jurisdictional.—
14 Cyc. 662, and authorities supra. This must be shown
by the allegata and probata.—*Joiner v. Winston*, 68
Ala. 129; *McCreary v. Remson*, 19 Ala. 430. Under
these authorities, it must be held that the decree was
void and the complainant was denied the right to show
these defects to her injury.—*Ingram v. Ingram*, 143
Ala. 130.

KNOX, ACKER, DIXON & BLACKMON, for appellee. As
to the construction to be given to the allegation of residence and non-residence in the bill for divorce, see *King
v. Kent*, 29 Ala. 542; *Pollack v. Hamrick*, 74 Ala. 334;
Whitlow v. Echols, 78 Ala. 208. On collateral attacked
the allegation should be construed as alleging sufficiently the necessary jurisdictional facts, and when so
construed they uphold the judgment and decree granting the divorce. A decree rendered upon service by publication in the manner prescribed by the statute, unless
controverted in the manner pointed out thereby and set
aside, is equally as binding and obligatory on the absent
defendant as if he had been served with process and had
appeared in answer to the bill.—*Harrison v. Harrison*,
19 Ala. 510; *Thompson v. State*, 28 Ala. 12; *Thompson
v. Thompson*, 91 Ala. 594. While a foreign judgment

may be impeached by showing a want of jurisdiction by
evidence dehors the record, a domestic judgment is not
subject to impeachment on collateral attack, unless its
invalidity appears upon the record.—*White v. Simpson*,
14 Ala. 238, 240; *Edgerton v. Edgerton*, 12 Mont. 122,
23 Am. St. Rep. 557, 574; *Perry v. King*, 117 Ala. 533;
Whitlow v. Echols, 78 Ala. 206; *Massey v. Smith*, 73
Ala. 173. In case of a judgment rendered by a domestic
court of general jurisdiction, there is presumption on
collateral attack that the court had jurisdiction both of
the person and the subject matter, and proceeded in the
due exercise of that jurisdiction.—*White v. Simpson*,
124 Ala. 238; *Robison v. Allison*, 97 Ala. 596; *Weaver v.
Brown*, 87 Ala. 533; *Wilson v. Wilson*, 18 Ala. 176; 23
Cyc. 1078, and authorities cited. Where a court of general jurisdiction has conferred upon it special powers
by statute and such special powers are exercised judicially, that is, according to the course of common law
and proceedings in chancery, the same presumption will
be indulged to uphold its judgments as prevails in the
exercise of its common law jurisdicion.—Black on Judgments, sec. 279; *Harvey v. Tyler*, 2 Wall. 328; *Galpin v.
Paige*, 18 Wall. 350; 28 Gratt. (Va.) 82. In case of a
judgment of a court of limited jurisdiction, or statutory
jurisdiction, if the jurisdictional facts are ascertained
by the court, or they appear of record, the judgment is
not subject to collateral attack. In determining whether
or not the jurisdictional facts appear of record, the language must be construed most favorably for the maintenance of the judgment or decree.—*King v. Kent*, 29
Ala. 542; *Landford v. Dunklin*, 71 Ala. 594; *Whitlow v.
Echols*, 78 Ala. 206; *Pollard v. Hamrick*, 74 Ala. 334;
May v. Marks, 74 Ala. 249; *Neville v. Kenney*, 125 Ala.
149.

McCLELLAN, J.—The jurisdiction of courts of equity to dissolve the bonds of matrimony is purely statutory.—Nelson on Div. §§ 10, 17, 18, 19; 1 Pom. Equity Juri. §§ 98, 112 (subd. 10); 14 Cyc. pp. 581, 582; 9 Am. & Eng. Ency. Law, p. 726. Accordingly, the power to grant divorce a vinculo is not of the general jurisdiction of courts of equity; but they are in that respect, courts of limited and special jurisdiction. "Where a special authority, in derogation of the common law, is conferred by statute on a court of general jurisdiction, it becomes quoad hoc an inferior or limited court."—*State v. M. & G. R. R. Co.*, 108 Ala. 29, 18 South. 801; *Goodwater Warehouse Co. v. Street*, 137 Ala. 621, 34 South. 903; *Gunn v. Howell*, 27 Ala. 663, 62 Am. Dec. 785.

With respect to the judicial acts of courts exercising special and limited jurisdiction, the existence of jurisdictional facts is not inferred from the mere exercise of jurisdiction, but must affirmativly appear from the record.—*Goodwater Warehouse Co. v. Street*, 137 Ala. 621, 625, 34 South. 903, and authorities there cited. In such cases "a compliance with the requisitions of the statute is necessary to its jurisdiction, and must appear on the face of its proceedings."—*State v. M. & G. R. R. Co., supra*. It follows, as of course, that such jurisdiction cannot be obtained or conferred by the proclamation thereof positively or by invited necessary inference, in the order or decree of a court assuming to exercise a limited special authority.—*Neville v. Kennedy*, 125 Ala. 149, 28 South. 452, 82 Am. St. Rep. 230; *Pollard v. Hanrick*, 74 Ala. 334.

On collateral attack of a judgment or decree, no presumption of the existence of jurisdictional facts can be indulged.—*Whitlow v. Echols*, 78 Ala. 206; *Pollard v. Hanrick, supra*. But, where the judgment or decree is collaterally assailed, every reasonable intendment, *as a matter of construction only*, will be made in favor of the validity thereof.—*King v. Kent*, 29 Ala. 542, 554; *Pollard v. Hanrick, supra; Whitlow v. Echols, supra.* On such an inquiry, the determination of the question whether the pleading contained the averment of *jurisdictional facts* will be undertaken with a motive, *in construction*, favorable to the validity of the judgment or decree; and where the pleading is reasonably susceptible thereof. that construction will be adopted that will support the judgment or decree, guarding, of course, against the supplying thereby of omitted essential averments.—*King v. Kent, supra.* The pleading will be understood "as it is reasonable to infer that the party who made it and the judge who acted upon it did understand it, and not as they were bound to understand it."—*King v. Kent, supra; Whitlow v. Echols, supra.*

Code 1896, § 194 (Code 1907, § 3802), provides "When the defendant is a non-resident, the other party to the marriage must have been a *bona fide* resident of this state *for one year next before the filing of the bill,* which must be alleged in the bill and proved." (Italics supplied.) Residence within the state, the powers of the courts of which are invoked to grant divorce, of at least one of the parties to the marriage, is a jurisdictional prerequisite to a valid decree in the premises.— Nelson on Div. § 21, and notes; *Bell v. Bell,* 181 U. S. 175, 21 Sup. Ct. 551, 45 L. Ed. 804, among others. The provision of the quoted statute, with respect to the residence of the complainant, in cases within the requirement of the statute, establishes a bona fide residence in this state "for one year next before the filing of the bill" as a jurisdictional prerequisite to a valid decree of divorce.—14 Cyc. p. 663; *Pate v. Pate,* 6 Mo. App. 49;

Collins v. Collins, 53 Mo. App. 470; *Cheatham v. Cheatham,* 10 Mo. 296; *Kruse v. Kruse,* 25 Mo. 68; 9 Am. & Eng. Ency. Law, p. 732, and notes; *Greenlaw v. Greenlaw.* 12 N. H. 200; *Batchelder v. Batchelder,* 14 N. H. 380.

The adoption in the pleading of the exact terms of the statute in this regard is not essential. It is sufficient if the averments convey the same idea in equivalent terms.—*Needles v. Needles* (Tex. Civ. App.) 54 S. W. 1070; *Collins v. Collins, supra;* 14 Cyc p. 663.

In the bill for divorce a vinculo, filed by M. J. Martin against Gussie Martin in the then existing county court of Cleburne county, Ala., these allegations, comprising all of them presently pertinent to the inquiry submitted for review here, appear: "Your orator, M. J. Martin, a resident of Cleburne county, Ala., over the age of 21 years, respectfully shows unto your honor: That on or about May 3. 1906, orator intermarried with said Gussie Martin, in the state of Georgia, Polk county, and that they lived together until about June 4, 1906, as man and wife, most of the time residing in Cleburne county, Ala., and orator has been a bona fide resident of Cleburne county for more than three years. * * * That Gussie Martin is over the age of 21 years and resides in the state of Georgia, but her particular place of residence is unknown to orator," etc. The decree of divorce to which that cause progressed is collaterally assailed by the bill inceptive in the cause now appealed from; a decree sustaining demurrer taking the objection that the jurisdiction of the Cleburne county court (since abolished by law) was not invoked in the cause of *Martin v. Martin,* for that the bill in that cause did not contain the jurisdictional allegation of bona fide residence of the complainant therein in this state "for·one year next before the filing of the bill,"

according to the requirement of the statute above
quoted.

The statute (section 3802), in the particular now
important, requires of the complainant the allegation
(and proof, after jurisdiction obtained) of three distinct, yet concurring, facts, viz.: (a) Bona fide residence in the state; (b) that residence for one year; (c)
and that year to run back, continuously, from "the filing of the bill." In this particular the statute is incapable of any other construction. Even though the
rule of favor to judgments and decrees collaterally
assailed, to which we have adverted and which we have
approved as upon the authority of *King v. Kent,
supra,* is extended to the bill exhibited in *Martin v.
Martin,* we are constrained, after most cautious consideration, to the conclusion that the bill omitted jurisdictional averments, thereby wholly avoiding the decree of
the Cleburne court.

Unless by construction we supply vital omissions in
the bill—a process not allowable—it is seen that the
bill is entirely silent as to the relation of the "more
than three years" bona fide residence of complainant *to*
the date of "the filing of the bill." Such bona fide residence could have existed in all perfection, and yet not
have included "one year next before the filing of the
bill." It might have comprehended a period terminating more than "one year next before the filing of the
bill," or have continued within the period of "more
than three years," but a part, *only,* of the "one year
next before the filing of the bill." The verb *"has been,"*
descriptive of past action, added nothing to the allegation in respect of the relation of the three-year period
averred *to* the essential fact of residence for the requisite period of "one year next before the filing of the
bill." The verb did, of course, refer the · residence

alleged to a period *before* the bill was filed, but did not
make a part of the period so averred the year *next*
before the bill was filed. And this construction is
strengthened, if not expressly confirmed, by the allegation "that they lived together until June 4, 1906, as
man and wife, *most* of the time residing in Cleburne
county, Ala." The period referred to was within one
year before the bill was filed. "Most" signified, not *all*,
but *nearly all*, of the time elapsing between the date of
the marriage and June 4, 1906. The view indicated, on
like inquiries, was taken and approved in the following
decisions of other tribunals: *Haymond v. Haymond*, 74
Tex. 414, 12 S. W. 90; *Collins v. Collins, supra; Johnson v. Johnson*, 95 Mo. App. 329, 68 S. W. 971.

Where from the face of the record it appears that the
judgment or decree is wholly void, delay or inaction of
the party whose rights would be affected thereby will
not, cannot, invest the judgment or decree with power
and vitality.—*Sweeney v. Tritsch*, 151 Ala. 242, 44
South. 184. It is a nullity under all circumstances. It
appearing from this bill that the decree of divorce of
the Cleburne county court in the cause of *Martin v.
Martin* was void for want of jurisdiction, the demurrer
of the defendants, raising the objection that according
to this bill complainant was not the *widow* of M. J.
Martin, deceased, should have been overruled. The
decree of divorce being void, she survived as his *widow*.
In this particular the decree sustaining the demurrer
of the defendants is, we think, erroneous.

The separate demurrers of the defendants Hanson
and Studdard were properly sustained. They are sureties on the administrator's bond merely, and are not
proper parties to this bill to remove the administration
of intestate's estate from the probate into the chancery
court.

The decree appealed from is reversed to the extent and in the respect indicated, and affirmed in the particular that the demurrer of Hanson and Studdard is sustained. The cause is remanded.

Reversed in part, affirmed in part, and remanded.

DOWDELL, C. J., and SIMPSON and MAYFIELD, JJ., concur.

Birmingham Securities Co.
v. Southern University.

Quieting Title.

(Decided April 5. 1911. Rehearing denied April 27, 1911.
55 South. 240.)

1. *Words and Phrases; Constructive Possession.*—Constructive possession is used to denote. sometimes, that legal fiction which extends actual possession of a part of a tract of land to the whole tract. where possession is held under color of title describing the whole tract.

2. *Quieting Title; Evidence.*—The evidence in this case stated and held to establish title to the land in the respondent.

APPEAL from Jefferson Chancery Court.

Heard before Hon. A. H. BENNERS.

Bill by the Birmingham Securities Company against the Southern University to quiet title to a particular piece of land. Decree for respondent, and defendant appeals. Affirmed.

FRED S. FERGUSON, for appellant. The map of Forest Hill was an essential part of the description to the same extent as if it had been incorporated in the deed. —*Miller v. Cullum,* 4 Ala. 576; *McGoun v. Lapham,* 21 Pick. 133; *Lampley v. Kennedy,* 25 Wis. 223; *Cov x.*

Hart, 145 U. S. 376; Devlin on Deeds, Sec. 1020. Parol evidence was inadmissible to vary the boundary shown in the plat or map.—88 N. C. 336; 23 Wis. 99; 122 Mass. 305; 18 Howard 150. If the description is erroneous a reformation should be sought.—*Brown v. Powers*, 52 South. 647; *Page v. Whatley*, 162 Ala. 472. There was a variance between the answer and the proof of the respondent.—*Meyer Bros. v. Mitchell*, 75 Ala. 475; s. c. 77 Ala. 312. The variance was fatal.—*Marx v. Threeat*, 131 Ala. 341. By giving a description of the land sold at the mortgage sale appellee has estopped itself from saying that it was any other land or lot than that described in its deed to Horton, and in Horton's deed to it.—6 Me. 364; 82 Miss. 372; 75 Mass. 445. A patent ambiguity cannot be helped by averment.—*Chambers v. Ringstaff*, 69 Ala. 140; *Webb v. Elyton Land Co.*, 105 Ala. 471. Where the right is equal, the claim of the party in actual possession should prevail.—Sec. 5995, Code 1907.

HARRY UPSON SIMMS, and DEGRAFFENREID & EVINS, for appellee. Possession actual or constructive is essential, and such possession must be definitely averred.—*Smith v. Gordon*, 136 Ala. 495; *Gallaway v. Hendon*, 131 Ala. 280. To aver one sort of possession and prove another does not establish the bill.—*Holland v. Coleman*, 50 South. 128, and authorities supra. Constructive possession follows the title and so an averment of constructive possession is equivalent to averring that the complainant had the legal title.—*Ladd v. Powell*, 144 Ala. 495, and authorities supra. Upon a statutory answer the defendant is entitled to an adjudication of title in him if his answer and proof so shows.—*Interstate B. & L. Asso. v. Stocks*, 124 Ala. 109; *Collier v. Alexander*, 138 Ala. 245; *Whittaker v. VanHoose*, 157

Ala. 286; *N. C. & St. L. v. Proctor*, 160 Ala. 450. It is immaterial whether the complainant alleges actual possession and fails to prove it, or constructive possession and fails to prove the legal title, the decree will be for the defendant if he sets forth a good title and establishes it.—*East B'ham Realty Co. v. B'ham M. & F. Co.*, 160 Ala. 461; *Vandergrift v. S. M. Land Co.*, 51 South. 983; *Johnson v. Johnson*, 147 Ala. 543. The statute of limitation is not applicable.—*Driver v. Hudspeth*, 16 Ala. 348.

MAYFIELD, J.—Appellant filed its bill against appellee under sections 5443 et seq., Code 1907, to quiet and determine title to lot No. 9, on the south side of Cherry street, in Forest Hill, Jefferson county, Ala.

It has been repeatedly held by this court that a bill under this statute must allege that complainant is in the peaceable possession of the land—peaceable, as distinguished from scrambling. The possession, if peaceable, may be actual or constructive. The complainant, of course, may allege either actual or constructive possession, but must prove the character which he alleges, in order to be entitled to recover. If he alleges possession to be actual, proof of constructive possession would not support the averment; for the same reason, if he alleges his possession to be constructive, proof of actual possession would not support the averment. If the bill alleged peaceable possession only, then proof of either actual or constructive peaceable possession would support the averment. The possession, and the character thereof, are material averments in the bill, and, of course, must be proven as alleged. It is axiomatic that proof of material facts, without allegations thereof, is as fatal to relief as are allegations of such facts without proof. The averment of this bill as to possession is "that the complainant is the owner, and is now in the constructive possession peaceably" of the lot in question. This is an allegation of the legal title in complainant, which was unnecessary, but, the allegation having been made, proof thereof was necessary to relief, because upon this averment depended the equity of the bill. Besides, alleging that complainant was the owner, it also alleged that it was then in the "constructive possession." As was said by this court, speaking through Dowdell, J. (now Chief Justice): "It is a legal impossibility for a constructive possession under the statute of uses to vest in the complainant under a deed from one who had no legal estate to convey; the theory of the law being that constructive possession accompanies the legal title."—*Smith v. Gordon*, 136 Ala. 498, 34 South. 839.

Constructive possession follows the legal title; the rightful owner being deemed in possession until he is ousted and disseized. Possession follows the title, in the absence of actual possession adverse to it.—*Woolfolk v. Buckner*, 67 Ark. 411, 55 S. W. 168. The phrase is also sometimes used to denote that legal fiction which extends actual possession of a part of a tract of land to the whole, when the possession is held under a color of title describing the whole tract.—See 2 Words & Phrases. This phase of the definition, however, is not important to this case or decision. It is true that complainant proved actual possession at the time the bill was filed, but that is not what was alleged. It was alleged that it was the owner and had the constructive possession. Mr. Greenleaf says that it is an established rule that the evidence offered must correspond with the allegation and be confined to the point in issue. This rule, of course, supposes the allegations to be material and necessary. Surplusage, therefore, need not be proven, though averred. Surplusage, some authors say, comprehends whatever may be stricken from the record, without destroying the plaintiff's right of action. "But," continues the writer, "it is not every immaterial or unnecessary allegation that is surplusage; for, if the party in stating his title should state it with unnecessary particularity, he must prove it as alleged."— Greenl. Ev. § 51, appendix 11, citing a number of English authorities, including Stephens on Pleadings, 261, 262. Mr. Daniel says that it is only necessary that the substance of the case made by each party should be proven; but it must be substantially the same case as that which he has stated upon the record.

These rules have been strictly followed by this court as to variance, both in courts of law and of equity. In the case of *Gorce v. Clements,* 94 Ala. 337, 10 South. 906, which was a bill to declare an absolute deed a mortgage and to redeem, the allegation was that the mortgage allowed the mortgagor to repurchase "within a reasonable and convenient time," while the proof showed the time agreed on to be, "until he was able to pay," and the variance was held fatal. In the case of *S. & N. A. R. R. Co. v. Wilson,* 78 Ala. 589, it was held that where the allegation relies on a nonfeasance of a certain duty, but the proof shows a malfeasance thereof, the variance is material and fatal. Likewise in the case of *Webb v. Robbins,* 77 Ala. 177, in which it was alleged that complainant owned the lands as her statutory estate, but the proof showed that they constituted her equitable estate, the variance was held material and fatal. Again, in the case of *Munchus v. Harris,* 69 Ala. 506, where the estate was alleged to be a fee, and the proof showed it to be a lesser estate, the variance was held to be fatal.

The case nearest in point is that of *Helmetag v. Frank*, 61 Ala. 67. This involved a bill to foreclose a mortgage against Helmetag and his wife. The bill alleged that the husband was seised in fee. Therefore he and his wife both alleged that he was so seised. But the proof showed that the husband had conveyed to the wife, thereby vesting an equitable estate in her. The equity of the bill was undoubted, and the right to relief under the proof was undoubted, but the allegation and the proof were different, and relief was denied solely upon that ground. Brickell, C. J., in that case said: "To support a final decree, the pleading and proof must correspond, and a variance between them, however clear may be the equity of the complaint, is fatal." The variance was therefore fatal to any relief on final decree.

It is true, as argued by appellant, that a deed containing a description and referring it to a map having lines drawn upon it, and marking natural boundaries, and the natural objects delineated on its surface, should be construed as giving the true description of the land, as much as if the map were marked down in the deed.—2 Dev. Deeds, §§ 1020, 1021. And, when such a map is thus referred to, it is considered a part of the conveyance, and may be referred to for the purpose of aiding the identification, showing the form, and location of the tract.—*Miller v. Cullum*, 4 Ala. 581. It is likewise true as is argued that in case of a patent ambiguity parol proof is not admissible to show what was intended by the writing, but that, if it is a latent ambiguity, the uncertainty may be explained or cleared up by the same kind of proof as that by which the ambiguity is made to appear. The law has been clearly and accurately stated by Stone, C. J., in the familiar case of *Chambers v. Ringstaff*, 69 Ala. 143, 144, as follows: "The distinction between latent and patent ambiguity has long existed, and the general rule applicable to each class of cases should not be disturbed. *When a contract or conveyance, on its face, or aided by judicial knowledge, equally describes two or more persons, things, etc., this is patent ambiguity, or ambiguity apparent. In such case the rule is clear, and we do not wish to depart from it, that parol proof of what was intended by the contracting parties will not be received. Latent ambiguity exists when, on the face of the paper, no doubt or uncertainty exists, but by proof aliunde the language is shown to be alike applicable to two or more persons, things, etc.* When this is the case, the uncertainty or ambiguity may be explained or cleared up by the same character of proof as that by which it is made to appear. These are familiar principles. But there are cases involving principles which are scarcely referable to either of these heads. They may be styled exceptional shadings of patent ambiguity. They arise when on mere inspection there does appear to be an uncertainty or ambiguity. This frequently grows out of a careless use of language, and sometimes results from the many shades of meaning usage and provincial habit accord to the same word or expression." The respondent's deeds each referred to others and to the map, and some referred to the lots in question (8 and 9), as on "S. Cherry street" and otherwise described the parcel as being "known as the C. B. Rencher lot." We do not think this such a patent ambiguity as to render the deeds void for uncertainty.

It results that the decree of the chancellor must be affirmed.

Affirmed.

SIMPSON, MCCLELLAN, and SAYRE, JJ., concur.

On Rehearing.

PER CURIAM.—All the concurring Justices are of the opinion that a rehearing should be denied, and approve the conclusion affirming the decree of the chancellor; but they do not concur in what is said in the opinion as to a variance between the allegations and the proof, and base their concurrence in the conclusion for affirmance, upon the ground that the respondent established title to the land in controversy, as was decreed by the chancellor.

The application is overruled.

Rosenau *v*. Powell.

Bill for An Accounting and to Declare a Deed Void.

(Decided May 18. 1911.   55 South. 789.)

1. *Discovery; Statutory Provisions.*—The remedy given by Section 3135. Code 1907, is cumulative to the right of discovery previously existing and implies a right to exhibit such interrogatories and have them answered, although the bill waives answer under oath.

2. *Same; Filing.*—Under section 3136, Code 1907, where a complainant places his interrogatories to the respondent in the official custody of the register he does not lose his right to have them answered although such officer does not indorse the same as his duty requires.

3. *Same; Order Fixing Time to Answer.*—Under section 3136. Code 1907, it is enough that a formal order in writing fixing the time for answer was made, and a copy of same served on respondent. though the order was not placed on the minute book of the court.

4. *Same; Failure to Answer; Decree.*—On failure to answer interrogatories within the time fixed. the provisions of section 3135. Code 1907. became operative, and under it a decree granting relief to complainant means such a decree as may be proper in the then condition of the cause. and hence authorizes a decree pro confesso. if that is the only proper decree in the case at the time of the default.

5. *Appeal and Error; Harmless Error; Amendment to Prayer.*—Where the relief given by the decree against the respondent in default was authorized by the facts and the general prayer con-

tained in the bill error cannot be predicated on the allowance of an amendment which was only the addition of a special prayer, without notice.

APPEAL from Tuscaloosa County Court.
Heard before Hon. H. B. FOSTER.
Bill by M. E. Powell against D. L. Rosenau for an accounting and to declare a deed null and void. Judgment for complainant and respondent appeals. Affirmed.

JONES & PENICK, for appellant. The court was in error in rendering a decree pro confesso against the defendant. First, because interrogatories were never filed, and no order was made by the register requiring and fixing a time for answer. Sections 3135, 3136, Code 1907. The court erred in permitting the amendment. Sections 3126, 3127, Code 1907; Rules 40, 41, 42 and 44, Chancery Practice; *Holley v. Bass*, 63 Ala. 387; *McCluny v. Ward*, 80 Ala. 243; *Howton v. Jordan*, 152 Ala. 428.

P. B. TRAWEEK and E. L. CLARKSON, for appellee. The respondent was in default for failure to answer interrogatories, and the court properly entered a decree pro confesso.—Sections 3135 and 4055, Code 1907. There was no error in allowing the amendment, as the complainant was entitled to relief granted under the averments and prayer of the original bill—*Sharpe v. Miller*, 7 South, 701; *McDonald v. Finch*, 131 Ala. 85; 130 U. S. 684; 165 U. S. 358; *Kelly v. Payne*, 18 Ala. 371.

SAYRE, J.—In her original bill complainant (appellee) waived answer under oath. The bill was fully and properly answered. Afterwards complainant lodged with the register interrogatories requiring sworn answer by the defendant. The register failed to mark the interrogatories filed, nor does he seem to have made any formal order upon the minute book of the court fixing the time within which they should be answered. However, he prepared duplicate notices to the defendant, reciting the fact that complainant had filed interrogatories, and notifying defendant that he had 65 days from date in which to answer them. On the same day one copy of the notice, along with a copy of the interrogatories, was served on the defendant by the sheriff of Tuscaloosa County; the other, with the sheriff's indorsement of service thereon, being returned into court, where it remains upon the file. On a day 75 days later the presiding judge passed a decree pro confesso in default of an answer to the interrogatories. Thereafter the court allowed the cause to proceed to a decree ascertaining the rights of the parties on the theory that the defendant was in contempt in failing to answer the interrogatories as shown by the decree. The question of controlling importance is whether the decree pro confesso was properly allowed.

The remedy given to complainant in chancery by section 3135 of the Code of 1907, which permits the complainant to exhibit interrogatories to the defendant and call upon him to answer the same, is culminative to the right of discovery which complainants have always had. It implies the complainant's right to exhibit interrogatories to his adversary, although answer under oath to the averments of the bill may have been waived when the bill was filed. The further provision is that, on the defendant's failure to answer "within such time as may be prescribed by the register, the court may, by attachment, compel him to answer, or may render a decree granting relief to the complainant, or may extend the time for such answers to be made." Section 3136 pro-

vides that: "Upon the filing of interrogatories * * *
the register must issue a copy thereof which, together
with a copy of the order of the register fixing the time
for answering them, must be served upon the party to
whom the interrogatories are propounded, or his solicitor, not less than sixty days before the expiration of
such time."

It is objected to the validity of the decree pro confesso that it was without authority of law for the following reasons: (1) The interrogatories were not filed;
(2) the register made no order; (3) the statute does
not authorize a decree pro confesso.

1. The proceeding is statutory and its validity depends upon an observance of the statutory requirements. But in ascertaining the meaning of the statute we are not required to stick too closely to the bark
of its language. The statute contemplates a filing of
interrogatories by the complainant. The register's indorsement of the fact of filing is appropriate, of course,
and should not be omitted. "Accordingly we find that
filing a paper is now understood to consist in placing it
in the proper official custody, on the part of the party
charged with the duty of filing the paper, and the making of appropriate indorsement by the officer." But,
"as was said in the case cf *Holman v. Chevaillier,* 14
Tex. 337, where the law requires or authorizes a party
to file a paper, it simply means that he shall place it in
his official custody. That is all that is required of him.
The party cannot be prejudiced by the omission of the
officer to indorse the paper filed."—*Phillips v. Beene,*
38 Ala. 248; *Ex parte State ex rel. Stow,* 51 Ala. 69.

2. Much of the same considerations dispose of the
second objection. The register did make a formal order
fixing the time within which the interrogatories were
to be answered. And perhaps he transferred the order

to the permanent records of the court. At any rate, the order was made in writing and a copy duly served upon the defendant. This was a compliance with the letter of the statute.

3. The statute provides that, in default of an answer, the court may render a decree granting relief to the complainant. Conceding that the court may in ordinary cases grant complete relief, appellant seems to say that a decree pro confesso is not complete relief, and is not therefore authorized by the statute. Prior to 1907 the articles of the Codes dealing with the subject of the examination of parties by interrogatories were limited to a definition of the procedure in cases at law. In the Code of 1907 notwithstanding the process in courts of equity for the identical purpose was elsewhere regulated sections 4049-4057 undertake, by interpolating "suits in equity" and "decrees and decrees pro confesso," to accommodate their procedure to courts of equity. The result is that some language is used which is wholly inapt to suits in equity, while other language is used which is equally inapt to suits at law. But the distribution of the language used to those subjects to which it properly relates can give rise to no difficulty. Section 4055 provides that decree or decree pro conconfesso may be rendered, if answers to interrogatories are not filed within 30 days after service of a copy. We take it that the provision of section 3136, which allows the party interrogated 60 days in which to answer, being the language used by the Legislature while it had its mind directed particularly to the subject of the proceeding as it was to be administered in the court of chancery, ought to prevail in that court. In other respects, the two statutes not being in conflict, effect must be given to all provisions found in either and appropriate to the procedure of the court in which the

cause is pending. And the language of section 4055 expressly authorizes decrees pro confesso. But we would reach the same conclusion without the aid of section 4055. Section 3135 authorizes a decree on failure to answer. This section was framed in view of the well-known practice of the chancery court and can mean only such a decree as may be proper in the then posture of the cause. The language is broad enough to include a decree pro confesso. Such was the only proper decree in this case at the time of the defendant's default, and there was no error in taking the bill as confessed.

But, subsequently and without notice to the defendant, the prayer of the bill was amended, and it is insisted that this was error infecting the final decree of relief rendered in accordance with the amended prayer. It is error to proceed to a final decree against a party in default on a bill which has been amended so as to change the issues between the parties or authorize relief different from or more extensive than that prayed in the original bill, unless notice has been given to the defendant or his counsel, or entered upon the register's order book for such time as the chancellor or register may direct.—Code Ch. R. 44, p. 1504; *Holly v. Bass*, 63 Ala. 387; *McClenny v. Ward*, 80 Ala. 243; *Howton v. Jordan*, 154 Ala. 428, 46 South, 234. Here the original bill contained a prayer for specific and general relief. The relief to be awarded is determined by the facts alleged in the bill.—*McDonnell v. Finch*, 131 Ala. 85, 31 South. 594. The fact that a bill contains a prayer for specific relief not authorized by the facts averred will not destroy its equity.—*Bledsoe v. Price*, 132 Ala. 621, 32 South. 325. Nevertheless a prayer for relief is essential to the equity of a bill, and, if it contains only a prayer for specific relief, the decree will go no further than the terms of the prayer require.—*Driver v. Fort-*

ner, 5 Port. 9; *Rice v. Eiseman,* 122 Ala. 343, 25 South.
214.   Under the general prayer the complainant may in
the ordinary case have the relief authorized by the facts
averred, although he may be mistaken in the special relief prayed.—*May v. Lewis,* 22 Ala. 646; *Munford v.
Pearce,* 70 Ala. 452. It is not denied that the complainant was on the facts entitled to the relief awarded in the
general prayer. The special prayer added by the amendment served only to call the chancellor's attention to the
appropriate relief, a suggestion that might have been
made at the bar, and was immaterial as affecting the
equities of the bill or the relief to be rendered under the
bill as originally framed. Error cannot be predicated
of its allowance without notice.—*Masterson v. Masterson,* 32 Ala. 437.

Affirmed.

DOWDELL, C. J., and ANDERSON and MAYFIELD, J. J.,
concur.

Casey *v.* Bryce.

*Bill to Enjoin Taking Possession of the Office of
Sheriff.*

(Decided June 16, 1911.   55 South. 810.)

1. *Evidence: Judicial Notice; Public Records.*—The issuance of a
commission to a public officer by the Governor is a public act of
public record of which the courts must take judicial notice.

2. *Same.*—The courts take judicial notice of the declared results
of a general election and of the fact that one has been declared
elected to the office of sheriff of a county and has received the Governor's commission.

3. *Same; Conclusiveness.*—The courts take judicial notice of matters of public record and the facts disclosed by such records are
conclusive.

[Casey v. Bryce.]

4. *Officers; Title to Office; Certificate of Election.*—A commission from the Governor based on a certificate of election, confers prima facie title to the office, and entitles one duly qualified holding such commission to enter on the discharge of the office; hence his title under such conditions is conclusive until determined on statutory contest, and no inquiry as to his title to the office will be entertained in any collateral proceedings.

5. *Same; Right of Outgoing Officer; Injunction.*—An officer whose term of office is about to expire cannot bring a bill in equity to prevent one who has received a certificate of election and a commission from the Governor to occupy said office, from taking possession of said office pending a contest brought by his opponents to determine his right thereto.

6. *Same; Bill; Sufficiency.*—An outgoing officer may not sue for an injunction to restrain a candidate who has a certificate of election and a commission from the Governor, from taking the office to which his commission entitles him, and an allegation in a bill by an outgoing officer that a third person, who was a candidate for the office, has instituted a contest of the election of such commissioned officer, according to the statutes, shows that such candidate has been declared elected to the office and is entitled to a commission from the Governor, and in the absence of a contrary allegation it will be presumed that a commission has been issued in due course.

7. *Same; Right of Incumbent; Injunctive Relief.*—Equity will protect by injunction the incumbent of a public office against the intrusion of an adverse claimant out of possession and whose title has not been established; but to obtain such relief the complainant must show a continuing prima facie right to occupy the office, or show prima facie that there is no other person authorized by law to hold the office.

APPEAL from Cullman Chancery Court.

Heard before Hon. W. H. SIMPSON.

Bill by A. J. Casey, the outgoing sheriff of Cullman County, against C. W. Bryce, the sheriff declared elected and commissioned, to enjoin him from taking charge of the office of sheriff of Cullman County. From a decree sustaining demurrers to the bill and dissolving the temporary injunction on the denials to the answer, complainant appeals. Affirmed.

KYLE & HUTSON, for appellant. The facts stated in the bill must on the motion and demurrers be taken as true.—*First Ave. C. & L. Co. v. Johnson*, 54 South. 599. These facts show appellant to be a de jure officer. 29 Cyc. 1399; 18 A. Rep. 321. If not a de jure officer, he certainly is a defacto officer.—*Casey v. State,* 76 Ala. 85; *Stephens v. Davis,* 39 South. 831; *Heath v. State,* 36 Ala. 276. This being true, he holds until his successor is elected and qualified, and the office does not become vacant on the expiration of his term.—*Plowman v. Thornton,* 52 Ala. 599; sec. 1464 Code 1907; 30 Am. St. Rep. 208; 22 Am. St. Rep. 629; Mecham on Public Offices, secs. 128-397. As the bill was filed before January 16, 1911, and as it alleges that the defendant was not elected sheriff of Cullman County on November 8, 1910, these allegations must be taken as true on the demurrer and motion to dismiss, and there cannot, and could not have been a legal vacancy in said office.—48 N. E. 1025, 5 Pom. Eq. sec. 235; 86 Am. St. Rep. 215; 47 Ohio St. 570; 22 Cyc. 887; 6 South. 507. Under these authorities and under the authority of *Driver v. Fortner,* 5 Port. 9; *Rice v. Eisman Bros.* 122 Ala. 348, and 2 High on Injunctions, sec. 1215, the bill must be held to contain equity. Where the question arises incidentally in a suit in which the court has rightful jurisdiction, and the granting of relief depends upon its decision, a chancery court will pass upon the question of an election.—*Crow v. Florence I. & C. Co.,* 143 Ala. 543; *Nathan v. Tompkins,* 82 Ala. 437; *Perry v. Tuscaloosa,* 93 Ala. 364.

J. B. BROWN and F. E. ST. JOHN, for appellee. The allegation of the bill brings the case clearly within the condemnation of section 459 Code 1907. Independent of the statute, however, the incumbent of a public office cannot invoke the powers of the court of equity to enjoin another who holds a certificate of election to such office from using such certificate, which is conclusive of his right to the office against all persons except such as have a right under the law to contest the election, and even as to them, such certificate is prima facie evidence, and casts the burden on the one questioning the right.— *Moulton v. Reed,* 54 Ala. 323; *Little v. City of Bessemer,* 138 Ala. 128; *Goodwin v. Sate,* 145 Ala. 399. The bill shows that the election has already been held; that the candidates for the office are contesting the election, and that respondent was declared elected to the office and has received his commission therefor, and hence complainant cannot urge that the perquisities thereof are probable, and that hence he is entitled to protection. —*Moulton v. Reed,* supra; *Gulf Compress Co., v Harris,* 158 Ala. 351; *Deegan v. Neville,* 127 Ala. 417. If complainant has any right, he has a complete and adequate remedy for its protection under sections 5450-5452 Code 1907.—Authorities supra. The complainant fails to bring his case within any principle of equity jurisdiction, and hence the action of the lower court will be affirmed.—*Terrell v. South. Ry. Co.,* 164 Ala. 433.

SOMMERVILLE, J.—This is a bill filed by the appellant, A. J. Casey, on January 12, 1911, seeking to enjoin the appellee, C. W. Bryce, from taking possession of the office of sheriff of Cullman county, or any of the paraphernalia thereof, and from interfering in any manner with complainant's possession of said office until a judicial determination of said Bryce's right to do so.

The bill shows that the complainant, Casey, was elected to the office of sheriff of Cullman county in 1906, and was the legal incumbent thereof for the term ending on January 16, 1911—a fact of which all courts must take judicial notice. It further shows that, within 15 days after the result of the general election of November, 1910, was declared, one C. C. Scheuing instituted a contest, in accordance with the law, against the said C. W. Bryce, for the office of sheriff of Cullman county, which contest was then pending in the probate court.

The real gravamen of the bill seems to rest upon the notion that, as complainant is entitled to hold office until his successor is elected and qualified, he is therefore entitled to hold until this contest between Scheuing and Bryce is settled by the judgment of the probate court; and that, if Bryce, who "pretends" that he is entitled to the office, be allowed to enter into the office, as he is threatening to do, complainant will suffer irreparable injury, in that Bryce will get the fees and emoluments of the office and complainant will lose them. The bill avers, on information and bleief, that Bryce was not elected to the office, which averment, however, construed in conection with the averment that Scheuing had filed a contest of Bryce's election "duly instituted in all respects as required by law," can only mean that the pleader's conclusion is that Bryce was not *legally* elected. A temporary writ of injunction was issued in accordance with the prayer of the bill.

The respondent Bryce answered the bill under oath, setting up that he was elected to the office at said election, which result had been regularly and duly declared by the authorized officers, and that he had been commissioned, and had qualified by filing his bond and taking the oath of office. A copy of the respondent's commission from the Governor, dated November 28, 1910, is attached as an exhibit to his answer. In the answer there was incorporated a demurrer to the bill for want of equity; and a motion was filed to dissolve the injunction for want of equity in the bill, and also upon the denials of the answer. The chancellor sustained the demurrer; and granted the motion to dissolve the injunction on the denials of the answer, and the appeal is from this decree.

1. The issuance of a commission to a public officer, by the Governor of the state, being a public act of pub-

lic record which is prescribed by law, must be judicially noticed by courts.—*White v. Rankin,* 90 Ala. 541, 8 South. 118; *Sandlin v. Anderson,* 76 Ala. 403; *Cary v. State,* 76 Ala 78. The declared result of a general election is also a matter of judicial knowledge.—4 Wigmore on Ev. § 2577, note 3. We therefore judicially know, as did the chancery court, that C. W. Bryce was duly declared elected to the office of sheriff of Cullman county at the general election of November, 1910, and that a commission was duly issued to him therefor by the Governor of the state on November 28, 1910.

In *White v. Sandlin,* supra, it is said: "The clerk being a commissioned officer the court was authorized and bound to take judicial knowledge that he was clerk, and also of his term of office, when it commenced, and when it expired. If the cognizance extends beyond actual knowledge, the judge may resort to any authoritative sources of information, and inform himself of the fact in any way he may deem best in his discretion; but he is not required to receive oral evidence to disprove a fact, the existence of which is judicially known to the court." And in *Cary v. State,* supra, it is said: "The dates of these commissions are matters of public record in the executive department of the state government, being accessible to inquiry by all who may be concerned, and the law fixes the duration of each official term."

A commission from the Governor, issued on a certificate of election, confers a clear prima facie title to the office, entitling the person commissioned, after due qualification, to enter upon the discharge of the duties of the office; and his title is conclusive until the ultimate right to the office is determined on quo warranto (or now on statutory contest); and no inquiry as to the truth or falsity of the certificate upon which the commission is based can be entertained in any mere collateral proceeding.—*Plowman v. Thornton,* 52 Ala. 559; *Moulton v. Reid,* 54 Ala. 320.

It results that judicial knowledge of matters of public record, fixed and certain as they are, is not only compulsory upon the court, but is also conclusive of the fact and exclusive of ulterior inquiry.

It is evident, then, that in considering the allegations of complainant's bill, and determining upon its equity, the chancery court could not close its eyes to the publicly recorded fact that Bryce was the regularly commissioned sheriff-elect of Cullman county, and was bound to reckon with that fact as though it were solemnly alleged in the bill. In this connection, it is proper to say, we aprehend that this consequence of the rule of judicial notice does not follow as to ordinary matters not of record, and not fixed and certain.—4 Wigmore on Ev. § 2567.

The bill of complaint, thus viewed, presents a singular and sinister aspect. It proposes, not that the chancery court shall consider or determine the merits of the pending contest, but that, so long as that contest remains undetermined, the complainant shall be allowed to occupy the office and harvest its perquisites to his own use. And it asks the mandatory aid of a court of chancery to keep in office one whose lawful term has expired, and to keep out one who has been duly elected thereto and commissioned therefor; in other words, to halt him upon the threshold, and command him to wait until the claims of his competitor, a stranger to complainant, have been disproved.

There is not, and cannot be, any such right in an outgoing public officer, and we are cited to no principle of law that even tends to support the proposition.

2. But, if we consider the bill of complaint without the aid of judicial knowledge at all, the result is the

same. It shows a contest, instituted by Scheuing, of Bryce's election to the office, "duly instituted in all respects according to law." This must mean, ex vi terminorum, that Bryce has been declared elected to the office by the duly authorized election officers; and it follows that he was entitled to a commission from the Governor, and it will be presumed, at least in the absence of express denial, that a commission was issued to him in due course.

3. We do not controvert the proposition of law so vigorously argued by complainant's counsel that in proper cases a court of chancery will by injunctive process protect the incumbent of an office against the intrusion of adverse claimants out of possession, and whose title is not yet established. This principle is well established, and is supported by many text-writers and cases.—2 High on Inj. (2d Ed.) § 1315; 5 Pom. Eq. Jur. § 335, and cases cited; *Guillotte v. Poincy*, 41 La. Ann. 333, 6 South. 507, 5 L. R. A. 403. But an examination of these authorities will show that the essential condition to injunctive relief is the complainant's continued prima facie right to occupy the office, or a prima facie showing that there is no other person as yet authorized by law to do so, and an adversary claim as between the complainant and the respondent

If it be conceded, for the sake of the argument, that the bill in this case shows that Bryce was not elected sheriff, and has no right to occupy the office as such, yet complainant fails to bring himself within the protection of the equitable principle above stated, because he does not show that some legally authorized person will not appear and qualify upon the expiration of his own term, nor that there is no such person; and hence he does not show any right in himself to remain in the office. He shows there was an election, and that some

person, other than himself, was unquestionably entitled
to the office. In such a case he cannot appear as the
guardian and protector of the true claimant, whoever he
may be, and vicariously appropriate the valuable perquisites that should inure to the other.

4. Section 459, Code 1907, is as follows: "No jurisdiction exists in or shall be exercised by any chancellor,
chancery court, or any officer exercising chancery powers, to entertain any cause or proceeding for ascertaining the legality, conduct, or results of any election,
except so far as authority to do so shall be specially and
specifically enumerated and set down by statute; and
any injunction, process, order, or decree from any chancellor, chancery court, or officer in the exercise of chancery powers, whereby the results of any election are
sought to be inquired into, questioned, or affected, or
whereby any certificate of election is sought to be
inquired into, or questioned, save as may be specially
and specifically enumerated and set down by statute,
shall be null and void, and shall not be enforced by any
officer or obeyed by any person; and should any chan
cellor or other officer hereafter undertake to file, or in
any wise deal with any person for disobeying any such
prohibited injunction, process, order, or decree, such
attempt shall be null and void, and an appeal shall lie
forthwith therefrom to the Supreme Court then sitting,
or next to sit, without bond, and such proceedings shall
be suspended by force of such appeal; and the notice to
be given of such appeal shall be five days."

It may be, as argued by counsel for the appellee, that
by the injunctive process here invoked the results of an
election are *questioned or affected*, within the inhibition
of this statute. We prefer, however, to place our conclusions upon the simpler and surer grounds above discussed.

5.   In view of what has already been said, it is not necessary to discuss the decree of the chancellor sustaining the motion to dissolve the injunction.   It was fully justified, not only for want of equity in the bill, but also by reason of the sworn denials and showings of the answer, which completely refuted the alleged equity.

The decree of the chancellor is accordingly in all things affirmed.

Affirmed.

SIMPSON, ANDERSON, and SAYRE, JJ., concur.

Bulke *v.* Bulke.

Bill for Divorce and Alimony.

(Decided May 11, 1911.   55 South. 490.)

1. *Divorce; Temporary Alimony.*—The provisions of section 3803, Code 1907, do not require the allowance of temporary alimony if the husband has already provided for such support.

2. *Same; Attorney's Fee.*—The allowance for attorney's fees in a divorce suit, in the absence of the statutory provisions, is governed by the general principles of law as to the propriety of such allowance, which depends upon the good faith of the proceedings, the probability of success, etc.

3. *Same; Bill; Condoning Derelictions.*—Where the cross-bill of the husband in answer to the wife's suit for a divorce alleges that subsequent to the wife's dereliction, he received her back into his home and supported her, it is not subject to demurrer, though not alleging that he lived with her as his wife so as to condone her former dereliction.

4. *Husband and Wife; Support; Contract; Abrogation.*—Even if a husband not only received his wife back into his home, but lived with her as his wife, thereby condoning the wife's dereliction, this would not necessarily abrogate the contract by which she had received a definite amount from him in lieu of all obligations of support.

APPEAL from Shelby County Court.

Heard before Hon. E. S. LYMAN.

[Bulke v. Bulke.]

Bill by M. E. Bulke against Paul Bulke for divorce
and alimony. From a decree granting temporary alimony and attorney's fee, and ordering a reference,
respondent appeals. Reversed and rendered.

SAM WILL JOHN, for appellant. Under the facts in
this case the wife had accepted a lump sum in lieu of
all further support and was not entitled to temporary
alimony and attorney's fee.—*Ex parte Jones*, 172 Ala.
186; *Brindley v. Brindley*, 121 Ala. 450; *Spilter v. Spilter*, 108 Ill. 124. The wife had a right to contract with
her husband as though she was sole.—Secs. 4492-4497,
Code 1907; *Osborne v. Cooper*, 113 Ala. 405; *Sample v.
Guyer*, 143 Ala. 410.

JOHN E. MILES, for appellee. The court properly
allowed temporary alimony and attorney's fee.—Sec.
3803, Code 1907; *Jeter v. Jeter*, 36 Ala. 392; *Brady v.
Brady*, 144 Ala. 415; *Edwards v. Edwards*, 80 Ala. 97;
Rast v. Rast, 113 Ala. 319; 5 A. & E. Ann. cases, 230.

SIMPSON, J.—The appellee filed a bill for divorce
and alimony, and the appeal is from a decree ordering
a reference and allowing temporary alimony and attorney's fees pendente lite.

The answer, which is made also a cross-bill, denies all
of the grounds set up in the bill for a divorce; alleges
immorality and lewdness on the part of the wife; that
she lived with him for about a year and three months
from her marriage in February, 1902, when she abandoned him and went away with another man, led an
open and notoriously lewd life; that she returned in
March, 1908, when, on her promise of reformation, he
"received her and her daughter back into his home, and
supported and maintained them, as best he could, till
March, 1909, when they voluntarily left him and have

ever since remained away." It also alleges that, after the complainant left him the first time, she instituted proceedings for divorce, and thereupon a written contract (which is made an exhibit to the bill) was entered into, by which, in consideration of $500, the receipt of which is acknowledged in the contract, said complainant acknowledged "satisfaction and payment of all claims against the said Paul Bulke of every kind for alimony, support, and maintenance," and released all interest, right, and title in all property owned by the respondent.

It is insisted by the appellee—and such seems to be the basis of the decree—that under section 3803 of the Code of 1907 the allowance is a matter of right, without regard to the circumstances of the case. This contention is sustained as a general proposition by our decisions; but, if the husband has already provided for the "support of the wife," the statute cannot mean that she is entitled as a matter of right to additional support. To hold so would be to say that, although the husband has conveyed all of his property and assets to provide for the support of the wife, yet she is entitled to an additional decree for the temporary alimony and attorney's fees. The contract explicitly releases him from further liability for her support, and there is no allegation that the wife was overreached. It was clearly a settlement of her demand for divorce and alimony, and if it had not been for her subsequent return to his home no one would hold that she could institute another suit for divorce, and demand, as a matter of right, "an allowance for her support."

It is contended that, by receiving the wife and her daughter (his stepdaughter) back into his home, all former causes of divorce were condoned, and with the condonation went the agreement. It will be noticed

[Bulke v. Bulke.]

that the answer does not state that the defendant ever
lived with her as his wife again, but only that he
received her and her daughter into his home and supported them. Of course, if he did receive and live with
her, by cohabitation, as a wife, it would be a condonation of those causes of divorce; but that would not necessarily abrogate the contract by which she had received
a definite amount in lieu of all obligation to support
her. The temporary allowance is only for her support,
and the statute cannot have the effect of impairing the
obligation of the contract, by which the complainant
has bound herself, for an adequate consideration, not to
claim anything more for that purpose. In a case where,
by previous agreement, provision for the support of the
wife had been made, it was held that alimony pendente
lite should not be allowed, but that on the final hearing
of the case the court would inquire whether the provision was sufficient. It is not shown whether there
was an express release of liability for support, but
under the peculiar circumstances of that case counsel
fees were allowed.—*Collins v. Collins*, 80 N. Y. 1, 11,
12; 14 Cyc. 754, 755.

Our statute does not specifically provide for an allowance for attorney's fees. The propriety of allowing for
the same must be governed by the general principles of
the law, according to which such allowances depend
upon the good faith of the proceedings, the probability
of success, etc.—14 Cyc. 749, 753, 754, et seq., 761, 762;
Brindley v. Brindley, 121 Ala. 429, 431, et seq., 25
South. 751. On the whole, taking into consideration all
the circumstances of this case, we think the temporary
alimony and attorney's fees should not be allowed pendente lite.

While it is true, as stated in the opinion of the judge,
that an allegation of what the cross-complainant

"believes" is not sufficient basis for a claim for divorce, yet, since, as before stated, the answer does not allege that the cross-complainant lived with the complainant as his wife, so as to condone former derelictions, the demurrer to the cross-bill should not have been sustained.

The decree of the court is reversed, and a decree will be here rendered, declaring the plea sufficient, denying the motion to strike the answer of respondent, overruling the demurrer to the cross-bill, and denying the motion for alimony and allowance pendente lite.

Reversed and rendered.

DOWDELL, C. J., and McCLELLAN and MAYFIELD, JJ., concur.

Ellis *v*. Vandergrift, *et al.*

Bill for Dissolution of Corporation and Relief Against Fraudulent Practice.

(Decided May 11, 1911.   Rehearing denied June 8, 1911.
55 South. 781.)

1. *Equity; Pleading; Bill.*—Where the bill is by a shareholder in a corporation to dissolve the corporation and seeks relief against the alleged fraudulent conduct of the directors and officers, and seeks the disallowance of the claim assigned by the directors or officers to a respondent, with the alternate prayer that if such claim be found valid, it should be paid out of the assets of the corporation, then such respondent is not concerned with those phases of the bill relating to the dissolution of the corporation, and the fraud of the directors, unless the entire equity of the bill depends on the solution of those questions.

2. *Same; Demurrer; Office.*—The purpose of a demurrer in equity is to accelerate the decision of the complainant's right upon the confessed averments of his pleading, and a demurrant cannot obect to imperfections in the bill not related to the cause of action asserted against him.

3. *Same; Bill; Multifariousness.*—A party not prejudiced thereby cannot object to a bill on account of multifariousness.

[Ellis v. Vandergrift, et al.]

4. *Same; Bills; Multifariousness.*—Where the bill was by the minority stockholders seeking to dissolve a corporation and to relieve it from the effect of fraudulent acts of its directors and majority stockholders and also to have relief against a claim held by a respondent, alleged to have been created by the directors and assigned to him that he might file a petition in bankruptcy against the corporation, and also seeking reimbursement of the sums expended by the minority stockholders in resisting the bankruptcy petition, it was not multifariousness with respect to the respondent holding the alleged fraudulent claim, either because he was not interested in winding up the corporation, or that the necessary parties are different in the different phases of the bill, or that it sought reimbursement for the sums expended in resisting the petition in bankruptcy, as such relief was not sought against the respondent, but against others.

5. *Same.*—As it is not necessary that all the parties to a bill should have an interest in all the matters in controversy, it being sufficient that each respondent has an interest in some of the matters involved, and if they are connected with the others, a bill is not multifarious as to a respondent because he has no connection with a large part of the record, or that the same defense is not applicable to the different aspects, or that no common relief is sought as against him.

6. *Same; Pleading; Adoption of Demurrer.*—Where a respondent by most general terms adopts the grounds of demurrer of another respondent such adoption does not entitle him to rely upon the waiver of the bar of the statute of limitation which was set up in the demurrer adopted.

7. *Same; Jurisdiction; Disposal of Entire Matter.*—Where the jurisdiction of the court of equity has been properly invoked it will dispose of all the questions involved in the controversy and a respondent cannot object that some of these questions could have been adjudicated in an action at law.

8. *Appeal and Error; Objection Below; Necessity.*—An appellate court will not pass upon a ground of demurrer not presented in the lower court although argued in brief on appeal.

9. *Corporation; Stockholders; Suit on Behalf of Corporation.*—While a corporation is primarily entitled to sue to redress corporate wrongs, stockholders may sue for that purpose, where the corporation refuses to act, or where the litigation would be in the control of the wrong doers.

10. *Same; Conditions Precedent.*—A stockholder suing on behalf of a corporation to redress corporate wrongs need not make a demand or request of the corporate authorities to act where such a demand or request will be refused.

11. *Same.*—The facts made by the bill stated and examined and held to authorize suit by the minority stockholders on behalf of the corporation to redress corporate wrongs without demand or request of the corporate authorities to do so; also held that as against the appealing respondent the cause of action against him did not depend upon the dissolution of the corporation, and hence that he could not complain of any defects in the cause of action for the dissolution of the corporation.

APPEAL from Birmingham City Court.

Heard before Hon. H. A. SHARPE.

Bill by A. B. Vandergrift and others, minority stock-holders in the Three Rivers Coal & Iron Company, against J. E. Ellis, the corporation and the corporate officers to dissolve the corporation, correct certain fraudulent acts and for other purposes. From a decree overruling his demurrer to the bill the respondent Ellis appeals. Affirmed.

BLACK & DAVIS, and BARNEY L. WHATLEY, for appellant. The court erred in overruling the first ground of demurrer to the bill.—*Bishop v. Bishop*, 13 Ala. 475; *McDonald v. Life Ins. Co.*, 56 Ala. 468; Sec. 3094, Code 1907. The bill was multifarious and that ground of demurrer should have been sustained.—*Gordon v. Ross*, 63 Ala. 364. The stockholder could not bring the bill against the corporation and its officers for the purposes sought.—*Tutwiler v. Tus. C. I. & L. Co.*, 89 Ala. 391; Cook on Corporations, 246; *Church v. Citizens R. R. Co.*, 78 Fed. 526. The bill seeks alternative and inconsistent relief.—*Bellview Cemetery Co. v. McEvers*, 53 South. 274. The bill is multifarious for misjoinder of parties.—*Adams v. Jones*, 68 Ala. 117; *A. G. S. v. Prouty*, 43 South. 354; *Bentley v. Barnes*, 47 South. 159. The bill is rendered multifarious by the further fact that no common relief is sought against the respondents.—*Am. R. Co. v. Linn*, 93 Ala. 610; *Siglan v. Smith*, 53 South. 260; *Henry v. Tenn. Live Stock Co.*, 50 South. 1029. The necessary parties are different in the different phases of the bill.—*Kennedy v. Kennedy*, 2 Ala. 609; *McIntosh v. Alexander*, 16 Ala. 87; *Nowlin v. McAfee*, 63 Ala. 364; *Bolman v. Lobman*, 74 Ala. 507; *McDonald v. Turnipseed*, 51 South. 758, and authorities supra.

TILLMAN, BRADLEY & MORROW, JOHN D. STRANGE, and WARD & RUDOLPH, for appellee. The bill contains equity: (a) Because of the breaches of the fiduciary obligations on the part of the directors.—*Legarde v. Anniston L. & S. Co.*, 126 Ala. 496; *Montgomery Traction Co. v. Harmon*, 140 Ala. 505; *Luther v. Luther Co.*, 99 Am. St. Rep. 977; *Pacific Vinegar Co. v. Smith* (Cal.), 104 Am. St. Rep. 42; 15 Cyc. 790. (b) Because the claims of the directors and officers were not legal liabilities against the company Directors and officers serve without compensation in the absence of a prior agreement therefor The payment of the claims were frauds against which equity will relieve.—*Branch Bank v. Collins*, 7 Ala. 95; *M. & K. C. R. R. v. Ownes*, 121 Ala. 505; *Jones v. Morrison*, 16 N. W. 854; *McConnell v. Com. M. & M. Co.*, 30 Mont. 239; 104 Am. St. Rep. 703; *Taussig v. St. L. etc. R. R.*, 166 Mo. 28; 89 Ab. St. Rep. 674; *Von Armin v. Am. Tube Works*, 188 Mass. 515; 74 N. E. 680; *St. L. R. R. v. O'Hara* (Ill.), 52 N. E. 734; Decennial Digest, Vol. 5, Sec. 308 of Corporations; Cook on Corporations, Sec. 657 and citations; Thompson on Corporations, Vol. 4, Sec. 4682; Thompson on Corporations, Vol. 7, Sec. 8504; 10 Cyc. 952; *Notley v. First State Bank* (Mich.), 118 N. W. 486; *Lowe v. Ring* (Wis.), 101 N. W. 699; *Fitzgerald Constr. Co. v. Fitzgerald*, 137 U. S. 98. (c) Because the issue of stock of the company in part payment of such claims was contrary to the constitution and laws of Alabama. —Constitution 1901, Sec. 234; Constitution 1875, Art. 14, Sec. 6; *American Ice & I. Co. v. Crane*, 142 Ala. 620; *Fitzpatrick v. Dispatch Co.*, 83 Ala. 607. (d) Because the issue of stock of the company in part payment of such claims was contrary to the articles of incorporation and by-laws of the company.—10 Cyc. p. 760. (e) Because the demands paid by stock and notes of the

company were unreasonable and excessive.—*Ala. C. &
C. Co. v. Shackleford,* 127 Ala. 224; *Decatur M. L. Co.
v. Palm,* 113 Ala. 531; *Donald v. Mfg. Ex. Co.,* 142 Ala.
578. (f) Because the demands paid by the stock and
notes of the company were barred by the statutes of limitation at and before the time of payment.—Thompson
on Corporations, Vol. 3, Sec. 4015; *Montgomery L. &
P. Co. v. Lahey,* 121 Ala. 131. (g) Because the assignment to Drennen cannot be set aside except by a court
of equity.—*Tillis v. Brown,* 154 Ala. 403; *Allen v.
Montg. R. R. Co.,* 11 Ala. 437. (h) Because of the mass
of fraud shown by the issuance of fictitious stock and
the execution of the negotiable notes in payment of
simulated claims, and the continued and repeated
efforts of the guilty directors to perfect their frauds by
a general assignment and by bankruptcy proceedings
and by the suit in the circuit court, etc.—*Jefferson
County v. Francis,* 115 Ala. 317; *Howard v. Corey,* 126
Ala. 283. (i) Because under the facts alleged, the complainants are entitled to a dissolution of the company.
—*Noble v. Gadsden L. & I. Co.,* 133 Ala. 250; *Ross v.
Am. Banana Co.,* 150 Ala. 268; *Central Land Co. v. Sullivan,* 152 Ala. 360; *Minona Portland Cement Co. v.
Reese,* 52 South. 523. The complainants are entitled to
an attorney's fee for their successful services in the
bankruptcy cause.—*Cowdrey v. G. H. & H. R.,* 93 U. S.
352; *Trustees v. Grenough,* 105 U. S. 527; *McCourt v.
Singers,* 145 Fed. at p. 114. The bill is not prolix. A
complainant may aver additional cumulative facts if
he so desires.—*Noble v. Moses Bros.,* 81 Ala. 530; *First
National Bank v. Tyson,* 144 Ala. at p. 469. The bill is
not multifarious.—Code 1907, Sec. 3095; *Montgomery
I. Works v. Capitol C. Ins. Co.,* 137 Ala. 134; *Smith v.
Smith,* 153 Ala. at p. 520; *Northwestern L. Co. v. Gra-
dy,* 137 Ala. 219; *Bentley v. Barnes,* 155 Ala. at p. 663;

Ex. Natl. Bank v. Stewart, 158 Ala. 218; *Lebick v. Fort Payne Bank,* 121 Ala. 447; 16 Cyc. p. 239, et seq., and citations. An appeal to the stockholders or directors for redress was not required under the facts alleged.— *Tillis v. Brown,* 154 Ala. 403; *Montgomery Traction Co. v. Harmon,* 140 Ala. 505; *Minona Portland Cement Company v. Reese,* 52 South. 523.

McCLELLAN, J.—This appeal is prosecuted alone by J. E. Ellis, one of a number of defendants. His complaint here is that his separate demurrer (he was concerned in no other) to the bill was overruled.

The general purposes of the bill—stating them without effort at particularity—are dissolution of the Three Rivers Coal & Iron Company, a corporation, and relief against averred fraudulent conduct on the part of a majority of the directorate, and of some of the officers, and a majority of the shareholders, of the corporation.

The only relation J. E. Ellis appears from the bill to have to the subject-matter of the bill is that of a creditor—the holder, by assignment and transfer, of a note against the corporation. He is not shown to be a stockholder. His claim is traced, in particular averment, to S. A. Ellis, his transferror.

In formulating his demurrers, appellant appropriated the grounds of the demurrer interposed by C. B. Powell, another defendant. To these appellant added, in his demurrer, grounds addressed to those phases of the bill, wherefrom it is sought to invalidate his alleged claim against the corporation. While the amended bill assails the validity of his claim (note) against the corporation and invokes the powers of the court to annul his claim, yet it carries, also, the alternative in its prayer that, if the appellant's claim is found to be

valid, it be paid out of the assets of the corporation—
an entity unequivocally alleged to be solvent in any
event.

In this state of averment—of limited relation of
appellant to the subject-matter of controversy—he is
not concerned with those phases of the amended bill
which relate to the establishment vel non of the invalidity of stock issued to others described therein, or with
the approval vel non of other (than his) claims or
charges against the corporation. Nor can his rights be
affected in any degree by the inquiry whether the dissolution of the corporation should be effected, since in
any event his claim is assured of payment, unless the
equity of the bill as amended depends wholly upon the
solution of that question.

Only a party who is prejudiced thereby can avail of
the objection of multifariousness.—16 Cyc. p. 263; 14
Ency. Pl. & Pr. pp. 212-213; *Stone v. Knickerbocker
Ins. Co.*, 52 Ala. 589.

The office of demurrer in equity is to accelerate the
decision of the complainant's right, upon the confessed
averments of his pleading, to maintain the bill as
against the demurrant. If the phases of a bill to which
the demurrant objects as defective cannot affect any interest or right the demurrant is impleaded to defend, he
will suffer no prejudice by the retention of the bill, having equity notwithstanding. He cannot invoke his ex-
oneration because of imperfections, not related to the
cause or right of action, asserted against him. In
short, he must be prejudiced by the defect; else he is
unharmed and unconcerned.

Does the equity of the bill depend wholly upon the
dissolution vel non of the corporation: We think not.
We think its equity, so far as to conclude against appellant's demurrer in this regard, may be rested upon that

phase of the bill whereby fraudulent conduct on the part of those before mentioned is particularly and sufficiently charged. Out of this conduct came, according to the bill, the claim (note) now held by appellant.

From the allegations of the amended bill, these general conclusions, avoiding unnecessary reiteration of the detailed averments thereof, must be deduced; that a majority of the stockholders and a majority of the directorate, together with some, if not all, of the officers of the corporations entered upon a scheme to wrongfully increase the capital stock of the corporation, to wrongfully create, in their personal behalf, liabilities against the corporation, to dissolve and wind up the corporation by means of a general assignment by them to a trustee of their own selection, and to have the corporation adjudged an involuntary bankrupt, when it in fact was entirely solvent. The phase of the conspiracy to wreck the corporation, charged by the bill, with which appellant is, by averment, connected thus appears: S. A. Ellis, from the year 1887 (the year the corporation was organized) until the year 1907, was at times secretary, president, and secretary and treasurer of the corporation. July 10, 1907, he presented an account for services in these respective capacities to the corporation. Therein he also included items for taxes paid by him on the corporate property for 20 years; for special and extraordinary services under the resolutions of a specified date; and for advertising meetings, and interest thereon. The aggregate of the whole account was $4,003. The aggregate of the items last described was.$903. The directorate, of which he was one, allowed his account in toto. At this meeting accounts of other directors and officers for services were allowed, though in each instance the alleged creditor of the corporation did not, as the minutes show, vote upon the allowance of his particular claim. The account allowed to S. A. Ellis was ordered paid, half in stock issued at par, and half in a note maturing in 30 days. This was accepted by S. A. Ellis. On August 10, 1907, the bill alleges S. A. Ellis assigned this note for $2,001.50 to his son (appellant). It is further alleged that the purpose and scheme in so assigning the note was to arm appellant to invoke the United States District Court's power to adjudicate the corporation an involuntary bankrupt; the general assignment before mentioned having been that day executed.

It is further alleged that the transfer and assignment was without consideration; that appellant "at said time had notice that these complainants and other stockholders denied that said corporation justly owed the debt for which the note was given, and that they had filed said former bill in this court for the purpose, among other things, to prevent the payment of said alleged debt, and he had notice at said time of the rights and equities of said corporation and these complainants as against the payment of the same."

"Orators aver that the transfer of said note, the adoption of said resolution, and the execution of said assignment were parts and parcel of a conspiracy on the part of said members of said board of directors, and said persons whose said claims had been allowed, to defraud orators and other stockholders of said corporation, not members of said conspiracy, by having said claims alleged to be due satisfied from the assets of said corporation, as a bankrupt, and thereby defraud its remaining stockholders; that it was the purpose of said persons, in furtherance of said conspiracy and their efforts to wreck said corporation, to deprive this court of jurisdiction of this cause, to have said bankruptcy cause instituted by a pretended innocent creditor, so

that the defense of said bankruptcy proceedings could
be undertaken and controlled by said majority of said
board of directors, to the end that said fictitious and
invalid claims might be allowed as legal and subsisting
debts against said corporation in said bankruptcy proceedings, and there paid out of the assets of said corporation, and that further counsel fees incurred by
said persons holding said claims and said members of
the board of directors, since the last meeting of said
board, for services in their additional efforts to wreck
said corporation, might be worked in as additional
debts against said corporation, and then and there allowed and ordered paid. Orators further aver that in
further pursuance of said conspiracy said majority of
said board of directors authoried the said C. B. Powell, as attorney for said corporation, to file an answer to
said petition in bankruptcy, admitting its allegations,
which was done."

The bankruptcy proceeding having been dismissed
by the United States court, appellant instituted his
action at law to enforce the payment of the note. It
is averred that the governing body of the corporation
and its officers took no steps to defend against the action, until the time had about arrived when judgment
by default could be taken. The bill was amended, setting forth the facts indicated, whereupon the further
prosecution of that action was restrained.

Primarily only the corporation may seek relief from
or redress for corporate wrongs. This rule has, however, found exception in those cases, among others perhaps, where the corporation actually or virtually refuses to institute or prosecute such a suit, or where the
wrongdoers themselves would be in control of the litigation necessary to enforce or protect corporate rights.
—*Montgomery Traction Co. v. Harmon*, 140 Ala. 505,

37 South. 371; *Tillis v. Brown,* 154 Ala. 403, 45 South. 589. No demand or request of the corporate authorities is required to be made, as a condition to suit by the stockholder, where it can be inferred with reasonable certainty that it would be refused, actually or virtually, or where, being the wrongdoers, a majority of the governing body would control the litigation so requested or demanded.—Author. supra. The acts and conditions shown in the amended bill leave no sort of doubt of the right of complainants to maintain this bill on the theory we have indicated. Whether the bill is maintainable upon the theory that dissolution of the corporation should be effected is not decided, since, as we view the record, that question is not presented by one necessarily entitled to contest it.

Coming down more particularly to the grounds of demurrer interposed by appellant, it is insisted, first, that the remedy at law was adequate and complete to determine in the action then pending the validity of the appellant's claim. It will suffice to say in response to this contention that equity, having been warrantably invoked, upon the theory indicated, to redress corporate wrongs, was in duty bound to draw within its jurisdiction every phase of the controversy involved in the wrongs charged in the amended bill. Under the charges of the amended bill, it is evident that the claim asserted by appellant was one of the immediate products of the wrongs charged therein.

It is next insisted that the bill is multifarious. Numerous grounds for this contention are stated in brief for appellant. The chief ground urged is that the amended bill seeks reimbursement of complainants for sums expended by them in resisting the petition to have the corporation adjudicated a bankrupt.

In *Bentley v. Barnes,* 155 Ala. 659, 47 South. 159,
Simpson, J., writing for the court, many of our previous decisions dealing with multfariousness were reviewed. It is not every defendant who can complain
of bills to which he is a party on that ground. In *Stone
v. Knickerbocker Insurance Co.,* 52 Ala. 589, Stone and
others, creditors of Drake, deceased, filed the bill to
subject the proceeds of insurance policies on Drake's
life to the satisfaction of their demands. Drake was
insolvent. The insurance companies and Sheppard, a
son-in-law of Drake, were among the parties defendant.
They demurred to the bill for multifariousess, in that
the bill should not, as was done, have sought to subject
the proceeds of both policies, written by separate companies, in *one* suit. What right or interest Sheppard
had in the subject-matter was not shown by the bill.
Notwithstanding, the lower court was held to have
erred in sustaining the demurrer of Sheppard. Speaking to multifariousness in general, the court said
(Brickell, C. J., writing) "that a bill is not multifarious which unites several matters distinct in themselves,
but which together make up the complainant's equity
and are necessary to complete relief." But to the point
in mind it was said, as to Sheppard's demurrer: "The
bill may be multifarious as to one or more defendants,
without being so as to others. When such a case is
presented, the objection can only be taken by the defendants who are *affected by it,* on the same principle
that a misjoinder of defendants is available only to the
parties improperly joined." (Italics supplied.)

This appellant is within this doctrine as to the feature of the bill seeking reimbursement as stated. In no
event could he be concerned in the allowance of this
claim for reimbursement. It does not appear that the
payment of his note, if found a valid charge against the

corporation, will be in any wise affected by an allowance of the claim for reimbursement. He is without interest in the corporation, except as an alleged creditor. A finding favorable or unfavorable to that claim can in no event affect his rights in the premises. Those interested in the corporation, and the corporation itself, are affected by the plea for reimbursement, and these have the right to raise the inquiry whether that feature of the bill renders it multifarious.

It is further insisted that the bill is multifarious because (a) appellant has no connection with a large part of the record; (b) the same defense is not applicable to the different aspects; (c) no common relief is claimed against defendant; (d) he is not interested in winding up the corporation; and (e) the necessary parties are different in the different phases of the bill. What has been said before disposes of the contentions we have lettered "d" and "e."

The others are not predicated upon accepted tests of multifariousness. There are doubtless expressions in the decisions some of which are noted in appellant's brief suggesting the lettered grounds as supporting the conclusion that the bill under review was multifarious. While this is true, it is evident that these expressions were but reinforcing *reasons* for the conclusions attained upon the status of averment presented in each, rather than—instead of—the announcement of a substantive proposition of pertinent law controlling the inquiry of multifariousness vel non. Such appears to have been the case in *Tutwiler v. Tuscaloosa Coal Company,* 98 Ala. 391, 7 South. 398, and *A. R. & C. Co. v. Linn,* 93 Ala. 610, 7 South. 191. In each of these cases there was no legitimate connection or relation between distinct matters which, when blended, went to constitute the complainant's equity, to effectuate complete

relief in respect of which the distinct matters shown
were necessary to be brought before the court. Other
of the decisions noted in brief for appellant on this
point fall within the same category. The effect of the
rule against multifariousness is to forbid the inclusion
in one bill of distinct, disconnected, independent, matters—matters that do not contribute to a single equity
the complainant would enforce.

If the three first lettered contentions of appellant
were sustained this undoubtedly sound and pertinent
observation, by Brickell, C. J., in *Truss v. Miller,* 116
Ala. 494, 505, 22 South. 863, would be departed from:
"When, as in the present case, the objection in that distinct and unconnected matters are joined against several defendants, it is not necessary that all the parties
should have an interest in all the matters of controversy; it is sufficient if each defendant has an interest in
some of the matters involved, and they are connected
with the others."

Upon general principles, without recourse to the provisions of Code 1907, § 3095, the opinion is entertained
that the bill is not multifarious on any ground available
to this appellant.

We find no ground of appellant's demurrer definitely
taking the objection that the bar of the statute of limitations, against the claim to which appellant is alleged
to have succeeded, was waived by the directorate of the
corporation. Doubtless the demurrant conceived that
the demurrer of Powell took the point. If it did so, as
to the claims asserted by him, the adoption, by most
general terms, of the grounds of his demurrer was not
sufficient to point appellant's demurrer on that score.

After a careful review of the whole amended bill, we
cannot approve appellant's insistences that the amended
bill is prolix; that it is indefinite in its averments of

improper conduct; that the appellant's connection with the wrongful scheme and conduct charged is not sufficiently, denitely, averred in the amended bill; or that the essential allegations to give the bill equity in the aspects with which appellant is concerned are but conclusions of the pleader. The bill is ample in averments of fact.

The contention of curative ratification by the directorate or of laches by the complainants, under the averments of the amended bill, cannot prevail.—*Montgomery Light Co. v. Lahcy,* 121 Ala. 131, 25 South. 1006.

We find no ground of appellant's demurrer assailing that feature of the amended bill, whereby the claim of appellant (assigned by S. A. Ellis to him) is asserted to be invalid, under the doctrine that corporate officers are presumed to serve without pay, unless a previous agreement is made or the circumstances reasonably invite the conclusion that compensation was contemplated. Not being raised, we cannot treat the question ably discussed in brief of the respective solicitors.

No error appearing in overruling appellant's demurrer, the decree in that particular is affirmed.

Affirmed.

SIMPSON, SOMERVILLE, and MAYFIELD, JJ., concur.

[Swope. et al. v. Swope.]

Swope, *et al. v.* Swope.

Bill to Remove an Estate from the Probate to the Chancery Court and for Final Settlement.

(Decided Feb. 1. 1911. Rehearing denied May 5, 1911.
55 South. 418.)

1. *Courts; Priority of Jurisdiction; Settlement of Estate.*—As Probate and Chancery courts have concurrent jurisdiction of the settlement of an estate, the court first acquiring jurisdiction should be allowed to continue unless some special reason arises for equitable interference.

2. *Infants; Next Friend; Removal.*—While any one can act as next friend for an infant in bringing a suit, and while it requires no authority from the court to bring such suit, the court may and should revoke the authority of the next friend when it appears that he is not a proper party to prosecute the suit.

3. *Same; Party.*—While a next friend is not technically speaking a party to a suit. he is a party in the contemplation of the statutes. and the practice of courts as to the conduct of the suit.

4. *Actions; Same Person as Plaintiff and Defendant; Sale of Infant's Land.*—An administrator could not as next friend of his infant ward prosecute a suit chiefly against himself both as administrator and as his guardian for the sale of lands of an estate.

5. *Executors and Administrators; Sale of Lands.*—Under sections 2619. 2620 and 2621. Code 1907, a sale is authorized only at the suit of the personal representative. and not at the suit of an heir or legatee. and hence an infant heir could not by next friend maintain a bill to have land of the estate sold for distribution.

(McClellan. J., dissenting.)

APPEAL from Lawrence County Court.

Heard before Hon. W. H. SIMPSON.

Bill by Carter Swope, pro ami against Clay Swope and others as guardians, etc., to remove an estate from the Probate to the Chancery court, and to wind up the estate. From a decree for complainant respondent appeals. Reversed and remanded.

KIRK, CARMICHAEL & RATHER for appellant. The probate and chancery courts have concurrent jurisdiction in the matter of estates, and the court first taking jurisdiction should retain it, unless cause for equitable interference should arise.—*Warren v. Lewis*, 53 Ala. 622; *Ligon v. Ligon*, 105 Ala. 464; *McNeil v. McNeil*, 36 Ala. 115. After an administration has been pending more than eighteen months the distributees have a prima facie right to ask for a settlement.—*Hooper v. Smith*, 57 Ala. 557; *Cook v. Cook*, 69 Ala. 294. There is no privity between a resident and a foreign administrator. The doctrine is the same where the same person is administrator in both States.—*Johnson v. McKinnon*, 129 Ala. 226; *Jefferson v. Beard*, 117 Ala. 436. It is not necessary that settlement should be made in a chancery court because of the fact that the administrator of the estate and guardian of the infant distributee is the same person.—Section 2684 Code 1907. The purchase of the notes and mortgages on a tract of land belonging to the estate does not bring about any matter of complication or special equity.—*Moore v. Winston*, 66 Ala. 296; *Shackleford v. Bankhead*, 72 Ala. 476; *Draper v. Draper*, 64 Ala. 547. The Tennessee claim not having been filed against the Alabama estate is barred and is not a charge upon the property.—Section 2667, Code 1907. It therefore follows that the demurrers to the bill should have been sustained. The motion to dismiss for want of equity should also have been sustained.—*Tenn. C., I. & R. R. Co., v. Hayes*, 97 Ala. 209; 2 Johns Chan. 542; I. N. Y. Chancery, 482; 22 Cyc. 631; Pom. Equity. Secs. 1305, 1307 and 1309.

C. M. SHERROD and E. W. GODBY, for appellee. The filing of the bill by Carter Swoope, through his general guardian and next friend, rendered him the ward of the court whose jurisdiction over him thereby attached;

giving to the court a general superintendency and control over his affairs.—3rd Ed. Pomeroy's Eq. Jurisprudence, Sec. 1305; *Proctor v. Scharpff,* 80 Ala. 229-230; *Rivers v. Durr,* 46 Ala. 422; *McGowan v. Lufburrow,* 14 Am. St. Rep. 181. As there had never been any removal or resignation of the guardian it was impossible that the probate court could have had any sort of jurisdiction over the final settlement of his accounts.— *Lewis v. Allred,* 57 Ala. 632; *Glass v. Glass,* 76 Ala. 371; *Lee v. Lee,* 67 Ala. 419. The knowledge or consent of the infant to file a bill in his name by his next friend is entirely immaterial; upon suggestion the court will investigate whether it be to his interest to proceed with the bill or whether the next friend is a fit and proper person to champion his cause.—Tyler on Infancy, Sec. 139, P. 204 and 205 and Sec. 138, P. 204; Sims Chancery Practice, Sec. 64. E. C. Swoope's dual capacity as guardian and administrator necessitated the exercise of jurisdiction by the chancery court over his accounts in both capacities, in order in each instance to award the proper charges and credits, and to fix his liability in each capacity.—*Johnson v. Porterfield,* 43 South. 231. The bill of Carter Swoope, an infant and distributee of the estate, was sufficient to confer jurisdiction upon the chancery court, even if it had stated no ground of equitable jurisdiction.—*Hurt v. Hurt,* 47 South. 262; *Pearson v. Dorrington,* 21 Ala. 176; *Glenn v. Billingslea,* 64 Ala. 345; *Baker v. Mitchell,* 109 Ala. 490. It is impossible for the jurisdiction of the probate court to attach to the final settlement of the administration until the administrator has filed his accounts and vouchers for settlement and until the date has been set for the hearing and passing upon the same.—*Ligon v. Ligon,* 17 South. 90, 105 Ala. 460; *Glenn v. Billingslea,* 64 Ala. 345; *Gamble v. Jordan,* 54 Ala. 432; *Dimmick v. Stokes,* 43 South. 854; *Hurt v. Hurt,* 47 South. 260. The settlement of the Tennessee ancillary administration did not deprive the adminis-

trator of the right to resort to Tennessee lands to pay
any judgment rendered against him after said settlement, in a suit brought against his intestate there which
was pending at the date of said settlement; and this
feature renders it equitable to withhold sufficient Alabama funds to meet such prospective judgment.—*Reynolds v. Reynolds,* 11 Ala. 1026; 18 Cyc. 634-635, and
670-671; *Sellars v. Smith,* 11 Ala. 265. The administrator is entitled to credit for the Alabama funds invested in the unmatured Sledge & Norfleet notes to
enable him to advantageously dispose of the intestate's
equity in the Mississippi plantation.—18 Cyc. 1140;
634-635. The right to reimbursement for the saving to
the estate and the right to hold Annie responsible for
personal assets received by her from Alabama is an
additional ground of equity.—*Stewart v. Stewart,* 31
Ala. 212-213; *Bellamy v. Thornton,* 103 Ala. 104; *Spin-
dle v. Blakeney,* 144 Ala. 196; 18 Cyc. 634-635. The
estate and the parties and the administrator all alike
constitute a unity and the equity of the domiciliary
administration has jurisdiction.—18 Cyc. 670-671; *Mc-
Namara v. Dwyer,* 32 Am. Dec. 629; *Greenhood v.
Greenhood,* 29 South. 300; 18 Cyc. 1248; *Cureton v.
Mills,* 36 Am. Rep. 702 to 711.

MAYFIELD, J.—William C. Swoope, a resident of
Lawrence county, Alabama, died intestate February 17,
1907, leaving four minor children, Annia, Temple, Clay
and Carter, as his sole heirs. He left a considerable
estate in Alabama, Mississippi and Tennessee, but was
largely indebted. Edgar C. Swoope, a brother of intestate and main actor in this suit, was appointed administrator of the estates in all three of the states, and
guardian of the wards and their estates in Alabama.
The letters of administration and guardianship were

[Swope, et al. v. Swope.]

granted by the probate court of Lawrence county, Ala., and the estate of the intestate in Alabamaa was being administered in that court, as well as the estates of the wards. Annie, the oldest of the children, became of age October 26, 1908, and on the 29th of March, 1909, 18 months having elapsed from the granting of the letters of administration, she filed a petition in the probate court of Lawrence county to compel the administrator to make a final settlement of the estate; and that court entered an order directing the administrator to file his accounts and vouchers for a final settlement.

The administrator appeared and filed objections, upon various grounds, to then making final settlement; and the consideration of his objections was several times continued by the court. While this proceeding was thus pending, the administrator filed a petition in the probate court, to sell lands belonging to the estate of his intestate, which petition was resisted by all the heirs. While both of these proceedings was thus pending in the court, the minors, acting through Annie, filed a petition in the probate court, asking that the administrator, who was their guardian, be removed from the guardianship of their property. Soon after this, the administrator, acting as next friend of the youngest child, filed in the chancery court of Lawrence county a bill against himself, as administrator and as guardian and the other children and heirs, seeking to remove the administration of the estate from the probate court into the chancery court.

The administrator, as such, answered this bill filed by himself as next friend, made his answer a cross-bill against all the children including his ward, and sought to enjoin the proceedings in the probate court, instituted to compel him to make a final settlement of the decedent's estate and of his guardianship of the children's estate, and to remove the same into the chancery court for settlement there; and also sought an order of the court directing that all of the lands of the estate in Alabama be sold for distribution among the heirs. The children, including Carter,. the one for whom the administrator had filed the original bill as next friend, by their attorney and guardian ad litem, demurred to the original and cross-bills and filed a motion to dismiss same, setting up facts which were not stated in the bills, showing that the probate court had taken jurisdiction to finally settle the estate of the decedent; and prayed the removal of the guardian, and that he be required to make final settlement of his guardianship before the filing of the bill.

Probate and chancery courts are given concurrent jurisdiction of the settlement of estates of decedents, and the court first acquiring jurisdiction should be allowed to continue in the settlement unless (the case being in the probate court) some special reason arises for equitable interference. This is always true as to suits to remove, filed by the personal representative, or any person other than the heir, distributee, legatee or devisee. And, after the probate court has acquired jurisdiction for the special purpose of final settlement of the pending administration, there can be no removal into chancery at the suit of the heir or distributee except upon some ground of exclusive equity cognizance, or it be shown that the powers of the probate court are inadequate.—*Ligon v. Ligon*, 105 Ala. 17 South. 89.

While the bill in this case is technically filed by one of the heirs and distributees, who is not required to show special equities as against the personal representative or creditors, yet, in fact, it is practically filed by the personal representative. While the infant is the real party in law, and the next friend is only the nomi-

nal party, yet it is the next friend—and not the infant—
who decides upon the policy and the propriety of the litigation, and who selects and determines the course of
the litigation, subject of course to the supervision of
the chancellor. So far as the policy of propriety of
maintaining this suit is concerned, it is and was determined by the personal representative, and not by the
infant heir.

The undisputed facts in this record show that the
administrator was not a proper person to prosecute this
suit as next friend for the infant, Carter. His interests in the whole matter were adverse and antagonistic.
As the next friend for the infant, he files the bill against
himself and others; and then answers his own bill and
makes it a cross-bill against the complainant, his ward
and client, and the other respondents to the original
bill. The rights of the infant could not be properly represented and protected in such a proceeding.

While any one can act as next friend for an infant,
in bringing a suit, and while it requires no permission or
authority from the court to so bring such a suit, yet the
court can and should revoke the authority of a next
friend, when it appears—as it does in this case—that he
is not a proper person to prosecute the suit, whether
from incompetency or from having interests conflicting
with those of the infant.—*Barwick r. Rackley,* 45 Ala.
218, 219; *Dowty r. Hall,* 83 Ala. 168, 3 South. 315. See
5 Port.

It is said in *Barwick's Case, supra,* that "on a proper
application, which may be made by the infant, by a
next friend, the general guardian, or any near relative
of the infant, the court will institute an inquiry whether
the suit is for the benefit of the infant, or whether it is
for his interest that it should be prosecuted by the person named as next friend; and if, on such inquiry, it

shall appear that the suit is not for the benefit of the infant, or that it is not for his interest that the suit should be prosecuted by the person named as next friend, in either case the court would order the proceedings to be stayed; and in the latter case will remove the next friend and appoint another in his stead." Page 219, 45 Ala.

The facts in this case are similar to those of *Dowty v. Hall, supra,* and some of the purposes of the bills in the two cases are the same. In that case, the court, speaking through Stone, C. J., after pointing out some other defects in the bill, said: "Nor should William Sandford be allowed to prosecute this suit as next friend of William Dowty. Their rights and interests according to the averments of the bill are antagonistic, and they should not be co-complainants."—83 Ala. 168, 3 South. 317.

For much stronger and more convincing reasons in this case, E. C. Swoope should not be allowed to prosecute this suit as next friend of his infant ward, when the suit is chiefly against himself, both as administrator and as guardian. This record presents the anomalous condition of one person instituting a suit in equity in two representative capacities. This condition appearing affirmatively on the face of the proceedings, the chancellor should not have allowed the suit to proceed as far as it has done. While there is no statutory inhibition against any one person's acting as next friend for another, and while, as before said, the next friend is not the real party, yet it is incongruous that the same person should direct and conduct both the prosecution and the defense of the same suit in a court of either law or equity, no matter in what capacity he may appear. Especially is this true when such person is necessarily liable to the person whom he represents, as to both the subject-matter and the result of the suit.

It was not necessary in this case to institute any inquiry as to the propriety of E. C. Swoope's representing the infant, Carter Swoope, as next friend, for the reason that the bill of complaint affirmatively showed that he was not a proper person. The interest of the next friend and that of the ward or client were directly conflicting as to all relief or redress sought by the bill. The chancellor should have at once removed the next friend, and appointed another in his stead. The chancellor in his opinion says that he will in the future substitute another next friend for the complainant if it is necessary; but he should have done this at once upon the first hearing. Some of the evils of this delay or failure are shown by the subsequent proceedings of the suit. The chancellor, of course, had to appoint a guardian ad litem to defend for the infant, Carter, as to the cross-bill filed against him by his friend and guardian. This guardian ad litem, who must be presumed to be impartial and to properly represent the interest of the infant, answered and demurred to the cross-bill. In this answer he denied all the facts set up in the original and cross-bills, which are claimed to give them equity. To further confuse matters, we find the guardian ad litem of Carter Swoope both denying and demurring to the original bill filed by Carter Swoope. This infant by one of his representatives is affirming a certain state of facts, and by his other representative is denying these same facts and affirming the contrary. How can any court proceed correctly and certainly in such a state of the pleadings? How can the court properly protect the rights of such infant when it is so represented?

While a next friend is any one who will undertake to prosecute the suit of an infant or person under legal disability, and is not, technically speaking, a party to the suit, yet he is a party within the contemplation of the statutes, and the practice of courts, as to the conduct of the suit.—*Thomas v. Safe Deposit Co.*, 73 Md. 451, 21 Atl. 367, 23 Atl. 3.

The original practice as to the next friend seems to have been that the next friend and the infant went before the judge at chambers, in person, or presented a petition to him, praying that the person intended be assigned by the judge as the infant's prochein ami. The judge, if he thought the proposed person a proper one, issued a fiat to the clerk, on which the clerk drew up a rule admitting such person to sue in the particular case mentioned, as the next friend. This ancient and formal practice, however, has become obsolete; and the next friend now sues in any case without previous permission of the court or of the infant. But the reason still exists that the next friend should be a proper person to prosecute the suit. He should be competent and should have the interest of the infant at heart, and his own personal interest should not conflict with or be opposed to the interest of the infant. It is just as necessary that a next friend should be personally disinterested in the result of the infant's suit as it is that a guardian ad litem should be; the only difference of function being that the one prosecutes, and the other defends, for the infant. It is true that we have statutes regulating the appointment of guardians ad litem and none as to next friends; but the importance of having proper persons is no greater in the one case than in the other. The statute as to the appointment of guardians ad litem prohibits even the suggestion of a person, as such, by the adverse parties or their attorneys. Code 1907, § 4484. When the law thus regards the rights of the infant, when defending, with such jealousy, surely it ought not to allow the prosecution of the infant's rights to be conducted by the same person who is defending

against such rights. That part of the original and cross
bills which seeks to sell the lands of the estate of the
intestate is wholly bad and subject to the demurrers.
There is no pretense that the sale is necessary to pay
the debts of the estate, but the contrary is alleged. In
fact, the specific purpose of the sale is alleged to be a
distribution among the heirs.

(5) The statutes authorizing the sale of lands of the
estate of a deceased person as a part of the administration of the estate are sections 2619, 2620 and 2621 of the
Code, respectively, as follows:

"Sec. 2619. * * * Sale for payment of debts when
there is a will.—Lands may be sold by the executor, or
by the administrator, with the will annexed, for the payment of debts, when the will gives no power to sell the
same for that purpose, and the personal estate is insufficient therefor.

"Sec. 2620. * * * Sale in case of intestacy.—In
case of intestacy, lands may be sold by the administrator for the payment of debts, when the personal estate is
insufficient therefor.

"Sec. 2621. * * * Sale for division.—Lands of an
estate may be sold by order of the probate court having
jurisdiction of the estate, when the same cannot be
equitably divided among the heirs or devisees, when any
adult heir or devisee files his written consent that the
land be sold."

Here it is not averred that the personal property is
insufficient to pay debts, without which averment and
proof there could be no sale to pay debts. These statutes as to the administration of estates only authorize
the land to be sold at the suit of the personal representative, and not at the suit of an heir or legatee. Sales of
lands are thus made as part of the administration of the estate. The original bill in this

case professes to be filed by an infant heir against the
person representative et al., and, of course, the infant
heir in such bill cannot seek to have the lands sold for
distribution. His right to maintain a bill for the sale
of the lands in question would be under the statutes as
to sales for partition, and not under those for the administration of the estate of the deceased person. While
the cross-bill is by the personal representative, the proper party to sell lands of the estate, it shows no reason or
necessity therefor, and makes no attempt to show that
an adult heir or devisee consented to the sale, as is required by the statute, but, on the contrary, shows that
the only adult heir was opposed, and objected to the
sale. In other words, it seeks to have the lands sold
as a part of the administration of the estate in express
violation of the statute. It may be that, when the chancery court removes the next friend and appoints a suitable person to act in such capacity, such substituted next
friend may not deem it to the interest of the infant to
prosecute the main suit.

For the error in overruling the demurrers to the original and cross-bills, the decree is reversed and the cause
is remanded.

Reversed and remanded.

DOWDELL, C. J., and SIMPSON, ANDERSON, SAYRE, and
SOMMERVILLE, J. J., concur.

McCLELLAN, J.—(dissenting).—The chancellor
should not be put in error for overruling the demurrer
of the guardian ad litem of Carter Swoope to the original bill of Carter Swoope, for the obvious reason that a
party cannot demur to his own pleading. Nor can the
chancellor be put in error for overruling the motion of
the guardian ad litem of Carter Swoope to dismiss Car-

ter Swoope's own original bill for want of equity; and
so, for two reasons: First, motion to dismiss for want
of equity was "abolished" by Code 1907, § 3121; second,
a party cannot, as in case of demurrer, before stated,
thus invoke the court to test his own pleading. Again,
no appeal lies from an interlocutory decree overruling a
demurrer to a cross-bill.—*Bickley v. Bickley,* 129 Ala.
403, 29 South. 854; *Summer v. Hill,* 157 Ala. 230, 47
South. 565; *Herndon v. Gilreath* (mem.) 165 Ala. 669,
51 South. 601. When review may be had of such ruling
is pointed out in *Bickley v. Bickley,* and in *Summer v.
Hill,* namely, upon appeal from the final decree in the
cause. Accordingly the assignment of error from 33
to 47, inclusive, invoking review of the ruling on the
demurrer to the cross-bill, "cannot * * * be considered."—*Summer v. Hill,* 157 Ala. 233, 47 South. 566.
So it may be just here suggested that the majority are
in error in pronouncing erroneous, and reversing the
chancellor for "overruling the demurrers to the * * *
cross-bills."

This process of elimination, which seems to the writer
to be incontestable, winnows the review, on this appeal,
to the two questions: (a) Whether the demurrer to the
original bill (of respondents other than Carter Swoope
whose bill it was) should have been sustained for want
of equity therein; and (b) whether the demurrer, taking
objection to E. C. Swoope's serving as next friend to
Carter Swoope in Carter Swoope's original bill, was, by
the chancellor, erroneously overruled. If E. C. Swoope
was competent, as next friend of Carter Swoope, to present the original bill, it is clear that the original bill
possessed equity to invite the removal of the administration of the estate in which Carter Swoope was one of
the heirs from the probate into the chancery court.
Where the probate court has not taken jurisdiction for

final settlement of the estate (and it had not in this instance)' an heir's bill to remove the administration
from the probate court possesses equity, without showing any other lead to invoke that jurisdiction. If perchance the heir's bill should pray for relief, in the course
of administration of the estate, not grantable by the
chancery court, that would not, could not, denude his
bill of the equity inhering in his (heir's) right to remove the administration. This proposition finds apt authority in *Bromberg v. Bates*, 112 Ala. 363, 20 South.
786 (the decision, on this matter, being summarized in
the first head note), and in *Bresler v. Bloom*, 147 Ala.
504, 41 South. 1010. The decision in *Kirkbride v. Kelly*,
167 Ala. 570, 52 South. 660, may be opposed to the doctrine underlying the rulings in *Bromberg v. Bates* and
Bresler v. Bloom, but that decision does not take account of those cases, and hence does not overrule them.
Upon reason, principle and authority, in the particular
under consideration, *Bromberg v. Bates* and *Bresler v.
Bloom*, do not admit, it would seem, of question of their
soundness. The nature, office and purpose of a prochein
ami is amply yet accurately amply stated in *T. C. I. &
R. Co., v. Hayes*, 97 Ala. 201, 209-210, 12 South. 98,
102: "In theory a prochein ami is an officer of the
court in which a minor sues by him. His only functions
are to put his capacity to sue in the place of the infant's capacity, and thus set the machinery of justice in
motion. *The court is not asked to pass upon any right
of his, for he has no rights in the premises*, but only to
determine the claims of the minor which he *perfunc-
torily* brings before it. The character of the necessity
for his appearance marks the limitations of his powers.
* * * The next friend has no interest in the result of
the proceeding. * * * His being an officer of the

court is basis for the court's powers over him in the litigation." (Italics supplied).

Will demurrer lie to test the competency of a next friend, an officer of the court with powers, as defined in the case quoted, limited to the necessity for his appearance? That that inquiry may be instituted on proper application "by the infant of a next friend, the general guardian, or a near relative," is, of course, well recognized.—*Barwick v. Ruckley, pro ami,* 45 Ala. 215; *Bethea v. McCall,* 3 Ala. 449; *Hayes' Case, supra; Railroad v. Hanlon,* 53 Ala. 70, 82; 22 Cyc. p. 662 et seq. If it appears that the suit is not for the benefit of the infant, or that the named next friend should not prosecute the suit, the court will stay the proceeding; and, in the latter alternative, remove the named next friend and appoint another.—Authorities supra. The mere statement of this approved practice as well as the purposes to be subserved by the inquiry denies, in the writer's opinion, any possibility of recourse to demurrer to test the matter, to invite the inquiry. On demurrer, no investigation of fact, outside the averments of the pleading assailed, is possible. On the "application" contemplated by the long approved practice, fully stated in *Barwick v. Ruckley.* opportunity to present and have considered matters dehors the pleading, as well as the pleading itself, is afforded. But, aside from this approved practice, the consequence of suffering demurrer to supplant this practice demonstrates the total inappropriateness of demurrer to avail to test the competency, etc., of the next friend. After demurrer sustained to an original bill, even on a single ground, the litigation cannot proceed, unless it is amended to avoid the points taken by the demurrer and upon which the demurrer is sustained. —*Kinney v. Reeves & Co.,* 139 Ala. 386, 36 South. 22; *Coleman v. Butt,* 139 Ala. 266, 30 South. 364. In the

closing lines of the controlling opinion, it is said: "For
the error in overruling the demurrers to the original and
cross-bills the decree is reversed and the cause is remanded." But this is also said in the opinion of the
majority: "It may be that, when the chancery court
removes the next friend and appoints a suitable person
to act in such capacity, such substituted next friend may
not deem it to the interest of the infant to prosecute the
main suit." If the chancellor erred in overruling the
demurrer objecting to the competency, etc., of E. C.
Swoope as next friend, then upon the return of the cause
to his court, ordinarily, usually, he must, in deference
to the ruling here, sustain the demurrer. If that decretal order is entered, E. C. Swoope will be stricken as
next friend; and, unless amended, the bill will not permit further procedure upon it.—*Kinney v. Reeves & Co.,
supra; Coleman v. Butt, supra.* So that in that view
the quoted statement in the opinion that the chancery
court may remove E. C. Swoope would seem to be entirely vain, since the sustaining of the demurrer will
have immediately effected that. However, it may be
well concluded from the opinion that since this court
has not seen proper to itself sustain the demurrer the
chancery court may first observe its suggestion of substitution of another next friend, and thus avoid the
point of the demurrer in this particular. Whether this
anomalous situation may be worked out consistently
with orderly procedure and proper regard for the rights
of the demurrants is not now to be anticipated. It
would seem, however, aside from reversing the decree
mentioned, that this court has merely advised in the
premises without ruling to finality upon the demurrers.

If the decree here compels the chancery court to first
sustain the demurrer to the original bill in its objection
to the continuance of E. C. Swoope as next friend, it is

obvious that, unless amended, the original bill will not
support further proceedings. Who may amend the bill?
Surely, the court, of its own motion, cannot amend
pleadings. The infant complainant, incapacitated to
sue, certainly cannot perfect this imperfect pleading.
While the court may "upon proper application" remove
one prochein ami and appoint another instead, it cannot,
first hand, furnish a next friend. It has no such unin-
vited initiative. Logically and ordinarily, sustaining a
demurrer to an original bill, whereby the next friend is
ejected from the cause, would operate to end the proceeding; there being no one to amend to avoid the effect of the demurrer. Such a consequence cannot, it
seems to the writer, flow from any sound rule of procedure; and a rule of procedure that so concludes must
in the writer's opinion be totally inappropriate. Apart
from these considerations, the demurrer to the original
bill in respect of objection to the competency, etc., of the
next friend, was in my opinion properly overruled by
the chancellor. Carter Swoope was not, as before stated, a respondent in the original bill; and hence his guardian ad litem appointed for him as one of the respondents to the cross-bill was, of course, without right to demur to the original bill, whatever objections he might
have interposed to the cross-bill. May the respondents
to the original bill assume by demurrer the protection of
Carter Swoope (infant complainant in the original bill)
from a next friend who, it is claimed, is antagonistic to
the interests of Carter Swoope? It seems to the writer
that the question admits of but one response, and that
is in the negative. The relation to the original bill of
the next friend is that of an officer of the court. No
interest or right of his is litigable or determinable in
the cause.—*T. C. I. & R. R. Co. v. Hayes, supra.* So the
objection by the demurrant points alone to protecting

the infant complainant from an (alleged) antagonistically interested next friend. The demurrant is without
concern, in any way, in that asserted danger to the
complainant. If the relation between the interests of
the complainant and of the next friend was as asserted,
it could not affect in any degree or event the rights of
the respondents. If existing, the asserted relation concerned the next friend and the complainant only. If
existing, it was a matter that did not go to the perfection as to the parties or subject-matter of the original
bill. The next friend is not a party to the cause.—*T. C.
I. & R. R. Co. v. Hayes, supra.* Nor did the alleged antagonistic relation affect or bear upon the subject-matter of the original bill as far as the respondents were
concerned; for no right or interest of the next friend
was litigable as upon the original bill.

Dowty v. Hall, 83 Ala. 165, 3 South. 315, does not in
my opinion, sustain the controlling opinion in the particular under consideration. In that case the statement of facts on page 168 recites: "The chancellor sustained a demurrer to the bill on account of *misjoinder*
of Chess Carley & Co., Deitrich and others, and so far
as it sought a settlement of the administration in chief;
but he held that it contained equity so far as it prayed
a settlement of Hall's administration. The complainants appeal *from this decree,* and here assign as error
the sustaining of the demurrer." (Italics supplied.)
As appears, the demurrer was sustained for misjoinder.
That is not the matter involved or ruled upon in this
appeal. Carter Swope was the sole complainant in
the original bill, so there could be no question of misjoinder. A full reading of the decision in *Dowty v.
Hall* will emphasize its want of bearing on this appeal.

Upon the foregoing considerations, I am unable to
concur in the opinion disposing of the appeal.

Irwin, *et ux. v.* Coleman, *et ux.*

Bill to Declare a Deed a Mortgage and to Redeem.

(Decided May 11, 1911.　Rehearing denied June 8, 1911.
55 South. 492.)

1. *Pleading; Amendment; Departure.*—Where both bills relate to the same subject matter, or transactions between the same parties, an amended bill is not a departure from the original bill, under section 3095, Code 1907.

2. *Mortgages; Deed as Mortgage; Character of Transaction.*—Where the relation of debtor and creditor exists at the time of the execution of a deed absolute on its face, or where the transaction commences in a negotiation for the loan of money, or where there is a great disparity in the value of the property conveyed and the consideration paid, or where there is a debt continuing for the payment of which the grantor is liable, the transaction is regarded as a mortgage rather than a conditional sale unless the purchaser overcomes these facts by clear and convincing proof.

3. *Same.*—As between a conditional deed and a mortgage, in case of doubt, the court will always lean toward the mortgage.

4. *Same; Fraud.*—Where the complainants, ignorant people, applied to the repondent for a loan and executed an agreement that in consideration of the loan and the interest to be charged thereon they had sold certain property to defendant, which agreement contained stipulations as to interest and payment, and a stipulation by the defendant to reconvey the land to complainant upon payment of the loan, and complainants executed notes to the defendant, and ignorantly signed a paper represented as a copy of their agreement, but which was in fact a deed conveying the property to the defendant, complainant was entitled to have the deed cancelled and declared to be a mortgage.

5. *Same; Existence of Debt.*—Where the complainants, on execution of a deed to respondent procured respondents to assume their indebtedness to a loan association, the existence of a debt on the part of the respondent to be secured by the conveyance, is to be considered in determining whether the conveyance was a deed or mortgage.

6. *Landlord and Tenant; Estoppel; Title; Dealings With.*—The fact that while in ignorance and in distress at her husband's illness, one of the complainants agreed to pay a d did pay rent to a grantee of respondent, who had notice of the transaction between defendant and complainant, and of complainant's interest and equities in the land conveyed, does not estop complainants from seeking a cancellation of their deed to defendant, and to have the deed declared a mortgage.

[Irwin, et ux v. Coleman, et ux.]

APPEAL from Morgan Chancery Court.

Heard before Hon. W. H. SIMPSON.

Bill by Daniel Coleman and wife against S. W. Irwin and wife for the cancellation of a deed, to declare it a mortgage, and for other relief. Decree for complainants, and respondents appeal. Affirmed.

The agreement noted in the opinion is dated March 26, 1909, and is executed by S. W. Irwin and Daniel and Mattie Coleman, and asserts in effect that for and in consideration of the sum of $300 Irwin has sold to Coleman and wife certain described land in the city of Decatur, for which the parties of the second part have executed several promissory notes bearing even date therewith, and due and payable at S. W. Irwin's office, with interest at 8 per cent per annum, payable monthly, to be paid $10 per month, with interest for 30 months. Then follow covenants, stipulations, and agreements on the part of Irwin to convey to the complainants the land upon full performance by them in the payment of the notes and interest. Then follow certain stipulations on the part of Coleman to keep the house insured, to pay all state, county, municipal, school, or other taxes, to keep the premises in good repair, and upon failure on their part to keep and perform all the conditions contained in the agreement the same shall work a forfeiture, with the right in Irwin to re-enter and take possession of the property. Exhibit B is a deed, executed on the 26th day of March, 1909, by Mattie and Daniel Coleman to S. W. Irwin, to the lands described in the contract heretofore set out. Exhibit C is a deed, dated September 9, 1909, from S. W. Irwin and wife to B. J. Brown, to the land. Then follow other deeds not necessary to be here set out.

WERT & LYNNE, for appellant. The amendment worked an entire change and the court erred in allowing it.—*Ward v. Patton*, 75 Ala. 207; *Patterson v. Patterson*, 1 Abb. Prac. 262; *Brown v. Hunter*, 121 Ala. 210; *Ray v. Womble*, 56 Ala. 32. The chancellor erred in his finding on the facts.—*Rogers v. Burt*, 47 South. 230. There was no misrepresentation, or if there was, complainants were willingly deceived and the maxim volunti non fit injuria applies.—*Monroe v. Pritchett*, 16 Ala. 785. Complainants were guilty of negligence.—*Monroe v. Pritchett*, supra: Smith on Fraud, secs. 3, 77, 78; *Guy v. Blue*, 45 N. E. 1052. The complainants ratified the transaction and estopped themselves by agreeing to pay and paying rent.—16 Kan. 312; 104 N. W. 845; 57 S. W. 584. There was no special inadequacy of consideration.

KYLE & HUTSON, for appellee. The bill undoubtedly contains equity.—*Smith v. Smith*, 153 Ala. 508; *Brown v. Hunter*, 121 Ala. 212. There was actual fraud.—*Johnson v. Cook*, 73 Ala. 540; *Peek v. Houpert*, 104 Ala. 506; *Tillis v. Austin*, 117 Ala. 262; *Leonard v. Roebuck*, 44 South. 290. This being true, and the complainants being in possession, they had a right to have the deed cancelled.—*Eufaula v. Pruitt*, 120 Ala. 470; *Curry v. Peebles*, 83 Ala. 225; *Lehman v. Shook*, 69 Ala. 286; 6 Cyc. 287; 4 Pom. Eq. 1399. The deed being void, there is no question of bona fides.—13 Am. Rep. 679; Howard, 495; 26 Am. Rep. 600; 1 Am. St. Rep. 241; 1 A. & E. Dec. & Eq. 105; 9 Cyc. 142. The deed and contract will be construed together.—*Sims v. Gaines*, 64 Ala. 392; *Cosby v. Buchanan*, 81 Ala. 574; *Elston v. Comer*, 108 Ala. 76; *Glass v. Heironemous*, 125 Ala. 141. The court's attention is called generally to the following cases as sustaining the view taken by the chancellor.—*Robers v. Burt*, 157 Alt. 91; *Harrison v. Murry*, 157 Ala. 227; *Rose v. Gandy*, 137 Ala.

330; *Turner v. Williamson,* 72 Ala. 361; *Reeves v. Abercrombie,* 108 Ala. 588; *Thomas v. Livingston,* 147 Ala. 216; *Maxwell v. Herzfelt,* 149 Ala. 69; *Vincent v. Walker,* 85 Ala. 337. As to the rules of evidence, see authorities supra, and 3 Pom. Eq. sec. 1195.

SIMPSON, J.—The bill originally filed by the appellees, sought the cancellation of a deed on account of misrepresentations—the allegations being that complainants, who are ignorant negroes, applied to de-defendant S. W. Irwin to borrow $175; that he agreed to lend that amount if complainants would pay him $125 in addition as interest, the whole amount to be paid in 30 months at $10 per month, with interest; that thereupon complainants entered into the written instrument, which is made Exhibit A to the bill (the substance of which will be set out in the statement of the case), and complainants executed notes in accordance therewith, and have since paid three of the notes; that said Irwin presented to complainants another paper, which complainants thought was a mere copy of Exhibit A, said Irwin so stating to them, and they signed the same, but that it was really a deed conveying the property to said Irwin, as shown by the copy attached to the bill, marked "Exhibit B"; that about September 9, 1909, said Irwin conveyed the property to Bennett J. Brown, who had notice of the contract between complainants and said Irwin, and of complainants' interest and equities in the land; that shortly after said date one Dix came to complainants' house, professing to be the agent of said Brown, and informed the complainant Mattie Coleman that the property belonged to said Brown, and demanded that she agree to pay rent for the same; that at said time said Daniel Coleman (her husband, the other complainant) was very sick, and said Mattie Coleman, without the knowledge of said Daniel, being in distress about the illness of her husband, and being ignorant, agreed to pay rent, and did afterwards pay $3 rent; and that an attachment has been levied for rent. Complainants offer to pay whatever is due to Irwin, submit themselves to the order of the court, and pray for an injunction of the attachment proceedings, and that the deed (Exhibit B) and also the deed from Irwin to Brown (Exhibit C) be cancelled.

A demurrer was sustained to the original bill, on the grounds that the paper, "Exhibit A," is a complete refutation of complainants' contention, and an admission of title in Irwin, and that a tenant cannot assail the title of his landlord, while holding possession. The complainants then amended the bill so as to allege that the contract (Exhibit A) as well as the deed (Exhibit B) was obtained by misrepresentation and fraud, and that it was intended only as a mortgage, and prayed that upon the payment of the amount due the contract and deed (Exhibits A and B) be declared to be null and void. A demurrer to the bill as thus amended was overruled, and the answer filed, the testimony taken, and another amendment to the bill filed to meet the evidence, setting out the transactions more in detail, reasserting that the papers were intended as a mortgage, and praying that they be declared a mortgage, that a reference be ordered to ascertain the amount due, excluding usury, and that complainants be allowed to redeem, that the title be divested out of Brown, etc. The demurrer to the bill as amended was overruled, and the decree rendered in accordance with the prayer of the bill.

The original bill and amendments all relate to the same subject-matter, the same contract or transaction, and to the same property, between the same parties. Consequently, under our statute, the objection that the amendment constitutes a departure is not well taken. Code 1907, § 3095.

This court has said that: "Although it is difficult to establish fixed rules by which to determine whether a particular transaction is a mortgage or a conditional sale, there are some facts which are regarded as of controlling importance in determining the question. Did the relation of debtor and creditor exist, before and at the time of the transaction? Or, if not, did the transaction commence in a negotiation for a loan of money? Was there great disparity between the value of the property and the consideration passing for it? Is there a debt continuing, for the payment of which the vendor is liable? If any one of these facts is found to exist, in a doubtful case it will go far to show a mortgage was intended. If all of them are found concurring, the transaction will be regarded as a mortgage rather than a conditional sale, unless the purchaser, by clear and convincing evidence, removes the presumption arising from them."—*Turner v. Wilkinson*, 72 Ala. 366; *Winn et al. v. Fitzwater et al.*, 151 Ala. 171, 178, 44 South. 97. See, also, 3 Pomeroy, Eq. Jur. (3d Ed.) 1195.

The appellants do not contend that the deed and contract created an unconditional fee in the respondents, but that the effect was to vest the title in respondents, and then to vest in the complainants only a conditional title, dependent upon the performance of the conditions by paying the installments of purchase money. It has been universally held that, as between a conditional fee and a mortgage, in cases of doubt the court will always lean towards the mortgage, as that secures the interests of all parties and works a hardship to none.—*McNeill v. Norsworthy*, 39 Ala. 156, 160; *Glass v. Hieronymus Bros.*, 125 Ala. 147, 148, 28 South. 71, 82 Am. St. Rep. 225; *Rose v. Gandy*, 137 Ala. 329, 34 South. 239.

This court has always emphasized the principle that, when a man of superior intelligence has a transaction with one who is ignorant, the utmost good faith must be observed.—*Abercrombie v. Carpenter et al.*, 150 Ala. 294, 43 South. 746. What was the situation of these . parties at the time of this transaction? The complainants owed, on a mortgage to the Building & Loan Association, $177.83. The transaction with the respondents created a debt of $300, with interest, payable in installments of $10 per month. If the mortgage had been foreclosed with the statutory right of redemption of two years, $10 per month would have fully paid the redemption money within the two years. It does not seem reasonable that the complainants would have conveyed away their rights by making a conditional deed, under which they would forfeit their property on failure to pay promptly the $10 per month until the amount of $300, with interest, was paid.

The transaction originated in a proposition to borrow the money to pay off the mortgage, and the evidence shows that the respondent Irwin still holds the notes against the complainants, and he explains this by saying that he holds them because he had to make the title good to Brown. While there is some conflict in the evidence, yet on the whole evidence we hold that the chancellor correctly held "that the method adopted in this transaction was for the purpose of securing a loan of money and to evade the law against usury." The assumption of the debt to the Building & Loan Association created the relation of debtor and creditor between complainants and Irwin.—*Shrere v. McGowin*, 143 Ala. 668, 42 South. 94.

Brown bought with notice, and the fact that the wife agreed to pay rent, under the circumstances, does not constitute an estoppel.—*McNeill v. Norsworthy, supra,* 39 Ala. 159.

The decree of the court is affirmed.

Affirmed.

McCLELLAN, MAYFIELD, and SOMMERVILLE, JJ., concur.

McHan v. McMurry.

Bill to Enjoin the Erection of a Dam.

(Decided May 9, 1911.   55 South. 793.)

1. *Injunction; Right; Equity.*—A bill without equity will not support an injunction of any character under any circumstances.

2. *Same; Application; Bill; Intendments.*—Where an application for an injunction is presented under section 4528, the complainant is the actor, and his bill, when attacked for want of equity, cannot be aided by presumption that amendable defects have been cured, as is the case on a motion to dissolve an injunction already granted for want of equity in the bill.

3. *Same; Threatened Injury.*—The allegations examined and held to contain no facts from which it could be reasonably inferred that the threatened injury was likely to happen and that the application was devoid of equity as such application sought relief merely from a prospective nuisance, concerning which the injury was contingent.

APPEAL from Cullman Chancery Court.

Heard before Hon. W. H. SIMPSON.

Bill by H. R. McMurry against James McHan seeking an injunction to restrain the erection of a dam. Decree for complainant and respondent appeals. Reversed, rendered and remanded.

J. B. BROWN for appellant. Where an injunction is granted on a bill which is wanting in equity it should be dissolved whether the allegations of the bill are admitted or denied.—*Satterfield v. John*, 53 Ala. 127; *Hart v. Clark*, 54 Ala. 490; *Bishop v. Wood*, 59 Ala. 253; *Chambers v. Ala. Grain Co.*, 67 Ala. 356. The principle on which equity grants relief in such a case as this is that there is a permanent continuing nuisance, and that the damages arising therefrom is continuous and constantly recurring, and the legal remedy inadequate.—*Ogletree v. McQuagg*, 67 Ala. 584; *Ninninger v. Norwood*, 72 Ala. 280; *Roberts v. Vest*, 126 Ala. 255; *Nixon v. Bolling*, 145 Ala. 277. Under these authorities it must be held that the bill was without equity, and that the court improperly granted the injunction.

F. E. ST. JOHN, for appellee. The granting or refusing of a temporary injunction is within the discretion of the trial court, and will not be disturbed where the bill contains equity.—*Chambers v. Ala. Iron Co.*, 67 Ala. 353; *Davis v. Sowell*, 77 Ala. 262; *Whorton v. Hannon*, 101 Ala. 558. The rule is the same as formerly that on motion to dissolve an injunction for want of equity in the bill all amendable defects are treated as supplied.—*Jones v. Bright*, 140 Ala. 268. The bill undoubtedly contains equity.—High on Injunctions, 714; *Ninninger v. Norwood*, 72 Ala. 277; *S. A. & M. R. R. Co., v. Buford*, 106 Ala. 303; *A. G. S. R. R. Co., v. Prouty*, 149 Ala. 71; *Crabtree v. Baker*, 75 Ala. 91; 67 Am. Dec. 666; 26 Penn. St. 417; 55 Am. Dec. 734.

McCLELLAN, J.—This bill is by a lower riparian proprietor against the adjacent upper proprietor, and seeks his restraint from the erection of a proposed dam, on his own lands, across a stream coursing through the farms of each. In the third paragraph of the bill must its equity be found, if at all. That paragraph reads:

"That defendant erected a dam across said Thacker's
creek and dammed up the creek, and on several occasions said dam broke or washed away, and caused the
water to come down said creek with such force and in
such volume that it overflowed complainant's farm,
which is and was in cultivation, and washed away the
dirt and soil, and washed great gulches or ditches in
complainant's field, and damaged complainant's farm
in the sum of $1,000; and said defendant is now erect-
ing another dam across said creek above complainant's
farm, against the objections of complainant, and is
building said dam in such way that it will not hold the
water which flows in said creek during the heavy rains,
and said dam will break or be washed away, and complainant's farm will again be overflowed with water,
and the dirt and soil will be washed away from said
farm, and great gulches or ditches will be washed in
said farm, until it will be rendered useless for cultivation, unless the defendant is restrained by this court
from erecting said dam."

Upon hearing (Code, § 4528), a temporary writ of
injunction was granted, as prayed. From this order
the appeal is prosecuted. Code, § 4531.

The hearing provided by Code, § 4528, is new to our
law. So this preliminary inquiry is mooted by the solicitors: Whether, under the new procedure for the issuance of injunctions, all amendable defects will be
treated as perfected, consistent with the rule applicable where *dissolution* of an injunction, for want of
equity in the bill, was the matter invoking the court's
ruling.— *Chambers v. Ala. Iron Co.*, 67 Ala. 353; *E. &
W. R. R. Co., v. E. T. V. & G. R. R. Co.*, 75 Ala. 275;
L. & N. R. R. Co., v. Bessemer, 108 Ala. 238, 18 South.
880.

One of the two sole grounds for dissolution is the want of equity in the bill. As will be seen from our decisions, the two first cited being among them, it was well conceived that motion to dismiss for want of equity was not, and could not be allowed to become, a substitute for a demurrer. Hence it was held, where the objection rested on the assertion of a want of equity in the bill otherwise than by a demurrer, that amendable defects should be taken as cured; the implication being, of course, that objections in that form confessed the bill *as so perfected.* To what extent the assumed amendment of the bill, so assailed, should go, was again determined, following *Seals v. Robinson,* 75 Ala. 368, in *Blackburn v. Fitzgerald,* 130 Ala. 584, 30 South. 568. No such condition for the assumption of amendments made obtains where the issuance of an injunction, upon application of the complainant, is the question for determination. On dissolution, vel non, the respondent is, of course, the movant. On the hearing of the application stated, the complainant is the actor. He can be aided by no rule of favor, like that of assumed amendment, to his initial pleading.

The Nebraska court, in *Bishop v. Huff,* 81 Neb. 729, 116 N. W. 665, dealing with injunctive process, said of complainants: "The court cannot aid their allegations by construction; but, unless their right to the writ is made clearly to appear, it must be denied." A fortiori, a complainant should be denied assistance by assumed amendment of his bill. His bill must be determined, as to its equity, upon the averments contained in it, unaided by construction and unamplified by assumed amendment. This requirement consists with the view, firmly established in this court, that this extraordinary power should be cautiously and sparingly exercised, and that, in cases of private nuisance, generally, it will

not be used, unless "there is a strong and mischievous
case of pressing necessity."—*Rouse v. Martin*, 75 Ala.
510, 51 Am. Rep. 463. "Where the injury complained
of is not a nuisance per se, but may become so by reason of circumstances—being uncertain, indefinite or
contingent—equity, as we have said, will not interfere.
* * * It is a rule of universal recognition that *in
doubtful cases* an injunction will always be denied, or
dissolved on motion when granted ad interim. A very
strong case must therefore be made by the bill, and if
there be a reasonable doubt as to the probable effect of
an alleged nuisance, either on proof, affidavits, or on
the construction of the facts stated in the bill, there
will be no interference until the matter is tested by ex-
periment in the actual use of the property."—*Rouse, et
al., v. Martin, et al., supra; Amer. T. & T. Co., v. Morgan County Tel. Co.*, 138 Ala. 597, 604, 605, 36 South.
178, 100 Am. St. Rep. 53; 1 High on Inj. § 742, and
note; *Rhodes v. Dunbar*, 57 Pa. 274, 98 Am. Dec. 221,
224; *Lake Erie & W. R. Co., v. City of Fremont*, 92 Fed.
721, 730, 731, 34 C. C. A. 625; 2 Joyce on Inj. § 1069,
and note.

In the last-cited new and excellent work on the subject of Injunctions, it is pertinently said: "Equity
will not afford relief against a merely prospective or
threatened nuisance, where the injury is apprehended,
doubtful, or contingent. A mere prospect or possibility of future annoyance or damage is insufficient."
From *Lake Erie & W. R. Co., v. Fremont, supra*, Judge
Taft, writing for the Court of Appeals, where it appeared from the bill that the flooding, *if concurring,*
would result in irreparable injury, incapable of adequate compensation in damages, this expression is appropriated: "But it is well settled that an injunction
does not issue in such cases unless the probability of

danger is clearly shown, and the existence of the nuisance clearly made out upon determinate and satisfactory evidence, and that in no case will the chancellor interfere by injunction where the nuisance sought to be abated or restrained is eventual or contingent. * * *"

The application of the stated principles convinces us that the temporary injunction should not have issued; for, as we construe the bill, presented solely for the injunctive relief indicated, it is without equity. A bill without equity will not support an injunction of any character, under any circumstances.—*E. & W. R. R. Co., supra; Bishop v. Wood,* 59 Ala. 253.

The presently material averments of the bill assign themselves to two categories, viz., those descriptive of the breaking or washing away of a previously created dam across Thacker's creek, whereby water, in devastating volume, was caused to rush down on complainant's cultivated land, washing away the soil, cutting gulches and ditches therein, and entailing damage in the sum of $1,000; and, secondly, those charging that defendant is now erecting another dam that will not withstand floods in the creek, which, breaking, will entail like damage to complainant's lands.

The relief the complainant seeks is from the anticipated menace of injury to his property, created by the inefficient dam *as proposed,* and from the apprehended damage to his property consequent upon the breaking of the dam. Evidently the apprehensions relied upon for injunctive relief are grounded, in complainant's pleaded view, upon the previous failure of the other dam to withstand the floods in the stream. In the averments of the bill—and to those we are confined—we are unable to find any sufficient support for the alleged apprehended damnifying result prophesied as from the

occurrences with respect to the other dam. It is not
averred that the proposed dam is similar to the other
dam. It is not averred that the proposed dam is located at the same point on the creek as the other dam. It
does not appear that the proposed dam is to be of the
same material as the previous dam, nor that its base,
height and thickness will be the same as that of the
other dam. It is not alleged that the proposed dam will
be subjected to floods of like force and volume to those
to which the other dam was exposed. It is not asserted that the surface conditions, affecting the area of territory drained into the creek at the time the writ was
sought or issued, were the same, or substantially the
same, as they were when the elder dam was pressed
down and the damage described inflicted. So it must
be concluded that the apprehension averred cannot be
predicated upon the occurrences described with respect
to the other dam. This leaves the bill to stand alone
upon the allegations of the second category, viz., that
defendant is proposing to erect a dam that will not
withstand the floods to which it will be subjected,
which, breaking, will entail the damage anticipated.

Obviously a private nuisance is not shown, as threatened of creation, by averments inherently suggestive
alone of contingency and doubtfulness, and a mere apprehension founded only upon opinion of the pleader.
Whether the proposed dam will in all reasonable probability withstand the floods must at least depend upon
its character—in material of construction, in durable
plan of construction, and in place of construction, as
well as upon the measure of flood pressure to which,
in reasonable probability, it will be subjected. But the
pleader has assumed a greater obligation than the mere
fact the dam will not survive the floods. He has predicated his theory for the relief sought upon the notion,

[McHan v. McMurry.]

evidently thought by him to be essential to make out
a case of private nuisance, that the dam as proposed
will restrain the flow of water, thereby accumulating
it, until the pressure against the dam will be such that,
suddenly released, it will wreak the damage he antici-
pates. Whether this conclusison is justified must, in
its turn, depend upon the restraining character of the
proposed dam. If it were so weak, in material and
manner and in place of construction, as to yield to
slight rise in the creek, and it is to the flood tide therein he refers, and in consequence hold behind it, until its
failure, a small volume of water, it is readily conceiva-
ble that the menace and apprehension the pleader asserts would not be well founded. So it is to be concluded that the water, the more unresisting to flood
pressure, the structure as proposed should be, the less
pent-up water it would accommodate, and, in consequence, if sleazy to the extreme, the menace, the apprehension, asserted would be deprived of reasonable justification and support.

When it is considered that the abstract right of the
defendant to put a dam across this creek, on his own
land, is not questioned by the bill, and when it is noted
that the challenge is only against the *character* of the
dam, and when it is borne in mind that the process proposed is not a nuisance per se, and when, as appears,
the pleader has not excluded, by proper averments in
his bill, the numerous elements of contingency and
doubt, and of apprehension merely, to which we have
in part adverted, the conclusion before stated seems to
be inevitable, viz., that the bill as now framed is without equity. Accordingly the order granting the temporary injunction is reversed, and the application
therefor is denied.

The cause is remanded.

Reversed, rendered, and remanded.

DOWDELL, C. J., and SIMPSON and MAYFIELD, JJ., concur.

Smith v. Young.

Bill to Set Aside Conveyance as Fraudulent and Void.

(Decided May 11, 1911. 55 South. 425.)

1. *Assignments; Benefit of Creditor; What Constitutes.*—Under section 4295, Code 1907, the word "creditor" is used in its broad and general sense, and includes a surety who has not paid the debt; hence a conveyance by the debtor of substantially all of his property to the surety in consideration that the surety would pay the debt was a general assignment for the benefit of all the creditors.

2. *Principal and Surety; Right of Surety; Accrual of Action.*—A surety cannot maintain an action against his principal on a liability created by his suretyship until he has paid part or all of the debt, the right of action not accruing until such payment.

3. *Fraudulent Conveyance; Creditor; Surety as Creditor.*—A surety is a creditor within the provisions of section 4295, Code 1907, from the inception of his contingent liability, and after he has paid the debt he may maintain a creditor's bill against his principal and other creditors to set aside a conveyance as fraudulent, made while the liability was contingent, or to have such conveyances declared a general assignment.

4. *Equity; Bill; Multifariousness.*—Under section 3095, Code 1907, a bill to have an assignment of substantially all a debtor's property to his surety in consideration that the surety would pay the debt, declared a general assignment for the benefit of all the creditors, or an alternative that it be declared fraudulent as to such creditors, was not multifariousness.

APPEAL from Anniston City Court.

Heard before Hon. THOS. W. COLEMAN, JR.

A bill by C. H. Young as trustee in bankruptcy of R. P. Thomason against J. F. Smith to declare a conveyance a general assignment, or as a fraud on creditors.

WILLETT & WILLETT for appellant. Section 4295 Code 1907, is in derogation of the common law and must be strictly construed, for at the common law a debtor had the unquestioned right to prefer one or more of his creditors by a sale of even all of his property in payment of a prior debt.—*Inman v. Sloss,* 122 Ala. 461; *Sheally v. Edwards,* 75 Ala. 418; *Webb v. Mullen,* 78 Ala. 111; 2 Lewis Sutherland Stat. Cons. 573; *Cook v. Meyer Bros.,* 73 Ala. 590. Under this rule of construction section 4295 takes away the common law right of preference, and must be strictly construed and its terms and provisions must not be enlarged by intendment or construction.—*Murphy v. Bank of Mobile,* 5 Ala. 421, and 465; *Nations v. Roberts,* 20 Ala. 543; *Danner v. Brewer,* 69 Ala. 191; *Cook v. Meyer Bros., supra; Lanier v. Youngblood,* 73 Ala. 587. Smith was not a creditor of Thomason under section 4295. 55 Minn. 130; 43 Ill. App. 424. Words and phrases. A surety is not a creditor of the principal until the debt or part of it is paid by him.—*Foster v. Trustees,* 3 Ala. 302; *Martin v. Ellerbee,* 70 Ala. 326; *Lanc v. Westmoreland,* 79 Ala. 372; *Smith v. McCadden,* 138 Ala. 284; Norton on Bills and Notes, 173. He could not have set off the debt from Thomason to him because he had not paid it to Cooper.—*Stallworth v. Pressler,* 34 Ala. 505; *Tyree v. Parham,* 66 Ala. 424. It would not have been subject to garnishment.—*White v. Hobart,* 90 Ala. 368; *Askew v. Hale Co.,* 54 Ala. 639. If the conveyance is an assignment inuring to the benefit of creditors, Smith's claim would not be provable.—*Danner v. Brewer, supra; M. & F. Bank v. Paulk,* 124 Ala. 591; 3 A. & C. Encyc. Law, 139; 23 S. E. 947; 144 S. C. 406. The bill was multifarious.—*Henry v. Tenn. L. S. Co.,* 164 Ala. 376.

[Smith v. Young.]

Knox, Acker, Dixon & Blackmon, and Blackwell
& Agee for appellee. A surety is a creditor within the
meaning of section 4295 Code 1907.—*Smith v. McCadden*, 138 Ala. 284; *Smith et als., v. Pitts*, 52 South.
402; *Watts v. Eufaula Nat. Bank*, 76 Ala. 474; *White
v. State*, 134 Ala. 197; *Bibb v. Freeman*, 59 Ala. 612;
Gannard v. Eslaba, 20 Ala. 732; *Keel v. Larkin*, 72 Ala.
493. The bill was not multifarious.

MAYFIELD, J.—This appeal presents two questions only for the decision of this court—one, a question of chancery pleading. The one of law is this: Is
a conveyance by a debtor of substantially all his property to his surety, in consideration that the surety will
pay the debt owing to one creditor for which the guarantee is surety, a general assignment within the meaning and operation of section 4295 of the Code of 1907?
The question of pleading is this: Is a bill of equity
multifarious which seeks in the alternative to declare a
given conveyance a general assignment for the benefit
of all the grantor's creditors; and, if not, then to declare it fraudulent as to such creditors? Under our
existing statutes we are constrained to answer both of
these questions as did the chancellor—that is, the first,
in the affirmative; the latter, in the negative.

Section 4295 of the Code, which is most material to
the first question, is as follows: "Every general assignment made by a debtor, 'or a conveyance by a debtor, of
substantially all of his property subject to execution in
payment of a prior debt; by which a preference or priority of payment is given to one or more creditors, over
the remaining creditors of the grantor, shall be and inure to the benefit of all the creditors of the grantor
equally.' * * * A general assignment within the
meaning of this section shall include, in addition to the

conveyances now defined as such by law, every judgment confessed, attachment procured by a debtor, or
other disposition of property by which a debtor conveys
all or substantially all of his property subject to execution, in payment of, or as the security for a prior debt,
or charges such property with the payment of such
debt." This statute first appeared as section 1556 of
the Code of 1852. It there read like the first sentence,
with the omission of that part above indicated by single quotation marks. It has reappeared in all subsequent Codes, each time with amendments added to it
by acts of the Legislature, code commissioners, or code
committees. It has been three times, if not oftener,
amended by special acts of the Legislature—that of
February 23, 1883 (page 189), February 21, 1893 (page
1046), and February 16, 1897 (page 1089). Each
amendment has evidently been for the purpose, with
the effect, to extend the scope and provisions of the act,
to include additional conveyances and transactions not
heretofore included. This statute in all its stages of
evolution has been many times construed, and these
constructions are uniform from the first, that of *Holt
et al. v. Bancroft, et al.,* 30 Ala. 193, to this, the last,
to the effect that the statute was to prohibit all dis-
criminaion by a debtor, if he made a general assignment of all his property. "It does not aim to deny,
and does not deny, to a debtor the power of securing a
creditor's debt by a conveyance of a part of his property. The right of preferring creditors by partial assignments is untouched by the section of the Code quoted. It is not the preference of itself, but the preference
as a feature of a general assignment, which the statute
condemns." "Neither an evasion nor a direct violation
of the statute prohibiting preference in general assignments can render absolutely void the deed or deeds by

which the preference is attempted to be given, because
the statute itself prescribes the effect of its violation.
The assignment 'shall be and inure to the benefit of
all the creditors of the grantor equally.' Visiting,
therefore, the act of evading the statute with the consequences of a direct violation, we can only annul the
preference, and place the beneficiary of the first deed
on a footing with the other creditors."

In this first case the statute was held to apply to a
conveyance of a part only of the debtor's property, on
the ground that he contemplated a general assignment
at the time he conveyed, and did subsequently make the
general assignment, and that the first was only a part
of the general assignment. This court has uniformly
held that a surety is a creditor of his principal from
the inception of the contingent liability; that he is a
creditor in such sense that he may maintain a creditor's
bill against his principal as to fraudulent conveyances
of the principal's property with intent to defraud creditors, one of whom is the surety.—*Smith v. Pitts*, 167
Ala. 461, 52 South. 403; *Keel v. Larkin*, 72 Ala. 493, 500.
If the surety can file a creditor's bill against the principal and other creditors to set aside a conveyance made
by his principal either as fraudulent or as a general assignment, while his liability is only contingent, we can
see no reason why other creditors cannot file such a bill
against him, when he is the grantee of the fraudulent
conveyance, or when it is a general assignment, as in
this case, and the one to be held as a trustee. In fact,
a number of such bills have been filed, and in each case
was held to have been properly filed. Such were the
causes of *Watts v. Eufaula Bank*, 76 Ala. 474, and
Crawford v. Kirksey, 50 Ala. 590. In the case of *Smith
v. McFadden*, 138 Ala. 284, 36 South. 376, the transaction assailed was removed one degree further from the

letter of the statute, in that the conveyance by the debt-
or in that case was made to a third party, in consideration that he would mortgage or convey it to the surety
for the purpose of paying the debt for which the principal debtor and surety were both liable; whereas, in
this case, there is only one conveyance, and that is directly to the surety by the principal in consideration
that the surety would pay the debt for which both
were liable—the one as principal and the other as surety. The transaction in neither case—that of *Smith v.
McCadden,* and the one at bar—would have been different in effect or in a court of equity if the conveyance
had been made directly by the principal debtor to the
preferred creditor. The third party and the surety
are only made conduits through and by which the debt-
or passes all of his property to one preferred creditor;
and it is this and this only that the statute was intended to prevent. It is true that the writer of the opinion
in the case of *Smith v. McCadden* did not concur in the
conclusion reached by the majority of the court, and he
wrote a very strong argument to the proposition that a
surety was not a creditor within the meaning of the
statute now under consideration, and counsel for the
appellant here makes a strong and persuasive argument
to the same effect; but this does not convince us that it
is unanswerable, and more especially in view of the fact
that the statute has been so often re-enacted with a
construction upon it different from that contended for.
It is argued that as the surety could not, at the time
the conveyance was made, sue the principal in assumpsit on the contingent liability, and could not have pleaded it as a set-off if sued by the principal, and that as
the principal could not have been garnisheed as to such
liability, and that, if a general assignment had been
made by the principal, he would not have shared in the

distribution of the trust fund, that these facts are conclusive to the effect that the surety is not a creditor of his principal within the meaning of the statute, and that the conveyance to him in question was not within the statute as to general assignments. The answer to this contention is that the words, "creditor" and "debtor" each has a general and specific definition—a broad and a narrow signification. The words as used in the statute should have their general and broad meaning, and not be restricted to specific meaning which appellant would have us accord to them.

Although a surety cannot maintain an action against his principal on the liability created by the suretyship, until such surety has paid the debt or a part thereof, it is because the right of action does not come into existence until such payment, and not because the relation of debtor and creditor did not theretofore exist. The same thing is true as to the creditor or payee of a note signed by the principal and surety. The payee cannot sue the principal or the surety until the note is due, yet the relation of debtor and creditor certainly exists from the making of the note. While a surety probably could not file a creditor's bill as to conveyances by his principal until he had paid the surety debt, yet he is a creditor within the protection of the statutes from the inception of his contingent liability; and, after he has paid the surety debt, he may maintain his creditor's bill against the principal and other creditors to set aside fraudulent conveyances made while the liability of the surety was contingent, or to have them declared general assignments. As before said, if he can maintain such bills against other creditors, surely the other creditors ought to be able to maintain them against him, if he happens to be the one preferred or benefited by the transaction. If the debtor in this case had conveyed all of his property to one of these complainants in payment of his debt, then certainly appellant Smith could have paid the debt and have maintained this identical bill against such grantee. The fact that his right of action does not accrue until he pays the debt does not prevent his being a creditor within the statute as to fraudulent conveyances or general assignments. If protected by the statute, it is but equitable that he be subject to it. If he receives the benefits conferred, he ought to bear the burdens imposed.

To the second question, the one of procedure, whether a creditor's bill can be filed in the alternative—in one aspect assailing a conveyance as fraudulent, and, in another, asserting its validity, and that it was a general assignment—it was at first held that such a bill could be maintained— (*Crawford v. Kirksey*, 50 Ala. 590), but that case was subsequently overruled in the case of *Lehman v. Meyer*, 67 Ala. 397, and the decision has been often reaffirmed down to the case of *Green & Gray v. Wright et al.*, 160 Ala. 476, 49 South. 320. Since the bills were filed in these last cases, but before the filing of the bill in the case under consideration, the statutes as to chancery pleading and practice have undergone changes more or less radical by the adoption of the Code of 1907. The one as to multifariousness now reads: "Unless taken by demurrer, objection to a bill because of multifariousness must not be entertained. A bill is not multifarious which seeks alternative or inconsistent relief growing out of the same subject-matter or founded on the same contract or transaction, or relating to the same property between the same parties." Section 3095. The effect of this statute was to allow a bill like this to be filed, which seeks alternative reliefs, though inconsistent, if they be founded upon the same transaction and grow out of the same subject-matter, and are

contested between the same parties. The statute therefore restores the rule to this effect, as first announced
in the case of *Crawford v. Kirksey, supra.* No error
appearing, the decree of the lower court is affirmed.
   Affirmed.

   DOWDELL, C. J., and SIMPSON and McCLELLAN, JJ.,
concur.

Cartwright, *et al. v.* West.

Bill to Cancel Certain Conveyances as Fraudulent.

(Decided May 16, 1911.   Rehearing denied June 27. 1911.
55 South. 917.)

1. *Equity; Pleading; Verification.*—Where pleas are received without verification the lack of verification is not a ground for holding
them insufficient.

2. *Same; Sufficiency.*—A respondent in equity cannot be denied
the benefit of his defense of the statutory bar by limitation set up by
way of special plea based on facts averred therein, by complainant's
amendment of his bill alleging a state of facts contrary to those
averred in the pleas.

3. *Same; Plea to Part of Bill.*—In chancery practice a plea may
be filed to a part of a bill.

4. *Appeal and Error; Questions Presented; Record.*—Where the
record showed that pleas 1 and 2 were not refiled to the substituted
bill as last amended but that pleas 3 and 4 were filed to such bill,
and the decree recites that the cause was then submitted for decree
upon the sufficiency of the plea, it did not affirmatively appear that
the cause was set down for hearing on pleas 1 and 2 to the bill as
amended.

5. *Bankruptcy; Capacity of Trustee; Fraudulent Conveyance.*—
While ordinarily the trustee in bankruptcy is a representative of
both the bankrupt and the creditors, yet when he files a bill to set
aside a fraudulent conveyance made by the bankrupt, he represents
the creditors alone.

6. *Same; Action by Trustee; Limitations.*—Where a trustee in
bankruptcy files a bill to set aside certain conveyances of the bankrupt as being fraudulent, the respondents are entitled to set up by
way of plea, that certain creditors named in the bill had not filed
their claims within the time allowed. and hence were barred by limitation, as creditors entitled to participate in distribution of the
estate.

[Cartwright, et al. v. West.]

7. *Limitation of Action; Pleading; Necessity.*—As a bar to an action limitations must be pleaded, else it is waived.

8. *Same.*—Although under section 3115, Code 1907, the bar of the statute of limitation may be asserted as a defense by answer, yet that does not deprive a respondent of setting it up by special plea.

APPEAL from Morgan Chancery Court.

Heard before Hon. W. H. SIMPSON.

Bill by Marvin West as trustee in bankruptcy of the estate of Herbert Cartwright against Cartwright and others to cancel certain conveyances as fraudulent and void, made by the bankrupt. From a decree holding certain pleas insufficient respondents appeal. Reversed and rendered.

KYLE & HUTSON, for appellant. Pleas may be filed to a part of a bill. Sims Chan. Prac. Sec. 457; 2 Daniels Chan. Prac. 685; Story's Eq. Plead. Sec. 647. The pleas were submitted on a test of their sufficiency, which was an admission of their truth.—*New Decatur v. Scharfenburg,* 155 Ala. 651; 17 Pick. 129; 49 Md. 516. This being true, some of the creditors had not filed their claims within the time, and hence were barred from participating in the estate. A trustee is an officer of the court, and is limited strictly to the powers conferred by the act under the orders of the court.—Loveland's Bankruptcy 351; 280 and 190; *in re Ryan,* 21 Fed. Case, 182. In a case of this character he only represents creditors in provable claims under the bankrupt act; authorities, supra. Claims cannot be proven after the expiration of one year from the date of the adjudication of bankruptcy.—100 Fed. 270; 104 Fed. 982; 105 Fed. 231. Verification was not necessary. —*New Decatur v. Scharfenburg, supra; Tyson v. Land Co.,* 1212 Ala. 414; *Glasser v. Meyrovitz,* 119 Ala. 152; *Wright v. Evans,* 53 Ala. 107.

CALLAHAN & HARRIS, for appellee. Only pleas 3 and 4 were pleaded to the bill as last amended. The pleas were technically insufficient.—*Scharfenburg v. New Decatur*, 47 South. 95; 16 Cyc. 288; 16 Encyc. P. & P. 603. The presentation within that period is not negatived by the pleas.—*Andrews v. Huckabee*, 30 Ala. 143. The pleas were in substance if not in form pleas since the last continuance.—*Sanche v. Webb*, 110 Ala. 220. Such pleas must be verified.—Sec. 5333 Code 1907; *Smith v. Hiles, et al.*, 107 Ala. 275. The respondents could not plead the statute of limitation or non-claim as to the creditors.—204 U. S. 536; 122 Fed. 558; *Stutz v. Huger*, 107 Ala. 253.

DOWDELL, C. J.—The appeal in this case is taken from the decree of the chancellor holding certain pleas filed to the bill insufficient; the cause having been set down for hearing on the sufficiency of said pleas.

Waiving the question as to the character of the pleas, whether or not pleas puis darein continuance and requiring verification at the time of their filing, or at the time the cause was set down for hearing on their sufficiency, "The oath is not a part of the plea, but a preliminary to its reception, and when the plea is thus received it cannot be rejected by the court because it is insufficient."—*McCall v. McRae*, 10 Ala. 313-316. In *Wright v. Evans*, 53 Ala. 103-107, it was ruled: "If verification is necessary, the want of it is not cause of demurrer, but ground of objection to the filing of the plea, or, if filed, on motion to strike it from the files." "The setting down of a plea to a bill for hearing on its sufficiency is an admission of the truth of all the facts alleged for the purpose of invoking judgment as to whether the facts constitute a defense."—*Town of New Decatur v. Scharfenburg*, 147 Ala. 367, 41 South. 1025, 119 Am. St. Rep. 81; *Tyson v. Land Co.*, 121 Ala. 414, 26 South. 507; *Glasser v. Meyrovitz*, 119 Ala. 152, 24

South. 514. The contention of appellee that a want of verification rendered the pleas insufficient, when set down for hearing on their sufficiency, as was done in the present case, is without merit.

In chancery practice and pleading, a plea may, the same as a demurrer, be filed to a part of the bill, as well as to the whole bill.—Sims' Chan. Prac. & Plead. (Ala.) § 57; Story's Eq. Pl. (Redfield's Ed.) §§ 647, 659; Dan. Chan. Prac. (4th Am. Ed.) vol. 1, p. 685.

The record in the present instance fails to show with any degree of certainty that particular pleas numbered 1 and 2 were set down for hearing on their sufficiency. All that is shown in this respect is found in the decree of the chancellor, wherein it is stated that the cause "was submitted for decree upon the sufficiency of the pleas filed by Emma D. Cartwright and Anna Cartwright." Pleas numbered 1 and 2 were filed to the substituted bill as amended July 2, 1908, but were not refiled to the substituted bill as last amended on September 12, 1908. To the substituted bill as last amended, pleas 3 and 4 were filed, and then it was that the cause was set down for hearing on the sufficiency "of the pleas." From this it does not affirmatively appear that the cause was set down for hearing on pleas 1 and 2 to the bill as last amended, and on appeal error must be affirmatively shown. The court cannot be put in error for ruling on pleas, when the record does not clearly show that action was had by the court on them. A submission and hearing on pleas 3 and 4 filed to the bill as last amended fully respond to the above-quoted recital contained in the decree.

This brings us to a consideration of pleas 3 and 4, and the ruling had thereon. Plea 3 sets up as a defense that certain persons, alleged in the bill to be creditors of the bankrupt, and whose names are set forth in the plea, failed to file their said claims in the bankruptcy proceedings within 12 months from the adjudication in bankruptcy, and were therefore barred as creditors entitled to participate in any distribution of the bankrupt's estate, and hence there could be no recovery by the complainant in the present bill as trustee in bankruptcy for the benefit of such creditors.—Collier on Bankruptcy (8th Ed.) pp. 612-613. The defense set up in plea 4 is the same as that in plea 3, and is not restricted to any particular creditors or their claims named in the bill, but is directed against all of the creditors mentioned in the bill.

We digress here to state the purpose of the bill. The bill is exhibited by the appellee, Marvin West, as the trustee in bankruptcy of the estate of Herbert Cartwright, who had theretofore been adjudicated a bankrupt, and has for its object the annulment and setting aside of certain conveyances alleged to have been made by the said Herbert Cartwright to the appellants, respondents in the bill, with the intent to hinder, delay, or defraud his (the said Cartwright's) creditors. The complainant in his bill undertakes to set out the names of the various creditors of the bankrupt, and the amounts of their respective claims. The prayer of the bill in the alternative, among other things, is for personal decrees against the alleged fraudulent grantees for the value of the property so fraudulently conveyed.

The trustee in bankruptcy in a sense is a representative of both the bankrupt and the creditors. As such he succeeds in right and title to the bankrupt's estate for the benefit of his creditors. He may, as a general rule, maintain all actions, both at law and in equity, for the recovery and preservation of the assets, both real and personal, of the bankrupt's estate that the bankrupt himself, but for the bankruptcy, could have maintained. Even more, he may maintain an action the bankrupt could not, where, as in the present case, he seeks to avoid conveyances made by the bankrupt in fraud of his creditors. In this latter instance it cannot be said that the trustee is a representative of the bankrupt, for he (the bankrupt) could not maintain such a bill, nor in any legal or equitable proceeding become a beneficiary of his own fraudulent act.

The bill before us is in the nature of a creditor's bill to set aside fraudulent conveyances made by the debtor, and the trustee in filing it in reality represents the interests of the creditors alone. The object of a recovery is for distribution among the creditors of the bankrupt. If in such a case the bill was exhibited by the creditors themselves, all of whose claims were barred by the statute, and this defense should be set up by plea, it is evident there could be no recovery. Why, it may be asked, should not the same principle be applicable here? If the creditors are barred by the statute of the right of participation in a distribution of the bankrupt's estate by reason of a failure to file their claims within the 12 months prescribed by the bankrupt statute, and a recovery should be had in a bill like the present one, to whose benefit would the recovery inure? There would be no one else to receive the benefits but the bankrupt himself, and by such a proceeding he would become the beneficiary of his own fraud.

Recurring to pleas 3 and 4 which the chancellor held to be insufficient for reasons stated in his decree. These pleas are what are termed in chancery practice as pure pleas. They are each directed to parts of the bill only, and profess to answer such parts by setting up as a defense a statutory bar to any right of recovery under the bill. The theory of the chancellor in overruling the

[Cartwright, et al. v. West.]

pleas, as shown in his decree, was that the bill as last amended met the objections raised by the pleas; that is to say, that the bill as amended averred that the claims of the creditors were filed in the bankruptcy proceedings within the time prescribed by the statute. This may be so in respect to plea 4, which avers a failure by the creditors generally to file their claims, but not so as to plea 3, which specifies the creditors failing to file. The bill as amended does not aver that any one of the creditors named in plea 3 ever filed his claim at any time in the bankruptcy proceedings. So, as to plea 3, the bill as last amended stood just as it did before amendment. The bill as amended undertook by averment to meet the facts stated in the pleas, namely, that the mentioned creditors had failed to file their claims within the prescribed time by affirming that the claims had been filed within the prescribed statutory period. The defense set up in the pleas was the statutory bar predicated on the statement of the facts as averred in the pleas. The question is, Can the respondent be denied the benefit of his defense of the statutory bar by way of special plea, based on facts averred in the plea, by the complainant's amendment of his bill, alleging a contrary state of facts to those averred in the plea? We are of the opinion that such is not the rule. There is such a thing as a purely negative plea recognized in chancery practice and pleading.—See Story's Eq. Pl. 660, where it is stated, by way of illustration: "Thus, if a bill calls for an account of partnership transactions, and alleges a partnership between the plaintiff and defendant, the latter may, by a negative plea, deny there was any partnership, and the plea will be good." —See, also, Story's Eq. Pl. § 668.

At common law the statute of limitations as a bar to an action may be waived, and is considered as waived,

unless set up defensively by proper plea. It may likewise be waived in equity, if not in some manner pleaded
as a defense. It may be that under our present statute,
section 3115, Code of 1907, this defense could be set up
in the answer, but this does not take away the right of
the defendant to specially plead it. A mere denial in
the answer of the averment in the bill that the claims
of creditors were filed within 12 months of the adjudication in bankruptcy, without more, would not, in our
opinion, sufficiently invoke the defense of the statutory
bar of the claims. Our conclusion is that the defense
set up was proper subject-matter of a special plea, notwithstanding the affirmative statement in the substituted bill as last amended, and the chancellor erred in
overruling the pleas.

The decree of the chancellor is reversed, and one is
here rendered sustaining the pleas.

Reversed and renderd.

ANDERSON, MAYFIELD, SAYRE, and SOMERVILLE, JJ.,
concur.

Newell *v.* Manley.

A Bill to Quiet a Title.

(Decided May 9, 1911. 55 South. 495.)

1. *Quieting Title; Action; Requisites.*—Under the statutes authorizing a bill to quiet title a complainant is not required to show title.
or such adverse possession as would ripen into title, but to show
peaceable possession.

2. *Same; Possession; Character.*—In a bill to quiet title. where
the land involved was a continuous tract of but eighty acres, and
plaintiff's possession was shown to have covered at least five acres,
and at one time thirteen or fourteen acres. and was accompanied by
actual ownership. the possession was not so slight as to deprive him
of the benefit of his title.

[Newell v. Manly.]

APPEAL from Tuscaloosa Chancery Court.
Heard before Hon. A. H. BENNERS.

Bill by George W. Newell against Chas. Manley to quiet title to certain land. Judgment for respondent and complainant appeals. Reversed and rendered.

RICHARD B. KELLY and MAUDE McCLURE KELLY, for appellant. The statute makes it the duty of the court to consider and determine the title to the land involved, and to finally adjudge and decree whether the defendant has any right, title, interest in or incumberance upon the same.—Code 1907, section 5443, et seq. This statute gives to parties in bills like this the right to have a determination by the court of the status of the title to the land as between them.—*Interstate v. Stocks*, 124 Ala. 111; *Ward v. Janney*, 124 Ala. 122; *Cheney v. Nathan*, 110 Ala. 254; Code 1907, 5443 et seq. and cases cited. If appellant was in the actual, peaceable possession of the land, claiming it, at the time the original bill was filed, he was entitled to a decree adjudging that he had the legal title to said land, unless the defendant by his answer alleged and by his evidence proved either that he himself or some predecessor in interest was in the prior actual possession of said land, claiming to own the same, or that he had the legal title to said land.—*Brand v. U. S. Car Co.*, 128 Ala.; *Redlick v. Long*, 124 Ala. 260; *Mills v. Clayton*, 73 Ala. 359; *Strange v. King*, 84 Ala. 212; *Anderson v. McLear*, 56 Ala. 621; I. Am. & Eng. Ency. 2 Ed. 870.

HENRY FITTS, for appellee. No brief reached the reporter.

SIMPSON, J—The original bill in this case was filed (August 28, 1905) by the appellant against the appellee to quiet the title to W. ½ of N. W. ¼ of section

15, township 21, range 7 W., in Tuscaloosa county. The
respondent denies that the complainant is in possession
of the land claimed, within the meaning of the statute,
and deraigns his title through a tax deed to Basil Manly, dated September 14, 1849, the will òf Basil Manly,
made in 1858, devising his lands generally, without description, to his wife, Sarah M. Manly, and a deed by
said Sarah M. Manly (July 7, 1892), to the appellee,
as trustee.

The complainant introduced in evidence deeds from
J. R. Dailey to him, dated March 6, 1883, recorded October 22, 1903, and also from several parties previously
to Dailey. It was shown that the land was entered from
the United States, in 1830, by George N. Stewart and
Thomas Raiser. The evidence on the part of the complainant, including that of Dailey himself and of the
justice who took the acknowledgment, tended to show
the execution of the deeds on the day of their dates;
that the complainant took possession of the land at
once, cleared up a portion of it, built a fence around
said portion, and cultivated it for years, claiming the
entire tract under the deed; that although there were
some years when the fence was allowed to go down, yet
in 1903 it was rebuilt; and that complainant has been in
possession ever since; also that no one by the name of
Manley has ever been in possession of any part of the
land.

No effort was made by the respondent to prove the
validity of the tax deed, and in fact the brief of respondent admits that it is not valid. There is no proof of any
acts of possession by either of the Manlys, and the respondent rests his case on the denial of possession by the
complainant. To this end very voluminous testimony
is introduced, most of which is irrelevant to this case,
such as suits between other parties involving other lands

claimed to be near these lands, hearsay statements made
by persons not connected in any way with this complainant, and the fact that, about the time the deeds introduced by said complainant were said to have been made,
a number of other deeds to other parties for lands in
the same neighborhood, known as railroad lands, were
claimed to have been made, but were not recorded for
many years thereafter. In fact, the general trend of
the testimony brought forward by the respondent is
avowed to be that about that time there was a general
agreement or conspiracy, among a number of persons,
to enter and claim lands belonging to other persons,
and that the deed of Dailey to the complainant is a forg-
ery. It must be remembered that this is not an action
of ejectment, but simply a bill to quiet title under the
statute, and it must stand or fall under the evidence
revelant to the issue in such a case.

The statute requires, in the complainant, not a title,
nor such adverse possession as would ripen into a title,
but merely peaceable possesssion; the theory of the
statute being that if a party is in possession of land,
whether his possession be rightful or not, he cannot
force the other party to sue him, and he has a right to
inaugurate the litigation by calling on the other party to
propound and prove his title. The complainant does
not have to prove his title at all, and if he is in peaceable possession the sole inquiry is whether the respondent has proved any title in himself.—*Geo. E. Wood
Lumber Co. v. Williams,* 157 Ala. 73, 76, 77, 47 South.
202; *Whitaker v. Van Hoose et al.,* 157 Ala. 286, 289,
47 South. 741; *Dickinson v. Harris,* 155 Ala. 613, 615,
47 South. 78.

There is no force in the suggestion that the possession, under color of title, was so slight and disconnected
as not to entitle the complainant to the benefit of his

[Oates v. Whitehead, Tax Collector.]

color of title, under the remarks made in *Lawrence v. Alabama State Land Co.*, 144 Ala. 524, 529, 41 South. 612. The land involved is a continuous tract of only 80 acres, and the possession shown covered at least 5 acres, and at one time 13 or 14 acres, connected with acts of ownership. Nor do the facts in this case come within the principal of the case of *Belcher v. Scruggs*, 125 Ala. 336, 340, 27 South. 839, where the party, on the advice of his counsel, built a fence around an acre, planted corn and peas, and then "abandoned it." The fact that his residence was on another tract has no bearing on his possession of a part of the land in question.

The decree of the court is reversed, and a decree will be here rendered declaring that the respondent has no right, title, or claim in the land in controversy.

Reversed and rendered.

ANDERSON, SAYRE and SOMMERVILLE, JJ., concur.

Oates *v.* Whitehead, Tax Collector.

Bill to Enjoin Raise of Taxes.

(Decided June 13, 1911. 55 South. 803.)

Taxation; Assessment; Injunction; Equity Jurisdiction.—A bill is without equity that seeks to restrain the collection of a tax levied on the increased assessment made by the State Tax Commission, which alleges that the increase was illegal for want of notice. and charging that if the complainant was forced to pay the difference he would be without any remedy to force the refunding thereof, and further alleging that the acts creating the Alabama Tax Commission, in so far as they authorize an increase of valuation without notice to the tax payer, were unconstitutional.

APPEAL from Henry Chancery Court.

Heard before Hon. L. D. GARDNER.

Bill by W. S. Oates against W. J. Whitehead, as Tax Collector, for injunction. Decree sustaining demurrer to the bill, and complainant appeals. Affirmed.

The bill alleges proper residence and age of the complainant; that Whitehead is over the age of 21, is a resident of Henry county, and tax collector of said county, together with his duty as to the collection of taxes; that complainant is a taxpayer, and as such taxpayer he listed his property for taxation with the tax assessor of Henry county, Ala., giving the date, and attaching the assessment as an exhibit of the bill, showing that the total amount of his real estate was $27,900, and his personal property $440; that the tax rate for both state and county taxes for that year was $1.40 per $100, and that his total tax, state and county, amounted to the sum of $397.26. He then avers his readiness and willingness, on the day the tax became due and since that time to pay said amount to the tax collector, but that the tax collector refuses and declines to accept said sum in full payment of the taxes, but is demanding and is required by his records to demand and collect of the complainant the sum of $587.81, which complainant refuses to pay, as not being due. It is then averred that legal steps have been or are about to be taken to enforce the collection of the last named amount, as the amount due by complainant for taxes. It is then averred that the State Tax Commission of Alabama met with the board of county commissioners of Henry county, on the 5th day of February, 1910, and then and there raised or reassessed complainant's real estate, not embracing his city property, to the sum of $41,500, or an additional sum of $13,710 to that assessed by complainant, and that said board set aside and held for naught the assessment made by the tax assessor, and ordered said assessor to enter upon the tax assessment books of Hen-

ry county the assessment as there made by them, which
order is attached to the bill and marked "Exhibit B."
It is then averred that the complainant had no legal
notice of the meeting of said tax commission, and was
not present at their meeting. It is further averred that
no notice was given them as required by section 2228,
Code 1907, before the assessment was made by said tax
collector and entry of record thereof made; that no time
was set apart for hearing objections to said reassess-
ment or revaluation, nor personal notice given, and no
notice mailed to complainant, or left at his dwelling,
describing the property and assessment in valuation
fixed by the commission, and notifying complainant to
appear at a time specified to show cause or reason why
the assessment or revaluation should not be made. On
these facts it is alleged that the acts and doings of the
commission were void and of no effect. It is then alleged that he is forced to pay the difference, and that he
will be without legal or equitable remedy to enforce the
collection or refunding of the same. It is then alleged
that the act creating the Tax Commission of Alabama
is unconstitutional and void, wherein it authorizes or
empowers such commissioner to reassess or revalue complainant's property, and to order the same to be entered
upon the tax assessment books of Henry county, without notice to complainant, in that it is in violation of
plaintiff's constitutional right of appearing and defending in every court empowered to take or incumber complainant's property with the lien. It is further alleged
that the order was void, and Whitehead was without
authority to take any action in the premises, because of
the fact that the order is void. On this statement an
injunction is asked, restraining the collection of the
excess, and for general relief. The demurrers take the
point that the bill is without equity, and that it appears

that the assessment referred to in the bill was in all respects regular and valid, and that the complainant has a full, adequate, and complete remedy at law.

A. E. PACE and W. L. LEE, for appellant. The bill has equity.—*Gold Life Ins. Co., v. Lott,* 54 Ala. 508; *City of Ensley v. McWilliams,* 145 Ala. 159. The act creating the State Tax Commission is unconstitutional in so far as it allowed the raise in value without notice to the taxpayer.

ROBERT C. BRICKELL, Attorney General, WM. L. MARTIN, Ass't. Atty. Gen., and B. B. HAYES, for appellee. No brief came to the reporter.

McCLELLAN, J.—If it be assumed (for the occasion only) that this bill shows illegality and hardship and irregularity in respect of the sum (tax) against the collection of which, by the tax collector, complainant invokes injunctive process, still his bill is not maintainable, because the case made thereby does not show, in addition, any lead to the application of recognized principles of equitable jurisdiction.—*Ala. Gold Life Ins. Co. v. Lott,* 54 Ala. 499, 508, 509; *City of Ensley v. McWilliams,* 145 Ala. 159, 41 South. 296, 117 Am. St. Rep. 26; *Town of New Decatur v. Nelson,* 102 Ala. 556, 15 South. 275.

The chancellor, in sustaining the demurrer, followed and correctly applied the principles announced in the cited decisions of this court—decisions amply and accurately setting forth the reasons supporting the conditions therein entertained. There is no occasion to reiterate them. The decree is, hence, affirmed.

Affirmed.

SIMPSON, ANDERSON and MAYFIELD, JJ., concur.

City of Birmingham *v*. Coffman.

Bill to Enjoin Enforcement of Lien.

(Decided April 13, 1911. Rehearing denied June 8, 1911.
55 South. 500.)

1. *Quieting Title; Grounds; Illegal Assessment.*—An ordinance framed for the improvement of streets, which is void on its face for want of the requisite formalities, and which seeks to create a lien on property for the improvement done under such ordinance creates such a cloud on the title as will support a bill to remove same.

2. *Equity; Pleading; Demurrer.*—The allegations of a bill must be accepted as true on demurrer.

3. *Same; General Demurrer.*—If the bill contains any equity, a general demurrer is properly overruled.

APPEAL from Birmingham City Court.

Heard before Hon. H. A. SHARPE.

Bill by R. D. Coffman against the City of Birmingham to enjoin the enforcement of a lien and to remove same as cloud upon title. From a decree for complainant respondent appeals. Affirmed.

R. H. THACH, for appellant. The improvement ordinance was passed under and by virtue of the act of the Legislature approved March 5, 1907, and before the adoption of the Political Code, and the cause should be reversed and remanded on the authority of *City of Ensley v. McWilliams*, 41 South. 296. The chancellor's opinion is in direct conflict with the case of *M. & A. of Birmingham v. McCormick*, 40 South. 111. See also *Strenner v. City of Montgomery*, 5 South. 115; *City of Ogden v. Armstrong*, 168 U. S. 444.

FELIX E. BLACKBURN, for appellee. The ordinance was void, but pretended to fasten a lien upon the property.—*Foss v. Chicago*, 56 Ill. 354; *Bryan v. Chicago*,

60 Ill. 507. Sec. 1361 Code 1907. The bill contained
equity and the demurrer was properly overruled.—
Woodstock Iron Co. v. Fullenwider, 87 Ala. 587. Equity
does not work by piecemeal and having acquired jurisdiction for one purpose, will grant full relief.—*Whaley
v. Wilson*, 112 Ala. 697. The bill was not multifarious.
—*Gorce v. Dickins*, 98 Ala. 363.

MAYFIELD, J.—Appellee filed this bill to enjoi :
appellant from foreclosing an alleged lien upon his
property for street and sidewalk improvements and to
remove such alleged or pretended lien as a cloud upon
his title.

The bill alleges that the municipal ordinances by
which the assessment and levy was made upon this
property in question are of no effect so far as this property is concerned, for that it was not included in the
ordinances or notices required by the statute for such
purposes. The statute under which the assessment was
made (Code, § 1361) in part reads as follows: "It shall
adopt an ordinance or resolution to that effect, describing the nature and extent of the work, the general character of the materials to be used, and the location and
terminal points thereof, and the streets, avenues, alleys
or other highways, or parts thereof," etc. It is alleged
in the bill that both the property in question and the
streets bounding it were not included or embodied in
the ordinance as required by the statute, and that therefore the assessments made against it are void. It is also
alleged that the grades of the streets or avenues had not
been fixed or established as required by law, before the
adoption of the ordinance providing for the improvements of such streets. If the averments of the bill are
true, and on demurrer they must be so treated, the bill
did contain equity, and the chancellor ruled correctly

in overruling the general demurrer based on that ground. There was no special demurrer interposed to the bill. Consequently neither the trial court nor this court could pass upon its sufficiency, except as to whether or not it contained equity.

The case at bar is distinguishable from that of *Ensley v. McWilliams*, 145 Ala. 159, 41 South. 296, 117 Am. St. Rep. 26. In that case it was an act of the Legislature, enlarging the territory of Ensley, that was alleged to be unconstitutional, and the bill there sought to enjoin the collection of taxes assessed upon the property included in the void act of the Legislature, and to remove cloud from and to quiet title. In that case the bill showed that the levy and assessment was void on its face, and that a levy and sale with no semblance of legality constituted no cloud on title, and that the remedy at law was complete and adequate. The levy, assessment, and sale under that case was had under a void statute, of which all courts will take judicial notice; hence the proceedings would be void on their face.

In this case the assessment and sale is not under a valid statute; but it is the municipal ordinance (of which courts do not take notice), and a failure to fix the grades of the streets and avenues before the assessment, that renders it void. It was the failure of the officers to comply with a valid statute that rendered the proceedings void. It has been expressly ruled by the Supreme Court of California that a suit may be maintained to remove, as a cloud upon title, a street assessment, like this, void upon its face, but void because of informalities in the proceedings of the officers in making the assessment.—*Bolton v. Gilleran*, 105 Cal. 244, 38 Pac. 881, 45 Am. St. Rep. 33. Our own case of *City of Ensley v. McWilliams*, 145 Ala. 159, 41 South. 296, relied upon by appellant, is reported and annotated in 117 American State Reports, 26, and in a note thereto there are collected many cases which show the distinction between this case and the one relied upon. Affirmed.

SIMPSON, ANDERSON and McCLELLAN, JJ., concur.

Caldwell, *et al. v.* Caldwell.

Bill to Ascertain Amount Due on Mortgage and to Apportion It on Several of Certain Lots, and to Redeem.

(Decided May 11, 1911. 55 South. 515.)

1. *Mortgages; Foreclosure; Right of Mortgagee to Purchase.*— Where a mortgagee forecloses a mortgage upon real estate. which had been partitioned among the joint owners, subject to the lien of the mortgage. the mortgagee may purchase at such a sale and acquire title subject only to the right of redemption.

2. *Tenancy in Common; Right of Co-Tenants; Acquisition of Outstanding Title.*—The facts in this case stated and examined and held not to show such fraud in the acquisition of the title of the mortgagee by one of the co-tenants as to entitle the other co-tenant to relief by being permitted to come in and redeem their part of the property.

3. *Same; Confidential Relation.*—Where a co-tenant verbally agreed with his co-tenant that he would purchase all the property under the mortgage foreclosure sale and give each of his co-tenants time to redeem. and in pursuance of the said agreement said other co-tenant did not bid at the sale. a confidential relation existed between all the co-tenants. which precluded the one acquiring title to the entire land under a deed from the mortgagee who purchased at his foreclosure sale, and authorizing and empowering the other co-tenants to demand within a reasonable time that the purchase should inure to their benefit on their contributing their proportion.

4. *Same; Laches.*—Where heirs who inherited land incumbered by a mortgage, agreed with one of the heirs that he should purchase the land at the foreclosure sale and give the others time to redeem, and the purchasing heir acquired the entire title for himself. a delay by the others of five years before demanding that the purchaser should permit the purchase to inure to their benefit was not such laches as would deprive them of their right. However, they could not dispossess bona fide purchasers of the heir acquiring title, but could only compel such purchasing heir to account for the proceeds.

5. *Same; Rights of Co-Tenant.*—Where real estate was incumbered by a mortgage executed by the owner before his death and his heirs after his death, partitioned the property subject to the mortgage so that each owned and occupied a distinct part; they were tenants in common as to the mortgage.

6. *Descent and Distribution; Obligation of Heirs.*—Where real estate descended to heirs incumbered by a mortgage, and was partitioned among them subject to the mortgage the debt could not be said to be the personal obligation of the heirs and they were under no duty to pay.

APPEAL from Jackson Chancery Court.

Heard before Hon. W. H. SIMPSON.

Bill by Geo. B. Caldwell and others against D. K. Caldwell and others to apportion a mortgage debt as to several parcels of land and for redemption. From a decree overruling demurrers to the bill respondents appeal. Corrected and affirmed.

The case made by the bill is substantially as follows:

The bill avers that complainants and defendants, D. K. and S. Alema Caldwell, were the only heirs at law of one Hamlin Caldwell, who died September 3, 1895, seised of the real estate described in the bill, which was subject to two mortgages to J. E. Butler, who had also purchased the lands at sheriff's sale under execution against said Hamlin Caldwell. On December 28, 1896, Butler transferred his mortgages to Sallie B. Brown, and on December 24, 1896, conveyed the lands by quitclaim deed to Sallie B. Brown, who in turn conveyed them, on November 21, 1898, by quitclaim deed to defendant A. H. Moody, and also transferred the Butler mortgages to him. On September 26, 1895, defendant D. K. Caldwell was appointed administrator of Hamlin Caldwell. On February 8, 1897, an agreement in writing was made, between complainants and defendants D. K. and S. Almena Caldwell, for D. K. Caldwell to make a final settlement of his administration of the estate of Hamlin Caldwell; paragraph 5 of the bill averring in regard thereto: "* * * Without taking ac-

count of the lands of the estate, except account for the
rents thereof for the years 1895 and 1896, nor without
taking account of the debt covered by the Butler mortgage transferred to Sallie B. Brown, and by her to the
defendant A. H. Moody, and by the terms of said written agreement the said settlement was to be made without regard to the land and the debt covered by the said
Butler mortgages, and no debt that any of the heirs
might owe the said estate of Hamlin Caldwell was to
be charged as against any interest the heirs had or might
have in the lands belonging to the said Hamlin Caldwell estate that had been transferred or conveyed by
J. F. Butler to Sallie B. Brown, and it empowered William B. Bridges, who was then judge of probate of Jackson county, Ala., to appoint one or more commisssioners
to value all the lands, and to take from the whole a sufficient quantity of land to bring within three years an
amount sufficient to meet the Sallie B. Brown debt, and
place the same in the hands of a trustee, and control
and sell within three years to pay said debt, and the remainder of said lands, after taking out the said lot or
parcel to be sold to pay the Sallie B. Brown debt, the
commissioners were to divide into four equal lots or
parcels, and to set apart to each heir one of the same,
in case the heirs could not agree among themselves. A
correct copy of the said written agreement is hereto attached, marked 'Exhibit A,' and made a part hereof, as
if here set out in full."

The final settlement was made and a decree rendered
by the probate court discharging the administrator.
The probate judge, William B. Bridges, appointed W.
W. McCutcheon, P. W. Keith, and the defendant A. H.
Moody commissioners, and issued to them a commisssion
in pursuance of the agreement. The commissioners
made a division of the lands into five lots, numbered 1,

2, 3, 4, and 5. Lot No. 1 to be put in the hands of a
trustee to control and sell to pay off the debt of Sallie
B. Brown (the Butler mortgages and debt); lot No. 2
to S. Almena Caldwell; lot No. 4 to George B. Caldwell,
and lot No. 5 to Europe H. Caldwell. On the division,
each heir went into possession of his or her respective
lot, and, the bill avers, became the owner thereof. On
October 11, 1902, the Aultman Company filed a bill
against the complainants herein and defendants D. K.
Caldwell and A. H. Moody praying to have the mortgages held by Moody and the quitclaim deed from Sallie B. Brown, held and treated as a mortgage, and to
ascertain the amount, etc. A decree of sale was rendered by agreement; the decree directing a sale in separate lots. The lands were all sold by the register. A.
H. Moody, defendant herein, purchased all of them for
$16,000, being the amount of the mortgages, etc., held
by him, plus the amount of the decree in favor of the
Aultman Company, the costs in the chancery court, and
the fee of defendants' solicitor in that case, and received a deed from the register.

In paragraph 11 of the bill it is averred: "At the
time of said sale, and shortly before, the defendant D.
K. Caldwell, agreed with the complainant herein that
he would procure the defendant A. H. Moody to purchase said lands at and for the amount due upon said
mortgages, transferred by Sallie B. Brown to the said
A. H. Moody, added to the amount of said decree and
the cost in the case in which it was rendered, and that
such purchase would be for the benefit of all the heirs
of Hamlin Caldwell, deceased, to wit, the complainants
herein and the defendants D. K. Caldwell and S. Almena Caldwell, and allow the said heirs five years in
which to redeem said property; and the said D. K.
Caldwell assured these complainants that he had made

such agreement with the said Moody, and thereby induced these complainants not to bid at said sale on said
lands, and to make no further effort to procure a purchaser in the interest of the heirs of Hamlin Caldwell,
deceased, although they had made arrangements to this
effect."

It is averred in paragraph 12 that: "At the time of
the agreement, referred to in the last paragraph, of the
said D. K. Caldwell, the said A. H. Moody was fully advised as to the agreement which had theretofore been
made between these complainants and the defendants
D. K. Caldwell and S. Almena Caldwell, providing for
the settlement of the administration of D. K. Caldwell
of the estate of Hamlin Caldwell, and had been one of
the commissioners appointed by the probate judge of
said county to divide said lands and allot the several
tracts thereof of the said lands. And by reason of the
agreement and understanding between the said D. K.
Caldwell and these complainants, which is hereinbefore
set forth, all of said lands were sold in one body, instead of separate tracts, as provided for in the said decree in the case of *Aultman Company et al., v. E. H.
Caldwell et al.,* which is made an exhibit hereto."

The bill alleges that defendant D. K. Caldwell con-
spired with A. H. Moody to deprive complainants of
any interest in the lands, by causing Moody to purchase
the lands and convey the same, and all interests in them,
to said D. K. Caldwell. Said Moody executed to said
D. K. Caldwell, on May 4, 1905, a conveyance of all of
said lands, which was filed for record June 16, 1905.
D. K. executed to Moody a mortgage on the lands for
$16,000, the amount of Moody's bid, which, upon the
records, is dated January 16, 1905, and appears to have
been acknowledged May 4, 1905, and was filed for record June 1, 1905. D. K. procured the conveyance to

himself from Moody without the knowledge, consent, or approval of complainants. They were not aware that he had procured the legal title until they discovered the deed in the probate judge's office in the latter part of the summer of 1905. It is averred on information and belief, that D. K. and Moody have conveyed to defendants Charles E. and William Webb a portion of the lands. D. K., after the conveyance to him from Moody, for some time recognized the rights of complainants to participate in a redemption, but now denies their rights, and refuses to confer with them in regard thereto. Complainants have each requested D. K. Caldwell to join with them in a redemption from the mortgage held by defendant Moody, and he has refused to join with them, or to negotiate with them in any way. Since the conveyance from Moody to him, defendant D. K. Caldwell has collected the rents of all the lands, except lot No. 5.

The prayer is for "a decree fixing and ascertaining the total amount due upon said mortgage upon all the said real estate executed by D. K. Caldwell and wife to the defendant A. H. Moody, and recorded in the probate court of Jackson county in Mortgage Book 41, page 377; second, ascertaining and declaring what part of and how much of said mortgage indebtedness is a charge upon that part of said real estate included in said mortgage, and known as lot No. 5, described in said report of the commissioners which is Exhibit C hereto, and which was allotted and assigned to complainant Europe H. Caldwell; third, fixing and declaring what part and how much of said mortgage indebtedness is a charge upon that part of said real estate included in said mortgage and known as lot No. 4, allotted and assigned to the complainant George B. Caldwell, and described in said report of said commissioners which is marked 'Exhibit C" hereto, commanding and requiring said A. H. Moody, in foreclosing said mortgage, to sell, first, that part of said lands included in said mortgage, and known as lot No. 1, described in said report of the commissioners, which is Exhibit C hereto, and permitting these complainants to pay off and discharge each that part of said debt which is a charge on his part of said real estate; fourth, ascertaining and determining what part and how much of said mortgage indebtedness shall be payable to the defendants T. E. Morgan, C. W. Webb, and William Webb, and these complainants now submit this to this honorable court, and offer to do equity in the payments of said debt, or securing any part thereof which is proper charge against their respective tracts, including in said mortgage, and offer to do whatever may be required by the court in the premises;" and for general relief.

The causes of demurrer noted as overruled are as follows: (1) "There is no equity in the bill." (3) "The bill fails to show that the respondent A. H. Moody was a party to the agreement referred to in section 11 of said bill." (10) "For that complainants' rights, if any, are barred by laches." (12) "For that the bill shows that respondent D. K. Caldwell, as the administrator of the estate of Hamlin Caldwell, deceased, made a final settlement of his administration, and that it was agreed between complainant and said Caldwell that the respective amounts ascertained to be due by complainants, respectively, on said settlement, should be a charge upon that part of the estate respectively allotted to them by the said commission, and the bill fails to show that on said settlement nothing was ascertained to be due by complainants, or either of them, or that such amount so due has been paid." (14) "The bill fails to show that complainants, either of them, before this bill was filed,

[Caldwell, et al. v. Caldwell.]

tendered to said Moody or Caldwell the charges fixed
by law for the redemption of said land." (15) "It fails
to show payment into court of the charges fixed by law
for the redemption of said land, or that before the filing
of the bill complainants made any effort to ascertain
such charges and offered to pay the same."

MILO MOODY, for appellant. The agreement set out
in the bill upon which complainant seeks relief is void
under one or both of sub-divs. 1 and 5, sec. 428, Code
1907.—*Jenkins v. Lovelace*, 72 Ala. 303; *Stringfellow v.
Ivey*, 73 Ala. 209. Apart from this void agreement, the
bill to redeem is without equity as the requirements authorizing redemption has never been complied with, and
the complainants have been guilty of laches.—*Bube v.
Barton*, 99 Ala. 117; *Beatty v. Brown*, 101 Ala. 695;
Murphree v. Summerlin, 114 Ala. 54; *Long v. Slade*, 121
Ala. 269. Several of the respondents are shown to be
purchasers without notice of any alleged equity of complainant, and the bill is without equity as to them.—
Randolph v. Webb, 116 Ala. 135; *Hoots v. Williams*,
116 Ala. 372; 5 Cyc. 719.

TALLY & FRICKE, R. W. CLOPTON and S. S. PLEAS-
ANTS, for appellee. All persons interested in the premises who would be prejudiced by a foreclosure have a
right to redeem, and this includes grantees, assignees,
devisees and heirs.—*Butts v. Broughton*, 72 Ala. 294;
Homer v. Boyer, 89 Ala. 280; *Raney v. McQueen*, 1212
Ala. 191; *Howzer v. Cruickshank*, 122 Ala. 263. When
such person redeems, he must redeem from the entire
mortgage by paying the entire debt, however small his
interest.—*McQueen v. Whetsone*, 127 Ala. 417; s. c. 137
Ala. 417; 121 Ala. 191. Such redemptioner becomes
the equitable assignee of the mortgage and may be com-

pelled to permit his co-tenants to redeem their portion.
—*Jones v Matkin*, 118 Ala. 348; 3 Pom. Eq. Secs. 1220
to 1222. The equity of the bill does not depend upon the
agreement set up in par. 11. That simply gives it additional equity by way of an equitable estoppel.—*Nelson
v. Kelly*, 91 Ala. 565; *Goetter v. Norman Bros.*, 107 Ala.
585. The bill has equity outside of the agreement.—
Authorities, supra. No laches is shown.—*Caldwell v.
Caldwell*, 47 South. 268. If it is necessary that the purchasers have notice the bill sufficiently avers their constructive notice of the condition of the title.—*Truss v.
Miller*, 116 Ala. 494; Pomeroy Eq. secs. 630, 626 and
613; *Campbell v. Roach*, 45 Ala. 667; *Thompson v.
Sheppard*, 85 Ala. 611; *Corbitt v. Clenny*, 52 Ala. 480;
Dudley et al. v. Witter, 46 Ala. 664; *Milhouse v. Dun-
ham*, 78 Ala. 48; *Johnson v. Thweat*, 18 Ala. 741.

SIMPSON, J.—The bill in this case was filed by the
appellees against the appellants. The material parts
of the bill are that the complainants and the respondent, D. K. Caldwell were owners of the lands described
in the bill, which lands had been partitioned among
them, subject, however, to an outstanding mortgage on
the same, which was held by A. H. Moody, one of the respondents; that said mortgage was foreclosed by decree
of court, and at the sale under said decree said Moody
became the purchaser for the amount of the mortgage
debt; that a few days thereafter said Moody conveyed
said land to said D. K. Caldwell, and took from him a
mortgage on said lands for the purchase money. The
bill alleges that, previous to said sale, the complainants
had a verbal agreement with said D. K. Caldwell, by
which they were to refrain from bidding at said sale,
said Caldwell was to purchase the land, and allow complainants five years within which to redeem the land,

that the land was conveyed by said Moody to said D. K. Caldwell on January 20, 1905, and complainants did not know that said D. K. Caldwell had acquired to himself the legal title to the lands, until they discovered the deed on record in the probate judge's office "in the latter part of the summer of 1905," and that said D. K. at first recognized the right of complainants to redeem, but has since denied them said right.

It is acknowledged that said verbal agreement is void under the statute of frauds (Code 1907, § 4289); and section 3412 also provides that "no trust concerning lands, except such as results by implication or construction of law, or which may be transferred or extinguished by operation of law, can be created, unless by instrument in writing, signed by the party creating or declaring the same, or his agent or attorney lawfully authorized thereto in writing." The complainants disavow any attempt to enforce the parol agreement, but insist that, regardless of the parol agreement, the act of said D. K. Caldwell, which it is alleged was the result of a fraudulent agreement between him and said Moody to defeat their right of redemption, amounted in equity to a mere redemption by said D. K. Caldwell, which would inure to the benefit of all the several owners of the lands covered by the mortgage. There is no controversy in regard to the proposition that a redemption by one joint owner inures to the benefit of the other joint owners, who have a right to be let in to redeem by paying their aliquot part of the incumbrance; but, without the aid of the parol agreement, it is difficult to see how this transaction can be held to be a redemption.

It cannot be controverted that, under the decree of sale, the holder of the mortgage could become the purchaser, and thereby acquire title to the land, subject only to the right of redemption according to law. When Moody purchased at the sale under the decree, he acquired said title subject to said right; and when he conveyed to Caldwell he conveyed simply the interest held by him, subject to the same equities, unless the relations between D. K. Caldwell and the complainants were such that he could not purchase the property in his own right. As above stated, the bill shows that the complainants were apprised of the fact that D. K. Caldwell had acquired the legal title to himself within less than a year after the conveyance, so that they had ample time to exercise their right to redeem under the statute, in place of which they waited five years before filing this bill. Pomeroy says: "There are many instances in which equity thus compels the owner of land to forego the benefits of his legal title and to admit the equitable claims of another, in direct contravention of the literal requirements of the statute; but they all depend upon the same principle. The rule under consideration is strictly analogous to another familiar rule that a legal owner of land cannot be turned into a trustee ex delicto by any mere words or conduct. A constructive trust ex delicto can never be impressed upon land as against the legal title by any verbal stipulation, however definite, nor by any mere conduct. Such trust can only arise where the verbal stipulation and conduct together amount to fraud in contemplation of equity." 2 Pomeroy's Eq. Jur. (d Ed.) § 807, p. 1433. And he further states that the misrepresentation must be of a fact or facts, as disinguished from a mere promise. "A statement concerning future facts would either be a mere expression of opinion, or would constitute a contract, and be governed by rules applicable to contracts." Id. § 808, pp. 1435, 1436. Again: "A statement of intention merely cannot be a misrepresentation amounting to fraud, since such a statement is not the affirmation of any external fact, but is, at most, only an assertion that a present mental condition or opinion exists," although "the statement of matter in the future, if affirmed *as a fact,* may amount to a fraudulent representation." Section 877, p. 1561. In the case of *Jones v. Matkin,* 118 Ala. 341, 343, 24 South. 242, in which the opinion of the majority prevailed over the dissent of Coleman, J., and Brickell, C. J., it is stated distinctly that the money was paid "to redeem said real estate."

It cannot be said, then, that there was such fraud in the statements made by D. K. Caldwell as would entitle the complainants to relief. It remains, then, only to consider the question above suggested, to wit: Did D. K. Caldwell occupy such a relation of confidence to the complainants as to preclude him from acquiring title to the entire land, so that any purchase he may have made, either directly or indirectly, under the judicial sale, would necessarily inure to the benefit of the others. It will be noticed that they had all originally occupied the property as tenants in common, having received it from the common ancestor with the mortgage incumbrance on it, but they had made a partition, each owning and occupying a distinct, separate part; but under the facts of this case we hold as to this mortgage they can be considered as being tenants in common, although they had agreed on a partition subject to the mortgage. This court has held that a purchase at tax sale, by one whose duty it is to pay the taxes, operates only as a payment of the taxes.—*Johnston & Seats v. Smith's Adm'r.,* 70 Ala. 108.

It is true that in the present case, while the property was received by the parties subject to the mortgage incumbrance, yet it cannot be said that the debt was the personal obligation of either of the parties, or that he

was under any duty to pay the same. It is stated that,
"as a general rule, any person may become a purchaser
at a mortgage foreclosure sale who does not stand in
such a relation of trust or confidence to the mortgagor
as to make his purchase a fraud or breach of duty."—27
Cyc. 1482. Chancellor Kent said: "I will not say,
however, that one tenant in common may not, in any
case, purchase in·an outstanding title for his exclusive
benefit. But when two devisees are in possession, under
an imperfect title derived from the common ancestor,
there would seem naturally and equitably to arise an
obligation between them, resulting from their joint
claim and community of interests, that one of them
should not affect the claim to the prejudice of the other.
It is like an expense laid out upon the common subject,
by one of the owners, in which case all are entitled to
the common benefit."—*Van Horne v. Fonda,* 5 Johns.
Ch. (N. Y.) 388, 406, 407. It is true that in that case
one of the heirs, who purchased, and the question was
whether he bought *as executor,* or not, and the defendant
purchased from him, and the court further said: "I
have no doubt, therefore, that in a case like the present,
and assuming that the evidence warrants us to assume
that the deed of May, 1794, was taken by the defendant
for trust purposes, that the purchase from Moses Johnson ought in equity to inure for the common benefit."

This court expressed a doubt as to whether one tenant in common would be allowed to set up, as against
the others, a title acquired at tax sale (*Howe v. Dew,*
90 Ala. 184, 7 South. 239, 24 Am. St. Rep. 783) ; and
other cases hold that he cannot (*Donner v. Quartermas,*
90 Ala. 164, 169, 170, 8 South. 715, 24 Am. St. Rep. 778;
Bailey's Adm'r. v. Campbell, 82 Ala. 342, 346, 2 South.
646). The *Van Horne-Fonda Case, supra,* and others,
are cited; but we do not find in them any distinct deci-

sion that one tenant in common may not acquire title to
the entire tract, by purchase at a judicial sale, under
a foreclosure decree. The decisions in other states are
not as distinct and harmonious as they might be. In
one case where a tenant in common purchased an outstanding mortgage, taking an assignment of it, the
court said: "It is then objected that one tenant in
common cannot purchase an outstanding title, or incumbrance upon the joint estate, for his exclusive benefit,
and assert the same to the prejudice of his cotenant in
any way. That principle cannot be properly applied
to a purchase of an outstanding mortgage upon the
joint estate. Such title may temporarily inure to the
benefit of a cotenant who elects to make such a purchase. But it leaves the other party in the full enjoyment of the right of redemption that he previously enjoyed." And it was held that, until the cotenant elected to contribute his share, the title, as assignee of the
mortgage, was sufficient to prevent a partition.—*Blodgett et al. v. Hildreth,* 8 Allen (Mass.) 186, 188.

The Supreme Court of Pennsylvania holds that "a
conveyance to one of several tenants in common, or a
deed to one of two devisees of the same land, shall inure to the benefit of all who came in under the same
title and are holding jointly or in common"; the court
saying further that, "where several persons have a joint
or common interest in an estate, it is not to be tolerated
that one shall purchase an incumbrance or an outstanding title and set it up against the rest for the purpose
of depriving them of their interests," and, quoting from
Chancellor Kent, in the *Van Horne-Fonda Case, supra,*
says: "Such a proceeding would be repugnant to a
sense of refined and accurate justice, and would be im-
moral, because it would be against the reciprocal obligations to do nothing to the prejudice of each other's

claim, which the relationship of the parties created."—
Weaver v. Wible, 25 Pa. 270, 64 Am. Dec. 696, 697.

In a case where one of the heirs of an estate purchased
the land at a foreclosure decree based on a mortgage
made by the ancestor, and had sold a part of the lands,
it was held that a bill was sustainable to require said
purchaser to account for the moneys received by him,
deducting the amount paid out by him, and to establish titles in the coheirs as to the unused portions of the
land —*Tisdale v. Tisdale,* 2 Sneed [Tenn.] 596, 599, 64
Am. Dec. 775, 777); the court saying: "Tenants in
common by descent are placed in a confidential relation
to each other by operation of law as to the joint property, and the same duties are imposed as if a joint trust
were created, by contract between them, or the act of a
third party." Upon the same principle, where one of
the tenants in common acquired a patent from the government, it was held to inure to all of the tenants in
common.—*Roberts v. Thorn,* 25 Tex. 728, 78 Am. Dec.
552, 554. And the like result was held where one tenant
in common purchased the lands, at a sheriff's sale, under execution on a judgment against all.—*Gibson v.
Winslow,* 46 Pa. 380, 84 Am. Dec. 552.

While these cases may be differentiated from the one
now under consideration, in some particulars, yet all
hold that, under the broad equitable principle laid down
by the great chancellor in the *Van Horne-Fonda Case,*
there is a confidential relation existing between tenants
in common, by which a purchase such as is shown in
this case entitles the other tenants in common, within a
reasonable time, to demand that the purchase inure to
their benefit, on their contributing their proportion.

We hold that under the circumstances of this case
the complainants were not guilty of such laches as to deprive them of this remedy, but if, before they elected to

demand that the purchase inure to their benefit, any parts of the lands had been sold to bona fide purchasers, their remedy is to require D. K. Caldwell to account for the money received, and not to dispossess such purchasers. From what has been said, it results that the bill has equity, though some of the causes of demurrers should have been sustained.

The decree will be corrected, so as to overrule causes 1, 3, 10, 12, 14 and 15, of the demurrer, and to sustain the remaining causes; and, as corrected, the decree of the court is affirmed.

Corrected and affirmed.

ANDERSON, SAYRE and SOMMERVILLE, JJ., concur.

Horton, *et al.* *v.* Southern Railway Co.

Bill to Enjoin Removal of Depot.

(Decided May 11, 1911.　55 South. 531.)

1. *Railroads; Location of Station; Legislative Powers.*—If such requirement is not so unreasonable as to amount to confiscation of property, or destruction of the business of the carrier, the legislature may require the railroads to establish depots at particular points.

2. *Same.*—The legislature may confer on the railroad commission power to determine the location of depots and make the conclusion of the commission final, or permit its action to be reviewed by the courts.

3. *Same; Judicial Power.*—The courts may compel a carrier to perform the duties imposed upon it by law and may restrain acts in excess of the power granted.

4. *Same; Regulation; Statutory Power.*—The matter of locating depots is legislative and within the power of the railroad commission to determine, under section 243, Constitution 1901, and sections 5651, et seq. Code 1907, and hence, the court of chancery will not entertain jurisdiction of a bill by a private individual against a carrier to restrain it from moving its passenger depot from one location to another.

[Horton, et al. v. Southern Railway Co.]

5. *Same.*—One seeking to enjoin a railroad from removing its depot from one location to another in the city, on the ground that the carrier owes a duty to the public and to the complainants to continue to maintain the depot at its present site, has the burden to show both in allegation and in proof some special injury different in kind and degree from that sustained by the general public.

6. *Same; Injunction; Evidence.*—The evidence in this case examined and held not sufficient to show such irreparable injury to complainant as to warrant a temporary injunction, complainant's right not having been established by law, and the railroad commission having declined to interfere after a full hearing.

7. *Nuisance; Public Nuisance; Relief by Private Individual.*—To entitle private individuals to an injunction against the construction of buildings, or the operation of agencies performing duties to the public generally, or to a considerable part thereof, such individuals must allege that the construction or alteration complained of will be a nuisance in fact, and that they will suffer some substantial injury different in kind and degree from that suffered by the public generally.

8. *Municipal Corporations; Duty Not Enjoined by Law; Power of Courts.*—Unless the duty is enjoined by a charter or other statutory law the courts will not compel a municipality to perform such duty.

APPEAL from Colbert Chancery Court.

Heard before Hon. W. H. SIMPSON.

Bill by T. B. Horton, and others, against the Southern Railway Company, to enjoin the removal of its depot from one point to another in the city of Tuscumbia. From a decree denying the temporary injunction, and dismissing the bill, complainants appeal. Affirmed.

KIRK, CARMICHAEL & RATHER, and E. W. GODBEY, for appellant. The railway company is without right to inflict injury upon the public by removing its station for the purpose of advancing its own emolument or convenience.—33 Cyc. 142; 2 Elliott R. R. 931 Ala. p. 414; *People v. L. & N. R. R. Co.* 10 N. E. Rep. 657; Purdy's Beach on Corporations, Sec. 1038; 26 Am. & Eng. Encyc. of Law, 497, 499; *State v. M. J. & K. C. R. R. Co.*, 38 So. 738-739 (Miss.); *State v. Republican Valley R. R.* 52 Am. Rep. 426; 2 Elliott on R. R., Sec. 930, p. 406; 931; *C. & A. R. Co. v. Suffern*, 21 N. E. Rep. 825; 23 Am. Eng. & Eng. Encyc. of Law, 690; *Brown V. A. &*

B. R. Co., 55 S. E. 26; 2 Elliott on R. R. Sec. 930, p. 404-5; *People v. Albany & V. R. Co.* 19 How. Prac. (N. Y.) 523; *Leverett v. Middle Ga. & A. R. Co.* 24 S. E. 156; *Coe v. L. & N. R. Co.* 3 Fed. Rep. 775; *State v. Northern Pac. R. Co.* 95 N. W. 301. The power of the railroad commission extends only to supervising the original location of a station, and not to the changing of a station.—Code, Sec. 5543. A railroad commission is not a judicial tribunal; its actions are not binding upon the courts nor upon the parties who resort to the courts.—2 Elliott on R. R. 675, 677, 682, 683; 33 Cyc. 45-46; 2 Elliott on R. R. Sec. 694; 33 Cyc. 51; 33 Cyc. 53; *State v. M. J. & K. C. R. Co.,* 38 So. 738.

The railway company cannot justify the change of this station by reason of its proposal to install a new and unauthorized main line, in order to lengthen rather than straighten said main line as provided by statute. —*Brown v. Atlantic Etc. R. Co.,* 7 Am. Eng. Ann. cases, 1032, Note; *State v. M. J. & K. C. R. Co.,* 38 So. 738; 33 Cyc. 135; 2 Elliott on R. R. Sec. 923; Code, Sec. 3484; 2 Elliott on R. R. Sec. 930, p. 407; 33 Cyc. 132; 23 Am. & Eng. Enc. of Law, p. 692; *Brown v. Atlantic Etc. R. Co.,* 7 Am. Eng. Ann. cases, p. 1034, Note. The original location is a question for legislative and administrative bodies; a change of existing conditions, interfering with the vested interests, provokes a judicial question, and there has been frequent judicial interference with changes of railway stations and tracks to the prejudice of local interests.—*People v. L. & N. R. R. Co.,* 10 N. E. 657. The following authorities hold that a writ of injunction is the remedy to prevent a threatened wrong of this kind.—33 Cyc. 136. *People v. Albany etc. R. Co.,* 19 How. Prac. 523; *People v. Albany etc. R. Co.,* 37 Barb. (N. Y.) 216; *Leverett v. Middle Ga. etc. R. Co.,* 24 S. E. Rep. 154; *State v. M. J. & K. C. R.*

Co., 38 So. 732 (739); 22 Cyc. 897. The following authorities hold that mandamus is the remedy to compel the performance of public duties which have been abandoned; and that injunction is the remedy to prevent abandonment where the duties are still being performed but a cessation thereof threatened.—*People v. Albany etc. R. Co.*, 37 Barb. (N. Y.) 216; *Coal Co., v. Coal & Navigation Co.*, 88 Am. Dec. 538, Note; Morawetz on Corporations, Sec. 1132. Private parties may bring suits against quasi public corporations for dereliction in the performance of their duties to the public.—*U. P. R. Co. v. Hall*, 91 U. S. 343; *Brown v. Atlantic etc. R. Co.*, 7 Am. & Eng. Ann. cases, 1034; *Macon etc. R. Co. v. Gibson*, 21 Am. St. Rep. 144; Beach on Injunctions, Sec. 353; *Toledo etc. Co. v. Pennsylvania Co.*, 19 L. R. A. 393; High on Injunctions, Sec. 16; 2 Thompson on Corp. Sec. 468; *Messenger v. Pa. R. Co.*, 13 Am. Rep. 462-3; *State (Grinsfelder) v. Spokane S. R. Co.*, 41 L. R. A. 517; *First Nat. Bank of Montgomery v. Tyson*, 39 So. 561.

ALMON & ANDREWS, for appellee. The proceedings were instituted in the wrong court.—*State ex rel Mead v. Dunn*, Minor, 46; *Ex parte Jones*, 1 Ala. 15; *Travers v. Commissioners Court*, 17 Ala. 527; *Ex parte Huckabee*, 71 Ala. 421; *M. & G. R. R. Co. v. Comm. Ct.*, 97 Ala. 105; *Weatherly v. Water Works Co.*, 115 Ala. 175; *Montgomery v. Capital City Water Co.*, 92 Ala. 361; 4 Mayf. 167. There is no pretension that the court has jurisdiction because of the avoidance of a multiplicity of suits.—*Turner v. Mobile*, 135 Ala. 108; *Jones v. Hardy*, 127 Ala. 221. The questions presented are decided more nearly in *Jacquelin et al. v. Erie Ry. Co.*, 61 Atl. 18, than in any other case coming within our observation. See also in this same connection.—*Fritts et al. v.*

D. L. & W. R. R. Co., 73 Atl. 92; *U. P. R. R. Co. v. Hall,*
91 U. S. 343; *State v. Hartford R. R. Co.,* 29 Conn. 538.
The parties seeking this injunction were private individuals and must show an interference with some substantial right differing in kind and degree from that suffered by the general public, before they can be heard to
complain.—*Baker v. S. S. & S. R. R. Co.,* 135 Ala. 552;
First Nat. Bank v. Tyson, v33 Ala. 459; 10 Cyc. 1340;
see also 30 Ala. 238; 55 Ala. 421; 87 Ala. 157; 124 Ala.
162; 138 N. Y. 179; 14 Enc. P. & P. 1145. The court
had no jurisdiction of the subject-matter.—Sec. 243,
Constitution 1901; Secs. 5650, et seq., Code 1907; *N. P.
R. R. Co. v. Washington,* 142 U. S. 492; *People v. Railroad Co.,* 104 N. Y. 58, and authorities supra.

MAYFIELD, J.—Appellants filed this bill to enjoin
the appellee railway company from removing its passenger depot from its present location to another, some
3,600 feet distant. The bill alleges that the present site
is centrally located in Tuscumbia, which is a city of
4,000 or more inhabitants, and contains property assessed at a valuation of $2,000,000; that about 42,000 tick-
ets are annually sold from this depot over the main and
branch lines of the railroad; that the present depot is
located very near that of the Louisville & Nashville;
that it has been so located for about 65 or 70 years; that
within a radius of 600 feet are located the hotel of the
complainants and the principal business houses of the
city, including two banks, the post office, city hall, court
house, etc., and that within a radius of 1,000 feet are
located the Methodist, Presbyterian, Baptist, and Epis-
copal churches, and within 1,500 feet is the public school
building; that the defendant proposes to remove the station to a locality 3,600 feet distant, and that the newly
selected and proposed site is inaccessible; that leading

to and from it are no macadamized streets nor paved
sidewalks, no water mains, electric car lines, etc. The
bill alleges that the station is on the present ancient
main line of the Southern Railway, and that said railway proposes to remove the depot to the outskirts of
the city in order to put it upon the new main line, which
the bill alleges will make a circuitous detour, and not
tend to strengthen the line of the railway. The bill alleges, further, that complainants' hotel, the Parshall
House, is near the depot, and is a convenient stopping
place for many passengers coming to and going from
Tuscumbia; that both the hotel and depot have been
maintained at their present sites for many years, for
at least two generations; and that to change the location
of the depot would entail great loss upon the complainants, and would inconvenience the traveling public. The
bill was accompanied by affidavits in support of the allegations of the bill.

Upon the hearing of the application for a temporary
writ of injunction, and after notice to the defendant, it
filed a number of affidavits for the consideration of the
court, which affidavits were to the effect that the Railroad Commission of the state had passed upon and approved the proposed change; that the Commercial Club
of the city of Tuscumbia had filed a protest with the
Railroad Commission against the location of the depot
at the place designated in the bill; that the commission
went upon the proposed site, and, in company with the
complainants and others, examined the entire situation;
that, after having once passed upon the question, they
granted a rehearing, and after due consideration the
commission unanimously entered an order declining to
interfere in the matter of the proposed change. A copy
of the order of the commission was made an exhibit of
the affidavit used upon hearing. Upon the hearing of

the application for the temporary writ of injunction, the chancellor reached the conclusion that the chancery court was without jurisdiction and power to entertain the bill, and to grant the relief sought.

The chancellor in his opinion which accompanies his decree dismissing the bill states that the bill makes no pretense that the court's aid can be invoked under any provision in the charter under which the defendant operates its road, and that there is no common-law principle upon which the jurisdiction of the court can be rested; that the Legislature of Alabama had undertaken to regulate the business of common carriers (in this state), and to this end had created a railroad commission, upon which it had conferred power to supervise the location of passenger and freight depots, etc.; that the location of such depots should be left to the discretion of the commission; that, while the railroad company was charged with the duty of furnishing reasonably adequate and suitable facilities, this matter was referred to the Railroad Commission by the Legislature, and that the proposed change had met with the approval of said commission; that the chancery court should not interfere unless it clearly appeared that there was gross and arbitrary abuse of the authority. The chancellor further expressed the opinion that, if the court's aid could be invoked in such a case as made by the bill, it should be by a public proceeding in the name of the state, and not by individuals; otherwise there would be no end to the litigation, as every individual affected in the slightest degree by the change of the site of the depot could maintain a suit. It is said on high authority that it is a part of the common-law duty of railroad companies, which are common carriers, to establish and maintain stations and depots along their roads sufficient to furnish reasonable facilities for the use of their lines by the public who may desire to use the same as travelers or shippers.—*State v. Republican Valley R. R.*, 17 Neb. 647, 24 N. W. 329, 52 Am. Rep. 424; *Id.*, 18 Neb. 512, 26 N. W. 205.

There is no doubt that the Legislature may require such railroads as are common carriers to establish depots or stations at particular points, if not so unreasonable as to amount to a confiscation of the property or destruction of the business of the railroad.—*Commonwealth v. Eastern Co.*, 103 Mass. 254, 258, 4 Am. Rep. 555.

The Legislature may also confer this power upon a railroad commission which may determine whether stations shall be located at certain places, and their conclusions may be made final, or they may be made reviewable by the courts.—*Com'rs v. Portland Railroad Co.*, 63 Me. 269, 18 Am. Rep. 208. The court of New York, in the case of *People v. N. Y. R. R. Co.*, 104 N. Y. 66, 9 N. E. 856, Am. Rep. 484, refused to grant a mandamus to compel a railroad company to construct and maintain a station and warehouse sufficient to accommodate a town of more than a thousand inhabitants, and which supplied a large passenger and freight business to the road, although the Railroad Commission of New York had recommended such station and warehouse. The court in that case said: "A plainer case could hardly be presented of a deliberate and intentional disregard of the public interests and the accommodation of the public. No doubt, as the respondent urges, the court may by mandamus also act in certain cases affecting corporate matters, but only when the duty concerned is specific and plainly imposed upon the corporation. Such is not the case before us. The grievance complained of is an obvious one, but the burden of removing it can be imposed upon the defendant only by legislation."

[Horton, et al. v. Southern Railway Co.]

The Supreme Court of Nebraska held that it was a part of the common-law duty of a railroad company as a common carrier of passengers to maintain a station at a town of 1,500 people, such as would afford reasonable facilities to the people, and issued a mandamus to compel the location of the station.—*State v. Republican Valley Co.*, 17 Neb. 647, 24 N. W. 329, 52 Am. Rep. 424; *Id.*, 18 Neb. 512, 26 N. W. 205. The Illinois courts also have gone a long way towards holding that mandamus will lie at the suit of the state to compel railroads to locate stations where they are needed, and are almost in line with the Nebraska court.—*People v. Louisville & Nashville Railroad Co.*, 120 Ill. 48, 10 N. E. 657; *Vincent et al. v. C. & A. R. R. Co.*, 49 Ill 33; *People v. Chicago Ry. Co.*, 130 Ill. 175, 22 N. E. 857; *Mobile Ry. Co. v. People*, 132 Ill. 559, 571, 24 N. E. 643, 22 Am. St. Rep. 556. The above case (reported in 130 Ill.) held that mandamus would lie to compel the relocation of a station at a county seat, where there had once been a station, on the ground that being once located there the railroad company had no authority to change it; but these cases are all reviewed, criticised, and some of them disapproved by the Supreme Court of the United States in the case of *Northern Pacific Ry. Co. v. Washington Territory*, 142 U. S. 492, 12 Sup. Ct. 283, 35 L. Ed. 1092. The case last referred to was similar to the one at bar. In that case the railroad when first constructed stopped its trains at Yakima City, which was the county seat; but it built no depot there, and subsequently the company obtained lands four miles north of the town, and was interested in building up a city on its own land and established a passenger depot at this new site, and ceased to stop its trains at Yakima City. The courts were applied to in that case to compel the railroad company to make Yakima City a station.

Before the litigation terminated, the new city rapidly increased and the old one retrograded. The new one became the larger, and was subsequently made the county seat. The case finally went to the Supreme Court of the United States, where it was held by a divided court that mandamus could not issue in such case; that courts could not attempt the supervision of railroads; and that the remedy in such cases should be sought in proper legislation.

The case nearest in point to the one in hand which we have been able to find, and probably as near as could be found, is that of *Jacquelin et al. v. Erie Ry. Co.*, 69 N. J. Eq. 432, 61 Atl. 18. In most of the cases we have examined mandamus seems to have been the remedy pursued to compel the location, or to prevent the removal, of stations and depots; but in the Jacquelin Case the remedy sought was by injunction, as in the case at bar, and the bill was filed by property owners and citizens of the town to prevent the removal of the station and depot, and practically the same condition of facts was alleged in that bill to exist that we have in the case at bar, and the damages and inconveniences there alleged to be the necessary consequence of the change in the location of the depot were similar to those here set up. Consequently there can be no doubt that it is an authority in point, unless the Constitution and statutes regulating railroads in the two states or those pertaining to pleading and practice render it not an authority. The case seems to have been fully and well considered, and a great number of authorities are cited in support of its holdings. The bill in the New Jersey case was originally filed by one Jacquelin, and it was subsequently amended by the addition of a number of other parties as complainants, including a great number of business firms and associations, and the borough of Orville. The bill sought an injunction to restrain the railroad company from discontinuing the use of its station at Hobokus, and require it to retain and maintain a station at that point. The bill alleged that the station at that point was the only station within the limits of the borough of Orville, and that the nearest stations thereto were those of Undercliff (about four-fifths of a mile distant) and Waldick (about a mile and a half distant). In this respect the case corresponds very closely with the one at bar, where the proposed new site is some 3,600 feet from the present location. Affidavits accompanied the bill in that case, and others by the respondent railroad company were filed upon the hearing—all bearing upon the propriety of the proposed change of site of the station, and showing a similar state of affairs to that made by the bill and affidavits under consideration. In that case, as in this, the exact question for determination was whether a court of equity could grant a preliminary injunction, requiring a railroad company to continue to furnish railroad facilities at a station which the company desired to abandon; there being no charter or statutory requirements as to continuing the station at such point.

One point of difference in regard to the law of the two states; it being decided in that case that there were no statutes in New Jersey defining the duties of railroads with respect to the establishment and maintenance of such railroad stations, whereas there are numerous statutes of that nature in this state. The contention was made in that case, as in this, that the equity of the bill depended upon either of two theories—that the complainants had a legal right which, under peculiar circumstances, the court of equity would protect, or that they had an equitable right which the court would respect. The equitable right is based on the contention

that the railroad company by its conduct had induced
the complainants and other people to purchase property, build homes, and establish businesses at or near the
station; that it had advertised the place as one where
the public would be served, and that it would be inequitable to permit the railroad company to decline to
make good its implied promise to continue to so maintain the station. The court in that case held that, if
any such right as this existed, it was a legal, and not
an equitable, right, and that the court of equity had no
jurisdiction to enforce specifically such implied contract; that a court of equity could not specifically enforce such contract if it were an express instead of an
implied one, because such an agreement would be
against public policy; and that the railroad company
and such contracting parties would have to be remitted
to a court of law to a suit for damages, rather than to
a court of equity for a specific enforcement of such contract, upon which proposition many authorities were
cited. In that case the court declined to consider the
question whether or not the -complainants were the
proper parties to enforce the specific performance of
such contract or duty, if it existed, and was capable of
such performance; or whether such suit should be
brought by the Attorney General on behalf of the state
as a necessary party complainant. It will be observed
that, while the relief here sought is in form to restrain
by prevention, it is in effect to compel performance;
that is, to compel the railroad company to continue to
use its present station. While railroads are quasi public
corporations, and may be compelled by courts to perform the duties enjoined upon them by law, the difficult
question presented is, Can a court compel a railroad
company which is a common carrier to perform a duty
which is not enjoined upon it by its charter nor by any
other express statutory provision?

[Horton, et al. v. Southern Railway Co.]

The law is well settled that a public corporation, such as a municipal one, cannot be compelled to perform any duty that is not enjoined upon it by its charter or other statutory law. It has been held by the great majority of the courts, in both England and America, state and federal, that the subject of regulating the operation of railroads and common carriers, in both the matter of locating and maintaining depots, warehouses, and like accommodations for passengers and patrons, and that of schedules, speed, and mode of operating trains, etc., is a question for the legislative department of the government, and not for the judicial; that the courts cannot originate provisions with respect thereto, but can only interpret and apply to these subjects the law as it may have been ordained by the legislative departments.

It is certainly true, however, that, wherever there is a positive duty imposed by law upon such common carriers, the courts have the power to enforce its performance or discharge, and to restrain actions in excess of the powers and rights granted to such public service corporations. It must be conceded, however, that the authorities are in conflict upon the proposition as to the power of courts to interfere with, or to direct or control, the management and operation of a railroad as to the location and maintenance of depots, stations, etc., and the line of its road, where there is no statutory or legislative requirement upon the subject. As has been before pointed out, the decisions of the courts of Nebraska and Illinois seem to hold that the courts have power and jurisdiction to interfere with the management and operation of railroads in these matters, and certainly so, in extreme cases, where the public would otherwise suffer irreparable loss. But, as held by the New Jersey court and by the Supreme Court of the United States, the correctness of these decisions may well be doubted; and

the decisions of the court of Illinois upon the subject
are very much in conflict with one another. It has,
however, become the declared policy of a great number
of states that this question should be dealt with by the
Legislature, and many of them have constitutional provisions relative to conferring powers and enjoining duties upon such public service corporations in these matters which so much concern the public. These provisions require that the Legislature shall provide by law
for the construction and operation of railroads; and in
pursuance of these powers (and sometimes without
them) the Legislatures of the several states have provided by statute for the settlement of many questions
which arise between the railroad companies and the
public; and such is the law in this state.

Section 243 of our Constitution of 1901 provides,
among other things, that the power and authority of
regulating railroad freight and passenger tariffs, the
locating and building of passenger and freight depots,
the correcting of abuses, preventing of unjust discriminations, etc., are conferred upon the Legislature, whose
duty it shall be to pass laws from time to time for such
regulation. The Constitution makers could, of course,
have committed this subject to the courts, but they have
seen fit to commit it to the Legislature. The Legislature, for the evident purpose of carrying out these constitutional provisions, has passed a great number of
statutes upon this subject, which· have been repeatedly
changed, at nearly every session, and sometimes completely twice revised at one session of the Legislature.
But in the main, as to the power and authority of regulating railroad passenger and freight tariffs, of locating depots, of correcting abuses, of preventing unjust
discriminations and extortions, and of requiring reasonable rates, etc., the Legislature has conferred these

powers and duties upon a railroad commission created
by act of the Legislature, and provided for their enforcement.   A part of these statutes are now embraced
in various sections of the Code.   Those provisions pertinent for reference here are as follows: Section 5651 of
the Code of 1907 provides that the Railroad Commission
is charged with the duty of supervising, regulating, and
controlling all transportation companies doing business
in this state in all matters relating to the performance
of public duties, and of correcting abuses by such companies, and requiring them to establish and maintain
all such public service conveniences as may be reasonable and just.   Section 5652 of the Code, almost copying the constitutional provision above referred to, provides that common carriers shall be subject at all times
to the control of the Legislature, which may regulate
freight and passenger tariffs, the locating of depots,
etc., correct abuses, prevent unjust discriminations, and
establish and regulate reasonable and just rates of passenger and freight tariff.   Section 5667 of the Code
provides for a complaint which any person or association may make against a transportation company as to
any service in connection therewith in any respect unreasonable, unjustly discriminatory, or inadequate, such
complaint to be made to the commission, which may notify the transportation company of the same; and 10
days after such notice the commission may proceed to
investigate the complaint; the conduct of such investigation being provided for in other sections of the Code.

We are of the opinion that it is the declared policy of
this state to commit the regulation of matters such as
are complained of in this bill to the Legislature, and
that the Legislature, in turn, has committed it to the
Railroad Commission, which has power to act in the
premises, and is the proper and appropriate tribunal in

which to right such wrongs, and that for a chancery
court to attempt to determine which of two sites in a
certain town a railroad depot should be located on or
maintained upon would be usurping the functions and
powers which the Legislature and Constitution have
·seen fit to repose in another tribunal, which is given
legislative, judicial, and administrative functions necessary to perform the duties enjoined upon it by law. In
the case of *Nashville, Chattanooga and St. Louis Railway v. State*, 137 Ala. 439, 34 South. 401, this court,
speaking through Dowdell, J., its present Chief Justice,
said: "The demurrer to the bill raised the question as
to the jurisdiction and power of the court to entertain
the bill and grant the relief sought. There is no pretense of authority for the filing of the bill under any
provision of the charter of the defendant company. We
must therefore look to the statutes alone or authority
of the Railroad Commission to make the order, and for
the jurisdiction of the court to entertain a bill for its
enforcement. It seems that there is no common-law
principle upon which such jurisdiction can be vested.
While a corporation which is quasi public in its character and owes duties to the citizens which the court
can and will in appropriate remedies compel it to respect, yet the location of stations and the building of
depots is not within such duties when not imposed by
the Legislature." The bill in that case was filed to compel the railroad company to obey an order of the Railroad Commission, requiring it to locate a station and
erect a depot, suitable for the accommodation of passengers and the handling of freight, in the town of Guntersville, the county seat of Marshall. It was shown in
this case that the depot had been located just outside of
Guntersville, in the town of Wyeth, and that the depot
was maintained for the two towns jointly. What was

[Horton, et al. v. Southern Railway Co.]

said in that case is in part applicable to the facts made
by the bill in this case. This court further held in that
case that the statutes of this state at that time conferred nothing more than advisory functions upon the Railroad Commission, with no power to compel performance; it being authorized only to notify the railroad
company what the commission deemed to be necessary
changes, and to report such action to the Governor, that
such authority to advise the company and report to the
Governor fell far short of power to order and compel
the performance of their advice. But since the rendition of this decision these statutes have been several
times revised and amended by the Legislature, and much
more extended powers are now conferred, and more important duties enjoined, upon the Railroad Commission. It now has authority to act and require where before it had authority only to suggest and advise, and report its action to the Governor. It now has power to
hear and determine the question of locating and maintaining depots and stations; and the Legislature has
gone very far toward conferring upon it the powers and
duties reposed in the Legislature by the Constitution.
These additional powers and duties were no doubt suggested to the Legislature by the decision of this court in
the case above referred to, and, whatever defects the
statutes may yet have, they have not those above mentioned. It was also declared by this court in the case
of *Page v. L. & N. R. R. Co.,* 129 Ala. 237, 29 South.
676, (which was quoted with approval in the case of *N.
C. & St. L. Ry. v. State, supra*) that there was no common-law duty resting upon a railroad company to establish and maintain comfortable waiting rooms at its
stations. While this is not the exact question now under consideration, it is one closely akin. It was further
held in Page's Case that no such duty exists unless im-

posed by the charter of the railroad company, or by
statute or some other legislative authority.

It has been repeatedly decided by this court that, to
entitle a complainant to an injunction against the construction or operation of certain buildings or agencies,
it was incumbent upon the complainant to show by averment that such construction or operation would be a
nuisance in fact, and that the complainant would suffer some special injury, different in kind and degree
from that sustained by the general public. This is particularly true where the duty is one that is assumed toward the public generally, or toward a considerable portion thereof in the aggregate.—*Baker v. Selma Railway
Co.,* 130 Ala. 474, 30 South. 464; *First Nat. Bank v. Tyson,* 133 Ala. 459, 32 South. 144, 59 L. R. A. 399, 91 Am.
St. Rep. 46.

While the complainants in this case do not seek to
enjoin the construction or erection of any structure or
business which constitutes a nuisance, yet they do seek
to restrain the defendant from removing its depot, and
allege that the company owes a duty to the public as
well as to the plaintiffs to continue to maintain the depot at its present site. But we can see no reason why
the rule should be different as to the rights of a party to
maintain the injunction in either case. The mere fact
that it is a nuisance in the one case and not in the other
is not the test, but it is rather whether the duty owed
by the respondent is to the public, and is one, the performance or discharge of which the public could and
should require of the respondent.

It was shown upon the hearing of the application for
temporary injunction, by the affidavits and exhibits introduced in evidence on the part of the complainants
that irreparable injury would ensue if the preliminary
injunction did not issue; and we confess that the bill

and these affidavits make a very strong case that injury
will result to the complainants and other residents of
the town of Tuscumbia, which cannot be easily repaired, if the railroad company does not continue to maintain its depot at its present location, and this showing
would be a very strong appeal to a court of equity if
such court had jurisdiction to confer the relief requested. But, on the other hand, the railroad company insists, and has introduced affidavits and exhibits to show,
that it will continue to maintain reasonable railroad facilities for the accommodation of the people of Tuscumbia and the public generally, and that a change of sites
will be beneficial and not detrimental to the interests
of the people of the town as alleged in the bill. It further appears from this record that all these matters have
been twice heard by the Railroad Commission, and that
it has declined to interfere with the railroad company in
consummating the proposed change in the location of
its depot in Tuscumbia.

Therefore, notwithstanding the strong showing made
by the bill, it is evident that the complainants' rights
have not been established at law, nor are their rights
clear and indisputable in such sense that a court of
equity would grant relief by injunction. Under all the
authorities above referred to, we are constrained to hold
in this case that the decree of the chancellor dismissing
the bill and denying the temporary injunction sought
was proper. To hold otherwise and grant the relief
prayed would be to hold that the chancery courts of this
state may locate the stations and depots of the railroads
at such points as the court shall determine best, or, at
least, to hold that the railroad companies cannot discontinue stations at points once established, when it is
decided by such court that it would be better for the
public or some individual that the station be not removed.

[Guesnard, et al. v. Guesnard.]

It is unnecessary for us to decide in this case whether injunction or mandamus would be the proper remedy, and we merely refer to the case of *Jacquelin et al. v. Erie Co., supra,* which fully discusses the question.

It follows that the decree of the chancellor should be affirmed.

Affirmed.

DOWDELL, C. J., and SIMPSON and McCLELLAN, JJ., concur.

Guesnard, *et al. v.* Guesnard.

Bill for Partition and to Construe Will.

(Decided May 11, 1911. 55 South. 524.)

1. *Wills; Construction; Per Capita or Per Stirpes; "Between;" "Heirs."*—The will considered and held that the word "heirs" as used in the will meant children, and that the devisees under such clause took per capita and not per stirpes; the word "between" not being used in its technical sense as a reference to two only, but as applying to a division among many.

2. *Perpetuities; Will; Heirs.*—A will devising the income from certain real estate to testators' daughter during her life, and on her death one-half of the income to go to her issue, if any, and the balance to testator's surviving heirs, was not objectionable as creating a perpetuity; the word "heirs" being used in the sense of children, and the devise of the income, not being limited, carrying the property itself.

APPEAL from Mobile Law and Equity Court.

Heard before Hon. SAFFOLD BERNEY.

Bill by Theodore L. Guesnard against Theodore H. Guesnard and another for sale of land for division, and incidentally to construe a will. From a decree overruling demurrer to the bill, respondents appeal. Affirmed.

The bill alleges that orators own a fee-simple undivided interest in certain property therein; that he and

Alcide F. Guesnard are the grandchildren of Theodore Guesnard, deceased, being the only children and heirs at law of Alcide Peter Guesnard, who died intestate prior to the death of Lea Marie Guesnard; and that the said Theodore S. Guesnard was the son of the said Theodore Guesnard, deceased. The bill further alleges that Lea M. Guesnard, in whom a life estate vested by the will, has recently died, unmarried and without issue; that William Charles Guesnard and Marie Victoria Craft, named in the will as the children of said Theodore Guesnard, have all died without issue; and that the three named in this will are the only surviving heirs. It is then averred that the provision of the said will that the said real estate should never be sold is an attempt to create a perpetuity, and is therefore ineffective and void. It is then alleged that the land cannot be equitably divided. The following are the sections of the will directed to be set out:

"(2) I devise, give and bequeath to my daughter, Lea Maria the income that may be derived from that two-story brick building on the south side of Dauphin street, second east of Conception, known as 103 Dauphin street, during the term of her natural life, free from the control, liability or incumbrance of any husband she may have hereafter. At her death, should she leave any issue, said issue to receive one-half of the said income, the other half to be equally divided between my other heirs as hereinafter mentioned. But should there be no issue left by my said daughter, then the property to revert back to my estate, and said income to be divided equally between my surviving heirs and the children of such of my heirs who may have died leaving issue. It is further my will and desire that said property No. 103 Dauphin street, should not be sold, but be kept as a source of income to my heirs.

"(3) The balance of my real estate of which I shall die seised and possessed, or to which I shall be entitled at my decease, I devise and bequeath by equal division among my sons, William Charles, Theodore H., Alcide Peter, and my daughter, Marie Victoria Craft."

"(6) I give, devise and bequeath all the balance of my personal property to my five children mentioned above, to be divided between them as they may determine between themselves. Provided, however, that the provisions of article 7 shall not be included in this provision."

INGE & MCCORVEY, for appellant. The only question involved is as to whether or not the real estate described in the first paragraph of the bill shall be distributed or divided under the second item of the will per capita or per stirpes. The first thing to ascertain in construing a will is to arrive at the intention of the testator.—*Thrasher v. Ingram*, 32 Ala. 645; *Alford v. Alford*, 56 Ala. 350. Under the will, the property reverted back to the estate, the daughter having died without issue.—*Ballentine v. Foster*, 128 Ala. 638; *Sharpe v. Sharpe*, 35 Ala. 574; *Bethea v. Bethea*, 116 Ala. 265; *Billingsley v. Abercrombie*, 2 S. & P. 24; *Thomas v. Miller*, 161 Ill. 60; *Slingluff v. Johns*, 39 Atl. 872; *Kelly v. Vigas*, 112 Ill. 242; *Raymond v. Hillhouse*, 29 Am. Rep. 688; 33 Conn. 222; 15 N. E. 457; 11 B. Monroe, 32; 59 L. R. A. 125; 79 N. E. 260; 64 Atl. 460.

SHELTON SIMS, for appellee. The word "heirs" as used in the will means children.—*English v. McCreary*, 157 Ala. 487; *Van Zant v. Morris*, 25 Ala. 291. The gift of the income was tantamount to a devise of the land itself.—*Stein v. Gordon*, 92 Ala. 535; *Earl v. Grimm*, 1 Johns Ch. 494. The will must be construed as not attempting to create a perpetuity.—*Robertson v. Hayes,* 83 Ala. 298; *Trammell v. Chambers County,* 93 Ala. 390. The parties to this suit take per capita and not per stirpes.—*Wilds' Case,* 6 Code, 16a; *Nimmo v. Stewart,* 21 Ala. 691; *Smith v. Ashurst,* 34 Ala. 208; *Williams v. McConnico,* 36 Ala. 28; *Varner v. Young,* 56 Ala. 285; s. c. 56 Ala. 283; *Moore v. Lee,* 105 Ala. 436; *Furlow v. Merrill,* 23 Ala. 705; *Cox v. McKinney,* 32 Ala. 461. The will creates a contingent remainder converted by statute into an executory devise after the life estate of Leah Guesnard had determined to be divided equally between the surviving children.—*Terrill v. Reeves,* 103 Ala. 264; *Phinizy v. Foster,* 90 Ala. 262; *Ballentine v. Foster,* 128 Ala. 638.

SIMPSON, J.—The bill in this case was filed by the appellee for a sale of property for partition, alleging that the complainant is entitled to a one-third interest in the property. A demurrer was interposed on the ground that the will of Theodore Guesnard, the grandfather of the complainant, shows that the complainant is entitled to only one-fourth of the property. The reporter will copy sections 2, 3, and 6 of the will in the statement of the case.

The complainant and Alcide S. Guesnard are grandchildren of Theodore Guesnard, being the children of Alcide Peter Guesnard, deceased. Lea Marie Guesnard died without issue, and the other children of Theodore Guesnard died before her decease; none leaving issue, except said Alcide Peter, as above shown. The appeal is from the decree overruling the demurrer to the bill, and the question at issue depends upon the construction of the second section of the will, to wit, whether the devisees take per stirpes or per capita.

This is a question which has been much discussed by
the courts of various jurisdictions. The decisions of
the courts of other states are not harmonious, and the
question is not free from difficulty. In arriving at the
intention of the testator, we must be governed by the
provisions of the will itself, and not by what would be
a reasonable and proper disposition of the property, according to our own notions. It may be that, generally
speaking, grandfathers, taking their ideas from our
statutes of descent and distribution, may not intend to
place the children of deceased children on an equality
with their children; but it cannot be affirmed as a universal proposition. Mr. Jarman states that: "Where
a gift is to the children of several persons, whether it be
to the children of A. and B., or to the children of A. and
the children of B., they take per capita and not per
stirpes. The same rule applies where a devise or be-
quest is made to a person and the children of another
person, or to a person as standing in a certain relation,
as to 'My son A. and the children of my son B.,' in which
case A. takes only a share equal to that of the children
of B., though it may be conjectured that the testator
had a distribution according to the statute in his view."
—2 Jarman on Wills (6th Ed.) p. 265 (1050).

It cannot be doubted that the plain wording of the
section calls for this construction, if there were no relationship between the parties, and no field for the operation of our own views as to what would be a proper disposition of the property. From a careful examination
of the numerous authorities which have been called to
our attention by the diligence of counsel on both sides
of this controversy, and others which have been referred
to, we think that the weight of reason and authority sustains Mr. Jarman's views. From the multitude of authorities we cite a number which explain and illustrate

this principle, and others to the contrary may be found, among the cases cited by counsel for the appellant.— *Collins v. Feather,* 52 W. Va. 107, 43 S. E. 323, 61 L. R. A. 600, 94 Am. St. Rep. 912; *Hill v. Bowers, et al.,* 120 Mass. 135; *Wills v. Folz,* (W. Va.) 12 L. R. A. (N. S.) 283, and notes; *Farmer v. Kimball,* 46 N. H. 435, 88 Am. Dec. 219; *Crow v. Crow,* 1 Leigh (Va.) 72; *Howton v. Griffith,* 18 Grat. (Va.) 574; *Senger v. Senger,* 81 Va. 687.

We refer to the decisions of other states because they are entitled to great respect and carry weight with them, though they are not, strictly speaking, authority to be followed, unless in our opinion they are supported by the reason and analogies of the law. When our own court has made a deliverance on a subject, it is our duty to follow it, unless it is so plainly erroneous as to call for a decision overruling it. We think our case of *Smith v. Ashurst and Wife,* 34 Ala. 208, is conclusive of this case. In that case this court distinctly adopts the language above quoted from Jarman on Wills, and states that it is well sustained by authorities, and refers to the case of *Duffee v. Buchanan,* 8 Ala. 27, 30, in which the court holds that the word "equally" plainly shows the intention for a per capita distribution. .

Counsel for appellant seek to differentiate the Smith-Ashurst Case from the one now under consideration, stating that in that case "there is no devise to the burden, but a devise directly to the children of the brother." In the present case the devise is equally direct. It is not to his children, and, in case any of them shall die, then to their children; but the will seems to take it for granted that some of them will die and the devise is directly "to be divided between my surviving heirs (which clearly means children in this will) and the children of such of my heirs, who may have died, leaving issue."

So far from there being anything in the will itself to indicate any intention other than that suggested by the plain wording of this section, it is noticeable that this is the only section which mentions the children of a deceased child. Section 3 leaves the balance of his real estate to his children by name, and makes no mention of the children of those who may die, thus evidently leaving it to the law to provide for that contingency; and section 6 makes the same disposition of his personal property. The testator, or the scrivener, evidently understood that, if the second section had stopped with the provision that at the death of the life tenant without issue the property should revert back to his estate, it would have been distributed in the same manner as the property provided for by said residuary clauses; but, to avoid that conclusion it is specifically stated that it is to be divided equally between the parties named. The words *pro rata* in the *Smith-Ashurst Case* do not add anything to the word *equally*.

There is no significance in the use of the word "between," as indicating a reference to only *two*. Whatever may be the strict philological propriety of the use of the word, it is frequently used as applicable to more than two. The original Articles of Confederation were declared to be a league "between" the states, and the last section of the Constitution of the United States declares that "the ratification of the conventions of nine states shall be sufficient for the establishment of this Constitution 'between' the states so ratifying the same." The testator also himself provides for the division of his property, real and personal, "between" his five children.

There is nothing in our subsequent decisions tending to qualify the principles laid down in the *Smith-Ashurst Case*. In the case of *Sharp's Administrator v. Sharp,*

35 Ala. 574, the only question decided was that the administrator of a child who died before the widow was not entitled to any portion of the assets. The court makes no remarks on the difference in meaning between the use of the words "or" and "and," saying that the court will not substitute one for the other, except "in cases where it is clearly authorized by the intention and meaning of the testator, as collected from the whole will," and goes on to quote with approval the principle announced in the *Smith-Ashurst Case,* 34 Ala. 579. The case of *Bethea et al. v. Bethea et al.,* 116 Ala. 256, 22 South. 561, distinctly recognizes the correctness of the principle laid down by Jarman, and by the *Smith-Ashurst Case,* but simply recognizes also the further principle, stated in both, that the court may give the other construction "on faint evidence," and holds that in that case "the word *each,* as here employed, is clearly distributive of the grandchildren of the testator referred to into classes or stirpes."

In the case of *Ballentine et al. v. Foster et al.,* 128 Ala. 638, 644, 30 South. 481, 483, the property was devised "to be divided equally among the children of P. J. W. and my daughter, E." (P. J. W. being a son of the testator) ; and it was held that the devise was to the children of the son and of the daughter, and this court says: "The language employed, 'to be equally divided among,' * * * is opposed to the idea of an intention on the part of the testator to divide the estate into moieties, one to the children of P. J. W and the other moiety to his daughter, E.; for this construction would necessarily involve the idea of a still further division of one of the moieties among the children of P. J. W. Nor, on the other hand, is it reasonable to conclude that it was the intention of the testator to place his daughter, E., upon an equal footing with the children of P. J., who

were his grandchildren, in a division of the estate; that
is to say, to give her a portion equal to a grandchild's
portion. By the use of the words 'equally among,' according to the definitions given to them by standard
lexicographers, * * * it is wholly improbable that
the testator could have intended other than a per capita
distribution among the several grandchildren."

While that case is not, in all points, analogous to
the one now under consideration, yet it is a clear expo-
sition of the words "equally divided," and while it led
the court in that case to construe the intention to be to
devise the property to the children of E., and not to herself, yet if there had been no room for construing it to
be a devise to her children in place of herself, the definition of the words, as given, would necessarily have indicated a per capita distribution.

We do not construe the will as attempting to create
a perpetuity, because, as before indicated, the testator,
in using the word "heirs," intended *children;* and, reading the words "children" in the place of "heirs" in the
concluding clause of item 2 of the will, it does not create a perpetuity. The devise of the income of the property, without limit, carried with it the property itself.—
Stein v. Gordon, 92 Ala. 532, 535, 9 South. 741, and case
cited; 1 Jarman on Wills (6th Ed.) p. 758 (741).

The decree of the court is affirmed.

Affirmed.

DOWDELL, C. J., and MCCLELLAN and MAYFIELD, JJ.,
concur.

[Maben v. Gulf Coal & Coke Co., et al.]

Maben *v.* Gulf Coal & Coke Co., *et al.*

Bill by Stockholder to Declare Conveyance Null and Void.

(Decided May 9, 1911. 55 South. 607.)

1. *Corporations; Sale of Assets; Power; Rights of Stockholders.*—In the absence of fraud, breach of duty or bad faith, minority stockholders were not entitled to avoid or invalidate a sale made by the majority stockholders of all the lands and minerals which constituted all the property of the corporation, on the ground that the corporation was thereby denuded, where it appeared that the corporation was authorized to rent or purchase mineral lands and to sell and lease the same.

2. *Same; Sale of Property; Effect; Franchise.*—A sale of all of a corporation's property does not necessarily terminate the corporation nor operate as a transfer of such corporate powers or franchises as it had.

APPEAL from Walker Chancery Court.

Heard before Hon. A. H. BENNERS.

Bill by J. C. Maben against the Gulf Coal & Coke Company and others, to annul and set aside a conveyance of the corporation's property in mineral lands. From a decree dismissing the bill on demurrer, the complainant appeals. Affirmed.

TILLMAN, BRADLEY & MORROW, and L. C. LEADBEATTER, for appellant. A corporation cannot divest itself of all its property in such a manner as to deprive it of the power to continue to exercise the corporate functions against the dissent of a single stockholder.—*Tillis v. Brown,* 45 So. 589; *Keen v. Johnson,* 9 N. J. E. 401; *Gabriskie v. Hackensack,* 18 N. J. E. 178. The principle is analogous to that of the consolidation of the corporation against the dissent of the stockholder.—*McMahon v. Morris,* 79 Am. Dec. 424; *Botts v. Simpsonville Co.,* 10 S. W. 134; *Rabe v. Dunlap,* 25 Atl. 959.

It follows that the court erred in overruling the demurrers to the bill.

BROOKS & STOUTZ, for appellee Gulf Coal & Coke Company, BANKHEAD & BANKHEAD, for appellee Hanson and Empire Land Company. In the absence of fraud, bad faith, or breach of duty on the part of the majority of stockholders, the bill is without equity.—10 Cyc. 969; *Smith v. Prattville Mfg. Co.*, 29 Ala. 503; *Tuscaloosa Mfg. Co. v. Cox*, 68 Ala. 71; 53 Am. Dec. 624; 9 L. R. A. 530. The corporation had the power to acquire by purchase and lease, and to sell or rent the property acquired, and being a private corporation, could make the contract even to the extent of selling all its property.— *Woolf v. Underwood*, 91 Ala. 523; 10 Cyc. 1265 and 1302; 85 Am. Dec. 516; 99 Id. 300; 66 Id. 490; Thompson on Corporations, sec. 5441; 114 Mass. 37; 45 L. R. A. 560.

MAYFIELD, J.—This bill was filed by appellant against appellees, seeking to have a certain conveyance, executed by the Gulf Coal & Coke Company to the respondant, Hanson, as trustee for the Empire Land Company, conveying all the lands and minerals belonging to the said Gulf Coke & Coal Company, decreed to be null and void and of no effect, and to have the legal title to the lands and minerals conveyed thereby declared to be in the said Gulf Coke & Coal Company, and to have the said company return to the said Hanson all the consideration received by it from the attempted sale. The complainant filed the bill as a stockholder of the Gulf Coke & Coal Company.

The equity of the bill is sought to be supported upon the contention that the lands conveyed constituted the entire holdings of the corporation (Gulf Coke & Coal Company) of which the complainant was a stockholder, and that the corporation was thereby denuded of all its property and deprived of all means of carrying out the purposes for which it was organized; that the sale was not for the purpose of reinvesting the funds, but to terminate the existence of the corporation in that way, which was claimed to be in contravention of the laws made and provided in such cases.

The bill alleges that all of the members of the board of directors, except one, voted in favor of the sale and conveyance of the lands to Hanson as trustee, and that it would therefore be useless to appeal to the board of directors of the corporation for the redress sought by the bill. The bill avers that on July 5, 1906, the board of directors of the Gulf Coke & Coal Company passed resolutions authorizing and providing for a sale of all the lands and mineral holdings of the said company to Hanson, in consummation of the contract theretofore made to that end. All of the stockholders, except the complainant and L. B. and J. C. Musgrove, voted their stock in favor of the sale; 6, 876 shares being voted in favor of the sale, and 2,203 shares against it, and complainant owning 138 shares of those voted against the sale. The complainant, at the meeting of the stockholders, protested against the sale.

Among the powers and purposes of the corporation was that to rent or purchase known mineral lands and to sell or lease them. The corporation was organized under the general statutes providing for the organization of mining and manufacturing corporations, on December 22, 1887. It was given many powers besides those above mentioned.

The respondent, the Gulf Coke & Coal Company, demurrer to the bill, assigned grounds too numerous to be mentioned; but among them was the general demurrer that there was no equity in the bill. The cause was heard on this demurrer, which was sustained by the chancellor, and from his decree thereon this appeal is prosecuted.

The proposition of law insisted upon by the appellant, and the theory upon which the bill was filed, is that a solvent corporation which is a going concern cannot, against the objection of a single stockholder, sell its entire property and thereby denude itself of the means and powers necessary to carry on the purposes for which it was organized.

We think the law upon this subject applicable to a corporation like the one in question, and to transactions or sales like the one involved in this suit, has not been better stated by any of the authorities than by that great justice, Bigelow, of the Supreme Court of Massachusetts, in the case of *Treadwell v. Salisbury Manufacturing Company*, 7 Gray, 393, s. c. 66 Am. Dec. 499. This case has been followed, if not quoted literally, by many text-writers on the subject. It is sustained by both the great weight of authority and the majority of the adjudicated cases. The law is so well stated in that decision, and is so in accord with our views on the subject in this case, that we shall quote it at length:

"We entertain no doubt of the right of a corporation, established solely for trading and manufacturing purposes, by a vote of the majority of their stockholders, to wind up their affairs and close their business, if in the exercise of a sound discretion they deem it expedient so to do. At common law the right of corporations, acting by a majority of their stockholders, to sell their property is absolute, and is not limited as to objects, circumstances or quantity.—Angell & Ames on Corp. § 127 et seq.; 2 Kent's Com. (6th Ed.) 280; *Mayor, etc., of Colchester v. Lowton*, 1 Ves. & B. 226, 244; *Binney's Case*, 2 Bland (Md.) 142. To this general rule there

are many exceptions, arising from the nature of particular corporations, the purposes for which they were created and the duties and liabilities imposed on them by
their charters. Corporations established for objects
quasi public, such as railway, canal, and turnpike corporations, to which the right of eminent domain and
other large privileges are granted in order to enable
them to accommodate the public, may fall within the
exception; but also charitable and religious bodies, in
the administration of whose affairs the community, or
some portion of it, has an interest to see that their corporate duties are properly discharged. Such corporations may, perhaps, be restrained from alienating their
property, and compelled to appropriate it to specific
uses, by mandamus, or other process. But it is not so
with corporations of a private character, established
solely for trading and manufacturing purposes. Neither the public nor the Legislature have any direct interest in their business or its management. These are committed solely to the stockholders, who have a pecuniary
stake in the proper conduct of their affairs. By accepting a charter, they do not undertake to carry on the
business for which they are incorporated indefinitely,
and without any regard to the condition of their corporate property."

There are many recent cases to the same effect, to
wit: "A corporation, while solvent and a going concern, holds property like an individual, free from lien
or trust in behalf of its general creditors, and may dispose of the same as it deems best, subject to the provisions of its charter and those other restraints upon the
conveyance of property which the law imposes alike on
corporations and individuals."—*New Hampshire Sav-
ings Bank v. Richey*, 121 Fed. 956, 58 C. C. A. 294. "A
corporation organized under the laws of West Virginia

has power, under the Code of West Virginia 1899, c. 53, §56, to sell and transfer all of its property and discontinue its business by the action of the holders of a majority of the stock, taken at a general stockholders' meeting."—*Metcalf v. American School Furniture Co.,* (C. C.) 122 Fed. 115. "A private corporation, unless restrained by statute, may legitimately deal with its property as an individual deals with his."—*Levering v. Bimel,* 146 Ind. 545, 45 N. T. 775. "Where the majority members of a corporation have sold its entire property, the sale will not be set aside at the instance of a minority stockholder on the sole ground that the corporation was doing a fairly good business, and that some of the stockholders did not consent to the sale."—*Tanner v. Lindell Ry.* Co., 180 Mo. 1, 79 S. W. 155, 103 Am. St. Rep. 534.

We think that the cases cited and relied upon by the appellant are not applicable to the case under consideration. The New Jersey case of *Kean v. Johnson,* 9 N. J. Eq. 402, is distinguishable from this case upon two grounds pointed out by Justice Bigelow in the Massachusetts case quoted from above. The New Jersey case involves a sale by a public service corporation of all its property and franchise rights, and also involved the construction of a New Jersey statute, which the court in that case held to expressly prohibit such sale without the consent of all the stockholders. This case is also distinguishable from the line of cases shown by the note in 79 Am. Dec. 424, relied upon by appellant. Those cases involved the rights and powers of two or more corporations to consolidate, without the assent of all the stockholders. This it was held, could not be done in the absence of a statute providing for such consolidation; and it was also held that stockholders could not be compelled, in this manner, to invest their capital in other corporations against their protest, and thus be required by other stockholders to embark in new and different enterprises from those undertaken by the original corporation in which they had invested their money. The line of cases referred to hold that such consolidation might be authorized by the Legislature, provided compensation be made to the dissenting stockholders.

So far as appears from the record in this case, the Gulf Coke & Coal Company had never engaged in the business of mining or manufacturing, though authorized so to do under its charter. The only business shown to have been carried on by it during its lifetime of more than 20 years was the buying and selling of real estate. This being true, we can see no reason why it could not make the sale of its lands in question. It must be remembered that there was no attempt to allege fraud, duress, or overreaching on the part of the majority stockholders, directors, or other officers of the corporation. The equity of the bill seems to rest solely upon the lack of authority of the majority of the stockholders and directors to make a sale of the company's lands.

Under the facts as shown by this bill, and in the absence of allegation of violation of the charter powers of the corporation, or of fraud, neglect, breach of duty, or of bad faith, we find no ground upon which to rest the equity of this bill. A court of chancery should not usurp the direction of a private corporation at the instance of a man whose only complaint is one against the acts of the managers and of the majority of the stockholders, done in good faith, and which are authorized by its charter powers.—*Smith v. Prattville Co.*, 29 Ala. 503; *Tuscaloosa Mfg. Co. v. Cox*, 68 Ala. 71.

The sale of the lands in question would not have the effect of terminating or annihilating the corporation. A corporation may continue to exist after all its property is gone.　It was not a transfer of its corporate powers or of its franchise rights, if such it had.　The particular property sold, though it was all the land owned by the corporation under its charter powers as shown by the bill, was not at all essential to the existence of the corporation.—*Miners' Ditch Co. v. Zellerbach*, 37 Cal. 543, 99 Am. Dec. 300.　Mr. Thompson, in his work on corporations, vol. 3 (2d Ed.) § 2415, says: "A private corporation has power to sell and dispose of all its property, except its franchise of existence, without express authority from the Legislature."　In section 2417 of the same book, he says: "A rule of general application is that a corporation of a purely private character, and one which owes no special duty to the public, when the exigencies of its business require it, or when the circumstances are such that it can no longer continue the business with profit, may sell and dispose of all of its property, pay its debts, divide the remaining assets, and wind up the affairs of the corporation."

For these reasons, and others which might be assigned, we are of the opinion that the decree of the chancellor is correct and should be affirmed.

Affirmed.

SIMPSON, MCCLELLAN and SOMERVILLE, JJ., concur.

[Dawson, et al. v. Copeland, et al.]

Dawson, *et al.* v. Copeland, *et al.*

Bill to Remove Estate from Probate to Chancery Court, for an Accounting, and to Sell Lands for Partition.

(Decided May 11,. 1911. Rehearing denied June 8, 1911.
55 South. 600.)

1. *Attorney and Client; Fiduciary Relations; Effect.*—While transactions between an attorney and client should be strictly scrutinized, and the attorney should give to the client the benefit of all the information he has regarding the value of property purchased by him from the client, yet such purchases are voidable only upon timely application.

2. *Cancellation of Instruments; Conveyance to Attorney; Laches.* —A client is not entitled to cancellation of a conveyance to his attorney where the client did not act promptly but awaited the termination of the litigation affecting the property, even if such conveyance was obtained without a disclosure by the attorney of his information.

APPEAL from Jefferson Chancery Court.

Heard before Hon. A. H. BENNERS.

Bill by F. P. Dawson and others, against W. B. Copeland and others, to remove the administration of an estate from the probate to the chancery court, for an accounting, and to sell lands in a foreign jurisdiction for partition. From a decree denying relief, complainants appeal. Affirmed.

C. B. POWELL, for appellant. The burden was upon the trustee to show that the transaction was fair and just, and the consideration adequate.—*James v. James,* 55 Ala. 525; *Holt v. Agnew,* 67 Ala. 360; *Walker v. Nicrosi,* 135 Ala. 353. To be available laches must be pleaded.—*Solomon v. Solomon,* 81 Ala. 505. No estoppel was pleaded, and nothing from which an estoppel would arise is alleged.—*Hall & Farley v. Henderson,*

126 Ala. 490; *Jones v. Peebles*, 130 Ala. 273; *Scruggs v. Decatur Co.*, 86 Ala. 173. There was no laches shown. —*Scruggs v. Decatur Co., supra; James v. James, supra; Montgomery v. Lahey*, 121 Ala. 136; *Walker v. Nelson*, 18 So. 154.

L. J. HALEY, and BOWMAN, HARSH & BEDDOW, for appellee. Counsel discuss the errors assigned, but without citation of authority.

SIMPSON, J.—The bill in this case was filed by the appellants, seeking the removal of the estate of Harriet B. Parker, deceased, from the probate into chancery court, seeking an accounting by the representatives of R. H. Kerr, the original executor of said estate, and an order to the trustee to sell certain lands in Texas, to distribute, etc.

The bill alleges that said R. H. Kerr, a short time before his death, purchased a one-third interest in the lands in Texas from E. P. Dawson, one of the complainants and one of the beneficiaries under the will, for an inadequate consideration, that the conveyance by said Dawson is void by reason of the trust relation, and prays that said sale and conveyance be declared null and void.

The chancery court took jurisdiction, the settlement was made, and a reference made to the register, directing him to take testimony and report (1) whether said deed from Dawson to Kerr is valid, and (2) whether said Dawson is entitled to a one-third interest in the proceeds of the lands of said estate. The register reported, among other matters, that the deed from Dawson to Kerr is invalid, and that Dawson is entitled to a one-third interest in the proceeds from the sale of said lands, upon refunding $134 paid to Dawson by Kerr, subject to certain charges. Exceptions were filed to this item of the report of the register, which exceptions were sustained by the chancellor, and the report otherwise confirmed. The only controversy raised by this appeal is as to the correctness of the decree of the chancellor in sustaining the said exceptions.

The evidence shows that said Kerr has been, as executor and attorney, corresponding with attorneys in Texas in regard to said lands, also with real estate men; that there were various reports as to the value of the lands, ranging from $1.50 to $2 and $3 per acre; that a suit had been instituted in Texas, by other parties claiming said lands, which suit was undetermined at the time of the making of said deed by Dawson May 13, 1904; that in February, 1901, one of the parties in interest had received a letter from a man in Texas, stating that the land was worth more than $3 per acre (the value at which the purchase from Dawson had been made), although he did not know any one who would buy it, though other lands near it had been sold at from $10 to $25 per acre. This letter, according to the testimony of Dawson's sister, who received it, was shown to Kerr shortly after received, but was not shown to Dawson until just after he had sold to Kerr.

Dawson testifies (subject to the objection of incompetency, as being a transaction with a deceased party whose estate is interested) that he had, on the same day as that on which the deed was made, returned to th office of Kerr, and offered to return the money; that his wife had refused to sign the deed, and that Kerr said it was not material for her to sign it; that his knowledge of his rights in the estate was that he "thought the thing was gone; Mr. Kerr had it for eight years, and he thought his charges would take it up," and that Mr. Kerr did not say anything to him about the value of the land at the time the deed was delivered;

that he is a white man; was born in 1854; is of reasonable intelligence and moderate education, and engaged in business.

Dawson's wife also testified that she went to Kerr's office with her husband on the same day; told him that she would not sign the deed because she thought the land was worth more; that Dawson offered to pay the money back; that Kerr said he would return the deed, if they would secure him for the expenses necessary to recover the land. The deed in evidence shows no name of Mrs. Dawson in the body thereof, and no place left for her signature.

The witness Haley testifies that he heard the conversations between Kerr and Dawson which resulted in the sale of Dawson's interest in the land, one about a week before, and the other at the time the deed was signed; that Kerr explained to Dawson that some one would have to raise the money to pay the expenses of the litigation in Texas; that they figured out what they thought the land was worth, the amount of expenses, etc., and finally agreed on the amount; that Kerr stated to Dawson, on two occasions, that he did not want Dawson's interest in the land, and would much prefer that Dawson raise his share of the amount for expenses, and that if they succeeded in winning the suit he thought the land would become valuable at some time, and that Dawson stated that he preferred to sell out, at the amount stated in the deed, as he had recently purchased some property in Birmingham, or was about to purchase same, and needed the money for that purpose. Also that Kerr informed Dawson who the parties in Texas were with whom he had corresponded in regard to the land; that Kerr showed Dawson the correspondence, including a letter from one Hensley, offering $3 per acre for the land, being the same name

[Dawson, et al. v. Copeland, et al.]

as that signed to the letter of February 1, 1901, which was written to Dawson's sister, Mrs. Beasley, one of the parties to this suit. Also that the suit in Texas was not terminated until April, 1907.

It is true that the principles of our law require a strict scrutiny of transactions between attorney and client, and the attorney is required to give his client the benefit of all the information he possesses in regard to the value of property which he purchases from his client. In fact, to be above suspicion, and preserve the high ethical position of the attorney, in observing that uberrima fides which he should preserve, he should rarely, if ever, purchase from his client the property which is the subject of litigation, yet the transaction is not necessarily void, but voidable, on proper and timely application.

While the letter from Texas which was produced by Mrs. Beasley related to the supposed value of the property free of litigation, yet, if Kerr had that information at the time of the purchase from Dawson, and Dawson did not have it, Kerr should have told him of it. But the evidence shows that Dawson received the information shortly after the transaction, and in order to enforce his rights he should have made timely application to cancel the deed. It would be inequitable to allow him to speculate on the chances, by waiting until after the litigation had terminated, and then claim a cancellation of the deed.—*Sheffield Land, I. & C. Co. v. Neill,* 87 Ala. 158, 161, 162, 6 South. 1; *Goree v. Clements,* 94 Ala. 337, 343, 10 South. 906; *Connely v. Rue,* 148 Ill. 207, 35 N. E. 824, 828; 6 Cyc. 302.

The decree of the court is affirmed.

Affirmed.

DOWDELL, C. J., and McCLELLAN and MAYFIELD, JJ., concur.

Tallapoosa County Bank *v.* Wynn.

Bill for Injunction and Accounting.

(Decided June 15, 1911. 55 South. 1011.)

1. *Banks and Banking; Deposits; Right to Set-off.*—Unless the claim of the bank is certain, definite and liquidated, or capable of liquidation by calculation without the aid of the jury to determine the amount, such claim cannot be set off as against the depositor, and his deposit.

2. *Injunction; Proceedings at Law.*—A bank is not entitled to an injunction restraining the maintenance of a suit by the depositor's administrator against it to recover the deposit, where there was no claim that the depositor's estate was insolvent, or not amply able to answer any claim that might be established against it by the bank, nor that the bank had applied the amount of the deposit or any part of it to any debt or demand owing by the depositor or his estate to the bank.

3. *Same; Dissolution in Vacation.*—Where a final decree granting a perpetual injunction was reversed on appeal, and the cause remanded, the cause in the trial court stood in the same situation as though there had never been any final decree, and the respondent was entitled to move to vacate the injunction on ten days' notice in vacation under section 4526, Code 1907.

APPEAL from Tallapoosa Chancery Court.

Heard before Hon. W. W. WHITESIDE.

Bill by Tallapoosa County Bank against W. H. Wynn as administrator to enjoin a suit, and to set off certain claims against deposits. From a decree dissolving the injunction restraining the action, complainants appeal. Affirmed.

LACKEY & BRIDGES, and J. M. CHILTON, for appellant. It is improper where the cause was submitted for final hearing merely to dissolve the injunction without rendering a final decree.—*Trump v. McDonnell*, 112 Ala. 256; Sec. 4535, Code 1907. The bank had the right to set off the claim it held against the estate against the deposits claimed by the estate.—*Clear Creek L. Co. v.*

Nixon, 150 Ala. 602; *Lehman v. Tallassee F. M. Co.*,
164 Ala. 567; Moss on Banking, 91.

JAMES W. STROTHER, for appellee. The motion was
authorized by section 4526, Code 1907, as the cause
stood after remandment just as if there had been no
final decree. The court has decided that complainant
was not entitled to an injunction in this case.—*Wynn v.
Tallapoosa County Bank*, 53 So. 228; Counsel discuss
the cases cited by appellant, and concludes that they
are without application to the case at bar.

MAYFIELD, J.—This appeal is from a decree dissolving an injunction. The cause was submitted in the
lower court on respondent's motion to dissolve the injunction; the submission being had under a written notice, served on complainant's solicitor. The proceeding
in the lower court was had, in vacation, under section
4526 of the Code of 1907, which is as follows: "A defendant may in vacation, upon ten days' notice to the
complainant or his solicitor, move before the chancellor
of the division in which the bill is filed, to dissolve an
injunction for want of equity in the bill or on the coming in of an answer, or to discharge an injunction, to
be heard on the original papers or certified copies thereof; and motions to discharge and dissolve may be made
and heard at the same time, without prejudice to
either."

On the former appeal in this case (168 Ala. 469,
South. 228), which was from a final decree, the bill was
held to be without equity in so far as it sought to enjoin
an action at law, brought to recover the amount of the
intestate's deposit in the bank of the appellant, and also
without equity in so far as it sought to have the court
to declare and enforce a lien in favor of the bank

against the deposit. What was then said on this subject we think is strictly applicable to, and conclusive of,
the question involved on this appeal. It was then said:
"The bill, in so far as it attempts to have the court declare and enforce a lien against the deposit of the intestate in its bank, is without equity. The lien, claim or
right, whatever it may properly be called, which a bank
has upon a deposit in its vaults, as against the deposit-
or—its creditor to that amount—cannot be enforced by
a court of equity, though in a proper sense it might be
declared or recognized. The word 'lien' is inaptly applied to a general deposit in a bank; it is the property
of the bank itself. It can be properly applied to special
specific deposits of chattels, choses in action, valuables,
etc. As to a general deposit, the bank has a right to
set-off as for the balance of the general account of the
depositor, and of course so long as that balance is in
favor of the depositor the lien or right has neither existence nor validity; but the moment any advance or
loan by the bank is made to the depositor—in the form
of an overdraft, a discount, acceptance, etc.—then the
lien or right is born, and may be applied by the bank
(and the bank only) to the payment of such indebtedness till it is fully discharged.—Morse on Banks &
Banking, §§ 324, 334; *Lehman's Case*, 64 Ala. 567; *Dean
v. Allen*, 8 Johns. (N. Y.) 390. The bill does not attempt to charge respondent with any debt or account
as to which the bank could apply the deposit. If it did,
it could do so without the aid of the court and in fact
the court could not aid it to do so; the most it could do
for it would be to say it did no wrong in so doing if it
showed it had properly so applied the deposit. But this
is not here done—the court is asked to do that only
which the bank can do. In a proper case the court
might declare that a certain claim or demand was one

to which it might be applied; but clearly this is not such a case. It therefore follows that the injunction of the action at law to recover the amount of this deposit was improperly granted. No reason except that of the lien was attempted to be offered, to authorize the issuance of the same; and, this ground being clearly without merit, the right to the injunction did not exist."

It is therefore not shown by the bill in this case that the bank had any such lien, upon the deposit of the deceased cashier, as could be declared or enforced in this suit.

Mr. Morse, in his work on Banks and Banking, § 335, speaking of the claims of the bank against the depositor, for which it has a lien upon, or which it may set off with, his funds on deposit, says: "The claims set off must be certain, i. e., either already reduced to precise figures, or capable of being liquidated by calculation without the intervention of a jury to estimate the sum. And when the claim sought to be used as an offset requires the decision of a jury on the question of negligence before the claim is established, it cannot be offset, even though the amount of the judgment is very clear, provided there should be any judgment of the claim. As where a bond deposited as collateral for a note was lost, and in suit by the bank on the note the maker tried to offset the loss of the bond. A judgment, or contract claim, that can be sued in debt, assumpsit, or covenant, may be set off. But a demand that must be sued upon in tort, or by bill in equity, cannot be set off."

The claim or demand sought to be set off in this suit is not within the class or classes as to which a bank has a lien upon the deposit of its customer, or as to which it has the right to set off such deposit. The claim

is not certain, but very uncertain, and unquestionably
requires the decision of a jury or of a court of equity to
establish it.   The only claims or demands sought to be
enforced in this suit are those based upon actions in
tort, or which could only be reached by a bill in equity,
and they are consequently not subject to set-off.

There is no pretense in this case that the depositor
or his estate was insolvent, or that it would be necessary, in order to obtain satisfaction on any decree that
might be rendered herein, to proceed against this deposit; nor is there any claim in the bill that .the bank
had applied the amount of the deposit, or any part
thereof, to the payment of any debt or demand owing by
the depositor or his estate to the bank; nor is there
shown any reason whatever why the action brought in
a court of law to recover this deposit should be enjoined.
Had it been averred that the estate was insolvent, and
that the complainant's judgment or decree against the
personal representative could not be satisfied without
resorting to the deposit, and that, if it were compelled
to pay to the personal representative that deposit, it
would lose the benefit of its judgment or decree against
such representative pro tanto, there might be some reason why the action at law should be enjoined; but, in
the absence of such allegation or proof, it is made to
fully appear that the injunction in this case was unwarranted, and that the chancellor properly dissolved
it on motion of the respondent.

A case very similar to the one at bar is that of *Irvine
v. Dean*, 93 Tenn. 346, 27 S. W. 666.   Therein a creditor
of the cashier sought by garnishment to reach the deposit of the latter in the bank.   The bank, in its answer,
sought to hold the deposit as partial indemnity for an
alleged unascertained and unliquidated claim for damages, amounting to $5,000, the result of the cashier's

alleged gross mismanagement of its affairs, as in discounting worthless paper and doing other acts of gross
recklessness.   Held, that this claim being unascertained and unliquidated, and a matter of future litigation,
the bank had no right to apply the deposit of the cashier to its payment, and no lien upon, nor right to hold
the deposit as indemnity against such alleged liability
of the cashier.

The bank in this case having no lien upon the deposit,
because there was no ascertained or liquidated debt due
the bank, to which it could be applied, and the estate of
the depositor not being shown to be insolvent, of course
there was shown no right, on the part of the complainant, to an injunction of the law suit, brought against
the bank to recover this deposit; and the chancellor
therefore properly dissolved the injunction on the respondent's motion.

It is insisted by appellant that the chancellor had no
jurisdiction in vacation to entertain a motion to dissolve
the injunction under section 4526 of the Code; and that
this case having been submitted for final decree, and
such decree having been rendered, this statute does not
apply, for the reason that it is intended only to enable
a respondent to dissolve an injunction in advance of
submission for final decree. If injunction were the only
relief sought in this bill, the argument would possibly
be applicable, as the final decree would either perpetuate or dissolve the injunction. It is true that the former decree upon the final hearing would perpetuate the
injunction, but on appeal from that final decree it was
reversed by this court; but, for the reason set forth in
the opinion on the former appeal, it was deemed im-
pacticable for this court to render a final decree, as is
usually done on appeals from such decrees.

It is possible that this court could have rendered a decree, on that appeal, dissolving or discharging the injunction for want of equity in the bill or upon the denials in the answer; but, as the cause had to be reversed for other reasons, the court did not render such a decree, but left the parties to take such action in the further proceedings, after the reversal and remandment, as they might be advised. The decree of this court had the effect of entirely destroying the final decree of the court from which the appeal was taken, and, after the reversal, the cause stood in that court as if there had never been any final decree. The respondent therefore had a perfect right, under section 4526 of the Code, to proceed as he did; and the bill not having been amended, and it not being made to appear by the bill, or otherwise, that the bank had any lien upon the deposit, or any right to enjoin the action of the administrator against the bank, to recover the deposit, the chancellor properly granted the motion to dissolve the injunction.

The appellant discusses in its brief a number of other questions which were considered by this court on the former appeal, but which cannot be raised on this appeal. They might be raised on appeal from a final decree, but not on appeal, as in this case, from an interluctory decree dissolving an injunction, except in so far as they may support or deny the right to grant or maintain the injunction.

No error appearing, the decree of the chancellor heretofore, dissolving and discharging the injunction, must be affirmed.

Affirmed.

SIMPSON, ANDERSON, and McCLELLAN, JJ., concur.

.

Albes *v.* Southern Railway Co., *et al.*

Bill to Enjoin Vacating Street, and to Declare Ordinance Void.

(Decided June 6, 1911. 55 South. 816.)

Eminent Domain; Compensation; Closing Streets; Abutting Owners.—Although the bill alleges that the property abutted on the street, but failed to allege that it abutted on the part vacated, and the description of the boundaries and the diagram made an exhibit to the bill, showed that the complainant's lots did not abut on the portion vacated, it was not sufficiently shown that the plaintiff was an abutting owner and entitled to damages against the city for closing the street and permitting the railway to acquire it.

APPEAL from Morgan Chancery Court.

Heard before Hon. W. H. SIMPSON.

Bill by C. Edward Albes against the Southern Railway Company, and the city of Decatur to enjoin the closing of a street, and for damages to abutting property. Decree for respondents and complainant appeals. Affirmed.

KYLE & HUTSON, for appellant. Section 235, Constitution 1901, should be liberally construed in favor of the citizens.—*City Council of Montgomery v. Townsend,* 80 Ala. 489. The court should be liberal in holding that the appellant's property abutted on the street vacated. —*Chicago v. Soburcky,* 48 Am. St. Rep. 142; *Gargan v. L. N. A. & N. R. R. Co.,* 6 L. R. A. 340. If the appellant is an abutting owner, then his injury would be peculiar to himself, and not suffered by the public at large.—*In re Mellonstreet,* 182 Pa. 397; *Walsh v. Scranton,* 23 Pa. S. C. 278; *Chicago v. Baker,* 86 Fed. 763. If complainant is an abutting property owner, and has suffered some special damages not suffered by the general public, then as a property owner, he is entitled to complain of the vacation of the street.—*Dantzler v. L. & M.*, 50 Am. St. Rep. 343; *Chicago v. Soburcky, supra; Smith v. Boston*, 7 Cosh. 254; *Brannan v. Rohmeisher*, 90 Ky. 48. The complainant has no adequate remedy at law.—*Wadsworth v. Goree*, 96 Ala. 227; *Wilson v. Mycr*, 144 Ala. 402.

CALLAHAN & HARRIS, for appellee. The street was vacated under a duly passed ordinance which the city had authority to pass, and none of complainant's constitutional rights were infringed.—*So. Ry. v. Albes*, 153 Ala. 523; *Albes v. So. Ry.*, 164 Ala 356; *Transportation Co. v. Chicago*, 99 U. S.; *Crofford v. A. B. & A.*, 48 So. 367; *Montgomery v. Maddox*, 89 Ala. 183. It follows then from these authorities that being authorized by law, the vacating of the street cannot be said to be a public nuisance. The injury claimed was not different in kind from that suffered by the public at large, but was different in degree only.—Authorities supra.

SIMPSON, J.—This is the third appeal in this case. See *Southern Ry. Co. et al. v. Albes*, 153 Ala. 523, 45 South. 234, and *Albes v. Southern Railway Co. et al.*, 164 Ala. 356, 51 South. 327.

While the bill has been amended in a few particulars, we cannot see that said amendments add equity to the bill. While the bill does allege that complainant's property abuts on the streets, a part of which have been vacated, yet it does not allege that they abut on that part which has been vacated, and, even if it did so allege, the description of the boundaries of the lots, and the diagram which is made an exhibit to the bill, show that complainant's lots do not abut on that portion of the street which has been vacated, but merely corner on it, as stated when the case was last before this court.

As to the inconvenience from having to cross the railroad tracks to reach complainant's hotel, the claim for damages is not on account of the building of the railroad; but, on the contrary, the bill shows that the railroad company and its predecessor have owned and occupied the right of way for many years, apparently before the hotel was built, as the description of the lot shows that, when it was originally platted, it was described as being bounded on one side by the railroad right of way. The only part of the street vacated is that which was already occupied by the railroad company as its right of way.

The case being substantially as it was when before this court at a previous term, after a re-examination of the law as heretofore enunciated, we see no reason to depart from the principles heretofore laid down in this case, and, as those principles have been fully argued before, we do not deem it necessary to rehearse them here. In the case of *Dennis v. Mobile & Montgomery R. Co. et al.*, 137 Ala. 649, 658, 659, 35 South. 30, 33, 97 Am. St. Rep. 69, referred to in appellant's brief, the bill was held to be without equity; this court holding that, even if it were assumed that the city council was without authority to authorize the warehouse to be erected, there was no warrant for the interposition of equity to abate a nuisance, and stating: "Nor has there been had, or threatened, such taking of or proximate injury to the lot as entitles complainant to compensation, or injunctive process, under the constitutional provisions relating to eminent domain." The case of *Baltimore & P. R. R. Co. v. Fifth Bap. Ch.*, 108 U. S. 317, 2 Sup. Ct. 719, 27 L. Ed. 739, was an action at law for damages, not for the mere vacating of a street and permitting the erection of a depot, but for creating a nuisance by erections which rendered the property of complainant uninhabitable.

We have shown in our previous decision that the city
had authority to vacate the street, and that, therefore,
that act could not be claimed to be the authorization or
creation of a nuisance, even though it was accompanied
by a contract authorizing the erection of a depot, with
appropriate facilities, both because the motives of the
city council in passing the ordinance cannot be inquired into, and because it was not, as appellant contends,
a mere act for the benefit of the railroad company, but
for the purpose of providing for the comfort and convenience of the traveling public, in accordance with the
orders of the Railroad Commission of Alabama.

The decree of the court is affirmed.

Affirmed.

DOWDELL, C. J., and ANDERSON, MAYFIELD, SAYRE,
and SOMERVILLE, JJ., concur.

Coleman, *et al. v.* Coleman, *et al.*

Bill for Accounting, and to Declare a Trust.

(Decided June 13, 1911. 55 South. 827.)

1. *Tenancy in Common; Termination; Foreclosure of Mortgage.*—
The foreclosure of a mortgage on property owned by tenants in
common, or a failure to redeem before the expiration of the period
allowed, vested the title in the purchaser and terminated the tenancy in common and all the rights of persons claiming as co-tenants.

2. *Trusts; Resulting Trusts.*—The fact that a tenant in common
in possession promised to pay certain debts and advanced money to
the common source of title, for which such tenant was given a second mortgage on the land, and out of such advances the first mortgage was to be satisfied, and the first mortgage was foreclosed, and
after the time to redeem had expired, the mortgagee having purchased at the sale, conveyed to the promising tenant, the lands so
purchased, who then mortgaged the land to secure his own debt,
was not sufficient to raise a resulting or constructive trust in the
land.

[Coleman, et al. v. Coleman, et al.]

3. *Same; Creation; Persons in Possession; Recognition of Trust Character.*—Where a trust is regularly fixed on land, the fact that the person in possession recoguizes the trust character thereof is important in determining the question of laches, but is not effective to fix a trust on the land where none previously existed.

4. *Same; Oral Agreement.*—An oral agreement by a tenant in common in possession to advance money to pay a mortgage on the common property and other debts of a common source of title is not sufficient to create a trust on the land.—(Sections 3412 and 4289, Code 1907.

APPEAL from Autauga Chancery Court.

Heard before Hon. W. W. WHITESIDE.

Bill by Kate Coleman and others, against Claude Coleman and others, for an accounting, and to declare a trust. From a decree sustaining demurrers to the bill, complainants appeal. Affirmed.

W. A. GUNTER and A. A. EVANS, for appellant. The right, if any, is against the legal title, and therefore, equitable, and must be asserted in equity.—*Berry v. Webb*, 77 Ala. 507; *Donnor v. Quartermaster*, 90 Ala. 164; 1 Pomeroy, 137. Being in possession the co-tenant could not change his tenancy without notice to the other tenants.—*Ashford v. Ashford*, 136 Ala. 632; *Walker v. Wyman*, 157 Ala. 478; *Alexander v. Wheeler*, 69 Ala. 340; *Parks v. Barnett*, 104 Ala. 443. A sale without a debt is void, and a mortgage is dead as to right and title when the debt is paid.—Sec. 4899, Code 1907. If there is a debt, and the requirements of the sale are not observed, the sale is void as to the mortgagors and his heirs.—*Sanders v. Askew*, 79 Ala. 443; *Wood v. Lake*, 62 Ala. 489. The purchase of Claude of the legal title inured to the benefit of his co-tenants.—*Bailey v. Campbell*, 82 Ala. 342; *Howse v. Due*, 90 Ala. 184; 23 Cyc. 492; 45 Cent. Dig. 2669. A co-tenant out of possession may rest on the possession as being for all until an actual ouster is shown.—*Williams v. Avery*, 38 Ala. 115. The trust character was recognized.—*Hockensmith v.*

Small, 158 Ala. 232. The bill appears to be perfectly free from every objection, and laches never applies to a period short of the statute of limitations.—*First Nat. Bank v. Nelson,* 106 Ala. 535; *Scruggs v. Land Co.,* 86 Ala. 172; *Shorter v. Smith,* 56 Ala. 208. The bill was not multifarious.—Section 3095, Code 1907.

RAY RUSHTON and W. M. WILLIAMS, for appellee Georgia Loan & Trust Company, WILLIAM H. & J. R. THOMAS and EUGENE BALLARD, for appellee C. E. Thomas. The complainants are not in possession, and cannot maintain the bill to remove cloud from title.—*Rhea v. Longstreet,* 54 Ala. 29; *Daniel v. Stewart,* 55 Ala. 278. One tenant in common cannot maintain an action against another tenant in common for use and occupation.—*Fielder v. Childs,* 72 Ala. 567. Courts of equity obey and apply in suits in equity the limitations provided for in the Code.—*Johnson v. Johnson,* 5 Ala. 90; *James v. James,* 55 Ala. 525. The bill shows on its face that complainants' claim to title had been lost by an adverse holding of ten years under color of title, and that the right of action is barred by the statute.—Sec. 2830, Code 1907; *Ambercrombie v. Baldwin,* 15 Ala. 363; *Moulton v. Henderson,* 62 Ala. 426; *Fielder v. Childs, supra; Hamby, v. Folsom,* 42 So. 548; *Crampton v. Rutledge,* 47 So. 214. No recognition of the trust character is shown.—*Berry v. Laveratta,* 63 Ala. 374; *Phillipi v. Phillipi,* 61 Ala. 41; *Fowler v. Ala. I. & S. Co.,* 163 Ala. 417. The bill falls far short of being a good bill for partition.—*Russell v. Beasley,* 72 Ala. 190; *Berry v. Tennessee Co.,* 134 Ala. 618. Equity will not grant relief because complainait's claim is stale.—*Nettles v. Nettles,* 67 Ala. 599; *James v. James,* 55 Ala. 525; *Harrison v. Heflin,* 54 Ala. 552; *Phillipi v. Phillipi,* 61 Ala. 41; *Greenless v. Greenless,* 62 Ala. 330;

Gordon v. Ross, 63 Ala. 363, 367; *Abernathy v. Moses*,
73 Ala. 381; *Heflin v. Ashford*, 85 Ala. 125; *Duncan v.
Williams*, 89 Ala. 341; *Willis v. Rice*, 141 Ala. 168, 174.
The bill clearly shows on its face that the complainants
have no legal or equitable interest in the property,
either jointly or severally.—*Lewis v. Robinson;* 10
Watts 354; 29 Pa. St. 137; 50 Ia. 192; 13 Barb. 561.

SIMPSON, J.—The bill in this case was filed by the
appellants, alleging that on January 12, 1895, Elizabeth
S. Coleman, who was the mother of some of the complainants and of the respondent Claud Coleman and
the grandmother of the other complainants, died intestate; that said intestate owned the land in controversy; that in 1887 she had executed a mortgage on said
lands to the New England Mortgage Company, which
mortgage, on the 14th day of December, 1894, covered
an indebtedness of $700; that on said last-named day
said intestate executed a mortgage to said respondent
Claud Coleman for nominally $1,300, due by promis-
sory note of that date; that at the death of said intestate
said Claud Coleman went into possession of the land
as tenant in common with the other heirs which he has
held to and including 1907 and has had the use and benefit of the results of said land ever since (about 15
years); that the nominal $1,300 note was intended to
cover money thereafter to be paid by said Claud Coleman which was never paid, or, if there really was any
amount paid, it was more than offset by the value of the
rents, while said tenant in common was in the possession, to wit, during the years 1895, 1896, and 1897, so
that in September, 1907, nothing was due on said mortgage of December 14, 1894, on which day said Claud
Coleman undertook to foreclose said mortgage; that the
proceedings for said foreclosure were not in accordance

with the terms of the mortgage, but at said sale mortgagee bought the property; that, on the 21st day of September, 1897, said New England Mortgage Company foreclosed its mortgage and purchased the property; that afterwards, on the 23rd day of January, 1901, said New England Mortgage Company, for a consideration of $891, conveyed said property to said Claud Coleman, who had been in possession since January, 1895, enjoying the use and occupation thereof; that up to and after said purchase said Claud Coleman never pretended that said land belonged to him, but recognized the rights of said cotenants in common, and that said purchase inured to the benefit of his said cotenants; that on December 1, 1902, said Claud Coleman mortgaged said lands to the Georgia Loan & Trust Company for $3,500, and on November 29, 1907, conveyed the lands to C. E. Thomas and Major M. Smith, whose heirs, together with said Thomas, are the other respondents to the bill; that the consideration of said sale was the assumption by said Thomas and Smith of said mortgage debt to said Georgia Loan & Trust Company of $3,500, and the security of about $3,500, due by said Claud Coleman to said Thomas and Smith and to third persons, "taken up by said Thomas and Smith for said Claud Coleman; that said transaction was intended to be a security for money, and not an absolute deed; that neither said Thomas and Smith nor said Georgia Loan & Trust Company is a bona fide purchaser without notice; that said Thomas and Smith took up and assumed for said Claud Coleman a debt held by the Prattville Mercantile Company, of $3,500, as part of the consideration of said deed, which was composed largely of usurious interest, of which Thomas and Smith had notice;" that "the conveyances of said Georgia Loan & Trust Company and to Thomas and Smith in equity operate only on the one-

fifth interest in said lands held and owned by Claud W.
Coleman, since neither of said conveyances were taken
without notice of the claims and rights of complainants
in and to said lands."

The prayers of the bill are that complainants be decreed to be entitled to such interest in said lands as if
the mortgages and deeds had never been made; that an
account be stated between said Claud Coleman and
complainants, charging him with rents and profits, use
and occupation, and waste; that any balance found to
be due by said Claud W. Coleman be applied to reimburse him for amount paid out in acquiring the outstanding title, etc.; that an account be taken of the
amount due to said Georgia Loan & Trust Company and
said Thomas and Smith, and the same be held to be a
lien on the one-fifth interest of said Claud W. Coleman
in said lands, and that the shares of complainants be free
of all lien or incumbrance, and that said lands be sold
for division. This bill was filed December 13, 1910.

A demurrer to the bill was sustained, and an amendment was filed, adding a section alleging that said Claud
Coleman, at the time of the execution of the mortgage
to him, December 15, 1894, agreed to advance the money
necessary to pay off the New England Company mortgage, which was the consideration of said mortgage to
Claud Coleman; that it was his duty to pay said mortgage and protect the estate; that, in making the purchase, said Coleman merely discharged his duty, etc.
The demurrer to the bill as amended was also sustained,
and it is from that decree that this appeal is taken.

It will be observed that the New England Mortgage
Company regularly foreclosed its mortgage, buying the
property at the sale under the mortgage, and that after
the time for redemption had expired, the title to the
property having vested absolutely in said New England

Mortgage Company, it sold the same to Claud W. Coleman. Upon the sale and purchase by said company, the tenancy in common ceased, if it ever existed, and whatever might have been the rights of the complainants, if Claud W. Coleman had redeemed the property before the expiration of the two years allowed for redemption, certainly there was no tenancy in common after the property had become absolutely vested in said company, without any right of redemption. Each former tenant in common (if they had been such) had an equal right to purchase that property, just as might have been done in any other property in which they had no title or right. The reciprocal rights of tenants in common necessarily cease when they cease to be tenants in common.

In addition to this the complainants had notice that Claud W. Coleman was claiming the property, in his own right, whether the sale was regular or not when he bought the property on foreclosure of his mortgage, December 14, 1894; they had notice that on the 21st day of September, 1897, the New England Mortgage Company had foreclosed its mortgage and bought the property at such sale, yet they made no effort to redeem, and did not even (in so far as there are any allegations in the bill) request the said Claud Coleman to advance the money to redeem the land, but waited until after the title to the property had become vested absolutely in said New England Mortgage Company, after said company had sold the property, on January 23, 1901, to said Claud Coleman, after he had mortgaged it for a present debt to the Georgia Loan & Trust Company, December 1, 1902, after he had sold the property to Thomas and Smith, on November 29, 1907, and for more than three years beyond that time, before filing the bill in the present case.

[Coleman, et al. v. Coleman, et al.]

This court has said, even in referring to a case where one tenant in common had redeemed, "In ordinary cases, such as this is, by analogy to the term fixed for the exercise of the statutory right of redemption, two years is the limit of time within which election by a cotenant should be made, in order to avail himself of the redemptioner's act."—*Savage et al. v. Bradley,* 149 Ala. 169, 173, 43 South. 20.

The facts as stated in the bill are not sufficient to raise either a resulting or a constructive trust in the land.—*Butts v. Cooper,* 152 Ala. 375, 44 South. 616. And the verbal agreement could not have the effect to create a trust on the land.—Code 1907, §§ 3412 and 4289; *D. K. Caldwell et al. v. E. H. Caldwell et al. infra,* 55 South. 515. In fact the agreement as set out in the bill does not indicate any intention to fix a trust on the land, but is obviously a mere personal promise by Claud Coleman to loan money to his mother.

It is true that, where there is legally fixed a trust on lands, the fact that the party in possession recognized the trust character of his possession may be important in determining the question of laches, yet such recognition could not fix a trust on the lands, where none existed before. This is the distinction between such cases as *Small et al. v. Hockinsmith et al.,* 158 Ala. 234, 48 South. 541, and the present case.

The decree of the court is affirmed.

Affirmed.

MCCLELLAN, MAYFIELD, and SAYRE, JJ., concur.

Johnson *v.* Gartman, *et al.*

Bill to Annul Deed, and for Partition.

(Decided June 8, 1911. 55 South. 906.)

1. *Equity; Bill; Amendment; Footnote.*—Amendments to a bill made by interlineations in red ink do not require an additional footnote pointing out the particular statements or interrogatories which the complainants desire the respondents to answer.

2. *Equity; Trial; Submission.*—Where a suit was submitted for a decree on Oct. 29th, 1907, under an agreement allowing ninety days to take testimony, and the case was continued from time to time, and amendments, demurrers, etc., were filed, and submissions and decrees on demurrer, and other proceedings had indicating that the parties were treating the case as if the submissions had been set aside, the respondent even examining a witness whose depositions were filed Feb. 6, 1908, the court did not err in entering a decree on Nov. 18, 1909, setting aside the former submission, and declaring that the order had effect from the adjournment of the April term, 1909, admitting the testimony regularly taken in the meantime, although the respondent objected to the issuance of a commission to take testimony on Nov. 2, 1909, since the original submission had in fact ceased to be effective.

3. *Partition; Distribution; Adverse Claim.*—The provisions of section 3176, Code 1907, have no application to a sale for distribution as authorized by section 3178.

4. *Executors and Administrators; Sale of Land; Nature of Proceeding.*—Proceedings for the sale of lands in the probate court are in rem.

5. *Lis Pendens; Proceedings in Probate Court.*—The doctrine of lis pendens applies as fully to the proceedings in the probate court in which land is disposed of and the title and interest of the parties must be determined, as to proceedings affecting the land in other courts.

6. *Same; Purchaser Pending Probate Proceedings.*—The decedent purchased and occupied as a homestead the lots in controversy, but later removed to other lands in the country on which he lived till his death. His wife refused to go to the country but continued to reside on the land in controversy and after the husband's death the wife remarried. She obtained a deed to the lot from her deceased husband's vendor, and in proceedings by the husband's administrator to sell the lots for the payment of debts and for distribution claimed that she had paid the purchase money and had acquired title by purchase from the vendor, and that if her husband had acquired any interest in the land they were his homestead. But the probate court found that the lands occupied by decedent in the country were his homestead, and that he had the equitable title to the lots in controversy, and that it was subject to sale. Pending these

proceedings in the probate court the widow conveyed the lots to
J. Held, that J. was a pendente lite purchaser and was concluded
by the determination of the probate court under the doctrine of lis
pendens, and therefore, acquired by his purchase only the widow's
dower interest.

7. *Same; Enforcement of Decree; Laches.*—Where a probate decree for the sale of lands for the payment of debts was rendered
August 2, 1909, pending the proceedings leading thereto, decedent's
widow had conveyed the lots to J. on March 30, 1905, and a decree
for sale of the lots for division was filed May 10, 1905, the complainant alleging that the property was advertised to be sold under the
decree Sept. 19, 1904, and that no bidders could be obtained because
the widow appeared on that day ,and gave notice that she claimed
the property, the complainants were not barred by laches under the
rule that a party claiming the benefit of lis pendens must prosecute
his actions to final judgment without such unreasonable delay as
would amount to abandonment of the action and terminate the lis
pendens.

APPEAL from Mobile Chancery Court.

Heard before Hon. THOMAS H. SMITH.

Bill by Paul Gartman and others, against Anna R.
Johnson, to declare a deed void, and to sell lands for division. Judgment for complainant and respondents appeal. Affirmed.

FREDERICK G. BROMBERG, for appellant. Appellant
was bona fide purchaser for value without notice of the
claim of the heirs of Gartman and entitled to protection as such.—*Center v. P. & N. Bank*, 22 Ala. 743;
Crosky v. Smith, 126 Ala. 120; *Eley v. Pace*, 139 Ala.
293; *Nolan v. Farrow*, 154 Ala. 269. Appellees have
been guilty of laches.—*Center. v. Bank, supra; First
Nat. Bank v. Nelson*, 106 Ala. 535; *Galliher v. Cardwell*,
145 U. S. 358. The purchaser was not required to examine the records of the probate court for any proceedings against the land as the record showed a deed to the
land in the name of a living person.—*Center v. P. & M.
Bank, supra*, 25 Cyc. 1452; Wade on Notice, secs. 350,
351, 357, 359; Code 1907, sections 2579-2582. The husband has no rights in real property which survive his
death where the legal title is in the wife, of which a

bona fide purchaser for value is legally required to take notice.—*Cook v. Cook*, 125 Ala. 583. The written agreements of counsel in a cause are binding upon the court. —Sec. 2988, Code 1907; *Roden v. McAfee*, 160 Ala. 564; *Ingram v. Gill*, 145 Ala. 666; *Winter v. City Council of Montgomery*, 79 Ala. 481.

D. B. COBBS, for appellee. The decree of sale was jurisdictional and valid.—*Gartman v. Lightner*, 160 Ala. 209. The probate court had jurisdiction of the equitable title, separated from the legal, and had equity powers correspondingly.—*Todd v. Flournoy*, 56 Ala. 106; *Inman v. Gibbs* 47 Ala. 311; *Jones v. Woodstock Co.*, 95 Ala. 558. And had jurisdiction in this particular case. —*Gartman v. Lightner*, 160 Ala. 209. The widow was not an heir, but a stranger here, as the holder of the outstanding legal title.—*Snedecor v. Morley*, 47 Ala. 523. Her legal title, acquired after her husband's death, was no obstacle to the jurisdiction over the equitable title of descent at his death; and the claim of the legal title was no defence to the probate petition.—Code of 1896, sec. 3176; *Sherer v. Garrison*, 111 Ala. 231; *Layton v. Campbell*, 155 Ala. 222. The probate court was obliged to receive evidence of the equitable title and of the homestead questions raised by the widow, else her mere denial of the petition's averment would defeat it. —*Guilford v. Madden*, 45 Ala. 292. The court must exercise the power it has, omitting that it has not.—3 Brickell, page 181, secs. 74, 75. The probate court could not sell a greater interest than decedent left.—*Ford v. Garner*, 49 Ala. 603. Any party interested in the estate may contest a petition to sell decedent's lands.— Code of 1896, sec. 158. The allegations of the petition must be proved.—Code of 1896, sec. 166. The quantum of interest left by decedent is involved.—*Ford v. Garner*,

45 Ala. 603. The widow claiming homestead, or her
vendee, is such interested party, and could either contest, or appeal after the decree of sale.—*Newell v. Johns,*
128 Ala. 588-9. And appeal within a year.—Code of
1896, sec. 457. They cannot attack the probate decree
collaterally.—*Lyons v. Hamner,* 84 Ala. 197; *Chardavoyne v. Lynch,* 82 Ala. 377. That within its limited
jurisdiction, the probate court's decrees are as binding
as those of any other court.—*Wyman v. Campbell,* 6
Porter, 219; *Whitlow v. Echols,* 78 Ala. 210; *Farley v.
Dunklin,* 76 Ala. 530; *Caperton v. Hall,* 83 Ala. 171.
That being *in rem* proceeding, the decree bound all persons interested, including heirs, administrator, widow
and her vendee.—*Bank of Decatur v. Pullen,* 29 So. Rep.
685; *DeBardeleben v. Stoudenmire,* 48 Ala. 644. Especially the widow, who contested the petition.—*Davis
v. Tarver,* 65 Ala. 100. And the heirs, complainants.—
Lyons v. Hamner, supra; Chardavoyne v. Lynch, supra.
Binding Johnson, her vendee.—*Newell v. Johns,* 128
Ala. 588, and other authorities supra. To the effect that
the decedent (and his heirs) owned the equitable title,
in lots not his homestead, at his death and after; and
all other questions within the jurisdiction of the probate court, and involved actually or necessarily.—
Cromwell v. County of Sac., 94 U. S. 350; 114 U. S.
619. Johnson was also bound as a privy of the widow
who contested, and from whom he bought.—*McCalley
v. Robinson,* 70 Ala. 433; *Shamblin v. Hall,* 123 Ala.
545; *Coles v. Allen,* 64 Ala. 105; *Woods v. Montevallo
Co.,* 84 Ala. 564. Other authorities that the heirs are
bound.—85 Ala. 582; 114 Ala. 327; 128 Ala. 583. On a
point established by a judgment or decree wide enough
to include the point.—119 Ala. 152; 72 Ala. 371; 71 Ala.
186; 121 Ala. 626; 80 Ala. 459; 84 Ala. 508. Whether
the two forms of suit were the same or not.—1 Porter,

215. That the form of the *lis* claimed to have been pending when Johnson bought, was immaterial.—*Kelly v.
Turner,* 74 Ala. 523. Lis pendens doctrine applies to
all sorts of suits that can affect real property, and to
every court of competent jurisdiction to affect it.—25
Cyc. page 1454, A; *Whitfield v. Riddle,* 78 Ala. bottom
of page 107; *Greenwood v. Warrana,* 120 Ala. 76; 19
Am. & Eng. Encyc. pp. 602-3. Including the probate
court in a proceeding to sell a decedent's or ward's real
estate.—21 Am. & Eng. Encyc. p. 630. This results
from the necessity of preserving property in its situation at the beginning of the litigation, to give effect to
decrees.—19 Am. & Eng. Encyc. pp. 602-3; *Warren v.
Hearne,* 120 Ala. 76; 2 Pomeroy's Eq. secs. 632-3-4. Lis
pendens notifies the world of equities and equitable titles concerned in it.—19 Am. & Eng. Encyc. p. 596.
Law courts apply the doctrine of lis pendens as notice,
but equity courts especially—wherever it can be applied
it is applied, whether the lis itself was in one court or
another.—8 Ala. 570; 13 Ala. 119; 63 Ala. 250; 78 Ala.
573; 59 Ala. 315; 70 Ala. 253; 4 Ala. 592; 84 Ala. 587.
And without regard to any sort of supposed hardship;
the courts adhere to the rule inflexibly.—*Trustees Univ.
of Ala. v. Kellar,* 1 Ala. 408. It is a firmly established
rule of property.—*Rooney v. Michael,* 84 Ala. 587. It
is notice, like a recorded conveyance, "with like effect as
the registration of a deed."—19 Am. & Eng. Encyc. p.
596, note.

SIMPSON, J.—The bill in this case was filed by the
appellees for a sale of lands for division, and also to
cancel a deed made to the ancestor of appellant. The
lands in question, being certain lots in Citronelle, were
originally the property of one Loper. About 1888 the
possession of said property passed from Loper to George

[Johnson v. Gartman, et al.]

W. Gartman, and was occupied by him as his homestead. In 1895 said Gartman removed to other lands in the country, on which he lived until his death in 1896; but his wife, Susannah J. Gartman, refused to go to the country, and continued to occupy said homestead, and after his death remarried, becoming Susannah J. Lightner.

Gartman took possession of the land under a verbal contract of purchase, and the witnesses for the respondent testify that he had paid the purchase money, but he never received any deed to the land, and, after his death, to wit, on October 21, 1898, his said widow paid Loper $50, and received from him and his wife a deed conveying to her said property, she still continuing to reside thereon. On the 6th day of August, 1903, R. M. Sendd, as administrator of the estate of said George W. Gartman, filed in the probate office of the county a petition for the sale of the lots in question and the land in the country for the payment of debts of the estate and for distribution, making, as parties defendant, a number of heirs, and the said widow, Susannah J. Gartman. Said widow filed an answer to said petition, denying that said George W. Gartman owned said property, stating that he had entered under a verbal contract of purchase, that he had paid no part of the purchase money, at the time of his death, and that she had acquired the title to the same by the purchase from Loper, if he had acquired any interest in the property, it was his homestead, and, as said property and all other land owned by him at the time of his death was of less value than $2,000, the lots vested in her and her minor children as a homestead. Said probate court decreed that the land in the country constituted the homestead of George W. Gartman at the time of his death; that he had the equitable title to the lots involved in this suit;

that the widow and her minor children were entitled to homestead in the land in the country, but not in the lots in Citronelle. It was accordingly ordered that said lots be sold in conformity to the prayer of the petition. No sale having been made under the decree, on the 30th day of March, 1905, said Susannah J. Lightner and her husband, E. K. Lightner, conveyed the lots in question to E. H. Johnson. The amended bill of June 5, 1906, made said E. H. Johnson a party defendant to the bill in this case, and, his death being afterwards suggested, his widow and heirs were substituted as parties defendant.

The contention of the appellant is that said E. H. Johnson, being the purchaser of the legal title, as it appeared of record, and having no notice of any other claim to the property, was an innocent purchaser, without notice, as claimed in the cross-bill of respondents, and they are entitled to have their title to said lots declared to be valid and free from all incumbrance. The appellees claim that the proceedings in the probate court operated as notice to said Johnson, under the doctrine of lis pendens, and that all the interest which the Johnsons are entitled to claim is the dower interest of said Susannah J. Lightner in the property in question.

This case was before this court at a previous term on an appeal from an order of the probate court, setting aside and vacating the decree of sale of August 2, 1904, and it was held that said original decree was valid, and that said probate court could not, at a subsequent term, vacate the same.—*Gartman et al. v. Lightner et al.*, 160 Ala. 202, 209, 49 South. 412.

As preliminary to the main issues in this case, the amendments to the bill made by interlineations in red ink did not require that an additional footnote be made. —3 Mayfield's Digest. p. 301.

Although it is true that this case was submitted for decree October 20, 1907, under an agreement allowing 90 days within which to take testimony, yet the case was continued over from time to time, amendments, demurrers, answer, cross-bill, etc., were filed, submissions and decrees on demurrers, etc., were had, and various proceedings, indicating that the parties were treating the case as if the submission had been set aside, and the respondents had examined a witness, whose testimony was filed February 6, 1908. While it would have been more regular and proper to have had the submission formally set aside before taking testimony, although the respondents, on November 2, 1909, objected to the issuance of a commission to take testimony, yet there was no reversible error in the order of the chancellor setting aside the former submission on the 18th of November, 1909, and declaring that the order have effect from the adjournment of the April term, 1908, and consequently admitting the testimony which had been regularly taken in the meantime.

The submission had really ceased to be effective.

The appellant insists that the doctrine of lis pendens does not apply to proceedings in the probate court, partly because the deceased, George W. Gartman, did not hold the legal title to the land in question, and partly because, under our statutes, the administrator does not make any inventory of the lands, nor assume to dispose of them except in certain cases. It is nevertheless true that the lands of the deceased can be, and often are, disposed of by proceedings in the probate court, in which the title and interest of the various parties must necessarily be determined. Hence no good reason appears why the doctrine does not apply as fully to proceedings in the probate court as to any other.

[Johnson v. Gartman, et al.]

The proceedings in said court for the sale of lands are
in rem against the land itself.—*Wyman et al. v. Campbell et al.*, 6 Port. 219, 232, 31 Am. Dec. 677; *Lyons v.
Hamner*, 84 Ala. 197, 198, 4 South. 26, 5 Am. St. Rep.
363.

While it is true as a general proposition that the
probate court is not a proper tribunal in which to litigate questions as to title to lands, yet it necessarily results from its functions in selling lands, making distribution of the proceeds, setting apart homesteads, etc.,
that it must ascertain whether the lands belong to the
decedent, what the interests of the various parties are,
etc.   This court has said: "It is obliged to receive the
ordinary evidence of a claimant's right to his property,
otherwise every proceeding of this sort would be defeated by a simple denial of his title, on the part of the con-
testant."—*Guilford v. Madden*, 45 Ala. 290, 293; *Ford
v. Garner*, 49 Ala. 601, 602, 603; *Hillens v. Brinsfield*,
108 Ala. 605, 615, 616, 18 South. 604; *Layton v. Campbell*, 155 Ala. 220, 222, 223, 46 South. 774, 130 Am. St.
Rep. 17.

The provisions of section 3176 of the Code of 1896
have no application to sales under section 3178.—*Sherer
v. Garrison*, 111 Ala. 228, 231, 19 South. 988; *Layton v.
Campbell, supra.*   In the case of *Greenwood v. Warren
et al.*, 120 Ala. 71, 76, 23 South. 686, this court recognized the application of the doctrine of lis pendens in proceedings in the probate court, but it was held not applicable in the case only because the matter being tried in
the subsequent equity case, to wit, undue influence in
the execution of a mortgage, was not and could not be
before the probate court.   One who purchases property
from one of the parties pending a bill filed (in chancery)
for sale and division takes it subject to the hazard of
the pending litigation, and the decree against the parties

litigant is equally binding against the purchaser.—
Stein et al. v. McGrath et al., 128 Ala. 175, 180, 181, 30
South. 792. There can be no reason why the mere fact
that the proceeding were in the probate court should
change the rule, and the courts have so held.—*Draper
v. Barnes,* 12 R. I. 156; *Mowry v. Robinson,* 12 R. I. 152,
155; *Parks v. Smoot's Adm'r,* 105 Ky. 63, 48 S. W. 146;
Harris v. Davenport, 132 N. C.697, 44 S. E. 406.

There is a case in which the Kentucky Court of Appeals held that a proceeding by the heirs of an estate
for a sale of lands for division among themselves was
not such a lis pendens as would authorize the chancellor
to entertain jurisdiction to turn out one who entered,
claiming the land as his own, pending the litigation.—
Clarkson v. Barnett's Heirs, 14 B. Mon. (Ky.) 164,
165; but, without deciding whether that case is not contrary to our own decisions above cited, the facts are entirely different from the case now under consideration,
in that the intruder did not claim by purchase from one
of the parties to the suit, and the court differentiates
it from a case "where a suit is brought to subject it to
sale for the payment of a debt, and, pending the suit, a
person has gained the possession by purchasing the right
of the original defendant."

In the present case the proceedings in the probate
court were to subject the lands for the payment of debts,
and the widow (the vendor of respondents), being a
party to the proceedings, presented to the court for determination the very question upon which depends the
title of the respondents, to wit, that the entire title to
the land had been acquired by her and that the land did
not belong to the estate of the decedent; also, the alternate proposition that, if the land did belong to the estate of the decedent, it constituted his homestead, and
vested in her and children, at his death, both of which

contentions were decided against her. The court subjected to the sale the equitable interest held by George W. Gartman at his death, which it had the right to do. —*Jennings v. Adm'r of Jenkins et al.*, 9 Ala. 286, 290; *Evans, Adm'r v. Matthews*, 8 Ala. 100, 102, 103; *Vaughn & Hatcher, Admr's, v. Holmes et al.*, 22 Ala. 593, 594, 595; *Jones v. Woodstock Iron Co.*, 95 Ala. 551, 558, 559, 10 South. 635. Under the case last cited, the equitable title was all that the probate court could subject. It is true that a party claiming the benefit of the doctrine of lis pendens is required to prosecute his action to final judgment, and such an unreasonable delay as would amount to the abandonment of the action would terminate the lis pendens.—25 Cyc. 1470.

In the present case the decree of sale was rendered August 2, 1904, the conveyance by Mrs. Lightner to Johnson was made on March 30, 1905, the original bill in this case was filed May 10, 1905, and it alleges that the property was advertised to be sold under the decree on September 19, 1904, and that no bidders could be obtained on account of Mrs. Lightner's appearing on that day and giving notice that she claimed the property. We hold that the facts of this case do not authorize the invocation of the principle last referred to; nor was there such laches as to preclude the complainants from filing this bill.—*Shorter et al. v. Smith et al.*, 56 Ala. 208, 210; *First National Bank v. Nelson*, 106 Ala. 535, 542, 18 South. 154; *Pratt Land & Imp. Co. v. McClain*, 135 Ala. 452, 459, 33 South. 185, 93 Am. St. Rep. 35.

From what has been said, it results that the probate court properly directed the equitable interest in said lots to be sold, yet the legal title remained in Mrs. Lightner and passed to Johnson by her conveyance, and as the evidence shows that the purchase money was fully paid by George W. Gartman, making a "perfect equity," his widow held the dower interest, which was conveyed by her deed to Johnson. While there is no appropriate prayer in the bill, yet under the general prayer of the bill the decree will be corrected so as to declare that the legal title being in the Johnsons, for the benefit of the complainants, the same is divested out of them and invested in the complainants.

The decree of the court as corrected is affirmed.

Corrected and affirmed.

McCLELLAN, MAYFIELD, and SAYRE, JJ., concur.

Goodson *v.* Dean, Judge, *et al.*

Bill to Enjoin Issue of Bonds.

(Decided June 15, 1911.　55 South. 1010.)

1. *Counties; Limitation of Indebtedness; Time of Incurring Debt.*—Under section 224, Constitution 1901, and section 158, Code 1907, it is held that the inhibition is against the indebtedness and not against the preliminary steps to ascertain the wishes of the voters, and hence, the validity of the bond issue would depend on the condition of the county indebtedness when the bonds were issued, and not at the date of the election.

2. *Same; Bond Issue; Illegal Act.*—A tax payer cannot maintain a suit to enjoin the county judge and the county commissioners from issuing bonds for which authority had been voted, on the ground that the issue of the bond would create an unconstitutional indebtedness, since such officers are charged with ascertaining first, whether the authority has been granted for the proposed issue, and second, whether the issue will create an unconstitutional indebtedness, before authorizing an issuance of the bonds, and it will not be presumed that they will issue them illegally.

3. *Same; Issuance.*—Section 168, Code 1907, must be construed in connection with section 224, Constitution 1901, and does not authorize or require the issuance of bonds, although voted for if the issue would be in contravention of the constitution limiting a county's indebtedness to 3½ per cent of the assessed value of its property.

4. *Same; Commissioner's Court; Order; Effect.*—An order of the commissioner's court directing an election to determine whether certain bonds of the county should be issued, was complete when passed and was not defective because the probate judge did not record the order until after the court had adjourned.

[Goodson v. Dean, Judge, et al.]

APPEAL from Conecuh Chancery Court.

Heard before Hon. L. D. GARDNER.

Bill by I. F. Goodson against F. J. Dean, probate judge, and the members of the commissioner's court of Conecuh county seeking to restrain the issuance of certain bonds. From a decree sustaining demurrers to the bill complainants appeal. Affirmed.

MILTON A. RABB, and EDWIN C. PAGE, for appellant. The issuance of the bonds would create an indebtedness.—*Hagan v. Commissioner's Court,* 160 Ala. 544, and authorities cited. The county had already reached the amount of indebtedness authorized by section 224, Constitution 1901, and to this must be added the aggregate amount of the bond issue.—*Culberson v. City of Fulton,* 127 Ill. 30; *Hedges v. Dixon County,* 150 U. S. 182. The section authorizing the election, must be construed in connection with the Constitution, and cannot authorize or require issuance of bonds beyond the constitutional limit.—Authorities supra, and yet, when this power has been granted there is no discretion in the court, but to follow the plain mandate of the statute, and issue the bonds so voted.—128 U. S. 102; 30 N. Y. Supp. 375; 14 U. S. 304; 94 U. S. 248. Being a taxpayer, complainant could maintain the bill.—*Inge v. Mobile,* 135 Ala. 195; 22 Cyc. 894. The order was insufficient because not entered when made.—*Crenshaw County v. Sykes,* 113 Ala. 627.

HAMILTON & CRUMPTON, for appellee. The election was authorized by section 158, Code 1907, and the bonds may be issued if not exceeding the limitation fixed by section 224, Constitution 1901 as to indebtedness. For what is indebtedness, see.—25 Pac. 508; 49 Supp. 606. It follows that the computation of indebtedness must be made at the time of the issuance of the bond and not at the time of the election which merely authorizes them.—*Corning v. Meed County*, 42 C. A. A. 158. The mere vote did not create an indebtedness, but merely authorized its creation.—*Thompson E. Co. v. Newton*, 42 Fed. 728. The Board of Revenue had the power only to order the election, to determine the result of the election, and to issue the bonds, if by so doing, the constitutional limitation was not exceeded.—*Dudley v. Board of Commissioners*, 80 Fed. 675; *Rathbone v. Commissioners*, 83 Fed. 130. It will be presumed that the commissioners will do their duty. The order was valid when made, and was not rendered invalid by failure to enter the order.—*L. & N. v. Perkins*, 152 Ala. 141; 1 Black on Judgments, secs. 100, 106; 1 Enc. P. & P. 422.

SIMPSON, J.—The bill in this case is filed by the appellant, as a taxpayer, to enjoin the probate judge and county commissioners from issuing county bonds, after an election had, providing for said bonds. The claim set forth in the bill is that the county of Conecuh is already indebted up to the amount allowed by the Constitution, according to its taxable values, as shown by the assessment books of 1910. The bill alleges that the complainant does not know the exact amount of the debts of the county, over and above a bonded indebtedness which does not reach the limit, and seeks a discovery to ascertain the exact amount of said indebtedness, which it is claimed is over the limit allowed. The bill does not allege that any steps have been taken towards issuing the bonds, but only that "the court of county commissioners of Conecuh county will order issued the negotiable bonds of the county of Conecuh under the supposed authority obtained by virtue of the

election held on the 8th day of November, 1910." Demurrers were interposed to the bill; the gravamen being that the election is shown to have been held according to law, and the bill does not show that any steps
have been taken towards the issuing of the bonds.

Section 158 of the Code of 1907 provides for the holding of such elections.

Section 224 of the Constitution of 1901 provides that
"no county shall become indebted in an amount, including present indebtedness, greater than three and
one-half per centum of the assessed value of property
therein."

The prohibition of the Constitution is against the
indebtedness, and not against the preliminary steps
thereto, in ascertaining the wishes of the voters.

It is evident that the validity of the issue of the bonds
must depend upon the condition of the county indebtedness at the time of the issue of the bonds, and not
upon its condition at the time of the election.—*Corning
v. Board of Com'rs*, 102 Fed. 57, 42 C. C. A. 154, 158;
Thompson-Houston Elec. Co. v. City of Newton (C. C.)
42 Fed. 723, 728; *Redding et al. v. Esplen Borough et al.*
207 Pa. 248, 56 Atl. 431, 432; *Rathbone v. Board of
Com'rs*, 83 Fed. 125, 130, 27 C. C. A. 477; *Dudley v.
Board of Co. Com'rs*, 80 Fed. 675, 677, 26 C. C. A. 82;
28 Cyc. 1584.

An injunction should not be issued upon the mere apprehension of the complainant that some illegal act will
be done. The county commissioners are charged with
the duty of ascertaining, first, whether a majority of
the electors have voted in favor of the issue of the
bonds; and, second, before the issue of the bonds, whether their issue will create an indebtedness beyond the
constitutional limit. In the absence of allegations of
any steps taken towards the issue of the bonds, we can-

not presume that the commissioners will do an illegal act.—1 High on Inj. (2d Ed.) § 591, p. 391; *Troy v. Com'rs of Doniphan Co.*, 32 Kan. 507, 510, 4 Pac. 1009; 1 Joyce on Inj. § 17, p. 35.

Section 168 of the Code of 1907, which makes it the duty of the commissioners, when the majority of the voters have declared in favor of the bond issue, to issue the bonds, must be construed in connection with the Constitution, and cannot intend that they shall issue the bonds in contravention of the Constitution.

There is no force in the contention that the order of the commissioners' court for the election is invalid because not recorded by the probate judge until after the commissioners' court had adjourned. The action of the court was complete when they passed the order, and the bill alleges that they did make the order.

Section 3314 of the Code requires the judge of probate to record the proceedings of the court, but does not provide when he shall enter them on record. Even as to his own official acts and proceedings, he is allowed three months thereafter within which to record them.— Code, § 5421, subd. 2. At any rate, that would be no cause for granting the injunction, on the principles above announced.

The decree of the court is affirmed.

Affirmed.

ANDERSON, MAYFIELD, SAYRE, and SOMERVILLE, JJ., concur.

Rutledge, *et al. v.* Cramton, *et al.*

Partition.

(Decided June 29, 1911. 56 South. 128.)

1. *Bills and Notes; Interest; Payment.*—Where the payor of the note which was deposited with a stranger as custodian pending litigation, had the right to pay off the note and stop interest at the time he paid it to the custodian, and would have paid it into court had not the custodian accepted payment, by accepting the payment the custodian did not prejudice the rights of the litigant entitled to the proceeds of the note so as to be chargeable with interest beyond the time the note was paid.

2. *Depositary; Duties.*—A custodian of a note pending litigation is not bound to earn profis in the way of interest upon the amount paid him on the note beyond that called for by the note.

3. *Contempt; Depositaries; Acts Constituting.*—The custodian of a note in litigation who received payment thereof according to its tenure before the litigation was finally terminated, was not guilty of a contempt or breach of duty by seeking to review final decree which directed him to turn over the note itself in order to obtain judicial confirmance of his receipt of payment, there having been no final accounting of the money received by him until thereafter.

(Simpson and Mayfield, JJ., dissent.)

APPEAL from Montgomery City Court.

Heard before Hon. ARMSTEAD BROWN.

Bill by T. J. Rutledge and others, against F. J. Cramton and others, for partition. From a decree denying interest on a note deposited with a custodian pending litigation beyond the time of payment, complainants appeal. Affirmed.

W. A. GUNTER, for appellant. The appellants were entitled to interest on the note while in the hands of Ball, or rather the money paid on it from the date it was due until the termination of litigation as it appears that Ball the custodian used it in his own affairs and made profits thereon.—*Phillips v. Toles*, 73 Ala. 406; *Cowan v. Jones*, 20 Ala. 128; *McCalley v. Otey*, 105 Ala.

472. A wrong doer deals with trust funds at his peril. —*Tharmes v. Herbert*, 61 Ala. 346; *Whaley v. Whaley,* 71 Ala. 159; *Oliver v. Piatt;* 3 How. 333. The proposition that the appeal should be dismissed is fully answered by the case of *Phillips v. Toles, supra.*

BALL & SAMFORD, for appellee. The appeal should be dismissed.—*Phillips v. Toles*, 73 Ala. 411; *Hanson . v. Todd*, 95 Ala. 328. Counsel discuss the merits, but without citation of authority.

McCLELLAN, J.—The original proceeding was in equity and sought, among other things, the partition of real property. During the pendency of the cause the parties agreed to and did sell the property, and, by agreement, one-third in value of the purchase-money notes—corresponding to the interest claimed by the Rutledges in the real estate and payable upon the termination of the litigation, and bearing interest at 8 per cent—was turned over to Fred S. Ball to await the event of the litigation. This court, in *Crampton v. Rutledge,* 169 Ala. 486, 53 South. 922, in definition of Ball's relation to the court and to the subject-matter of the controversy said: " * * * He thereby became the custodian of the subject of the litigation. He was, in effect, an officer of the court, and subject to its orders and decrees in dealing with the subject of the suit—just as. much so as would be a commissioner who sold the land for division and held the proceeds of the sale, as the purpose and effect of the transaction was to substitute the fund for the land and make Ball a stakeholder.. * * *"

Under the circumstances shown by the record, it is. entirely safe to say that Ball's act in accepting payment of the Epperson note after the rendition of the final decree of March 4, 1910, and in surrendering it,

wrought no just prejudice to appellants in respect of
the interest the obligor had engaged to pay up to the
termination of the litigation. Ball accepted payment
of the note in question on March 12, 1910. The testimony leaves no room for doubt that the payor of the
note had then determined to pay the obligation and to
stop the running of interest against him, as was his
right to do. Indeed, it was shown that the solicitor for
the appellants had suggested to the attorney of the
payor of the note that the note be paid. The attorney
of the payor almost immediately secured from his client
the fund (or check) to pay the note. It may not have
been stipulated, or even implied in the suggestion indicated, to whom the payment of the note should be made.
However this may be, it was at least reasonable that
the offer of payment should have been made to the custodian of the note (Ball) designated by the written
agreement of the parties to the cause; and this is especially true, since it was known to the parties that
another note, held by Ball under the agreement, had
been satisfied by a payment to Ball—a payment that
does not appear to have been questioned at any time.
Aside from this, it does appear, with reasonable certainty, that had Ball declined to accept the payment of
the note, the sum then due upon it would have been paid
into the registry of the court; and, hence, the accrual
of interest, against the payor, would have then ceased.
So, in either event it cannot be ruled, under the evidence
before us, that Ball's act in accepting payment of the
note, when he did, deprived appellants of any obligation of the payor of the note to longer pay interest. The
contingency upon which the note was payable had occurred.

Ball was required, by the court in decree appealed
from, to account for, all sums *received by him* in his re-

lation as custodian—a relation that did not lay upon
him any duty to earn profits upon the subject of his
custody. He, it affirmatively appears, secured no financial benefit from the possession of the money. The deposit interest, from the bank, was paid in by him.

The decree of March 4, 1910, directed Ball to turn
over the *note,* the payment of which he accepted on
March 12, 1910. Of this decree he sought revision in
this court. It was not until the pronouncement of the
decree from which *this* appeal is prosecuted was there
any affirmative and final account taken of the *money,*
the proceeds of the note so paid to Ball.

Certainly the exercise by Ball and Cramton of the
conceived right of revision in this court, of the decree
of March 4, 1911, was no contempt of court or breach
of duty.—28 Am. & Eng. Encyc. Law, p. 1083. The acceptance by Ball of the payment of the note preserved
the principal thereof; and it is only upon the theory
that appellants lost interest, as upon the payor's obligation, by Ball's acceptance of payment that a contention could be made to charge Ball therewith. According to the evidence, a refusal by Ball to have accepted
the payment as made by the payor's attorney would not
have prolonged the period of the payor's obligation to
pay interest. Hence, if it was error of judgment, on
the part of Ball and of the payor's attorney in effecting the delivery and acceptance of the money to and by
Ball, and thereupon the surrender of the *note* to the attorney of the payor, it wrought no prejudice to the appellants.

In consequence, the declination of the court to charge
Ball with interest on the proceeds of the Epperson note,
additional to that accruing from its deposit in bank,
was not error to the prejudice of appellants.

The decree, in the particular it is assailed on this appeal, is therefore affirmed.

Affirmed.

ANDERSON, SAYRE and SOMERVILLE, JJ., concur.

MAYFIELD, J.—(dissenting).—The questions for decision in this case are: (1) Is a trustee liable for interest upon failure to pay money to beneficiary in accordance with the terms of the trust? (2) Is a trustee liable for interest upon failure and refusal to deliver property to the beneficiary in accordance with the terms of the trust? (3) Is a trustee liable for interest for failure to pay money in accordance with the decree of a court of equity administering the trust? (4) Is a trustee liable to his beneficiary for interest upon failure to pay money, or to deliver a promissory note in accordance with the terms of the trust, and with the decree of a court of equity administering the trust?

Until the decision in this case, I thought the decisions were uniform to the effect that a trustee was liable to his beneficiary for interest, upon and after a failure and refusal to deliver trust property or to pay money in accordance with the terms of the trust, or in accorrdance with the decree of the court of equity administering the trust. The effect of the judgment of this court in this case is to deny the beneficiary interest when both of the above mentioned conditions exist.

The facts are undisputed in this case that Ball received the trust fund, which consisted of notes and money collected thereon, as trustee under an express trust, and that he both failed and refused to pay over the money or to deliver the notes in accordance with the terms of the trust, and with the decree of the court of equity which was administering the trust; and yet the lower court and this court decline to make him pay interest on the amount due upon the note, or for the money collected thereon, held and retained by him in violation of the express terms of the trust, and in utter disregard of the decree of the lower court and of this court.

The lower court and this court seem to have acted upon the theory that, because there was no mala fides on the part of the trustee in failing and refusing to pay the money or to deliver the note, and because his failure and refusal was in the hope and anticipation of reversing the decree of the lower and of this court as to the distribution he should make of the trust fund, he should not be required to pay interest, either for *failure to deliver the note* as agreed or decreed, or *failure to pay the money* as agreed and decreed.

The error which the lower court and this court have fallen into is in forgetting the principle of law that neither the trial court nor this court has any discretion in the matter as to whether the trustee under the disputed facts in this case, should be required to pay interest. The facts undisputed, the law fixes the liability both in character and extent, and the court has neither the right nor discretion to relieve the trustee from this liability to the beneficiary as to any amount, nor to any extent.

This court said, in the case of *Broughton v. Mitchell,* 64 Ala. 211, that interest attaches as a matter of right to all contracts for the payment of money from the day on which it becomes due, and that no court of law or equity has discretion as to its amounts. Interest is given by statute as a compensation for the detention of the money, and no court has any discretion in its allowance.

Our statute is plain and mandatory, that no court, whether of equity or of law, has the right to avoid the statute nor enforce it. Our statute upon the subject reads as follows: "All contracts, express or implied, for the payment of money, or other thing, or for the performance of any act or duty, bear interest from the day such money, or thing, estimating it at its money value, should have been paid, or such act, estimating the compensation therefor in money, performed."—Code 1907, § 4620.

The facts in this case are undisputed that the trustee did make a contract, both for the payment of money and for the performance of acts and duties, and the statute expressly declares that he shall be liable for interest from the day the money should have been paid or the · act performed. Why the lower court or this court should decline to follow or to enforce this express statute, I am unable to conceive.

According to the trustee's own answer and evidence, he is clearly liable for interest, both for a failure to pay over the money, and failure to deliver the note. Moreover, it is undoubtedly the law that if the beneficiary had sued the trustee in a court of law, instead of moving for the decree in the chancery court, he would have been liable for interest, both for the amount of money he failed to pay, and for the amount of the notes he failed to deliver, and for the amount of money he collected on the note which he declined to deliver in accordance with his agreement, and with the decree of the court. This being true, he was clearly and certainly liable, and should have been made to pay the same by the chancery court.

That there is no distinction between the right to recover interest in courts of equity and that to recover in courts of law is well established. This court, in the

case of *Crocker v. Clements*, 23 Ala. 296, 312, said:
"Courts of chancery upon this, as upon the subject of
the application of the statute of limitations, follow the
law, and allow interest in all cases where it would have
been recoverable had the suit been instituted in the
common-law court." It was likewise held in that case
that where a sum of money to be refunded was certain,
then the law implied a contract and raised a promise
to pay it and the interest, and that in such case interest was properly allowed.

Another error which the trial court and this court
fell into was in treating the trustee as if he were acting
in pursuance of the trust, and not in disregard and violation of it as the undisputed evidence in this record
shows he was doing. It is an undoubted principle of
law that a trustee who is a bare stakeholder (as was
the trustee in this case) is not liable for interest so long
as he acts in accordance with the terms of the trust, or
unless he uses or realizes profit from the trust fund;
and then, if he use it and act in good faith, and without negligence, he is liable only for the profit which he
actually realizes; but when he acts in violation and disregard of the express terms of the trust, and in rebel-
lion against the decree of the court which is administer-
tering the trust, this rule no longer applies. He is then
not only liable for legal interest but may under certain
conditions be made liable for compound interest and
for other damages in addition thereto. For example:
If the trustee in this case had paid over the money to
the parties, in accordance with the terms of the trust,
and with the decree of the court, or if he had paid it
into court on taking the appeal, to await final adjudication, he would not then have been liable for legal interest, but merely for the amount he actually received
and was decreed by the lower court to be liable for;

but, having declined to pay in accordance with the agreement, and with the decree of the court, he was no longer protected from liability to interest by such rule, and was at least liable as for the minimum amount of damages, which the law says is legal interest for the time the money and notes of the beneficiary were withheld.

It was well said by this court, in the case of *State v. Lott,* 69 Ala. 154 (speaking of interest), as follows:

"Interest, in this state, has been long regarded not as the mere incident of a debt, attaching only to contracts, express or implied for the payment of money, but as compensation for the use, or for the detention of money. Wherever it is ascertained that at a particular time money ought to have been paid, whether in satisfaction of a debt, or for the failure to keep a contract, interest attaches as an incident.—*Whitworth v. Hart,* 22 Ala. 343; *Boyd v. Gilchrist,* 15 Ala. 849; *James v. Governor,* 1 Ala. 605. The true and just doctrine is expressed in *Dodge v. Perkins,* 9 Pick. (Mass.) 368, approved in *Boyd v. Gilchrist, supra,* that 'the inquiry is, whether the party has done all that the law has required of him in the particular case, whether acting on his own account, or as agent, executor, administrator, or trustee for others. If he has, he is not accountable for interest; if he has not, he is accountable for it, as a compensation for the nonperformance of his contract.' "

In the case of *Godwin v. McGehee,* 19 Ala. 474, a case similar to the one under consideration, the court, in speaking of the liability of a trustee for interest upon failure to pay over the money or funds in accordance with the decree of the court, said: "The fund being called for in the court of chancery, it was the obvious duty of the defendants who desired to rid themselves of the payment of interest upon their unpaid bonds, to

[Rutledge, et al. v. Cramton, et al.]

have tendered the money in court, and, if instead of doing so, they engaged in a protracted, expensive, but fruit-
less litigation concerning it, and hold onto it until obtained at the extremity of the law, it is but equitable and
right that they should be required to pay interest."

In the case of *Kirkman v. Vanlier*, 7 Ala. 218, in
speaking of the liability of the trustee for interest, the
court said:

"Any trustee will be chargeable for interest if he has
made interest, used the money, or is guilty of laches or
neglect. * * * And * * * if an agent does not
in a reasonable time apply money to the purposes for
which it was received, he will be liable to pay interest.
* * * So if one man retains the money of another,
the presumption is that he kept it for the purpose of
profit, and that he should therefore pay interest on it."
It was further held in that case "that a trustee was liable to pay interest on the trust money in his hands, unless he can show that it was necessarily kept in hand
for the purpose of the trust; this he may do upon oath,
subject to be controlled by other testimony and the circumstances of the case; and in such case interest is calculated from the time the money was received. But the
case more strikingly analogous to the one before us is
Shackelford v. Helm, 1 Dana (Ky.) 338, in which it was
determined that a debtor is not excused from the payment of interest, because the debt is attached in his
hands by bill in chancery; unless he bring the money
into court, or is enjoined from using it. So it has been
decided that an officer of court who has money in his
hands, raised by sale of attached effects, which the court
forbade him to pay over, shall pay interest, unless it
appear that he kept the principal by him."

SIMPSON, J., concurs.

J. Loeb Grocery Co. *v.* I. Brickman & Co., *et al.*

Bill to Declare a Preference a General Assignment.

(Decided June 29, 1911. 56 South. 119.)

1. *Fraudulent Conveyance; Preference.*—At the common law, a debtor had a right to prefer one or more of his creditors even to the entire exclusion of others.

2. *Assignments; Benefit of Creditors; Constructive Assignment.*— Section 4295, Code 1907, makes an assignment thereunder a general one for the benefit of all creditors regardless of the character of their debts or securities, and hence, where a debtor had had a thousand dollars exempted to him in a bankruptcy proceeding, and had paid it out to certain creditors holding waive notes against him, a creditor of the same class could not require or maintain a bill against the debtor and the preferred creditors to declare said payment a general assignment for the benefit of a class, the remedy being to declare it a general assignment for the benefit of all creditors.

3. *Same; Lien; Effect.*—Where a transfer or assignment of property is declared to be a general one for the benefit of all creditors, under the provisions of section 4295, Code 1907, it does not destroy or affect any existing lien which any creditor or class of creditors had upon the property at the time of its assignment.

4. *Same; Liens; Waiver of Exemptions.*—Where creditors held notes in which the debtor waived his exemptions to personal property, the mere fact that they could have subjected such property to the payment of their debts under execution, and that such property could not be so subjected by other creditors, gives them no lien upon the property assigned or any greater rights than other creditors.

APPEAL from Montgomery City Court.

Heard before Hon. ARMSTEAD BROWN.

Bill by J. Loeb Grocery Company, against I. Brickman & Co., and others, to declare a preference a general assignment for the benefit of all creditors holding waive notes. From a decree sustaining demurrer to the bill, complainants appeal. Affirmed.

STEINER, CRUM & WEIL, for appellant. The money paid in this case is such property as comes within the

meaning of section 4295, Code 1907.—*Barnett v. Bass,*
10 Ala. 951; *Hall & Farley v. Ala. Term. Co.,* 143 Ala.
481. Means or instrumentalities adopted to circumvent
the statute will not be permitted.—*Smith v. McCadden,*
138 Ala. 284; *Anniston Carriage Works v. Ward,* 101
Ala. 675. All the creditors were properly joined and
the several amounts received by them are to be taken
together as forming one general assignment under the
statute.—*Danner v. Brewer,* 69 Ala. 191; *Bank v. Paulk,*
124 Ala. 595. The exempt property of the debtor is subject to execution in favor of a creditor as to whom exemption had been waived.—Sections 4172, 4231, and
4234, Code 1907. A creditor holding waiver of exemption has the same equity to complain as to the disposition of property exempt to the debtor as an ordinary
creditor would have with reference to the general property of the debtor.—*Tillis v. Deane,* 118 Ala. 645. In
construing the statute, the court will look to the legislative intent and not to its literal expression.—*Davis v.
Thomas,* 154 Ala. 279; *Sunflower Co. v. Turner,* 158
Ala. 191. The exempt property can be disposed of by
the debtor at his will as against any of his creditors except those in whose favor he has waived his exemptions,
and we submit the debtor had no creditors as to this
fund except such as held his obligation waiving his exemption.—*Wright v. Smith,* 66 Ala. 516. The court has
no jurisdiction over the property claimed by the bankrupt as exempt and creditors holding instruments in
which the debtor waived his right of exemptions are
relegated to the state court for the enforcement of their
rights.—*Lockwood v. Exchange Bank*s 190 U. S. 294.
Of course, there can be no dispute as to the equity of
the bill aside from the fact that it seeks a general assignment for the benefit of a class of creditors.

JOHN V. SMITH, for appellee. In attempting to create a general assignment for a class complainants are proceeding in direct contravention of the provisions of section 4295, Code 1907.—*Eley v. Blacker & Flynn,* 112 Ala. 311. The cases cited by appellant are not in contravention of this principle, the complainants had a clear and adequate remedy at law.—*Lockwood v. Exchange Bank,* v90 U. S. 294. The failure to exercise this right cannot justify the reading of equity into the present bill.

MAYFIELD, J.—In the bankruptcy proceeding instituted to adjudicate J. S. Oppenheimer (one of the respondents) a bankrupt, $1,000 in money was set apart to said bankrupt, as his exemption as to personal property, in accordance with exemptions in bankruptcy statutes. Subsequently, the bankrupt paid this $1,000 to five of his creditors, distributing it pro rata among them. The debts due these five creditors were secured by waive notes signed by the bankrupt. Shortly thereafter, appellant, another creditor of the bankrupt, whose debt was secured by waive notes, filed this bill in behalf of itself and all the other creditors whose debts were evidenced or secured by waiver of the debtor's right to claim exemption as to personal property; and sought to have the payment of this $1,000 by the bankrupt to the five preferred creditors, declared a general assignment for the exclusive benefit of those creditors, to secure whose debts the assignor or payor had waived his right of exemption as to personal property. The respondents demurred to this bill on the ground that it sought to have the $1,000 declared a general assignment or payment, for the benefit of only one class of creditors, and not for the benefit of all. The trial court sustained the demurrer to the bill, and from that decree this appeal is prosecuted by the complainant.

The abstract question of law involved on the appeal is this: Can an assignment by a debtor of the personal property exempt to him, to some of his creditors, be declared a general assignment under section 4295 of the Code, for the benefit of those creditors only, against whose debts the assignor had waived his right of exemption? The trial court answered this question in the negative, and we are inclined to the opinion that the answer was correct.

Our statute (section 4295 of the Code), which was intended to prevent a debtor from preferring some of his creditors to the exclusion of others, by conveyance, assignment or transfer of substantially all of his property to such preferred creditors, is in derogation of the common law, which recognized the right of a debtor to prefer one or more of his creditors, even to the entire exclusion of others.

But for the statute in question, it is conceded that there would be no equity in this bill, there being no contention or suggestion that there was any actual fraud other than a violation of this statute. To be more exact, the only contention is that the transaction falls within the provisions of the statute. The statute does not make such a transaction fraudulent, but merely converts it into a general assignment for the benefit of all creditors, instead of a special one for the benefit of preferred creditors.

The statute makes the assignment a general one for the benefit of all creditors—regardless of the kind, character, or extent of their debts, or of the security given for the payment; and we do not feel justified in limiting it to those creditors only, who could subject the property assigned to the payment of their debts by attachment, execution, or other process. If the assignment or payment of the thousand dollars in question was a general assignment, within the meaning of the statute (a question we do not decide), and it should be declared such under the statute in question, it would inure to the benefit of all the creditors by virtue of the statute, irrespective of class, or the character of security held by the creditors. The statute is not intended to destroy or otherwise affect any lien that any creditor or class of creditors had upon the property transferred or assigned by the debtor.

If a transfer or assignment of property be declared a general one for the benefit of all creditors, it in no manner destroys any existing lien which any creditor had upon the property at the time of the assignment.

It is not claimed, and cannot be plausibly contended, that the complainants had any lien upon this property by virtue of the fact that the debtor had waived his right of exemption as to his personal property against the payment of the complainant's debts. The mere fact that the complainant could have subjected his property to the payment of its debt under an execution and that such property could not have been subjected by creditors as to whose debts the debtor had not waived his right of exemption, does not confer any greater right upon the complainant under the statute in question, than is conferred upon the other creditors. The statute in question makes no distinction between creditors on account of the character or class of the security for, or evidence of, their debts.

For the reasons pointed out in the demurrer, the bill was defective, and the trial court properly so decreed.

Affirmed.

SIMPSON, ANDERSON and MCCLELLAN, JJ., concur.

[Stocks v. City of Gadsden.]

Stocks *v.* City of Gadsden.

Bill to Enjoin Change of Grade of Street.

(Decided June 29, 1911. 56 South. 134.)

1. *Eminent Domain; Necessity of Payment; Entry on Making Payment or Deposit in Court.*—Under section 235, Constitution 1901, the rights of an owner who files a bill to enjoin a street grade improvement until he shall be compensated for the injury to his abutting property, are protected by an order of reference to ascertain full indemnity to the owner and costs, and a deposit with the register of the amount so ascertained, to abide the results of the suit.

2. *Constitutional Law; Contemporaneous Interpretation.*—Where a constitutional provision has been interpreted by judicial decision and has been re-enacted, it will be presumed that it was re-enacted with the interpretation put upon it by such decisions.

3. *Municipal Corporations; Streets; Change of Grade.*—It is the duty and the right of the municipal corporation to make its streets safe and convenient by establishing grades or changing grades already established.

4. *Same; Improvements; Discretion; Review.*—Where the bill alleged that the grading proposed would not add to the safety or convenience of the street, but would cause the street to be four or five feet lower than the grade of complainant's property, and would render ingress and egress difficult, and the sworn answer did not take issue as to the difficulty of ingress or egress but averred that the grade would not lower the street more than one or one and one-half feet for a short distance and that the cost of making the property conveniently accessible would be small and that the grading would enhance its value it is held that even if the court had power to control the discretion of the city in a case where a great abuse was shown no construction of the answer in this case would require such a review.

5. *Costs; Appeal; Records; Agreement as to Contents; Presumptions.*—Construing section 2848, and rules of practice 27 and 28, it is to be presumed that the appellant might have had an agreement for an abridgement of the record, and in the absence of such an agreement, the court will not strike out any part of the record so as to deny the register his costs.

APPEAL from Etowah Chancery Court.

Heard before Hon. W. W. WHITESIDE.

Bill by A. T. Stock against the city of Gadsden to enjoin the change of the grade of a street. From an order dissolving the preliminary injunction, complainant appeals. Affirmed.

A. E. GOODHUE, and A. R. BRINDLEY, for appellant. Although reference be had and the amount ascertained and paid into court the injunction should not have been dissolved, as no public necessity is shown.—*Town of New Decatur v. Scharfenburg,* 41 South. 1025; *City Council v. Townsend,* 84 Ala. 486. The averment that the change of the grade would not render the street any more safe or convenient is nowhere denied in the answer, and therefore, must be taken as true, and hence, no necessity is shown for the exercise of this right by the city, and the injunction should have been retained.

CULLI & MARTIN, and M. C. SIVLEY, for appellee. The court properly dissolved the injunction upon a payment into court of the damages ascertained by the register.—*C. & W. R. Co. v. Witherow,* 82 Ala. 190. This will not interfere with the power of the chancellor to direct an issue to be made up for a final determination by a jury as to the amount of damages to which complainant is entitled.—*Town of New Decatur v. Scharfenburg,* 147 Ala. 567. The execution of a sufficient bond to be approved by the chancellor would have authorized the dissolution of the injunction.—*M. & W. R. Co. v. Fowl R. L. Co.,* 152 Ala. 326. As to whether the matter of damages will be referred to a jury is a question within the irrevisable discretion of the chancellor. —*Norwood v. L. & N.,* 149 Ala. 159.

SAYRE, J.—The city of Gadsden was proceeding to reconstruct the grade of Haralson street when appellant filed his bill to have the work enjoined until he should be compensated for the injury which would be caused thereby to his abutting property. Preliminary injunction was ordered. After a motion to dissolve on the sworn answer had been overruled, the defendant amended its answer by incorporating a prayer for a reference to ascertain an amount which would secure to complainant full indemnity for the probable damages to his property, and the costs, and that it be allowed to pay over to the register the amount so ascertained to abide the result of the suit. That course was taken and the deposit made. Thereafter the defendant moved the court to dissolve the injunction, and the court so decreed. From that decree, this appeal is taken.

The court followed the precedent set by the decree of this court in *C. & W. Ry. Co. v. Witherow*, 82 Ala. 190, 3 South. 23. In that case this court ordered a reference to ascertain what sum of money would be sufficient to secure a full indemnity for the probable damage that might ensue to complainant's property by reason of the construction of a railroad track along a street in front of complainant's property, and that, upon the deposit of the sum so ascertained, the injunction should be dissolved. The court said: "This will be security for the damage done, such as will conform to our constitutional requirements. * * * Nor will it at all interfere with the power of the chancellor to direct an issue to be made up for the final determination by a jury, of the amount of damages to which complainant may be entitled, if any, on final hearing of the cause." That practice seems to have had the approval of the court in *New Decatur v. Scharfenburg*, 147 Ala. 367, 41 South. 1025, 119 Am. St. Rep. 81, and *M. & W. Ry. Co. v. Fowl River Lumber Co.*, 152 Ala. 320, 44 South. 471. Section 7 of article 14 of the Constitution of 1875 provided that: "Municipal and other corporations and individuals invested with the privilege of taking private property for public use, shall make just compensation for the property taken, injured, or destroyed by the construction or enlargement of its works, highways, or improvements, which compensation shall be paid before such taking, injury, or destruction." And in *Southern Ry. Co. v. B. S. & N. O. Ry. Co.,* 130 Ala. 660, 31 South. 509, it was held that the right of prepayment secured to the property owner, in cases where his property was taken by municipal or other corporations or individuals invested with the privilege of taking private property for public use, was inseparably connected with the right to have the amount determined by a common-law jury. To meet this state of the law, the Constitution of 1901 provided that "municipal and other corporations and individuals invested with the privilege of taking property for public use, shall make just compensation, to be ascertained as may be provided by law, for the property taken, injured or destroyed by the construction or enlargement of its works, highways or improvements, which compensation shall be paid before such taking, injury or destruction." It then secures the right of appeal and the right to have the amount of damages determined, on appeal, by a jury according to law, but provides that "such appeal shall not deprive those who have obtained the judgment of condemnation from (sic) a right to enter, provided the amount of damages assessed shall have been paid into court in money, and a bond shall have been given in not less than double the amount of damages assessed," etc.—Const. 1901, § 235. These changes in the Constitution make plain the purpose in all cases to divorce prepayment from the right to have damages assessed by a jury, and in cases where a right of entry, a taking, is sought, permits prepayment by a deposit of money and a bond. In respect to all cases of injury without a taking, it must be presumed that the constitutional provi-

sion for prepayment was ordained anew with the interpretation which had been put upon it in the Witherow
Case. These considerations lead us to the conclusion
that the order of the court in this cause was made with
due regard for the constitutional rights of the appellant.

In his bill appellant charges that the contemplated
removal of earth is not necessary to make the street safe
and convenient and extends entirely beyond the requirements of the public safety and convenience. The specific averment is that "the removal of said dirt or earth
will result in lowering the grade of said Haralson street
opposite complainant's said property to such an extent
as to cause said street to be five feet or more below the
surface of said complainant's said property, thereby rendering difficult the ingress and egress to and from complainant's said property." The sworn answer does
not take issue with the specific averment, but explains
the situation by showing that the surface of the street
is already from two to three feet below the surface of
complainant's property, and that the proposed excava-
tion will lower the present surface one and one-half feet,
and this for only a few feet along the street. It concludes that the cost of making complainant's property,
which is unimproved, conveniently accessible after the
change will be insignificant, and that the net result of
the proposed work will be an enhancement in its value.
It shows the defendant's purpose is to improve the
street and make it more convenient for travel. On this
state of the pleading, appellant bases a contention that
the defendant has admitted a case of abuse of municipal authority in that the proposed change of grade extends entirely beyond the requirements of public safety
and convenience, as is alleged in the bill. It is both the
right and the duty of a municipal government to make

its streets safe and convenient by establishing grades or
changing grades once established.—*Montgomery v.
Townsend,* 84 Ala. 478, 4 South. 780. The rule is ordinarily stated to be that the municipality is the sole judge
as to when and how a street shall be improved, and its
determination in that regard is legislative and irrevisable by the courts.—2 Dill. Mun. Corp. (4th Ed.) §§
686, 941; Lewis Em. Dom. (2d Ed.) § 107. Some cases
show an inclination to control the discretion of the municipal authorities in such matters, where great abuse
is shown. But if it should be admitted that there is
such power in the courts, we are of the opinion that no
fair construction of the answer can place this case within hailing distance of it.

The record contains a transcript of the evidence taken
by the register on the reference. The appellant moves
to strike. There was no exception to the register's report, and this evidence might well have been omitted
from the transcript. But it was not for the register to
take the initiative in this. The statute requires that
"the register * * * must, on the application of the
appellant or his attorney, make and deliver to him in
time to be returned to the Supreme Court, a full and
complete transcript of the record and proceedings in
the case."—Code, § 2848. Rule of Practice 27 specifies
what papers and orders are to be omitted from the record by the register. Rule 28 authorizes parties, or their
counsel, to "make an agreement in writing, specifying
what part of the proceedings shall be inserted in the
transcript." It is to be presumed that the appellant
might have had an agreement in this cause for an abridg-
ment of the record by the omission of the proceedings
on reference. In the absence of such agreement we are
not prepared to say that the register improperly includ-

ed those proceedings, or that he ought to be denied his costs. The motion is overruled.

Affirmed.

SIMPSON, ANDERSON, and SOMERVILLE, JJ., concur.

Carroll *v.* Draughon, *et al.*

Bill to Declare a Resulting Trust in Land.

(Decided June 29, 1911. 56 South. 207.)

1. *Public Lands; Homestead; Resulting Trusts.*—No trust results in favor of a married woman in public land homesteaded by her husband merely because she furnished the money to purchase a prior entrymen's relinquishment.

2. *Same; Patent; Effect.*—A patent to public land presumptively vests the legal title in the parties to whom it was issued.

3. *Same.*—A patent to public lands is prima facie evidence of a compliance with all preliminary requirements to its issuance.

4. *Same; Homestead; Title of Entryman.*—Under the United States statute, title cannot inure to the benefit of or in trust for any one but the entryman.

5. *Trusts; Resulting Trusts; Innocent Purchasers.*—Even if a wife could enforce a resulting trust in lands acquired by her husband with money furnished by her, as against him and his heirs, she cannot as against bona fide purchasers for value.

6. *Same; Establishment; Resulting.*—The occupancy of the land jointly with her children, heirs of decedent, without claiming a resulting trust, though having furnished money for the acquisition of the land, does not charge purchasers from the heirs with notice of the widow's equity.

APPEAL from Geneva Chancery Court.

Heard before Hon. L. D. GARDNER.

Bill by D. S. Carroll against J. W. Draughon and others, to establish a resulting trust in land. Decree for respondent and complainants appeal. Affirmed.

R. H. WALKER, for appellant. The application to have the land set apart to the widow as a homestead

does not estop her or her vendee to seek the redress here
sought.—*Faircloth et al. v. Carroll*, 137 Ala. 243. She
was left in possession in her own right, and by no act of
the husband, and hence her possession was notice of her
claim.—*McLeod v. Bishop*, 110 Ala. 645. The several
declarations of her husband and herself while in possession were admissible in evidence.—*Goodbar v. Daniel*, 88 Ala. 583; *Dyces' Case*, 88 Ala. 225. It was the
homestead, and hence, not subject to alienation.—*Mc-
Guire v. Van Pelt*, 55 Ala. 344. The action taken by the
wife in the probate court cannot affect her title or
claim.—*Tyler v. Jewett*, 82 Ala. 93; *Winston v. Hodges*,
102 Ala. 304; *Marks v. Wilson*, 115 Ala. 563.

W. O. MULKEY, for appellee. There is no specific
prayer to declare or establish a resulting trust, nor is
there prayer for general relief. Hence, that relief cannot be granted.—*Patterson v. Bragg*, 95 Ala. 58; 58
Ala. 221; 5 Port. 9; Sec. 3094, Code 1907. Under the
revised statute, the alleged sale by Kelly was void, and
conferred no rights whatever on the purchaser, and could
not have the effect of stamping the land with any trust
in favor of the person furnishing the money for that
purpose.—*Cox v. Donelly*, 34 Ark. 762. Under the facts
in this case, if the money was furnished by the wife the
presumption is that it was furnished as an advancement,
and no presumption of trust arises.—*Hatton v. Landman*, 28 Ala. 135; *Long v. King*, 117 Ala. 423. The idea
of a trust is barred by the doctrine of laches and the
statute of limitation.—*Bracken v. Newman*, 121 Ala.
311; *Martin v. Kelly*, 132 Ala. 201. No knowledge on
the part of the purchaser of the existence of the trust
is shown, and it is shown that they paid value for the
land.—*Walker v. Elledge*, 65 Ala. 51; 71 Ala. 220. There
is no reason why the administrator of Mrs. Carroll

should be restored to the possession of the land involved
in this suit, as the administrator is not shown to have
been deprived of anything to be restored.—3 Cyc. 462;
Ex parte Weldon, 148 Ala. 430; *Crocker v. Clemmons,*
29 Ala. 296.

SOMERVILLE, J.—The primary purpose of the
bill of complaint is to declare a resulting trust in certain lands. The following essential facts are shown by
the record: In 1888 one Kelley was living on the land
in question, claiming it under a homestead entry, the
status of which does not appear. In that year he sold
and turned over his claim, possession, and improvements
to one Delaware Peacock, the consideration for which
was $185, which was paid out of money belonging orig-
inally to Ophelia Peacock, his wife; the intention being
to provide a home for himself, his wife, and his children. No written transfer is shown. Delaware Peacock then entered on the land and occupied it until his
death in April, 1894. Presumptively he made the final
proofs required by law, as testified to by one of the witnesses, for a few days after his death a patent, issued
by the government, came to his address. The patent was
returned, with the explanation that the patentee was
dead, leaving heirs, and on February, 1895, a patent was
issued granting the land to "the heirs of Delaware W.
Peacock, deceased," and reciting that their claim had
been "established and duly consummated in conformity
to law." This patent was received and kept by the widow, said Ophelia Peacock, who, with her said Delaware's
only two children, Emma and Chaldee, continued to
reside on the place. The respondents acquired and now
own the interests of the said two children, by deeds executed by them after they became sui juris, and prior to
the filing of this bill. The recital in each deed is for a

grant of an undivided half interest in the land, and the purchasers had no knowledge or notice of the fact that Ophelia Peacock's money was used in the purchase of Kelly's claim, nor of any claim to any interest in the land on her part. For Emma's half interest, purchased in May, 1901, $225 was paid; and for Chaldee's, purchased in January, 1907, $1,000 was paid. Ophelia Peacock married the complainant, Carroll, and prior to her death executed a deed conveying to him all her interest in the land, and he now claims the land in his own right. Much other evidence was introduced, and several other issues raised, in the court below, which, in our view of the case, need not be here considered.

The facts and conditions which will support a resulting trust have often been considered and declared by this court, and we shall not restate them.—*B. & A. R. Co. v. L. & N. R. R. Co.*, 152 Ala. 422, 44 South. 679; *Butts v. Cooper*, 152 Ala. 375, 44 South. 616. Had complainant's wife furnished the money with which her former husband actually bought this land from the owner, he taking the title in his own name, it may be conceded that a trust would have resulted in her favor, such an implication not being rebutted by the accompanying circumstances.

But the facts of this case clearly do not come within this principle. At best, the money was furnished to the husband to remove an impedient to his own entry and acquisition of the land as a homestead under the laws of the United States, and he so used it. Neither the land nor any interest in the land was bought or acquired from Kelley, and the entry was made and the proof proceeded in the name of the husband, entirely independent of the arrangement made with Kelley.

Presumptively, the patent vests the legal title in the parties to whom it is issued, and, prima facie, all the pre-

[Carroll v. Draughon, et al.]

liminary requirements to its granting had been complied
with.—*T. C. & R. Co. v Tutwiler,* 108 Ala. 483, 485, 18
South. 668. And if, upon any state of facts, the law authorized the issue of the patent to the heirs of Delaware
Peacock, upon collateral attack courts must presume the
existence of these facts.

The title to the land entered cannot inure to the benefit of any other person than the entryman, nor can
trust relations legally exist between the entryman and
any other person in respect to the land entered. This
results from section 2290, U. S. Rev. St., 6 F. S. A. 290
(U. S. Comp. St. 1901, p. 1389). *Shorman v. Eakin,* 47
Ark. 351, 1 S. W. 559; *Clark v. Bayley,* 5 Or. 343. And
where an agreement was made by a son to secure a title
from the government for his father's use and benefit, the
father could not sustain a bill in equity to impress a
trust on the homestead entry which had been patented
to his son.—*Moore v. Moore,* 130 Cal. 110, 62 Pac. 294,
80 Am. St. Rep. 78. The title acquired by the heirs of
Delaware Peacock, by patent from the government, is
founded upon no privity with the transaction between
him and said Kelley; and, whatever this latter transaction may have been, it cannot affect the government
grant to said heirs, and fasten upon it a resulting trust
as against them. The simple statement of the proposition sufficiently refutes complainant's contention in
this regard. The government grant to Emma and Chaldee Peacock vested in them a perfect title to the homestead tract; and it results that Ophelia Peacock, their
mother, never had any interest therein, and hence complainant has shown no right thereto, either legal or
equitable.

We agree with the chancellor, also, that the respondents have shown that they are bona fide purchasers for
value, without any notice whatever of the equitable claim

of Ophelia Peacock; and, whether or not she might have enforced a resulting trust against her husband or his heirs, she cannot do so against these respondents.— *Walker v. Elledge,* 65 Ala. 51; *Dixon v. Brown,* 53 Ala. 428.

Nor would the fact of her joint occupancy of the land with her two children, after her husband's death, without openly asserting her alleged equity against them, be at all suggestive of such a claim on her part, since it was perfectly natural and consistent with the legal title and possessory rights of her children, who were living with her.—*Traun v. Keiffer,* 31 Ala. 136, 145.

We are satisfied the decree of the chancellor is correct on the facts shown, and it is therefore affirmed.

Affirmed.

DOWDELL, C. J., and ANDERSON and SAYRE, JJ., concur.

Powell *v.* Union Bank & Trust Co.

Bill for Partition.

(Decided June 29, 1911. 56 South. 123.)

1. *Insane Persons; Guardian; Appointment; Collateral Attack.*—The fact that the jury which pronounced a person insane was composed of ten instead of twelve persons, was an irregularity merely, which would not make the appointment of the guardian void, it not being necessary that the records of the probate court show such facts; hence, that question cannot be raised on collateral attack by a stranger to the proceedings, so as to question the authority of the guardian to maintain a bill for patition. Such questions should be raised by appeal or in direct proceedings.

2. *Judgment; Collateral Attack; Probate Court.*—Where the jurisdiction of the probate court had attached and it had proceeded to exercise that jurisdiction, irregularities in the subsequent proceedings will not subject the decree rendered to collateral attack; this rule being extended to a failure to make interested persons parties or to notify necessary parties.

APPEAL from Montgomery City Court.

Heard before Hon. GASTON GUNTER.

Bill by the Union Bank & Trust Company as guardian of Virginia Powell, against Bolling R. Powell, and others, for the sale of certain lands for partition. From a decree for complainant the respondent named above appeals. Affirmed.

DANIEL W. TROY, and EDWARD S. WATTS, for appellant. The appointment of a guardian without inquisition is void.—*Moody v. Bibb,* 50 Ala. 248. The jury holding the inquisition was not in accordance with the statute, and the judgment rendered was not valid.— Sections 2258-9, Code 1907. An infant cannot be bound by the admissions of his guardian ad litem, unless they are for his benefit, and this rule applies to insane persons as well.—15 A. & E. Enc. of Law, 12; 24 Cyc. 132; *Bell v. The State,* 44 Ala. 393.

JAMES F. PARRISH, for appellee. The right of trial by jury is purely statutory, and the failure to empanel a jury of twelve was but a mere irregularity.—*Reynolds v. Reynolds,* 11 Ala. 1023; *Willis v. Willis,* 9 Ala. 330; 24 Cyc. 104. While there are no cases in point in Alabama, the court's attention is directed to the following cases: —*Nealy v. Shepherd,* 190 Ill. 637; *State v. Kilborn,* 68 Minn. 320. The guardian ad litem is a full representative of the rights and interests for the particular case in which he is appointed.—23 Cyc. 661. The only way an insane person can be served is that prescribed by statute. —Sec. 5313, Code 1907. If the matters complained of may be considered as irregularities, they should have been raised by appeal, or a direct proceeding should be had to annul the judgment. It was not subject to this collateral attack.—*Simmons v. Craft,* 118 Ala. 625.

MAYFIELD, J.—As stated in brief of counsel for appellant, "the sole question in this case is whether or not the proceedings by which the Union Bank & Trust Company claims to have become the guardian of Virginia Powell were void." It is admitted by the appellant that, if such proceedings were regular, the bill is well filed and the injunction properly granted.

The fact that the jury that made the inquisition and rendered the verdict pronouncing Virginia Powell insane was composed of 10, instead of 12, persons, was a mere irregularity in the proceedings, and did not render the appointment of a guardian by the court absolutely void. Such question cannot be raised on collateral attack, for the purpose of denying or disputing the authority of the guardian so appointed to maintain or defend an action by or against such ward. The validity of the appointment and the authority of such guardian to represent the ward cannot be raised by a stranger to the proceedings in the probate court, and certainly not by a stranger to the proceedings in another and different court, and in a collateral proceeding on which the question arises only incidentally, as in this case.

If the appointment of such guardian and the proceedings of the probate court for that purpose are voidable, the matter should be corrected by appeal, or by a proceeding, instituted in that, or the chancery court, to rectify the same, or reversed and avoided in a direct proceeding for such purpose. Otherwise the proceeding will be still standing in the probate court, and, so far as concerns the appointment or the grant of letters of guardianship, will be perfectly valid, though liable, on collateral attack, to be by some courts pronounced voidable or void, and by others valid—valid for some purposes, and void or voidable for others. It is not at all necessary that the records in the probate court shall disclose that the inquiry was made by a jury of 10 persons, instead of 12. It is a mere incident, in that particular case, that such fact appears of record in the probate court, which record, without this irregularity, affirmatively and conclusively shows that the probate court acquired jurisdiction for the purpose of appointing a guardian, and that a jury of 12 persons was ordered and summoned, as directed by the statute; that the jury impaneled and sworn made the inquiry and returned a verdict in all respects according to law, with the exception that the parties consented to a trial by a jury of 10. And this recital of an unnecessary fact touching the organization of the jury, being matter which could be stricken without affecting the validity of the proceeding, cannot render it void on its face.

It has been ruled frequently and repeatedly by this court that, in all proceedings in the probate court where it is made to appear that the jurisdiction of the court has attached, and that the court has proceeded in the exercise of that jurisdiction, no irregularity in the subsequent proceedings can avail to avoid or annul the decree rendered, on collateral attack. This rule has been so extended that even the failure to make interested persons parties to the proceedings, or the failure to notify necessary parties, will not be held to render void the decree of the probate court on collateral attack-

It was held by this court, in the case of *Craft v. Simon,* 118 Ala. 635, 24 South. 380, that mere irregularities and errors in the appointment of guardian for insane persons, must be corrected by appeal, certiorari, or other direct proceeding; and that if the probate court acquires jurisdiction to proceed, and the error or irregularity occurs thereafter, the proceedings cannot be assailed on account thereof by collateral attack.

We therefore conclude that the court properly overruled the demurrer to the bill.

Affirmed.

SIMPSON, ANDERSON, MCCLELLAN, and SOMERVILLE, JJ., concur.

Foley, *et al. v.* Brock.

Bill for Partition.

(Decided June 29, 1911.   56 South. 207.)

1. *Partition; Pleading; Sufficiency.*—A bill for partition of land which describes the land, states the interest of each party and alleges that it could not be equitably divided between them, and prays for a division, states a case for relief by sale for division.

2. *Same; Incumbent Property.*—Where six tenants in common owned land over which a railroad right of way passed, and the railroad company had not acquired the rights of two of the tenants, the land should be sold, which was not encumbered by the right of way, and the proceeds distributed, and the two tenants whose interest was not acquired by the railroad should be left to obtain such relief as they could against the railroad.

APPEAL from Jefferson Chancery Court.

Heard before Hon. A. H. BENNERS.

Bill by D. P. Brock against Sam Foley and others for partition of land.   From a judgment overruling a demurrer respondents appeal.   Affirmed.

GASTON & PETTUS, for appellant.   The bill was subject to the demurrers interposed for the reason that the railroad company is a joint owner or tenant in common of the land, under the averments of the bill.

SUMTER LEA, and F. D. NABORS, for appellee.   The bill was sufficient under the statute.—Section 5205, Code 1907.

SAYRE, J.—This is a bill for sale for division among tenants in common. The bill is defective in respect to formalities which it would have been better to observe, but it states a case for relief. It avers that complainant and five others own the land in equal undivided parts. The further averment is that the Atlanta, Birmingham & Atlantic Railroad Company owns an easement of way across the land, "subject to the one-sixth interest" of each of two named defendants. We take this averment to mean that the railroad company has never acquired its right of way by conveyance from or condemnation proceedings against the two named tenants in common. It seems to have been for this reason that the railroad company is made a party defendant along with the five who own in common with the complainant. The defendant Foley, against whom the railroad company must be taken to have secured its right of way, alone complains on this appeal from the chancellor's decree overruling a demurrer to the bill, and the case as affecting his interest alone has been considered.

The bill or petition describes the land, shows the interest of each party, avers that the land cannot be equitably divided among the owners, and prays for a sale for division. We are of the opinion that, as for any objection here urged against the bill, it sufficiently states a case for relief by a sale for division.—*Edwards v. Edwards,* 142 Ala. 267, 39 South. 82; *Berry Lumber Co. v. Garner,* 142 Ala. 488, 38 South. 243. No reason is perceived why so much of the land as remains after carving out that part which is incumbered by the right of way should not be sold for division, leaving the two owners in common, as against whom the easement has not been established, to such remedy as they may have against the railroad company for the recovery of their undivided interest in the land covered by the easement. In that the other cotenants have no interest.

The decree of the chancellor will be affirmed.

Affirmed.

SIMPSON, McCLELLAN and MAYFIELD, JJ., concur.

Carroll v. Draughon.

Bill for Restitution and for an Accounting.

(Decided June 29, 1911. 56 South. 209.)

1. *Restitution; Appeal; Reversion.*—One who pays money or is dispossessed under a judgment afterwards reversed on appeal, is entitled to restitution as a general thing.

2. *Same; Enforcement.*—The right to restitution, upon reversal of the judgment under which money was paid, or possession taken, may be enforced by provision in the judgment on appeal, or by motion in the trial court.

3. *Same; Restitution.*—Where it appears that it was finally determined in another suit that a person had no interest in the land, such person was not entitled to restitution of land of which he was dispossed, under a sale in partition, although the decree was reversed and the suit dismissed on appeal.

APPEAL from Geneva Chancery Court.

Heard before Hon. L. D. GARDNER.

Bill by D. S. Carroll, as administrator, against J. W. Draughon for restitution, and for an accounting for rents and profits. From a decree dismissing the bill complainant appeals. Affirmed.

R. H. WALKER, for appellant. The application to have the land set apart to the widow as a homestead does not estop her or her vendee to seek the redress here sought.—*Faircloth et al. v. Carroll*, 137 Ala. 243. She was left in possession in her own right, and by no act of the husband and hence, her possession was notice of her claim.—*McLeod v. Bishop*, 110 Ala. 645. The

[Carroll v. Draughon.]

several declarations of her husband and herself while
in possession were admissible in evidence.—*Goodbar v.
Daniel*, 88 Ala. 583; *Dyces' Case*, 88 Ala. 225. It was
the homestead, and hence not subject to alienation.—
McGuire v. Van Pelt, 55 Ala. 344. The action taken by
the wife in the probate court cannot affect her title or
claim.—*Tyler v. Jewett*, 82 Ala. 93; *Winston v. Hodges*,
102 Ala. 304; *Marks v. Wilson*, 115 Ala. 563.

W. O. MULKEY, for appellee. There is no specific
prayer to declare or establish a resulting trust, nor is
there prayer for general relief. Hence, that relief cannot be granted.—*Patterson v. Bragg*, 95 Ala. 58; 58
Ala. 221; 5 Port. 9; Sec. 3094, Code 1907. Under the
revised statute, the alleged sale by Kelly was void and
conferred no rights whatever on the purchaser, and
could not have the effect of stamping the land with any
trust in favor of the person furnishing the money for
that purpose.—*Cox v. Donnelly*, 34 Ark. 762. Under
the facts in this case, if the money was furnished by
the wife, the presumption is that it was furnished as
an advancement, and no presumption of trust arises.—
Hatton v. Landman, 28 Ala. 135; *Long v King*, 117 Ala.
423. The idea of a trust is barred by the doctrine of
laches and the statute of limitation.—*Bracken v. Newman*, 121 Ala. 311; *Martin v. Kelly*, 132 Ala. 201. No
knowledge on the part of the purchaser of the existence
of the trust is shown, and it is shown that they paid
value for the land.—*Walker v. Elledge*, 65 Ala. 51; 71
Ala. 220. There is no reason why the administrator of
Mrs. Carroll should be restored to the possession of the
land involved in this suit as the administrator is not
shown to have been deprived of anything to be restored.
—3 Cyc. 462; *Ex parte Weldon*, 148 Ala. 430; *Crocker
v. Clemmons*, 29 Ala. 296.

SOMERVILLE, J.—In a former proceeding in the chancery court at Geneva, the respondents herein procured a sale of certain land for division among tenants in common, they claiming a one-third interest, and alleging that the respondents therein—Ophelia Carroll and her minor child, Chaldee Peacock—owned the other two-thirds. At this sale respondents herein purchased said land, received a deed, and were put in possession under a writ issued by said court, ousting therefrom said Ophelia Carroll and Chaldee Peacock. These two parties had in the meantime appealed from the chancery decree under which said sale was had, but without superseding same, and the Supreme Court reversed said decree and dismissed the bill of complaint without prejudice. See *Carroll v. Fulton,* 41 South. 741. Shortly afterwards the complainants in that suit acquired by purchase the interest of Chaldee Peacock. After said reversal by the Supreme Court, Ophelia Carroll died, and, claiming title to the land by deed from her, D. S. Carroll, her surviving husband, filed his bill against these respondents for restitution to possession and an accounting for mesne profits, including also a prayer to set aside said partition sale. On demurrer the bill was held to show no right to relief, and on appeal this ruling was affirmed. See *Carroll v. Draughon,* 154 Ala. 430, 45 South. 919. Said Carroll, having qualified as administrator of his said wife's estate, now files the present bill, as such administrator, against the same respondent, praying that restitution of said land be made to the estate of Ophelia Carroll, through himself as administrator, and that an account be taken and decree rendered against respondents for rents, profits, and waste. Simultaneously he filed a bill in his own right against these same respondents setting up an alleged title in himself through his said wife, and seeking

[Carroll v. Draughon.]

to quiet his title as against the claim of these respondents. The chancellor heard and determined the latter cause first, and rendered a final decree that complainant was not entitled to relief, and that his bill be dismissed. On appeal to this court, the decree of the chancellor has been affirmed. See *Carroll v. Draughon et al. Infra* 56 South. 207. He then proceeded to hear the instant cause; and, holding that restitution, though usually a matter of right upon the reversal of a judgment, may in exceptional cases be refused, rendered a final decree denying the relief prayed for, and dismissing the bill of complaint.

It must be regarded as the settled law of this state that a party who pays money, or is dispossessed of property by process on a judgment or decree afterwards reversed on appeal is in general entitled as of right to restitution of the money paid or the property taken, so as to be placed in statu quo with respect to his rights and advantages previous to the erroneous judgment.— *Marks v. Cowles*, 61 Ala. 299; *Ex parte Walter Bros.*, 89 Ala. 237, 7 South. 400, 18 Am. St. Rep. 103; *Florence C. & I. Co. v. Louisville Banking Co.*, 138 Ala. 588, 36 South. 456, 100 Am. St. Rep. 50; *Lehman-Durr Co. v. Folmar*, 166 Ala. 325, 51 South. 954.

The right may be enforced by the incorporation of an appropriate order in the judgment or decree of reversal. —*Marks v. Cowles, supra; Lehman-Durr Co. v. Folmar, supra;* or summarily by motion in the trial court (*Ex parte Walker Bros., supra; Cowden v. London, etc., Bank*, 96 Am. St. Rep. 142, note); or by supplemental bill of review, if in equity.—*McCall v. McCurdy*, 69 Ala. 71; or, if by a distinct, independent action *Haebler v. Myers*, 132 N. Y. 363, 30 N. E. 963, 15 L. R. A. 588, 28 Am. St. Rep. 589; *Cowdery v. London, etc., Bank, supra*, 96 Am. St. Rep., note p. 143. As the result, apparently, of these different modes of securing restitutional relief, conflicting views have found their way into the decisions of this court as to the nature of the right of restitution—that is, whether it is an absolute right enforceable in every case as a matter of course, or whether considerations of equity or practical inconvenience may in particular cases justify its denial.

In the case of *Duncan v. Ware's Ex'rs*, 5 Stew. & P. 119, 24 Am. Dec. 772, it was said: "By a judgment which was irregular, and for that reason reversed, the amount of a debt, justly due, was recovered and paid to the decedent. In this situation he was not authorized to renew (prosecute?) his suit; his debt was paid, and if Lawrence & Co. were permitted to recover against him, would it not place him in a worse situation than if the money had not been collected? He must wait until they recover from him, before he sues them; or, without suit, he must refund to them money to which he is justly entitled, and which they owe him, that he may be authorized to institute a suit against them, and recover the same money back again. This cannot be tolerated. If an irregular judgment has been obtained, and the money recovered, for a debt justly due, proof that the debt was due affords a good defense in an action of assumpsit brought to recover the money back."

This decision was afterwards followed or approved in *Dupuy v. Roebuck*, 7 Ala. 484; *Stewart v. Conner*, 9 Ala. 803; *Ewing v. Peck*, 26 Ala. 413; *Crocker v. Clements' Adm'r*, 23 Ala. 307—all of which were actions in general assumpsit. These cases were seemingly criticized in *Florence C. & I. Co. v. Louisville Banking Co.*, 138 Ala. 592, 36 South. 456, 100 Am. St. Rep. 50, as being inconsistent with other authorities, but were not overruled.

In *Traun v. Keiffer*, 31 Ala. 136, Keiffer had recovered a judgment on verdict in detinue for eight slaves, and had coerced satisfaction under process issued thereon, receiving from the defendant four slaves and the alternate value of the others in money. The judgment was afterwards reversed and the cause remanded, and, when the case was again called for trial, the defendant moved the court that the plaintiff be required, before the trial proceeded, to place him in statu quo by refunding the money and restoring the slaves to him, or at least to bring them into court pending the suit. The motion was overruled, and on appeal this court said: "The defendant's motion * * * was properly overruled. * * * Here the defendant has obtained a reversal of the judgment, and he may fully protect himself by pleading in an appropriate manner the facts upon which his motion is predicated. If the property and money belong to the plaintiff, it would be extremely unjust to compel the restoration of them to the wrongful possession of the defendant. Whether they belong to the plaintiff or defendant can only be judicially ascertained upon the trial of the case." No authorities are cited, and the controlling factor undoubtedly was that the motion for restitution was not made until the case was called for trial, and was about to be determined on its merits.

In *Ex parte Walter Brothers*, 89 Ala. 237, 7 South. 400, 18 Am. St. Rep. 103, the most extreme view is entertained and declared, the court saying per McClellan, J.: "We can conceive of no case in which a party, who pays money on a decree which is subsequently reversed, is not entitled to have restitution of what he had paid, and to be thus reinstated in the position and to all the rights he had prior to the erroneous decree. * * * He (the plaintiff) had no right to the money involved in the litigation, in contemplation of law, until there should be a correct determination of the matters involved in dispute, however clear his rights may have been in point of fact. * * * We entertain no doubt, therefore, of the absolute right to have restitution made on the one hand, and the absolute correlative duty to make restitution on the other, wholly regardless of considerations looking to the final equities of the parties. * * * The facts which constitute the only predicate for such an order (of restitution)—a decree, payment under it, and its reversal—are a part of the cause itself. There can be no mistake or dispute about them. On them the order for restitution goes as a matter of course. It does not involve the exercise of judicial functions. There is no remedy for the refusal to grant the order, except mandamus." The writ was granted to compel the chancellor to enter the appropriate order, but no authorities are cited or discussed.

In *Florence C. & I. Co. v. Louisville Banking Co.*, 138 Ala. 588, 36 South. 456, 100 Am. St. Rep. 50, the plaintiff had paid off a judgment recovered against him which was afterwards reversed on appeal; and, after remandment of the cause, the defendant—then plaintiff—dismissed the suit. In assumpsit to recover back the money so paid, this court, per Sharpe, J., after disapproving the doctrine of *Duncan v. Ware's Ex'rs,* and other like cases, supra, at least partially approved the rule of "absolute right" declared in *Ex parte Walter Bros.*, and said: "We adopt this latter expression as applicable to this case, and accordingly hold that the existence of the debt claimed by Fields in the suit he dismissed is not a defense to this suit, and this without regard to the merit of the suit."

But in *Ex parte Wellden*, 148 Ala. 429, 42 South. 632, the case of *Traun v. Keiffer, supra,* is seemingly approved, and under the peculiar conditions shown—the suit being statutory detinue in which the defendant was protected against loss by the plaintiff's bond, and the mule sued for and taken having been sold by plaintiff to a third party—it was held that the petitioner did not show a clear legal right to the relief prayed for, and mandamus to the circuit judge was denied. After recognizing the general rule as expounded in previous cases, the court, per Denson, J., said: "In applying the doctrine, consideration must be given to the nature of the action in which the judgment reversed was rendered, the facts of the case, and the forum and procedure resorted to, to effectuate the right." This statement seems to be in accord with the rule announced in *McCall v. McCurdy*, 69 Ala. 70: "The restoration of parties to the plight and condition in which they were, at and prior to the rendition of an erroneous judgment or decree, and the restitution of all advantages the party obtaining it may have acquired by its enforcement, upon reversal, it is the spirit and policy of the law to promote and compel, when there are no facts or circumstances which may render restitution inequitable."

In the case of *Carroll v. Draughon*, 154 Ala. 430, 45 South. 919, heretofore referred to, the same Carroll now asking for restitution as the representative of his deceased wife's estate, there sought restitution as her successor in estate. And, although the bill showed that Ophelia Carroll had been ejected from these same premises by process issued under a reversed decree (the circumstances being identical with the instant case), it was ruled, on demurrer to the bill, that it showed no right to relief because, on its own showing, complainant's wife, Ophelia Carroll, had but a life estate in the land; and, she being dead, complainant's interest ceased upon her death. The effect of this decision, as we construe it, is to recognize another exception to the rule of "absolute right."

We have thus fully, and perhaps tediously, reviewed the Alabama cases dealing with the right of restitution, not only to show the general state of the law, but more especially to illustrate the distinguishing features of the present case.

Here, before this petition was heard, the rights of the parties, and necessarily also of complainant's intestate, had been fully and distinctly adjudicated adversely to her and to complainant's claim, the decision being that Ophelia Carroll did not own any interest in the land. If possession of the land had been restored to complainant, with a decree for rents and profits, respondents could have immediately recovered them back in a separate action or actions. Such judicial juggling with the rights of parties would discredit the science of jurisprudence, and, indeed, would violate an ancient and salutary maxim of the law.—"Circuitus est evitandus."

We are of the opinion that the chancellor did not err in denying restitution to the complainant in this cause; and we further hold that the case of *Ex parte Walter Bros.*, 89 Ala. 237, 7 South. 400, 18 Am. St. Rep. 103, in so far as it declares that the right of restitution is absolute and invariable, and follows as of course in every case where there is a judgment, satisfaction, and reversal—is not in harmony with the general current of our decisions, and must in this respect, and to this extent, be overruled.

The decree of the chancery court is therefore affirmed.

Affirmed. All the Justices concur.

Roanoke Guano Co. *v.* Saunders.

Bill to Enjoin Action at Law and to Determine Damages.

(Decided June 29, 1911. 56 South. 198.)

1. *Equity; Jurisdiction; Multiplicity of Suits.*—To give equity jurisdiction on the ground of preventing a multiplicity of suits, a community of interest in the subject matter of the several actions is necessary; community of interest in the question at law and facts involved in the several actions not being enough.

2. *Injunction; Restraining Action.*—In a bill by one maintaining a guano factory, sulphuric fumes from which injure the lands owned separately, to enjoin their separate actions for damages, and have the damages assessed and determined in one suit is not given equity by the additional prayer that if the factory be found to be a nuisance, it be abated; for, while those injured could have maintained a joint bill to abate the nuisance, they could not have recovered damages therein, and they and not the wrong doer, have the right to elect whether they will maintain such a suit or separately sue for damages.

APPEAL from Randolph Chancery Court.

Heard before Hon. W. W. WHITESIDE.

Bill by the Roanoke Guano Company against Hattie Saunders and others, to enjoin several actions at law, and to ascertain and determine the damage suffered by respondents. From a decree by respondents complainants appeal. Affirmed.

LACKEY & BRIDGES, for appellant. Every question presented by the demurrers from 1 to 11 inclusive, is fully answered by the opinion in the case of *Southern Steel Co. v. Hopkins,* 47 South. 274; *Cleveland v. Ins. Co.,* 151 Ala. 191; *Morgan v. Morgan,* 3 Stew. 383; *Kennedy's Heirs v. Kennedy,* 2 Ala. 571; 45 South. 861; 44 South. 161; Pom. Eq. secs. 245-274. Equity has jurisdiction also to prevent a multiplicity of suits where there is a single party on each side of the case, and also of liability to several suits growing out of the same transaction or subject matter between the same parties. —*Whaley v. Wilson*, 112 Ala. 627. If liable in suits already filed, then complainant will be liable for successive actions of damages by each of the plaintiffs in the suits at law.—*C. of Ga. v. Wyndham*, 126 Ala. 552; *S. & N. v. McLendon*, 63 Ala. 266; *Sloss- S. S. & I. Co. v. Mitchum*, 49 South. 851. It constituted no infringement of the constitutional right of trial by jury.—*Cook v. Schmide*, 100 Ala. 582; *Southern Steel Co. v. Hopkins, supra.*

BARNES & DENSON, and N. D. DENSON, for appellee. The court properly sustained the demurrers to the bill. A demurrer is not an admission of facts not pleaded. or of statements of legal conclusion.—*Sheffield Ry. v. Rand*, 83 Ala. 294; *Manning v. Pippin*, 86 Ala. 357. Community of interest in the subject matter is absolutely necessary in order for equity to take jurisdiction on the ground of multiplicity of suits.—*Turner v. City of Mobile*, 135 Ala. 73; *Hale v. Allison*, 188 U. S. 56; L. R. A. 6 0; 101 Ill. App. 523. This doctrine rests upon the inadequacy of a legal remedy.—140 Fed. 666. A bill in the alternative is no stronger than the weakest of its alternatives.—75 Ala. 363; *David v. Shepherd*, 40 Ala. 587.

MAYFIELD, J.—The appellant owns and operates a fertilizer factory, and uses large quantities of sulphuric acid in manufacturing such fertilizers. The natural and necessary result of the use of these acids is that sulphuric fumes and vapors in large quantities are emitted from the factory, and these gases and vapors are noxious and offensive to the inhabitants of the immediate vicinity, and are more or less injurious, if not destructive, to vegetable life near the said plant.

The appellees, each of whom was the owner of land near the appellant's factory, brought actions in the circuit court of Randolph county, to recover damages for injury to their crops and timber growing upon their lands near the appellant's factory. Thereupon the appellant filed this bill in the chancery court of Randolph county, to enjoin the actions at law and to have the damages of the several plaintiffs assessed and determined in one suit. A temporary injunction was issued, to this effect, upon the filing of the bill. The respondents then demurred to the bill, assigning many grounds thereto, among them, one for want of equity and one for multifariousness. Upon the hearing of the demurrer, it was sustained. Thereupon the complainant amended its bill by making the allegations fuller, and adding to the prayer that, if on final hearing it should be decreed that complainant's plant was a public nuisance, it should be abated. To the amended bill, the respondents again interposed demurrer, assigning the same grounds which were assigned to the original bill, which demurrer was sustained, the bill dismissed, and the temporary injunction dissolved, and from that decree this appeal is prosecuted by the complainant. It was attempted to rest the equity of the bill upon two grounds of equity jurisdiction; first, to prevent and enjoin a multiplicity of suits, and, second, to abate a nuisance.

It has been stated by this court that it has never undertaken to define the jurisdiction of equity to prevent a multiplicity of suits, nor even to lay down the general principles governing the several categories of cases in which that jurisdiction may be invoked, but this court has evinced an inclination toward confining this jurisdiction to a narrow field, in order to conserve and preserve the right of trial by jury.—*Turner v. Mobile*, 135 Ala. 124, 33 South.. 132, and cases there cited. Bills of this character are called bills in the nature of bills of peace, to quiet the rights of parties and to put an end to further litigation.

It was said by this court, in the case of *Turner v. Mobile, supra*, that equity will not take jurisdiction to prevent a multiplicity of suits in order to lessen its own labors or those of other courts; that the court itself has no equity, but that equity must reside in the party filing the bill. It has been said by other courts that to avoid a multiplicity of suits is a ground of equity jurisdiction, but that multiplicity of suits does not mean multitude of suits. The mere fact that many persons have similar or like independent rights or causes of action does not confer the right to invoke equity jurisdiction. Equity has no power to amalgamate several independent legal rights so as to constitute but one equitable right, and thereby allow all to join in equity, on the ground of preventing a multiplicity of suits. The rule is different from that governing cases in which one party is subjected to, or threatened with, a multitude of vexatious actions at law, or is threatened with numerous and continued wrongs, so that many and repeated actions will be necessary; in such cases the multitude of the possible actions at law is, of itself, sufficient to give him the right to redress such wrongs, and to create the equity jurisdiction of multiplicity of suits.

Prior to the publication of Mr. Pomeroy's inestimable work on Equity Jurisprudence, it was thought to be a requisite to the equity of a bill which rested solely upon the ground of preventing or enjoining a multiplicity of actions at law that there should be a mutuality among the many complainants or defendants, as the case might be, as to the subject-matter of the suit; that a mere mutuality as to the facts and the law, in the many cases, was not sufficient. In this work, Mr. Pom-

eroy, after stating the general rule theretofore announced in the text-books on the subject, and in many, if not
all of the adjudicated cases, that there must be a mutuality of title to, or a community of interest in, the subject-matter involved, proceeded to state another rule,
viz., that there is a class of cases in which a mere community of interests in the questions of law and of fact
involved in the general controversy is sufficient to warrant the interposition of equity to settle, in one suit,
the several controversies.

Mr. Pomeroy was first taken to task as to the correctness of this proposition by Chief Justice Campbell, of
the Supreme Court of Mississippi, in *Tribette's Case,*
70 Miss. 182, 12 South. 32, 19 L. R. A. 660, 35 Am. St.
Rep. 642, wherein a great number of property owners
had brought suit against the Illinois Central Railroad
Company, to recover damages for destruction of their
property by fire emitted from that company's locomo-
tives, and wherein the railroad company had filed its
bill to enjoin the many actions and to settle the entire
controversy, as to liability vel non, and the extent of
the damages to the several plaintiffs, in one suit. The
equity of the bill was denied by Chief Justice Campbell, who held that the community of interest in the
facts and the law involved was not sufficient.—1 Pom.
255-269.

This text was again criticised and declared unsound
by this court, in the case of *Turner v. Mobile*. 135 Ala
73, 33 South. 132, in which it was said that the decisions
cited by Mr. Pomeroy did not sustain the proposition
announced in the text; that mere community of interest
in questions of law and of fact was sufficient. These
two opinions—one by McClellan, Chief Justice of Alabama, and the other by Campbell, Chief Justice of Mississippi—are certainly among the leading and best-con-

sidered cases, on the subject of the equity of a bill to prevent a multiplicity of suits, appearing in the reports since Mr. Pomeroy's publication on Equity Jurisprudence.

Unfortunately, however, the text announced by Mr. Pomeroy has been followed in a great number of adjudicated cases, and probably in the majority of the cases in which the exact proposition involved has been passed upon. Among such cases are those of *Southern Steel Co. v. Hopkins,* 157 Ala. 175, 47 South. 274, 20 L. R. A. (N. S.) 848, 131 Am. St. Rep. 20, and *Whitlock v. Yazoo County,* from the Supreme Court of Mississippi, reported in 91 Miss. 779, 45 South. 861. The last two cases clearly support the text announced by Mr. Pomeroy, which was declared unsound by the Supreme Court of Mississippi, in *Tribette's Case,* and by this court in *Turner's Case.* But the decision by the Supreme Court of Mississippi did not overrule its pioneer case of Tribette nor those which cite it or refer to it; neither did this court in *Hopkins' Case,* overrule *Turner's Case;* but Chief Justice Tyson, who wrote the opinion, did say that there are expressions in the opinion of McClellan, C. J., in *Turner's Case,* that are in conflict with what was decided in *Hopkins' Case,* notwithstanding that there are others which support the conclusion in the *Hopkins Case.* He then quotes from the opinion in *Turner's Case,* and concludes by saying that the questions in *Hopkins' Case* comes directly within the fourth class, as defined by Mr. Pomeroy and Judge McClellan. See 1 Pom. Eq. Jur. 255-269. It appears, therefore, that there was no intention on the part of the writer, nor on that of the court, in the *Hopkins Case,* to overrule the *Turner Case;* but, on the other hand, that the court considered the *Turner Case,* or a part thereof, as authority for the decision in the *Hopkins Case.*   .

After a careful review and comparison of these two cases, we are of the opinion that they conflict. While, of course, they are distinguishable in many respects, yet they are in direct conflict as to the fundamental proposition that a bill to prevent a multiplicity of suits contains no equity, if the parties have a community of interest only in the question of the fact and of law involved, and none in the subject-matter. In other words, the *Turner Case* holds that a community of interest in the subject-matter of the several actions is necessary to give equity jurisdiction, when it is based solely upon the ground of preventing a multiplicity of suits, and that community of interest in the questions of law and of fact involved in the several actions alone is not sufficient; whereas, in *Hopkins' Case,* the exact converse of this proposition is held. In fact, the sole ground of equity cognizance in the *Hopkins Case* was rested upon the community of interest in the questions of fact and of law involved in the 110 suits brought against the complainant in courts of law. There was confessedly and concededly no community of interest in the subject-matter of any two of such actions at law, much less among all. It was for this very reason that the bills in the *Turner Case* and the *Tribette Case,* 70 Miss. 182, 12 South. 32, 19 L. R. A. 660, 35 Am. St. Rep. 642, were held to be without equity. Therefore, after a careful consideration of these two cases, and of the decisions of this court upon this question, as to the necessity of showing mutuality and community of interest in the subject-matter involved, to give equity jurisdiction, we are of the opinion that the two cases are in conflict; that the case of *Turner v. Mobile* announces the correct rule, while that announced in *Hopkins' Case* is not sound; and that the latter case should be, and it is, overruled.

As we find the decisions of this court and those of the Mississippi court to be in direct conflict as to this question, and find also like conflict among the decisions of other courts, it may not be out of place to state, as briefly as possible, the reasons which induce us to over-rule the *Hopkins Case*. In the first place, the reason and logic, as well as the authorities cited by Chief Justice Campbell in *Tribette's Case,* and those by Chief Justice McClellan, in *Turner's Case,* we have found to be unanswerable. We cannot hope to add to the force of the logic or the reasoning of either of these opinions, but will attempt to review some of the decisions relied upon therein, holding to different views from those expressed in the *Turner* and *Tribette Cases, supra.* We have examined all the cases cited in the opinion in the *Hopkins Case* as being in support of the conclusion therein announced, and in our opinion they do not support it. In nearly all of the cases cited, in which the equity of the bill was supported, the decision rested upon an equity independent of that of multiplicity of suits; and while the bills in those cases were held to contain equity, it was not that alone of preventing a multiplicity of suits. The decision in the case of *Crawford v. Mobile Railroad Co.,* 83 Miss. 708, 36 South. 82, 102 Am. St. Rep. 476, was rested upon the independent equity of the cancellation of an instrument which was obtained by fraud. Likewise the decision in the case of *Sheffield Waterworks v. Yoemans,* L. R. 2 App. Cas. 8, cited and strongly relied upon in the *Hopkins Case,* was based upon an independent equity, to wit, the cancellation of instruments which had been issued to the representatives of 7,315 persons who lost their lives, or who had property injured, and were prosecuting claims against the waterworks company on account of a burst pipe. The actions in that case were not in tort, to recover damages for the negligence of the waterworks company, but were brought upon the certificates which had been issued to the persons injured, or their representatives, and the bill sought to have these certificates canceled because issued or obtained through fraud; consequently cancellation of the instruments and fraud afforded sufficient equity to the bills in those cases; and only the question of multifariousness was involved, and not the question whether the jurisdiction of the court depended upon the equity of preventing a multiplicity of suits.

The writer of the opinion in the *Hopkins Case* failed to distinguish between cases in which the sole ground of equity jurisdiction depended upon the question of preventing a multiplicity of suits, and those cases which rest upon some other independent equity. The real question involved is multifariousness because of the number of parties, complainants or respondents. In most all the cases cited in the opinion in *Hopkins' Case* the real question involved was multifariousness, and not equitable interference to prevent or enjoin a multiplicity of actions at law. If a bill in a given case rests firmly upon some independent equity, such as the cancellation of instruments, accounting, discovery, or the like, then a community of title or of right or interest in the subject-matter is not requisite to the maintenance of such a bill; but in such case as community of interest in the questions of law and of fact in controversy among the several defendants may save the bill from being objectionable on account of multifariousness, though it does not follow that such a bill would contain equity solely on account of the community of interest in the question of law or fact, and without any community of interest in the subject-matter among the several defendants.

We have found but few cases which support the doctrine announced in the *Hopkins Case,* among which may be mentioned that of *Whitlock v. Yazoo*, 91 Miss. 779, 45 South. 861, as being probably the nearest in point. So far as appears from the report of that case, there was no independent equity upon which to rest the bill, yet it was upheld as containing equity; for, while there was no community of interest in the subject-matter, there was a community of interest in the facts and the law involved. The decision in that case was written by Chief Justice Whitfield, of the Supreme Court of Mississippi, and while it is very brief, and does not mention or refer to to *Tribette Case*, it is directly opposed to the holding in that case.

. It has been pointed out by the annotators, in notes to the report of the *Hopkins Case*, 157 Ala. 175, 47 South. 274, 20 L. R. A. (N. S.) 848, 131 Am. St. Rep. 20, that the cases and authorities cited by this court as supporting the conclusion reached are inapt, and that some of them announce the opposite conclusion. We therefore refer to these notes, which we think conclusively show the error of our former holding in the *Hopkins Case*, and establish the correctness of the holding in the *Turner* and *Tribette Cases, supra*.

While we have examined many cases on this vexed and disputed question, we have not examined all; but we have reached the conclusion that the principles announced in the *Turner* and *Tribette Cases* are correct, and should be adhered to by this court. While it is true that the facts and the principles of law involved in the *Hopkins Case* are different, to some extent, both in kind and degree, from those involved in the *Turner* and *Tribette Cases,* and also different from the facts and the law involved in the case now under consideration, we are convinced that the decision in the *Turner Case* was largely, if not wholly, based upon the doctrine that equity has no jurisdiction to prevent a multiplicity of

suits, in the absence of some community or mutuality
of interest in the subject-matter involved, and when
there is no other independent equity upon which the
bill can rest. We have also reached the conclusion that
many of the cases cited in the text and in the opinions
of the adjudicated cases, holding to the contrary, have
failed to note the distinction which we have tried to
point out in this case, and clearly appearing in the
Turner and *Tribette Cases.*

In Mr. Pomeroy's work the rule is stated to be that
care should be taken not to confound the jurisdiction of
equity to prevent a multiplicity of suits with the general principle of equity that, when a court of equity has
acquired jurisdiction for one purpose, or of a part of a
general subject-matter, it may then go on and determine the whole controversy and give complete relief.
The failure to observe this distinction is, in our opinion,
the cause of the many conflicting decisions upon the
question as to the sufficiency of a bill to prevent a multiplicity of suits. The conflict and variance of authorities, both text-books and adjudicated cases, upon this
question, occasioned by the failure to observe this distinction, pervades even the statements of the law by
the same text-writer and the decisions of the same
court.

It often happens that equity takes or acquires jurisdiction of a certain subject-matter or controversy for
one purpose, and, in order to grant complete relief, finds
it necessary to add other parties to the suit, or maybe
to enjoin the prosecution of other suits which would
prevent complete relief or embarrass the court in administering such relief; but it does not follow that in such
case a bill would have equity if filed for the sole purpose of preventing the prosecution of such suits. Multifariousness in equity pleading and practice and equity

jurisdiction to prevent a multiplicity of suits are kindred subjects, but not the same subject. A given bill may not be objectionable as for multifariousness, although had to prevent a multiplicity of suits, if it rests solely upon this one equity jurisdiction.

We therefore conclude that the safer rule is to adhere to the former doctrine that, in order to support a bill in equity upon the sole ground of preventing a multiplicity of suits, the bill must show some community or mutuality of interest in the subject-matter of the controversy in which the various litigants are interested; that a mere community of interest in the questions of law and of fact involved is not sufficient in such cases.

It is not to be doubted that there are many and high authorities to the contrary; but it seems to have been uniformly held that a community of interest in the law involved is not alone sufficient to confer equity jurisdiction to prevent a multiplicity of suits, and we think that adding thereto a mere community of interest in the facts involved, without any community or mutuality of interest between the litigants in the property rights or other subject-matter involved, should not confer jurisdiction.

It was said by the English court, more than a hundred years ago, that a court of equity will not take cognizance of distinct and separate claims of different persons in one suit, though they stand in the same relative situation as to both the facts and the law involved.—1 East, 220, 227. It was also held by the same English court that where a number of persons claimed one right in one subject, as a bill of peace, or a bill in the nature thereof, it might be maintained to prevent a multiplicity of suits and to put an end to the litigation; but that such a bill could not be maintained where the demands claimed against the defendants, although of the same nature, were entirely distinct from and unconnected with those of any other defendant, and that in such cases each defendant had a right to object to the joining of any distinct and unconnected causes of action.— 2 Ans. 469.

It was also decided at an early date, by the Supreme Court of New Jersey, that a plaintiff could not maintain an action against several defendants, as to matters of different natures, where there was no community of interest in the subject-matter; and that the mere fact that the plaintiff had a common interest with all the defendants in questions of fact and of law involved gave that court no jurisdiction upon any principle of equity. —*Marselis v. Morris Canal & Banking Co.*, 1 N. J. Eq. 31. It was also held by that court that several persons could not maintain a bill in equity against one defendant, even to restrain a nuisance by such defendant, in consequence of the special injury done to each particular defendant; but that they might enjoin a nuisance, such as a slaughter-house in a populous district, because in such case the injury was a common one, and the object to be obtained was to give protection to each suitor in the enjoyment of common rights.—*Demarest v. Hardham*, 34 N. J. Eq. 469. These New Jersey cases, we think, clearly illustrate the rule and show the community of interest necessary to support such bills.

It should be constantly borne in mind that the single fact that a multitude of suits may be prevented by the assumption of jurisdiction by equity is not, in all cases, enough to sustain the equity of a bill. It may be that, while such a bill will prevent a multitude of suits, it will nevertheless be attended with greater inconvenience and detriment to the defendants than benefit or convenience to the single plaintiff.

In determining this vexed question, courts should keep in mind the question whether such consolidation of many suits at law, by one bill in equity, will confuse the issues to be there tried; and see to it that too many questions of interest are not brought into one case, and that the constitutional guaranty of the right of trial by jury shall not be denied. Every citizen has, or should have, the right to try his case with the issues made clear and well defined. If a consolidation can be had without interfering with this right, and the other requisites of such bills shall be made to appear, the bill should be allowed; otherwise it should be denied.

The inability of litigants who are residents to pay costs should not prevent them from having their rights adjudicated in courts of law, and tried by a jury of their peers. It is not the purpose of our government, nor the effect of our laws, to measure a citizen's liberty or privilege to litigate his rights in the courts of this state by his financial or pecuniary condition. Justice should be administered in orderly and due course, alike to the rich and to the poor.

While courts of equity may and should exercise some discretion as to when they will take jurisdiction to prevent a multiplicity of suits, yet this discretion is not arbitrary, but depends upon the question of the rights of all the litigants, as well as upon that of the convenience and expedition of the court. But the constitutional right of the citizen should be always placed beyond and above considerations such as the convenience, expedition, of court or litigant, or even the pecuniary loss of the complainant. Neither the convenience of, nor the saving of costs to, a tort-feasor, should be allowed to be set off against the constitutional right to a jury trial of the persons who are injured in consequence of this tort, though they all suffer similar injuries as the result of one and the same tort. The law is fixed and settled that, in order to avoid a jury trial to recover damages in each of several cases, the result of one and the same tort, the case made by the bill seeking to avoid or prevent a multiplicity of such actions must be brought within one of the well-recognized and established grounds of equity jurisdiction as to which the right of trial by jury does not now exist and had never existed.

The amended bill is sought to be given an additional claim to equity by consenting to, or requesting that, complainant's fertilizer factory be declared a nuisance, and abated as such, if the court, upon a final hearing, should find the law and the facts to justify such a decree. These allegations as to declaring or abating a nuisance cannot serve to give the bill equity upon this ground. The petition and prayer comes from the wrong party and source. A tortfeasor who is sued in a court of law to recover damages for his wrongs will not be heard in a court of equity, when he asks that court to enjoin the actions thus brought against him in the court of law, upon the ground that his torts or wrongs constitute a nuisance. Neither his convenience, nor the saving to him of the costs of a number of suits, can be set off against the right of the persons who have suffered in consequence of his wrong, to recover damages of him in a court of law, nor against their right to have a jury of their peers award and fix the amount of damages to which they are entitled, even though such wrong could and should be held to constitute, and be abated as, a nuisance. The persons injured in consequence of such wrong are the ones who have the right, if such right exists, to elect as to whether they will proceed in a court of law to recover damages, or in a court of equity to abate a nuisance. They also (and not he) have the right to elect whether they will proceed jointly to abate the nuisance in a court of equity, or whether they will proceed severally, in actions at law and before a jury, to recover their damages. Certain it is that the wrongdoer cannot make the election, nor is he in position to ask a court of equity to enjoin the actions at law, in order to serve his convenience and to save costs of litigation to him, or to expedite the business of the courts.

This bill is anomalous, in that the complainant is the party who created and maintains the nuisance, and who asks that a court of equity take jurisdiction to abate it and to award damages, in order to prevent a multiplicity of actions from being brought or prosecuted against him to recover damages for the nuisance. The maxim that "He who does iniquity will not be awarded equity," is certainly applicable to such a bill as this. Moreover, it is settled law that, if the parties were reversed, and the bill sought both to abate the nuisance and to award damages to a multitude of parties who were injured in consequence of the nuisance, the complainant could not then maintain the bill against the wrongdoer. The law is well settled to the effect that, where two or more persons, having separate and distinct tenements, are injured by a common nuisance which affects each in the same way, they may properly join as complainants in a bill filed solely for injunctive relief, but they cannot recover damages in such suit; and that where there is no community of interest in the subject-matter, and the object of the suit is to restrain something which works a distinct and special, but not separate, injury to the property of each, they cannot join in such suit.—*Demarest v. Hardham*, 34 N. J. Eq. 469; *Rowbotham v. Jones*, 47 N. J. Eq. 337, 20 Atl. 731, 19 L. R. A. 663; *Brady v. Weeks*, 3 Barb. (N. Y.) 157.

While the bill in this case is distinguishable in some respects from the bill in the *Hopkins Case*, yet in both the bills rest upon the same fundamental propositions that community of interest among the several respondents, as to the questions of fact and of law involved in the numerous actions at law, is sufficient to confer equity jurisdiction to prevent or enjoin such actions as a multiplicity of suits; and that community or mutuality of interest between the respondents, in the subject-matter or property rights in the several suits, is necessary to the equity of a bill which rested solely upon the ground of preventing a multiplicity of suits. This, we believe, is not the law. The decision in the *Hopkins Case* was therefore wrong, and it is hereby expressly overruled; which necessarily results in the affirmance of the decree of the chancellor, dismissing the bill in this case for the want of equity. Since this case was decided, but before it was put out, the *Hopkins Case*, on second appeal, has been decided in accordance with this opinion.

Affirmed.

DOWDELL, C. J., and MCCLELLAN and SOMERVILLE, JJ., concur.

Cook, *et al. v.* Atkins.

Bill to Enforce Vendor's Lien.

(Decided June 29, 1911.   56 South. 224.)

1. *Vendor and Purchaser; Lien; Waiver.*—The receipt of payments of interest by a vendor on a purchase money note from an heir of the vendee would not be the acceptance of an independent security from such heir so as to waive the vendor's lien.

2. *Same; Suit to Establish; Decree.*—The fact that the bill so vaguely described a small part of the land that a decree with respect thereto could not be made, would not prevent the granting of relief since the final decree could provide for the rights of the parties with respect thereto.

3. *Same; Right to Lien.*—In the absence of satisfactory evidence of a purpose to exclude it equity raises a vendor's lien by implica-

tion, and the formal acknowledgment in the deed of the receipt of the consideration for the conveyance would not prevent the grantor from claiming the existence of a vendor's lien if the price was not in fact paid.

4. *Same; Action to Establish; Burden of Proof.*—In the enforcement of a vendor's lien, where the purchase price has not been paid, the burden rests on the resisting vendee to show that a lien was intentionally waived or relinquished by the parties; the lien attaching if doubtful.

5. *Same; Collateral Security.*—The recital in a purchase money note that it was given to secure the purchase price evidenced the intention of the parties to retain a vendor's lien.

6. *Same.*—An agreement by the vendee that if he could not pay the principal he would pay the interest, and deliver up the land to the lawful holder of the purchase money notes, was not a collateral security in such sense as to waive the vendor's lien, being a mere option of discharging the principal of the debt by reconveying the land.

7. *Same; Limitation.*—An action to enforce a vendor's lien against the personal representative of the vendee was barred where brought forty years after the accrual of the lien and the death of the vendee.

8. *Appeal and Error; Assignment; Joint.*—Where error is jointly assigned injury must be shown to all parties joining in the assignment to sustain it.

9. *Limitation of Action; Suspension of Statute; Payment.*—If an heir of the vendee acted as agent for the other heirs in making payment of interest on the purchase money note, his payment operated to toll the statute as to all of them.

10. *Same; Payment of Interest.*—As analagous to the rule in case of a mortgage lien where heirs of a vendee who inherited the land subject to a purchase money lien paid interest on the purchase money notes before an action to establish the lien was barred, they acknowledged the debt as a lien, and the lien was continued by such payment for twenty years thereafter. (Section 4850, Code 1907.)

11. *Executors and Administrators; Vendors' Lien; Action to Enforce; Parties.*—Where a debt had long been barred so that a deficiency decree could not be rendered, the personal representative of a deceased vendee is not a necessary party to a bill against the heirs to enforce a vendor's lien.

APPEAL from Cherokee Chancery Court.

Heard before Hon. W. W. WHITESIDE.

Bill by Fanny Atkins, against James A. Cook and others, to enforce a vendor's lien. From a decree overruling demurrers to the bill, respondents appeal. Affirmed.

McCONNELL & CONNER, for appellant. Under the conveyance the lien of Atkins on the lands in controversy

could be but a mere creation of equity.—*Hester v. Hun-
nicutt*, 104 Ala. 282; *Sykes v. Betts*, 87 Ala. 537. The
unambiguous consideration recited in the deed is as between the parties prima facie correct.—*Hall v. Love-
man*, 85 Ala. 284. The provisions in the note constituted a collateral security.—*Tedder v. Steele*, 70 Ala. 351;
Foster v. Trustees, 3 Ala. 302. The right was barred
by laches and limitation.—*Watts v. Burnett*, 56 Ala.
344; *Espy v. Comer*, 76 Ala. 505; 27 Ala. 411; 108 Ala.
527. The personal representative was a necessary party.—*Moore v. Alexander*, 81 Ala. 509; *Dooley v. Villalonga*, 61 Ala. 129; *Bell v. Hall*, 76 Ala. 546; *Smith v.
Murphy*, 58 Ala. 630. The bill was vague and indefinite as to the description of the land.—*Page v. Bradford*,
100 Ala. 610; 86 Ala. 611. Neither James Cook nor
any other heir could make any payment on the note nor
obligate themselves in writing so as to prevent the bar
of the statute of limitations.—Sec. 4850, Code 1907;
Warren v. Hearn, 82 Ala. 556; *Stark v. Wilson*, 65 Ala.
580; 67 Ala. 146. It was essential to the equity of the
bill that the pleader aver with definiteness, the time
of Cook's death and the payments made by him.—
Shields v. Sheffield, 79 Ala. 91; *Goldsby v. Goldsby*, 67
Ala. 563; *Cockrell v. Gurley*, 26 Ala. 405.

BLACKWELL & AGEE, for appellee. Complainants had
a lien enforceable in equity.—*Chapman v. Peebles*, 84
Ala. 283; *Thomason v. Cooper*, 57 Ala. 560. Cook not
having reconveyed or offered to reconvey the land when
the note was due, became absolutely liable for the
amount of the note.—35 Cyc. 253. By the payment the
doctrine of laches and the statute of limitations was
tolled.—*Reynolds v. Lawrence*, 147 Ala. 216; *Phillips v.
Adams*, 78 Ala. 227; *Hughes v. Thomas*, 11 L. R. A.
(N. S.) 744; *Lisle v. Esser*, 73 N. W. 1008; *Taylor v.*

Perry, 48 Ala. 240; 25 Cyc. 1373; 13 A. & E. Enc. of Law, 794. The personal representative was not a necessary party, as the debt was barred, and no deficiency judgment could be rendered.—*Boyle v. Williams,* 72 Ala. 353; *Eslava v. N. Y. N. B. & L. Assn.,* 121 Ala. 480; *Chapman v. Peebles, supra; McCall v. McCurdy,* 69 Ala. 65.

SAYRE. J.—The bill in this case is filed by appellee against the heirs at law of William C. Cook, deceased, and seeks the enforcement of an alleged vendor's lien. The facts shown by the amended bill are as follows: In 1865, David Atkins sold and conveyed to William C. Cook a certain tract of land in Cherokee county. The purchase money was secured by a note in words and figures as follows: "$3,000. On or before the first day of January, 1866, I promise to pay to David Atkins, or order, three thousand dollars ($3,000.00) in gold, for certain parcels of land lying in Cherokee county, which I have this day purchased of him, known as the Solomon and Robert McGhee places, containing three hundred (300) acres more or less. The interest of the above amount, I promise to pay annually in the paper currency of the country, but if that currency is at a greater discount than fifty per cent. (50 per cent), I promise to pay an amount greater in proportion to that discount. I also promise that if I find that I cannot pay the principal of the note, I will pay up the interest and deliver the land up again to the lawful holder of this note. Witness my hand and seal, the 25th day of September, 1865. [Signed] William C. Cook. [Seal.]" Cook died in the year 1867, leaving as his heirs children, the survivors of whom, and the children and heirs at law of others who have died in the meantime, are made parties defendant to the bill. After the death of Cook,

[Cook, et al. v. Atkins.]

his son, James H. Cook, paid interest on the debt secured by the note. These payments, made at intervals
of one and two years and averaging about $240 a year,
cover the period from Cook's death to the year 1910,
when this bill was filed. The averment is that they were
made for and on account of the heirs at law of William
C. Cook. Complainant claims in virtue of her ownership of the note and all rights accruing therefrom, be-
queathed to her by the last will and testament of her
deceased husband, David Atkins.

Questions of controlling importance are: Whether
a lien was reserved; whether, if there was a lien, it has
been lost by laches or the statute of limitations; and
whether the presence of a personal representative of
William C. Cook is necessary to a proper disposition
of the cause. It is suggested that the receipt of interest
payments from James H. Cook may have constituted
the acceptance of independent security; but it seems obvious that there is no merit in the suggestion, and we
will not refer to it again. It is also said that the land
is not accurately described. We are unable to find that
this point was taken by the demurrer. But if, as the
brief seems to assert, some small part of the land is so
vaguely described that no decree in respect to it can be
safely made that is a matter which does not affect the
equity of the bill, and will be properly cared for in the
event a final decree is rendered for complainant.

Was there a lien? The formal acknowledgment in
the deed of the receipt of the consideration for the conveyance does not conclude the grantor or those claiming under him, if in fact the purchase price remains unpaid.—*Bankhead v. Owen,* 60 Ala. 457; *Wilkinson v.
May,* 69 Ala. 33. Equity raises the lien by implication,
unless there is satisfactory evidence of a purpose to exclude it, and the vendee who resists its enforcement as-

sumes the burden of showing that it has been intentionally displaced or waived by the consent of parties. If the question remains in doubt, the lien attaches.—*Wilkinson v. May, supra*. The recital of the note that it was given to secure the purchase money of the land evidenced the intention of the parties that a vendor's lien was retained, even though it showed a collateral security in some sort, in that the vendee promised that, if he could not pay the principal, he would pay the interest and deliver up the land to the lawful holder of the note. —*Tedder v. Steele*, 70 Ala. 347; *Hood v. Hammond*, 128 Ala. 569, 30 South. 540, 86 Am. St. Rep. 159. This promise did not provide for that contingency in which the vendee might be able, but unwilling, to pay. It was in truth no security to the complainant.or her assignor, but an option by which the promisor reserved the privilege of discharging the principal of the debt by a reconveyance of the land. We conclude that there was a lien.

It does not appear that defendant's position in opposition to the asserted lien has suffered impairment or embarrassment in any respect by mere delay. So, then, the imputation of laches to complainant by the demurrer must find support in the general policy of repose which the law adopts without reference to the hardships or difficulties of individual cases, and must be measured by the legislative declaration of that policy to be found in the statute of limitations. At the time of filing the bill, more than 40 years had passed since the accrual of the lien and the death of the vendee. If the case for a lien stood upon the original transaction, without more, there could be no question but that the lien had been lost long before this suit was commenced. What effect, then, is to be assigned to the continuous payments of interest by the heirs during this period? This question must be

[Cook, et al. v. Atkins.]

answered in the shape in which it is presented by the record. All the defendants demurred jointly and separately. But the defendants, other than James H. Cook, for themselves advanced a ground of demurrer which asserts a difference in their position and that of James H. in respect to the effect of payments made by him upon the running of the statute of limitations. James H. could, of course, take nothing by that ground of objection to the bill. If there was error in overruling this ground of demurrer, it was not error of which James H. could complain. The appeal is taken jointly by all the defendants. There has been no severance in the assignments. The joint assignments attack the decree as to all the defendants. It is a perfectly familiar rule in this court that, where error is jointly assigned, injury must be shown to all joining in the assignment, or an affirmance must follow.—*Lehman v. Gunn,* 154 Ala. 369, 45 South. 620, and the authorities there cited. Counsel for appellants, speaking at this point for the defendants, other than James H. Cook, as we assume, seem to say that in making payments of interest James H. was a volunteer, so far as concerns the other heirs, and that their rights under the statute of limitations are not to be prejudiced thereby. But, as has been heretofore noted, the averment of the bill is that these payments were made by James H. Cook for and on account of the heirs at law of William C. Cook. We have taken this to mean that James H. was acting as the agent of the other heirs by the appointment in fact, express or implied. In that case, it would be clear that his payments operated upon the interest of all of them alike.—*Murdock v. Waterman,* 145 N. Y. 55, 39 N. E. 829, 27 L. R. A. 418. But, if the intention was to assert the proposition of law that James H. Cook was the agent of the other heirs by reason of the mere fact that he and they were coheirs, a question of some difficulty, it may be, would be presented. We have thought it well to pretermit decision of this question, because, for reasons indicated above none of the appellants could take anything by its determination in their favor, because the argument on this point scarcely amounts to more than a suggestion on either side, and because, under the unusual circumstances shown by the bill, we suppose it to be hardly probable that the solution of the question will depend upon the bare fact that the defendants became coheirs more than 40 years ago.

The debt on which the heirs made payments of interest was not their debt, but that of their ancestor. That a suit against the personal representative of the deceased vendee on the debt, under the conditions here shown was barred long before this bill was filed is admitted, and is beyond controversy.—*Starke v. Wilson,* 65 Ala. 576; *Lewis v. Ford,* 67 Ala. 143; *Warren v. Hearne,* 82 Ala. 554, 2 South. 491. These cases show that in the absence of a specific lien complainant would be remediless. They show nothing in respect to the survival of the lien. The statutory period of limitation of an action on a vendor's lien differs from that provided for the bar of an action on the debt, so that, if these periods run uninterruptedly to a conclusion, the remedy on the lien long outlives the remedy on the debt. In the case of a mortgage lien, it is stated in Jones on Mortgages to be the universally recognized rule that a payment of interest or part of the principal renews the mortgage, so that an action may be brought to enforce it within 20 years or other period of limitation after such last payment. Code § 1198. The rule stated has been recognized in this court.—*Phillips v. Adams,* 78 Ala. 225. These authorities afford a strict analogy for complainant's case, except for the fact that payments in her case were made, not by the debtor, but by his heirs. But the heirs inherited the property, subject to the lien. They became, in this way and to the extent of the value of the property, payors of the debt, and their payments of interest from time to time before the bar was complete can be construed only as acknowledgments of the debt as a lien—as evidence of a continuing liability within the clear intendment of the statute, which provides that a partial payment, made upon a contract by the party sought to be charged, before the bar is complete, is evidence of a new and continuing contract. Code § 4850. We hold, therefore, that the payments shown in this case operated to continue the lien for 20 years thereafter as against the land in the possession and ownership of the heirs.—*Murdock v. Waterman,* supra.

The debt having been long since barred, and, no deficiency judgment being sought or possible, there is no reason why the personal estate of the deceased vendee should be represented in this litigation. The reasons stated in *Moore v. Alexander,* 81 Ala. 509, 8 South, 199, *Dooley v. Villalonga,* 61 Ala. 129, and that line of cases, why the personal representative should be made a party, to wit, that the personal estate was interested in the ascertainment of the amount of the debt, fails in this case.

The decree of the chancellor overruling the demurrer to complainant's bill was free from error, and will be affirmed.

Affirmed.

SIMPSON, ANDERSON, and SOMERVILLE, JJ., concur.

Robinson *v.* Griffin, *et al.*

Bill to Cancel Deeds and to Surrender Property.

(Decided June 29, 1911. 56 South. 124.)

1. *Cancellation of Instrument; Bill; Incidental Relief.*—The bill examined and under its allegations, it is held that, though the money was procured at a different time from the execution of the deed, the money having been secured after intestate's death, yet sufficient connection was shown between the two wrongs so as to authorize relief as to the money if a cause of action for cancellation of the deeds was established.

2. *Equity; Demurrer; Good in Part.*—Where a demurrer went to the bill as a whole, it was properly overruled, though a part of the relief demanded was obtainable in a court of law, and could only be granted in equity as incidental to purely equitable relief, also prayed for.

3. *Evidence; Burden of Proof.*—Where the answer seeks no affirmative relief, the burden is on complainant to prove the material allegations of his bill.

4. *Deeds; Validity; Undue Influence.*—Where the action was to cancel a deed to respondent by complainant's intestate, the burden of proof shifted to the respondent after proof by complainant of confidential relations existing between intestate and respondent.

5. *Same; Fraud and Undue Influence; Sufficiency of Evidence.*— The evidence in this case stated and examined and held not to show undue influence or fraud in procuring the deed.

APPEAL from Mobile Law and Equity Court.

Heard before Hon. SAFFOLD BERNEY.

Bill by William Griffin and others, against Allen Robinson, to cancel certain deeds and to require a return of property. From a decree for complainant respondent appeals. Reversed and rendered.

WEBB & MCALPINE, for appellant. It is never sufficient to aver fraud as a legal conclusion, but facts must be set out which are legally sufficient to show fraud.— *Kidd v. Morris*, 127 Ala. 393; *Bell v. Southern Home Co.* 140 Ala. 377; *Pinkston v. Boykin*, 30 South. 398. This question was properly raised by demurrer.—*Flewellen v. Crane,* 58 Ala. 627. Counsel insist that the evidence did not justify the decree annulling the deed on account of undue influence.—*Lyon v. Campbell,* 88 Ala. 462; *Jackson,* 87 Ala. 685; *Dunlap v. Robinson,* 28 Ala. 100. Fiduciary relationship alone does not raise presumption of fraud.—*Eastis v. Montgomery,* 93 Ala. 293; *Bancroft v. Otis,* 91 Ala. 279; *McLeod v. McLeod,* 137 Ala. 270; *Woods v. Craft,* 4 South 649. Being without power to annul the deeds, of course, the court was without jurisdiction to render a money judgment.

BOYLES & KOHN, for appellee. Having acquired jurisdiction for one purpose, equity will proceed to grant complete relief.—*Gulf G. Co. v. Jones C. Co.* 157 Ala. 32. The allegations of fraud and undue influence were sufficient.—*McLeod v. McLeod,* 137 Ala. 267; *Cronk v. Cronk,* 142 Ala. 214; *Brisler v. Broom,* 147 Ala. 504; *So. Ry. v. Hayes,* 150 Ala. 212; *Worthington v. Miller,* 134 Ala. 420. Having shown a fiduciary relation, the burden was upon the respondent to show that no undue influence was exerted.—*Tyson v. Tyson,* 37 Md. 583; *Bancroft v. Otis,* 91 Ala. 279; *Shipman v. Furniss,* 69 Ala. 565. This burden was not carried, and the court very properly annulled the deed and rendered the decree complained of.

MAYFIELD, J.—Appellee filed this bill, individually and as administrator of the estate of Carrie Woods, alias Carrie Robinson, deceased, against the appellant; and seeks the cancellation of two deeds by Carrie Woods to the respondent, and the surrender and delivery, by the respondent, of $1,500 belonging to the estate of complainant's intestate, which sum, the bill alleges, was fraudulently appropriated by the respondent to his own use. The bill further alleges that the intestate,

Carrie Woods, died on March 9, 1908, leaving complainant, appellee, as her sole heir and next of kin—he being
her half-brother, and having been appointed administrator of her estate.   The bill then alleges that in the lifetime of the intestate she was seised and possessed of
considerable money and real estate; that complainant
as such administrator had taken possession of said real
estate, but had been unable to obtain possession of
either the money in question or the lands conveyed by
the deeds sought to be canceled, because of the wrongs
of the respondent complained of in the bill.   The bill
then alleges in substance, that the respondent, through
fraud and deceit, procured the conveyance to himself,
from Carrie Woods, of the money in question, which belonged to the estate and converted it to his own use.
Demurrer having been sustained to the original bill, it
was amended by adding the paragraph numbered 8, alleging that if the deeds were executed by Carrie Woods,
the grantor and grantee at the time of their execution,
were living together in an unlawful state or relationship, and that her signature to such deeds was procured
by fraud and undue influence on the part of the respondent.   A demurrer being sustained to the bill as last
amended, it was further amended by adding that the
complainant and his two children were the only blood
relations of Carrie Woods; that complainant had been
reared, from childhood, by Carrie Woods, who was his
half-sister.   The bill then alleges that notwithstanding
this blood relationship between complainant and decedent and the respondent; that during that time she asisted for many years prior thereto, a much closer relationship—that of illicit intimacy—between the decedent and the respondent; that during that time she assumed the name of Robinson, instead of her own name,
Woods; that the deeds sought to be canceled were made

without any consideration and constituted a gift by the
intestate to the respondent; that her signature to the
deeds was not of her own free act, and volition, but was
procured and superinduced by undue influence on the
part of the respondent. If this bill had been filed merely
to recover the $1,500, or to compel its payment, or to
recover that amount from the respondent, it would be
without equity and subject to demurrer, for the reason
that it would affirmatively show that the complainant
had a complete and adequate remedy at law; but the restoration of the money is sought, for that it was obtained in furtherance, and as a part of the alleged fraudulent scheme and purpose of the respondent to procure
the property of the intestate; and this feature of the bill
is sought to be maintained only upon the ground that
the court, having acquired jurisdiction for one purpose,
should proceed to do complete justice between the
parties in one suit.

The bill does allege some connection or relation between the acts of the respondent in procuring the deeds,
and those in procuring the money; and while, of course,
they are separated by a considerable lapse of time (the
one culminating during the lifetime of the intestate, and
the other, after her death), yet the relation or connection shown between the two wrongs complained of,
is sufficient to authorize relief as to the taking of the
money, provided the main equity of the bill is made out
as for the cancellation of the deeds. Moreover, the demurrer did not go to this part of the bill only, but went
to the entire bill, to the effect that it showed that the
complainant had a complete and adequate remedy at
law. Had the demurrer been directed to that part of the
bill only which seeks the recovery of the $1,500, we are
not prepared to say that it should not have been sustained. If the fourth ground of demurrer could be said

to go to that part of the bill only, which seeks to recover the money, it is sufficient to say that it is not insisted upon. The only grounds insisted upon by counsel are the first and sixth. The entire demurrer to the original and the amended bills, however, was addressed to the bills as a whole, and not to any particular part.

The address of each of the demurrers was as follows: First demurrer: "Comes now the respondent and demurs to the original bill." Second: "Comes the respondent and demurs to the amended bill heretofore filed." Third: "Comes the complainant and demurs to the amended bill heretofore filed."

The word *complainant* is here used evidently as meaning "respondent," and we treat it as a clerical error.

Each of the demurrers was addressed to the bill as a whole, and not to any part of it and the bill as a whole was clearly not subject to any one of the grounds of demurrer insisted upon in the argument of counsel for appellant. The court therefore committed no error in overruling the demurrer to the bill as last amended. After the demurrers were overruled, the respondent answered, denying the equity of the bill, paragraph by paragraph, and set up few if any affirmative facts as a defense—thereby placing the burden of proof upon complainant.

A great many witnesses were examined on behalf of each party; and the case was submitted for final decree, upon the bill, the answer, and the proof as noted by the register. The chancellor rendered a decree granting the relief prayed in the bill; and from that final decree the respondent prosecutes this appeal. After a careful reading of all the evidence shown in this record, we are unable to concur in the conclusion reached by the chancellor that the complainant was entitled to the relief prayed in his bill and awarded in the chancellor's decree.

The burden was on the complainant, of course, to prove the material averments of his bill, but we do not think that he has discharged that burden, either as to all the material facts alleged, or as to those which would be necessary to support the relief sought and awarded.

It is true that after complainant proved the confidential relation between the grantor and the grantee, the burden of proof as to undue influence was shifted; but the evidence of respondent discharged this burden.

We do not mean to say that none of the averments of the bill are made out—some of them are not even controverted; but a number of others, material and necessary to the relief prayed and granted, are not proven to our satisfaction, while some are actually disproven.

It is shown that Carrie Woods, the intestate, otherwise known as Carrie Robinson, many years ago intermarried with one Lem Woods, who committed a serious crime—a capital offense—and in consequence thereof, absconded, leaving Mobile, the home of the parties concerned in this litigation; that he left about 20 years ago; that Carrie, his wife, and the appellant, Allen Robinson, thereafter lived together as man and wife, though Carrie never obtained a divorce from Woods, that they lived in this manner for a number of years, and Carrie for a long time was known by the name of Carrie Robinson. It is also shown that the complainant was a half-brother of Carrie, and therefore inherited her property, subject to the rights of her husband, Lem Woods, she having no children or other next kin. It is shown by some of the witnesses who boarded with Carrie and the respondent during the time they lived together as husband and wife that they were deemed to be husband and wife, and were accordingly treated by the public; though it is undisputed that there was never any lawful marriage between them.

It was shown by the testimony of the complainant himself, and by several of his witnesses, that Carrie repeatedly said, during her lifetime, that she desired to leave the house in which she was then living to Allen Robinson, and a boy they had raised and by other witnesses that she said she had already so willed the property and so fixed it that Willie Griffin (the complainant) could not get it. It is shown by the testimony of the complainant himself that he and his half-sister were not on speaking terms at the time of her death, and had not been for some time before; that they had often had serious disputes and differences; that Carrie had on several occasions expressed the wish and intention that the complainant should not have any of her property.

While the complainant testifies to the bad state of feeling between his sister and himself, and to the intimate relations between her and the respondent, he also claims, in other parts of his testimony, that she had said she intended to leave her property to him and his children, and that she had declared that the respondent should not have her property. But he contradicts himself, flatly and repeatedly, as to many of these declarations attributed to his sister, as to conversations between them, and those between her and the respondent.

It is shown by the depositions of the witnesses George J. Sullivan, of the accuracy of whose testimony there seems to be no dispute, who appears to have been disinterested, and who was introduced by the complainant, that the respondent, Allen Robinson, and Carrie Woods, otherwise called Carrie Robinson, had lived together, at one place near the residence of the witness, for 15 or 20 years; that they rented the house in which they lived from his mother, and that he thought they were husband and wife—they being generally so regarded in the community; that the respondent was a hardworking, industrious man; that he paid his rent promptly, and was a first-class tenant; that he and Carrie were always at their business, and that during the time they lived in his mother's house they carried on a cookery and boarding house, working together in the business as husband and wife; that Allen was not engaged about that business all the time, but was also engaged as a teamster, doing public hauling, and witness thought he sold wood at a woodyard.

It was shown by one of the complainant's witnesses, Alfred Jenkins, who seems to have been favorably inclined to the complainant, that Carrie told him, the night she died, that she and complainant had fallen out and that complainant had talked of beating her; that witness tried to get her to make up with complainant, and she said she would if he would beg her pardon, etc. Yet it was admitted by the complainant himself that he was not speaking to his sister at the time of her death, nor just prior thereto. It is shown by this record—by plaintiff's own testimony—that notwithstanding this, and the fact that complainant had not visited his sister during her last illness, he went to her home and into her room about twenty minutes after her death, in order to get a chest which he thought contained her money, and carried the same to his house where he broke it open and took out some papers; and that he delivered this chest to respondent who demanded it as the property of his wife.

As before stated, it is shown by the testimony of the complainant himself and by that of a number of the witnesses, that Carrie had often expressed the intention of leaving her property to Allen; though it should be stated that at other times they testified that she had said she did not want Allen and his people to get any of her property.

We think it is shown by this record and partly by the evidence brought out in behalf of the complainant, that the respondent paid Carrie Woods, the intestate, $1,000 for one piece of property, and $800 for the other, and that the purchase was made and paid in cash. It is further conclusively shown that after the death of Carrie, the defendant took $1,100 from the house and deposited it in the First National Bank of Mobile, which money is claimed to be the property of the intestate and not that of the respondent.

While the evidence does not fully satisfy us as to whether this eleven hundred dollars was the separate property of Carrie, or that of Allen, we are inclined to the opinion that the complainant has failed to discharge the burden of proving that it was Carrie's money. We find that the proof contained in this record conclusively shows that Allen purchased the property from Carrie, and paid her a valuable consideration therefor in cash; and we find nothing to show that these conveyances were obtained from Carrie by undue influence, fraud, or force. To the contrary, it appears that it was the act of her free will and accord. And there can be no doubt that she had the right to make these conveyances upon the consideration of money paid by Allen, nor for that matter, the right, if she so desired, to give him the property; and we think the proof shows that it was her desire that he should have the property—which was only natural, under the circumstances.

While it is shown that the relation between intestate and respondent was unlawful, yet it is undisputed that they did live as husband and wife for a great number of years, and they seemed to have treated their business and property as that of legal husband and wife. They were both industrious and frugal, and desired to save and accumulate property, in which they were successful in some degree; and what each had, no doubt, was the result of the joint efforts of both, through a long life spent together as husband and wife, and it was but natural that each should have desired the survivor to have what was left by the other.

This record satisfies us that such was the intention and purpose of Carrie in making these conveyances to Allen. It may be that the whole of the consideration was not paid, or that the money which passed was the money of both grantor and grantee, or that it was the property of Carrie alone. As to this there is no proof. However, even conceding that the proof had shown that there was in fact no consideration paid by Allen, yet it nevertheless conclusively appears, we think, that the conveyances were voluntary, there being absolutely no proof to show any persuasion, threats, undue influence, or fraud on the part of Allen to induce Carrie to make them. And the intestate being at the time of her death on unfriendly terms with her half-brother, her sole next of kin, it was but natural that she should prefer that Allen should have her property.

It was shown by the testimony of Dr. Sullivan that the respondent was an industrious negro, and had ac-cumulated considerable money, he having left with witness, at different times, various sums, amounting to more than 1,700 at the time witness paid it over to respondent. So it is not at all improbable that he had, or could have obtained, the $1,800 with which, as testi-fied, he purchased this property. In fact, the testimony of Dr. Sullivan, who attested the conveyances, and that of the notary who took the acknowledgments, is to the effect that the money was actually paid over at the time of the making of the conveyances. There is no proof whatever to contradict this, and considering all the evi-dence and all the circumstances connected with the transaction, we are unable to find proof sufficient to support the material allegations of the bill, that these deeds sought to be canceled were forgeries, or that they were obtained by undue influence on the part of Allen, or that he had been guilty of any fraud in the matter of obtaining such conveyances, such as would authorize a court of chancery to cancel the deeds; but, on the other hand, we are persuaded that the evidence in this record shows that these conveyances were voluntarily made by the grantor; that they disposed of her property in exact accordance with her wishes, and that the title to the property should be allowed to remain where she has so voluntarily placed it. Indeed, if the testimony of the attesting witnesses and of the notary who took the acknowledgments (and this is all that appears in reference to them) is to be believed—and we find nothing to discredit the same—the transactions involving these conveyances were free from fraud, undue influence, or coercion.

It follows that the decree of the chancellor must be reversed; and a decree will be here rendered dismissing the bill of complaint.

Reversed and rendered.

SIMPSON, McCLELLAN, and SAYRE, JJ., concur.

[Grubbs, et al. v. Hawes.]

Grubbs, *et al. v.* Hawes.

Bill to Foreclose Mortgage.

(Decided June 29, 1911. 56 South. 227.)

1. *Fixtures; Questions.*—It is a mixed question of law and fact whether a chattel has become a part of the realty.

2. *Same; Intention of Parties.*—The intention with which a chattel is attached to the realty is of great importance in determining whether it had become a fixture.

3. *Same; Mortgagor and Mortgagee; Foreclosure.*—A mortgagor of a lot and building in which machinery was erected after the execution of the mortgage was not prejudiced by permitting the mortgagee to pay off the balance due upon the machinery which had become a fixture so as to permit the building and machinery to be sold as a whole on foreclosure, since the machinery could be treated as between the mortgagor and mortgagee as a fixture, although as between the mortgagor and the original seller, it was a chattel.

4. *Same; Pleading.*—The bill examined and held to sufficiently allege that the machinery was a part of the realty so as to be covered by the mortgagee.

5. *Pleading; Demurrer; Construction.*—On demurrer, the allegations of the pleading are taken most strongly against the pleader.

6. *Equity; Bill; Numbering.*—Although rule of practice No. 8, requires bills of equity to be numbered, the fact that the paragraphs were lettered instead of being numbered was not objectionable where the purpose of the rule was effectuated by the course pursued.

APPEAL from Morgan Chancery Court.

Heard before Hon. W. H. SIMPSON.

Bill by Walker A. Hawes against Walter M. Grubbs and others. From a decree for complainant on demurrer, defendants appeal. Affirmed.

The respondents named in the bill are Walter M. Grubbs, Hallie Grubbs, Dodson Printers' Supply Company, a corporation, C. Ed Albes, W. N. Hall, and J. W. Mulligan. Paragraph 1 alleges the execution of a mortgage to orator by Walter M. and Hallie Grubbs, on May 15, 1905, or on or about May 23, 1905, in the sum of $1,250, which deed was duly acknowledged and recorded, and conveyed lot C, in block 312, of the Decatur M. & L. Co.'s addition to Decatur, Ala. Paragraph 2 alleges the execution, contemporaneous with the execution of the mortgage, by Walter Grubbs to orator, of eight promissory notes, each for the sum of $150, except the one maturing May 15, 1914, which was for the sum of $200; each note being payable as follows: One on May 15, 1907, and one on the 15th day of each succeeding May thereafter, until all of said notes should be paid, and the notes provided payment with interest semi-annually. Paragraph 3 alleges that Walter M. Grubbs had paid nothing whatever on said notes or mortgages, nor had any one paid him anything whatever, except four installments of interest at $50 each, paid by Walter Grubbs on the following dates: May 15, 1907, November 15, 1907, May 15, 1908, and November 15, 1908—and that the remainder of said notes and mortgages, counsel fees, insurance, premiums, taxes, assessments, etc., hereinafter set forth, are all past due and unpaid, and said Walter M. Grubbs is in default. Paragraph 4 alleges the provisions of the mortgage as to keeping the property insured against loss by fire in favor of orator, the payment of all taxes or other legal charges, and, on the failure of Grubbs to pay the same, that orator might pay or cause the same to be paid, which would then become a part of the indebtedness secured by the mortgage, and bear the same rate of interest as the principal debt secured thereby, and payable upon the security of the next maturing note thereafter. It also alleges the further provision that in case of default in the payment of said notes, or any one of them, and in the payment of any premiums of insurance, any taxes, or other charges that should have accrued, for a period of 60 days after maturity, then orator might declare the whole indebtedness payable immediately, take possession, advertise for sale, etc. Paragraph 5 alleges the agreement to pay the expenses of foreclosure, including reasonable attorney's fees, any balance of principal and interest, together with any amount expended for insurance, taxes, or other charges, which might have been paid as therein agreed. It is further alleged that the note referred to contained an agreement to pay all costs of collection, including a reasonable attorney's fee, in case the note should not be paid at maturity, and the said note also waived the rights of exemption as to personal property. Paragraph 6 alleges that upon said lot of land above described there was afterwards erected a small one-story brick structure, planned, designed, and built for use as a printing office; and it was agreed at the time the money was loaned, for the payment of which said mortgage was executed, that said money should be expended in erecting said structure, and said building, after it was erected, was by the said Walter M. Grubbs equipped with the following machinery, which was to be used and which has been used in conducting a printing plant, and which constitutes a part of the printing outfit for which said structure was erected, to-wit: One Eclipse folding machine, No. 2383; also one 37x-inch rebuilt Campbell cylinder printing press; one No. 1 Eclipse folder, with steel runs and trimmers; one $14\frac{1}{2}$x22-inch Chandler & Price press, No. K-82; one 8x12 Jones-Gordon jobber press; also one large electric motor for running said presses, and one long shaft and pulley connecting said motor and presses. Paragraph 7 avers that all of said machines above described are firmly fastened and fixed to the building; that they were installed and attached with especial reference to the building, and in furtherance of the purpose for which the building was erected, and with the object and intention that the same should be permanent, and that, as between your orator and the said Walter M. Grubbs, the said articles, etc., were fixtures, and are and always have been, since their installation and connection, a part of the realty embraced within the lien of your orator's mortgage aforesaid. Paragraph 8 alleges that the said fixtures above mentioned, except the said motors and pulleys and shafts, and except, also, the said Jones-Gordon press, were purchased by the said Walter M. Grubbs from the Dodson Printers' Supply Company, on which a part of the purchase money, just how much is to your orator unknown, is past due and unpaid, and to secure the same Grubbs executed, contemporaneously with said purchase, certain instruments in writing, in substance and effect stipulating that the title to said machine should remain in the said Dodson Printers' Supply Company until said articles and others should be paid for in full. Copies of said agreements are made exhibits to the bill. It is then alleged that the Dodson Printers' Supply Company had brought detinue for said machines, which is now pending and undetermined in the Morgan law and equity court, of Morgan county, and that Walter M. Grubbs had executed the statutory bond enabling him to remain in custody of said property pending the determination of said suit, and that upon each of said bonds said W. N. Hall, C. Ed. Albes, and J. W. Mulligan were and are sureties. Paragraph 9 alleges Grubbs' insolvency, and that the mortgaged property and said machines above referred to as being a part of the realty, taken in connection with the incumbrances on said machines, altogether are much less in value than the amount of complainant's debt and the unpaid charges on said property hereinafter set out. Paragraph 10 alleges that on July 24, 1909, W. H. Drinkhard, as tax collector of Morgan county, Alabama, assumed to levy upon, and

did assume to make sale of, and did as tax collector
execute substantially a statutory bill of sale of, a large
amount of the printing outfit in said building, including
the above-named Campbell roller press, for delinquent
state and county taxes due and owing and assessed
against the said Walter M. Grubbs and his property,
and the purchaser at said sale was the said Hallie M.
Grubbs, and the subject-matter of said sale was, or was
recited to be in the said bill, after mentioning the number of articles, "all other printing material, fixtures, etc.,
belonging and appertaining to the office of the said
Decatur News, belonging to said Walter M. Grubbs.
It is further averred that on the 19th of July, 1909,
Marvin West, as register in chancery in and for Morgan county, Ala., did as such register sell and convey
to E. L. Simpson and J. D. Orr said house and lot
above mentioned and described at and for the sum and
price of $83.30, which was the amount of taxes due and
owing and assessed against said Walter M. Grubbs by
and in favor of the city of Decatur, Ala., for the preceding tax year; said Grubb being delinquent. Said
sale was made under and by virtue of a decree rendered
by the chancery court on May 17, 1909, in the case of
City of Decatur v. Walter M. Grubbs, in a delinquent
tax proceeding, which decree is here referred to and
asked, if necessary, to be taken as a part of this bill
of complaint. It is then alleged that orator considered
himself compelled to and did purchase of and from said
vendees, Simpson and Orr, all right, title, and interest
which they held, and which they had acquired under
said sale under said decree, at and for the sum of $90.81,
taking from them a quitclaim deed to said property. It
is further alleged against said property there are now
past due, delinquent, unpaid, and interest-bearing
taxes, which were of right due and payable October 1,

1909, in the amount of $13.50 with the further sum of
$1 fees, and also the sum of $8 further taxes due the
city of Decatur by the said Walter Grubbs, with interest and 50 cents fees, and also the following improvement assessment against said property for street and
sidewalk improvements: Sidewalk improvements,
$31.43, with interest since July 14, 1908, and street
paving assessment of $173.10, with interest from No-
vember 6, 1908, and curbing assessments of $7.80, with
interest from September 1, 1908. Paragraph 11 alleges the insurance premiums paid by orator to be
$11.50, and that in this respect Grubbs is also in de-
fault. Paragraph 12 alleges divers and sundry other liabilities against the said W. M. Grubbs, with respect to
which he is in default, and that his assets are far less
in value than his liabilities, and that orator has no further security for the claim and indebtedness against
the said Grubbs than is above set forth. Paragraph
13 alleges certain outstanding judgments against
Grubbs, executions issued thereon, and returned no
property. Paragraph 14 alleges that the building is of
cheap construction and material, that it is in a leaky.
condition, on account of the defective roof, and that
it is becoming generally dilapidated for want of ordinary care and attention; that it is decreasing in value,
and is liable to decrease to a greater extent unless the
court will take charge of the same through the instru-
mentality of a receiver, and unless a receiver is appointed there is liable to be and is danger of great loss
and injury to the complainant. Paragraph 15 alleges
demand for and refusal of possession of the real estate
mentioned in the mortgage. Paragraph 16 annexes as
exhibits to the bill the various judgments, bills of sale,
decree, etc., previously set forth in the bill. Paragraph
17 offers to redeem from the Dodson Printers' Supply

Company, and paragraph 17a states the residence of all of the defendants. Then follows an appropriate prayer for special and general relief, for the appointment of a receiver, etc.

The amended bill alleges in paragraph A the ages of the parties, complainants and respondents. In paragraph B that, in addition to the appliances named in the original bill as being situated in the building on the land involved in this suit, there are two shorter shafts, with pulleys attached thereto, which shafts revolve in collars which have braces or other supports fastened to the building by bolts, nails, or other means, and are part of the real estate. In paragraph C it is alleged the tax sale to Hallie M. Grubbs, mentioned in the bill, was void for the reason that said Walter M. Grubbs willfully and purposely defaulted in the payment of the taxes, in order that the property might be sold for taxes and be purchased in the name of the wife, and in pursuance of such purpose the property was sold and purchased in the name of the wife with the funds or resources of the said Walter M. Grubbs, or the proceeds thereof. Paragraph D alleges the same sale to be void for the reason that the machines and appliances had become affixed to the freehold and were real estate, but were assessed by the assessor as personal property and condemned to be sold as such; that the necessary steps for the sale of real estate were not taken (setting out the statutory requirements); and alleging that the tax proceedings were an illegal effort to dismember the freehold by selling a part of the corpus thereof. Paragraph E avers that at the time Walter M. Grubbs made default with respect to the payment of taxes he was operating a printing plant known as the Decatur Weekly News, which he continued to operate after having supplied his wife, the said Hallie M. Grubbs, with

money to purchase said property, or after having supplied it to some one else for her; and that ever since,
until the enterprise was abandoned after the filing of
the original bill, he has with the acquiescence and consent of Hallie M. Grubbs, continued to operate said
plant to his own benefit, without the payment of rent
or taxes. Paragraph F alleges that the defendant Dodson Printers' Supply Company is a nonresident of the
state of Alabama, and has no property in this state, except, perhaps, some few liens or mortgages for the purchase money of machinery, and that it proposes to sell
or make way with or dispose of said property as soon
as it can obtain a judgment against the same, either by
selling to somebody in the state of Alabama, or by
transporting the property outside of the state; that it
claims and contends that the property is worth more
than its debts held thereof; that if the said detinue
suits are tried in the law and equity court a large bill
of costs will be incurred, and that the said printing
company will insist upon the costs of these suits being
paid before allowing complainant to redeem, and that
this will work an additional burden upon complainant;
that such parts of said property as are not fixtures
should be first ordered sold or subjected to the Dodson
Supply Company's debt, before resorting to that part
of the machinery which is a part of the freehold. Then
follows a list of the machines and property alleged to
be not a part of the freehold. Paragraph G amends by
striking from paragraph 7 the following words: "Is
firmly fastened and fixed to the building; that." Paragraph I further amends by averring that said printing
presses are heavy and ponderous; that the larger press
rests and was originally installed after its acquisition
by Grubbs, and before the filing of the original bill,
upon piers constructed of brick and mortar, which start

below the surface of the ground, underneath the floor
level of said building, and are built up solidly to about
the floor level, with special reference to the support of
said machine and its operation, and that said machine
is rested upon said brick piers let into the ground as
aforesaid, and has been firmly held in place while and
when in operation by its own ponderous weight; that
all the shafts are attached to the building in the same
manner as are the shorter shafts in this amendment
referred to; that said Grubbs acquired the lot and
erected the building for the special avowed purpose of
installing the printing plant upon the ground, or
ground floor, in order that the operation thereof might
not produce vibration and jarring of the building, and
imperil the enterprise and the occupants of the house
where he might be located. Paragraph I further amends
the bill by averring that the two job presses and folders
are ponderous, and are held in place when being run
by their own weight; that the entire outfit of machinery
was operated by an electric motor, which was firmly
fastened to the brick wall by long bolts running through
said motor, or the rims or edges thereof, let into and
firmly embedded in the wall; and the said motor and
said machines were all connected by belts running from
one pillow to another, and by power communicated
from the motor to the shafts, and from the shafts and
pulleys to the belts, and from the belts to the machines.
Paragraph J further amends the bill in paragraph 12
thereof with the added averment that Grubbs' assets
and resources are insufficient for the payment of
his liabilities, and that the names and amounts of other
creditors to whom liabilities are owing are unknown
to complainant. Paragraph K amends the prayer by
asking that the Dodson Printers' Supply Company be
enjoined and restrained from prosecuting its detinue

suits in the law and equity court; that it be enjoined
from selling or disposing of the machines; that it be enjoined and restrained from removing any of said property out of the state, or from dislocating or removing
it from the building; that the court order a sale of all
that part of the property covered by the reservation of
title of the Dodson Printers' Supply Company that
may be ascertained to be chattels and not fixed to the
freehold; that the proceeds be applied on the debt of
the said Dodson Printers' Supply Company; that complainant be allowed to pay off and discharge the remainder of said debt, when ascertained; and that the
building and machines which are a part of the realty be
sold as an entirety.

KYLE & HUTSON, for appellant. The property was
not so attached as to become a part of the freehold, and
pass under the mortgage lien.—*Tillman v. DeLacey,*
80 Ala. 106; Jones on Mortgages, 49; *Rodgers v. Prattville M. Co.,* 81 Ala. 487. Having acquired jurisdiction
of the case of the *Printers' Supply Co. v. Grubbs,* the law
and equity court will be permitted to proceed to a final
determination thereof, and hence, there was error in enjoining this suit.—1 Pom. Eq. §638. On the question as
to when chattel becomes part of the realty, in addition
to the authorities cited above, see.—87 Am. St. Rep. 266;
16 Am. St. Rep. 471; 27 Vt. 428; 59 Am. Dec. 648; 45
Am. St. Rep. 285; 26 N. J. E. 568; *Capital C. I. Co. v.
Caldwell,* 95 Ala. 90; 92 Am. St. Rep. 261; *Parker v.
Blount County,* 148 Ala. 277; 127 Mass. 125; 19 Cyc.
1041, et seq.

D. F. GREEN, and E. W. GODBEY, for appellee. The
paragraphs of the bill may be as appropriately designated by letters as by figures; and *an amendment to the*

bill need not recite that it is an amendment to any particular part. Machines held in place by gravity and connected with other machines firmly fixed to the freehold are part of the realty if installed as part of the plant to which the realty is permanently devoted, capable of such use and actually so used.—*Voorhis v. Freeman*, 37 Am. Decs. 490; *Higman v. Humes*, 40 So. Rep. 128, 145 Ala. 215; *Winslow v. Merchants Ins. Co.*, 38 Am. Dec. 368; *Ottumwa W. M. Co. v. Hawley*, 24 Am. Rep. 719 (725); *Giddings v. Freedly*, 128 Fed. 355 (359); *McLaughlin v. Nash*, 92 Am. Dec. 741; *Dudley v. Hurst*, 1 Am. St. Rep. 368 (372-3); *Thompson v. Smith*, 50 L. R. A. 780 (782); *Brigham v. Overstreet*, 10 L. R. A. N. S. 452 (454); *Equitable G. & T. Co. v. Knowles*, 67 Atl. Rep. 961 (697); *Cavis v. Beckford*, 13 Am. St. Rep. 554; *Union B. & T. Co. v. F. W. Wolf Co.*, 108 Am. St. Rep. 903 (906-7). Appellant's cases either involve trade fixtures between landlord and tenant; or outfits that are *ex-vi-termini* portable; or articles that are not annexed to the realty and also not connected with any other machine that is so connected; —or else are opposed to the overwhelming weight of authority. If the machines are fixtures as between mortgagor and mortgagee, the former cannot plead to a foreclosure suit, the pendency of an action of detinue brought by a third party.

SAYRE, J.—Appellee filed his bill to foreclose a mortgage which conveyed a lot in the city of Decatur by descriptive boundaries only. The principal subject of controversy between the parties is whether certain machinery put into a building upon the lot after the execution of the mortgage is to be included in the security. The question is doubtfully raised, but the parties have treated it as properly raised, and since its

determination will in the end be important, we would
be willing to pretermit any objection which might perhaps be taken to the manner in which the demurrer
presents the issue, and decide the question if that could
be done at this stage of the cause. We will not repeat
the averments of the original and amended bills in ex-
tenso. They will be set out in the report of the case.
Nor do we intend to undertake any elaborate review of
the many cases cited; nor to formulate any general
statement of the tests to be applied in such cases.
The author of the chapter on "Fixtures" in 19 Cyclo-
pedia of Law and Procedure states it to be a mixed
question of law and fact whether a chattel has become a
part of the realty. He submits that from a consideration of the cases no more specific formula is possible,
and very justly observes that "it is the effort to compress the tests of whether there has been such annexation as will change the status of the thing in question
into a compact and specific formula that has rendered
inevitable the contradictions in the decisions." Page
1038.

Appellant borrowed money from the appellee upon
the express stipulation that it should be used in the
erection of a permanent structure or building upon the
mortgaged premises. There is, of course, no contention
that the mortgage does not cover the building thus
erected. Nor will appellant understand that the stipulation to which we have referred above has been permitted to be influential in determining the question
whether the machinery was subsequently attached to
the freehold in such manner and under such circumstances as to indicate an intention that it should become permanently a part thereof. This we say for the
reason that while the intention with which a chattel
is attached to realty is everywhere considered to be of

great importance, and while it would require no far-
fetched inference to support the conclusion that the
parties to the mortgage contemplated that the machinery should be located, as well as the building constructed, for the benefit of the inheritance, still it is
not precisely so alleged in the bill. It is now referred
to for the sole reason that appellant in his brief desires
it to be noted that the mortgage makes no mention of
the building. Our conclusion has been reached upon
consideration of the averments of the original and
amended bill. We cannot as yet know what the proof
may show. As we understand appellant's brief, he insists that on the facts alleged the court must say as
matter of law that as between the parties to this appeal
the machinery has never become a part of the realty.
Now complainant's general averment is that "all of
said machinery above described was installed and attached with specific reference to the building, and in
furtherance of the purpose for which the said building
was erected, and the object and intention that the same
should be permanent, and that as between your orator
and the said Walter M. Grubbs, the said articles, etc.,
are fixtures, and are and always have been since their
installation and connection, a part of the realty embraced within the lien of your orator's mortgages aforesaid." But appellant contends that this general, and
as we think, sufficient averment of the original bill,
though retained in the amended bill, is unsupported,
is in fact eviscerated and destroyed by certain affirmative averments of the bill in its last shape, and by its
failure to aver some other facts which will be mentioned, so that, upon the whole, the machinery in controversy, as between the parties to this appeal, cannot
be held to have become a part of the freehold except by
the exercise of unwarranted favor to the mortgagee,

whereas the requirement of the law is that on demurrer
the averments must be taken most strongly against the
pleader. In this connection appellant observes that the
bill contains no allegation that the machines could not
be removed from the building without doing injury
thereto; nor any that they are so ponderous as that by
reason of that fact alone they ought to be considered
as permanently placed; nor any that they could not be
used as effectively in some other building; nor that the
placing of the machines in the building enhanced the
value thereof; nor that any of the machinery except the
motor is actually attached to the building. No one
nor all together of these omissions prevented the machines from being fixtures as they are alleged to be,
though some or all of them may be of significance in
the final determination of the question. But in addition to the general averment already noted it is averred
that the building was planned and built for use as a
printing office; that the machinery is ponderous and
held in place by its own weight while being operated;
that the large press rests upon brick piers that are built
from the ground underneath the floor so as to prevent
vibration; that the machinery is operated by an electric
motor which is fastened to the wall by bolts; and that
power is furnished "from the motor to the shafts (themselves fastened to the walls of the building), and from
the shafts and pulleys to the belts, and from the belts
to the machines." On this statement of the contents
of the bill, and upon consideration of the principles of
law declared, and the authorities cited and quoted, in
Humes v. Higman, 145 Ala. 215, 40 South. 128, for the
mere repetition of which at this time there seems to
be no occasion, we conclude that the machinery in question is averred to be a part of the realty and within
the lien of the mortgage, whatever the proof in that re-

gard may develop on a final hearing. So, after all, we
can do no more than respond to the specific question
raised by the demurrer which avers the bill to be inconsistent, repugnant, and self-contradictory in respect to
the connection of the machines with the realty. We
do not find the demurrer to be well taken.

The machinery in question was bought by Grubbs
from the Dodson Printers' Supply Company, which
company retained title as security for the unpaid balance of purchase money. Before the bill was filed that
company had brought statutory detinue for the machinery, and it had been claimed and replevied by Mrs.
Grubbs. The amended bill contains a prayer that the
detinue suit be enjoined, and that upon final hearing
complainant be allowed to pay off and discharge the
balance of the debt due to the Dodson Company, and
that the building and the machines be sold as an entirety. To this part of the bill the appealing defendants demurred and now complain that their demurrer
was improperly overruled. The machines may be fixtures as between complainant and appellants, though,
as between the Dodson Company and all others, they
may be mere chattels. But the Dodson Company has
made no complaint of this feature of the bill either
here or in the court below. On the assumption that as
between appellants and appellee the machines do form
a part of the realty, as the bill alleges the case to be,
it is not perceived how the relief here sought can prejudice any right of the appellants. The court of equity
has power to make the complainant's mortgage security
completely effective according to the intent and purpose of the parties. If the Dodson Company were objecting to this feature of the bill, an entirely different
question would be presented.

The original bill was divided into paragraphs numbered from 1 to 17a. By amendment, paragraphs lettered from A to K were added to the bill. The effect of one of these paragraphs was to strike certain words from paragraph 7 of the original bill. It is urged that by lettering the amendatory paragraphs, instead of numbering them, there was a violation of Rule of Practice No. 8, which directs that "the stating part of all bills must be divided into sections, and numbered consecutively, 1, 2," etc. We see no reason why a substitute should be sought for so plain a direction. But the fact that every purpose of the rule has been met is so evident that we would not be satisfied to affirm error of the ruling below which sustained the bill against the demurrer taking objection to the bill for a departure from the practice indicated by the rule.

We are of opinion that the decree must be affirmed. Affirmed.

DOWDELL, C. J., and ANDERSON and SOMERVILLE, JJ., concur.

Hall & Farley *v.* Alabama Terminal & Improvement Co., *et al.*

Bill by Judgment Creditors to Subject Equitable Assets of an Insolvent Corporation to the Payment of Their Debts.

(Decided June 29, 1911. 56 South. 235.)

1. *Corporations; Creditor's Action; Remedy; Fraud.*—Upon return of execution nulla bona, a bill in equity may be maintained by a judgment creditor of an insolvent corporation to reach amounts alleged to be due the corporation from its original stockholders on unpaid stock subscriptions and fraud in the transfer or withholding the assets from the creditors is not necessary to equity jurisdiction.

[Hall & Fariey v. Alabama Terminal & Improvement Co., et al.]

2. *Same; Creditor's Action; Adequate Legal Remedy.*—The jurisdiction of a court of equity to subject the indebtedness of the stockholders on their unpaid stock subscription to the payment of judgments against an insolvent corporation after execution returned nulla bona, is founded upon the inadequacy of the legal remedy, and not on fraud vel non, and the inadequacy of the legal remedy is the better test of equity jurisdiction in such cases.

3. *Same; Stockholder's Liability; Fraud.*—Where a corporation purchases shares of its own capital stock in an attempt to discharge the liability of its original stockholders on unpaid subscriptions by the use of assets of the corporation, there is a fraud on the creditors.

4. *Same; Effect of Transfer; Bona Fide.*—Where a subscriber to the capital stock of the corporation, while the corporation was solvent, and while a balance was due on his subscription, transferred his stock in good faith to other stockholders who were solvent, and who, as part of the considerations for said transfer, assumed the liability to the corporation for the balance due, and with full knowledge of all the facts the corporation accepted the purchasers in the place of the original subscribers as the owners of said stock, and agreed to look to them for the balance due, such original subscribers were discharged from any liability for a fraud upon a subsequent creditor resulting from transactions between the corporation, and the purchasers of his stock. since a subsequent creditor cannot complain of the disposition of the property by a corporation unless such disposition was made with the intent to hinder, delay or defraud subsequent creditors, and actually had that effect.

5. *Same; Burden of Proof.*—Where subscribers to the capital stock of a corporation have transferred their stock in good faith to purchasers who have been accepted by the corporation, a subsequent creditor of the corporation who seeks to enforce the former's liability to the corporation on the grounds of fraud in the transfer has the burden of proof.

6. *Same; Effect of Transfer.*—Where the purchaser of stock agrees expressly to assume all the transferor's liability thereon, and when such agreement is acceded to by the corporation on making the transfer, the rule that a stockholder. on a bona fide transfer of his stock, is only discharged from liability as to future calls for payment on stock, and not from liability for amounts due upon previous calls, has no application.

7. *Same; Powers; Purchase of Own Stock.*—Unless so authorized, a corporation may not buy its own capital stock.

8. *Same; Capital Stock; Nature of Property in Shares.*—Stock in a corporation is only evidence of the right of the holder or owner to share in the proceeds of the corporation's property, and a share of stock only represents an aliquot part of the corporation's property, or the right to share in the proceeds to that extent when distributed according to law and equity.

9. *Same; Transfer of Shares; Registration.*—Section 1262. must be construed with sections 1263 and 1265, Code 1907. and is for the protection of creditors of and purchasers from the stockholders. and not for creditors of the corporation; hence a failure to register a bona fide transfer will not render the transfer void as to creditors

[Hall & Farley v. Alabama Terminal & Improvement Co., et al.]

of the corporation so as to entitle them to sue the transferor to recover on unpaid subscriptions on the stock.

10. *Same; Officers; Representation; Ratification.*—Where a corporation, without express authorization at a regular meeting, leaves the entire management of its affairs to its president, and the president assents to a transfer of stock by the subscribers to the capital stock, on which a balance is unpaid, and accepts the purchases instead of the subscribers, as owners of the stock, and liable for the unpaid balance, such acts, when ratified, become the acts of the corporation as they were such acts as could have been regularly authorized.

11. *Same; Officers; Nature of Office.*—So far as the creditors of the corporation are concerned, the directors of the corporation have the right to leave to the president the entire management and discretion as to the transfer of stock of a subscriber, on which a balance is unpaid, and as to accepting the purchaser as owner of the stock and liable for any unpaid balance, as the officers of the corporation are trustees for the stockholders and not for the creditors.

12. *Appeal and Error; Review; Questions Presented.*—Where it affirmatively appears from the record that all of the testimony of witnesses on their several examinations is not set out, any difference in their testimony on different examinations cannot be considered on appeal with reference to their credibility.

13. *Depositions; Examination without Order; Waiver.*—By cross examining the witnesses without objection, the adversary party waived the fact that the witnesses were examined after their depositions had been taken without an order of court first obtained.

14. *Same; Suppression.*—Whether depositions should be suppressed, because taken without special order is discretionary with the trial judge according as he thinks the right of the parties would be best subserved.

15. *Judgment; Estoppel of.*—Since there should be an end to litigation the doctrine of estoppel by judgment is not disfavored.

16. *Same; Pleading.*—Where a creditor sought to reach sums alleged to be due to an insolvent corporation on their unpaid stock subscription, a plea in estoppel or defense, by such stockholders, that a former judgment was rendered in a suit by such creditor against respondents as garnishees of the same indebtedness or chose in action in favor of the respondent, after its answer was contested and after a trial and determination of the case on its merits, is sufficient as to its averments.

17. *Same; Burden of Proof.*—The burden is upon the respondent to prove a special plea of res judicata as alleged.

18. *Same; Conclusiveness; Requisites as Estoppel.*—The judgment of a court of concurrent jurisdiction directly upon the point is a plea in bar, or is evidence conclusive, between the same parties upon the same matter directly in question in another court, but in the absence of any one of these ingredients, the defense fails.

19. *Matters Concluded.*—A judgment is conclusive between the same parties when rendered on a verdict on the merits not only as to the facts actually litigated and decided, but as to all the facts

necessarily involved in the issue; and although a particular matter
is not necessarily involved in the issue, yet if the issue is broad
enough to cover it, and it actually arose and was determined, it may
then be connected with the record by evidence aliunde.

20. *Same; Present Case.*—Held by an equally divided court in a
subsequent proceeding in equity that the judgment therein was res
judicata of complainant's right to recover in that proceeding.

APPEAL from Birmingham City Court.

Heard before Hon. A. D. SAYRE.

Bill by Hall & Farley as trustees, against the Alabama Terminal and Improvement Company and others,
to subject equitable assets of the insolvent corporation
to the payment of certain judgments, execution thereon
being returned "no property found." Decree for respondent and complainant appeals. Affirmed.

GUNTER & GUNTER, and J. M. CHILTON, for appellant.

ROBERT L. HARMON, for appellee.

MAYFIELD, J.—The bill in this case is by the judgment creditors, to subject equitable assets of an insolvent corporation to the payment of their judgments,
after the return of execution, "No property found."
The particular assets sought to be subjected are debts
or choses in action alleged to be due the insolvent corporation from its original stockholders, for their unpaid
subscriptions to its capital stock. The equity of the
bill for this purpose has once been doubted (if not denied) by this court; but we take it that it has now been
settled affirmatively.

This suit, in one form or another, has been many
times before this court. For its history, and a full
statement of the facts and the law of the case, we refer
to the reports of former decisions of this court in this
particular case. See *Hall v. Henderson,* 134 Ala. 455,
32 South. 840, 63 L. R. A. 673; *Ib.,* 126 Ala. 449, 28

South. 531, 61 L. R. A. 621, 85 Am. St. Rep. 53; *Hall v. Alabama Terminal & Imp. Co.*, 104 Ala. 557, 16 South. 439, 53 Am. St. Rep. 87; *Ib.*, 143 Ala. 464, 39 South. 285, 2 L. R. A. (N. S.) 130; *Ib.*, 152 Ala. 262, 44 South. 592. The last decision above referred to settled the questions as to the propriety of the various amendments to the bill, and that they did not constitute a departure from the original.

Since the last appeal in this case, it appears that some of the respondents have compromised their liabilities. The bill was dismissed as to these, but retained against the other three respondents, to-wit, O. C. Wiley, Wiley & Murphree, and J. M. Henderson & Co.

The claim against each of these three respondents is for unpaid subscriptions to the capital stock of the insolvent judgment-debtor corporation, the Alabama Terminal and Improvement Company. These respondents admit subscriptions for stock in the corporation as alleged, and admit original liability to the corporation as for such stock, but set up, as defenses, that the liability had been satisfied and discharged before the filing of the bill.

They also set up the defense—heretofore urged before this court—that a court of equity, at the suit of creditors, is without jurisdiction to pursue and condemn choses in action of an insolvent corporation, such as are sought to be subjected in this suit, which are withheld from the creditors, provided they are so withheld, "without fraud"; that is, in the absence of active fraud, equity is without jurisdiction. This question has been much and ably discussed in former opinions of this court and in briefs of counsel, to be found in the former reports of this case.

The law as contended for by respondents was announced in the case of *Donovan v. Finn,* Hopkins, Ch. (N. Y.), 59, 14 Am. Dec. 531, and probably by a dictum of Lord Thurlow, in *Dundas v. Dutins,* 1 Ves. Jr. 196. And this court was at first inclined to follow these cases to the extent contended for by respondents. But, after extended and mature consideration of this question, we are inclined to recede from the position first taken by this court on the question, and now hold that fraud in the transfer or in the withholding of the assets from the creditors is not necessary to equity jurisdiction in cases like this.

We are now inclined to the opinion, and hold, that the jurisdiction of equity to subject choses in action to the payment of a judgment, after the return of execution, "No property found," is founded upon the necessity for supplying a remedy, where that of the common law is inadequate, and therefore that inadequacy of a legal remedy, and not fraud vel non, is the better test of equity jurisdiction in such cases.—*Public Works v. Columbia College,* 17 Wall. 530, 21 L. Ed. 687; *Watson v. Sutherland,* 5 Wall. 4, 18 L. Ed. 580; *Scott v. Neely,* 140 U. S. 106, 11 Sup. Ct. 712, 35 L. Ed. 538; *McConihay v. Wright,* 121 U. S. 220, 7 Sup. Ct. 940, 30 L. Ed. 932; 1 Pom. Eq. §§ 294, 295, 297; 1 Bates, Fed. Pro. § 188; *Brown v. Bates,* 10 Ala. 432; *Spader v. Davis,* 5 Johns. Ch. (N. Y.) 280; *Hadden v. Spader,* 20 Johns. (N. Y.) 554; 1 Story, Eq. Jur. § 53.

The complainants' demand against the insolvent corporation being founded upon a judgment, and the insolvent corporation's claim against the other respondents, sought to be subjected, being founded upon subscriptions to capital stock of the corporation, and the amount of this subscription and the original liability therefor being undisputed, and the equity of the bill,

and the questions as to pleadings and departure, being
settled in favor of complainants, there remains for decision only the liability of these particular respondents
as for their subscriptions at the time of the filing of
the bill.

The special defenses to the bill set up by these respondent stockholders are, first, that they had paid
their subscriptions and thus discharged their liabilities; second, that they had sold their stock to third parties, who had assumed the original liability of the respondents, and who were accepted by the corporation
as debtors in lieu of the respondents, and that the transferees of the stock had paid the debts or discharged the
liability; third, they, or some of them (O. C. Wiley and
Wiley & Murphree), set up res judicata, in that they
were sued as garnishees by complainants, and were discharged after contest and trial on the merits. Either
of these defenses, if well and sufficiently pleaded and
established, is good. We will first treat the cases of O.
C. Wiley and Wiley & Murphree, as to the defenses of
res judicata; they being the only ones who set up this
defense.

The ancient doctrine announced by Coke, that estoppels were odious, is not now regarded as correct; and
it is certainly not so, when applied to estoppels, by
judgment, such as that attempted to be set up in this
case. There should be an end to, as well as a right of,
litigation. A plea of res judicata, or estoppel by judgment, to be sufficient, must be well pleaded. The true
rule in such cases, both as to the sufficiency of the
pleadings and of the proof, has been thus quoted and
stated by this court: "In the opinion of the Judges,
given in the *Duchess of Kingston's Case*, 2 Smith's
Lead. Cas. 609 (573), is the following language, given
as the result of the numerous decisions relative to judg-

ments being given in evidence in civil suits: 'That the
judgment of a court of concurrent jurisdiction, directly
upon the point, is, as a plea, a bar, or as evidence conclusive, between the same parties, upon the same matter, directly in question in another court.' It cannot
be overlooked that this language lays down a strict rule;
yet it is supported alike by reason and authority. The
parties must be the same, the subject-matter the same,
the point must be directly in question, and the judgment
must be rendered on that point. Any of these ingredients wanting, the defense fails. The sentence quoted
above has been adopted, both by text-writers and judicial tribunals, and has come to be recognized as a judicial axiom.—*McCravey v. Remson,* 19 Ala. 30, 54 Am.
Dec. 194; *Miller v. Jones,* 29 Ala. 174; 1 Greenl. Ev. §§
528, 529; Freem. on Judgments, § 258. In *Chamberlain
v. Gaillard,* 26 Ala. 504, this court said: 'The rule is that
judgments are final and conclusive between the parties,
when rendered on a verdict on the merits, not only as
to the facts actually litigated and decided, but that they
are equally as conclusive upon all the facts which were
necessarily involved in the issue; and, although the particular matter is not necessarily involved in the issue,
yet, if the issue is broad enough to cover it, and it actually arose, and was determined, it may then be connected with the record by evidence aliunde. * * *
In the plea we are considering, however, there is no allegation that the question of ownership entered into the
issue of the former action.' "—*Gilbreath v. Jones,*
66 Ala. 132, 133.

The rule has been thus stated by the Supreme Court
of the United States: "To render the judgment conclusive, it must appear by the record of the prior suit, that
the particular matter sought to be concluded was necessarily tried or determined—that is, that the verdict

in the suit could not have been rendered without deciding that matter; or it must be shown by extrinsic evidence, consistent with the record, that the judgment
necessarily involved the consideration and determination of the matter."

Unless otherwise provided by statute or rule of practice of courts, such as rule 28, chancery practice (Civ.
Code 1907, p. 1537), one requisite to the sufficiency of
such pleas and the proof thereof is that the former judgment, set up as an estoppel or res judicata, must have
been decided or rendered upon the merits of the case
involved in the second suit.

The plea of res judicata interposed in this case would
have met the requirements as above quoted, and would
have been sufficient if the records which were made exhibits and parts thereof had supported the conclusion
of the pleader; but if it be said that it averred facts,
and not conclusions, then the plea was inconsistent in
its averments, and was not proven. It averred that the
answer of respondents was contested, as provided by
law, and that the case was tried and determined on its
merits, in favor of the garnishees, the respondents here;
but unfortunately it made the record of that garnishment proceeding a part of the plea, and the record was
inconsistent with the other averments of the plea.

The burden of proof was, of course, upon these respondents to prove this special plea as alleged. In this,
we are of the opinion they failed. While they proved
that a judgment was rendered in the former suit in
favor of the garnishess, and in the very one which was
made a part of the plea, they did not prove that the case
was heard or tried upon the merits involved in *this* suit,
nor even upon the merits of the other action—that in
which it was rendered. The record as to this matter
shows that, after the answer of the garnishees and the

affidavit of contest by the plaintiff in garnishment were filed, the case was continued from 1893 to 1895, without any issue having been made up or tendered, as the statute requires, for a contest, and that no trial of contest was ever had. After the affidavit for contest was filed, nothing more appears to have been done, except to continue the case from time to time, until the 15th day of March, 1895, when (so far as the record shows) without any issue being made up or joined, the following order or judgment was entered: "This day come O. C. Wiley and Clarence Murphree, two of the garnishees herein, and move the court to be discharged, and upon consideration it is ordered and adjudged that said garnishees be and they are hereby discharged on their respective answers filed in this cause, that they go hence and recover of the plaintiffs the costs in this behalf expended for which execution may issue."

This shows affirmatively that the judgment was rendered on the ex parte motion of the garnishees, and without an issue of contest having been made up, though proper affidavit for contest had been filed by plaintiffs; that there was not in fact any judgment rendered on the merits, though a judgment of dismissal or nonsuit, as it were, was rendered against the plaintiffs. This judgment does not show or tend to show that they were not then indebted to the defendant corporation. Their answer was the only evidence tending to show this, and it of course was not conclusive upon the plaintiffs; they had the right to contest this answer, and had made the affidavit necessary to contest it, and until there was a contest of the answer, and a judgment thereon, the indebtedness vel non of the garnishees to the corporation, nor the right of plaintiffs (if such they had) to subject the assets to their claim against the corporation, was not determined. A judgment in favor of the garnishee

is never a bar to an action by the defendant, even upon
the same demand; a judgment against him is not a bar
until it is paid, and if not for the full amount due the
defendant it is then only pro tanto a bar.—Rood on Garnishment, § 212; Drake on Attachment, § 707.

The judgment in a law court, discharging the garnishees, attempted to be set up as res judicata to this
suit in equity, to be efficacious to such end, must of necessity be a judgment upon the merits of the issue involved in this suit—that is, the garnishees' indebtedness
or liability to the defendant—which could be enforced
in this suit but for that judgment. That the debt or
demand sought to be recovered in the two suits is the
same, and that the parties are the same, is not alone
sufficient. A debt or demand might be reached in this
suit that could not and should not have been reached
in the former. The plaintiffs might have failed in the
former action in a law court, for the very reason that
the particular demand sought to be enforced was an
equitable, and not a legal, one. It may be that the
judgment in the law court was in favor of the garnishees merely because the plaintiff should have proceeded, as he has done in this suit, in a court of equity,
in which event, of course, the former judgment is not
res judicata.

This very condition is pointed out by this court in the
case of *Teague et al. v. Le Grand*, 85 Ala. 494, 495, 5
South. 287, 7 Am. St. Rep. 64, which, like this, was an
action to subject the unpaid subscriptions of stockholders to the claims of the creditors of the insolvent corporation; and Stone, C. J., in that case, said: "Garnishment, such as was resorted to in this case, is purely a
legal remedy, a species of statutory attachment. When
invoked for the purpose of condemning credits, or legal
liabilities due to the defendant in the attachment, it is

not every species of liability that can be reached. It is
such as the defendant in attachment can recover of the
garnishee in an action of debt, or indebitatus assumpsit,
that are subject to this process.—Code 1886, § 2976, and
note. True the debt need not be due and presently de-
mandable; but there must be a contract, express or implied, out of which a money liability will certainly
spring, in the usual course of things. Many contracts,
from which money liabilities may possibly arise, are
not subject to garnishment at law. * * * Chancery
might have taken jurisdiction, the corporation being insolvent, and itself made calls, and enforced their collection, for the benefit of creditors.—*Glenn v. Semple*, 80
Ala. 159, 60 Am. Rep. 92. A common-law court—the
more especially under statutory garnishment—is without the power to do so."

One of the tests as to the sufficiency of a plea of res
judicata is, Does the plea show that the identical matter
in controversy in the second suit was determined and
concluded by the former judgment between the same
parties? It is the matter involved in the second, not
that involved in the first, which must be concluded by
the first judgment. The identity of the parties and of
the subject-matter in the two suits is always necessary;
but this alone is not sufficient. Nor is the fact that
the judgment pleaded was final, and was on the merits
of the case in which it was rendered, sufficient; it must
have been on the merits of the case in which it is interposed as a bar. The particular issue or matter of controversy involved in the second suit must or should
have been determined and concluded in the first.

A plaintiff may have a good cause of action, and may
sue in the wrong court, or bring the wrong action, and
in either case he will necessarily fail; but the judgment
against him in either case will be no bar to a proper

action in the proper court, though each judgment be final and on the merits involved in the particular suit, and the parties to the suits be the same. For examples: A. converts B.'s horse; B. sues A. in detinue therefor, and fails, because A. was not in possession of the horse at the bringing of the suit; this judgment would not be a bar to B.'s action of trover.—*Gilbreath v. Jones,* 66 Ala. 129. Suppose B. takes possession of A.'s house and lot, and A. sues him in detinue therefor, of course he fails; but this judgment is no bar to his action of eject-ment. Suppose A. sells and conveys to B. a house and lot, in consideration of B.'s paying him $100 within 30 days, provided that, if not so paid, B. will pay A. $10 as rent and reconvey to him the house and lot. Then, if B. fails to perform any part of his agreement, and A. sues him in ejectment for the property, of course he fails; but this would be no bar to a proper suit in equity to recover the property.

Let us put the concrete case which is involved in this suit: These respondents subscribed for capital stock in the corporation, the Alabama Terminal and Improve-ment Company; they had paid a part of the subscrip-tion as it was called; the corporation became insolvent; it was sued in a law court by complainants as its cred-itors; judgment was obtained, and respondents were garnished, but answered, "Not indebted to the corpora-tion." This answer was contested, and plaintiff failed, because no call for the unpaid balance of the subscrip-tion had been made upon respondents; this would be no bar to this present suit, because chancery could make the call.—*Teague et al. v. Le Grand,* 85 Ala. 493, 5 South. 287, 7 Am. St. Rep. 64.

But the pleas in any of these cases would be sufficient, if it was or could be shown that any matter necessary to a recovery in the second suit had been finally concluded and determined in the first suit. Of course, res judicata would not be applicable or good, in some of the examples above put, for other reasons than the one we have assigned; but the examples serve to show that the plea in this case under consideration was not good.

Nothing that is said in this opinion is intended to deny the proposition that judgments in garnishment proceedings may not be as conclusive upon the parties thereto as are any other judgments; but we have only attempted to show that they, like all other judgments, are only conclusive as to the matters which were, or should have been, adjudicated thereby.

The plea of res judicata in this case was evasive or inconsistent in its averments. While it alleges, among other things, that the judgment set up as res judicata duly and legally discharged the garnishees and forever relieved them from all liability for and on account of their subscriptions to the capital stock of the Alabama Terminal and Improvement Company, and that the judgment was a final one upon the merits of the controversy, and in favor of the garnishees and against the complainants (who were plaintiffs in the former suit), which, if true, would be res judicata and a bar to this suit, yet the plea also alleges that all this will more fully appear by the records and the proceedings had in the garnishment proceeding, which are made exhibits to and a part of the plea; and on an inspection of the exhibits and records referred to it does not "more fully appear," as alleged, that that judgment is res judicata or a bar to this suit, but the contrary fully appears. To state it differently, that judgment did not relieve the garnishees from all liability for and on account of their subscription to the capital stock of the insolvent company, and the judgment was not rendered on the merits, but was rendered on the ex parte motion of the garnishees, and the garnishees were merely discharged on their answers, and there was no trial on the contest of the answers. So, construing the plea most strongly against the pleader, it was insufficient, and it should have been so held.

It is true that this identical plea was heretofore held sufficient by this court, in this particular case (134 Ala. 510, 32 South. 840, 63 L. R. A. 673). The error, however, in the first opinion, in one or more respects, was pointed out in a later opinion in the same case (143 Ala. 845, 39 South. 285 [2 L. R. A. (N. S.) 130]), by the same learned justice who wrote the first, in which last case he spoke as follows: "It is insisted for appelless that the decree on the motion to suppress depositions, and on the plea of Wiley and others, should not have been made below, inasmuch as the bill was dismissed. This may be so. We need not decide that; nor indeed definitely and absolutely whether those decrees were correct. It is likely, however that the decree on the motion to suppress was right; and that the decree on the sufficiency of said plea, wherein the chancellor followed the opinion of this court on the former appeal, which seems now to have proceeded on the mistaken notion that there *was a contest* of the answers in garnishment alleged in the plea, was erroneous."

However, the decision in the first case was not expressly overruled in this later decision quoted, and the first decision was subsequently followed, and probably extended, in the cases of *Montgomery Iron Works v. Roman,* 147 Ala. 441, 41 South. 811; *Roman v. Montgomery Iron Works,* 156 Ala. 606, 47 South. 136, 19 L. R. A. (N. S.) 604, 130 Am. St. Rep. 106, and *Montgomery Iron Works v. Capital, etc., Co.,* 154 Ala. 663, 664, 44 South. 1044, and it follows, and we now conclude, that upon this point all of these cases were wrong and should be overruled.

The defense of payment of the subscriptions by these respondents was only set up as a defense pro tanto, and was only so proven, and to that extent only is a defense. In fact, it is conceded that each had paid in good faith a part of his subscription to the corporation; and the defense, to this extent, is by appellants admitted to be good, though there is probably a difference between the litigants as to the exact amount so paid by each of the respondents.

The other and last defense we hold was made out. It is in substance that the respondents were not indebted nor liable to the insolvent corporation, the Alabama Terminal and Improvement Company, for any unpaid subscriptions for the shares of capital stock of such corporation issued by it to such respondents, for the reason that while the corporation was solvent these respondents, as such stockholders, in good faith sold their stock at par to other parties or stockholders, who were perfectly solvent, and who, as part of the consideration of such sale, assumed the liability of these respondents to the company, for the balance due on their subscriptions, and that the corporation, with full knowledge of all the facts, accepted the purchasers, in lieu of these respondents, as the owners of such shares of stock, and agreed to look to such purchasers for the balance due, and thereby released these respondents from all liability.

It is true that, in so far as this defense was specially pleaded, it was also alleged that the transferees of this stock had paid to the corporation such balances due as for the original subscriptions for such stock. It is also true that the proof failed as to this allegation as to a part of the respondents, in so far as it was necessary to discharge the transferees from liability to the creditors of the corporation, but not in so far as it was necessary to discharge the transferees from liability to the corporation or to its creditors.

While the proof shows that the balance due was paid, by the transferees, or was not paid in such way or manner as to discharge the liability of the transferees to the creditors, in that it appears that the payment, or a large part thereof, was made with the assets of the corporation; or the stock was in turn resold to the corporation, in payment of this subscription, which was of course, a fraud upon the creditors of the corporation, even if the corporation procured or assented to it. In other words, as against the creditors of the corporation, it could not lawfully purchase the shares of its own stock, nor could it discharge the liability of its stockholders, as for unpaid subscriptions, by paying such debts for the stockholders with the assets of the corporation.

It is the function of a corporation to purchase and sell its property, but not its stock, unless so authorized; and certainly not, if the effect is to defraud its creditors. It is said that corporations have no souls, but it has never been said that they can perform miracles.

Stock in a corporation is only evidence of the right of the holder or owner to share in the proceeds of the corporation's property. So a share of stock only typifies an aliquot part of the corporation's property, or the right to share in its proceeds, to that extent, when distributed according to law and equity. If stock of a corporation is paid, that which is paid, together with its proceeds, becomes the property and assets of the corporation. If not paid, the liability of the stockholder to pay forms the property of the corporation. The latter kind can be, and is intended to be, transformed into the former; but the corporation as an entity owns both, and hence can purchase neither, unless so authorized.

This much has been repeatedly decided in former appeals of this case. But it does not by any means follow that the original stockholders are not discharged from all liability to the corporation or to its creditors, by reason of these subsequent transactions between their transferees and the corporation or its officers. If the corporation or its officers and the transferees of such stock thus attempted to defraud the creditors and to shield the transferees from liability, by the corporation's buying its own stock or paying the subscriptions with the assets of the corporation, which would otherwise be available to the creditors, they could not thereby render the original subscribers liable, after they had in good·faith sold their stock and were released from all liability. To be liable as for this fraud, they would have to be parties to it, before or at the time they sold their stock and were thereby released from liability. They must have participated in the fraud, or have been chargeable with notice of it.

This last condition was evidently conceded by the complainants to be necessary to a recovery, and hence it was averred, in the bill as last amended, as to each of the respondents. The averment as to O. C. Wiley in this respect is as follows: "As your orators are informed and believe, and on such information and belief state the fact to be, the defendant Oliver C. Wiley asserts that he sold and transferred his stock in the said Alabama Terminal and Improvement Company to the defendant said Sarportas, the said defendant promising and agreeing to pay to said company his (said defendant Wiley's) subscription therefor and the promises in writing he had made for the payment thereof. Your orators aver that if said sale and transfer were made, it was with the intent to defraud said corporation, and to hinder, delay, and defraud the creditors thereof. The

said defendant Wiley was amply able to pay and satisfy said debt, but was desirous to relieve himself from
liability to pay the same, and if such sale and transfer
was made, it was a mere contrivance by which he sought
to evade and escape from such liability. He well knew
that said defendant Sarportas was not a resident of the
state of Alabama, and he did not believe and had no
good reason to believe he was of ability to pay for the
said stock. The said subscriptions and debt of the said
Wiley is yet due and unpaid to the said company; said
company has never agreed to accept any other person as
debtor in his place and stead."

There were averments of fraud as to each of the respondents, varying in details, but in substance the same.
These averments were evidently made in the amended
bill, either in anticipation of, or in reply to, the defense
of a transfer of the stock by the respondents, and release of them from liability for such unpaid subscriptions. In respect to these various allegations of fraud,
we think the proof fails as to all of these respondents
who are appellees here, whatever it may be said to show
as to other respondents, not now parties to this appeal.

The facts of the case as to the sale of the stock by
each of the three respondents O. C. Wiley, Wiley & Murphree and J. M. Henderson & Co. as shown by this
record, are practically without dispute, and are as follows:

O. C. Wiley, individually, subscribed for 95 shares
of the capital stock of the Alabama Terminal and Improvement Company, and gave his conditional note
therefor for $9,500, and Wiley & Murphree, a copart-
nership, subscribed for 120 shares, and gave their conditional note for the same for $12,000. Wiley & Mur-
phree sold their 120 shares of stock to A. C. Saportas
on June 30, 1890, and O. C. Wiley sold his 95 shares of

[Hall & Farley v. Alabama Terminal & Improvement Co., et al.]

stock to A. C. Saportas, on, to-wit, September 25, 1890. Saportas was accepted by the corporation as a shareholder in lieu of Wiley & Murphree and O. C. Wiley, and voted the stock at stockholders' meeting subsequent to his purchase, and was recognized as a stockholder. At the time of the sale of this stock, viz., on June 30, and on, to-wit, September 25, 1890, the Alabama Terminal and Improvement Company was solvent and in good financial standing, and A. C. Saportas was, by the respondents and most of the witnesses, regarded as solvent, and of high credit and financial standing in New York city, the place of his residence, and was the financial agent at that time of the Alabama Terminal and Improvement Company. This company did not become embarrassed until after May 1, 1891.

J. M. Henderson & Co., in the month of January, 1890, agreed to sell and did sell to J. C. Henderson $5,000 of the stock subscribed by them to said company, and J. C. Henderson executed and delivered to them his written obligation, by which, in consideration of $5,000 of the stock so subscribed by these defendants, which was to be issued to him, he agreed to pay or satisfy $5,000 of their said subscription. Said company was immediately notified of said sale of said stock to said J. C. Henderson, and his promise made to these defendants to pay the amount of $5,000, and J. W. Woolfolk, as president of the said company, with authority to bind said company in the premises, agreed to look to and to hold the said J. C. Henderson bound and liable for said sum, and to discharge and release J. M. Henderson & Co., from all liability on account of the same, and executed and delivered an agreement in writing to said J. C. Henderson, to issue to him $5,000 of the stock subscribed by these defendants, upon the payment of that amount of said stock subscription.

If all this was done in good faith on the part of these
respondents, at the times and in the manner shown, of
course these respondents are not liable, and ought not
to be so held, no matter what fraud in fact or in law
may have been subsequently perpetrated by the insolvent company or its officers upon the creditors of the
corporation.

There is no direct evidence whatever to show that the
first transfer was not in good faith, so far as these respondents were concerned. And there are no facts or
circumstances from which it could be reasonably inferred that they acted in bad faith in the matter. In
fact, they all tend to show the contrary, in that, at this
time and for some time thereafter, the corporation and
all the parties to the contract were perfectly solvent,
and all had almost unlimited credit, and were apparently prosperous, so far as the evidence shows.

At that time neither these complainants nor their
assignors were creditors of the Alabama Terminal and
Improvement Company. This company did not open
up an account with the Farley National Bank until October 12, 1890. So these complainants are subsequent
creditors, and not existing ones as to these transactions; and hence the sales are not void as to them, unless tainted with actual intent to hinder, delay, or defraud them or other subsequent creditors. This court
has spoken and quoted as follows on this subject: "A
subsequent creditor cannot complain of a disposition
of its property by a corporation, unless such disposition
was made with intent to hinder, delay, or defraud subsequent creditors, and actually had that operation and
effect.—*Graham v. La Crosse & M. R. Co.*, 102 U. S.
148, 26 L. Ed. 106; *Porter v. Pittsburgh Bessemer Steel
Co.*, 120 U. S. 649, 7 Sup. Ct. 1206, 30 L. Ed. 830; *Dick-
son v. McLarney*, 97 Ala. 388, 12 South. 398; *Rollins v.*

Shaver Wagon Co., 80 Iowa, 380, 45 N. W. 1037, 20 Am.
St. Rep., 434; *Schrever v. Scott,* 134 U. S. 405, 10 Sup.
Ct. 579, 33 L. Ed. 955; 2 Morawetz on Corp. §§ 795,
800. And the burden is upon the complainant to allege
and prove such fraud.—*Yeend v. Weeks,* 104 Ala. 339,
16 South. 165, 53 Am. St. Rep. 50. Nor does a creditor,
existing or subsequent, occupy such relation to a corporation's directors as its stockholders."

We repeat that there is no evidence in this record
to show any such fraudulent intent on the part of any
of these respondents at the time these transfers were
made. It is difficult to see how, at this time and under
the conditions then existing, any one could have had
such intent. There is certainly no direct proof to show
that there was then any attempt or any intention to
defraud any one. The reasonable inference, from all
the known or shown facts at that time, is that these
transfers could not and would not injure or defraud
any one. True, as it subsequently turned out, the bank
or these complainants were injured and defrauded; but
it was not these transactions which so injured or defrauded them, nor were they alone capable of so doing;
it was subsequent transactions, with which these respondents had nothing to do, and could not have fore-
fended, had they tried, that caused losses to complainants. Of course, as we have before said, if these transfers were a part of the scheme of the corporation, or
its officers or stockholders, to defraud the creditors of
the corporation, and these respondents were parties to
it, or in their transfers they thereby aided or abetted
others to so subsequently defraud the creditors, then
they would be liable in this action, as claimed by the
appellees. But there is no proof to show this, and the
burden of proof as to such matters is upon the complainants; hence they fail in this feature of the case.

Appellants concede this in their brief, in which they say: "As to plea B, we *admit,* of course, that if the corporation or its agent, having authority to act for it in the premises, bona fide accepted a transferee of stock as its debtor for the outstanding note of the vendor, the latter would be released. But we *insist* that this alleged occurrence did not take place in January, 1890, and in a bona fide manner, but after all the Troy stockholders had agreed to betray the terminal company, and in pursuit of the general swindle of defrauding the creditors of the company by kiting with the Farley Bank and getting rid of their stock liability through the manipulations of Woolfolk and his coadjutors; and after the terminal company was really insolvent, all its assets having been, or being in the process of being, diverted by fraud to the buying of the subscribers' stock, or in the building of the M. T. & M. R. R." We find that the undisputed evidence in this case, so far as these respondents are concerned, shows the facts to be what appellants above "admit," and that there is no positive or direct proof of appellants' "insistence," and that the matters thus insisted upon cannot be reasonably inferred from any other facts which are proven.

It is also argued by appellants that, as there was no transfer of the stock in question entered upon the books of the corporation, as provided by the statute (Code 1896, §§ 1261-1263), the transfer was for that reason void, and the transferrors remained bound; that is, that such registration was necessary to respondents' release from liability to the creditors of the corporation. This we do not understand to be the law on this subject. This court has often decided the question as follows: "These statutes do not render the transfer void for a failure to comply therewith, except as to the class therein contemplated. This court has often held that a transfer, though not registered, was good as between the parties thereto.—*Duke v. Cahawba Co.* 10 Ala. 82, 44 Am. Dec. 472; *Fisher v. Jones*, 82 Ala. 117, 3 South. 13; *Campbell v. Woodstock Co.*, 83 Ala. 351, 3 South. 369. It has also been held that sections 1262, 1263, and 1265 should be construed in connection with each other. In the case of *Fisher v. Jones, supra*, it was said: 'The purpose of the statute on this subject is obviously to give notice of the title to creditors and purchasers, so as to prevent fraudulent transfers, and to protect the corporation itself in determining the question of membership, the right to vote, the payment of dividends, and other incident of ownership.' We do not think that these statutes were intended for the protection of creditors of the corporation, but creditors of and purchasers from the stock holders."

Shares of stock in a private corporation, in this state, are personal property, and may be sold and transferred as other personal property, though no certificates for the stock have been issued or registered.—See Code sections, supra, and cases there cited, and also *Henderson v. Mayfield Woolen Mills*, 153 Ala. 625, 45 South. 211.

It is likewise insisted by the appellants that the transfers of stock in question, with the assumption of the unpaid subscriptions by the transferees thereof and the release of the transferrors from liability, were inoperative or ineffective to this end, because the transactions in question were not first authorized at a regular meeting of the board of directors of the corporation; that the president of the corporation had no authority to assent to such transactions, unless he was first specifically authorized to do so by the board of directors. If the abstract proposition of law involved in this argument could be said to be sound, it is not applicable, either to the pleadings or proof in this case.

It is alleged in the bill as last amended "that the said Alabama Teminal and Improvement Company left the entire management of its affairs to J. W. Woolfolk, its president, and that he conducted all its affairs;" and this averment is supported by the proof, and it is shown that he assented to all the transactions in question, and approved them after they were consummated; and they were afterwards duly ratified by the corporation. A corporation can subsequently ratify whatever it could in the first instance have lawfully authorized. But here the pleadings and proof taken together show both au-thorization and ratification by the corporation. The directors of the corporation, so far as the creditors are concerned, had a right to leave to Woolfolk, as the president, the entire management and discretion as to these transactions in question. The officers of a corporation are trustees for the stockholders, but not for the creditors of the corporation. *Force v. Age-Herald Co.,* 136 Ala. 278, 33 South. 866; *O'Bear Co. v. Volfer,* 106 Ala. 205, 17 South. 525, 28 L. R. A. 707, 54 Am. St. Rep. 31.

It is insisted by appellants that the respondents J. M. and J. C. Henderson testified differently on their last examinations from what they did on their first, and that for this reason we should disregard all of their testimony showing good faith in this matter, certainly so far as the date of the sale of stock by J. M. Henderson & Co. to J. C. Henderson is concerned. It is a sufficient answer to this argument to say that it affirmatively appears from this record that all of the testimony of these two witnesses, on the two separate examinations complained of, is not set out. Hence we cannot know what that difference was, or that it was, as is argued. There is no reason shown by the record why we should disbelieve the testimony of these witnesses on the last examination.

It is argued that on the first examination, in 1895, they did not know the exact date of the sale of the stock; that they knew nothing more definite than that it was several months prior to December 13, 1890; and that on the last examination, 12 years thereafter, they say pat and positively that it was in January, 1890. If this were shown by the record, we would not think it alone a sufficient reason to conclude that they have sworn falsely on either examination, and there is no other reason assigned why they should be disbelieved. They might not, on the first examination, have rendered accurately the dates, and have subsequently refreshed their memories by referring to some memoranda or writing which fixed the date exactly, and enabled them thereafter to remember it. Moreover, we find a plea (Record, pp. 17, 18) which was sworn to by J. M. Henderson, on the 21st day of April, 1894, alleging that the transaction was had in the month of January, 1890—the exact date fixed by both the witnesses on their last examinations.

It is also insisted that appellees had no right to re-examine J. M. and J. C. Henderson as witnesses, and that the last depositions of these witnesses should have been suppressed. If the re-examination was had without first obtaining an order of the court to that effect, it was matter which could be waived, and the record shows that it was waived by an agreement of counsel, and by the fact that appellants cross-examined the witnesses without objection. If the trial court could have suppressed the depositions because taken without a special order of the court for that purpose, it was discretionary with the trial judge to do so or not, as he thought the rights of the parties would be best subserved thereby, and we see no abuse of that discretion.

The pleadings and proof in this case bring it squarely within the principles of law decided by this court a number of times, which are as follows: A stockholder of a solvent corporation is discharged from liability to the corporation as for the unpaid subscription on his stock by a bona fide transfer of such stock to a solvent transferee, if done with the consent of the corporation, or if it subsequently, with full knowledge of all the facts, assents to or ratifies the transaction. The transferee or purchaser in such case is thereby subrogated to all of the rights and powers, and subjected to all of the duties and liabilities, of the original stockholders. Cook on Corporations (5th Ed.) §§ 255, 256 and 258; 3 Thomp. on Corp. p. 1804; *Henderson v. Mayfield,* 153 Ala. 625, 45 South. 211; *Allen v. Montgomery,* 11 Ala. 437.

It is, however, insisted by appellants that this doctrine is only applicable as to future calls for stock, and has no application as to amounts past due as for previous calls. This is ordinarily true, and is not at all different from the doctrine stated above; in fact, it is the application of the same doctrine which is applied without any special agreement between the parties at the time of the transfer and sale, as to the respective rights, duties and liabilities of the transferror and transferee as to the unpaid subscriptions. This much is implied from the transfer and sale of the shares, in the absence of an express agreement as to such rights and liabilities. Appellants rely upon the case of *Webster v. Upton,* 91 U. S. 65, 23 L. Ed. 384, in support of their argument, in attempting to distinguish this case from the general rule, upon the ground that calls had been made for the full amount of the subscriptions before the transfers.

This decision relied upon is not at all different from those of our court above referred to, nor from the proposition as announced in the text-books upon the subject; in fact it quotes at length from such texts. But in that case the court was speaking of the *implied* promises to pay and release, and not to the *expressed* ones, which were made by the parties and formed a part of the sale or transfer, and which were consented or acceded to by the corporation. On this subject the court in that case said: 'But, if the law implies a promise by the original holders or subscribers to pay the full par value when it may be called, it follows that an assignee of the stock, when he has come into privity with the company by having stock transferred to him on the company's books, is equally liable. The same reasons exist for implying a promise by him as exist for raising up a promise by his assignor. And such is the law as laid down by the text-writers generally, and by many decisions of the courts." So the distinction contended for by appellants, and which is pointed out in the text-books, has no application here, for the reason that here there were expressed provisions and contracts as to the substitution of debtors, and change of rights, liabilities, and duties of the transferrors and transferees of the shares, and which were either consented or acceded to by the proper party—creditor corporation.

It follows from what is said above that none of the respondent appellees were shown to be liable to the Alabama Terminal and Improvement Company, nor to the complainants, at the time of the filing of this bill, nor thereafter, and that the bill was properly dismissed.

Affirmed.

DOWDELL, C. J., and SOMERVILLE, J., concur. SIMPSON, ANDERSON and MCCLELLAN, JJ., concur in the con-

[Sullivan, Trustee, v. Central Land Co., et al.]

clusion, but are of the opinion that the decisions in the cases of *Iron Works v. Roman,* 147 Ala. 441, 41 South. 811, and *Iron Works v. Capital City, etc.,* 154 Ala. 663, 44 South. 1044, are sound, and should not be departed from.

Sullivan, Trustee *v.* Central Land Co., *et al.*

Bill to Dissolve a Corporation, and to Wind Up Its Affairs.

(Decided May 18, 1911. 55 South. 612.)

1. *Corporations; Dissolution; Minority Stockholders.*—In a suit by minority stockholders to dissolve the corporation on the ground of an abandonment by the sockholders, the court must determine the right of the parties on the facts existing at the time of the filing of the bill, and the fact that since that time, efforts had been made to put the corporation on a better footing as to the conditions of its property, and as to the formality and regularity of the meetings of the stockholders, and the fact that the time fixed by statute for the life of the corporation has expired since the filing of the bill, cannot be considered.

2. *Same.*—In the absence of evidence of the insolvency of the corporation or bad faith in its management, the court will not order a sale of the property at the suit of the minority stockholders for the dissolution of the corporation.

3. *Same; Abandonment by Stockholders; Meetings Outside the State.*—Although the meeting of the stockholders of a domestic corporation are irregular, or illegal because of the absence of any statute authorizing such meeting, still they show that the stockholders retained an interest in the corporation, and are attempting to exercise its powers, hence, minority stockholders suing for a dissolution of the corporation on the ground of abandonment by the stockholders cannot relie thereon to show such abandonment.

4. *Same; Office in State; Agent in State; Object.*—The purpose of the statute in requiring corporations to keep its principal officer or agent in the state, is to aid the state in the supervision and control of the corporation, and has no regard to the financial interests of the corporation, and a failure to comply with this requirement may or may not evidence a purpose to abandon corporate functions, and hence, the mere fact that a corporation for a time failed to observe the statute, did not show an abandonment, where all the time it had agents in the state for the management of its property.

5. Same; Management of Business; Remedy of Minority Stockholder.—Where the question of corporate management is one of discretion, or of doubtful event in the undertaking in which the corporation is engaged, minority stockholders cannot resort to equity, their remedy being to sell their stock.

APPEAL from Birmingham City Court.

Heard before Hon. H. A. SHARPE.

Bill by C. B. Sullivan as trustee, against the Central Land Company, and others, to dissolve the corporation and wind up its business, and affairs. From a decree denying relief complainant appeals. Affirmed.

S. D. & J. B. WEAKLEY, for appellant. The equities of the bill were settled on a former appeal.—*C. L. Co. v. Sullivan,* 152 Ala. 360. Where a private business corporation has failed of the purposes and objects of its creation, a single stockholder may maintain a bill in equity for the sale of the assets and the distribution of the proceeds among those equitably entitled thereto.— *McKleroy v. Gadsden Imp. Co.,* 128 Ala. 190; *Noble v. Gadsden Land Co.,* 133 Ala. 250; (The opinion of the Supreme Court of Alabama in the Noble case is reprinted in 91 American Reports, page 27, with an extensive note, and the decision of the Court on the former appeal of this case is reprinted in Vol. 15, page 420-428 of the American and English Annotated cases, with a digest covering the entire subject under consideration. Reference is made to both of these cases.)— *Miner v. Belle Isle Ice Co.,* 17 L. R. A. 417-418, citing Morawetz on Corporations, 217-407; *Cramer v. Bird,* L. R. 6 Eq. 143. The election of trustees made apparently for no purpose but to keep the company in extension, will not prevent a dissolution of the company.—Wait on Insolvent Corp. p. 304; citing *Re the Jackson Marine Ins. Co.,* 4 Sand Ch. N. Y. 559; *Briggs v. Penniman,* 4 Cowan, N. Y. 387. Upon the dissolution of a corporation its stockholders become tenants in common of its property.—*Pewayic Mining Co. v. Mason*, 145 U. S. 349; *Craft v. Mining Co.* 6 Ga. 467. The existence of the corporation for nearly twenty years, the time limited for its existence, without having done anything to accomplish the purposes for which it was incorporated, is a circumstance to be considered by the Court in determining if the complainant is entitled to relief.—*Merchants, etc., Line v. Wagoner*, 71 Ala. 581.

TOMLINSON & McCULLOUGH, for appellee. Under the facts in this case, the court properly denied the relief sought.—*Central L. Co. v. Sullivan*, 152 Ala. 360.

SAYRE, J.—The considerations upon which a court of equity will intervene at the suit of a minority stockholder to dispose of the corporate property and distribute its proceeds, thus working a practical dissolution of the corporation, whatever in this last regard may be the precise legal effect of the decree, were well stated by Judge Tyson, in *Noble v. Gadsden Land Company*, 133 Ala. 250, 31 South. 856, 91 Am. St. Rep. 27, and by Judge Denson in this case on a former appeal (152 Ala. 360, 44 South. 644). Any further statement of the general principles involved is now unnecessary. The company in the Noble Case, like the one here, had for its leading, if not exclusive, purpose the realization of speculative profits out of a rapidly advancing market for lands. Then, as now, expectations had been disappointed by a quick subsidence of values to something like a true level. In that case many of the stockholders were nonresidents, the whereabouts of one-third of them unascertainable, and diligent efforts on the part of the president and secretary during a period of five years had failed to secure a meeting of the shareholders. The fixed charges which the corporation was bound to meet so far exceeded its income that annually a part of the corpus of its estate had to be sacrificed. The company was wholly without credit, and, by reason of the fact that a majority of its shareholders had lost all concern about its affairs, was unable to avert impending ruin. Under these circumstances, the court awarded relief. On the former appeal, Judge Denson, sustaining the bill in this case as against a demurrer, drew a parallel with the case of *Noble v. Gadsden Land Company* as follows: "The only difference between that case and the one in hand is that there the income of the corporation, at the time the bill was filed, was not sufficient to pay expenses, taxes, etc., and annually a portion of its land was sold on that account, and it was shown that the corporation was without credit and its assets were being sacrificed, the corporation, on account of the abandonment of it by the holders of the majority of its stock, being powerless to prevent it; while here it does not appear that any of the property of the corporation has been sacrificed, or even sold, to meet expenses, but the income is alleged to be the same as the outgo. Nevertheless it does appear from the bill in this case that the property from which income is derived is gradually deteriorating in value, and that in a short while the income will not be sufficient to meet the expenses. This being true, the inevitable result will be that, if the corporation continues, it will be in the same condition in this respect as was the one in the case cited."

We are now to say whether the complainant has established the allegations of his bill. Of controlling importance is the inquiry whether at the time of the bill filed the corporation had ceased to be a going concern. It is apparent that since the charges of the bill were preferred such efforts have been made to put the com-

pany on a better footing in respect to the condition of
its property and the formality and regularity of the
meetings of its shareholders as would hardly leave any
question as to its being a going concern at this time.
Meantime, also, the term fixed by statute for the life of
the corporation has expired. Both these considerations
are to be laid aside, and the rights of the parties under
the bill determined as of the date of its filing. The Central Land Company was organized under the laws of
this state. Between the time of its organization in February, 1887, and the filing of this bill, May 18, 1906,
the evidence shows that meetings of the stockholders,
attended by a majority of the stockholders in person
or by proxy, have been held on 24 occasions in 14 different years; the last five being held in the years 1902, 1904
and 1905. Seven of these meetings, the last on October
3, 1902, were held in this state in seven different years.
The rest were held in Kentucky, where the stockholders
lived. Appellant interprets the evidence to be in conflict
as to whether any meeting were held at all prior to
1900, but we are satisfied that the facts are as they have
been stated. Since 1901 stockholders of domestic corporations have been authorized to hold meetings outside
of this state upon certain conditions. Acts 1900, 1901,
p. 2099; Acts 1903, p. 310; Code 1907, § 3481. Prior
to the filing of this bill, the defendant corporation had
not complied with the conditions prescribed by the statutes. Appellant contends that such meetings as were
held outside of this state were therefore nothing more
than congregations from time to time of individuals
without corporate relations, without authority of law,
and that such meetings were utterly void for all constit-
uent purposes of the corporation. In Maine and Texas
it has been held that directors elected at a meeting of
shareholders convened outside the state are not even

directors de facto (*Miller v. Ewer,* 27 Me. 509, 46 Am.
Dec. 619; *Franco-Texan Land Co. v. Laigle,* 59 Tex.
339), but elsewhere it has been held that the preferable
view, and one more in accordance with modern ideas,
is that directors elected at such meetings are directors
de facto. *Humphreys v. Mooney,* 5 Colo. 282; *Wright v.
Lee,* 2 S. D. 596, 51 N. W. 706; 10 Cyc. 321. However
that may be, it is to be remembered that the complainant is proceeding, not for the specific purpose of vacating the charter of the defendant company, but for the
rescue of his individual share of its property. Nor does
he insist that things would have been any better for
him or for the company if all its meetings had been
held inside the state, but he refers to the fact of their
extraterritoriality as evidence of an abandonment of the
purposes of the company, whereas the plain fact is that,
however irregular or even unlawful these meetings may
have been, they satisfactorily prove that the stockholders retained interest in their company and were attempting to exercise its faculties.

The statutes to which we have referred have required
since 1901 that corporations must keep a principal office in this state and an agent thereat. This provision
is intended to serve the purposes of the state in the
supervision and control of corporations. It has no regard for the financial interests of corporations. A failure to comply may or may not evidence a purpose to
abandon corporate functions, depending upon attendant circumstances. In this case the company for a time
failed to observe the statute, but all the while has had
agents in this state for the management of its property.
The land had on it when bought by the company a
number of houses of an inferior sort. In 1888 and 1889
the company improved its property by building seven
new cottages at a cost of something more than $2,000.

The company has from time to time declared small dividends aggregating about 5 per centum on the price paid for its property. When the bill was filed, it had in the treasury about $450. The company's houses to some extent have fallen into decay, but the income has always been sufficient to meet the company's fixed charges. At the time of the filing of the bill, there was no indication whatever that a sacrifice of any of its property would be necessary during the remaining months it had to live under the law of its incorporation, or, for that matter, later. The company's agents during its entire life have paid taxes, collected rents, and rendered regular accounts to their principal. Soon after the investment, it became evident that the property had been bought at a greatly inflated price. And then the main avenue of communication with the business center of the city of Birmingham, a public street, was closed by an adjacent owner under the alleged authority of an act of the Legislature. For some years the company has had a suit pending for the purpose of opening this avenue, and upon the event of that suit, which seems to have been prosecuted with due diligence, the value of the property in considerable measure depends. Meanwhile the real value of property in that neighborhood has been advancing, and the great majority of the stockholders appear all along to have been of the opinion that the money invested in the company could best be retrieved by holding to their property yet a while. There seemed, when this bill was filed, small chance that stockholders would, within the life of the corporation, be able to recover the entire amount of their investment. The problem almost from the beginning seems rather to have been how to minimize losses which events quickly following the incorporation of the company brought about. That original loss cannot be repaired by a decree for the sale of the property. It cannot be said that to wait for a probable advance in a genuine market, when that may be done without further call upon stockholders will be an unprofitable business. And so long as a favorable event appears to be reasonably within the reach of ordinary prudence, and involves no further outlay, the effort to attain it seems to fall legitimately within the purposes had in contemplation when the company was formed and its entire capital invested in this property with the expectation that it would advance in value. The corporate purpose was not to sell merely to be selling, but to sell when that might be done to advantage. The venture was speculative. It may be assumed that the contract among the incorporators contemplated that the issue would be determined within the time fixed by law as the company's term of life. But that term had not expired when the bill was filed. So that the mere lapse of time without a sale of the property is not enough to demonstrate an abandonment of corporate purposes. Nor do the other facts show that the company's property will be consumed in the payment of fixed charges.

There are some other considerations of minor importance pro and con, but we think the merits of the controversy are shown by the facts stated, and that on them the conclusion ought to be that the defendant company was a going concern at the time the bill was filed.

There is no allegation or proof of insolvency or bad faith in the management of the company's affairs.

When the question is one of mere discretion in the management of corporate business, or of doubtful event in the undertaking in which the corporation has embarked, remedy cannot be had by application to a court of equity. *Benedict v. Columbus Construction Co.*, 49 N. J. Eq. 36, 23 Atl. 485. Under the circumstances shown, if the complainant was dissatisfied with the prospects and progress of his speculation when he filed his bill, his judgment in that regard differing from that of a majority of the stockholders, his only remedy was to sell his stock, whatever may be his rights now that the time set by law for the dissolution of the corporation has arrived. *Noble v. Gadsden Land Co., supra.*

Affirmed.

DOWDELL, C. J., and ANDERSON and SOMERVILLE, JJ., concur.

Mizell, *et al. v.* State *ex rel.* Gresham.

Quo Warranto.

(Decided May 16, 1911.   Rehearing denied June 27, 1911.
55 South. 884.)

1. *Quo Warranto.*—The validity of a municipal election authorized by section 1068 and 1164, and ordered by those in authority, cannot be determined on quo warranto, but the election may be contested under the provisions of section 1168, Code 1907, although the court may determine on quo warranto the validity of an election not authorized by a valid law, or an election in territory not included in the law, or an election ordered by those having no color of authority. (Section 5464, Code 1907.)

2. *Elections; Polling Places; Validity.*—The action of the council of a town in selecting a polling place after the mayor had given notice of the holding of the election at another place did not invalidate the election held at the place fixed by the council.

3. *Same; Selection; Contest.*—Where the qualified electors of a town had an opportunity to vote at an election, and a majority voted at the polling place fixed by the council of the town, and the minority cast their ballots at an unauthorized place, and the inspectors of the election were eligible to hold that office, the election was not void, but was subject to contest within section 1168, Code 1907.

4. *Same; Election Officers; Selection.*—While the law contemplates that inspectors of an election of a town shall be selected at the time the election was ordered, yet, the changing them at a subsequent date does not invalidate the election, and upon discovering that the inspectors appointed are unfit, the council of the town may appoint others, notwithstanding the provision of section 1164, Code 1907.

[Mizell, et al. v. State ex rel. Gresham.]

APPEAL from Geneva Circuit Court.

Heard before Hon H. A. PEARCE.

Quo Warranto by the state on the relation of W. J. Gresham, against Frank J. Mizell and others, seeking to oust them as mayor and council of the town of Samson. From a judgment for relator respondent appeals. Reversed and remanded.

W. O. MULKEY, and J. M. CHILTON, for appellant. Quo Warranto is not the proper remedy.—Sec. 5464, Code 1907; *Patton v. Watkins,* 131 Ala. 387. The election should have been contested under the provisions of section 1168, Code 1907.—*Parks v. State,* 100 Ala., 634; *Hilliard v. Brown,* 97 Ala. 92. There was a misjoinder of parties respondent.—32 Cyc. 1447; 17 Enc. P. & P. 440; *People v. DeMille,* 93 Am. Dec. 179. If quo warranto would lie, the question after all would be who received the greatest number of votes. *Echols v. The State,* 56 Ala. 137. The burden is on the challenger to show that the vote was not a qualified vote.—*Black v. Pate,* 136 Ala. 608. It appears that Mizell received the largest number of votes, and even if there was irregularity, and the council acted fraudulently and corruptly, then the election would not be set aside, unless the person declared elected was not elected in fact.—*Lee v. The State,* 49 Ala. 43. The resignation of Pinkard was complete when made, and he ceased to be a member of the council from the date of his resignation.—*William v. Fitts,* 49 Ala. 402; *Almon v. Fowler,* 160 Ala. 187. Hence, any acts in which he participated when his presence was required to make a quorum were irregular at least, and the subsequent appointment of inspectors made at a meeting of the council when an actual majority was present must be deemed the valid appointment. The failure to give the notice does not affect the

validity of the election.—*Wilson v. Pike County,* 144
Ala. 397; *Comm. Ct. v. Thurman,* 116 Ala. 209.

ESPY & FARMER, and C. D. CARMICHAEL, for appellee. Having answered that they held the office and exercised the powers thereof, the burden was on the respondents to show their authority and right.—*Montgomery's Case,* 107 Ala. 372. The inspectors were not properly appointed.—Secs. 1063 and 1164, Code 1907; 15
Cyc. 411; 29 Cyc. 1371. Quo warranto is the proper
remedy.—*Johnson v. Com. Ct.* 145 Ala. 557. The bal-
lost were not provided as prescribed by law.—Secs. 372
and 389, Code 1907. The storehouse election was nothing, and the election held in the council chamber was
the only election with any validity, as it was the only
one held according to law.

ANDERSON, J.—This is a proceeding by the statutory quo warranto to oust the respondents, as mayor
and council of the town of Samson. The respondents
set up a certificate of a majority of the then existing
town council, of September 20, 1910, certifying that they
were, on the 19th of said month and year, duly and legally elected to the offices held by them respectively.
    Section 1167 of the Code of 1907 provides that a cer-
tificate of election shall be given by the council, or a
majority of them, which shall entitle the persons so certified to the possession of their respective offices immediately upon the expiration of the term of their predecessors, as provided by law. Section 1068 of the Code
of 1907 fixed September 19 as the time for said election, and section 1164 gave the town council authority
to provide for the holding of the same, by appointing
the managers and clerks, and to designate the polling
place or places. The election was therefore authorized

by law and was ordered by those clothed with legal authority to do so. If it was not held or ordered in all respects according to law, those would be considerations going to the validity of same, and not the jurisdiction or authority for same, and when the certificate of election was shown by the respondents, from those having authority to issue same, of an election held at a time and for a purpose authorized by law, and ordered by those having the authority to do so, the regularity or validity of said certificate cannot be determined or adjudicated, without passing upon the validity of the election. Section 5464 of the Code says: "The validity of no election, which may be contested under this Code, can be tried under the provisions of this chapter." It should be observed that the word "validity," and not "regularity," is used in the statute, and that it is intended to prohibit inquiry, in quo warranto, into things connected with an election, beyond mere irregularities.

The word "validity" has a well-understood technical, as well as popular, acceptation, and must receive such meaning in the courts, if its use in the statute does not suggest a different one.—29 Am. & Eng. Ency. of Law, 573; *Sharpleigh v. Surdam*, 1 Flip. 489, Fed. Cas. No. 12,711. We think, however, the word "validity," as used in the present statute, does not mean that the court would not have the authority to determine that what purported to be an election was not sanctioned or authorized by law—that is, that the statute authorizing same was void, or that the law did not authorize an election for the office in question, or that it related to territory not included in the law, or that the election was called or ordered by those with no color of authority; but when the election is authorized by a valid law, and is ordered by the direction of those with authority to order same, the manner of conducting or ordering same, or of canvassing the returns, are questions that cannot be gone into in quo warranto, if the statute authorizes a contest of the election.

The election in question was authorized by law, was ordered by those in authority, and the manner of ordering same, the preparation of the ballot, the designation of the particular polling place, or places, relate to the validity or regularity of the election, and do not refer to jurisdiction or legal authority for the said election, and are questions which cannot be passed upon in quo warranto, if said election can be contested under the Code of 1907. Section 1168 of the Code of 1907 expressly authorizes a contest of the election in question. Nor does section 5464 prohibit inquiry only as to grounds for which a contest is provided, and authorize the consideration of grounds not covered by the statutory grounds for the contest of the election; but it excludes inquiry into the election, if the Code authorizes a contest, whether the grounds for contest include the things complained of or not. This was the construction given section 5464 in the case of *Park v. State,* 100 Ala. 634, 13 South. 756. This case was approved in the case of *State ex rel. v. Elliott,* 117 Ala. 150, 23 South. 1244, which held, however, that quo warranto was the remedy there, because the right to contest, in that instance, was given by the municipal act, and not the Code, and that section 3177 (5464 of the Code of 1907) did not apply. The present Code, however (section 1168), does give the right to contest the election in question, and section 5464 applies and cuts off the right to do so under quo warranto proceedings.

The case of *Blount Co. v. Johnson,* 145 Ala. 553, 39 South. 910, was not a quo warranto proceeding, and section 5464 had no application to same. Moreover the election there considered was not authorized by law, and there was nothing to contest. Here we have an election authorized by law, held at a time fixed by law, and ordered by those with the authority to do so, and if the law was not complied with as to ordering, conducting, and canvassing the returns these considerations would necessarily involve inquiry into the validity of said election, and which is expressly forbidden by section 5464 of the Code of 1907.

We hold that the circuit court erred in rendering judgment against the respondents, and in not dismissing the proceedings, and the judgment is reversed, and one is here rendered denying relief and dismissing the proceedings.

Reversed and rendered.

DOWDELL, C. J., and SAYRE and SOMERVILLE, JJ., concur.

On Rehearing.

ANDERSON, J.—While counsel make no war on the opinion, they claim that it overlooks or does not deal with the facts in the case. The facts were fully considered before and during the consideration of this case in consultation and if they were not dealt with or set out at lenth in the opinion it was because the writer thinks that legal opinions should not contain facts, except so far as it may be necessary to an understanding of the questions discussed, and that they should be set out by the reporter in the proper place. We did not overlook the fact that a previous meeting was held by the mayor and a majority of the council on September 2, when inspectors and clerks were selected, and that notice was given of said selection. The first meeting, however, did not select or name any special place for the election, and the action of the mayor in designating the council chamber as the place in his notice was unauthorized, except for the fact that it had been the place for holding previous elections, as the law (section 1164 of the Code of 1907) authorizes the council, and not the mayor, to direct the polling place or places.

The propriety of naming the Grimes store, after the mayor had given notice that the election would be held at the council chamber, may be questioned, but this did not render the action of the council void, as they, and not the mayor, were authorized to fix the place.

Nor can it be said that the council did not have the authority to change the inspectors and clerks before the day of the election. Of course the law contemplates that they be selected 10 days in advance of the election, but doing so at a subsequent day would not render the election void. If some of them should die or leave before the election, or if the council should discover that they were unfit, they would have authority to appoint others, and this authority is not taken from them, merely because section 1164 makes provision for what shall be done if the inspectors, or any one of them, do not appear on election day. This merely provides for a contingency in the event those selected by the council do not appear, but does not mean that the council exhausted their authority in the first instance.

Moreover the law contemplates that the election should be held by qualified electors, and if so held, and fairly so, it matters but little who they were, and the fact that one person or another served as an inspector or clerk does not render the election void. Therefore the polling place was fixed at Grimes' store by those who had authority to do so, and at the council chamber by one who had no authority to do so and, whether the inspectors were or were not selected under the letter of the law, they were eligible to hold same and they held

[Mizell, et al. v. State ex rel. Gresham.]

it under the authority of those having the power to appoint, and we cannot say that the election held in Grimes' store was void, and was not such an election as could be contested.

We repeat that whether the election was regularly held or not it was held under authority of law, and was not per se void, and was such an election as could be contested, and cannot be questioned by quo warranto. Had there been no attempted election at the city hall, and the one at Grimes' store was the only one held at Samson on September 20, it would scarcely be contended that the election in question was void. Therefore simply because a minority saw fit to cast their ballots at the unauthorized place fixed by the mayor, this fact should not operate to render null and void a perhaps irregular election, but one which had been ordered by those in authority, and at which a majority of the voters who voted or attempted to vote on that day saw fit to cast their ballots, and who do not appear to have been misled or deceived by the failure to give sufficient notice that the election was going to be held at the Grimes store, instead of the place selected by the mayor, and who had no authority to make the selection, except that he perhaps felt that he could arrogate unto himself the right, because of the fact that the city hall was the place for holding previous elections.

The application for rehearing is therefore overruled.

DOWDELL, C. J., and SIMPSON, MCCLELLAN, MAYFIELD, and SOMERVILLE, JJ., concur in the opinion, and in denying application for rehearing.

Commissioners Court of Pike County v. City of Troy.

Mandamus.

(Decided June 29, 1911. 56 South. 131.)

Highways; Taxation; Apportionment.—The special road tax collected under authority of section 215, Constitution 1901, cannot be apportioned among various parts of the county, and hence, acts 1909, pp 205 and 304, are inoperative as to special taxes so collected.

(Sayre, J., dissents.)

APPEAL from Pike Circuit Court.

Heard before Hon. H. A. PEARCE.

Mandamus by the City of Troy against the Commissioners' Court of Pike County. Order in favor of petitioner, and defendants appeal. Reversed and petition dismissed.

The petition alleges that there was levied and collected for Pike county by the commissioners' court thereof a road tax of one-fourth of one per cent. on the property assessed for taxes in said county. The said tax was levied for the years 1908-09, was due October 1, 1909, and delinquent January 1, 1910. It is alleged that the tax collector had collected and paid to the county treasurer on the property located in the city of Troy, for and on account of said road tax, the sum of $3,278.82, and that that amount was now held by the county treasurer. It is alleged that by virtue of the act of the Legislature approved August 26, 1909 (Acts Sp. Sess. 1909, p. 304), and by virtue of the act approved August 25, 1909 (Acts Sp. Sess. 1909, p. 205), one-half of said amount of money was due the city of Troy; that demand was made for it, and had been refused, etc. Demurrers were filed to said petition, and the answer was made, setting up that the acts in question were unconstitutional and void. The order of the court was that the commissioners' court of Pike county pay to the city of Troy $1,639.41, for the uses and purposes set forth in said petition, and said sum be charged by said commissioners' court to its fund raised and collected by it through and by its special road tax.

E. R. BRANNEN, for appellant. Appellant's contention is that the acts of 1909, pp. 205 and 304, are unconstitutional and void so far as the tax levied and collected under the provisions of section 215, Constitution 1901, as there is a direct conflict between the two, and the Constitution must prevail.—*McCain v. The State*, 62 Ala. 138; *Jeffersonian Pub. Co. v. Hilliard*, 105 Ala. 576; *State v. Street*, 117 Ala. 203; *Board of Revenue v. The State*, 54 South. 5757.

FOSTER, SAMFORD & CARROLL, for appellee. The court properly granted the mandamus requiring the county to pay the city its pro rata part of the tax.—Acts 1903, p. 412; Sec. 1335, Code 1907, Sec. 120, Municipal Code, *So. Ry. v. Cherokee County*, 144 Ala. 579. There is no conflict between the act in question and section 215 of the Constitution.—7 Ind. App. 309; 104 Fed. 833; 119 Ia. 619. A street is a public way or road.—27 A. & E. Enc. of Law, 102; *Perry v. N. O. & M. C. R. R. Co.* 55 Ala. 420; *Brace v. N. Y. C.* 27 N. Y. 269.

McCLELLAN, J.—Appeal from an order awarding mandamus to compel the court of county commissioners of Pike county "to pay to petitioner, the city of Troy, for the uses and purposes set forth in said petition, and said sum be charged by said commissioners' court to its fund raised and collected by it through and by its *special road tax. * * *"*

The sum in question thus appears from the record to have been the product of a *special road tax* within and under the influence and control of the second pertinent proviso of section 215 of the Constitution of 1901. Hence, for the reasons set down in the original opinion delivered in *Board of Revenue of Jefferson County v. State ex rel., etc.* 172 Ala. 138, 54 South. 757, and adopted as decisive of the appeal of *State ex rel. City of Tuscaloosa v. Court of County Commissioners, infra,* 54 South. 763, the Legislature was without power or right to direct or control the disposition, by delivery to the municipality, for the construction, maintenance, improvement, or repair of *streets,* of the product of such *special road tax.* On rehearing of *Board of Revenue of Jefferson County v. State ex rel., etc., supra,* the prevailing opinion was that the levy there involved did not constitute a *special road tax* for road purposes; and, hence, the pertinent proviso of section 215 of the Constitution did not apply to forbid legislative direction or control of the fund there in question, it being, on that levy, a part of the general fund to which the pertinent proviso of section 215 had no reference.

The order appealed from is therefore reversed, and the petition is dismissed.

Reversed, and petition dismissed.

DOWDELL, C. J., and SIMPSON, ANDERSON, and MAYFIELD, JJ., concur. SAYRE, J., dissents.

SAYRE, J. (dissenting).—I cannot concede the sufficiency of the reasons assigned for declaring the act unconstitutional. The provision of the Constitution is "that to pay any debt or liability now existing against any county, incurred for the erection, construction, or maintenance of the necessary public buildings or bridges, or that may hereafter be created for the erection of necessary public buildings, bridges, or roads, any county may levy and collect such special taxes, not to exceed one-fourth of one per centum, as may have been or may hereafter be authoried by law, which taxes so levied and collected shall be applied exclusively to the purposes for which the same were so levied and collected." The prevailing opinion, that the act is unconstitutional because it directs the application of funds raised by special county taxation to a purpose for which they were not levied and collected, rests necessarily upon the proposition that when the framers of the Constitution used the generic term "roads" they intended to exclude the species "streets." Reference is made to other sections of the Constitution in which the term "street" is employed as aptly descriptive of a thoroughfare in a municipality. The inference drawn is that the Constitution makers did not intend the inclusion of "streets" in the term "roads" when they used the latter iu Section 215. That "street," as the word is ordinarily used, has a more limited meaning than "road," is freely admitted. But in Section 215 of the Constitution deals with the subject of general taxation whereas in the other sections referred to it is dealing with a subject which called for the use of the narrower word. It is dealing with charges which are not considered as taxes in the ordinary sense or within the meaning and intent of constitutional provisions governing the levy, collection, or disposition of taxes; charges in the nature of compensation exacted for benefits peculiar to the owners of abutting property; charges which should be, and heretofore have been, confined to those densely populated districts, such as cities and towns, where the highways are ordinarily called "streets." "The authorities almost universally take such an imposition, though confessedly laid under the taxing power, out of the category of taxes and taxation, as those terms are employed in organic limitations on legislative power to levy or authorize the levying of taxes, and in general statutes."—*Birmingham v. Klein*, 89 Ala. 461, 7 South. 386, 8 L. R. A. 369. So that the use of different terms in different sections of the Constitution seems hardly to be convincing of anything more than that in dealing with different subject-matters the terms employed were aptly chosen to express the different purposes had in view.

For authority the main dependence for the theory of unconstitutionality is found in the case of *McCain v. State*, 62 Ala. 138. In that case the defendants, who were supervisors of the public streets of the town (then) of Anniston, were indicted for failing to keep a certain road or street in repair. The corporate authorities had passed an ordinance abolishing or discontinuing the road. The ruling was that the ordinance abolishing the street, was within the power of the municipal authorities. In the course of the opinion the court used this language: "To hold such public roads (referring to roads through rural districts which had been incorporated into the town), thus brought within the boundaries of an incorporated town, to be still under the jurisdiction of the court of county commissioners, would be very unnatural, and might lead to conflicts of authority, which should always be avoided. For the court of county commissioners to exercise jurisdiction over such highways as a road, and the corporate authorities to exercise jurisdiction over them as a street, would be impossible. They cannot be both a 'public road' of the county, as that phrase is understood, and a street of an incorporated village at one and the same time. One character must yield to the other." It is said, in effect, that this decision fixed a meaning for "roads" and "streets" which has become imbedded in the Constitution. That conclusion, in my opinion, overworks the doctrine that a Constitution, like a statute, may carry with it a construction of its phraseology by adopting terms which have acquired a definite and settled meaning. Constitutions are popular instruments, and "deal with larger topics and are couched in broader phrase than legislative acts or private muniments. They do not undertake to define with minute precision in the manner of the latter, and hence their just interpretation is not always reached by the application of similar methods."— *Houseman v. Commonwealth*, 100 Pa. 222, 232. The word "roads" had never been used in the same connection in previous Constitutions. In the Constitution of 1875 it occurs only once (section 21, art. 14), and then as meaning railroads. In the present Constitution it occurs in section 242, corresponding to section 21, art. 14, of the Constitution of 1875, and in section 104, which has to do with the subject of taxation the word occurs only in that section of the Constitution of 1901 here in question. It was and is of frequent occurrence in the statutes, and most often, as is conceded, in connection with the subject of county roads. But nowhere is there evidenced a fixed understanding and use of the word which would deny the propriety of a broader use as comprehending streets. To the contrary, in at least one case, *Gaston v. State*, 117 Ala., 23 South. 682, "public road" in a criminal statute was held to include "street." Recurring to *McCain's Case*, the expressions used by the court were proper enough in their application to the question then under consideration. But it does not seem to me that the court undertook to say that the word "road" might not have a broader meaning in other connections, nor was there any occasion for such a declaration. The present occasion seems rather to call for a recurrence to the rule for estimating the authority of judicial expressions which was stated by Chief Justice Marshall in this language: "It is a maxim not to be disregarded that the general expressions in every opinion are to be taken in connection with the case in which those expressions are used. If they go beyond the case, they may be respected, but ought not to control the judgment in a subsequent suit when the very point is presented."—*Cohens v. Virginia,* 6 Wheat. 399, 5 L. Ed. 257.

The word "road" has acquired no definite and fixed meaning in judicial decision or in ordinary use which makes necessary an interpretation of the Constitution against the power of the Legislature to pass the act in question. I have already referred to *Gaston v. State.* According to the lexicographers it is a general term, including highways, streets, and lanes.—24 Am. & Eng. Encyc. 985, 986. A street is nothing but a road in a city, town, or village, having houses and town lots on one or both sides. Cent. Dig. A road is specially a highway. Standard Dict. "Public road" and "highway" are commonly understood to mean the same thing, and include all ways which of right are common to all the people.—*Abbott v. Duluth* (C. C.) 104 Fed. 833. This court said, in *State v. Mobile,* 5 Port. 279, 30 Am. Dec. 564: "While the streets of a town are its highways, they may also be the public highways of the country." "The word 'road,' in a proper connection, may be fitly used to designate a city or borough street."—In re *Vacation of Osage Street,* 90 Pa. 117. In *Sharett's Road,* 8 Pa. 89: "It is, however, objected that a street or alley in an incorporated town is not a 'road' within the meaning of the resolution. But this objection, which is somewhat hypercritical, is fully answered by the decision of this court in the case of the *Moyamensing Road,* 4 Serg.

& R. (Pa.) 106, where it is shown the word 'street' is equivalent, in common parlance, to road or highway. Indeed, a street is strictly a road, and may be and frequently is so denominated without any violation of grammatical propriety." In *Northwestern Telephone Co. v. Minneapolis*, 81 Minn. 140, 83 N. W. 527, 86 N. W. 69, 53 L. R. A. 175, where a statute authorizing telegraph and telephone companies to use the public roads and highways was construed to include the streets of the city of Minneapolis, after noting that the word "highway," in actual use, embraces city streets as well as country roads, the court said: "We cannot, therefore, by looking through the charters of different cities where the words 'street' and 'highway' are used, respectively, in reference to urban thoroughfares, and by comparing the result, necessarily determine any distinction in this respect; for where a word of general import covers two classes, and another only one, the obvious and sensible inference would be that the general term was intended to embrace both." In *Stokes v. County of Scott*, 10 Iowa, 166, Webster's definiation of "road," as including "highway, street, and lane," is adopted. So in *People v. Commissioners of Buffalo Co.*, 4 Neb. 150; *Follmer v. Nuckolls Co.*, 6 Neb. 204; *So. Kansas Ry. Co. v. Oklahoma City*, 12 Okl. 82, 69 Pac. 1050. Whether the word is used broadly or in a restricted sense must be determined upon consideration of those principles which are usually observed in constitutional construction. It is to be conceded that, in the construction of statutes relating to the subject of roads and streets, attention must be given to the conflict and confusion which it may be presumed will arise from a division of control over the same subject between cities and counties—distinct and different governmental subdivisions of the state; but difficulties of that sort are by no means insuperable, and

it may be assumed that the Legislature will care for such
considerations (as it has in this case by intrusting to
the municipality the expenditure of that portion of the
special tax appropriated to the maintenance of streets
and bridges within the corporate limits), and they furnish no sufficient reason for limiting the power of the
Legislature, unless there be something in the nature of
the subject-matter which demands a construction of the
words "roads" in the Constitution as referring to rural
highways only. There is no such demand in the nature
of the subject-matter. On the contrary, the territory of
a county does not cease to be a part of the county when
it is included within an incorporated city or town. The
necessity for unbroken highways throughout the country remains, as it was, a matter of concern to all the
people of the county or state. One of the most important functions of the state is to make provision for public
roads for the use of the people. The powers intrusted
to the counties, including the erection, supervision, and
control of roads, are the powers of the state, delegated
for the purposes of civil and political organization, and
may be withdrawn by the state in the exercise of its sovereign will, and other instrumentalities or agencies
established. While, in the exercise of its quasi legislative authority over the roads of the county, the discretion of the commissioners' court in the application of
funds to particular roads and localities is not to be controlled by the courts, nor by evidence produced according to the ordinary rules of legal procedure, but by its
own knowledge of the geography of the county and the
needs of its people (*Askew v. Hale Co.*, 54 Ala. 639, 25
Am. Rep. 730; *Matkin v. Marengo Co.*, 137 Ala. 155, 34
South. 171), I have no doubt that the Legislature, in its
discretion, may itself direct such application or commit
it to other agents of its own selection. "To the common-

wealth here, as to the king of England, belongs the franchise of every highway as a trustee for the public."—
Perry v. N. O., etc., R. R. Co., 55 Ala. 413, 28 Am. Rep.
740.

No valid reason can be assigned, as I think, why the
people, in the adoption of the Constitution, and when
dealing with a fund to be raised by taxation upon all
the property of the county, including that within the
municipality, should be held to have used the word
'roads' in that narrow and restricted sense which would
deny to the Legislature the power to permit taxes levied
upon urban property to be expended in part at least in
the improvement of the highways which lie before the
doors of those who pay the tax. In the interpretation
of this section of the Constitution, designed to promote
the convenience of all the people, I see no occasion for
ignoring every equitable consideration by holding that
where there must be equality of burden there may not
be equality of benefit.

Further, what warrant can there be for holding that
the Legislature may not permit the levy of a special
county tax for the building of bridges within the limits
of towns or cities? There is none; and yet bridges and
roads are yoked together in the Constitution, as they
are in necessity, and identical considerations must influence legislation concerning them, for a public bridge
is nothing unless it be a part of a public road. "A public bridge is an essential part of a road, and the erection
of a bridge is but the laying out of a highway."—Elliott
on Roads and Streets, § 27.

The well-considered case of *Duval County Commissioners v. Jacksonville*, 36 Fla. 196, 18 South. 339, 29
L. R. A. 416, said by the editor of the series to be the
first case to present the constitutional question of the
power of a county under statutory direction to turn over

to the highway or street authorities of a municipal corporation situated in the county a part of the funds raised by taxation "for county purposes," affords an argument for my position. That was a proceeding by mandamus to require the commissioners to turn over to the municipal authorities one-half of the amount realized from a special tax for public roads and bridges levied and collected on the property within the limits of the municipal corporation as provided by a statute of Florida. The Constitution of that state provides that the Legislature cannot authorize counties to levy taxes for any other than county purposes, nor can counties be authorized to devote money so raised to any other than such purposes. Without following the court through its argument, which deals not with any mere words, but with the true meaning of such provisions, I quote its conclusion as follows: "It is true that there may be a distinctively municipal purpose, as distinguished from county purposes, and, in our judgment, the Constitution of the state recognizes such distinction; but in reference to the laying out and maintenance of public streets, or municipal highways, over which not only the people of the municipality, but of the entire county, can travel, it cannot be said, we think, that they are so distinctively and exclusively a municipal purpose as to render it impossible for the Legislature to authorize the counties to devote revenue raised by county taxation for public roads on the property situated within the municipalities to the maintenance of the public streets therein."

In response to the suggestion that under the construction which the Legislature has put upon section 215 of the Constitution a "county might levy and collect the special tax in order to discharge the county liability, as the Constitution clearly intends, and yet a part of the gross special tax sum would, by legislative action, be forbidden application to that constitutionally commanded purpose," I think it necessary only to say that no such result could follow, for the reason that a tax levied to pay a pre-existing debt or liability could not be applied for the "erection" of roads. The purpose to pay a pre-existing debt incurred for the building of roads and the purpose to "erect" or maintain other roads, whether in county or city, are different purposes, and the Legislature has evinced no purpose to break down or override the clear difference between them. It is perfectly plain that the act has relation to such special taxes as are levied for the purpose of constructing, repairing, or maintaining roads or highways. It can have no operation or effect upon special taxes levied to pay pre-existing debts.

In my judgment there is nothing in the word itself, nor in its context, nor in the policy of the state, nor in the justice and equity of the situation, which requires a construction of the word "roads" as excluding streets, which are but roads through thickly populated areas, whether incorporated or not, and I see no sufficient reason for so holding.

Touart *v.* State *ex rel.* Callaghan.

Quo Warranto.

(Decided June 29, 1911.　56 South. 211.)

1. *Officers; Creation and Abolition.*—The legislature may abolish any office that it can create, and the abolition of such office terminates the right of the incumbent to exercise the rights and duties thereof.

2. *Same; Removal; Term Fixed by Appointing Power.*—Where the appointing power is given the right to fix the term during which a officer is to hold office, the officer's right to his office terminates at the end of the will of the appointing power, by which he may be

removed at pleasure unless the act authorizing his appointment provides otherwise.

3. *Same; Special Provisions; Right to Notice and Hearing.*—Where a statute provides for the removal of an officer for cause, it contemplates notice of the charge and a judicial hearing of some character to determine whether cause for removal exists, and whether such officer can be removed, but a removal under section 2238, Code 1907, requires neither a notice nor a hearing.

4. *Same; Issuance of Commission to a Successor.*—Where the approval of the governor is required for the removal of a officer, his commission issued to another appointing him to that office is an approval of the removal.

5. *Same; Tenure; Evidence*—In a quo warranto proceeding to be admitted to an office of which another retains possession under claim of right, it is not necessary for the relator to introduce any other proof of his right to the office than his commission from the proper authority to that effect. (Section 5462, Code 1907.)

6. *Counties; Officers; Removal.*—Under Section 175, Constitution 1901, a county officer who has been elected or appointed to fill a fixed term cannot be removed from office during that term except by impeachment for cause enumerated in Section 173, Constitution 1901, in which proceeding he has the right of jury trial and appeal.

7. *Same; County Officer.*—A county tax commissioner is a county officer who may be removed under Section 175. Constitution 1901, by impeachment for cause specified in Section 173, Constitution 1901, but the section is not limited to county offices created or even mentioned in the Constitution, nor is it limited to those county officers who are elected by the people or the legislature, but extends as well as to those who are appointed. The provisions are for the protection of county officers from removal, except as authorized, during the term for which they were appointed or elected, and was not intended to apply to those county officers, the terms of whose incumbency is fixed or determined by the appointing power.

8. *Same; Removal.*—Construing Acts 1907, p. 425, and section 2238, Code 1907, it is held that the respondent was appointed for a term to be at the will of the governor, or appointing power, and that under section 2238, his removal by the governor with or without cause terminated his right to the office.

9. *Officers; Tenure; Removal.*—The power to appoint an officer carries with it as an incident, the right to remove such officer, in the absence of constitutional or statutory restraint.

10. *Quo Warranto: Relief; Judgment.*—Under section 5462, Code 1907. the judgement in a quo warranto proceeding may be rendered adjudging the relator entitled to the office as against the person continuing in occupancy. under a former appointment. where the relator appointed to office is found to be entitled thereto.

11. *Evidence; Judicial Notice; Appointment in Terms of Officers.*—Courts take judicial notice of the commissioned officers of the state and of the terms for which they hold and the extent of their authority.

12. *Same; Signatures.*—Courts will take judicial notice of the genuineness of the signature of the commissioned officers of the state.

[Touart v. State ex rel. Callaghan.]

APPEAL from Mobile Circuit Court.

Heard before Hon. SAMUEL B. BROWNE.

Quo warranto by the State on the relation of D. J.
Callaghan, against Stephen Touart, to oust him from
the office of Tax Commissioner of Mobile county. Judgment for relator, and respondent appeals. Affirmed.

BOYLES & KOHN, and TISDALE J. TOUART, for appellant. Section 2238, Code 1907, is violative of section
175, Constitution 1901.—*Nolan v. State ex rel. Moore*,
118 Ala. 154; *Hawkins v. Roberts*, 122 Ala. 130. If
said section of the Code is constitutional, the governor
must accord appellant a hearing before removing him.
—29 Cyc. 1409, and authorities cited in paragraph D.
The term of the office of the appellant is for a definite
number of years.—Section 2236, Code 1907; *State ex
rel. Yancey, v. Hyde*, 22 N. E. 644; *State v. Pearcy*, 44
Mo. 159; Mecham on Public Offices, sec 391. If his
term was not for a definite term of years, then the officer
holds until he is properly and legally removed under
the law.—3 Ill. 79; 7 Neb. 42; Secs. 2210-2267, Code
1907. It was proper to appoint appellant at the time
the appointment was made.—*Oberhaus v. State ex rel.*
55 South. 898; 23 A. & E. Enc. of Law, 347; *State v.
O'Reilly*, 66 N. W. 264. The court cannot award the
office of tax commissioner to relator without proof that
the relator is entitled thereto.—10 Enc. of Evi. 456; 32
Cyc. 1464-5; 4 Wis. 567; 14 Am. Rep. 312.

ROACH & CHAMBERLAIN, FITTS, LEIGH & RICKARBY,
and GREGORY L. & H. T. SMITH, for appellee. Where
the term is not fixed by law, the officer is regarded as
holding at the will of the appointing power, as the
power to remove is incident to the power to appoint.—
29 Cyc. 1396; *Ex parte Hennen*, 13 Peters 256; *State ex*

rel. Hawes v. Darrows, 73 N. W. 704; *Hard v. The State,* 79 N. E. 916. One appointed in the middle of a term because of a vacancy is not appointed for a longer term than the unexpired term.—29 Cyc. 1398; 108 Ky. 374; 100 Ky. 66; 99 Mo. 361; 86 Ark. 555. Sec. 2238, Code 1907, is not unconstitutional.—*Gray v. McLendon,* 67 S. E. 859. Appellant was not entitled to notice before removal.—29 Cyc. 1409; *Gray v. McLendon, supra;* 92 N. Y. 191; Mecham on Public Offices, sec. 454. The court had the power on determining that relator was entitled to the office to oust appellant, and render a judgment, putting relator in, upon proof of his commission, as the courts take judicial notice of the commissioned officers of the state, and the genuineness of their signature.—*Ryan v. Young,* 147 Ala. 660; *State ex rel. Foster,* 130 Ala. 154.

MAYFIELD, J.—This is a quo warranto proceeding, or one in the nature thereof, under chapter 128 of the Code of 1907. It is instituted to determine the right to exercise the duties and receive the emoluments of the office of county tax commissioner for Mobile county. The proceeding was instituted in the name of the state, on the relation of D. J. Callaghan, who claims to be entitled to exercise the duties and discharge the functions, and to receive the emoluments of said office; and was brought against Stephen Touart, appellant here, who was at that time, and had been, for a number of years, discharging the duties and receiving the emoluments of the office, under and by virtue of a commission, issued to him by the Governor of the State of Alabama on December 29, 1908, for the term commencing at the expiration of the term of his predecessor in office, H. M. Friend, which was on the first Monday in January, 1909.

[Touart v. State ex rel. Callaghan.]

The petition of the relator alleged that he was appointed to the office alleged to be usurped by the respondent, on the 16th of March, 1911, and that he gave bond, qualified, and was duly commissioned by the Governor of Alabama to discharge the duties of the office; that thereafter he made demand upon the respondent to be admitted to the office to which he had been appointed, which demand was refused and denied him by the respondent; that subsequently thereto, to wit, on April 12, 1911, the Governor of Alabama removed the respondent, Touart, and on April 26, 1911, the relator, Callaghan, was again appointed and recommissioned to the office of county tax commissioner for Mobile county, whereupon he again demanded the office of the respondent, and his demand was by the respondent again refused and denied. The petition then prayed that the respondent be declared not entitled to discharge the duties of said office, and that he be removed therefrom, and that the relator be declared entitled and admitted thereto.

The respondent demurred to this petition, assigning numerous grounds, among which may be mentioned the following: That the relator was not qualified to discharge the duties of the office; that the petition failed to set forth any facts showing or tending to show that the respondent was not qualified, or that he was not entitled to discharge the duties of the office, and that it wholly failed to show that the respondent was holding the office unlawfully, or that he was usurping the functions of such office; that it failed to show that the term to which the respondent was appointed or elected had expired, or in what manner or by what means the respondent had been rendered unfit or ineligible to discharge the duties of the office; that it failed to show that there was a vacancy in the office when the relator was appointed, and failed to show the beginning, duration, or ending of the term or terms to which the relator or respondent was respectively appointed or elected; that the petition showed that the attempted removal of the respondent by the Governor of Alabama was void and of no effect, for the reason that section 2238 of the Code of Alabama, under and by virtue of which the governor acted in attempting to remove the respondent, was in violation of section 175 of the Constitution of the state of Alabama of 1901, which prescribes a limitation upon the grounds for and modes of removing county officers, and limits the same to impeachment proceedings in the manner provided by law; that the petition also showed that the removal of the respondent was void. These demurrers being overruled, the respondent answered the petition or complaint by setting forth the facts as to the appointment of the respondent to the office, that his term had not expired at the time the relator was appointed, and claiming that the respondent was rightfully entitled to the office. To this answer the relator demurred, the demurrer being sustained by the court. The respondent declined to plead further, whereupon the court rendered judgment ousting the respondent from the office and awarding it to the relator; and from that judgment this appeal is prosecuted.

There are six propositions which the appellant insists upon on this appeal, and which, he says, render the decree of the lower court erroneous and prejudicial to the rights of the appellant. The first of these is that section 2238 of the Cole, authorizing the governor to remove tax commissioners, is unconstitutional and void; the second is that if the statute be valid, the tax commissioner is entitled to notice and a hearing before he is removed; and the third and fourth ask whether the term of the appellant is for a definite time, and, if not, for

what term he holds; the fifth questions the validity of
the appointment of relator, on the ground that it was
made prior to the expiration of the term of his predecessor; and the sixth, whether the court can award the
office to the relator without proof that he is entitled
thereto—that is, upon the mere petition and answer.

The first insistence is that section 2238 of the Code
is unconstitutional and void because in violation of section 175 of the Constitution of 1901, providing that certain officers mentioned, and "all other county officers,"
may be removed from office for any causes specified in
section 173 of the Constitution, under such regulations
as may be prescribed by law, provided the rights of trial
by jury, and of appeal, in such cases, shall be preserved.

Section 2238 of the Code, which is claimed to be unconstitutional, provides "that any county tax commissioner may be removed by the governor at his discretion,
or by the State tax commissioner, with the approval of
the governor, for any inefficiency or malfeasance in office; and of the sufficiency of the ground or cause of removal, the Governor shall be the sole judge." It thus
appears that this section of the Code attempts to confer
upon the Governor power to remove county tax commissioners at his discretion and without notice or trial.
We think there can be no doubt that this intention is
clearly expressed in this section of the Code, whether
construed alone or as a part of the original act of the
Legislature, of which it formed a part, or of that chapter and article of the Code in which it now finds its
place.

It was ruled by this court in the case of *Nolan v.
State,* 118 Ala. 154, 24 South. 251, that a statute which
authorized the Governor to suspend tax assessors and
to appoint commissioners to perform the duties of the
former, was unconstitutional and void, because in vio-

lation of section 3 of article 7 of the Constitution of 1875, which, for all purposes necessary to a decision on this appeal, is identical with section 175 of the present Constitution.

In the case of *Hawkins v. Roberts*, 122 Ala. 130, 27 South. 327, the doctrine announced in *Nolen's Case* was reaffirmed; but it was held in that case that neither the provision of the Constitution under consideration, nor the principles announced in Nolen's Case, would prevent the Legislature from abolishing certain offices which were not constitutional and which, therefore, it had the right to create and to abolish; that the Legislature having the right to abolish the office which it created, this abolition necessarily carried with it the term of the incumbent officer. There being no office, of course there could be no term of office, and there being no term of office, the incumbent at the time of the abolition of the office of necessity could not continue, or be continued, in office.

In other words, that case and a number of others of this state have decided that the Legislature may abolish an office which it is authorized to create, and that the abolition of such office terminates the right of the incumbent to exercise the rights and duties thereof.

It therefore follows that if a county tax commissioner is county officer, and he has been appointed or elected to fill a definite and fixed term, his removal from office during the term to which he was appointed or elected— except for the causes enumerated in section 173 of the Constitution, and by the method of impeachment—is inhibited by the Constitution; and that, in the impeachment proceeding provided, he has the rights of jury trial, and appeal, as guaranteed by section 175 of the Constitution.

We feel no hesitancy in deciding that a county tax commissioner is a county officer within the meaning of section 175 of the Constitution. See Words & Phrases, vol. 2, under subject, "County Officers."

It is clear from the decisions in the Nolen and Roberts Cases that this section of the Constitution is not limited to county officers created or even mentioned in the Constitution; nor do we think that the section is limited to those county officers that are elected by vote of the people or by the Legislature, but that it extends to those who are appointed, as well.

It is, however, likewise clear and certain that the provision is intended to protect county officers from removal, except in the manner authorized, during the term of office to which they are appointed or elected. It was not intended to apply to those officers, though county officers, the terms of whose incumbency is to be fixed or determined by the appointing power.

If the appointing power is given the right to fix the term during which the appointee is to hold office, then, of course, the right of appointee terminates at the end of the will of the appointing power; that is, the appointing power can remove him at pleasure, unless the act or statute authorizing his appointment provides otherwise.

It is certain that the statute here in question intended that the Governor might appoint and remove county tax commissioners at his pleasure, with or without cause. We think the section in question is incapable of any other construction.

. It has been uniformly ruled that the power to appoint an officer carries with it, as an incident, in the absence of constitutional or statutory restraint, the right to remove the appointee. *Taylor v. Kercheval* (C. C.) 82 Fed. 47; *Davis v. Filler*, 47 W. Va. 413, 35 S. E. 6; *Cam-*

eron v. Parker, 2 Okl. 277, 38 Pac. 14; *Sponogle v. Curnow*, 136 Cal. 580, 69 Pac. 255.

While it is very true that the power to oust an officer rightfully in office is essentially a judicial one, yet this rule does not apply, unless made applicable by constitutional or statutory provisions, where it is exercised by the appointive power. *Knox v. Johnson*, 124 Ind. 145, 24 N. E. 148, 7 L. R. A. 684, 19 Am. St. Rep. 88.

It was held by the Supreme Court of Louisiana, in the case of *Peters v. Bell*, 51 La. Ann. 1621, South. 442, that the power of appointment carries with it the power of removal, where the appointment is not made for a specified term.

It was ruled by the Supreme Court of Michigan, in the case of *Dullam v. Willson*, 53 Mich. 392, 19 N. W. 112, 51 Am. Rep. 128, that where the Governor is invested with the power to remove officers, he has the right to determine whether or not there exist the grounds specified by Constitution or statute as a cause for removal.

It was ruled by the Supreme Court of Minnesota, that when the law fixes no tenure of office, and even where no provision is made for the removal of the incumbent, the power of removal is a necessary incident of the power of appointment. *Parish v. City of St. Paul*, 84 Minn. 426, 87 N. W. 1124, 87 Am. St. Rep. 374.

It was ruled by the Supreme Court of Missouri that an officer who was appointed for a full term fixed by law, and who held over, after serving his term, was subject to summary removal at the pleasure of the appointing power. *Rife v. Hawes*, 177 Mo. 360, 76 S. W. 653.

It was held by the Supreme Court of New York that when the duration of an office is not provided by law, it should be held during the pleasure of the appointing power, where such authority is conferred in general

terms without restriction; that the power to remove at
pleasure impliedly exists unless restricted by law. *People ex rel. Fleming v. Dalton,* 158 N. Y. 175, 52 N. E.
1113, reversing 34 App. Div. 627, 54 N. Y. Supp. 1112;
People ex rel. Ray v. Henry, 47 App. Div. 133, 62 N. Y.
Supp. 102.

It was ruled by the Supreme Court of North Carolina,
in the case of *Greene v. Owen,* 125 N. C. 212, 34 S. E.
424, that the power to create vacancies in public offices
rests in the absence of express provisions to the contrary, in the body possessing the original power of appointment.

The office of county tax commissioner was first created in this state by the Acts of 1898-99, p. 195. Under
this statute the office was clearly made a county office,
and the term of incumbency definitely fixed at four
years.

On March 7, 1907 (Acts 1907, pp. 425-438), the entire
subject of state and county tax commissions was revised
by a single and complete enactment. This of course
took the place of, and therefore repealed, all of the prior
acts upon that subject, in so far as they were in conflict
therewith. This last act provided for a commission to
be known as the State Tax Commission, and that it
should consist of three members. It expressly abolished
the office of State Tax Commissioner created and provided by the former act, but recognized and provided
for the office of county tax commissioner, regulated the
manner of his appointment, and specified his duties.
This act of 1907, however, expressly provided that the
then county tax commissioners should be continued in
office for the term for which they were appointed, unless
sooner removed in the manner provided by the act. It
must be observed, however, that this last act, while continuing the then incumbents of the offices of county tax

commissioners for the term appointed, did not provide any term of office for their successors, nor fix any definite period for which any of their successors should hold office. It clearly appears from this act that it was not the intention of the lawmakers to fix any definite term for which subsequent appointees should hold office; but that it was intended that, under the new system and at the expiration of the terms of the incumbents, appointees should hold office at the pleasure of the governor and of the State Tax Commission. But whether it was so intended by the Legislature or not, this change of the statute was necessary, in order to make effective that provision of the law which authorized the governor to remove county tax commissioners at his discretion, in the light of the decisions in the Nolen and Roberts Cases, above referred to, to the effect that a county officer, appointed or elected for a definite and fixed period, cannot be removed at the pleasure of the appointive authority, except upon the ground and in the manner provided by the Constitution and statutes as to impeachment proceedings. But when a person is appointed to an office the term of which is not fixed by law, he is then and ever after regarded as holding subject to the will of the appointing power; and this upon the theory that the power of removal is incident to the power of appointment; and when he is removed he is not thereby deprived of any vested right or function, because the very condition of his appointment was that he could be removed at the pleasure of the appointing power.

Whether section 2238 of the Code, which authorizes the governor, at his discretion, to remove county tax commissioners, was unconstitutional as applied to the incumbents at the time of the adoption of the Code or of the statute, of which the Code provision is a substantial copy, is unnecessary to be decided here, for the reason that the appellant was not an incumbent at that time, but held under an appointment the term of which did not begin until the expiration of the term of his predecessor, who was in office in 1907, at the time of the passage of the last statute, and the adoption of the Code. He concedes that his term of office, of which he claims he is deprived, did not begin until after the first Monday in January, 1903. Therefore appellant was appointed, not for any definite term, but for a term at the will, pleasure, and discretion of the governor, or the appointing power, with the conditions specified in the statute. He could therefore have been removed by Governor Comer, during his term of office, with or without cause; and of course could be removed, at the time and in the manner he was removed, by Governor O'Neal.

While the county tax commissioners and the State Tax Commissioners are separate and distinct officers, and are assigned separate and distinct duties—the former not being the mere deputies of the latter—yet it is certain that it was the intention of the lawmakers that the county commissioners should be under the complete control and supervision of the State Commission. Many of the acts and duties of the county commissioners are made subject to the revision of the State Commission. Unquestionably the Legislature deemed it very necessary to the efficiency of the work of the State Commission that the county commissioners should be not only subject to its control, but that the latter officials should act in harmony with the officials of the higher commission. To this end the county tax commissioners are appointed by the State Tax Commission, and are subject to removal by that body, and being given no fixed terms of office, they can be removed without impeachment proceedings.

It is likewise evident from the statute of 1907, now embodied in the Code under the chapter "State Tax Commission" (Code 1907, §§ 2210-2241), that the governor should exercise control and supervision over both the state and county commissioners, and to this end he is authorized by statute to appoint or remove such officers; and in order that there might be no constitutional objection to this, the statute omits to fix any term for such officers, allowing this to rest in the discretion of the appointing power.

There is no question that when a statute provides for the removal of an officer for cause, it contemplates notice to the officer of the charge, and requires a tribunal of some kind to determine whether the cause for removal exists and whether such officer can be removed. But we think it certain that the statute in question authorizes the removal of county commissioners by the governor, without cause. If the removal is by the State Tax Commission, it must be with the approval of the governor, and must be for misfeasance or malfeasance in office; but in such case the statute makes the sufficiency of the ground for removal a question for the governor, rather than a judicial question. But as the removal in this case was by the governor, and the statutes in effect authorize the removal with or without cause, merely at the discretion of the governor, making him sole judge of the sufficiency of the cause for removal, notice to the officer of the intended removal was not necessary. The statute contemplates no hearing before removal can be made by the governor. The appellant in this case, not being appointed for any fixed term, could have no right to hold longer than at the will and pleasure of the appointing power, or of the governor, and consequently was not deprived of any right.

The appellant having no right to hold office at the time of his removal, nor at the time of the appointment, by the governor, of the appellee, the latter was clearly entitled to discharge the duties and functions of the office; and on the quo warranto proceedings instituted by the appellant, the trial court properly rendered a judgment adjudging that the appellee was entitled to the office. Section 5462 of the Code expressly provides for judgment in such cases.

When the governor issued his commission to the relator, that of itself operated as an approval of the removal of the incumbent.—*Ex parte Henen,* 13 Pet. 236, 259, 10 L. Ed. 138; 29 Cyc. 1408, 1373, 1474.

It is also said by Mechem (Public Officers, § 454) that where the Legislature has given authority to one officer to appoint another to an office which is created by the act of the Legislature, it may authorize the removal of the incumbent without notice or hearing; and such is the effect where it is provided that an executive is authorized to remove for any cause deemed sufficient by himself.

It was not necessary, on the hearing in the court below, for the relator, appellee here, to introduce any other proof that he was entitled to hold the office, than his commission, from the proper authorities, to that effect. The proceeding, while instituted by the relator, is in effect one by the state, and, the incumbent being properly removed, if the relator is entitled to the office, as before said, it was proper for the court to render judgment awarding the same to him, the Code authorizing such judgment.

It has been repeatedly held by this court that it will take judicial knowledge of the commissioned officers of the state, and of the length of the terms for which they hold, the extent of their authority, and the genuineness of their signatures, etc.—*Ryan v. Young,* 147 Ala. 660, 669, 41 South. 954.   And in the case of *Little v. Foster,* 130 Ala. 154, 30 South. 477, a contest between relator and respondent as to the right to hold office as trustee of the University of Alabama, this court held as follows: "Applying these principles to the facts of the case, the defendant's right to the office cannot be sustained for the reason that the governor was without warrant of law to appoint him.   As we judicially know that the defendant has since this proceeding was instituted been legally appointed as successor to the relator, it is unnecessary to adjudge the latter's rights in the premises." It was therefore not necessary to require the appellee to furnish proof of that fact, of which the court takes judicial notice.

There being no error in the record, the judgment of the lower court is in all things affirmed.

Affirmed.

DOWDELL, C. J., and SIMPSON and McCLELLAN, JJ., concur.

Dowling *v.* City of Troy.

Habeas Corpus.

(Decided June 1, 1911.   56 South. 118.)

1. *Statutes; Title; Sufficiency.*—The title of Act 1907, (S. S.) p. 179, is not sufficient to authorize the inclusion in the act of a provision requiring the court in imposing a sentence for cost to determine the time required to work out the cost at 40 cents per day, and hence, that provision of the act is violative of section 45, Constitution 1901.

2. *Costs; Criminal Prosecution; Sentence.*—Acts 1907, p. 179, in so far as it relates to costs on conviction of crime, being unconstitutional, in sentencing for costs, the rate should be 75 cents per day as provided by section 7635, Code 1907.

[Dowling v. City of Troy.]

APPEAL from Pike Circuit Court.

Heard before Hon. H. A. PEARCE.

Arch Dowling was convicted in the circuit court of a violation of an ordinance of the City of Troy, and he appeals. Reversed and remanded, and a constitutional question was certified to the Supreme Court for determination. Question answered.

See, also, 1 Ala. App. 508, 56 South. 116.

There was conviction in the mayor's court for a violation of the prohibition law, and the defendant was sentenced to pay a fine of $100 and $2 costs. On appeal to the circuit court there was a verdict of guilty, and a fine of $50 attached. A judgment was entered remanding the prisoner to the city authorities for punishment according to the judgment, and after having served his term with the city of Troy it was further ordered that he be delivered to the sheriff of Pike county to work out the costs incurred in the circuit court; the sentence being for 66 days of hard labor at the rate of 40 cents per day, the sentence to begin at the expiration of his term of service for the city of Troy.

A constitutional question having been raised, it was certified to the Supreme Court for determination under the practice act by the Court of Appeals.

A. G. SEAY, for appellant. The act fixing the rate of costs at 40 cents per day is violative of section 45 Constitution 1901.—*Brown v. The State,* 115 Ala. 74.

FOSTER, SAMFORD & CARROLL, for appellee. Even if the act is unconstitutional, the sentence should be corrected, and as corrected, affirmed.—*Johnson v. The State,* 94 Ala. 36.

SAYRE, J.—The Court of Appeals, acting under the authority of the act creating that court (Acts 1911, p.

95), as amended (Acts 1911, p. 449), has certified to
this court that the act of the Legislature of Alabama,
entitled "An act to provide for the hiring, management,
control and inspection of county convicts," and approved
November 30, 1907 (General Acts [Sp. Sess.] 1907, p.
179), has been assailed upon the constitutional ground
that the inclusion of the provision that "the court," in
the imposition of an additional sentence for the payment
of costs of conviction, "must determine the time required to work out such costs at the rate of forty cents
per day," is in violation of section 45 of the Constitution
of Alabama, 1901.   It is ordered by the Court of Appeals that the question, "Is the provision contained in
section 13 of the act of the Legislature of Alabama entitled 'An act to provide for the hiring, management,
control and inspection of county convicts,' approved
November 30, 1907, that 'the court,' in the imposition
of an additional sentence for the payment of costs of
conviction, 'must determine the time required to work
out such costs at the rate of forty cents per day,' in violation of the provision of section 45 of the Constitution
of the State of Alabama that 'each law shall contain but
one subject, which shall be clearly expressed in its
title?" be, and the same hereby is, certified to the Supreme Court for determination.

We are constrained by the decision of this court in
Brown v. State, 115 Ala. 74, 22 South. 458, to an answer
in the affirmative.   The title of the act is: "An act to
provide for the hiring, management, control and inspection of county convicts."   In the case referred to it was
said the sentence for costs "most clearly enters into, and
forms a part of the judicial disposition of the prisoner
creating and defining him as one amenable to the regulations provided by law for putting the sentence (meaning here the sentence for punishment primarily and the

further sentence for costs) into execution. When the sentence to hard labor is pronounced, the court pronouncing it must go further, and judicially ascertain that the costs have not been paid, when such is the case, and so declare upon its records, and (judgment therefore not being confessed) pronounced additional sentence provided by law. What this sentence shall be—whether it shall be limited to 6, 10, or 18 months—has, manifestly, no more natural or germane relation to a system of laws providing for the 'government, discipline and maintenance' of convicts, than has the sentence which the law requires the court to pronounce upon the prisoner as absolute punishment for the crime." So here, the judicial disposition of a prisoner which requires him to work out costs as a part of the punishment has no relation to his hiring, management, control and inspection after he has become a convict.

The section, in so far as it changes the rate at which convicts shall be credited for their labor, is unconstitutional, and appellant should have been sentenced for costs at the rate of 75 cents a day as provided by section 7635 of the Code of 1907.—*Ex Parte Gayles*, 108 Ala. 514, 19 South. 12, is also in point and to the same effect.

The clerk will certify this opinion to the Court of Appeals. All the Justices concur.

Sartain *v.* Gray, Sheriff.

Manadmus.

(Decided June 15, 1911.　55 South. 922.)

Mandamus; Eelection; Contest; Poll List; Duty of Sheriff.— Although the sheriff had custody of the poll list, he is not required to furnish a copy thereof except on the requisition of the judge of probate (section 458, Code 1907,) and as section 6806, Code 1907, makes it a misdemeanor for anyone to furnish such a list, the sheriff cannot be compelled by mandamus to furnish a poll list for one contesting an election.

APPEAL from Walker Circuit Court.

Heard before Hon. J. J. CURTIS.

Mandamus by Charles M. Sartain against John M. Gray, sheriff of Walker county, to require him to furnish poll lists of a certain election, which was being contested. From a judgment denying petition, petitioner appeals. Affirmed.

W. C. DAVIS, O. D. STREET, and R. A. COONER, for appellant. As a contesting claimant of the office it is the clear statutory right of appellant to have a certified copy of the poll list.—Section 458, Code 1907. The custody is in the sheriff, subject to requisition by the probate judge, unless by reading sections 415, 417, 420, 425 and 458, in pari materia, the probate judge is the legal custodian. The duty is a simple ministerial duty requiring no discretion, and hence, mandamus will lie.— 26 Cyc. 199, and 288; *Jackson v. Mobley,* 157 Ala. 411; *Phoenix Carpet Co. v. The State,* 118 Ala. 144; *Smith v. McCutcheon,* 146 Ala. 455; *Roney v. Simmons,* 97 Ala. 88.

BANKHEAD & BANKHEAD, for appellee. There is no statutory or other duty upon the sheriff to furnish poll lists of an election which the law places in his custody. In fact, he is expressly prohibited by section 6806, Code 1907. He cannot comply with the writ of mandamus without violating this criminal statute.

SOMERVILLE, J.—This is a companion case with that of *Charles M. Sartain v. James W. Shepherd, infra,* 55 South. 919, both being submitted and argued together.

In this case the petition for mandamus is directed against the sheriff of Walker county, while in the other it was directed against the probate judge; the object in each case being to compel the respondent to deliver to the petitioner a certified copy of the election poll lists of the several precincts of the county. The allegations of the petition, the rights of the petitioner, and the duties of probate judge and sheriff with respect to poll lists are stated and discussed in the opinion filed in *Sartain v. Shepherd, supra,* to which we need only add here that, not only is the sheriff not authorized or required to furnish such a copy, but, except upon the requisition of the probate judge under section 458, he is by penal statute expressly forbidden to do so. Section 6806, Code 1907.

The demurrer to the petition was properly sustained, and the judgment dismissing the petition must be affirmed.

Affirmed.

SIMPSON, ANDERSON and SAYRE, JJ., concur.

Sartain *v.* Shepherd, Judge.

Mandamus.

(Decided June 15, 1911. 55 South. 919.)

1. *Election; Contest; Registration List.*—While section 6806, Code 1907, makes it a misdemeanor to make a copy of the poll list, of any election, said section does no abrogate, but must be construed with section 458, which requires the probate judge to deliver to any party to an election contest a certified copy of such list.

2. *Same.*—The changes made in the election law from the Code of 1896, did not repeal section 458, and that statute by necessary implication gives the probate judge the right of access to such lists though they be in the custody of another officer.

3. *Same.*—Construing sections 415, 417, 420, 425 and 458, Code 1907, it is held that by necessary implication, the first poll list prepared by the election inspectors should be transmitted to the judge of probate who shall be the legal custodian of said lists.

4. *Pleading; Demurrer; Matters Not Appearing on the Face.*—Independent facts not appearing on the face of the pleading are not grounds for demurrer.

APPEAL from Walker Circuit Court.

Heard before Hon. J. J. CURTIS.

Action for mandamus by Charles M. Sartain against James W. Shepherd, as judge of probate. From a judgment sustaining demurrers to the petition, petitioner appeals. Reversed, rendered, and remanded.

See, also, Infra 55 South. 922.

The contents of the petition sufficiently appear from the opinion. The demurrers, other than those appearing in the opinion, are as follows: (1) "Because this defendant cannot furnish a list of voters who voted in said election without opening the ballot boxes." (2) "Because this defendant cannot furnish said list without opening the sealed envelopes containing the said list." (3) "Because there is no authority in law for this defendant to furnish said list." (4) "Because an election contest proceeding is strictly statutory, and does not provide for this defendant furnishing said lists." (5) "Because the law does not provide any compensation for furnishing said lists." (7) "Because it does not appear that it is reasonably necessary in the trial of this contested election case that said lists should be furnished to petitioner." (8) "Because said lists, if furnished, could not be used in evidence." (9) "Because said lists can only be used for the purpose of furnishing information to petitioner to enable him to search for evidence." (10) "Because the only effect of securing a copy of said lists would be to enable the petitioner to institute a fishing inquiry for evidence." (11) "Because this defendant is not authorized by law to tamper with the returns of said election, including the poll lists and ballots." (12) "Becuse it is the duty of this defendant to retain the poll lists in his possession in the condition in which they were delivered to him, and either to destroy them or to deliver them to some custodian of the court in which the contest proceeding is pending."

W. C. DAVIS, O. D. STREET, and R. A. COONER, for appellant. As a contesting claimant of the office it is the clear statutory right of appellant to have a certified copy of the poll list.—Section 458, Code 1907. The custody is in the sheriff, subject to requisition by the probate judge, unless by reading sections 415, 417, 420, 425 and 458, in pari materia, the probate judge is the legal custodian. The duty is a simple ministerial duty requiring no discretion, and hence, mandamus will lie.— 25 Cyc. 199, and 288; *Jackson v. Mobley*, 157 Ala. 411; *Phoenix Carpet Co. v. The State*, 118 Ala. 144; *Smith v. McCutchcon*, 146 Ala. 455; *Roney v. Simmons*, 97 Ala. 88.

BANKHEAD & BANKHEAD, for appellee. There is no stautory or other duty upon the sheriff to furnish poll lists for an election which the law places in his custody. In fact, he is expressly prohibited by section 6806, Code 1907. He cannot comply with the writ of mandamus without violating this criminal statute.

SOMERVILLE, J.—The petitioner, Charles M. Sartain, shows that at the general election held in November 1910, he and the respondent, James W. Shepherd, were opposing candidates for the office of probate judge of Walker county; said Shepherd being also the incumbent of that office, and being a candidate to succeed himself. Petitioner further shows that at the appointed time the election supervisors of the county regularly declared that said Shepherd had been elected to said office, and that within twenty days after such declaration petitioner filed in the circuit court of Walker county his contest of said election, in accordance with the statutes regulating the same; that thereafter, on December 15, 1910, he made application to the said Shepherd then probate judge of Walker county, to deliver to him a certified copy of the poll lists of the several precincts of said county used at said election, offering then and there to pay the fees prescribed by law for copying and certifying said lists; and that said Shepherd then and there refused, and still refuses to furnish him with said lists. The petition, which is addressed to the judge of the circuit court of Walker county, prays for the issuance of an alternative writ of mandamus, or other proper remedial writ, to the said Shepherd, commanding him to conform to petitioner's said request, or show cause why he should not do so. The respondent demurred to the petition, assigning numerous grounds, which will be found set out in the reporter's statement of the case. This de-

[Sartain v. Shepherd, Judge.]

murrer was sustained by the trial court, and the petitioner declining to plead further a judgment was entered dismissing the petition. The action of the trial court in both of these particulars is here assigned as error.

1. Section 458, Code of 1907, is as follows: "It shall be the duty of the judge of probate of any county, upon the application of either party to any contest, or his agent or attorney, to deliver to the party, his agent or attorney, a certified copy of the registration lists and poll lists (one or both) of his county, or of any election precinct therein, upon the payment of his fees for certifying and copying the same at the rate of fifteen cents a hundred words written by him in making such copy; and such copies, duly certified, shall be received as presumptive evidence of the facts therein stated, the registration lists that the persons therein named were duly registered, and the poll lists that the persons therein named voted at the election and precinct therein named." It is obvious upon the most casual consideration that the language of this statute refutes every ground of demurrer assigned, except the sixth, thirteenth, and fourteenth. We shall therefore not undertake to discuss the other grounds, as to which, indeed, no vindication seems to be now attempted by counsel for appellee.

2. The sixth ground of demurrer is: "Because it is made a misdemeanor by section 6806 of the Code for any election officer or any other person to make a copy of the poll lists or any memoranda therefrom or list of the persons voting." The section here referred to appears for the first time in the Code of 1907, and reads thus: "Sec. 6806. Unlawful Use of Poll List.—Any election officer or any other person who makes a copy of the poll list or any memoranda therefrom, or list of the persons voting, the number of their ballots, or discloses the number of such voter's ballot, shall be guilty of a misdeameanor,

and, upon conviction, shall be fined not less than two
hundred dollars." This ground is so patently bad as to
scarcely justify any comment. Section 6806 of the Criminal Code is, of course, designed to prevent in general
the making of copies of poll lists by any person, or for
any use or occasion, not authorized by law; and it must
be construed in connection with section 458, above
quoted. Each has its appropriate field of action, and
each is perfectly consistent with the other. Of course,
if the probate judge should make or deliver such a copy
otherwise than upon the application of one of the parties to an election contest, he would be liable to the penalty visited by section 6806; but that section is no obstacle to the petitioner in the present case.

3. The thirteenth ground of demurrer is, "because this
defendant is not the custodian of the lists of voters who
voted in said election." We interpret this objection as
meaning that respondent is not the person appointed by
law to receive and keep the poll lists, and therefore he
need not discharge the duty enjoined upon him by section 458 of the Code, even though he may be the de facto
custodian of such lists, or though, by reason of their
accessibility to him, the discharge of that duty may be
entirely practicable.

Conceding for the moment that the probate judge is
not the legal or titular custodian of election poll lists,
we can yet discover no good reason why he should not
be obedient to the mandate of the statute to the extent
at least that obedience lies within his power. If the lists
be in his own hands, his duty is imperative and its discharge easy. If they be in the hands of the sheriff or
any election supervisor, the statute by necessary implication arms the judge with the right of access and the
power of caption, and it is his bounden duty to get the
lists and obey the statute if it be physically and reason-

ably possible. That it is not reasonably possible to do so by reason of the loss, destruction, or inaccessibility of the lists would be a matter of defense to be presented by answer, and not by demurrer to the petition. The opposing argument is that section 458 is but an obsolete provision of the old law, nominally preserved by legislative inadvertence, but, in effect, repealed by certain provisions of the new election law as found in the new Code of 1907. This argument is unsound.

Section 1649, Code of 1896, required the election supervisors, after declaring the result of an election, to "file the poll lists and lists of registered voters in the office of the judge of probate, which shall be open to the inspection of any elector of the county." These lists thus became, after the election, public records accessible to any voter of the county. Under the new law, section 354, Code of 1907, requires that "each ballot shall be numbered by one of the inspectors to correspond to the number of the voter voting the same, on the poll list." Section 1649, Code of 1896, above quoted, is amended so as to exclude poll lists, becoming, as amended, section 425, Code of 1907, and section 6806, Code 1907, makes it a misedmeanor for any election officer or other person to make any copy or memoranda of the poll list, or any revelations with respect thereto. The legislative purpose is here perfectly plain. The new system of numbering the ballots is intended to furnish a means for the discovery of frauds and irregularities in election, but evidently to be used only in a legally instituted contest thereof. And since numbered ballots may in connection with correspondingly numbered poll lists result by misuse in destroying the secrecy of the ballot, which it is the policy of the law to carefully guard, these poll lists could no longer properly become public records, and a penal statute was necessary to protect them from unauthorized publication.

But in all of this there is nothing inconsistent with the preservation of the poll lists, and their subjection under statutory authority to the service of truth and justice, nor does there seem to be any good reason for their permanent immolation or ultimate destruction, in view of the early destruction by the sheriff of the numbered ballots themselves. In fact, as there is no provision of law for the destruction of poll lists, as there expressly is for the destruction of ballots in the absence of a contest, we would infer, even without reference to section 458, that they are not intended to be destroyed, and hence of necessity are intended to be preserved. And the only legislative inadvertence apparent to our minds is in the failure to counterbalance the amendment of section 1649, Code of 1896, by a new express provision for the preservation of the poll lists by the probate judge without publication, and subject only to the use authorized by section 458, Code of 1907.

4. In what we have said above we have tentatively conceded that probate judges are not appointed by law to be the legal custodians of election poll lists. We now recur to this question. By section 415, Code of 1907, the election inspectors are required to ascertain and certify the vote of each candidate, and to place their identifying certificate on one of the poll lists made by them, which, thus certified, must be sealed up in a box together with a list of the registered voters in such precinct. This box is directed to the sheriff of the county, to whom it is transmitted by the returning officer of the precinct. Under section 416 the inspectors are required, after counting the ballots, to roll up, label, and securely seal them, and then place them together with a sealed poll list, in the box from which they were counted, and de-

[Sartain v. Shepherd, Judge.]

liver the box to the returning officer, who must deliver
them to the sheriff.   It thus appears that two poll lists
go into the hands of the sheriff in these separate boxes;
and, other than by section 458, they are not again specifically referred to by any statute.   But unquestionably
one set of lists pass temporarily into the hands of the
county board of supervisors who are constituted and required to canvass the precinct returns by section 420.
This board is required by section 425 to file in the office
of the probate judge the lists of registered voters, which
accompanied the returns and poll lists; and the sheriff
is required by section 417 to keep the ballots for six
months, and then, if not notified of a contest, to destroy
them.   In neither case is any allusion made to the poll
lists. It seems most reasonable, therefore, that the sheriff
is and remains the custodian of the poll lists which
accompany the ballots; and it seems clear that he has no
authority to destroy them, at least during the period
within which he is enjoined to preserve the ballots.

What shall become of the other set of poll lists, which
are sealed up with the election returns and the lists of
registered voters?   No officer or other person is expressly required to take or keep or care for them; and
no officer, except the probate judge, has any duty with
respect to them.   We cannot assume that these lists, so
carefully certified, sealed, and returned, were intended
to have no responsible keeper merely because in the exigencies of statutory renovation express provision therefor was omitted.   Looking, therefore, to the important
duty enjoined upon the probate judge by section 458 of
the Code, a duty which seems to assume, if it does not
actually require, that the custody of these lists shall be
in him, we feel no hesitancy in holding that that section
by necessary implication makes of him the legal custodian of the lists; and authorizes and requires him to se-

cure them when they are removed from the sealed box by the canvassing board when they canvass the returns, to the end that they may not be lost or destroyed, and that he may, most promptly and conveniently, meet and discharge his statutory duty in the premises.

There are no real difficulties in the way, and it is our clear duty to give effect to section 458 by every reasonable intendment and implication, rather than to declare it abortive upon the consideration urged by the appellee, considerations which we cannot but regard as both fastidious and unsubstantial.

5. The fourteenth ground of demurrer sets up an independent fact, viz., that respondent "is unable to comply with said petition because he has not in his possession a copy of the lists of voters who voted in said election." It is, of course, bad as a demurrer, and, as we have seen above, is not per se a sufficient defense to avoid the duty imposed by the statute.

It results that the demurrer to the petition was improperly sustained, and the judgment of dismissal erroneous. The judgment is therefore reversed, and one will be here entered overruling the respondent's demurrer, and remanding the cause for further proceedings in accordance with the foregoing opinion.

Reversed, rendered, and remanded.

SIMPSON, ANDERSON, and SAYRE, JJ., concur.

[Oberhaus v. State ex rel. McNamara.]

Oberhaus *v.* State *ex rel.* McNamara.

Quo Warranto.

(Decided May 30, 1911. Rehearing denied June 23, 1911.
55 South. 898.)

1. *Courts; Jurisdiction; Quo Warranto.*—Construing Acts 1871-2, p. 109, and sections 3259, 3296, and 5455, Code 1907, it is held that the city court or Mobile had jurisdiction to grant a writ of quo warranto to determine title to the office of jury commissioner of Mobile County.

2. *Officers; Appointment; Expiration of Term.*—Where an officer's term would expire one day before the expiration of the term of office of the existing governor, the governor was authorized to fill the vacancy by appointment before the officer's term had, in fact, expired.

3. *Evidence; Judicial Notice.*—The courts will take judicial notice that the governor installed in 1907, was installed on January 15, and that his successor was inaugurated and installed on Monday, January 16. 1911, at 2:15 P. M.

4. *Time; Governor; Term of Office.*—Construing sections 115, 116 and 48, Constitution 1901, it is held that the legislature may count the votes on any day within seven days of their meeting, and that the governor's term expired at midnight on the first Monday after the second Tuesday in January, after the election of his successor, and that the incoming governor's term begins on the beginning of the third Tuesday in January after his election, notwithstanding the provision of section 1461 and 1570, Code 1907, and that the governor and other officers, are entitled to salary from the day on which they are inducted into office.

5. *Same; Jury Commissioners; Term.*—Under Acts 1909, p. 305, the jury commissioners appointed by the governor did not include any part, as to term of office, of the first Monday after the second Tuesday in January, 1911, and that since the term of the then governor did include that day, there was a vacancy in the office of jury commissioner which the then governor had power to fill by appointment.

APPEAL from Mobile City Court.

Heard before Hon. O. J. SEMMES.

Quo warranto by the State on the relation of J. E. McNamara against A. Z. Oberhaus, to determine respondent's right to the office of jury commissioner of Mobile county. From a judgment granting the writ, respondent appeals. Reversed and remanded.

RICH & HAMILTON, for appellant. The main point of
the controversy is the time for expiration of the defendant's first term as jury commissioner, and the point of
beginning of Governor O'Neal's term as governor. We
admit that if Comer's term had expired before the beginning of defendant's second term as jury commissioner, then Governor Comer had no authority to appoint.
On the other hand, if Governor Comer's term extended
beyond the beginning of defendant's term, he had full
power to make the appointment.—66 S. W. 264; 43 N.
E. 1103; 40 N. J. L. 468; 11 O. 46; 23 Am. Rep. 234; 49
N. E. 104; 19 S. W. 302; 23 A. & E. Enc. of Law, 347.
Under the statute (Acts 1909, p. 305), appellant's term
expired before the first Monday after the second Tuesday
in January, 1911.—*Richardson v. The State*, 142 Ala.
12; *Beebe v. Robinson*, 64 Ala. 172; 72 Pac. 208; 21 N.
E. 464; 91 N. Y. 630; 40 Ind. 16; 6 Ind. 335; 40 South.
571; 158 Ala. 458; 12 Ill. 302. Under all these authorities, the word "until" is excluded or used as a word of
exclusion. Where the statute provides an appointment
to be at the expiration of the preceding term, an appointment before its expiration or on the day of its expiration
was good.—Meechum on Public Officers, Sec. 111; 63
Cal. 333. In the absence of anything in the context to
the contrary, popular words are to be understood in
their popular sense.—*Harrison v. The State*, 102 Ala.
172; *Montgomery B. B. Works v. Gaston*, 126 Ala. 446;
Hagan v. Comm. Ct. 49 South. 419. The governor's term
exists through Monday after the second Tuesday in January, the succeeding term beginning on the third Tuesday in January.—Section 116, Constitution 1901;
Meechum on Public Offices, sec 391; *Best v. Polk,,* 18
Wall. 112; *Sheets v. Selden,* 2 Wall. 17; *Goode v. Webb,*
52 Ala. 452; *Cary v. The State,* 76 Ala. 78; *Prowell v.
State ex rel,* 142 Ala. 83; *Lang v. Phillips,* 27 Ala. 313;

Hall v. Streets, 112 Mass. 27. This construction is rendered certain by the provisions of section 48, Constitution 1901, as under that provision the legislature may at any time, within seven consecutive days after their meeting canvass the vote and declare the election.— *Evans v. Job,* 8 Nev. 322. The Constitution being plain, it must be implicitly obeyed.—*State v. McGow,* 108 Ala. 166; *State v. Foster,* 130 Ala. 162. And this is true, notwithstanding the provisions of sections 1461, and 1570, Code 1907.—*Lehman v. Robinson,* 59 Ala. 241; *Sadler v. Langham,* 34 Ala. 311, and authorities next above.

INGE & MCCORVEY, for appelle and ROBERT C. BRICKELL, Attorney General, amicus cure. The court's action in sustaining the demurrer to the pleas of respondent was free from error.—*Montgomery v. The State,* 107 Ala. 372; *State v. Waldrop,* 158 Ala. 86; *Jackson v. The State,* 143 Ala. 145; *State v. Foster,* 130 Ala. 154; *Fox v. McDonald,* 101 Ala. 51. It is a well settled rule that an officer clothed with the power of appointment shall not forestall the rights and prerogatives of his successor by making an appointment to fill an anticipated vacancy in an office, the time of which cannot begin until after his own term and power to appoint have expired. 26 L. R. A. (N. S.) 514; 8 L. R. A. 228; 40 Pac. 538; 39 N. J. L. 14; 45 *Ib.* 189; 16 N. E. 384; 29 Cyc 1373; 23 A. & E. Enc. of Law, 347. Under the Acts and the Constitution, the term of the governor and of the respondent expired at the same time.—Acts 1909, 305; Sec. 116, Constitution 1901; *Mont. T. Co. v. Knabe,* 158 Ala. 458. This construction is further strengthened by a legislative interpretation as found in sections 1461, and 1570, Code 1907. The terms begin on the first Monday after the second Tuesday in January, after the election.

—6 Mayf. 684; *Lane v. Kolb*, 92 Ala. 636; *Vogel v. The State*, 8 N. E. 164; *Arnold v. U. S.*, 9 Cranch. 104; *Carlise v. Yoder*, 12 South. 255; *Evans v. Sanders*, 8 Port. 497. Under the Act, the governor appoints successors only upon the expiration of the term, and hence, Governor Comer was without power to make the appointment.—*Bownes v. Meehan*, 45 N. J. L. 189; *Jackson v. State, ex rel.*, 143 Ala. 145. The city court had jurisdiction to grant the writ.—*Capital C. W. W. Co. v. State, ex rel.*, 105 Ala. 406; *State, ex rel. Goodgame v. Matthews*, 153 Ala. 646; Acts 1871-2, p. 109; Sec. 3296, Code 1907; *Lee v. State, ex rel. Locke*, 49 Ala. 43; *Ex parte Campbell*, 130 Ala. 171.

SOMERVILLE, J.—The appellee filed a petition in the nature of quo warranto in the city court of Mobile charging that the appellant was unlawfully usurping the office of jury commissioner of Mobile county, and was exercising the powers and duties of that office without warrant or authority of law. In accordance with the prayer of the petition, an alternative writ was issued to the appellant requiring him to answer and show cause why he should not be ousted and excluded from said office. Demurrers to the answer made by respondent were sustained by the trial court, and, the respondent declining to plead further, a judgment of ouster was rendered against him from which he appeals. The respondent's answer denies that he is usurping or unlawfully holding said office, and in support of his right thereto he sets out the following facts:

Under the act of August 31, 1909 (Laws 1909, p. 305), he was on November 12, 1909, duly and legally appointed as jury commissioner of Mobile county by Gov. B. B. Comer, his term of office being "till the first Monday after the second Tuesday in January, 1911."

On January 9, 1911, while still serving under this appointment, he was again duly appointed as jury commissioner of Mobile county for a term of three years from the expiration of his first term, as his own successor in said office. Immediately after his said last appointment, and prior to January 16, 1911, respondent duly qualified as such commissioner, as required by law, and has throughout his said first term and continuously since January 16, 1911, claimed to be and is a member of the jury commission of Mobile county, and has rightfully discharged the duties of said office, for which he possesses all the legal qualifications. On Monday, January 16, 1911, at 2:15 o'clock p. m., Emmet O'Neal, who had been previously elected Governor of Alabama for a period of four years from the first Monday after the second Tuesday in January, 1911, took the oath of office as Governor, and duly qualified as such.

The answer contains other matter, but the facts above recited are all that are material to a determination of the question as to respondent's right to the office of jury commissioner. The determination of the main question obviously depends upon (1) when the official term of Gov. Comer expired; (2) when the official term of Gov. O'Neal began; (3) when the term of the respondent as jury commissioner under his first appointment expired; (4) whether it expired during and before the expiration of Gov. Comer's term; (5) whether, if it did so expire, Gov. Comer could exercise the power of appointing his successor, as conferred on the Governor by section 1 of the act of August 31, 1909; and (6) if Gov. Comer could have so appointed respondent on Monday, January 16, 1911, after the expiration of respondent's original term, whether he might exercise the appointing power a week in advance of its expiration, in anticipation of that event.

The point is made by respondent's counsel on this appeal that the city court of Mobile was without jurisdiction to hear the petition or render judgment thereon. We now proceed to state our views and conclusions with respect to the several questions presented for our consideration.

1.   There is no merit in the objection to the jurisdiction of the city court of Mobile. Section 5455, Code 1907, provides, it is true, that "such action must be brought in the circuit court of the county in which the acts are done or suffered, or * * * in the circuit court of the county in which the corporation has its principal office," etc.   The caption of the statute, which first appears as section 3422, Code 1896, is "In what county action to be brought," and indicates that the statute was intended merely to fix the venue, and not at all to restrict the jurisdiction to the circuit court eo nomine.

Secion 2 of Sess. Acts 1871-72, p. 109, confers on the city court of Mobile "jurisdiction in civil causes (except in actions to try title to land)," as well as "all powers of a civil nature now exercised by the circuit courts of the state and the judges thereof"; and section 1 of Sess. Acts 1888-89, p. 210, with an exception not here material, confirms this jurisdiction and these powers.

Section 3296, Code 1907, is: "Unless otherwise provided by law, the city courts and judges thereof have and exercise all the jurisdiction and powers of the circuit court and the judges thereof; and, when invested with equity jurisdiction, have and exercise all the jurisdiction and powers of the chancery court and chancellors."   Section 3259, Code 1907, subd. 1, gives the circuit judges authority "to grant writs of certiorari, supersedeas, quo warranto, mandamus, and all other remedial and original writs which are grantable by judges at common law."

It is difficult to see how language could be more aptly chosen to comprehend and express the legislative intent to give to all city courts and judges jurisdiction and powers concurrent and coextensive with those of circuit courts and judges; and we hold that, whether under the special acts referred to, or under sections 3296 and 3259 of the Code, the city court of Mobile has jurisdiction of this proceeding. If authority were needed, we think the following cases are in point: *Tenn. M. B. & L. Ass'n. v. State,* 99 Ala. 197, 13 South. 687; *McDonald v. State,* 143 Ala. 101, 39 South. 257; *Lee v. State, ex rel. Locke,* 49 Ala. 43.

The case of *Moog v. Doe,* 145 Ala. 568, 40 South. 390, relied on by appellant, must be regarded as sui generis, and its operation limited to the special proceeding and statutes there dealt with, which, we think, clearly distinguish it from the present case. One essential difference is that a motion to sell land levied on in a justice court (as in the *Moog Case*) is not a civil action, and is strictly and purely statutory; while our statutory quo warranto is a civil action (*State ex rel. Goodgame v. Matthews,* 153 Ala. 646, 45 South. 307), and but a legislative substitute for its common-law prototype, with which it substantially accords (*Harris v. Elliott,* 117 Ala. 150, 23 South. 124), and by the general principles of which it is governed. Another feature of the *Moog Case,* apparently decisive of the conclusion reached, was the express mandate of the statute requiring the justice to return the papers to the clerk of the circuit court, this being the only means by which jurisdiction of the motion to sell was given or could be acquired.—*Johnson v. Dismukes,* 104 Ala. 520, 16 South. 424.

2. By section 116 of the Constitution of 1901 (Criminal Code, p. 92), it is provided that the Governor and other officers named shall hold their offices "for the

term of four years from the first Monday after the second Tuesday in January next succeeding their election, and until their successors shall be elected and qualified." It is evident that the term here prescribed must occasionally, by reason of the varying calendar position of the particular Monday indicated, be less than four years in duration. Hence the prescription of four years must be regarded as general only, and as controlled by the particular date mentioned as the beginning of each successive term. It is also evident that, for the same reason, the term between the two particular Mondays that mark the beginning and end of the term will sometimes be more than four years in duration. In such case the incumbent's term nevertheless runs until his successor "shall be elected and qualified."

Gov. Comer was inaugurated and installed in office, as we judicially know, on Monday, January 15, 1907; and Gov. O'Neal on Monday, January 16, 1911, at 2:15 o'clock, p. m. this being in each case "the first Monday after the second Tuesday in January next succeeding their election."

Whether the term of each incoming Governor includes this "first Monday after the second Tuesday," or whether this Monday is a part of, and the last day of, the term of the outgoing Governor, depends of course on the meaning to be given the word "from" as used in section 116 of the Constitution in the phrase *"from the first Monday,"* etc.

A review of the scores of English and American cases which have during the last 150 years undertaken to give judicial definitions of this and similar words well demonstrates the futility, if not the folly, of the attempt to prescribe a constant and uniform meaning for a word which in itself, and in popular use, is not thus restricted. The opinion of Lord Mansfield in *Pugh v.*

Duke of Leeds, 2 Cowper, 714, decided in the year 1777, throws a curious light upon the vacillations of the earlier cases between technical construction and reason. Referring to one of these cases (*Hatter v. Ash,* 1 Ld. *Raymond,* 84), involving a lease which ran *"from* the date of the indenture," he says: "After several arguments, Treby, Chief Justice, at first, from the strength of reason, was for supporting the lease; and then, staggered by the weight of authorities, changed his opinion. But when the judgment was given, he absented himself. Powell, Junior, Justice, at first followed the authorities; but afterwards came over to reason; and at last it was agreed, by Neville and the two Powells, that 'from the date' ought to be construed *inclusive,* and, therefore, that the lease was good."

Still earlier, the cases had settled upon the construction that "from" was always *exclusive.* "So it seems to have stood down to 24 Car. 1. At that time," quaintly observed the great jurist, "mankind began to revolt against such a doctrine." Lord Mansfield's own views are expressed in the following passages from his opinion: "In grammatical strictness, and in the nicest propriety of speech that the English language admits of, the sense of the word 'from' must always depend upon the context and subject-matter, whether it shall be construed inclusive or exclusive of the terminus a quo. And whilst the gentlemen at the bar were arguing this case, a hundred instances and more occurred to me, both in verse and prose, where it is used both inclusively and exclusively." And, in conclusion, "The ground of the opinion and judgment which I now deliver is, that 'from' may in the vulgar use, and even in the strict propriety of language, mean either inclusive or exclusive; that the parties necessarily understood and used it in that sense which made their deed effectual; that courts of justice are to construe the words of parties so as to effectuate their deeds and not to destroy them, more especially where the words themselves abstractedly may admit of either meaning." The ruling was that "from the date" meant the same as "from the day," and included the day of the execution of the lease.

It may well be doubted if the numerous judicial discussions of the subject since that time have added anything of value to the wise views of Lord Mansfield. Some courts have slavishly and unreasoningly followed the view that the word is always one of exclusion; while perhaps an equal number have more wisely held, where context, or popular usage or custom, so indicated, that it was inclusive. Many cases will be found collected in 4 Words & Phrases, pp. 2983-2986; and in a very comprehensive case note to *Halbert v. Live Stock Ass'n*, 49 L. R. A. 193, the entire subject of the computation of time is exhaustively treated. In this note the author, by way of general summary, says of the rule which excludes the first day and includes the last: "This rule, however, is subject to many exceptions, growing out of the language of the provisions for the period of time to be computed, and arising from peculiar facts and circumstances of the particular cases to which the rule is sought to be applied. And the question as to which of the first and last and last days of a period of time shall be included in the computation, and which shall be excluded, has not only given rise to much conflict of authority, but has also been determined differently and on different theories in different periods and jurisdictions; and this question, like the general one of inclusion of one day and exclusion of the other, has been variously decided with a view to the language of the particular provision for the period to be computed, and the peculiar facts and circumstances surrounding the particular case with reference to which the computation is to be made."

Where a statute fixes the time within which an act is to be done, section 11 of the Code provides that the first day shall be excluded and the last day included. This is in accord with the general law of the subject, which is that whenever the question is merely as to the computation of time the terminus a quo is excluded. 28 A. & E. Ency. Law, 215. This is especially true in commercial transactions.—*Bradley v. Northern Bank,* 60 Ala. 252; *Doyle v. Bank,* 131 Ala. 294, 30 South. 880, 90 Am. St. Rep. 41. The general rule undoubtedly grew out of the disposition of courts to avoid forfeitures against those who must act within a given time or lose their rights, by indulging them to the furthest time possible.

This court has held that a lease "for the term of one year *from* the 1st day of November, 1872, *to* the 1st day of November, 1873," excluded November 1, 1872, and included November 1, 1873.—*Goode v. Webb.* 52 Ala. 453. In that case, however, the court recognized the rule stated by Lord Mansfield that intention, when clearly apparent, must govern in every case, and the decision of the point was based on the general rule for computing time, and the absence of anything to show an inclusive intent; and we apprehend that if it had appeared that by common usage or acceptation leases began *on* November 1st in that community, "from" would have been held to be inclusive instead of exclusive, and "to" exclusive instead of inclusive.

In what we have said above, it is not our intention to unsettle the general rules which have been adopted by courts for the computation of time, nor to deny the propriety of the rule that "from" is prima facie exclusive of the terminus a quo; but rather to illustrate the unwisdom of the attempt to apply these rules to all cases indiscriminately.

Our conclusion with respect to section 116 of the Constitution is that "from the first Monday," as applied to a term of public office, though prima facie exclusive of Monday, might, agreeably to ordinary usage, be either inclusive or exclusive of that day, according to circumstances. Of the only two reported cases we find in point, *Best v. Polk,* 85 U. S. 112, 21 L. Ed. 805, holds "from" in this connection to be exclusive, while *Vogel v. State ex rel. Rand,* 107 Ind. 374, 8 N. E. 164, holds it to be inclusive. In *Best v. Polk* the only reason given is the general rule; and in *Vogel v. State,* while the general rule is recognized, it is said that the circumstances and reason of particular cases may remove them from the operation of the rule. We cite these cases only to show the inherent ambiguity in the meaning of "from," considered per se. We note, however, that both Mechem and Throop lay it down as a rule that where a term of office runs from a certain date the day of the date is excluded.—Mechem on Public Officers, § 386; Throop on Public Officers, § 315.

We do not regard the cases of *Cary v. State,* 76 Ala. 78, and *Prowell v. State ex rel. Hasty,* 142 Ala. 80, 39 South. 164, cited by appellant, as decisions on this point at all, since the exact duration of the official terms there considered was not in issue, and the termini were referred to with evident generality and inexactness.

Turning, now, to other sources for light, it is insisted for appellant that sections 48 and 115 of the Constitution unmistakably show that the particular Monday mentioned in section 116 was regarded as belonging to the term of the outgoing Governor. Section 48 provides that the Legislature shall meet on the second Tuesday in January next succeeding their election; and section

115 provides that the returns of every election for Governor and other State officers shall be transmitted to the Speaker of the House, "who shall *during the first week* of the session at which such returns shall be made, open and publish them," etc. The argument is that the "week" allowed for opening and publishing the returns, and declaring the result of the election, means, and can only mean, seven consecutive days, and hence they might properly be done as late as the Monday following the meeting of the Legislature, which is of course wholly inconsistent with the notion that the officers whose votes are to be canvassed, and whose election is to be announced, could be already in office.

We think this view is sound, and more persuasive of the constitutional intent than the opposing argument of a contrary legislative interpretation as indicated by sections 1461 and 1570 of the Code of 1907. Section 1461 provides that the Governor, and other State officers, shall hold their offices "for the term of four years from the time of their installation in office, * * * such installation to take place *on the first Monday* after the second Tuesday in January next after their election." And section 1570 provides that "the succeeding officer is entitled to the salary for the day upon which he is inducted into office."

That legislative interpretation of doubtful constitutional provisions may be looked to and be entitled to much consideration has been declared by this court.— *Farrior v. N. E. M. S. Co.*, 88 Ala. 279, 7 South. 200. However, the force of these statutes in that aspect is much weakened in view of the fact that both of them existed prior to the Constitution of 1901, and were merely carried over into the Code of 1907, although section 1461 was then modified in general accord with the change made by the new Constitution.

Upon a full consideration of the arguments in favor of each of these views, and regardful of the force of the general rules of construction, we are of the opinion that section 116 of the Constitution, read in connection with sections 48 and 115, must be construed as fixing the terms of the Governor and other State officers therein named as beginning on Tuesday, and as not including the Monday from which the terms begin to run; and that the meaning is too plain to permit of alteration by legislative enactment or popular usage.

We therefore hold that Gov. Comer's term of office de jure expired at midnight on Monday, January 16, 1911; and consequently Gov. O'Neal's term de jure began on and with the Tuesday following.

3. By the Act of August 31, 1909, the term of the respondent Oberhaus as jury commissioner, under the appointment made by Gov. Comer, ran *"till* the first Monday after the second Tuesday in January, 1911."

Webster's New International Dictionary defines "till" as meaning in relation to time "up or down to; as far as; until." "The words 'to,' 'till,' and 'until' are synonymous, and are sometimes ambiguous and equivocal in the particular connection in which they occur in provisions for a period of time for the performance of an act, and are therefore construed as exclusive or inclusive according as the subject-matter about which they are used may show the intention in using the words to have been the one or the other."—*Conway v. Smith Merc. Co.,* 6 Wyo. 327, 44 Pac. 940, 49 L. R. A. 201, and case note, 202. "Primarily, the word ('until') is one of exclusion, but this construction must yield to a manifestly contrary intent, and the word bears an inclusive meaning when manifestly so intended."—29 A. & E. Ency. Law, note 3, pp. 352, 353.

In *Johnson v. State,* 141 Ala. 7, 37 South. 421, 109 Am. St. Rep. 17, the court held that, under a statute providing that a term of court should continue *until* a certain Saturday, that day was excluded from the term, by force of the general rule of construction. But in *Montgomery Traction Co. v. Knabe,* 158 Ala. 458, 48 South. 501, a case involving the identical point, the Johnson Case was overruled, and "until" was held to include the Saturday named; the reason being that universal usage had thus interpreted that and similar statutes.

Contrary to what seems to be the weight of authority elsewhere, this court has held that in an order allowing *until* a certain day for the signing of a bill of exceptions, "until" was exclusive of the day named.—*Richardson v. State,* 142 Ala. 12, 39 South. 12; *Heal v. State,* 40 South. 571.

Upon a fair survey of the authorities here and elsewhere, we hold that "till" means the same as "until," and that as marking the end of a period of time it must be construed as prima facie exclusive of the terminus ad quem; although this construction will always yield to a clearly contrary intent when shown in any legitimate way.

Applying this rule to the word "till" as used in the act of August 31, 1909, defining the terms of jury commissioners, we can discover no clear legislative intent to extend the term in question so as to include Monday, January 16. It therefore results that the term of the respondent Oberhaus, under his first-named appointment, expired at midnight of Sunday, January 15.

4. The act above referred to provides that "upon the expiration of each of these terms (of jury commissioners), the Governor shall appoint successors, who shall hold office for three years, from the expiration of the

term of office of their respective predecessors." This
must be held to authorize the Governor, whoever he
might be, to appoint the successor of Oberhaus at any
time after the original term of Oberhaus fell in; and
this latter event happened, as we have seen, at midnight
of January 15th.   If, therefore, Gov. Comer's term
of office included Monday, January 16, 1911 (and we
have seen that it did), he could, while he was serving as
Governor on that day, appoint the successor of Oberhaus.

5. This being true, the question arises, could he validly
appoint him a week in advance of that day, without express confirmation of the appointment on January 16th
after the original term had actually expired?

We have carefully examined the authorities on this
proposition, and, as there is no material conflict among
them, it is not necessary to here reproduce their language or reasoning. They clearly settle the law to the
effect that the appointing power cannot forestall the
rights and prerogatives of its own successor by appointing successors to officers whose official terms expire contemporaneously with or after the expiration of the term
of the appointing power; but where, by law or personal
action, the office to be filled by appointment must become
vacant by the expiration of the incumbent's term or by
his withdrawal during the term of the appointing power,
a prospective appointment thereto, if not forbidden by
law, may be made at a convenient season before the
actual expiration.—Mechem on Public Offices and Officers, § 133; Throop on Public Officers, § 92; 23 A. &
E. Ency. Law, 347; 29 Cyc. 1373; *State ex rel. Morris v.
Sullivan*, 81 Ohio St. 79, 90 N. E. 146, 26 L. R. A. (N.
S.) 514, and note; *State ex rel. Whitney r. Van Buskirk*,
40 N. J. Law, 463; *State ex rel. Childs r. O'Leary*, 64

[Oberhaus v. State ex rel. McNamara.]

Minn. 207, 66 N. W. 264. And this we hold to be the law.

Nor do we conceive that it matters at all that the term of the appointing power projects beyond the term of the retiring officer by but a day or even the fraction of a day. We think, however, by way of distinction, that had Gov. O'Neal's term begun de jure *with* Monday, the 16th, a prospective appointment by Gov. Comer would have been invalid at least unless confirmed by him while holding over on the 16th. We might conjecture that the Legislature in framing the jury commission act intended to make the terms of the first of the series of commissioners synchronous with the Governor's term, so as to permit the incoming Governor to appoint their successors. If so, they failed to accomplish their design. But, by comparison with the act of the same Legislature in 1907, creating the State Tax Commission, and making their terms expire *on* the first Monday after the second Tuesday in January, 1911, we might equally conjecture that a difference was intended to be made in the appointing power.

It results from the foregoing views and conclusions that the respondent's answer to the writ showed that he was lawfully holding the office of jury commissioner of Mobile county, and the trial court erred in sustaining the relator's demurrers thereto.

Let the judgment be reversed and the cause remanded for further proceedings in accordance herewith.

Reversed and remanded.

DOWDELL, C. J., and ANDERSON and SAYRE, JJ., concur.

Farr, *et al*, *v.* Perkins, *et al.*

Ejectment.

(Decided June 16, 1911.   55 South. 923.)

1. *Deeds; Taking Effect; Death of Grantor.*—Notwithstanding the common law rule that an estate in remainder could be supported only by a prior freehold, an estate in land may be created to take effect in possession on the death of a grantor, with a reservation to the grantor of the intervening use and possession.

2. *Same; Remainders; Precedent Estate.*—Where a husband conveyed lands to his wife for life with all the privileges and appurtenances, and at her death to descend to the youngest son in fee, and in the event of the youngest son's death before he became of age, and in the event of his death without issue, then to the second youngest son, and so on to the next oldest child, and in the event of the death of all the sons without heirs surviving, then the remander after the li.e estate to his daughter Catharine, and her heirs forever, tne deed created in the wife an equitable separate estate, the legal title during her life, and the life of the husband vesting in the husband as trustee for the wife, and operating as a comp.ete divestiture of the grantor's estate, and creating a prior particular freehold sufficient to support the remainder in the youngest son.

3. *Same ;Construction; Base Fee.*—∪nder the deed above set forth, on the falling in of the widow's life estate, there was vested in the youngest son an estate in fee, which, however, was a base or qualified fee, since it was subject to be defeated by his death before arriving at the age of maturity without lawful issue.

4. *Same; Words of Limitation or Purchase.*—The above deed examined and held, that since the youngest son was never married, but survived his two older brothers, the oldest of which left children surviving uim, tne deed did not indicate an intent on the part of the grantor to engraft contingent remainder to possible grand children or to the conditional limitation to his several sons, nor to make such possible grandchildren joint purchasers with their respective fathers, but that the explanatory clause appended to the grant to each son was intended to restrict the descent in each case to the next youngest son "then alive," the varying phases referred to heirs or lawful heirs, or children, being understood as words of limitation intended only to convey a contingent bass fee to the son, and not as words of purchase to the grandchildren, so as to vest title to the entire property in the surviving children of the oldest son, on the death of the youngest son without issue.

5. *Same; Conditional Limitation; Construction.*—Since it was possible under the deed, as actually happened. that none of the successive contingent grantees would be alive and satisfy the conditions in the deed. either there was left in the grantor a quasi reversion, the possibility of ultimate interests not limited over by the deed, or else by reason of the impossibility of the conditional limitations

[Farr, et al, v. Perkins, et al.]

taking effect, a condition which arose during the lifetime of the youngest son by the death of his two older brothers, one of whom left children, which defeated the limitation to the daughter, so that the terminable fee in the youngest son became a fee simple, although he died after his two brothers, but without issue.

6. *Same; Life Estate; Limitations Over; Validity.*—Where a grantor conveyed property to his wife with remainder to their youngest son in fee except that if he should die before maturity without issue, then to the next youngest son, and so on to each son, and then to the daughter, were valid conditional limitations.

7. *Perpetuities; Limitation Over to Children.*—Under section 3417, Code 1907, a deed to a wife for life with remainder to the youngest son in fee except in case he died before maturity without issue, and in case none of them died leaving lawful issue, then to the grantor's daughter and her heirs, was not a limitation violative of the rule against perpetuity.

8. *Judgment; Against Landlord; Parties.*—Since the object of sections 3840, and 3844, is either to bind the landlord by the judgment, or to permit him as of right to effectually defend the suit in his own proper person, and since a judgment for possession in fact operates only on the tenant in possession, the intervention of a false landlord in such action could not give plaintiff a right either to a joint judgment against both the landlord and the tenant, or against the landlord separately, in case the tenant's possession was rightful.

9. *Ejectment; Defenses.*—Where defendant in ejectment was in possession under certain tenants in common, every defense available to them was equally available to the defendant.

10. *Same*—A tenant in common cannot maintain ejectment against a co-tenant in possession unless there has been an ouster of the plaintiff by the defendant before suit brought, or something equivalent thereto.

11. *Same.*—Where one tenant in common sues another in ejectment, the burden is on the plaintiff who asserts an ouster to overcome by proof the presumption of possession for the common benefit of all.

12. *Same; Ouster; Repudiation.*—A defendant's co-tenant's repudiation of the existence of the relation of tenant in common is sufficient evidence of previous ouster to excuse demand by plaintiff to be let into possession before suit brought.

13. *Same; Evidence.*—Formal demand by one co-tenant to be let into possession or enjoyment of his right as a co-tenant, and a refusal is clear evidence of ouster authorizing the bringing of ejectment.

APPEAL from Monroe Circuit Court.

Heard before Hon. JOHN T. LACKLAND.

Ejectment by Cammie Vera Farr, and others, against Lemuel Perkins and others. Judgment for defendants and plaintiffs appeal. Affirmed.

BARNETT & BUGG, and H. H. McCLELLAND, for appellant. At the time the deed was made, the husband could not convey the legal title directly to his wife(*Maxwell v. Gray*, 85 Ala. 577), and if the deed is to be held good as an executory devise (section 3398, Code 1907), then the wife acquired an equitable separate estate on which may be based the fee simple title of the youngest son, who it appears arrived at the age of maturity, but died without issue. The limitation over to the youngest son was void because not based on a sufficient freehold, and the property descended to the heirs as if there had been no devise.—3 S. & P. 28; 29 Ala. 76. All the limitations over on this equitable life estate were void, and hence, this property should descend according to the law of descent.—*Flynn v. Davis*, 18 Ala. 132; 29 Ala. 478; 34 Ala. 349; *Sherrod v. Sherrod*, 37 Ala. 537; *Phinizy v. Foster*, 90 Ala. 262; *Bibb v. Bibb*, 79 Ala. 437; *Newsom v. Holcsaple*, 101 Ala. 682; *Smaw v. Young*, 109 Ala. 528. The presumption prevails that the possession of the tenant in common is the possession of all until some open notorious act of ouster and adverse possession is brought home to the notice or knowledge of the cotenant out of possession.—*Fielder v. Childs* 73 Ala. 567; *Inglish v. Webb*, 117 Ala. 387; 98 Ala. 448; 2 Mayf. 78; 50 Am. St. Rep. 843. The court could have given the affirmative charge to the plaintiff on the theory that the heirs of Charlie Moore did not defend.

FITTS & LEIGH, for appellee. Being in possession as the agent of her children, it was the right of appellee to make any defénse that her children could make.— *Franklin v. Dorlan*, 87 Am. Dec. 111. Each tenant holds for himself and his co-tenant, and each is entitled to possession of the entire tract in which he was interested.—*Long v. Grant*, 50 South. 914. It is necessary to prove an ouster or its legal equivalent before one co-tenant can maintain ejectment against another—*So. C. O. Co. v. Henshaw*, 89 Ala. 448; *Jones v. Perkins*, 1 Stew. 512. Under the deed, the entire legal estate had passed to the children, the landlords of the tenant in this case.—Sec. 3417, Code 1907; *Gunn v. Hardy*, 107 Ala. 609; *Andrews v. Huckabee*, 30 Ala. 143. The reservation of the life estate did not in itself make the deed a will.—*Trawick v. Davis*, 85 Ala. 342;*Abney v. Moore*, 106 Ala. 131; *Hopper v. Reeves*, 132 Ala. 625. The deed must be interpreted as a whole.—*Hamner v. Smith*, 22 Ala. 433; *Sullivan v. McLaughlin*, 99 Ala. 60; *Overton v. Mosely*, 135 Ala. 599. When so construed it vested a fee in the defendants based on the original equitable separate estate of his wife, and the limitations therein are in no wise void.—*McWilliams v. Ramsey*, 23 Ala. 813; *Terrill v. Reeves*, 103 Ala. 264; *Mason v. Pate*, 34 Ala. 379; *Wilson v. Alston*, 122 Ala. 630; *Finlay v. Hill*, 133 Ala. 229; *Goldsby v. Golsby*, 38 Ala. 404.

SOMERVILLE, J.—L. R. Moore, the grandfather of plaintiffs and defendants, executed a deed in the year 1870, conveying the land sued for to his wife, Sarah Moore. The habendum clause of the deed was as follows: "To have and to hold unto said Sarah J. C. Moore, during the term of her natural life, with all the privileges and appurtenances thereto belonging, and at her death all the right, title and property interest therein to vest and descend to our youngest son, John Wheeler Moore, in fee simple. And provided in the event of his death before he arrives at the age of maturity and lawful marriage and before child born, or to be born, the issue and fruits of said marriage, then further, in consideration of love and affection of my said sons, said lands and tenements are to descend to and be inherited and enjoyed by my next youngest son, James Sylvester, to him and to his lawful heirs or children forever. But in case the said James Sylvester Moore, second youngest son of L. R. and Sarah J. C. Moore, should die without children lawfully begotten, then said lands and all interest therein to descend to my next youngest son and to his children, and so on to the next oldest son and their heirs forever, in case of the death or failure of issue lawfully begotten of the younger sons. But in the event of the death of all my sons without surviving children lawfully begotten, then I give the said lands, after the life estate of my said wife, to my daughter Catherine. It being the true intent and meaning hereof that my said wife, Sarah, shall have a life estate and interest in said lands first; then said lands to descend and be inherited and enjoyed by our youngest son then alive and his lawful children. But in case of his death without lawful children, the residue or remainder interest to descend and be enjoyed by my next youngest son then alive and his lawful children forever, and in the event of the death of all my sons during the life of my wife, Sarah, then I give my said lands to my said daughter then living and to her heirs forever."

The record shows that said L. R. Moore died in 1879; his wife, said Sarah Moore, died about 1885; John Wheeler Moore, the youngest son, died in 1906; James Sylvester Moore, the next youngest son, died in 1878; and Charles Moore, the next youngest (and oldest) son, died "prior to the death of John Wheeler Moore"; and Catherine Moore Farr, the daughter named in the deed, died before this suit was begun. John Wheeler Moore died at the age of 40 without bodily heirs, never having married; James Sylvester Moore died without bodily heirs; Charles Moore left surviving him a widow, Florence Moore (who was made a party defendant on motion), and "children," the number and ages of whom are not made to appear; and Catherine Moore Farr left surviving her six children, who are the plaintiffs in this action. The grantor's widow, Sarah Moore, held possession of the land from and after his death until her own death. And, when she died John Wheeler Moore took possession and held until his death in 1906. After this event, Charles Moore's widow, Florence Moore, took possession "for her children." She was the agent of her children (by Charles Moore), and "leased said lands to Lemuel Perkins as such agent." As shown by the record proper, this suit was brought against this Lemuel Perkins as sole defendant, but on defendant's suggestion that Florence Moore was his landlord, and on her motion to be made a party defendant, it was ordered by the court that she "is made a party defendant to this cause, and the landlord of said tenant." The only plea shown is the general issue filed by Florence Moore. On motion of defendants, the court excluded all of plaintiffs' evidence, and on request of the defendants the court gave the general affirmative charge for the defendants, and refused to instruct the jury to find for the plaintiffs for a one-sixth undivided interest in the land; both charges being requested in writing. There was verdict and judgment for the defendants, from which plaintiffs appeal and assign as error the giving and refusing of the two charges, respectively, above referred to.

The theory of plaintiffs' counsel is that the several remainder interests limited in the deed are void because (1) the estate of the life tenant—the grantors' widow—was under the law then in force but an equitable estate, and therefore incapable of supporting a remainder; or (2) the remainders to vest in James Sylvester Moore, or Charles Moore contingently upon the failure of issue in

John Wheeler Moore, necessarily failed because neither of those persons was in existence when the event happened upon which an estate could vest in him; and therefore, whether the estate became a fee simple in John Wheeler by the premature death of the two contingent remaindermen, or reverted to the grantor, or his heirs, it results that plaintiffs are the owners by descent of a one-sixth interest jointly with the other lineal heirs of their grandfather, the grantor. Although plaintiffs claim to own only a one-sixth interest, it is insisted that they were entitled to recover the whole property because the defendant Florence Moore is not shown to have any interest therein, nor any right to defend the suit in her own name. The theory of defendants' counsel, on the other hand, is that the grantor intended to make not only his several sons grantees in remainder, but their children as well, his chief intention as gathered from the whole deed being, it is argued, to keep the entire property in one of the male lines, if any there should be, to the exclusion of daughters and their children.

1. Under the principles of the common law, an estate in remainder could be supported only by a prior freehold estate. This was due, as Mr. Washburn says, to "that imperative feudal dogma of the common law, that a distinct independent freehold estate in lands cannot be created to commence in futuro."—2 Wash. on Real Property (5th Ed.) 582. And the basis of this dogma was that estates could be created only by livery of seisin, which operated strictly in præsenti.

Doubtless that ceremony as an incident of conveyances never prevailed in this country at all, being practically abolished by the English statute of uses (St. 27 Henry VIII), which was a part of our common law.—*Horton v. Sledge,* 29 Ala. 478. But it was formally abolished by the act of December 22, 1812 (Toulmin's Dig.

p. 247), and with it fell most if not all of its technical incidents. Accordingly it is the settled rule in this State that an estate in land may be created to take effect in possession upon the death of the grantor with reservation to the grantor of the intervening use and possession.—*Daniel v. Hill*, 52 Ala. 430, 436; *Hall v. Burkham*, 59 Ala. 349; *Sharp v. Hall*, 86 Ala. 110, 113, 5 South. 497, 11 Am. St. Rep. 28.

The deed now before us created in the wife of the grantor an equitable separate estate, the legal title during her life and his vesting in him as trustee for her. Hence, it would seem that in any view of the case there was a complete divesture of the grantor's estate and the creation of a prior particular freehold estate technically sufficient to support the remainder in John Wheeler Moore.

2. By the terms of the deed upon the falling in of the widow's life estate there was vested in the youngest son, John Wheeler Moore, an estate, "in fee simple;" but the qualifying clause that immediately follows makes of it in reality a base or terminable fee, since it may be defeated by the death of the taker before arriving at the age of maturity, and without lawful issue.

And the limitations over are not technically contingent remainders, but rather estates in fee upon conditional limitations.—2. Wash. on Real Prop. (5th Ed.) 590, 591; *Horton v. Sledge*, 29 Ala. 496. And under these authorities it is clear that the limitations over to the two other sons and the daughter, Catherine, were valid.

But, since it was possible, as actually happened, that none of these successive contingent grantees could or would be alive, and also meet and satisfy the condition upon which alone his estate would cease to be terminable and become one in fee simple, either there was left in the grantor a quasi reversion, a possibility of ultimate interest not limited over by the deed, or else, by reason of the impossibility of the conditional limitations taking effect, a condition that arose during the lifetime of John Wheeler Moore by the death of his two brothers, one of whom left children (which defeated the limitation to Catherine), the terminable fee in John Wheeler became eo instanti a fee simple.

It not appearing that John Wheeler left a will, we presume that he died intestate, and in that event the location of the ultimate fee, whether in him or his father, is of no practical consequence, since the descent of the land would in either case be the same. We therefore deem it unnecessary to decide this question.

3. Under section 1579, Code 1867 (section 3417, Code 1907), "lands may be conveyed to the wife and children, or children only, severally, suuccessively, and jointly." The limitations of the present deed are clearly within the terms of the statute, and do not violate the law against perpetuities.

4. It is insisted for the appellees that the children of Charles Moore are entitled, under a proper interpretation of the deed, to the entire estate, just as they would have been had their father survived John Wheeler, and died intestate. Looking to the language of the whole deed, we are unable to approve such a conclusion. In designating the successive beneficiaries he had in mind, the grantor nowhere uses the alternative *"or his chilren,"* or *"or his lawful heirs."* Indeed, he is explicit in the explanatory clause appended by him to restrict the descent in each case to the next youngest son *then alive;* and the varying phrases of reference to "heirs or lawful heirs," or "children," must be understood as words of limitation, intended only to convey the notion of a contingent fee to the son, and not as words of purchase to

the grandchildren. The use of the word "forever" several times in this connection adds force to this conclusion. It certainly cannot be that the grantor intended to graft contingent remainders to possible grandchildren onto the conditional limitations to his several sons, nor is the language consistent with the notion that he intended to make these possible grandchildren joint purchasers with their respective fathers. And upon no other theory can appellees' contention be sustained.

5. It is obvious that Florence Moore, the alleged landlord of Lemuel Perkins, was not his landlord at all; the real landlords being her children, for whom she merely acted as agent in the making of the lease. However, as the object of the statutes (Code, §§ 3840 and 3844) in making a landlord a party defendant is either to bind him by the judgment, or permit him as of right to efficiently defend the suit in propria persona, and as the judgment for possession in fact operates only on the tenant in possession, the intervention of a false landlord in this action could not give the plaintiffs a right to a separate judgment against her, if Perkins' possession was rightful; and still less could it entitle them to a judgment against both of them jointly. Hence the issue depended upon the rightfulness of Perkins' possession.

6. As we have seen, Lemuel Perkins occupied the land as the tenant of the children of Charles Moore, who, we hold, are tenants in common with the plaintiffs. Every defense available to them is equally available to him as their tenant.

It is a fixed principle of the law of tenancy in common that one tenant cannot maintain ejectment against a co-tenant in possession unless there has been an ouster of the plaintiff by the defendant, or something equivalent thereto, before suit brought.—*Jones v. Perkins*, 1 Stew. 512; *Foster v. Foster*, 2 Stew. 356; *Philpot v. Bingham*,

55 Ala. 435; *Southern Cotton Oil Co. v. Henshaw,* 89
Ala. 448, 7 South. 760.

In *Hamby v. Folsom,* 148 Ala. 224, 42 South. 549, it is
said, per Tyson, J.: "It is undoubtedly the law that, if a
person be a part owner, the presumption is that he enters as such part owner, intending, while enforcing his
own rights, to respect those of his cotenants, and until
by some act of an unequivocal character he indicates
that his possession is no longer the possession of his
cotenants, as well as himself, he cannot claim to have
acquired any rights against them based upon their dis-
seisin. The unequivocal act, however, may be shown by
acts and circumstances, and its existence need not be
established by direct evidence."

Whether there has been an ouster or not is generally
a question of fact for the jury, and various circumstances may be proved from which the jury will be authorized to infer it.—*Hamby v. Folsom, supra;* 7 Ency.
Pl. & Pr. 319.

The burden is upon him who asserts an ouster by his
cotenant to overcome by proof the presumption of a possession friendly to and for the common benefit of all.—7
Ency. Pl. & Pr. 317, 318.

Where, however, the defense interposed or any part
of it denies the plaintiff's title entirely, and repudiates
the existence of a cotenancy, this is, of course, sufficient
evidence of previous ouster, and no demand to be let
into possession need be made by the plaintiff upon the
defendant before suit brought.—*Southern Cotton Oil Co.
v. Henshaw,* 89 Ala. 448, 7 South. 760.

As remarked in *Newell v. Woodruff,* 30 Conn. 498, it
is "eminently proper and safe, before bringing an action
of ejectment against a tenant in common, to test the intent with which the property is holden by a formal demand to be let into the enjoyment of the right claimed;

[Bush v. Fuller.]

and a refusal furnishes that clear evidence of ouster
which a demand and refusal furnish of a conversion in
trover." The defense here interposed by defendants does
not in any way deny that plaintiffs have an interest in
the land, but only denies the allegation of the complaint
that defendants are unlawfully withholding the land;
plaintiffs suing for the whole, and not merely their
share.

Nor is there anything in the evidence which can at
all support an inference that the possession of Florence
Moore, as agent for her children, or of Lemuel Perkins
as their tenant, ever became hostile to plaintiffs' rights,
or exclusive of their claims, or ever resulted in an ouster
or anything equivalent thereto. In such a state of the
evidence, it is manifest that plaintiffs showed no right
to maintain ejectment against the defendants, who held
under lease from plaintiffs' cotenants, and for this reason the trial court properly gave the general affirmative
charge for the defendants. The judgment is therefore
affirmed.

Affimed.

SIMPSON, ANDERSON, and SAYRE, JJ., concur.

Bush *v*. Fuller.

Ejectment.

(Decided June 16, 1911. 55 South. 1000.)

1. *Landlord and Tenant; Vendor and Purchaser; Default.*—Where
a purchaser is let into possession under an executory contract, a default in the payment of the purchase money, though it destroys his
right as a purchaser does not make him a tenant of the vendor.

2. *Same; Tendency at Sufferance.*—Where a purchaser of land was
let into possession under an executory agreement, and made de-

fault, but remained in possession, he became a tenant by sufferance by operation of law, and was not entitled to notice to quit

3. *Same; Ejectment; Notice to Quit.*—Ejectment being a possessory action, the plaintiff must not only show title but right of possession at the commencement of the suit, and hence, ejectment cannot be maintained against a tenant at will, who has not been given ten days notice to quit as required by law.

4. *Same; Tenancy at Will.*—While a mistaken notion on the part of landlord that the tenant was a tenant at will, could not have the effect of changing a tenancy by sufferance to one at will, yet a notice by the landlord to the tenant wherein he recited that the tenancy was one at will, justifies an inference that the holding is in fact a tenancy at will.

5. *Same; Notice to Quit.*—Where a landlord serves notice on a tenant at sufferance demanding possession in ten days, such notice by necessary implication extended defendant's possession until the expiration of ten days, and nothing short of a demand could make the possession unlawful before the expiration of that time so as to authorize ejectment.

APPEAL from Bessemer City Court.

Heard before Hon. WILLIAM JACKSON.

Ejectment by W. D. Bush against F. D. Fuller. Judgment for defendant and plaintiff appeals. Affirmed.

PINKNEY SCOTT, for appellant. No brief reached the Reporter.

LONDON & FITTS, for appellee. No brief reached the Reporter.

SOMERVILLE, J.—The appellant sued the appellee in statutory ejectment, and the case was tried by the court without a jury on an agreed statement of facts.

B. H. Johnson, the former owner of the land sued for, sold it to the defendant on August 13, 1907, and executed to him on that day a bond for title in the usual form, undertaking, upon defendant's payment of all and the last of eight purchase-money installments as they became due, to convey the land to the defendant by sufficient deed in fee simple. The defendant did not pay any of these notes at any time, although he paid in monthly installments the interest on the entire debt of $3,500 down to January, 1909. In the meantime, on July 16, 1908, said B. H. Johnson executed a conditional deed, conveying the same land to the plaintiff, the deed being delivered in escrow, to be delivered to the plaintiff contingently on January 16, 1909. The grantor not meeting the condition, the deed was duly delivered by the holder to the plaintiff, and he became thereby invested with all the title of his grantor, which was a perfect legal title, subject to the equitable rights of the defendant under his bond for title. On January 29, 1909, the plaintiff, Bush, served on the defendant, Fuller, the following notice: "You are hereby notified *as a tenant at will* on the property hereinafter set out and described that the duration of the tenacy is hereby terminated, and that you are required, *within ten days* after this notice, on receipt of same, to vacate the premises hereinafter set out as follows: (describing the property sued for.)" On this state of facts the trial court rendered judgment for the defendant, which was duly excepted to, and is now appealed from by the plaintiff.

1. When a purchaser is let into the possession of land under an executory agreement of purchase, as in the present case, and makes default in the payment of the purchase money at the time or times stipulated, he loses his rights as purchaser (in a court of law), but he does not ipso facto become a tenant of the vendor. As said by Brickell, C. J., in *Tucker v. Adams*, 52 Ala. 254, 258: "If the vendor has not parted with the legal title, and the vendee fails to pay the purchase money, he has three remedies, all of which he may pursue at the same time, and cannot be compelled to elect between them. He may maintain ejectment on his legal title, sue at law for the recovery of the purchase money, and proceed in equity for the enforcement of his lien for the purchase money.

If he has parted with the legal title, the vendee cannot by possibility be treated as his tenant. If he has not parted with the legal title, treating the vendee as his tenant, liable for rent, would operate a destruction of the contract of purchase, and the substitution of a different contract the parties did not make."—See, also, *Gravlee v. Williams*, 112 Ala. 539, 543, 20 South. 952, where this relationship is discussed.

2. In the present case the defendant, on making default in the payment of the purchase price, did not become a tenant at will of the vendor, or his successor in interest, unless such person expressly or impliedly agreed that he might remain in possession after such default. In the absence of such permission, his tenure would be a quasi tenancy, called tenancy at sufferance, which arises purely by operation of law, when one who has come into possession of land by a lawful title keeps it afterward, without any right at all, before demand by the lawful owner.—24 Cyc. 1041. He holds without right, and yet is not a trespasser.—1 Wash. on Real Property, 648. But the moment the parties agree, the one to hold and the other to permit him to hold possession, it becomes a tenancy at will, or from year to year, and ceases to be one at sufferance.—Id. 651. And a tenant at sufferance is not entitled to notice to quit, or at least to more than is sufficient to enable him to vacate the premises.—Id. 660; Tiedeman on Real Property, § 227, note.

The trial court evidently gave judgment for the defendant on the theory that he was tenant at will of the plaintiff, and as such entitled to 10 days' notice of the termination of his tenancy by the plaintiff, as required by section 4732 of the Code of 1907. The notice to quit was given on January 29, 1909, and as shown by the agreed statement of facts this suit was begun on February 4, 1911, just *six* days after the notice was given.

3. As we have seen, if the defendant was merely a tenant at sufferance, the plaintiff could have terminated his tenure by simple entry or demand; while, if he was a tenant at will, plaintiff could terminate that tenure only by 10 days' notice in writing. Ejectment, both common law and statutory, is primarily a possessory action, and it is not enough that the plaintiff show title; he must also show a right of possession at the commencement of the suit.—*Williams v. Hartshorn,* 30 Ala. 211; *Goodman v. Winter,* 64 Ala. 410-437, 38 Am. Rep. 13; *Cofer v. Schening,* 98 Ala. 338, 13 South. 123. If, therefore, the evidence authorized the court to find that the relation between the plaintiff and the defendant, on or before January 29, 1909, the date of the notice, was one of tenancy at will, judgment was properly rendered for the defendant, for the obvious reason that the defendant's tenure and right of possession did not terminate until February 8, 1909, and plaintiff's suit was begun prematurely by four days.

4. While it is true that plaintiff's mistaken notion that a tenancy at sufferance was a tenancy at will would not make it so in fact, and while there is no direct evidence that by the plaintiff's permission or agreement it became such, yet the notice to quit given by him to the defendant expressly recites that the defendant was a tenant at will and authorizes him to remain in possession for 10 days thereafter. Hence it may, and in the absence of countervailing proof should, be inferred that the defendant's tenure had become in fact a tendency at will.

5. But, even if this were not so, the notice by necessary implication extended the defendant's permissive possession until February 8; and, conceding that it was revocable at any time by the plaintiff, nothing short of

a demand for possession could have made the defendant's tenure unlawful before the lapse of the 10 days, so as to authorize a suit for possession.

From the foregoing considerations, it results that the judgment must be affirmed.

Affirmed.

SIMPSON, ANDERSON, and SAYRE, JJ., concur.

Hardy *v*. Randall.

Ejectment.

(Decided June 6, 1911. 55 South. 997.)

1. *Trial; Argument of Counsel; Maps and Exhibits.*—Whether or not counsel shall be permitted against objection to explain the facts in controversy by reference in argument to a drawing which has not been proven to be correct nor admitted in evidence, is within the discretion of the court.

2. *Appeal and Error; Review; Discretion.*—The discretion of the trial court in excluding drawings offered by counsel in argument without formal offer as evidence with the statement that it was not a map but merely an illustrated drawing based upon the evidence in the case, will not be disturbed except upon abuse shown.

3. *Same; Review; Grounds; Specifications.*—Where matter was admitted in evidence under the rulings of the trial court, and was not palpably inadmissible, its admission will not be reviewed where no specific objections were taken.

4. *Charge of Court; Undue Prominence.*—Where the burden of carrying some of the issues was upon the plaintiff in ejectment, a requested instruction that the burden was upon the defendant to prove his plea of adverse possession is properly refused, as the effect would be to improperly contract the issue to that one upon which it was predicated.

5. *Evidence; Hearsay.*—Where a witness testified as to occupancy of land, and then added by way of explanation that he was too young to remember that now, such explanation rendered his evidence hearsay.

6. *Same; Intent or Mental Attitude.*—A claim to land as relating to its possession is a fact and not a statement of mental attitude or undisclosed intention.

7. *Same; Best Evidence.*—Since the deed is the best of evidence of what it describes, testimony of a witness on the issue as to whether

another had possession of certain land described in a certain deed
is inadmissible.

8. *Witnesses, Examination; Cross.*—Where a question is not confusing or unintelligible, though somewhat lengthy, and has reference
to what counsel supposed the witness had testied to in a certain particular, it is within the scope of a proper cross examination.

9. *Adverse Possessions; Instructions; Burden of Proof.*—The burden being upon the plaintiff to make out a prima facie right to recover, a charge asserting that the burden was upon the defendant
to prove his plea of adverse possession, is properly refused as misleading, where it is a question for the jury as to whether the prima
facie right to recover has been made out.

10. *Same; Claim or Color.*—A deed void for uncertainty or indefiniteness in description cannot operate as color of title; but a deed
may serve as color of title although it does not so describe the land
as from it alone the land may be identified, if the description can be
made so.

11. *Ejectment; Evidence; Deeds.*—Where the action is ejectment
and the defense adverse possession, and there is testimony tending
to show a long possession of lands described by deeds offered, such
deeds are properly received in evidence as color of title.

APPEAL from Shelby County Court.

Heard before Hon. W. W. WALLACE.

Common-law ejectment by F. H. Hardy against B.
T. Randall. Judgment for defendant, and plaintiff appeals. Reversed and remanded.

The following charges were refused to plaintiff: (1)
"I charge you that the burden of proof is on the defendant to prove his plea of adverse possession, and that if
the evidence is in equipoise—that is, equally divided—
you must find for the plaintiff." (2) "I charge you that
the burden is on the defendant to prove his plea of adverse possession."

The following constitute the fifth and sixth assignments of error: "State whether or not your father ever
claimed this land as his own while he was in possession"
(question propounded to defendant by his counsel), and
his answer, "Yes." The following are the other assignments of error mentioned:

"(8) In overruling appellant's motion to exclude the
statement of the witness W. H. Prestridge: 'I have never

claimed possession of it at all, except getting my fence a
few yards over the line, not knowing where the lines
were.' (9) Same witness: 'I never claimed any of it
anyway from George Randall.' (10) Question to same
witness: 'Where did you claim to? (11) Answer: 'I
claimed to where the line now is. I did not claim any
of the 40 involved in this suit.' (12) Question to the
same witness: 'How much did your father claim?' (13)
Answer: 'Sixty acres.' (14) Question to same witness:
'Did you ever hear your father say how much he
claimed?' (15) Answer: 'Yes.' (17) Question propounded by appellant to witness Bailey: 'I asked you a
while ago to discard the map and base your answer on
your own actual knowledge of the location of the land,
where in your best judgment the Richardson house
stood—on what 40; and did you not state in response
to that question that it lay in the S. W. ¼ of the S. W.
¼ of section 24, and, after you did so, did you not see
that that would put it in the 40 immediately west of the
section you have just put it in, since looking at your
private memorandum?" The deed referred to was the
deed from Elizabeth Y. and George C. Randall to B. F.
Randall and wife.

RIDDLE, ELLIS, RIDDLE & PRUET, for appellant. Witnesses who have a pecuniary interest in the result of the
suit are incompetent to prove transactions with, or statements by a deceased person whose estate is involved in
the suit.—Code 1907, section 4007; *McDonald v. Harris,*
131 Ala. 359. A witness who shows by his own statement that he does not know a fact of his own knowledge
can not testify that fact. Hearsay evidence is inadmissible.—Ency. of Evidence, pp. 443-4; *Buckley v. Cun-
ningham,* 34 Ala. 69. Declarations not shown to have
been made while the declarant was pointing out or mak-

ing boundaries or performing some duty with reference thereto, is hearsay and inadmissible.—*Southern Iron Co. v. Cen. of Ga. Ry. Co.*, 131 Ala. 649. A declaration which is a mere recital of something past is not an exception to the rule that excludes hearsay evidence.—Authorities supra. The owner of the legal title can not testify to a past unexpressed mental condition, can not testify to what he claimed while in possession of land, cultivating and fencing it, against a privy in title.—Authorities supra. Possession of land is a fact to which a witness may testify.—*Steed v. Knowles*, 97 Ala. 578; *Eagle Co. v. Gibson*, 62 Ala. 372; *R. R. Co. v. Corpering*, 97 Ala. 687. Great latitude is allowed on cross examination, and while this is left largely to the discretion of the lower court, it will be revised, if there is a palpable abuse of this discretion.—*Stoudenmire v. Williamson*, 28 Ala. 558. A deed not purporting to convey the land sued for is not admissible to show adverse possession under color of title.—*Ledbetter v. Borland*, 128 Ala. 418; *Morring v. Tipton*, 126 Ala. 350. Counsel in an ejectment suit may use drawings in arguing the case to the jury, to explain or illustrate his theory of the meaning of the evidence, and to show the location of objects testified about.—7 Cyc. 293. A plea of adverse possession under color of title is an affirmative issue, and the burden is on the defendant who pleads it.—*Dothard v. Denson*, 72 Ala. 541.

BROWNE, LEEPER & LAPSLEY, for appelle. The witnesses Randall were not incompetent as the estate of their father was not interested adversely to the witnesses, and they could testify as to his declaration of ownership or claim while in possession.—*E. & P. Co. v. Gibson*, 84 Ala. 208; *Woods v. Montevallo C. Co.*, 84 Ala. 560; *Dorlan v. Westervitch*, 37 South. 382; *Henry v. Brown*, 143 Ala. 446. The fact that a person enters under color of title does not dispense with the necessity for a claim of right. There must not only be color of title and actual possession of part of the land, but also a claim of title to the whole.—1 A. & E. Enc. of Law, 867. One may testify as to the existence and extent of his claim of title.—2 Cyc. 407, note 11; *Dorlan v. Westervitch, supra.* Counsel discuss the other assignments of error, but without further citation of authority.

McCLELLAN, J.—Common-law ejectment. The bill of exceptions contains this recital, which is the basis of an assignment of error: "The plaintiff rested his case. In opening his argument to the jury counsel for plaintiff handed about eight drawings, a copy of which is hereto attached marked 'Exhibit 5,' to the jury, without saying anything to the court or addressing counsel about it. When objection was made by adversary counsel, plaintiff's counsel stated to the court that it was a drawing based on the evidence of the case with which he desired to illustrate his argument, in the absence of a blackboard for that purpose. Counsel stated that it was not, nor did it purport to be a map; but that it was merely an objective illustration drawn from and based on the evidence in the case, which he desired to use in connection with his argument to the jury, in order to show the true location of the various houses and other things shown on the map introduced by defendant over the plaintiff's objection. Counsel for the defendant objected to the plaintiff using these drawings before the jury on the ground that it had not been identified as being a correct map of the land and appurtenances thereon. The court sustained the objection, and ordered that the jury return said drawings to plaintiff's counsel, and to this ruling of the court the plaintiff then and there reserved an exception."

It is a matter of discretion of the trial court whether counsel will be permitted on objection to explain the facts in controversy by reference to a map or drawing that has not been proven to be correct or that has not been admitted in evidence; for abuse only will it be revised.—5 Encl. L. & P. pp. 310-356; *Rand v. Syms,* 162 Mass. 163, 38 N. E. 196; *Zubc v. Weber,* 67 Mich. 52, 34 N. W. 264; *Hill v. Water Com'rs,* 77 Hun, 491, 28 N. Y. Supp. 805. No abuse of this discretion is shown in the instance under review.

Charge 1, refused to plaintiff, would have cast the result of the trial alone upon the failure of the defendant to carry the burden of his defense of adverse possession. Taking a view of the utmost (and perhaps on the evidence unjustifiable) favor to the plaintiff, there were other issues of fact the affirmative of which was on the plaintiff. The charge was hence well refused because its effect was to improperly contract the issues to the one only upon which it is predicated.

Charge 2, refused to plaintiff, would have, if given, tended to mislead the jury. Whether the burden of proof was upon the defendant to establish adverse possession depended upon the condition that plaintiff had made out a prima facie right to recover—a condition, upon this record, to be determined by the jury.

It is insisted in brief for appellant that the question propounded to B. T. Randall, and the answer thereto, set out in the fifth and sixth assignments of error, should have been disallowed and excluded on his objection and motion, because it invoked testimony affected with incompetency by Code, § 4007. The grounds of objection to the question, and those of the motion to exclude the answer, were general—not particularizing the ground argued in brief. In such cases the ruling of the court, the matter not being palpably inadmissible, will not be reviewed.—6 May. Dig. pp. 371, 372.

The motion to exclude the statement of the witness L. H. Randall, viz., "I know that Sessions cultivated some of this 40," should have been sustained. Immediately after making the quoted statement the witness added, "But I was too young to remember that now." This explanation put the affirmative statement in the category of hearsay evidence, and the plaintiff's objection took the point. It was error to overrule the motion to exclude.

The assignments numbered 8 to 15, inclusive, are argued together in brief for appellant. They rest upon the action of the court in allowing the witnesses, over appellant's objections, to testify to the absence of claim of ownership of the land in controversy. The sole argument in brief for appellant is that such testimony improperly permitted the recital of a postentertained and unexpressed mental attitude. It was ruled in *Dorlan v. Westervitch,* 140 Ala. 283, 37 South. 382, 103 Am. St. Rep. 35, in opposition to the argument now presented, that a claim to land, in relation to possession thereof, was a fact, and not a statement of mental attitude or undisclosed intention.

On the cross, appellant propounded this question to the witness Bailey: "Was ·W. H. Prestridge in possession of the land described in that deed?"—referring to deed of Hale to Prestridge. It was disallowed on objection of appellee. There was no error in this ruling. The only insistence to error in brief for appellant is that this ruling improperly limited the scope of appellant's right of cross-examination. The question was illegal in itself, and therefore not proper on examination at any stage, invited by preceding illegal examination in that particular. That was not the case here. The question could only invite in one phase the opinion of the witness,

whether Prestridge's possession was of the land described in the Hale deed. The deed was the best evidence
of what it described, and of what land Prestridge was in
the possession was a matter in issue and the subject of
necessarily separable proof. Aside from this, the witness had not been shown to know what lands were described in the Hale deed.

The question propounded on the cross to the witness
Z. R. Bailey, and set out in the seventeenth assignment,
should not have been disallowed. While somewhat
lengthy, due to its recitation of what counsel thought
the witness had previously testified in the particular indicated by the question, there was nothing confusing in
the question, nor was it unintelligble in any degree. It
was obviously within the scope of a proper cross-examination. The court erred in sustaining defendant's objection thereto.

The deeds referred to in the assignments numbered 18
to 21, inclusive, described lands, on either side, north
and south, of the railway, in that section. There was
testimony tending to show possession for a great period
under these instruments. They were offered and received in evidence as color of title only. There was no
error in this. It is true that a deed the description in
which is void for indefiniteness and uncertainty cannot
operate as color of title.—*L. & N. R. R. Co. v. Boykin,*
76 Ala. 460; *Black v. T. C. I. & R. R. Co.*, 93 Ala. 109, 9
South. 537; 2 Ency. L. & P. pp. 523-525.

On the other hand, the instrument may serve as color
of title notwithstanding it does not so describe the land
claimed as that from it alone the land may be identified.
The doctrine imported in the maxim, "Certum est quod
certum reddi potest," is applicable to such instruments
as it is to ordinary conveyances otherwise effectually
executed.—*Black v. T. C. I. & R. R. Co., supra; Dorlan*

v. Westervitch, 140 Ala. 283, 295, 37 South. 382, 103 Am.
St. Rep. 35; 2 Enc. L. & P. p. 525.

For the two errors indicated, the judgment is reversed
and the cause is remanded.   No other errors appear.

Reversed and remanded.

SIMPSON, MAYFIELD, and SAYRE, JJ., concur.

Marietta Fertilizer Co. *v.* Blair, *et al.*

Ejectment.

(Decided June 29, 1911.   56 South. 131.)

1. *Adverse Possession; Actual Possession; Occupation of Part.*—
As a rule, occupancy of a part of land entered upon in good faith
under color of title extends to the boundaries described in the color
of title, though a part of the land is not actually occupied; but this
rule does not apply where the conveyance is of two distinct tracts,
to only one of which the grantee has the legal title, and actual occupancy. However, each governmental subdivision or quartersection
does not of itself constitute a distinct tract within the exception.

2. *Same.*—Adverse possession of the whole of a tract, within the
boundaries described by the color of title, by actual occupancy of a
part thereof, is, in legal contemplation, actual and not constructive
possession, and may be restricted as to the part not actually occupied by the actual occupancy of another.

3. *Same*—In gaining by adverse possession title to the whole of
tract, by the actual occupancy of a part thereof, the relative proportion of the whole contiguous tract to the part actually occupied
is immaterial, and title to an entire half section was gained by the
adverse occupation, and actual cultivation of fifteen or twenty acres
thereof under color of title to the whole tract.

APPEAL from Clay Circuit Court.

Heard before Hon. JOHN PELHAM.

Ejectment by the Marietta Fertilizer Company against
R. W. Blair and others.   Judgment for defendants and
plaintiffs appeal.   Affirmed.

RIDDLE, ELLIS & KELLY, and TYSON, WILSON & MAR-
TIN, for appellant.   Under section 5361, Code 1907, the

appellant is entitled to have the conclusion and judgment of the lower court on the evidence reviewed without any presumption favorable to the court below. Under the facts in this case, the doctrine declared in *Lawrence v. Ala. St. L. Co.* 144 Ala. 524, must prevail. The plaintiff established a complete chain of title to the land, and under the doctrine established in the case of *Dothard v. Denson,* 72 Ala. 554, and followed in many cases which are collected in brief of counsel for appellee in *Lecroix v. Malone,* 157 Ala. 434, and referred to in the *Lawrence case, supra,* that plaintiff was entitled to a judgment. While possession of a part of a tract of land under color of title the possession ordinarily will extend to the boundaries described in the instrument constituting the color of title, but the principle had no application to a conveyance sought to be used as color of title, where the grantor is in possession of and owner of a tract of land and conveys the land thus in his possession and includes in that conveyance other lands adjoining the lands he actually has possession of and owns and the lands adjoining and there included in the conveyance would not be held by the grantee adversely and his possession of the adjoining lands would *not* be that character of adverse possession held under color of title as that same would ripen into title under the statute of limitations.—*Henry v. Brown,* 143 Ala. 446; *Woods v. Montevallo C. & T. Co.,* 84 Ala. 565; *Parks v. Barnett,* 104 Ala. 443; *Eureka v. Norment,* 104 Ala. 631.

WHITSON & HARRISON, for appelle. The deed from Bradford to Smith was essential to plaintiff's prima facie right to recover, and was not competent to establish a link to the lands sued for, and hence, defendants were entitled to a judgment.—*Christy v. Patton,* 148 Ala. 324; *Redmond v. L. & N.* 154 Ala. 311. Standing alone it did

not convey the land in controversy, and the terms of the
deed cannot be varied in a court of law by oral evidence.
—*Guilmartin v. Wood*, 76 Ala. 209;*Homan v. Stewart*,
103 Ala. 650; *Griffin v. Hall*, 115 Ala. 482; *Donahoo v.
Johnson*, 120 Ala. 438; *Hereford v. Hereford*, 131 Ala.
575. Before the contents of a lost deed becomes admissible, the execution of such deed must be shown, and by
the best evidence.—*Potts v. Coleman*, 86 Ala. 95. The
certified copies of the deeds introduced in evidence by
the defendant were properly admitted, as there is no presumption that the owner has possession of prior deeds
in his chain of title.—*Hendon v. White*, 52 Ala. 597;
Beard v. Ryan, 78 Ala. 37. These deeds were admissible
as ancient documents.—*Campbell v. Bates*, 143 Ala. 343;
Bernstein v. Humes, 75 Ala. 241. At the time the deed
from Smith to Jacobs was executed, defendant's tenants
were in adverse possession of the land, and this rendered
the deed inoperative and void as against the defendant.—
Mahan v. Smith, 151 Ala., 482; *City L. Co. v. Pool*, 149
Ala. 164; *Lowery v. Baker*, 141 Ala. 600; *Murray v.
Hoyle*, 92 Ala. 559. A tenant must surrender possession
to his landlord before he can question his landlord's title
—*Davis v. Williams*, 30 Ala. 530; *Duncan v. Guy*, 159
Ala. 524. He cannot make a valid attornment to another
while holding such possession.—*Brown v. French*, 148
Ala. 274; *Davis v. Wilson, supra*. The judgment by
Smith against Blair was not binding upon the landlord
of Blair, as they were not parties and had no notice.—
Stanley v. Johnson, 113 Ala. 344; *Doe v. Reynolds*, 27
Ala. 364. Under the facts in this case the defendants
established their right to recover by proof of the adverse
possession.—*Block v. T. C. I. & R. R. Co.* 93 Ala. 111;
Norment v. Eureka Co. 98 Ala. 182;*Goodson v. Brothers*,
111 Ala. 539; *Smith v. Keyser*, 115 Ala. 455; *Anniston
C. L. Co. v. Edmundson*, 127 Ala. 445; *Barrett v. Kelly*,

131 Ala. 378; *Chastang v. Chastang*, 141 Ala. 451; *Campbell v. Bates*, 143 Ala. 338; *Barry v. Madaris*, 156 Ala. 475; *Clak v. Dunn*, 161 Ala. 237. There is no question presented in this case as to any adversary actual possessin of any part of the land involved in this suit by parties claiming under different rights.—*Hughes v. Anderson*, 79 Ala. 209. A void deed may constitute color of title.—*Reddick v. Long*, 124 Ala. 261; *Hoyle v. Mann*, 144 Ala. 516.

McCLELLAN, J.—Statutory ejectment, by appellant against appellees, to recover the E. $\frac{1}{2}$ of section 6, township 22, range 6, in Clay county, Ala. The trial was by the court without jury. Upon the whole evidence there can be no reasonable doubt that since 1860 (and probably before) the predecessors, in asserted right, of the appellees Donaldson and the named appellees have been in the actual adverse possession, at least under color of title, of approximately 20 acres of the 320-acre tract in controversy. It is now urged upon the authority of *Lawrence v. Alabama State Land Co.*, 144 Ala. 524, 41 South. 612, that for want of evidence, to the particular effect stated in the cited decision, the adverse possession of a part of the half section in question cannot be extended to the boundaries described in the color of title under which such adverse possession was taken and held for more than 25 years before this action was instituted.

The general rule is, and has long been, that where one enters under color of title, in good faith, upon a tract of land his adverse occupancy of a part thereof will extend his adverse possession of that not adversely occupied, by another, to the boundaries described in the color of title.—*Black v. T. C. I. & R. R. Co.*, 93 Ala. 109, 110, 9 South. 537; *Henry v. Brown*, 143 Ala. 446, 39

South. 325; *Woods v. Montevallo Coal Co.*, 84 Ala. 560,
3 South. 475, 5 Am. St. Rep. 393; *Crowder v. T. C. I. &
R. R. Co.*, 162 Ala. 151, 50 South. 230, 136 Am. St. Rep.
17; *Clarke v. Dunn*, 161 Ala. 633, 50 South. 93; *Barry
v. Madaris*, 156 Ala. 475, 479, 47 South. 152; *Campbell
v. Bates*, 143 Ala. 338, 39 South. 144; *Stovall v. Fowler*,
72 Ala. 78; *Burks v. Mitchell*, 78 Ala. 63; *Lucy v. Tenn.
Co.*, 92 Ala. 246, 8 South. 806; *Childress v. Calloway*,
76 Ala. 133; *Farley v. Smith*, 39 Ala. 38, 44; *Bell v.
Denson*, 56 Ala. 444; *Torrey v. Forbes*, 94 Ala. 135, 141,
10 South. 320; *Normant v. E. Co.*, 98 Ala. 181, 12 South.
454, 39 Am. St. Rep. 45; *Ryan v. Kilpatrick*, 66 Ala.
332; *Smith v. Keyser*, 115 Ala. 455, 460, 22 South. 149;
Bailey v. Blacksher Co., 142 Ala. 254, 37 South. 827;
Baucum v. George, 65 Ala. 259, 268, 269; *Hughes v.
Anderson*, 79 Ala. 209, 215; *Watson v. Mancill*, 76 Ala.
600, 601. See, also, *Ellicott v. Pearl*, 10 Pet. 412, 413,
9 L. Ed. 475; Rose's Notes, pp. 593, 594; *Hicks v. Coleman*, 25 Cal. 122, 85 Am. Dec. 103, and note; and other
decisions of this court cited in them.

An exception to the general rule was recognized by
this court in *Woods v. Montevallo Coal Co., supra,* as
existing in those cases where the conveyance is of "two
separate and distinct tracts" of land, to only one of
which the grantee becomes invested with the legal title,
and the actual occupancy is of that tract. In such cases
the true owner of the other tract is *not* disseised and
the possession under the color of title thereto is not
extended to include such tract.—*Henry v. Brown,
supra; Crowder v. Tenn. Co., supra.* As is seen, one
of, if not the, controlling factors creating this exception lies in the separableness, the distinctness, of the
tracts conveyed. And this court has well determined
that each governmental subdivision or quarter-call does
not, in itself alone, constitute a separate, distinct tract

of land.—*Crowder v. Tenn. Co., supra.* The announcement, in respect of this exception, in *Woods v. Montevallo Coal Co., supra,* was bottomed on *Bailey v. Carlton,* 12 N. H. 9, 37 Am. Dec. 190. Reference to 5 Notes to Am. Dec. pp. 1216-1218, will show the consideration given *Bailey v. Carleton* by other jurisdictions.

Unless our decision in *Lawrence v. Alabama State Land Co., supra,* established *another exception,* than that to which we have referred, to the general rule before stated, this court has not, so far as we are advised, authoritatively done so. And it may be here pronounced that the case at bar does not present a status within the terms of the exception declared in *Woods v. Montevallo Coal Co.* and in the two recent decisions taking account of its doctrine in this particular.

The character of the extended possession to contiguous lands, under color of title, beyond that, within the boundaries defined by the color of title, actually occupied by the adverse claimant, is, in legal contemplation, *actual,* not *constructive.*—*Black v. Tenn. Co., supra; Stovall v. Fowler, supra.* Such possession, under color of title, may be restricted, as to area within the defined boundaries, by actual possession of another.—*Ryan v. Kilpatrick, supra; Ellicott v. Pearl, supra; Watson v. Mancill, supra.* So affirmatively is the general rule before stated that "color of title is sometimes said to be a substitute for a substantial and permanent fence around the premises claimed."—*Hughes v. Andersosn.* 79 Ala. 215; Sedg. & Wait on Land Titles, § 667.

The relative, proportionate area, of the whole *contiguous* tract, *actually occupied* by an adverse claimant, is not a factor, under our decisions—a qualifying element—in determining the effect of the application of the general rule previously reiterated.—*Watson v.*

Mancill, supra; Ellicott v. Pearl, 10 Pet. 412, 9 L. Ed.
475, followed by this court in *Baucum v. George*, 65
Ala. 269. Reason, if not the weight of authority in
other jurisdictions, confirms the soundness of this conclusion.—*Hicks v. Coleman*, 25 Cal. 122, 85 Am. Dec.
103, and notes thereto; 1 Cyc. 1127. To ingraft such a
qualification—exception—upon the general rule would
interpose a factor necessarily uncertain in application,
if, indeed, not requiring the exercise of a purely arbitrary discretion in establishing the boundaries of the
adverse claim. This qualification or exception to the
general rule seems to have been recognized in Vermont,
New York and Michigan, and perhaps Minnesota. The
Vermont court, in *Chandler v. Spear*, 22 Vt. 388, found
its authority, in part, in *Jackson v. Woodruff*, 1 Cow.
(N. Y.) 276, 13 Am. Dec. 525. Our court, in *Black v.
Tenn. Co.*, 93 Ala. 112, 9 South. 537, interpreted *Jackson v. Woodruff* as according with the general rule prevailing in this State; a rule that takes no account of
the proportion the actually occupied area bears to the
whole *contiguous* tract, or to the nature of the lands
adversely claimed or to the custom (if such there is
or could be) of the country in respect of the size of
landed holdings for the many purposes for which that
is done. We cannot be unmindful of the fact that very
large areas of land are and have been held in this State
by individuals and corporations for timber, farming,
and mineral purposes. What standard could be thereto
fixed as determinative of what area would, in such
cases, be subservient to or reasonable and proper for
use with, the area actually occupied, under color of
title, cannot, with any approach to definiteness, be pronounced. There is, in this State, no custom, in that
regard, of which we are aware. Ability to acquire a
landed estate, coupled with a desire to do so, fixes the

[Marietta Fertilizer Co. v. Blair, et al.]

only territorial limit to such activities, upon or in the
soil, as farming, timber gathering or culture, and mining. The open, notorious, actual, hostile possession of
a part of the contiguous lands described in the color of
title, with claim in good faith to the whole, is the basis
of the presumption of notice, of adverse claim, to the
true owner. Author, supra. The extent of the area
to which the true owner has title cannot be a satisfactory factor in determining the question of notice, of adverse claim by the adverse occupant of a part under
color of title, to the true owner. If that were accepted
as a factor, the question would at once arise, What relation, in proportion, must the land actually occupied
by the adverse claimant under color of title bear to the
true owner's entire contiguous tract? As appears, the
inquiry would submit a problem without definite min-
uend or subtrahend, and without rule whereby to ascertain them. Apart from this, however, it is but reasonable to assume, as the law does, that the true owner,
regardless of the extent of his contiguous area, cannot
be ignorant *for ten continuous years* of an open, notorious, actual, hostile possession, by another, under claim
to the boundaries defined in his color of title, of *any
part* of his lands.

Practically applying the pertinent doctrines we have
but restated, this court, in *Watson v. Mancill,* 76 Ala.
600, justified the right of the adverse claimant (Mancill) to 40 *acres of land,* notwithstanding the actual adverse possession was of 1 *acre only,* accompanying a
claim to the whole 40. The actual adverse possession,
in that case, was of 1-40th of the area adversely claimed.
Greater disproportion, in respect of the actual adverse
possession, of a part to the whole could rarely occur.

In the light of these considerations, the qualifications
of the general rule before stated, imported in some ex-

pressions, not necessary to the decision, in *Lawrence v. Alabama State Co.*, are dicta and are, hence, not authoritative; are not in accord with the settled rulings of this court.

In the case at bar the evidence fully justified the trial court in finding that from 15 to 20 acres of the half section in suit was actually cultivated, under adverse claim of ownership of the entire half section under color of title, for more than 25 years. Accordingly, the defendants (appellees) Donaldson were correctly adjudged to have acquired the title to the half section in question, and, in consequence, that the plaintiff should not recover.

We find no prejudicial error in the record. The judgment is therefore affirmed.

Affirmed.

SIMPSON, ANDERSON, MAYFIELD, and SOMERVILLE, JJ., concur.

Arnett *v.* Birmingham Coal & Iron Co.

Petition to Substitute Records.

(Decided June 7. 1911.   55 South. 831.)

1. *Guardian and Ward; Substitution of Records; Parties.*—Since a petition under section 5741. Code 1907, relates to the evidence of title to the land under a sale made by the guardian, and not to the proceeds, as to which the guardian was accountable, the personal representative of the guardian was not a necessary party.

2. *Records; Establishment of Title After Loss; Right of Action.*— Under section 5741. Code 1907, an action for substitution of probate records and of a guardian sale of land may be maintained by an owner who was not a party to the original proceeding where such records are material evidence of a link in petitioner's chain of title.

3. *Same; Evidence.*—The evidence in this case examined and held sufficient to authorize an order of substitution of the lost records.

[Arnett v. Birmingham Coal & Iron Co.]

APPEAL from Jefferson Probate Court.

Heard before Hon. J. P. STILES.

Petition by the Birmingham Coal & Iron Company for the substitution of records directed to William E. Arnett and others. From a judgment substituting the record, Arnett appeals. Affirmed.

ALLEN & BELL, and R. D. COFFMAN, for appellant. The guardian who made the sale having died, the personal representative of such guardian should be made a proper party by the proper notice.—*Davney v. Mitchell*, 56 Ala. It is insisted that the Birmingham Coal & Iron Company were not parties to the original proceeding, and that, therefore, they are incompetent parties to ask for an order of substitution, but no authorities are cited in support thereof.

PERCY, BENNERS & BURR, for appellee. The guardian who instituted the original proceedings was dead, and had no personal representative, and the wards were of full age, so there was no occasion to have a personal representative of the guardian appointed, and made a party to this proceeding. The petitioner offered a verified petition which was sufficient evidence to entitle them to have the records substituted.—*Stewart v. Oldacre*, 122 Ala. 676. Petitioners were entitled to bring the petition.—Sec. 5741, Code 1907; *Pruitt v. Pruitt*, 43 Ala. 73; *Peddy v. Street*, 87 Ala.

SAYRE, J.—This is a proceeding under section 5741, of the Code of 1907 for the substitution in the probate court of a petition by a guardian for the sale of land for the support of her wards and of the report of sale made in pursuance of an order of. sale made by the court in accordance with the petition. Except for the

papers referred to, there remains in the probate court
a perfect history of the proceeding under which the land
was sold. Petitioner avers his ownership of the land,
claiming under mesne conveyances from the purchaser
at the sale ordered by the court. The wards are now
of age and are made parties defendant to the petition
for substitution. Several objections are taken to the decree of substitution and the antecedent proceedings,
which will be noticed.

The guardian is now dead, and it is urged that her
personal representative ought to have been made a
party to the proceeding on the idea that her estate may
have to account for the proceeds of the sale. This proceeding has nothing whatever to do with the proceeds
of the sale ordered by the probate court. The question
now is about the evidence of title to the land. Whether
or not the land passed out of the wards by the proceeding in the probate court, the guardian was accountable
for the proceeds, not the land. If, perchance, she did
not account, and if her estate may after all this time
be brought to account through her personal representative, he must account for the proceeds of the sale, not
the land, in a proceeding in which the decree in this
case will be evidence of nothing.

It is said that the present owner of the title made
by the court is not a party in interest who may maintain the petition for susbtitution. The statute provides
that "if, after the determination of any civil cause or
proceeding, the original papers, or any part thereof,
pertaining thereto, which are not of record, are lost
or destroyed * * * any party in interest may, on
application in writing, stating the facts with the substitute proposed of such lost or destroyed paper or record,
verified by affidavit, obtain an order of substitution."
The petition and report of sale were not transcribed

[Arnett v. Birmingham Coal & Iron Co.]

upon the records of the court, as they should have been, though they remained in the files of the court until the year in which the petitioner acquired its title to the land. They are material evidence of a link in the petitioner's chain of title. The remedy does not seem to be confined to parties to the record of the original proceeding, but it is extended to parties interested in the matter evidenced by the record.

It is to be conceded that petitioner's case rests upon the affidavit of Brockman for proof of the contents of the papers sought to be substituted, and that in making orders of this character courts ought to move with great caution. But Brockman had made an abstract of the proceeding for the sale of the land, noting the substance of each paper and in part the language of the petition for the order of sale. No countervailing evidence was offered. Under these circumstances we discover no reason why his testimony should not be given credence. If believed it was sufficient to justify the order of substitution.

Accordingly, the judgment will be affirmed.

Affirmed.

. SIMPSON, MCCLELLAN, and MAYFIELD, JJ., concur.

Moore Bros., *et al. v.* Cowan.

Assumpsit.

(Decided June 16, 1911. 55 South. 903.)

1. *Bankruptcy; Forthcoming Bond; Action; Pleading.*—In an action against a surety on a forth coming bond, of an alleged bankrupt, pleas alleging that after the bankruptcy adjudication, a writ of error was duly sued out to review the same, but which failed to show whether or not, or when the decree was finally confirmed, or whether the writ was still pending and undetermined, or whether it had been dismissed, were insufficient either as pleas in abatement or in bar, under the bankruptcy statute.

2. *Same; Jurisdiction; Adjudication.*—The Federal Court has exclusive jurisdiction to adjudge a person a bankrupt, and to appoint a receiver, and such appointment and adjudication, cannot be collaterally attacked in a suit on the forthcoming bond, executed by the bankrupt.

3. *Same; Forthcoming Bond; Estoppel.*—A defendant who is surety or a principal in a forthcoming bond in bankruptcy executed to two persons named therein as receivers in the above cause, are estopped from questioning the validity of the receiver's appointment.

4. *Same; Defenses.*—Where a certain bankrupt was so adjudged in involuntary proceedings against him, and executed a forthcoming bond, for the purpose of retaining his assets, and then sued out a writ of error to review the adjudication, it was no defense to a subsequent action on the bond that after its execution, the property was taken from the alleged bankrupts pursuant to a voluntary bankrupt proceeding instituted by him, it not being denied that the voluntary proceedings were instituted for the bankrupt's benefit, and it not being shown that the assets were returned to and accepted by the person to whom they were surrendered as receiver in the bankruptcy proceeding.

5. *Pleading; Abatement; Verification.*—Under section 5332, Code 1907, a plea alleging the suing out of a writ of error to review the action of the court in adjudging defendants' bankrupt, was demurrable when not verified.

6. *Same; Special Plea; General Issue.*—Where matters set up in a special plea are available under the general issue, or are tantamount to a plea of the general issue, and the general issue is pleaded, it is not error to reversal to sustain demurrers to such plea.

APPEAL from Birmingham City Court.

Heard before Hon. H. A. SHARPE.

Action by A. S. Cowan, as trustee in bankruptcy of the firm of Moore Bros., against the individuals composing such firm, and the American Bonding Company, for breach of a forthcoming bond. Judgment for plaintiff, and defendants appeal. Affirmed.

The complaint alleged breach of a bond made by Moore Bros. in a proceeding in bankruptcy wherein it was sought to have the firm adjudged a bankrupt, and an order issued to the receiver to take possession of their property, under which the property was released to said Moore Bros. on the condition that, if the firm was adjudged bankrupt, they should turn such property over, or pay the value thereof in money to the trustee. The complaint alleges a demand for the property, the failure to deliver or to pay the value thereof, and the fact that Moore Bros. have been declared bankrupts.

The following are the pleas referred to:

"(1) Respondents say that this court ought not to maintain jurisdiction of this suit for this reason: That since the adjudication of H. C. Moore and Moore Bros. as bankrupts a writ of error has been sued out in said proceeding to the Circuit Court of Appeals of the United States for the Fifth Circuit, which said writ of error has been duly allowed, and upon said writ of error the said District Court has ordered the bond for a supersedeas of said decree of adjudication to be fixed at $6,500, and said bond has been filed in said cause and approved by the court or judge thereof and such supersedeas issued. The said writ of error was issued on the 21st day of November, 1908,, and filed in said cause on said date, and the said supersedeas bond was executed on the 28th day of Dacember, 1908, and approved and supersedeas issued thereon on said date. And these respondents aver that said decree of adjudication has been superseded by writ of error, and they pray that the suit may abate and be dismissed, at the cost of the plaintiff herein.

"(2) Come the defendants in this cause and specially appearing for the purpose of filing and presenting this plea and for answer to the complaint on said special appearance, they say that since the adjudication of the said H. C. Moore, T. A. Moore, and Moore Bros., bankrupts, a writ of error has been sued out on, to wit, the 21st day of November, 1908, and said proceedings sent to the Circuit Court of Appeals of the United States for the Fifth Circuit, which said writ of error was duly allowed and filed, and the cause of H. C. Moore and T. A. Moore and Moore Bros., in bankruptcy, is pending in the said Circuit Court of Appeals. That on, to wit, the 28th day of September, 1908, on the order of Hon. Oscar R. Hundley, judge of said court, a supersedeas bond was executed by said defendants in bankruptcy in said cause pending in said court, in the sum of $6,500, which said bond was duly filed in said cause in the District Court of the United States for the Northern District of Alabama, and was approved by the clerk, and a supersedeas issued in said cause of bankruptcy, and the said adjudication in bankruptcy has been superseded and suspended since the execution of said bond. The defendants aver that the Circuit Court of Appeals of the United States for the Fifth Circuit has assumed jurisdiction of said cause, and that the same is now pending therein. And the defendants aver that for the reasons set out in the foregoing plea this court ought not to maintain jurisdiction of this cause, but that the same should be evaded for the causes assigned." This plea is verified.

Plea 3 sets up the same state of facts, and on them alleges that the adjudication was suspended and superseded from the filing and allowance of said writ of error until the judgment of affirmance by the Circuit Court of Appeals, and, pending said appeal and the jurisdiction of the Circuit Court of Appeals, this cause was prematurely filed. This plea is not sworn to.

The complaint was afterwards amended so as to show the entire proceeding in the bankrupt court from the beginning thereof, and including the filing of the supersedeas bond referred to.

Plea A is as follows: "Plaintiff ought not to have and recover, for that, after the making of the bond sued on, the principal obligors therein returned the assets reclaimed by the making of said bond to the said A. S. Cowan, as receiver of the assets of T. A. Moore and A. C. Moore and Moore Bros., bankrupts, and said Cowan accepted the same." The above plea was filed by the American Bonding Company alone.

Plea Y is as follows: "Plaintiff ought not to have and recover, for that the said Cowan and Shelfer were never lawfully named as receivers of the estate of said Moore Bros., bankrupts, nor were they, as receivers, ever lawfully authorized or empowered to seize the assets of Moore Bros., or any part thereof. At a time prior to the making of the forthcoming bond sued upon said Cowan and Shelfer had wrongfully possessed themselves of certain merchandise belonging to said Moore Bros. At the time of said seizure they pretended to act as such receivers, under what purported to be an order of appointment signed by one Alex C. Burch, the referee in bankruptcy at Birmingham, and had no authority or power to make such seizure emanating from any such court or officer, having jurisdiction to appoint a receiver. Said Burch at the time of making said order had no jurisdiction to make the same, for that the proceedings in the course of which said alleged order was made were begun upon to wit, December 20, 1906, by certain creditors of Moore Bros. filing against them an involuntary petition in bankruptcy in the United States

District Court for the Southern Division of the Northern District of Alabama. Upon the same day upon which said petition was filed, and in the absence of any reference of said bankruptcy proceedings to him, the said Burch assumed to exercise jurisdiction to appoint receivers of the assets of said Moore Bros. In such unwarranted assumption of authority he signed a certain paper or papers, wherein he designated himself as referee, which purported to be an order or orders appointing said Cowan and Shelfer receivers of the assets of said Moore Bros. This alleged order of appointment was made wholly without notice to said Moore Bros., and directed or attempted to direct the said Cowan and Shelfer to take into their custody as receivers all property of every kind belonging to Moore Bros., or in their possession. Acting in pretended compliance of such order of appointment said so-called receivers by open trespass made seizures of certain merchandise belonging to Moore Bros., and were holding the same in their possession, claiming to be the receiver thereof under appointment from the court of bankruptcy. In order to save said Moore Bros. from the hardship of this tort, and under the duress of said trespass, the said bond sued on was executed, and upon its execution said assets were released by said so-called receivers to Moore Bros., and were thereby reclaimed, not from the custody of the court, but from the illegal graft of tortfeasors."

Plea B was filed by the American Bonding Company alone, and is as follows: "Comes the American Bonding Company, and for a special and separate plea says: That the assets for the reclamation (or withholding) of which the bond sued on is made were, after the making of said bond and before the bringing of this suit, taken from the possession of the principal obligors in said bond, under an order of the United States District

[Moore Bros., et al. v. Cowan.]

Court for the Southern Division of the Northern District of Alabama, whereby the said A. S. Cowan was appointed receiver of the very assets reclaimed (or withheld) by the said T. A. and H. C. Moore, under the bond sued upon in a proceeding in voluntary bankruptcy, wherein the said T. A. and H. C. Moore were adjudged bankrupts, and as such receiver said Cowan was expressly directed to take possession of said assets. Said Cowan, acting under said order and appointment, did take said assets into his possession, and said order and appointment were lawfully made by said court in the exercise of its lawful jurisdiction in that behalf. The cerditors represented by said Cowan in his appointment in the voluntary proceedings were the same represented by the plaintiff's receivers, and the said Cowan was so appointed the receiver at the instance of and upon the petition of one of said creditors, i. e., the American Skirt Company, and the appointment of said receiver and said taking possession of said property was without the knowledge consent, or procurement of this defendant."

Grounds of demurrer to plea B, numbered 2 and 4, are as follows: (2) "Because it is not denied in said plea that the voluntary proceedings were instituted for the benefit of the principal obligors in the bond sued on." (4) "Because it is not alleged in said plea that the said Moore Bros., or T. A. and H. C. Moore, did not permit said voluntary petition to be filed." Ground 4 of plaintiff's demurrer to plea A is as follows: "For that it is not alleged or shown that said assets were returned to and accepted by A. S. Cowan as receiver in the bankruptcy proceedings, in which said bond was given."

FRANK S. WHITE & SONS, for appellant. The court erred in sustaining demurrers to defendant's plea in abatement.—Subsection 2 of section 1, Bankruptcy Act; Brandeburg on Bankruptcy, 13; *In re Lee*, 171 Fed. 266. The court erred in sustaining demurrers to plea Y.— Section 22-a Bankruptcy Act; Brandenburg on Bankruptcy, 560. Counsel discuss other assignments of error, but without further citation of authority.

TOMLINSON & MCCULLOUGH, ESTES, JONES & WELCH, and TROTTER & ODELL, for appelle. There was no error in permitting the complaint to be amended.—*Cowan v. Campbell*, 31 South. 429; *Kaul v. Henderson*, 28 South. 531; *Leonard v. Starrs*, 31 Ala. 488; *Babcock v. Carter*, 117 Ala. 575; Section 2489, Code 1907. The referee had the right to make the appointment.—22 Enc. P. & P. 361; 184 U. S. 13; 102 Fed. 749; *McAfee v. Arnold,*, 155 Ala. 565. The plea should have been verified.—Section 5332, Code 1907. In order to exonerate them, the property must have been taken by the act of the obligee in the bond, a valid judicial proceeding, or the act of God. —*Bolling v. Vandiver*, 91 Ala. 379; *Watson v. Simmons*, 91 Ala. 568; *In re Diver*, 112 Fed. 777. Counsel discuss other assignments of error, but without further citation of authority.

ANDERSON, J.—The gravamen of plaintiff's complaint, was for the breach of a bond, in that Moore Bros. had been duly adjudged bankrupts before the commencement of the suit and had failed to restore the property reclaimed under the bond or to pay for same. Pleas 1 and 2, both before and after amendment, did not present any facts to abate the suit, because prematurely brought, nor did the facts therein set up a subsequent defense that should abate the action or that would bar a recovery, and, at most, merely set up suggestions that should suspend the action during the pendency of the

[Moore Bros., et al. v. Cowan.]

appeal and until a final determination thereof. Neither
of them set up a suspension of the adjudication in bankruptcy before the suit was brought, or whether or not,
or when the decree was *finally* confirmed, and, for aught
that appears, the appeal may have been subsequently
dismissed, and there may have been no final confirmation, on appeal, of the adjudication of bankruptcy, and
in which event it would date from the original rendition of same, October 8, 1908. Neither of these pleas
deny that the decree in bankruptcy did not exist when
the suit was brought, nor do they aver that said decree
had been suspended before the suit was brought, as plea
2 specifically avers that "said adjudication in bankruptcy has been superseded and suspended since the execution of said bond." It avers that the bond was executed on December 28, 1908, and which was subsequent
to the bringing of the suit. It is evident that the pleader
did not wish to deny that the order of adjudication was
made, as averred in the complaint, but wished to set up
facts to the effect that it became binding and effective
at a subsequent date, because the decree had been appealed from and the adjudication was not of the date as
averred in the complaint, but was subsequent to the
bringing of the suit. This brings us to a consideration
of subdivision 2 of section 1 of the bankruptcy act of
1898, and which reads as follows: "Adjudication shall
mean the date of the entry of a decree that the defendant, in a bankruptcy proceeding, is a bankrupt, or if
such decree is appealed from, then the date when such
decree is finally confirmed." We take this to mean, that
if there is no appeal from the decree adjudicating the
defendant a bankrupt, it dates from the rendition of
same, and if there is an appeal, and it is *finally confirmed*, the adjudication shall date from the confirmation. We do not think that the mere taking of an ap-

peal and the dismissal of same either by the appellant or the appellate court is a final confirmation so as to change the date of the adjudication from the time it is made to the dismissal of the appeal. The statute is too plain in the use of the words "finally confirmed," and the dismissal of the appeal is in no sense a final confirmation of the appeal.—*Ashly v. Brasil*, 1 Ark. 149. The pleas (1 and 2) only set up an appeal, and the pendency of same, and which fact should only suspend the trial until after the termination of said appeal. They do not aver that the adjudication had been confirmed or annulled, and until that was done the decree of adjudication would stand of the date of the rendition thereof. This would certainly be the result if the appeal was dismissed and the pleas do not show, with any degree of certainty, that the date of the original adjudication was or would be changed. We are aware of the fact that this statute received a different interpretation by McPherson, District Judge, in the case of *Re Lee* (D. C.) 171 Fed. 266, wherein it was held that an appeal not only suspended the original decree of adjudication, but changed the date from the rendition thereof to the time of the dismissal of the appeal, thus, in effect, holding that the dismissal of an appeal was a final confirmation of the decree from which the appeal was taken. We think this construction illogical and in the teeth of the statute, and prefer following the well-considered Arkansas case, supra. We do not question the correctness of the result in the *Lee Case, supra*, and think the claims were presented in time, but justify this upon the idea that the time between taking the appeal and the dismissal of same should have been deducted.—*Braun v. Sauerwein*, 10 Wall. 218, 19 L. Ed. 895. The trial court did not err in sustaining the demurrers to pleas 1 and 2.

Plea 3 was not verified, and was subject to the demurrer upon this ground, and which was properly sustained. —Section 5332 of the Code of 1907.

There was no merit in plea Y. The federal court has exclusive jurisdiction to adjudge a person a bankrupt and to appoint a receiver, and if the order was irregular, improvident, or unauthorized, it should be corrected or questioned in that forum and not in the state courts upon collateral attack.—*Turner v. Hudson,* 105 Me. 476, 75 Atl. 45; 18 Am. & Eng. Ann. Cas. 600, and many cases cited in note, among which will be found the cases of *Oates v. Farrish,* 47 Ala. 157, and *Jones v. Knox,* 51 Ala. 367. Moreover, the bond which was made a part of the complaint was signed by the defendants and made to Shelfer and Cowan, "the receivers in the above cause." Having made the bond to them as receivers, defendants were estopped from questioning their appointment as such.

In the case of *Watson v. Simmons,* 91 Ala. 567, 8 South. 347, it was held, in discussing when sureties on a forthcoming bond would be released, that if the property is taken from them under a paramount title or lien, or under valid judicial proceedings, this excuses them from the delivery of the property and discharges the obligation of the bond, so far as to render invalid a return of forfeiture by the returning officer. The law will not punish the failure to do that which itself has rendered impossible to be performed. The court intimates very strongly, however, that if the second seizure was caused through the collusion or fraud of the principal obligor in the forthcoming bond, that the second seizure though under legal proceedings could not operate to discharge the sureties. While this is but an intimation by the court, it is but a wise and salutary doctrine, for the sureties undertake to answer for the prin-

cipal obligor, and it would be unwise and unwholesome
to hold that they would be released by the action of the
principal obligor notwithstanding he took second legal
steps to put the property beyond his control. The very
purpose of the bond was to guarantee the conduct and
custody of the property of and in the principal, and it
would be a legal monstrosity to hold that he could make
a voluntary disposition of the property so as to release
the sureties and defeat the obligees in the bond, and
conditions cannot be helped because he resorted to legal
proceedings as a means of accomplishing such a feat.

Plea B shows that the property was seized under second bankruptcy proceedings instituted by the voluntary
action of the Moores, after the execution of the forthcoming bond, and a seizure of the property, under proceedings instituted by them, could not operate to discharge the bond company, whether instituted with or
without the knowledge of said company. Plea B, if not
otherwise bad, was subject to grounds 2 and 4 of the
plaintiff's demurrer.

Plea A fails to aver that the property was turned over
to or accepted by Cowan as receiver in the bankruptcy
proceedings in which said bond was given and was subject to ground 4 of plaintiff's demurrer. On the other
hand, if it sufficiently set up the capacity in which
Cowan received and accepted the property, it was but
a denial of the breach set up in the complaint and could
have been shown on the general issue. All special pleas
were eliminated and the judgment entry recites that,
issue being joined, etc., we must, therefore, assume that
the issue referred to was the general issue.

The judgment of the city court is affirmed.

Affirmed.

SIMPSON, MCCLELLAN, MAYFIELD, and SOMERVILLE,
JJ., concur.

Smith *v.* Smith, *et al.*

Assumpsit.

(Decided June 15, 1911.   53 South. 1009.)

1. *Bill of Exceptions; Presentation; Time; Motion to Strike.*—Where the bill of exceptions is not presented to the trial judge within ninety days, from the date of the judgment, a motion to strike such bill must prevail, under section 3019, Code 1907.

2. *Dismissal and Non-Suit; Agreement of Parties.*—Where an order was made on the agreement of the parties as recited in said agreement that the cause be dismissed if the plaintiff failed to give security for costs according to the agreement, the defendant was entitled to a dismissal of the cause upon an ascertainment by the court that there had been a non-compliance with the agreement.

APPEAL from Birmingham Cty Court.

Heard before Hon. C. W. FERGUSON.

Action by Alfred Smith against C. D. Smith and others. From a judgment dismissing the cause plaintiff appeals. Affirmed.

LONDON & FITTS, for appellant. The court erred in making the order of dismissal of Oct. 9th, and also in overruling appellant's motion to set aside and vacate such order.—Section 3687, Code 1907; *First Nat. Bank v. Cheney,* 120 Ala. 122; *Whittaker v. Sanford,* 13 Ala. 522; 1 Brickell's Dig. secs. 103-4; *Reese v. Billing,* 9 Ala. 263; *A. & T. R. R. Co. v. Harris,* 25 Ala. 232. Notice should have been given to appellant or counsel before the order of dismissal was entered.—*Stephenson v. Brunson,* 83 Ala. 455; *Duggan v. Taylor,* 60 Ala. 544; *Lide v. Park,* 132 Ala. 222; 14 Enc. P. & P. 122.

EDMUND H. DRYER, for appellee. The bill of exceptions should be stricken because not presented within ninety days after judgment.—Sections 3019, and 3020,

Code 1907. The court properly granted the order dismissing the cause.—Sec. 3687, Code 1907; *Ex parte
Jones,* 83 Ala. 587; *Patillo v. Taylor,* 83 Ala. 230 ;*Rogers
v. Prattville M. Co.* 81 Ala. 483; *Adler v. VanKirk L.
Co.* 114 Ala. 560. The motion to vacate the order of
dismissal was entered more than thirty days after the
granting of the order, and hence was barred so far as
the jurisdiction to entertain it was concerned.—*Ex parte*
Smith, 52 South. 895, and cases cited.

McCLELLAN, J.—This appeal is from a judgment
dismissing this cause for failure of the plaintiff (a non-
resident) to comply with an order of the court requiring
him to give security for costs, and adjudging that defendants have and recover of the plaintiff their costs
in that behalf expended.

This judgment was rendered October 9, 1909. The
bill of exceptions was *presented* to the trial judge on
June 21, 1910, more than 90 days after the entry of the
judgment to revise which this appeal is taken. The appellees move this court to strike the bill, because not
presented within 90 days after the judgment was entered. According to the express provisions of the statute (Code 1907, § 3019), the motion must prevail.—
Smith v. State, 166 Ala. 24, 52 South. 396; *King v. Hill
& Shaffer Co.,* 163 Ala. 422, 51 South. 15; *Edinburgh
American Land Mort. Co. v. Canterbury,* 169 Ala. 444,
53 South. 823.

On June 9, 1909, defendants moved that the plaintiff,
a nonresident, be required to give security for costs
"within such reasonable time as the court may prescribe,
or, in default of the giving of such security within the
time so prescribed by the court, that this suit be dismissed." The court records show this subsequent order
or judgment: "On this the 12th day of June, 1909, come

the parties by their attorneys and agree that this motion be granted and that plaintiff be allowed ninety (90) days within which to give security for costs and move for an order accordingly, whereupon it is ordered and adjudged by the court that this motion be and the same is hereby in all things granted and the plaintiff is allowed ninety days within which to give security for costs and in default of same this cause to be dismissed."

The judgment appealed from was entered October 9, 1909, more than 90 days after the just quoted order or judgment was entered. It reads: "On this the 9th day of October, 1909, come the defendants by their attorneys and show to the court that the plaintiff herein has not complied with the order of this court of June 12, 1909, requiring the said plaintiff to give security for costs in this cause, and move the court for an order dismissing this cause from this court, whereupon, it is ordered and adjudged by the court that this cause be and it is hereby dismissed from this court, and that the defendants go hence without day, and have and recover of the plaintiff their costs in this behalf expended, for which let execution issue."

The order or judgment of October 9, 1909, but effected the agreement, the recital of which appears in the minute entry of June 12, 1909, in connection with the motion to which it related. The only condition to the dismissal was that the costs should be secured within 90 days. The court, on October 9, 1909, ascertained that the condition had not been met by the plaintiff. Hence the dismissal was the defendants' due under the agreement. Accordingly, the judgment appealed from (that of October 9, 1909) is affirmed.

Affirmed.   .

SIMPSON, ANDERSON, and MAYFIELD, JJ., concur.

Pollak *v*. Winter.

Assumpsit.

(Decided May 18, 1911.   Rehearing denied June 27, 1911.
55 South. 928.)

Payment; Pleas; Burden of Proof.—Where the action is by an administrator on account for attorney's services, and the plea is payment, it will not be presumed from the mere evidence of the rendition of the service that the services were not paid for when rendered, the plaintiff being required, in order to establish a prima facie case. to prove not only the rendition of the service, but that they were not paid for when rendered. and this is true, notwithstanding the burden of proof of a plea of payment was on the defendant.

APPEAL from Cullman Circuit Court.

Heard before Hon. D. W. SPEAKE.

Assumpsit by Sallie Winter as administratrix, against Ignatius Pollak, for services rendered by her decedent. Judgment for plaintiff and defendant appeals. Reversed and remanded.

See also 166 Ala. 255, 51 South. 998.

J. B. BROWN, for appellant.   The court erred in permitting plaintiff to testify that she caused diligent search to be made through the papers of her decedent and found no evidence of payment having been made of the account sued for.—*Pollak v. Winter,* 166 Ala. 255. The statement was clearly a conclusion of the witness.— *Brandon v. Progress Distilling Co.* 52 South. 640 Ala.; *S. & W. Co. v. Thompson,* 52 South. 75; *Abingdon Mills v. Winter, supra;* *Cook v. Malone,* 128 Ala. 664; *Rice v. Kahn,* 90 Ala. 416.

W. A. GUNTER, for appellee.   It is a general proposition well settled that payment is an affirmative defense and will not, in the first instance, be presumed, but after the antecedent existence of the indebtedness has been proved by the creditor, the burden of proving its discharge is upon the person alleging the payment.—22 A. & E. Enc. of Law, 587 and cases cited. A party is not required to prove negative allegations which are merely necessary in pleadings, but constitute no part of this case.—*Carroll v. Malone*, 28 Ala. 521; *McAuley v. The State*, 26 Ala. 141; *Woolf v. Nall*, 62 Ala. 24; 1 Brick. 868-871; 4 Mayf. 585-596; 1 Greenl. secs. 78 and 80; 42 N. E. 223. Where services are shown to have been rendered, and are knowingly accepted, the law presumes an obligation to pay what such services are reasonably worth.—*Wood v. Brewer*, 66 Ala. 570; *A. G. S. v. Hill*, 76 Ala. 303; *McFarland v. Dawson*, 128 Ala. 561; *Hood v. League*, 102 Ala. 228.

SAYRE, J.—Plaintiff in the court below, appellee here, sued defendant for the value of work and labor done by her testator for the defendant at the latter's request. Defendant pleaded the general denial, payment, and the statute of limitations. Plaintiff offered evidence tending to show the performance of professional services by her testator as an attorney at law for the defendant on the latter's request, and their value. These services covered a period of about one year, at the end of which time Judge Winter, plaintiff's testator, accepted office as judge of the circuit court. About a year later on Judge Winter died. His acceptance of office presumptively took him out of the practice; but in order, as it seems, to create a presumption that there remained an unsettled account between him and defendant, or perhaps to strengthen a presumption which it is contended would have arisen in some shape without that fact, plaintiff showed that his services were continued after he went upon the bench. Lest, however, the matter be misunderstood, it must be stated that Judge Winter had been employed to represent the defendant in an arbitration which had been submitted to the arbitrator for decision prior to his being upon the bench, and that subsequently he did no more than to urge the arbitrator from time to time to decide the matters submitted. In the view we take of the case, the principle which must govern applies equally, whether the claim for services be assigned to the date when plaintiff's testator went upon the bench or the date of his death. There was no effort to show an express contract between the parties by which plaintiff's testator undertook to perform any definite service. Nor did the plaintiff or any other witness undertake to say that anything was due from defendant to plaintiff at the time of the trial or to state the account between plaintiff's testator and the defendant at that or any other time, nor was there any evidence to show that fact. The court charged the jury on plaintiff's request that the burden of proving payment was on the defendant. But the court refused the defendant's request for a charge in this language: "The court charges the jury that the burden of proof is on the plaintiff to show by the evidence to your reasonable satisfaction that the claim in suit for the services of Judge Winter was not paid for when rendered or when the compensation therefor was due and if, after considering all evidence in the case, you are not reasonably satisfied that such services were not paid for, then your verdict should be for the defendant." Appellant contends, on the authority of the decision rendered in this case when it was here on a former appeal, that these rulings were erroneous, while appellee renews her argument that the ruling on the former appeal was itself erroneous.—*Pollak v. Winter*, 166 Ala. 255, 51 South. 998, 52 South. 829,

53 South. 339. The first mentioned of these charges correctly stated the law in respect to the burden of proof on the issue raised by the special plea of payment—a plea in confession and avoidance, to which the charge was appropriately, if not necessarily, referred—as has been decided in perhaps a thousand cases, as counsel for appellee suggests, including this case as reported in 166 Ala. 255, 51 South. 998, 52 South. 829, 53 South. 339. No doubt the second of these charges was designed to state the other proposition of that case which is that, "when suit is brought upon an open account, the plaintiff does not overcome the burden by merely showing the rendition of service and the value of same, but must offer some proof that it was not paid for when rendered, or when due." On the trial which was under review when this case was here before, and on a state of the evidence substantially the same as that shown by the record on this appeal, the trial court had given the general affirmative charge for the plaintiff. The practical question is the same now as then, and is whether the evidence offered by the plaintiff was sufficient to make out a case. On both occasions the question has been discussed in briefs as if it related to payment generally, including payment as pleaded in confession and avoidance, rather than as we have stated it, thus evidencing some confusion of ideas. The question is as we have stated it.

In *Cook v. Malone,* 128 Ala. 662, 29 South. 653, defendants brought a cross-action for the price of six bales of cotton. The court instructed the jury that the burden of proof was on the defendants (cross-plaintiffs) to show that plaintiffs (cross-defendants) had bought the cotton and had not paid for it. This court said: "It is here insisted for defendants that the charge violated the rule stated generally in 3 Brick. Dig. 698, §§ 1 and 2, and applied to a cross-action of set-off in *Snodgrass v. Caldwell*, 90 Ala. 319, 7 South. 834, which subjects the party relying on the defense of payment to the burden of proof. That rule is applicable only where the issue is whether an indebtedness assumed to have been in existence has been discharged by payment. In this case the payment plaintiff sought to prove was not of a debt, but was one occurring in the consummation of a cash purchase. A sale wherein no credit is either expressly or impliedly given, but which is strictly for cash is not consummated until the consideration is paid.—1 Benj. on Sales, § 335 et seq.; *Shines v. Steiner*, 76 Ala. 458; *Blackshear v. Burke*, 74 Ala. 239. In such a sale payment concurs with the passing of ownership in the property, so that no indebtedness for the price can intervene." The judgment was affirmed. In order to take this case out of the influence of that decision, appellee insists that this is a case in which, from its very nature, the considerations could not pass simultaneously—is a case in which necessarily, from the very nature of the transaction, there was credit impliedly given for the work done. But there is in a transaction of the character here shown no such necessity. It does seem altogether reasonable to say that it cannot be presumed that the price or value of work and labor done by one for another, extending over a considerable period, has been paid in infinitesimal driblets pari passu as the work progressed. Nor is it reasonable to presume that the purchaser of a thousand bushels of corn stands by and pays for each bushel as it is delivered. Yet one may buy a thousand bushels of corn strictly for cash. There is no reason in the nature of things why one who does work and labor for another may not be paid in a practical way pari passu. It is in fact common. It is not open to us to assume that plaintiff's testator undertook

in the beginning to conduct the suit to a final judgment
on definite terms. That would be to assume a special
contract, whereas plaintiff's case proceeds as for money
due on a promise to be implied in order that justice may
be done. That would put the plaintiff out of court for
lack of evidence to prove the contract and its performance according to its terms. Defendant's promise to
pay, like his request for the services, is to be implied
from the fact that plaintiff's testator performed services
which were beneficial to the defendant and accepted by
him. In the absence of a special contract between the
parties fixing beforehand what services plaintiff's testator was to perform and on what terms, plaintiff's testator had a right to lay down the service at any time, and,
upon doing so, might have recovered the value of services
rendered so far as they were beneficial to defendant. If
a man shall show that he has worked in my field or at
building my house, why should the presumption be indulged, when he sues my administrator, that I did not
pay him before or at the time he did the work? Why
should it be assumed that he extended credit to me,
rather than that I credited him until the work could
be done? Or if one shall sue my administrator for
money had and received, and show that on an occasion
he handed me a sum of money, without more, why should
the presumption be that he lent me the money, rather
than that a consideration had moved, or did at the time
move, from me to him? The rule in such a case is that
the plaintiff is required to show a credit by excluding
the implication that a consideration had passed. He
must prove that the transaction was essentially a loan
of money.—2 Greenl. Ev. (16th Ed.) § 112. This question does not often arise, because parties are never willing and are seldom compelled, to rest their cases upon
the implication of such naked facts. Ordinarily there

will be something in the relations of the parties, the nature of the transaction, or other circumstances, capable
of proof, to show the terms on which the parties have
dealt with each other; but the principle of all such cases
is the same. It is that plaintiff must prove a credit. If,
therefore, the plaintiff, suing to recover the price of
merchandise, goods and chattels sold and delivered to
the defendant, or the price or value of work and labor
done at the defendant's request, proves a sale or the rendition of services and the value of his goods or services,
without more, he does not show a right to judgment;
for no presumption arises that the things bought or the
services rendered were not paid for when delivered or
rendered. The plaintiff in such case, as in all others,
must prove the allegations of his complaint. He must
show a credit, an indebtedness. Accurately speaking,
he must show, not a contract and its breach, but only
that there was at one time a contract, express or implied,
for the future payment of money, an obligation solven-
dum in futuro. This does not put upon plaintiff the
burden of proving a negative, but only requires that he
shall prove an express promise to pay in the future, or
that the nature of the transaction was such that out of
it there arose an implied promise to pay. An indebtedness once thus shown, the burden of proving a discharge
by payment devolves upon the defendant. These conclusions are in accord with "the principle that he who
alleges himself to be creditor of another is obliged to
prove the fact or agreement upon which the claim is
founded; * * * that, on the other hand, when the
obligation is proved, the debtor, who alleges that he has
discharged it, is obliged to prove the payment," which
is "one of those propositions in which every system of
jurisprudence must concur in general, whatever particular rules may be adopted, as to the mode and form of the

allegations by which the necessity of such proof is to be determined."—1 Phil. Ev. 810, note.

An inspection of the transcript of the record in the case of *Rice v. Schloss,* 90 Ala. 416, 7 South. 802, shows that all the transactions involved in that case were undisputedly credit transactions, and that, subject to plaintiff's claim that the account had been stated, the controversy was about the correctness of the account offered in evidence. The opinion in that case holds only this: That in a suit on open account the burden is on the plaintiff to show the balance due after allowing credit for all payments. It thus might appear on the surface to go in one respect even further than we have previously gone in this case, in that it seems to hold that plaintiff cannot discharge his burden by showing a debt to have been once due, but that he must show the amount due at the time of the suit brought or at the time of the trial; that is, must negative the fact that no payments have been made since the debt fell due. The language was no doubt used in view of the common practice in suits of this character, in which the plaintiff is not ordinarily content to show that the defendant was once indebted, but undertakes to show an indebtedness, a balance due, at the bringing of the suit or at the time of the trial. It may be conceded, however, that the case does not go to the precise proposition to which it was cited in 166 Ala. 255, 51 South. 998, 53 South. 339; for it does not in terms say that in common assumpsit for goods sold and delivered or work and labor done the plaintiff may not recover on proof of goods sold and delivered or services rendered on request, without more.

At page 179 of 16 Encyclopædia of Pleading and Practice it is said that "the true rule or principle is that the plaintiff should prove, not nonpayment generally, but nonpayment when due or at maturity, or in other words, a breach of the contract sued on."

In respect to the other cases cited in 166 Ala. 255, 51 South. 998, 53 South. 339, we think it may now be conceded that they have only a remote bearing on the question at hand.

Aside from the distinction which seems to have been attempted in respect to suits on open accounts and suits on accounts stated, and apart from some slight misleading tendency, perhaps, in the use of the word "maturity," which seems to imply a contract for future payment, a case which, once shown, would put the burden of proof of payment upon the defendant, we are of opinion that the gist of the decision in this case on former appeal is theoretically sound, and will be found to operate for the promotion of justice in practice. Counsel have cited a great number of cases to the effect that the burden of proving a plea of payment rests upon the defendant. We have not taken issue with that familiar proposition. If there are cases which assert that a plaintiff establishes a case in common assumpsit when he shows goods delivered or labor done and their value, without more, counsel, after evident great research, has been unable to cite them. Assuming in a way to know the accuracy and universality of the knowledge to which that research must have led, and applying in some sort the maxim, "De non existentibus et de non apparentibus eadem est ratio," we conclude there are no such cases. Fairly interpreted, the charge stated the law as we think it ought to be, and as it is.

If it be said that the use of the word "due" in the charge may have possibly produced the impression that the plaintiff carried the burden of proving payment of a debt which once existed, the judgment must still be reversed, for the reason that there was no evidence authorizing the inference that any sum was due from defendant to plaintiff, and the motion for a new trial should have been granted.

Reversed and remanded.

DOWDELL, C. J., and ANDERSON and SOMERVILLE, JJ., concur.

Hughes *v.* Albertville Mercantile Co.

Assumpsit.

(Decided Feb. 7, 1911. 56 South. 120.)

1. *Bill of Exceptions; Establishment; Grounds; Signature of Judge.*—Although under section 3021, Code 1907, a judge is not at default for a failure or refusal to sign the bill of exceptions, so as to enable the aggrieved party to establish the bill, until a correct bill is tendered, yet when a correct bill is tendered the judge, it is his duty to sign it as presented, and his signing it, after improperly changing it, is not a signing of the bill, but is in effect, a failure or refusal which will enable the aggrieved party to establish it under the statute, although it was signed after being changed.

2. *Appeal and Error; Conclusiveness of Record; Bill of Exceptions.*—Where a judge changes a bill of exceptions, whether properly or not, and without action to establish a proper one, the one so signed, is made a part of the record. It will be considered by this court, as the proper one, and cannot be changed or corrected by resorting to extraneous matters.

(McClellan, J., dissents.)

APPEAL from Marshall Circuit Court.

Heard before Hon. A. H. ALSTON.

Assumpsit by J. W. Hughes against Albertville Mercantile Company. From the judgment, Hughes appeals and submits a motion to establish a bill of exceptions. Motion granted.

Subsequently to the handing down of this decision the case was transferred to the Court of Appeals, for a decision on its merits, and will be found reported in 3 Ala. App. 462; 57 South. 98.

E. A. HAWKINS and JOHN A. LUSK, for appellant. No brief reached the Reporter.

STREET & ISBELL, for appellee. No brief reached the Reporter.

ANDERSON, J.—The preponderance of evidence shows that a correct bill of exceptions was presented by the movant to the presiding judge, who was no doubt actuated by an honest impression and good intentions, made a material but improper change in same before signing. Section 3021 of the Code of 1907, provides for the establishment of a bill of exceptions when the judge fails or refuses to sign same.

We have heretofore held that in order to put the judge in default for a failure or refusal to sign, so as to enable the aggrieved party to establish one, it must appear that a correct bill was tendered.—*Bradberry v. State*, 168 Ala. 141, 53 South. 266. On the other hand, we hold that, when a correct bill is presented, it is the duty of the judge to sign same as presented, and the signing of same, after improperly changing it, is not the signing of the bill of exceptions, but is, in effect, a failure or refusal which will enable the appellant to establish same under the statute.

Of course, if a judge should change the bill, whether properly so or not, and no action is taken to establish a proper one, and the one so signed is sent up and made a part of the record, the one so sent up will be looked to and considered by this court as the proper one, and it cannot be corrected or changed by resorting to extraneous matters. This rule has been repeatedly adhered to by this court in many cases, among which will be found the case of *Turner v. White*, 97 Ala. 545, 12 South. 601. It was there suggested, however, that if

the bill, as signed by the judge, was not a correct one
the appellant should have proceeded under the statute
to establish a proper one—a course adopted by this
movant, and the motion to establish the bill is hereby
granted.

In the case of *Gunter v. Pollack*, 169 Ala. 591, 53
South. 1002, the motion to establish the bill of exceptions was overruled, for the reason that the proof showed
that the one tendered the judge was not a correct one,
in that it purported to contain all the evidence, when
it did not in fact do so. The majority of the court did
not deny the motion, upon the idea that appellant was
precluded from establishing a true one, by the action of
the judge in signing a paper, deemed by him as correct,
but which was not in fact a correct bill of exceptions.
The majority wrote no opinion in this case, and an examination of the opinion of Justice MCCLELLAN will disclose the fact that he was not expressing the views of
the court, but was giving his invidual reasons for concurring, and which said views were not then and are not
now entertained by the court. We repeat that the
changing of a correct bill of exceptions, so as to make it
incorrect, notwithstanding the same is signed after the
change, is, in effect, a failure or refusal to sign a correct
bill, and gives the appellant the right to proceed under
the statute to establish the true one.

DOWDELL, C. J., and SIMPSON, MAYFIELD, SAYRE, and
SOMERVILLE, JJ., concur.

McCLELLAN, J.—(dissenting.)—When the minute
entry and the last paragraph of what purports to be a
bill of exceptions, in the transcript, are read together,
it appears that the judgment was entered on October 14,
1910, and tht the bill was *presented* to the *presiding*

judge on September 27, 1910, about 17 days *before* the
judgment entry expressly fixes as the date on which the
judgment was entered.   Since it appears that the court
adjourned sine die on July 22, 1910, it seems to be (indeed, it must be, to justify the entertainment of the motion here involved), assumed that the date of the judgment entry is self-correcting.

In view of the exacting statutory requirements (Code,
§ 3019) with respect to presentation of bills of exceptions (*Edinburgh, etc., Co. v. Canterbury,* 169 Ala. 444,
53 South. 823), the establishment of such a precedent .
may not ultimately prove to be safe or satisfactory.
More important consequences than the one here wrought
out may, upon occasion, argue against such an assumption, whereby the date of "judgment entered" is taken
as different from that specifically fixed in the minute entry of the court.   However, for the occasion only, the
writer assumes, with the majority, that a bill was seasonably presented to the presiding judge.   He altered
the bill tendered him, and then signed it within the period provided by the stateute.—Code, § 3019.

The majority now rule, in response to the motion to
establish the bill, that the signing of the bill, after its
alteration, by the presiding judge, was not a signing in
such sort as to deny to appellant the right to establish
the bill under the statute (Code, § 3021), which, as here
imporant, reads: "If the judge fail or refuse to sign a
bill of exceptions, the point of decision and the facts
being truly stated, he is guilty of a high misdemeanor
in office; and the Supreme Court must receive such evidence of the fact as may be deemed by it satisfactory,
and proceed to hear the cause as if the bill had been
signed by the judge.   *   *   *"

In *Gunter v. Pollack. supra,* mentioned in the
controlling opinion, the writer expresserd the view

that where the judge seasonably signs a bill of exceptions any inquiry into its correctness is wholly
foreclosed. This conclusion is rested upon three (to his
mind) well-established, main, legal propositions: First,
that the ascertainment of what took place on the trial is,
in nature, a judicial question, and is committed for determination, with necessary, though presently unimport-
ant, exceptions, to the presiding judge.—Code, § 3018;
Etheridge v. Hall, 7 Port. (Ala.) 47, 53; *Ex parte Nel-*
son & Kelly, 62 Ala. 380; *Weir v. Hoss,* 6 Ala. 881; *L.*
& N. R. R. v. Malone, 116 Ala. 600, 603, 22 South. 897;
3 Cyc. p. 31, and notes. Second, that the *act* of the presiding judge in seasonably signing a bill of exceptions
constitutes the instrument so executed a part of the
record of this court, and in consequence that it imports
absolute verity, "to contradict, add to, or vary" which
"parol evidence is inadmissible."—*L. & N. R. R. Co. v.*
Malone, 116 Ala. 600, 603, 22 South. 897; *Ex parte Nel-*
son & Kelly, 62 Ala. 376, 379, 380; *Pearce v. Clements,*
73 Ala. 256; *Chapman v. Holding,* 54 Ala. 61. Other
authorities might be added. Third, that the failure or
refusal, by the judge, to sign the bill *as presented by the*
exceptant is not the condition contemplated by or expressed in the statute (section 3021); on the contrary,
that condition is that the judge fail or refuse to sign "a
bill of exceptions."

These propositions, among others, were discussed and
some of the above-cited authorities were quoted in the
opinion of the writer, in *Gunter v. Pollack. supra.* It
follows from these propositions that the effort to show,
as in this instance, that the bill as signed by the judge
was incorrect should have been denied; that the evidence
offered was inadmissible for the reasons stated and under the authorities cited to the first and second propositions, ante.

Diligent investigation of our reported cases has not discovered any decision here supporting the ruling made in the majority opinion. Only two decisions are therein cited, viz., *Bradberry v. State*, 168 Ala., 141, 53 South. 266, and *Turner v. White*, 97 Ala. 545, 12 South. 601. Quotations from the opinion in the *Bradberry Case* will suffice to show the vital difference between the question there presented and decided, and that here involved: "A bill of exceptions was presented to the judge, *who refused to sign same*, because it was not correct, and, if it was not correct, he properly *refused* to sign same. It has been agreed that the *one sought to be established is correct, and, as it differs from the one presented to the judge, the one so presented was not correct.*" (Italics supplied.) Here the judge signed "a bill of exceptions." There the judge refused to sign, and did not sign, the bill presented, nor any other bill; and there the exceptant "admitted upon the submission of this cause that the two bills are not substantially identical, and that the one sought to be established is the correct one;" ergo, that he had not presented to the judge a correct bill.

The other decision cited (*Turner v. White*) brought to this court's view this status: "The opinion is based on two separate transcripts, one being ejectment by George C. White against Freeman Turner and others, to which case Marcia H. Turner was made defendant on her own motion, and, after judgment for plaintiff, by agreement, a separate cause was docketed for recovery of taxes paid by her subsequent to a purchase by her at tax sale of the lands sued for, and appeals were taken by the defendant in both cases, which appeals were heard together (97 Ala. 546, 12 South. 601). * * * On the 12th of May, 1891, the parties in open court consented. and the court accordingly ordered, that the matter of refunding said taxes be docketed separately from the ejectment suit, which the clerk, by the order of the court, did, entering the cause as Marcia H. Turner v. G. C. White and C. Alexander; and thereupon the court proceeded, upon an admitted state of facts set out in the record, to render judgment upon the petition of the said Marcia H. against said Geo. C. White and Charles Alexander for $153.05 for state and county taxes paid by her, and also for the costs of the proceedings. Afterwards the defendants prepared and tendered *a single bill of exceptions covering* the proceedings in the ejectment suit, and in the separate proceeding to ascertain the taxes paid by said Marcia H., *but the court refused to sign said bill of exceptions as one, embracing the facts, pleadings, and final judgment,* both in the ejectment suit and the separate judgment on the motion for the reimbursement of said taxes, *and for the refusal to sign the bill, as in one case the defendants excepted. The court, however, did sign separate bills as prepared and presented in each of said proceedings."*—97 Ala. 548, 12 South. 602.

There was no motion to establish a bill. The judge did not sign—he refused to sign—a "single" bill covering both proceedings. This refusal was attempted to be excepted to, and that was the sole question, in reference to the bill, presented to this court. The court ruled, and with obvious soundness, that the exceptants' remedy was by motion to establish the single bill, and not by *exception* to the judge's *refusal* to sign the "single" bill. There were *two separate bills signed by the judge,* and the court considered and decided the cases presented by "two separate transcripts." The court said: "The bill as signed by the judge is the one upon which this court must act until a new one is established in the mode pointed out by the Code.—*Hale v. Goodbar,* 81 Ala. 108, 2 South. 467; *Posey v. Beale,* 69 Ala. 32." That the court did not rule that a bill could be established when there was already a bill, a part of the record of this court, is plain when the facts quoted from the report are considered. The exceptants thought they were entitled to a "single" bill in both proceedings. The judge thought, and so ordered his acts, that there were two separate proceedings, requiring two separate bills. If the right vel non of the defendants to a "single" bill had been presented by a motion to establish the "single" bill presented to and refused signature by the judge (the only way it could be presented to this court), and, if this court had held that the "single" bill, instead of separate bills, should have been signed by the judge, then clearly the signature by the judge of the separate bills would not have negatived the existence there of the statute's condition, viz., "if the judge fail or refuse to sign a bill of exceptions," because upon that theory the judge had refused to sign a bill covering proceedings in which a "single" bill should have been signed by the judge. Not having attempted to establish the bill the judge *refused* to sign, this court said it would and did act on the *separate* bills to which the judge did affix his signature. There was no "single" bill signed by the judge. Had there been, the question presented would not have existed. If there had been a "single" bill signed by the judge, and motion to establish another "single" bill, and the court had made the remark before quoted, there might be semblance of reason to invoke the statement as authority on the present inquiry.

When we refer to the cases of *Hale v. Goodbar*, and *Posey v. Beale,* cited authoritatively in *Turner v. White,* it affirmatively appears that in both of them the judge had not signed "a bill of exceptions." And as emphasizing, in the writer's opinion, the correctness of the view to which he adheres, Justice Somerville, in *Posey v.*

Beale, defines the proper practice as requiring the seasonable tender of a correct bill to the presiding judge for his signature, "requesting him to sign or refuse to sign it as prepared." Obviously the necessity for the "request" stated by Justice Somerville would have been vain, idle, if the judge could only effect a signing, within our statutes, by affixing his signature to the bill "as prepared.' The office of the "request" was, as appears in the next sentence of the opinion, to avert the clothing of the bill (by the judge's *act* of signature) with all the attributes of a *record,* as expressly ruled in *Ex parte Nelson & Kelly,* 62 Ala. 379, 380, among others. So *Turner v. White,* does not, in the writer's opinion, support, in any sense, the ruling of the majority on this motion. No such question as we have here was presented on those appeals. The suggestion that a bill, altered and signed by the judge within the proper period, becomes a *record only* by some act of ratification or acquiescence on the part of the exceptant was treated by the writer in *Gunter v. Pollack.* To so hold is, in his judgment, in direct opposition to all the authorities in this state, some of which are noted under the first and second propositions, ante.

In *Ex parte Nelson v. Kelly,* 62 Ala. 379, 380, Judge Stone wrote: "Bills of exceptions, when signed by the presiding judge within the time prescribed by law, become a part of the record of this court when the case is brought here by appeal." The signing by the judge is the *act* constituting the signed paper "a part of the record of this court when the case is brought here by appeal.' No ratification, consent, or acquiescence on the part of the exceptant is a condition, precedent or subsequent, to the constitution of the bill a part of the record of this court, except that he appeal his cause to this court.

For these reasons (and other might be added, including the consequences to arise under the contrary view), the writer is constrained to dissent from the prevailing conclusion. He thinks the motion to establish should be overruled.

Jos. Joseph & Bros. Co. v. Hoffman & McNeill.

Assumpsit.

(Decided June 29, 1911. 56 South. 216.)

1. *Assumpsit; Action; Grounds; Counts.*—Where the contract has been fully executed by the plaintiff, and nothing remains to be done by the defendant except to pay the amount stipulated, an assumpsit on the common counts is proper, although the claim arose out of a special contract.

2. *Garnishment; Persons Subject; Plaintiff.*—The rule is not recognized in this state that permits the plaintiff to make himself a garnishee in his own action.

3. *Same; Nature of Remedy; Proceeding in Rem.*—A garnishment proceeding in a court of another state where a plaintiff may make himself a garnishee of his indebtedness to a non-resident defendant not personally served with process, and not appearing to defend, is a proceeding in rem.

4. *Same; Foreign Judgment; Constitutional Provision.*—Where a court of another state has jurisdiction and ascertains that a plaintiff, who has made himself the garnishee of his indebtedness to a non-resident defendant not personally served with process, nor appearing therein, is himself found indebted to the defendant in an ascertained sum, and that sum is reduced by the amount of the garnished indebtedness, thereby discharging any indebtedness from or liability of the plaintiff there to the defendant to the extent only of the sum condemned, this court is bound to observe and give effect to the judgment only so far as it is a judgment in rem, under the full faith and credit clause of the Constitution of the United States.

5. *Judgment; Process to Sustain; Personal Judgment; Garnishment.*—A court of another state which has jurisdiction to subject the indebtedness of the plaintiff there to the defendant to the satisfaction of the plaintiff's demand on plaintiff's garnishment of himself, in his own action against the defendant, has no jurisdiction to render a personal judgment over against a non-resident defendant, not personally served in the garnishment proceedings, and not appearing therein, and any such judgment is a nullity; the rule in

such cases being to ascertain the amount of the plaintiff's demand, and then render judgment only condemning the property or indebtedness of the defendant to the satisfaction of the ascertained demand.

6. *Same; Foreign Judgment; Fraud or Misconduct.*—Where an action by a seller against a non resident buyer is instituted in this state before an action brought by the buyer against the seller was begun in another state, where it went to final judgment there, before the judgment in the action here was rendered, and there is no evidence of fraud in the proceedings in the other state, the mere fact that the buyer knew that complaint had been filed against him in this state, does not show fraud or misconduct in obtaining a judgment in such other state.

7. *Same; Conclusiveness.*—The rule that the first judgment rendered controls, whether the action in which it is reached be instituted before the other or not, applies where the first judgment is rendered in another state.

8. *Same; Matters Concluded.*—Where an action for damages for a breach of contract is brought in another state, and the plaintiff garnishees his own debt due to a non-resident defendant, who had not been served with process, and who does not appear, and takes a judgment in personam for an amount reduced by the amount of the indebtedness condemned. a finding by that court of a breach of the contract is not conclusive on the issue of breach vel non of the contract declared on.

9. *Same; Discharge; Set Off.*—Where. in an action in this state, a plaintiff is shown to be entitled to a judgment for $2,517, for goods sold, and the defendant shows a right to recover $1,174, the amount of an indebtedness of plaintiff to defendant which was condemned in garnishment proceedings against the plaintiff as a defendant in another state, the judgment here should be reduced by setting off the indebtedness condemned by the foreign judgment, and hence, a judgment against a garnished fund of $2,000 in this state is excessive and erroneous.

10. *Court; Comity; Stay of Proceedings; Different States.*—Where a court of another state on an action brought therein is advised that the courts of this state in their jurisdiction has been first invoked by the parties, that court may, on the grounds of comity, stay its jurisdiction, but before judgment in the courts of this state, such action on the part of the court of another state is a matter of grace and not the observance of a legal duty.

11. *Appeal and Error; Objection; Bill of Particulars.*—To be available on appeal. an objection to a bill of particulars as being too indefinite. should be taken at the beginning of the trial.

(Dowdell, C. J.. and Mayfield and Sayre, JJ., dissent.)

Appeal from Jefferson Circuit Court.

Heard before Hon. A. O. Lane.

Assumpsit by Hoffman & McNeill against Joseph Joseph & Brothers Company,, a corporation. Judgment for plaintiff and defendant appeals. Reversed and remanded.

SMITH & SMITH, for appellant. The court should not consider items of the account not on the bill of particulars as objection was made at the time the evidence was offered.—Section 5326, Code 1907, and cases cited. The burden was on the plaintiff to show a compliance on their part and the defendant's breach, and the amount due.—*Winter v. Pollak,* 166 Ala. 255; 16 Enc. P. & P. 174-9, and this burden must be carried according to the terms of the written orders given by defendant and accepted by plaintiff.—*Rice v. Schloss,* 90 Ala. 416; *Cook v. Malone,* 128 Ala. 664; *Winter v. Pollak, supra.* Even if it be conceded that plaintiff made out their prima facie case, the transcript of the proceedings and judgment of the court of common pleas of Hamilton county, Ohio, which was introduced in evidence, is a complete defense.—*Kohn v. Haas,* 95 Ala. 478; *Bogan v. Hamilton,* 90 Ala. 454; *Semple v. Glenn,* 91 Ala. 245; *Pete v. Hatcher,* 112 Ala. 514; *Fauntleroy v. Lum,* 210 U. S. 230. There was sufficient notice to the plaintiff in this suit of the garnishment in the foreign state.—*C. & C. Groc. Co. v. Coleman,* 125 Ala. 158; *Cohen v. Portland Lodge,* 81 C. C. A. 483. Under the Ohio statute, a person may garnishee himself in his own action against another, and this will be looked to in order to determine the law of Ohio.—*Norton v. Norton,* 43 Ohio State, 509; *Beckley v. U. S. S. & L. Co.,* 147 Ala. 195. This is a collateral proceeding and the judgment in Ohio is conclusive and entitled to full faith and credit.—*Sample v. Glenn, supra; White v. Simpson,* 124 Ala. 238. There is no merit in the contention that the Alabama garnishment law governs instead of the Ohio law.—*L. & N. v. Deer,* 200 U. S. 176. The judgment should be reversed,

and a judgment here rendered discharging the garnishment.—*Montgomery v. Merritt*, 61 Ala. 534.

Z. T. RUDOLPH, for appellee. The proceedings in the
Ohio court were not sound.—*Woolridge v. Holmes*, 78
Ala. 570; 14 A. & E. Enc. of Law, 809. A plaintiff cannot garnishee himself in his own action.—Section 2171,
Code 1896. Where the law conflicts, our courts will determine in favor of its own statutes.—Minor Conflict
of Laws, sec. 5, et seq. The foreign judgment without
further proof was not evidence of the existence of the
debt on which the attachment issued.—*Moyer v. Lobengeir*, 28 Am. Dec. 723. Plaintiff was entitled to recover
on the common counts.—70 Ala. 389; 88 Ala. 328.

McCLELLAN, J.—On the trial, this cause was, by
agreement, "submitted on the plea of the general issue,
with leave on the part of the defendant to introduce evidence of any matters of defense it might have to the
action as though specially pleaded, and that the plaintiff might offer evidence of any matter on rebuttal as
though a special replication was filed."

The cause or causes of action were stated in the common counts. This form of claim for a recovery arising
out of special contract is well chosen when the contract
has been fully executed on the plaintiff's part, and nothing remains to be done on the part of the defendant but
payment of the amount stipulated.—*Holloway v. Tal-
bot*, 70 Ala. 389; *Maas v. Mont. Iron Works*, 88 Ala.
328, 6 South. 701.

On May 22, 1905, July 11, 1905, August 11, 1905,
August 14, 1905, September 13, 1905, and October 9,
1905, respectively, the plaintiffs (appellees) sold to defendant (appellant) "scrap" metals of various kinds at
stipulated prices. Because of defendant's failure to

pay the stipulated price as and when plaintiffs conceived the contracts obliged defendant, plaintiffs instituted this action in the circuit court of Jefferson
county, Ala., on December 1, 1905. The defendant was
and is a nonresident of this state. Writs of attachment
were issued and served in the action, and answers were
made by the garnishees, among them Republic Iron &
Steel Company which, according to the recitals of the
judgment entry, admitted an indebtedness of $2,000 to
the defendant. In this action it was ascertained on
April 23, 1910, that defendant was indebted to plaintiffs in the sum of $2,547; and the indebtedness of the
Republic Iron & Steel Company to the defendant (appellant) was condemned to its satisfaction.

On December 11, 1905, the Joseph Joseph & Bros.
Company (defendant in this action) instituted its suit
in the court of common pleas of Hamilton county, Ohio,
against the plaintiffs in the suit at bar, for breaches of
three several contracts of dates October 9, 1905, September 14, 1905, and August 11, 1905, respectively. The
defendants (plaintiffs in our circuit court) being nonresidents of the state of Ohio, publication of notice to
them was made as provided in the statutes of that state.
Writs of garnishment were prayed and issued, and
among those served therewith and answering thereto
was the plaintiff (the defendant, appellant here). It
confessed an indebtedness to the defendant (appellees,
plaintiffs here) of $1,174.87. On June 27, 1906, the
court of common pleas rendered a judgment, in solido,
in favor of the plaintiff for $2,093.71, being the aggre-
gate amount of damages claimed for the breaches declared on, with the interest, from December 1, 1905, included. The confessed indebtedness of plaintiff to the
defendants was, by the judgment, appropriated and allowed as a credit on the judgment for $2,093.71 leaving

a balance in plaintiff's favor of $918.84, aside from costs.

It appears from the evidence (Statutes of Ohio, § 5530; *Norton v. Norton,* 43 Ohio St. 509, 525, 2 N. E. 348) set out in the transcript on this appeal, that under the laws of the state of Ohio garnishment lies against the plaintiff in action to subject debts, due by the plaintiff to the defendant, to the satisfaction of the demand for which the action is instituted. It also appears from other statutes of that state, admitted in evidence on the trial, that service by publication may be had in cases of nonresidence of that state.—Statutes of Ohio, § 5045 et seq. It further appears, from like character of evidence admitted on the trial, that attachment or garnishment is serviceable, in that state, to subject debts due, or to become due, nonresidents under the circumstances our statement indicates.

While the right of a plaintiff to make himself a garnishee in his own action was denied by this court in a proceeding unaffected by the laws of another state (*Woolridge v. Holmes,* 78 Ala. 568), yet the rule is, as indicated, recognized and applied in Ohio, Pennsylvania, and other states.—Rood on Garnishment, § 39, and notes.

The Ohio court is shown to have had jurisdiction to subject and appropriate the indebtedness of the plaintiff (there), to the defendants, to the satisfaction of the plaintiff's (there) demands as declared on in the court of common pleas. Where, however, the defendant in attachment or garnishment is not *personally* served and does not appear (as was the condition of the cause in the court of common pleas), the court is without power—without jurisdiction—to render a personal judgment over against the nonresident defendant therein.—*Pennoyer v. Neff,* 95 U. S. 714, 24 L. Ed. 565;

Cooper v. Reynolds, 10 Wall. 308, 19 L. Ed. 931; *St. Clair v. Cox,* 106 U. S. 350, 1 Sup. Ct. 354, 27 L. Ed. 222; *Freeman v. Alderson,* 119 U. S. 185, 7 Sup. Ct. 165, 30 L. Ed. 372; *Exchange Bank v. Clement,* 109 Ala. 270, 280, 281, 19 South. 814; *De Arman v. Massey,* 151 Ala. 639, 44 South. 688; *Sweeney v. Tritsch,* 151 Ala. 242, 44 South. 184; *Planters' Chem. Co. v. Waller,* 160 Ala. 217, 225, 49 South. 89, 135 Am. St. Rep. 93; *Shuttleworth v. Marx,* 159 Ala. 418, 49 South. 83. The rule, in such cases, is to *ascertain* the amount of the plaintiff's debt or demand, and then *only* render judgment condemning the property or indebtedness to the satisfaction of the *ascertained* debt or damages.—*De Arman v. Massey, supra; Sweeney v. Tritsch, supra; Cooper v. Reynolds, supra.* Accordingly, the court of common pleas of Ohio was without authority or power to render a personal judgment against the nonresident defendants therein; and hence that feature of its proceedings is a nullity everywhere.

The proceeding in the court of common pleas was in rem only. It warrantably ascertained that plaintiff garnishee (there) was indebted to defendants (there) in the sum found; and condemned that sum to the benefit of the plaintiff (there), accordingly discharging any indebtedness from or liability by plaintiff (there) to defendants to the extent, only, of the sum ($1,174) so condemned.—*Planters' Chem. Co. v. Waller, supra; Shuttleworth v. Marx, supra;* and other authorities before cited. And in accordance with the "full faith and credit clause" of the Constitution of the United States, we are bound to observe and give effect to that judgment of the Ohio court having jurisdiction to deal with the res. In this instance jurisdiction of the Ohio court to so appropriate the mentioned admitted indebtedness appears from the evidence admitted on the trial of the case at bar.

Notwithstanding this action was instituted *before* the action in the court of common pleas of Ohio was begun, the proceedings there progressed to finality *before* the judgment in the cause at bar was rendered. We see no evidence of fraud or collusion in or about the proceedings in the court of common pleas. As before indicated, the laws of the state of Ohio, radically different in that regard from our own, contemplate and allow the employment of attachment and garnishment as was done in its court of common pleas. The mere fact, if so, that the plaintiff in the court of common pleas of Ohio was aware that the complaint in this action, in Alabama, had been filed, is no predicate for the imputation to it (plaintiff there) of improper conduct. The courts of that state were open to that plaintiff; and the fact that the jurisdiction of our courts had been theretofore, even shortly, invoked, but had not progressed to judgment, in the premises, between the like parties, could not denude the resident of the state of Ohio of his *right* to invoke the existent jurisdiction of the courts of that stae.

Comity might have appealed to the Ohio tribunal had it been advised of the fact that the jurisdiction of the courts of Alabama had *first* been invoked.—11 Cyc. pp. 1017, 1018. But that, before judgment rendered in our courts, would have been a matter of grace and not the observance of a legal duty.

It was said in *M. & C. R. R. Co. v. Grayson*, 88 Ala. 572, 579, 7 South. 122, 124 (16 Am. St. Rep. 69), by way of approving quotation, supported by abundant authority, that "the *first judgment rendered* controls, whether the action in which it is reached be instituted before the other or not; and the rule applies where the first judgment is rendered in another state."

The contention is that the proceeding in the court of common pleas *necessarily* adjudged, and to that end had jurisdiction, that defendants had breached the contracts there declared on; and so upon the conception that there could be no basis for a condemnation of the indebtedness of plaintiff garnishee to the defendants without an adjudication, by that court, of a liability from defendants to plaintiff, for the breach or breaches of the contract or contracts declared on.

The scope and effect of the jurisdiction acquired with respect to a nonappearing and a not personally served nonresident defendant, as well as the nature of the proceeding, have been stated, according to the controlling doctrine of the before cited decisions. If the proceeding in the court of common pleas was given an effect whereby the breach or breaches declared on was or were bindingly adjudicated in conclusion, in that regard, of the defendant, it is evident that the process would operate beyond the jurisdictionally limited scope of the proceeding, would effect a result, against such a defendant, beyond the restricted jurisdiction so acquired to condemn the res, the indebtedness of the plaintiff garnishee to the defendants. Such an adjudication, if allowed against a nonresident defendant only constructively, by publication, served and not appearing, would, of necessity, comprehend judicial action in personam; an action not possible with respect to the rights of a defendant over whom the jurisdiction is restricted to the power to conclude his rights in the res.--Author, supra.

In *Exchange National Bank v. Clement*, 109 Ala. 270, 280-281, 19 South. 814, it was said: "The judgment rendered must correspond to the nature of the proceeding. Of necessity, it must ascertain and declare the amount of the debt, claim, or demand sought to be enforced by the attachment; and this must be ascertained and declared in the same mode and form as if the suit were in personam. There must follow a condemnation of the property attached, or of the effects garnished, and the judgment may be enforced by any appropriate process pertaining to the court. Speaking of the judgment, its operation and effect, it was said by Miller, J., in *Cooper v. Reynolds, supra:* "The judgment of the court, though in form a personal judgment against the defendant, has no effect beyond the property attached in that suit. No general execution can be issued for any balance unpaid after the property attached is exhausted. No suit can be maintained on such a judgment in the same court or in any other, nor *can it be used in evidence in any other proceeding not affecting the attached property;* nor could the costs in the proceeding be collected of the defendant out of any other property than that attached in the suit.'" (Italics supplied.) The nature of the proceeding in the court of common pleas and the restricted jurisdiction acquired thereby lead, with certainty, to the conclusion that the phase of the finding by that court of breach or breaches of the contract or contracts there declared on did not, could not, conclude the not served and nonappearing nonresident defendants upon the issue of breach vel non of the contracts declared on.

The consequence, upon the concrete case, is that the plaintiff in the cause at bar must, to be entitled to a judgment against the defendant, assuming the pleading by defendant of the judgment of condemnation of the court of common pleas of the sum (indebtedness) of $1.174.87, show a right to recover, under their complaint in this action, a sum greater than $1,174.87, and the measure of their recovery must correspond to the excess above that sum ($1,178.87). If it be assumed that the trial court was correct in its finding of the amount for which defendant was liable to plaintiff in this action, that amount should have been tolled by the amount of the indebtedness ($1,174.87) condemned by the court of common pleas. In this respect the judgment appealed from is erroneous, and, accordingly, the appropriation, through the judgment against the garnishee of the defendant's indebtedness from its Alabama debtor, was, on the assumption stated, excessive, to defendant's prejudice.

The several contracts, between the parties as evidenced by the several letters, required, under the evidence in this bill, the defendant to pay the "balance" for the materials when it was "unloaded." We understand the trial court to have so interpreted the engagements in this respect.   .

The bill of particulars furnished may have been indefinite. The use therein of the term "cars" evidently referred to their contents, and consisted, as the evidence shows, with the practice of so describing their contents. If the bill was merely indefinite, the objection should have been taken at the beginning of the trial.

The view taken of the case is so different from that prevailing below, we think the adjustment of the rights of the parties litigant will be better conserved by remanding the cause, instead of finally determining it here.

Reversed and remanded.

SIMPSON, ANDERSON, and SOMERVILLE, JJ., concur. DOWDELL, C. J., dissents.

MAYFIELD, J.—(dissenting.)—This is really an anomalous case. The facts are substantially as follows:

Two residents of Birmingham, Ala., sold junk to a corporation of Cincinnati, Ohio. It is conceded that the Ohio corporation owed the Alabama parties a balance due as for the purchase price of the junk, though there was some difference as to the exact amount. The Alabama parties sued the Ohio corporation, in the courts of Alabama, to recover this balance due. The Ohio corporation pending the suit, and before final judgment, went into the courts of Ohio, and there sued the Alabama parties for a breach of contract in the sale of the junk. The only service had, or attempted to be had, upon the Alabama parties, was that the Ohio corporation summoned itself as garnishee, trustee, and debtor of the defendants. The corporation was therefore the only party in court, or attempted to be brought in. It was the plaintiff and the garnishee; and as trustee of the defendants' property (the debt it owed the defendants) it represented the defendants. This trinity of parties then proceeded to take a trinity judgment—one in favor of the corporation against the defendants, one in favor of the corporation and against the corporation itself as garnishee, and the third in favor of the corporation and against the defendants, for the difference between the other two judgments. In other words, the first two were set off one against the other, and the third was a judgment over for the difference; but all three judgments were rendered in one and the same decision and suit, and appear to have been rendered simultaneously. The Ohio corporation then obtained a certified transcript of the proceedings in the Ohio court, and brought it back to the Alabama court, setting up the Ohio proceedings as a defense to the suit in the Alabama court. The trial court in Alabama declined to recognize, as a defense, the judgments in the Ohio proceeding, and a trial was had upon the merits, the plaintiff obtaining a judgment apparently for the full amount due. The Ohio corporation appealed to this court, and this court holds that the trial court erred in declining to allow the judgment of the Ohio court as a defense; that while the judgment over against the defendants was not binding, the judgment against the garnishee was; that it was paid by being set off against the main judgment, and it was therefore a defense pro tanto to the suit in Alabama.

To this proposition I cannot give my assent for the following reasons: The trinity judgment in the Ohio court was not binding or conclusive upon the defendants for any purpose or any amount. So far as they are concerned the judgment proclaimed its own invalidity. To give it force and effect against the nonresident defendants is to deny due process of law. The Ohio judgment, introduced in the Alabama court, showed upon its face that it was not only an attempted fraud upon the rights of the plaintiffs, but a palpable and inexcusable attempt to defeat and evade the jurisdiction of the Alabama court.

On abstract principles, it seems clear to me that to allow a plaintiff in attachment against a nonresident defendant to garnish himself as a debtor, for the purpose of conferring jurisdiction upon the court, and thus represent three contending parties, is to permit a distortion of the process of garnishment; and that such a proceeding readily suggests some sinister or ulterior purpose. If two parties owe each other, the two debts offset each other as far as they go, and whenever the owner of one sues the other party, all courts allow the other to set off his debt.

In the concrete case, this record, to my mind, shows that the proceedings in Ohio were for no other purpose than to defeat the Alabama suit. The Ohio corporation

being sued in the Alabama court, it could have there
pleaded set-off or recoupment, and have obtained judgment over against the Alabama plaintiffs, if entitled
thereto; but, instead of doing this, it institutes another
suit, as to the same matter, in Ohio, by summoning
itself as garnishee, and is thus made the only real party
in court, and therefore, in a purely ex parte proceeding,
it takes judgment against the Alabama plaintiffs for
any amount desired—only being certain to take it for
more than it owes the Alabama parties; then takes
judgment against itself for itself, and applies this judgment in part payment of its judgment against the Alabama parties, and then has judgment over for the difference. It then hastens back to Alabama and says to
the Alabama plaintiffs and the Alabama court: "Since
the last continuance, and without your knowledge or
consent, I have had this matter all settled and adjudicated by the court of my own state, and here is a certified copy of the proceedings, which is an end to this
Alabama suit."

Is it possible that such a proceeding can be valid, and
binding upon the Alabama court and parties? This
court holds that it is not conclusive of nor binding upon
the Alabama parties, as to the full amount of the indebtedness due from the Ohio corporation, nor conclusive of the liability vel non of the Alabama parties to
the Ohio corporation; but that it is binding and conclusive as to the extent of the judgment rendered
against the garnishee, and that it has been paid and satisfied by crediting it upon the judgment against the
defendants—in other words, that the amount of the
judgment against the garnishee has been properly applied to the satisfaction of the Ohio corporation's
claims against the Alabama defendants, and that such
corporation cannot be compelled to pay it again.

I know that every state possesses exclusive jurisdiction and sovereignty over all persons and property within its territory, and hence has the power to determine, for itself, the civil status and capacity of its inhabitants, and to regulate the manner and conditions upon which property situate within its territory may be acquired, enjoyed, or transferred; but a corollary of this proposition is that no state can exercise jurisdiction or authority over persons or property without its territory.—Story's Conflict of Laws, c. 2. Mr. Story says that any exertion of a state's authority beyond its own territory is a mere nullity, and incapable of binding such persons or property in other tribunals.

It is true, as is said by the Supreme Court of the United States, in the case of *Pennoyer v. Neff*, 95 U. S. 71, 24 L. Ed. 565, that every state owes protection to its own citizens, and, when nonresidents deal with them, that it is a legitimate and just exercise of authority to hold and appropriate any property owned by such nonresidents, to satisfy the claims of its citizens. It is in virtue of the state's jurisdiction over the property of nonresidents, situated within its limits, that its tribunals can inquire into the nonresidents' obligations to its own citizens, but inquiry can be carried only sufficiently far to control the disposition of this property. If the nonresidents have no property in the state there is nothing the tribunal can adjudicate. Hence, except so far as the nonresidents' property is within the state, any attempt to exercise jurisdiction over them is coram non judice. This follows upon the principle that the jurisdiction can be acquired only in one of two modes: One against the person, by service of process or voluntary appearance; and the other, by a procedure against the property of the defendant within the jurisdiction of the court. In actions against nonresidents, com-

menced by attachment, the judgment of the court,
though in form a personal judgment against the defendant, has no effect beyond the property attached in
that suit. No execution can issue upon it, and no suit
can be maintained upon it, in the same court, nor in
any other court; nor can it be used as evidence in any
other proceeding not affecting the attached property.
Not even the costs can be collected, from any defendant, out of any other property than that attached in
the suit. The court cannot proceed unless the officers
find some property of the defendant upon which levy
of attachment can be made.

In the Supreme Court of the United States (*Pennoyer Case, supra*) it was said that if judgments obtained ex parte against nonresidents, upon mere publication, could be sustained as valid, they would be constant instruments of fraud and oppression; that judgments of all sorts, upon contracts and torts, real and
pretended, would be given, upon which property would
be seized, after the evidence of the transactions upon
which they were founded (if it ever existed) had pr-
ished. The only theory upon which the court has ever
upheld or given effect to substituted service by publication, is that in such cases the property is brought under the control of the court by seizure, or some equivalent act; and this theory rests upon the presumption
that the property is in the possession of its owner, and
that its seizure will inform him, and that he will then
look after it. Such service is held to be given in all actions which are substantially proceedings in rem. It is
said by the Supreme Court of the United States, in the
above-mentioned case, that where the entire object of
the action is to determine the personal rights and obligations of the defendants (and such was its undoubted
object in this suit), constructive service upon a non-

resident is ineffectual for any purpose. Process from the courts of one state cannot run into another, and service by publication cannot create any greater obligation upon a nonresident. Process sent to one out of the state, and process published within it, are equally unavailing to establish any personal liability.

The foregoing propositions, as I understand the majority opinion, are not denied nor disputed. The majority hold, however, that the Ohio court, by virtue of the statutes of that state, acquired jurisdiction of the property of the defendants in that suit, by the plaintiff's summoning itself as garnishee, and that, having thus acquired jurisdiction, it could wipe out and destroy all liability of the plaintiff and the garnishee (who were one and the same person) to the defendants, who were nonresidents.

While Mr. Rood (in his work on Garnishment) seems rather inclined to the opinion that a plaintiff may summon himself as garnishee, and thereby reach a debt owing from himself to the defendant, as he is so cited in the majority opinion in this case, yet the contrary is expressly decided in the text, both in Cyc. and American & English Encyclopedia of Law. In Cyc. (volume 20, p. 986) it is said (and it is all that is there said upon the subject): "The rule is well settled that the plaintiff in an action can neither summon nor charge himself as garnishee nor trustee in garnishment proceedings."

In said Encyclopedia of Law (volume 14 [2d Ed.] p. 809) it is expressed as follows: "The question has arisen whether the plaintiff may summon himself as garnishee, and thereby reach a debt owing from himself to the defendant, and though the decisions in regard to this point are in conflict, it is held by the best-considered cases, under statutes providing for summon-

ing as garnishees persons indebted, etc., to the defendant or providing for the attachment of indebtedness to
the defendant, that the plaintiff cannot summon himself as garnishee. In a great many jurisdictions, however, the courts, following the principle of the decisions
under the custom of London, which permitted a creditor to attach an indebtedness owing from himself, or
property in his hands, have held that the plaintiff may
summon himself as garnishee in regard to an indebtedness owing from him.

Mr. Drake, speaking on this subject in his work on
Garnishment (section 543), says: "By the custom of
London a plaintiff may by garnishment attach, in his
own hands, money or goods of the defendant; but can
a plaintiff charge himself as garnishee in respect to a
debt due from him to the defendant? or, can several
plaintiffs summon one of their own number with a view ·
to so charging him?" The author answers the question
by asking it; but adds that, in Pennsylvania and Ohio,
it is held that it may be done, though in New Hampshire and Rhode Island it cannot; and that Massachusetts had intimated that it could not. And some cases
are cited of Louisiana, Tennessee, and Vermont. But
an examination of these cases will show that it has
never been held that a debt due a nonresident defendant could be subjected by a resident plaintiff, in such
manner or by such process; in fact, the contrary has
been held by the courts of at least two of these states,
to wit, Pennsylvania and Tennessee.

In the case of *Moyer v. Lobengeir,* 4 Watts (Pa.)
390, 28 Am. Dec. 723, it is held that a judgment against
a garnishee in such case is not even prima facie evidence against the defendant when the plaintiff and garnishee, being the same, were thereafter sued by the defendant upon the debt sought to be subjected by gar-

nishment; that the judgment against the garnishee in such suit was not even prima facie evidence of the liability of the defendant to such plaintiff.

It was ruled by the federal court, in the case of *Rice v. Sharpleigh* (C. C.) 85 Fed. 559, that the statutes of Tennessee did not then, and never did, authorize a plaintiff to garnishee himself for a debt due a defendant.

Mr. Drake, speaking further on this subject (section 703b), said: "As we have seen, a plaintiff may by garnishment attach a debt due from himself to the defendant, but this will not authorize him to plead such garnishment, either in abatement or in bar, of a suit by the defendant against himself for that debt." Here the author seems to recognize such proceeding, but declares that it is not applicable nor binding in a case like the one under consideration.

The Supreme Court of Kansas, in the case of *National Bank v. Elliott,* 62 Kan. 764, 64 Pac. 623, 55 L. R. A. 353, holds that a plaintiff in an action can neither summon nor charge himself as garnishee therein, because a garnishment proceeding is an action by the plaintiff against the garnishee and defendant as parties defendant, and that the same person cannot be both plaintiff and defendant. A note to the report of this case in 55 L. R. A. 353, collects many authorities upon the subject.

The same was held by the Supreme Court of New Hampshire, in the case of *Hoag v. Hoag,* 55 N. H. 172, where the court decided that the same person cannot be both plaintiff and defendant, quoting from Dicey on Parties, § 220, "How can a man sue himself in a court of law? It is impossible to say a man can sue himself." In that New Hampshire case A. had brought suit against B., and summoned himself in the capacity of

administrator of the estate of C., and the court held
that it was a manifest absurdity to attempt to give
sanction to a proceeding whereby a party seeks to promote his own interests to the detriment and expense of
those he represents as trustee.

Chief Justice Shaw, in the case of *Belknap v. Gib-
bens*, 13 Metc. (Mass.) 473, speaking on the question
under consideration, said that the general tenor of the
law seemed to regard a garnishment suit as a suit between the plaintiff and the garnishee as a stakeholder
for the defendant; that it was, and should be, regarded
as an adversary proceeding, and should be brought
within the rule that a person cannot sue himself, nor
be both plaintiff and defendant in the same case. I do
not think the correctness of this proposition can be
doubted. This court, in the case of *Woolridge v.
Holmes*, 78 Ala. 568, speaking through Chief Justice
Stone, said: "There are authorities which hold that an
attaching creditor can constitute himself trustee or
garnishee, and condemn to the payment of his demand
a debt due from him to his debtor. * * * We do
not think them sound"—citing New Hampshire and
Massachusetts references. So this court is certainly
committed to the doctrine that no such proceeding
should be allowed, or, if allowed, that it is not valid.

While it is true that garnishment proceedings are
statutory, and therefore depend for their validity upon
the statutes of the various states, yet the statutes of
one state may authorize a proceeding which the statutes of another would not. But the statutes of no state
can authorize a proceeding which would deprive a citizen of any state of his property, without due process of
law. Both the federal and state Constitutions prevent
this. Nor will the courts of one state respect the statutes of another, as to notice and service upon nonresi-

dents, which would have this effect. Such was expressly held by this court in the case of *Foster v. Glazener*,
27 Ala. 391, where it was decided that a summary remedy given by statute of Georgia, to establish a lost note
or instrument, being predicated on a mere ex parte affidavit, and without notice to the party to be affected
thereby, could be assimilated to a proceeding in rem,
because the court had the custody of neither the person
nor the thing; and that it was a settled principle of international law, that every attempt, by any party or
state, to grant by its Legislature, jurisdiction to its
courts over persons or property not within its territory, is mere usurpation, and that all judicial proceedings in virtue of it are void for every purpose; that the
courts of one country are not bound to regard as notice
everything which may be made such by the statutes of
another.

It has been well said by the highest authorities in
England, and often quoted by high authority in America, that judicial power would be tyranny if it could be
exercised capriciously, without regard to the allegations of the parties, or on testimony given by one party,
and which the other had no opportunity to contradict.
—4 C. B. 567; 8 C. D. 275. A court of one state, therefore, cannot, without violating the Constitution, trans-
cend the known rules of judicial action, though authorized by statutes so to do, by rendering an ex parte judgment, because such course would not be due process of
law.

Mr. Webster, in his argument in the famous *Dart-
mouth College Case*, defined "due process of law" as "A
tribunal which hears before it condemns; which proceeds upon inquiry, and renders judgment only after
trial."

So far as the courts of Alabama, or those of any other state, are concerned, it is wholly immaterial whether the proceeding of the Ohio court, in question, was attempted to be authorized or justified by statute or by common law. The attempt would be equally futile in both cases, for the reasons shown.

It was said by the Lord Chief Justice of England, in the case of *Collins v. Blanton* (reported in 2 Smith, L. C. 717), that "statute law is the will of the Legislature in writing; the common law is nothing but the statutes . worn out by time; all law began by consent of the Legislature, and whether it is now law by usage or in writing, it is the same thing."

The judgment of the Ohio court must be given the same credence and the same effect by the courts of this state, whether it be authorized or sanctioned by the common law or by the statute law of Ohio. The "full faith and credit" clause of the federal Constitution does not require the courts of one state to give effect to the judgments and decrees of another, if, in so doing, the citizens of the one are thereby deprived of their property without due process of law. This would be to violate another provision contained in both the state and federal Constitutions, which is as binding as, and more sacred than, the other clause. A tribunal which decides, without hearing the defendant or giving him an opportunity to be heard, may claim the respect due a legislative or executive power, but cannot thereby give its decrees the weight of a judicial act. Hence, any judgment rendered without notice to or appearance of, the defendant, or a sufficient excuse for the want thereof, will be regarded as invalid by foreign courts. When the record of any court, whether superior or inferior, shows on its face, or by necessary implication, that it has proceeded without notice to the defendant and without having acquired jurisdiction of his person or property, and without any sufficient excuse for the want of such notice or service, the presumption in favor of such judgment is at an end, and it may be impeached collaterally as absolutely void.—*Foster v. Glazener*, 27 Ala. 391; *Hollingsworth v. Barkour*, 4 Pet. 475, 7 L. Ed. 922.

A judgment which strips the defendant of his property without giving him an opportunity to be heard cannot be justified by the mere pretext that the proceeding is in rem and imposes no obligation upon him. This was held by the Supreme Court of the United States, in the case of *Boswell v. Dickerson*, 9 How. 336, 13 L. Ed. 164. The court was speaking in that case of an Ohio statute which authorized the institution of proceedings against an absent defendant by publication, for the purpose of compelling the specific performance of a contract, and said that if the statute were valid, which it seemed to doubt, it could justify a decree in personam for the cost of the suit. At one time it was held by this court that judgments in personam could be entered after constructive service of process upon a nonresident, and that such judgments were valid in the state where rendered, to support a sale of the debtor's property situated in such state. But this doctrine was greatly modified, if not entirely overthrown, by the Supreme Court of the United States, in the case of *Pennoyer v. Neff*, 95 U. S. 714, 24 L. Ed. 565, which change of doctrine was announced and recognized by this court in the case of *Exchange Bank v. Clement*, 109 Ala. 279, 19 South. 814.

If the decision of the majority in this case is to stand as the law, any resident of Ohio may wipe out and cancel, at his pleasure, all liability to persons who do not reside in Ohio. Not only this, but any other person can go to Ohio and institute suit against his creditors, have himself summoned as garnishee, admit by his answer his indebtedness or liability, and have a judgment rendered against himself as garnishee, but in favor of himself as plaintiff; and then cancel such judgment against himself as garnishee by having it credited as payment against the judgment which he can take against his nonresident creditors. And it will be purely a matter of choice, whether he will be satisfied by entirely wiping out the debt he owes his creditors, or whether he will take the chance of having a personal judgment over against them for any amount that will suit his convenience or his notions as to propriety. As he represents all three of the parties, and nobody appears to oppose him, he may frame all the pleadings himself, make all the issues he desires, and admit, confess or deny any of them so made; and as he furnishes all the evidence that is to be received on the trial there can be no doubt that the judgments rendered will be to his liking.

In my opinion, the error into which the majority of the court have fallen, is that they have confounded or confused the situs of the debt garnished in the Ohio court, with the jurisdiction of the court over the garnishee.

Of course the Ohio court had jurisdiction over the plaintiff and over the garnishee, because they were one and the same person or corporation, and resided in Ohio, and invoked the jurisdiction of that court; but the court did not thereby acquire jurisdiction over the defendants' property the situs of which was in Alabama. The property held to be condemned by the garnishment in the Ohio court was no more within the jurisdiction of the Ohio court than was the person of the defendant. Both were equally beyond such jurisdiction. The property was that of the defendant, not of the plaintiff, nor of the garnishee.

The property thus condemned by the Ohio court (a chose in action) was Alabama property, and its situs—that is, all the situs it had or was capable of having—was that of its owner, who resides in Alabama. It is property which is taxable in Alabama, and not in Ohio. It was as much beyond the rights and powers of the Ohio corporation to confer on the Ohio court jurisdiction of this property, as it was jurisdiction of the person of the defendant. Neither the ownership, custody nor control was in the possession of the Ohio corporation, and how could it confer custody or control which it did not have ? It follows that the Ohio court had no more jurisdiction of the res than of the person of the defendant. In fact, in truth, and in law, the judgments of the Ohio court were nothing more nor less than personal judgments, which were absolutely void on collateral attack. One was a personal judgment in favor of the Ohio corporation, and against nonresidents, and this, the majority of this court concede and hold to be void ; the other, a personal judgment against the Ohio corporation and in favor of the Ohio corporation—which is not only void but absurd, and certainly has no more efficacy to bind the defendant than the personal judgment rendered against him.

There is another reason why this whole proceeding in the Ohio court is void and of no effect as a defense to the suit in Alabama (suggested by my Brother SAYRE), and that is this: If the judgment against the garnishee in the Ohio court was offered in the Alabama court as a set-off, it would not avail as such, because it is not shown that it had been paid by the garnishee. Surely it could not be paid by applying it to an absolutely void judgment against the defendant and in favor of the garnishee, because, to have the effect of payment, it must be applied in payment of a valid judgment against the defendant.

If the judgment against the defendant was absolutely void, even on collateral attack (as it undoubtedly was, and the majority opinion in this case holds), then certainly it was of no benefit to the defendant, and of no detriment to the garnishee, to apply payment to such a nullity; yet this is the effect that is accorded to the Ohio judgment by the decision of the court in this case.

The trial court was clearly right in denying any effect to the Ohio record introduced in evidence, and no other error appearing on the record, the judgment of the lower court should be herein affirmed.

SAYRE, J., concurs in dissent.

Oliver v. Kinney.

Assumpsit.

(Decided June 29, 1911. 56 South. 203.)

1. *Judgment; Attachment; Nature; Personal Judgment.*—Where the defendant is not personally served and does not appear generally, the court cannot render a personal judgment, but may only bind the property in an attachment proceeding, as such proceedings are in the nature or proceedings in rem; but a defendant becomes liable as on personal service where he executes a forthcoming bond or bond for the discharge of the garnishment in a suit begun by attachment, and thereafter the proceedings become a personal action, and proceeds as if the attachment was sued out in aid of a pending suit, except as provided by the statute, so as to authorize a personal judgment.

2. *Same; Record; Construction; Appearance.*—Notwithstanding the judgment in an attachment case recites defendant's appearance, that recital should be construed with the other parts of the record on that question.

3. *Appearance; Jurisdiction of Person; Special Appearance.*—An appearance made for a special purpose does not give the court jurisdiction over the defendant's person further than the determining

of the question presented to it for the determination on such appearance.

4. *Attachment; Purpose.*—The whole purpose of an attachment is to fix a lien upon specific property before the determination of the main suit; the attachment resting on its own facts, and not on the facts of the main action.

5. *Same; Affidavit; Failure to Make; Cure.*—The affidavit required by the statute in attachment proceedings is the foundation of the proceedings, and an abatement of the writ for want of affidavit, destroys the lien, although the defendant executed a forthcoming bond and bond to discharge the garnishment in order to regain possession of the property taken from him by the void process, the execution of such bond not having the effect of validating the attachment

6. *Same; Abatement; Grounds; Validity.*—Notwithstanding section 2964, Code 1907, provides that an attachment issued without affidavit and bond may be abated on defendant's motion, the lien could be destroyed for other reasons as by showing there had been no lawful levy.

7. *Same; Time of Filing Plea.*—So long as it is open to defendant to file the pleas in abatement prescribed by section 2964, Code 1907, he may also file other pleas having the effect of destroying the writ, provided that he has not already pleaded or otherwise challenged the validity of the lien, in which case, the cause stands for trial upon the day set by the clerk pursuant to section 5348, Code 1907, and cannot be called before that day except by consent.

8. *Same; Judgment; Time of Entry.*—Under section 2964, Code 1907, an attachment judgment nil dicit was premature when taken before the expiration of the third day of the return time.

9. *Appeal and Error; Record; Conclusiveness: Impeachment; Fraud.*—While a record imports verity, it may be attacked for fraud; hence, although the affidavit and bond required to be made in attachment proceedings appeared upon the fact of the record on appeal, the defendant could show that they were in the record illegally by fraud.

APPEAL from Cullman Circuit Court.

Heard before Hon. D. W. SPEAKE.

Assumpsit by E. C. Kinney against W. J. Oliver, with attachment and garnishment. Judgment for plaintiff and defendant appeals. Reversed and remanded.

GASTON & PETTUS, for appellant. The judgment was prematurely rendered.—Sec. 2961, Code 1907; see also sections 2962-4, and sections 5346-7. A plea in abatement must come before a plea in bar or demurrer.— *Brown v. Powell,* 4 Ala. 149; *Leiff's Case,* 101 Ala. 544.

[Oliver v. Kinney.]

A judgment by default or nil dicit in attachment proceedings cannot be rendered until after the expiration of three days of the return term.—*Woolsey v. R. R. Co.*, 28 Ala. 536; *Waggoner v. Turner*, 73 Ala. 197. A premature judgment will be reversed.—*Ivey's Case*, 97 Ala. 383; *Lawrence v. The State*, 160 Ala. 384; *Harris v. Herzberg*, 128 Ala. 474; *Ex parte Howard Harrison I. Co.*, 119 Ala. 484.

J. B. BROWN, and EYSTER & EYSTER, for appellee. The recitals shown by the record are conclusive on appeal, and cannot be questioned as to appellant's appearance in the court below.—*Greggs v. Gilmer*, 54 Ala. 430; *Burrough v. Wright*, 3 Ala. 43; *E. A. L. Co. v. Canterbury*, 53 South. 823. The motion to set the judgment aside was addressed to the discretion of the trial court and the action of the court in overruling that motion is not subject to review on this appeal.—*Ledbetter & Company v. Venton*, 108 Ala. 644; *Allen v. Lathop Hatton Lumber Co.*, 90 Ala. 490; *Truss v. Birmingham, La-Grange R. R. Co.*, 96 Ala.. 316; *Haygood v. Tait*, 126 Ala. 266; *Tuscaloosa Ice Mfg. Co. v. Williams*, 127 Ala. 110; *Ellis & Co. v. Brannon*, 161 Ala. 577; *Baggett v. Ala. Chemical Co.*, 156 Ala. 639; *Ex parte Parker et al.*, 54 South. Rep. (Ala.) 572. That when the defendant appeared and replevied the property by the execution of a replevy bond, and dissolved the garnishment by the execution of a refunding bond he waived the necessity for summons or other process, and all defects if any in the attachment proceedings.—*Merchants Laclede Nat. Bank v. Troy Groc. Co.*, 150 Ala. 131; *Rosenberg v. Claflin Co.*, 95 Ala. 252; *Lampley v. Beavers*, 25 Ala. 534; *Moore v. Easley*, 18 Ala. 619; *Peebles v. Ware*, 60 Ala. 413. The execution of the replevy bond was an admission of notice, and obverted the necessity of sum-

mons or other process, and after the execution of the
bond the defendant is conclusively charged with notice
of each and every step taken in the case.—*Chastain v.
Armstrong*, 85 Ala. 217; *Prickett v. Sebert*, 71 Ala. 197.
The demand made by the defendant for a bill of particulars under the provisions of § 5326 of the Code is in
the nature of a demurrer to a complaint, in that it requires the plaintiff to furnish a particular statement
of items constituting plaintiff's claim, and when furnished it is an amplification of the plaintiff's complaint, which restricts him to proof of the matters set
forth in the bill of particulars.—*Morrisette v. Wood*,
128 Ala. 505; *Boykin v. Pearson*, 95 Ala. 626. The record shows that the defendant not only appeared on the
record, but in open court by his attorney and by this
appearance the proceedings were transformed into an
action *in personam* and under the provisions of § 2963
of the Code, all the provisions of the Code, applicable
to actions commenced by, summons and complaint were
made applicable to this suit, including § 5347, of the
Code which is embraced in and a part of the same chapter as § 5326, the provisions of which were invoked by
the appellant in making demand for the bill of particulars, and in default of plea the case was subject to judgment *nil dicit*.—*Shields v. Barden*, 6 Ark. (1 Eng.) 459;
Merchants LaClede Nat. Bank v. roy Groc. Co., 150 Ala.
131; *Reynolds v. Williams*, 152 Ala. 491; *Hutcheson v.
Powell*, 92 Ala. 619; *Gidden v. Bowling*, 93 Ala. 92;
Rosenberg v. Claflin Co., 95 Ala. 249; *Peebles v. Ware*,
60 Ala. 413; *Hawkens v. Armour Packing Co.*, 105 Ala.
545; *Chastain v. Armstrong*, 85 Ala. 505; 4 Cyc., page
821, 2 Plea or Answer. We find on an examination into
the history of the statute, now Section 5347, of the Code
of 1907, that it originated in the act of December 14th,
1819, entitled An act to regulate the proceedings in the

courts of law and equity in this state," and that it has
been brought down through the several codes with various changes, and is the only statute regulating the time
of pleading in civil action that has ever been in force in
Alabama, and that it applies to actions commenced by
attachment as well as those commenced by summons
and complaint. In the absence of a plea on file, and
after the time for pleading had expired, the court owed
the defendant no duty.—*Nat. Fertilizer Co. v. Henson*,
103 Ala. 535. Appellant concedes both in argument
and brief, that if appellee had sued out a summons as
provided by section 962, which appears for the first
time in the Code of 1907, that then appellee's contention
that § 5347, of the Code, governed the time for pleading,
but, not having done this it does not apply. The answer
to this proposition is that the defendant by his appearance waived further notice and obviated the necessity
of a summons to bring him before the court.—*Buroughs v. Wright*, 3 Ala. 43; *Peebles v. Ware*, 60 Ala.
413; *Chastain v. Armstrong*, 85 Ala. 215; *Corley v.
Shropshire*, 2 Ala. 66; *Rosenberg v. Claflin*, 95 Ala. 249.
The purpose of the act "To regulate the trial of attachment cases" approved December 17, 1873, the provisions
of which were first brought into the Code of 1876,
placed suits by attachment on an equality as to time of
trial with other suits, commenced by process requiring
personal service.—*Rice v. Clements*, 57 Ala. 191; *Merchants Nat. Bank v. Troy Groc. Co.*, 150 Ala. 131; *Reynolds v. Willims*, 152 Ala. 492. The case of *Shields v.
Burden*, 6 Ark. (1 Eng.) 459, is on all fours with the
case at bar, and sustains the action of the trial court in
rendering judgment *nihil dicit*. The proceedings not
being void appellant is by these acts estopped to question the regularity of the attachment.—*Savage v. Russell*, 84 Ala. 103; *Fuller v. Fomin*, 108 Ala. 464. "At

the time the judgment was taken, the defendant ap-
peared by his attorney, W. E. James, but made no objec-
tion to the court proceeding to judgment further than
to say that the defendant reserved the right to make mo-
tion to set the judgment aside." This was clearly a
waiver of any defect in the process, and we contend a
consent to the judgment being rendered.—*Buroughs v.*
Wright, 3 Ala. 43; *Merchants Nat. Bank v. Troy Groc.*
Co., 150 Ala. 131; *Lamply v. Beavers,* 25 Ala. 534;
Moore v. Esley, 18 Ala. 619.

SAYRE, J.—Suit in this case was commenced in
April, 1910, by attachment on the ground that the defendant was a nonresident. The attachment was levied
upon goods and chattels and by the sheriff's writ of
garnishment to the Parker Bank & Trust Company.
Defendant replevied the goods and chattels by executing
a forthcoming bond, and secured a discharge of the garnishment, by giving bond as required by section 4312 of
the Code of 1907. On September 17, 1910, plaintiff
filed his complaint, and on September 21st, the same
being the third day of the fall term of the circuit court,
judgment nil dicit was rendered containing this recital:
"Come the parties by their attorneys." This appeal is
prosecuted on the theory that the judgment was prematurely rendered.

In the ordinary case of suits commenced by summons
and complaint the statute provides that: "When the
term of the court is but one week, the defendant must
plead or demur to the complaint within the first day;
and when the term of the court is more than one week,
by noon of the second day."—Code, § 5347. In cases in
which the suit is commenced by attachment on a demand due and payable at the time, "the plaintiff must,
within the first three days of the return term of the at-

tachment, file his complaint, and the cause stands for
trial at such return term, if the levy is made and notice
thereof is given twenty days before the commencement
of such term."—Code, § 2961. Section 2963 is as follows: "If the defendant appears and pleads, the cause
proceeds as in suits commenced by summons and complaint; if he fails to appear, or appearing, fails to plead
within the time required by law, the plaintiff may take
judgment by default or nil dicit, and may execute a
writ of inquiry, if necessary." This section was enacted at a time when the theory prevailed in this state that
actions by attachment were in personam and might lead
to binding personal judgments without actual personal
notice. It was frequently so interpreted in practice.
But since the decision in *Bank of Spokane v. Clement*,
109 Ala. 270, 19 South. 814, this court has followed the
doctrine of the Supreme Court of the United States,
which is that attachment proceedings, where the defendant is not brought in by personal service or fails to
appear generally in defense, partake of the nature of
proceedings in rem, and in such case the court is without jurisdiction to render a judgment of binding effect
in personam, but may proceed only to a judgment condemning the property levied upon to the satisfaction of
the plaintiff's demand, which, for that purpose only, is
to be ascertained and declared. In view of this state of
the law, section 2962 of the Code was enacted, as follows: "Whenever a complaint is filed in a suit begun
by attachment, whether at the time of suing out the attachment or subsequently thereto, upon the demand of
the plaintiff therefor, a summons shall issue upon the
complaint in all respects, and with the same effect as if
the suit had been begun by summons and complaint.
The issuance and service of such a summons and complaint shall in no manner affect the levy or lien of the

attachment, or the enforcement thereof." So that, where service of summons and complaint is subsequently had, actions commenced originally by attachment are put on the same footing with actions in which attachments are sued out in aid of a pending suit. There was in this case no summons served, for the reason, no doubt, that the defendant remained without the state.

But, by executing a bond for the forthcoming of chattels or for the discharge of garnishment, in a suit begun by attachment, the defendant acknowledges notice of the suit, and, if the attachment proceeding is sufficient to invoke the jurisdiction of the court, he thereby becomes bound to appear and defend, or becomes liable to be proceeded against as in case of personal service of process. From that time the proceeding becomes and is a personal action against the defendant, and, except in the respect provided by statute to be noticed, goes on as if the attachment had been sued out in aid of a pending suit, and the court is authorized to proceed to a judgment having like force and effect as in the case of an action commenced by summons personally served as well as a judgment condemning the property levied upon. It is clear that such was the legislative understanding of the effect of the execution of the bonds provided for by the statute, for it is enacted that, under certain conditions, judgment may be rendered against the sureties as to whom process is not required to issue.— *Peebles v. Weir*, 60 Ala. 413; *Chastain v. Armstrong*, 85 Ala. 215, 3 South. 788; *Hawkins v. Armour Packing Co.*, 105 Ala. 545, 17 South. 16; *Blyler v. Kline*, 64 Pa. 130; *Brenner v. Moyer*, 98 Pa. 274; *Richard v. Mooney*, 39 Miss. 357; *Wilkinson v. Patterson*, 6 How. (Miss.) 193; *Shields v. Barden*, 6 Ark. 459; Drake on Attachments, § 332.

The judgment recites an appearance by the defendant. But the recital is to be construed in connection with the appearance shown by the other parts of the record. The record shows only an appearance by the execution of the forthcoming bond and the bond for the discharge of the garnishment. The bill of exceptions, reserved on the motion to set aside the judgment, shows that by his appearance the defendant indicated no submission to the court's power to act at the time. It is obvious that an appearance made for a special purpose ought not to be held to give the court jurisdiction over the defendant, except to the extent of hearing and determining the question which he specially presents to it for consideration.—Freeman on Judgments, § 120a. In *Grigg v. Gilmer*, 54 Ala. 425, Chief Justice Brickell, speaking of the effect of an entry of an attorney's name on the margin of the docket of the court, opposite to the name of a party to the suit, accepted in practice as an appearance for such party, said: "The consequence resulting from an appearance thus made may be limited by the steps taken, or the pleadings interposed subsequently. If these refer to and are for the purpose of vacating an irregular service of process, or for showing to the court there has been no service of process, or for taking advantage of defects in the process, on error or appeal, such an appearance will not be deemed a general appearance, curing such irregularities or defects."

Where an effort has been made to confer upon the court jurisdiction in attachment by making affidavit in some sort, the law requires that "the plaintiff, before or during the trial, must be permitted to amend any defect of form or substance in the affidavit, bond, or attachment; and no attachment must be dismissed for any defect in the affidavit, if the plaintiff, his agent, or attorney, will make a sufficient affidavit, or for want of a

bond, if the plaintiff, his agent, or attorney is willing
to give or substitute a sufficient bond."—Code, § 2965.
The whole purpose and effect of the writ of attachment
is to fasten a lien upon specific property in advance of
the determination of the main suit. The action in personam to which it is auxiliary may, when personal service has been had or where the defendant obviates the
necessity for personal service by a general appearance,
proceed entirely without regard to whether a lien is secured. So, on the other hand, the lien sought depends
entirely upon the attachment proceeding. The attachment rests upon its own facts, and not upon the facts of
the main action.—*Reed v. Maben*, 21 Neb. 696, 33 N. W.
252.

Directing our attention, then, to the question of the
validity of the proceeding for a lien, for by that proceeding only has the defendant been brought into court,
it is to be noted that the affidavit required by the statute is "the initiatory step—the very foundation of the
whole proceeding. It alone can call into exercise the
extraordinary power of the court to command the seizure of the estate of the defendant, before he is heard,
and before judgment pronounced against him."—*Flex-
ner v. Dickerson*, 65 Ala. 130. An abatement of the attachment for want of affidavit destroys the attachment
and puts it beyond repair. If thereafter the plaintiff
would secure his debt by a lien in advance of judgment
and execution at the end of the main suit, he must begin ab initio. The execution of the forthcoming bond
and the bond for a dischcarge of the garnishment in order that the defendant might regain possession of his
property, if taken from him by void process, could not,
therefore, deprive him of the right to get rid of a levy
which had in law no more effect upon the rightful possession than if it had not been made, and did not have

the effect of validating the writ and its levy.—*Jones v. Baxter*, 146 Ala. 620, 41 South. 781, 119 Am. St. Rep. 54. And if the attachment had to be abated, in the absence of summons, the entire proceeding would fall to the ground. Now section 2964 of the Code provides that an attachment issued without affidavit and bond, as prescribed, may be abated on plea of the defendant, filed within the first three days of the return term. And on the last quoted section the appellant bases his contention that the judgment was prematurely rendered. To hold that a judgment, dependent altogether upon attachment proceedings for its validity and taken before the expiration of the first three days of the term, is not prematurely taken, would be to overturn the statute vi et armis, and to that we cannot feel ourselves equal.

But it is argued that a plea seeking to abate the attachment for the reason that no affidavit and bond were made must be based upon the record; that the record showed that no such plea could be successfully interposed; and, therefore, the court needed not to wait for the plea. But we think the argument hardly meets the situation. While the record imports absolute verity so long as it is not attacked for fraud, for fraud it may be set at naught; and, notwithstanding an affidavit and bond appeared upon the face of the record, it was open to the defendant to allege and prove they were there by fraud and were not the bond and affidavit required by law. And, besides, other defenses were open to the defendant, as, for example, he might destroy the asserted lien of the attachment by showing that there had been no lawful levy, for a lawful levy also was essential to the lien of the writ. That was the case in *Jones v. Baxter, supra*. True, the statute does not in terms lay down a rule in respect to the time for filing other pleas destructive of the lien. But, as long as the cause is open for the filing of the plea specified in the statute, the defendant may file other pleas having the same force and effect, provided, of course, he has not already pleaded, or taken other appropriate step challenging the validity of the lien of the attachment, in which event the cause stands for trial upon the day set by the clerk under the authority of section 5348 of the Code, and could not be called for trial before the day so set, except by consent. However lacking in merit may be any defense which may be hereafter interposed—though as to that we are not permitted to indulge presumptions—we feel constrained by the language of the statute to the conclusion that the defendant was acting within his rights when, as has been shown by the bill of exceptions, he refused to plead on the third day of the term, and that the premature judgment nil dicit was error for which the cause must be remanded.—*Hollis v. Herzberg,* 128 Ala. 474, 29 South. 582.

Reversed and remanded.

SIMPSON, ANDERSON, and SOMERVILLE, JJ., concur.

Pitts *v.* Campbell, *et al.*

Bill to Remove Settlement of an Estate from Probate to Chancery Court.

(Decided May 17, 1911. 55 South. 500.)

1. *Wills; Construction.*—Where the performance of a condition subsequent in a will has become impossible, without any fault of the devisee, the condition will not be regarded as broken, in law and there will be no defeasance.

2. *Same.*—Where a testator left his wife his farm during her natural lifetime subject to certain limitations, with remainder over to all his nieces in equal parts, and succeeding item of the will provided that certain legacies to two of his nieces should be paid in cash out

of his estate, whether real or personal, except the land left to his wife during her natural life, and the will further provided, that it was the intention of the testator to give to the two nieces named a certain amount more than to his other nieces, it constituted a special devise of the farm properties, and such property was not chargeable with such legacies.

3. *Same; Gifts.*—A clear gift under a will is not to be cut down by anything which does not with reasonable certainty indicate an intention to cut it down.

4. *Executors and Administrators; Wills; Claims; Claimant.*—The personal property of the testator is the fund primarily for the discharge of debts and legacies, and they are not chargeable upon the land, unless the intention to so charge them is manifested by the express word, or by fair implication from the will, read in the light of the environments of the testator and his estate.

APPEAL from Madison Law and Equity Court.

Heard before Hon. TANCRED BETTS.

Bill by J. C. Goodrich and others, as executors of the last will and testament of J. N. Hairston to remove the settlement of the estate from the probate to the circuit court and for a construction of the will. From the decree rendered, Pearl Pitts, one of the devisees, appealed. Affirmed.

WALKER & SPRAGINS, for appellant. The cardinal rule in the construction of a will is to ascertain the intention of the testator and to give it effect.—*Campbell v. Weakley*, 121 Ala. 64; *Woolf v. Loeb*, 98 Ala. 426. The testator may by express direction charge a legacy upon the real estate.—*Davidson v. Coon*, 9 L. R. A. 584. The intention of a testator should not be defeated by a construction of the will which will result in defeating a preference plainly manifested.—*Gorman v. McDowell*. 127 Ala. 549; *Newsom v. Thornton*, 82 Ala. 402.

PARKER & PARKER, and PAUL SPEAKE, for appellee. A gift in clear and positive terms should not be cut down by later vague and doubtful language.—1 Underhill on Wills, Secs. 358 and 689; *Flynn v. Davis*, 18 Ala. 132; 115 Tenn. 46; 39 S. W. 16; *Newsom v. Thorn-*

ton, 82 Ala. 402. The grant of the farm lands was a specific devise, and therefore not chargeable with legacies.—97 Am. St. Rep. 743; 82 Pa. St. 213, and authorities supra.

SOMERVILLE, J.—The bill is filed by the executors of the last will and testament of J. N. Hairston, deceased, and seeks to remove the settlement of his estate from the probate court of Madison county into the law and equity court. It prays for a construction of certain clauses of the will, and that two legacies, in the sum of $5,000 each, the one to appellant and the other to her sister, be contingently charged on particular lands described in the will as the testator's farm, and devised to the widow of the testator for her life, with remainder over to his nieces generally, including the appellees.

The testator died February 28, 1908, leaving about $37,000 of personal estate, his farm homestead, worth about $20,000, and several town lots, worth about $400. In September, 1905, and August, 1906, he had sold parcels of real estate for an aggregate of $6,300. From these facts it is inferable that at the date of the execution of the will, July 1, 1905, his personal estate amounted to about $30,000, and his real estate, other than the farm, to about $6,500. The chancellor held that the farm property was specifically devised in item 2 of the will, and was not chargeable with the said legacies, and denied the prayer that they be sold for their satisfaction.

The material items of the will, so far as this inquiry is concerned, are as follows:

"Second　I give and bequeath to my beloved wife, Jincy Rebecca Hairston, my farm about two miles east of Huntsville, in Madison county, state of Alabama, to have and to hold during her natural life, provided she pays the taxes on the land when the taxes are due and payable, and if she fails to pay said taxes and the land is sold to pay said taxes, then the land shall revert back to my estate and be equally divided between my nieces living at the time of said sale, if they will redeem in the time required by law. If my wife keeps the taxes paid up, at the time of her death the said lands shall be divided equally among my nieces living at the death of my wife. I also give and bequeath to my beloved wife all the household and kitchen furniture, all of the farming tools, and work stock on the place, and all provisions and feed of whatever nature, either for man or beast, that is on the place, also the milk cows

"Third, I give and bequeath to my two nieces, Jim Ruth Pitts and Pearl Pitts, the daughters of my sister, Pina Pitts, $5,000 each, to be paid to them in cash and to be paid out of my estate, either real or personal, except the lands left to my wife during her life. This $10,000 shall be over and above any of my other nieces and shall not be charged to Jim Ruth and Pearl in a division of my estate, but they shall share equally with my other nieces in the rest of my estate after the $10,000 has been paid, as it is my intention to give Jim Ruth Pitts $5,000 more than either of my other nieces, and to give Pearl Pitts $5,000 more than either of my other nieces.

"Fourth. All the rest and residue of my estate, real, personal and mixed, of which I shall die seised and possessed, or to which I shall be entitled at my decease, I give, devise and bequeath to be equally divided between all of my nieces living at the time of my death."

The widow, in the exercise of her statutory right, dissented from the will and was accorded dower and homestead out of the real estate, as well as all of the personal estate of $37,000, as allowed to her by the statutes, leaving no personal estate and practically no real estate, except the farm, out of which the legacies could be satisfied.

The authorities hold to three propositions of vital importance in the construction of wills:

1. Where the performance of a condition subsequent in a will has become impossible, without any fault on the part of the devisee (the remaindermen here), the condition will not, in contemplation of law, be regarded as broken, and there will be no defeasance.—*Lynch v. Melton*, 150 N. C. 595, 64 S. E. 497, 27 L. R. A. (N. S.) 684; *County of New Haven v. Parish of Trinity Church*, 82 Conn. 378, 73 Atl. 789; 17 Am. & Eng. Ann. Cas. 432.

2. The personal property of the testator is the primary fund for the discharge of debts and legacies, and they are not chargeable on lands, unless the intention so to charge them is manifested by express words, or by fair implication from the provisions of the will, read in the light of the environment of the testator and his estate.—*Gorman v. McDonnell*, 127 Ala. 549, 554, 28 South. 964; *Newsom v. Thornton*, 82 Ala. 402, 8 South. 261, 60 Am. Rep. 743.

3. A clear gift is not to be cut down by anything which does not, with reasonable certainty, indicate an intention to cut it down.—30 A. & E. Ency. Law, 688, and cases cited; 1 Underhill on Wills, § 358.

Item 3 of the will provides that the two legacies in question are to be paid to the legatees "in cash and to be paid out of my estate, either real or personal, *except the lands left to my wife during her life.*" Item 2 had left to his wife the farm, which is here sought to be charged, "during her natural life," subject to certain limitations, with remainder over to all his nieces in equal parts. It seems reasonably clear to our minds that the exception noted in item 2 was intended to include, by the ordinary words of description used, the farm *as a whole*, and not merely the wife's *life estate therein;* in other words, the testator was pointing out by a natural and convenient descriptive phrase a definite body of land to be excepted from the charge of the legacies which he was at the same time imposing upon the rest of his estate. Without the aid of such an exception, this court has apparently approved the doctrine that the presumption is against an intention to charge lands already specifically devised, and that a mere charge on "all my lands" is not sufficient to rebut the presumption.—*Newsom v. Thornton*, 82 Ala. 402, 406, 8 South. 261, 60 Am. Rep. 743. And this we regard as a sound rule.

It is ingeniously and forcibly argued, however, that other language in item 3 shows that the testator intended that these two legacies should be chargeable upon the *remainder* interests of the other nieces in the farm property, in that the $10,000 given was to be "over and above any of my other nieces, and shall not be charged to Jim Ruth and Pearl in a division of my estate;" and "it is my intention to give Jim Ruth Pitts $5,000 more than either of my other nieces, and to give Pearl Pitts $5,000 more than either of my other nieces." The insistence is that this language shows that these two nieces were highly favored objects of the testator's bounty, and that the predominating purpose of the will was to give to them the specified excess at all hazards out of any and all of his estate, except the life interest in the farm given to the wife. It is undoubtedly true that, if such an intent must be attributed to these preferential clauses, then it would be our duty to give it full effect, even to the extent of striking down, if necessary, previous specified devises. But we think the language is capable of a meaning which gives it a rational and appropriate field of operation consistently with the preservation of the specific devise already made—a result strongly favored by the principles of testamentary construction.

While the testator may have known that his widow could lawfully dissent from his will, there is nothing to show that he anticipated she would actually exercise this right. Hence the inference that he contemplated, and therefore intended, that these legacies should be satisfied from the personal property, which was ample for this purpose, and primarily liable in law; and his direction that they be paid out of his estate, either *real* or personal, may be reasonably referred to the other and substantial real estate then—when he made the will—presumably owned by him, and of the value of $6,000 or more, without necessarily involving the farm at all. This view is strengthened, we think, in the light of the testator's direction that the legacies should be paid in cash, and the strong improbability of his desiring or intending that a remainder interest should in any contingency be sold for that purpose—a proceeding that would be ordinarily both wasteful and unwise.

Keeping in mind that the testator's intention, as expressed in the language of the will, and as existing at the time of its execution, is the intention the court is required to gather from the four corners of the entire instrument, we are of the opinion that the conclusion reached by the chancellor was correct, and his decree is accordingly affirmed.

Affirmed.

DOWDELL, C. J., and SIMPSON and MCCLELLAN, JJ., concur.

Central of Georgia Ry. Co. *v.* Bagley.

Injury to Passenger.

(Decided May 9, 1911. Rehearing denied June 27, 1911.
55 South. 894.)

1. *Carrier; Passenger; Complaint.*—In an action for injury to a passenger, a complaint which alleges that the conductor negligently required the passenger to leave the train at a place highly dangerous for her to do so, on his refusal to accept her ticket, and which sets forth the facts as to danger of the place for an old and infirm person to disembark, states a cause of action as against the demurrer interposed.

2. *Same; Issues; Evidence.*—Where the action was for injury to a passenger who was required to disembark because her ticket was defective, and because she refused to pay fare, and the issues were the negligence of the carrier in requiring her to disembark at a dangerous place, and the plaintiff's contributory negligence, evidence that the passenger was old and infirm, that she was required to leave the train in the early morning before good daylight, that she carried a suitcase, that the conductor saw her but offered no assistance, that she left the car from the rear platform, and that the distance from the steps of the platform to the ground was from three to four feet, was competent under the issues.

3. *Same; Right to Eject Passenger.*—A carrier issuing a round trip ticket which needs to be validated to be good on the return trip need not carry a passenger on such ticket when the same has not been validated, and where such passenger refuses to pay fare, the passenger may be ejected.

4. *Same.*—In ejecting a passenger, which the carrier was authorized to do, the carrier must consider the safety of the passenger and not eject the passenger at a dangerous place.

5. *Same.*—Under the evidence in this case, it was a question for the jury as to whether in the justifiable ejection of the passenger, such passenger was ejected at a dangerous place resulting in injuries.

6. *Same.*—Whether an aged, female passenger was guilty of contributory negligence, in disembarking at a place designated by the carrier's agent, was under the facts in this case, a question for the jury.

7. *Same.*—Where a passenger believed in good faith that a ticket was good, and was required to leave the train because of a failure to present a good ticket or pay fare, such passenger could assume that the place selected by the conductor for her to alight with her baggage, was a safe place.

8. *Same; Existence of Relations; Obligation of Carrier.*—A person who boards a train in good faith believing that her ticket was good

is a passenger, and the carrier owes her a duty as such when requiring her to disembark.

9. *Same.*—A conductor who requires a passenger to disembark from the train because of the insufficiency of her ticket, and her refusal to pay the fare is required to know the perils of the place where he requires the passenger to disembark.

10. *Same; Misleading Instructions.*—Where the action was for injury to a passenger who was required to disembark because of the insufficiency of her ticket, and her refusal to pay fare, a charge asserting that if the jury were not reasonably satisfied that the conductor knew of the passenger's infirmity, and the peril attending her leaving the train at the time and place required, the carrier was not liable for injuries sustained in alighting, was misleading and properly refused.

11. *Evidence; Showing Purpose of Proof.*—Where the action was for injuries to a passenger ejected from a train, a question put to a witness as to whether he had not sworn as to the weight of a third person, was properly excluded in the absence of a showing of a purpose to lay a predicate to impeach the witness.

12. *Same; Opinion; Expert Testimony.*—An expert may not give his opinion as to whether the place at which a passenger was ejected from a train was a reasonably safe place for the passenger to alight; he may only state facts as to the nature of the place, and leave the determination of its reasonable safety to the jury.

13. *Witnesses; Cross Examination; Discretion.*—The latitude of cross examination to test the memory and sincerity of a witness rests largely within the discretion of the trial court.

14. *Charge of Court; Argumentative Instructions.*—A charge asserting that the jury cannot find that a person is old and infirm because fifty-six or fifty-seven years old, is properly refused as argumentative.

15. *Same; Invading Province of Jury.*—A charge asserting that if the jury believe the evidence they cannot find a particular fact, and one asserting that there is no evidence of a particular fact, may be properly refused as invading the province of the jury.

16. *Same; Conformity to Evidence.*—A charge predicated upon facts contrary to the evidence may be properly refused.

APPEAL from Birmingham City Court.

Heard before Hon. H. A. SHARPE.

Action by Mrs. W. W. Bagley against the Central of Georgia Railway Company for injury to her as a passenger. From a judgment for plaintiff, defendant appeals. Affirmed.

The second count is as follows: "The plaintiff claims of defendant the further sum of $10,000 as damages, for that heretofore, to wit, on the 28th day of December,

1904, defendant was a common carrier of passengers from Woodlawn Junction, in Jefferson county, Alabama, to Columbus, Georgia, by means of a train upon a railway; that on said day plaintiff boarded said train at said Woodlawn Junction with a ticket which plaintiff had purchased from defendant, purporting to be a ticket for one passage to said Columbus, Georgia, and plaintiff in good faith believed that said ticket entitled her to be carried by the defendant as its passenger from said Woodlawn Junction to said Columbus, and in good faith plaintiff boarded said train at said Woodlawn Junction to be carried by the defendant on said train as its passenger, and in good faith plaintiff tendered said ticket to defendant's conductor on said train as evidence of her right, as she believed, to ride thereon; that, notwithstanding said tender, said conductor required plaintiff to leave the train at a point at or near said Woodlawn Junction, which point was in Jefferson county, Alabama, and a long distance short of her said destination, to wit, said Columbus; that in or about requiring plaintiff to leave said train defendant's conductor negligently caused plaintiff, who was an old and infirm woman, to leave said train when the steps over which plaintiff was required to leave said train as aforesaid were a great distance from the ground, and by reason thereof it was highly dangerous to plaintiff to so leave said train at said point, and in or about attempting to leave said train at said point in obedience to said requirement of said conductor plaintiff slipped or fell, and her hip, knee, and shoulder were sprained, wrenched, broken, and otherwise injured, she was crippled and disfigured, suffered great mental and physical pain, her health and physical stamina were greatly and permanently impaired, she is likely for a long time to continue to suffer.

[Central of Georgia Ry. Co. v. Bagley.]

great mental and physical pain and to be crippled and disfigured, and she was put to great trouble, inconvenience, and expense for medicine, medical attention, care, and nursing in or about her effort to heal and cure her said wounds and injuries."

The demurrers are that the duty of defendant to carry plaintiff is a mere conclusion of the pleader, and no facts are shown making it the duty of the defendant to carry plaintiff as a passenger upon said train; that the wrongful ejection of plaintiff from said train is not shown to have proximately caused the injury. It is not alleged or shown that plaintiff, when she boarded said train, had any ticket which entitled her to be carried on said train; that the good faith of plaintiff in believing that she was entitled to be carried on said train would not constitute plaintiff a passenger thereon; that it is not alleged or shown how or in what manner the conductor was negligent in causing the plaintiff to do so. The complaint was afterwards amended by striking out the words "as defendant's passenger" where they first occur together in count 2.

The defense was contributory negligence in getting off on the side which she did, when by getting off on the other side, which was entirely safe and practicable for her to do, she would have gotten off upon the safe side. The other pleas set up the same facts in different ways, coupled with the allegation that she was incumbered with a heavy suit case.

The questions put to Moncrief, to which objection was sustained, are as follows: "Didn't you swear before, on the other trial, that Coyle weighed 160 pounds?" and "Will you tell the jury whether or not there was anything peculiar about his face when he left home that morning?" The question as to expert testimony to the witness Moncrief was as follows: "I will ask you as an expert whether there is any reason why a person, an ordinary person, not incumbered with any luggage at all, could not safely get off the train at that point?"

The following written charges were refused to the defendant: (20) "I charge you that, if you believe the evidence, the defendant's conductor was under no obligation or duty to assist the plaintiff in alighting from the train." (21) "I charge you that it is not the duty of the conductor to assist the plaintiff in carrying her baggage out of the car." (22) "I charge you that the fact that the plaintiff had with her a suit case would not impose upon the conductor any greater duty to assist her in leaving the train than if she did not have any baggage." (26) "I charge you that you cannot find that the plaintiff was old and infirm, merely because she was 56 or 57 years old." (27) "I charge you that if you believe the evidence, you cannot find that the conductor knew that the plaintiff was old and infirm." (28) "I charge you that there is no evidence that the conductor knew that the plaintiff was old and infirm." (12) "I charge you that, if you are not reasonably satisfied from the evidence that the conductor knew of the infirmity of the plaintiff and the peril attending her leaving the train at that time and place, the defendant would not be liable for any injuries she may have sustained in alighting from the train." (14) "I charge you that, if you believe from the evidence that the plaintiff was not a passenger on defendant's train on the 28th day of December, 1904, the conductor in charge of the train had a right to notify plaintiff to leave said train at said time and place, and the defendant is not liable for injury the plaintiff may have sustained, unless the conductor knew or ought to have known that for the plaintiff to get off the train at that time and place would be attended with danger to the plaintiff." (6) "I charge you that, under the undisputed evidence in this case, defendant's conductor had the right to require plaintiff to leave its train, and unless the jury is reasonably satisfied from the evidence that the conductor knew that the place where plaintiff alighted was dangerous or likely to injure plaintiff, then the plaintiff cannot recover." (17) "I charge you that the burden is upon the plaintiff to reasonably satisfy the jury by the evidence that the servants of the defendant knew that the place where the plaintiff alighted was dangerous or likely to produce injury." (19) "I charge you that the relation of passenger and carrier did not exist between the plaintiff and defendant on the morning of the 28th of December, 1904, at the time of the alleged injury, and that the defendant owed the plaintiff no duty as a passenger, and cannot be held liable for any injury she may have received in alighting from the train, unless the servants of the defendant intentionally caused or required the plaintiff to leave said train with knowledge or notice that it would be dangerous to the plaintiff to leave the train at that point." (24) "If the jury believe from the evidence that at the place where the plaintiff alighted there was a long step down from the steps of the car to the ground, which was obvious, and the plaintiff attempted to alight from the car with a heavy bag or dress suit case in her hand, without calling for assistance, and as a consequence fell and was injured, she cannot recover."

There was verdict and judgment for $4,000.

LONDON & FITTS, for appellant. The demurrers should have been sustained to the complaint.—*City Council v. Hughes*, 65 Ala. 201; *Lacy v. Holbrook*, 4 Ala. 88; *Lovell v. DeBardeleben C. & I. Co.*, 90 Ala. 13; *Patrick v. Hutchison*, 91 Ala. 320; *M. & O. v. George*,

94 Ala. 214; *Ensley R. Co. v. Chewning*, 93 Ala. 26; *Bescemer L. & I. Co. v. Campbell*, 121 Ala. 50; *Montgomery St. Ry. Co. v. Armstrong*, 123 Ala. 233. It must appear from the pleading that the servant knew that the time or place was not suitable for the ejection of passengers. —*Johnson v. L. & N.* 104 Ala. 241; *So. Ry. v. Williams*, 143 Ala. 212; *C. of G. v. Foshee*, 125 Ala. 199. The court erred in refusing charges 20, 21, and 22.—4 Elliott on Railroads, sec. 1628-a; 5 A. & E. Enc. of Law, 579; *So. Ry. v. Hobbs*, 63 L. R. A. 68; *Yarnell v. R. R. Co.* 18 L. R. A. 599. Plaintiff was conclusively presumed to have known the contents of the ticket, and to have agreed to the conditions on which it was sold.— *McGee v. Reynolds*, 117 Ala. 413; Hutchinson on Carriers, sec. 1028. The person was not old and infirm.— *Johnson v. L & N. supra; Sims v. S. C. Ry. Co.* 3 S. E. 301. An intruder is not a passenger.—*McGee v. Reynolds, supra; L. & N. v. Johnson*, 92 Ala. 204. There was no duty on the conductor to assist plaintiff from the train.—Authorities, supra. A conductor rightfully ejecting one from a train is not required to choose a place suitable to the age and infirmity of such person, of which he does not know, and which is not reasonably apparent to him.—*L. & N. v. Johnson*, 104 Ala. 241; s. c. 108 Ala. 62. The court erred in the admission of evidence.—*Ortez v. Jewett*, 23 Ala. 662; *Blakey v. Blakey*, 33 Ala. 661; *Bivens v. Brown*, 37 Ala. 424; *Beall v. Folmar*, 122 Ala. 414; *Scales v. Chambliss*, 35 Ala. 19; *Martin v. The State*, 104 Ala. 71; *Crawford v. The State*, 112 Ala. 17.

BOWMAN, HARSH & BEDDOW, for the appellee. The court properly overruled demurrers to the complaint.— 3 Thomp. on Neg. secs. 3244-5; *L. & N. v. Johnson*, 108 Ala. 62; *Haug v. Great N. Ry. Co.* 42 L. R. A. 664; 4

Enc. P. & P. 759, 760 and 762. When facts are stated out of which a duty arises, it is not necessary to state more than the negligent failure to do or perform.—*So. Ry. v. Burgess,* 143 Ala. 364; *C. of G. v. Edmundson,* 135 Ala. 336. 2 Hutchinson or Carriers, 1002. Having actually undertaken to eject a passenger, the conductor was required to do so with due care, all of which is sufficiently alleged.—*L. & N. v. Weathers,* 50 South. 270. Honesty and good faith are presumed.—1 Jones on Evid. sec. 12; 30 Conn. 559. Counsel discuss the charges refused, but without citation of authority.

DOWDELL, C. J.—The second count of the complaint, to which a demurrer was interposed and overruled, states a good and sufficient cause of action. The wrong complained of in this count and from which the alleged injury resulted consisted in the averred negligent act of the defendant's servant, the conductor on "said train," in requiring the plaintiff, an old and infirm woman, to leave "said train" at a place "highly dangerous" for her to do so. There is a general averment of negligence and facts stated as to the dangers of the place for an old and infirm person to disembark. The complaint we think was unobjectionable as to any of the stated grounds of demurrer, and in overruling it the action of the court was free from error.

The cause was tried on the plea of not guilty, and special pleas of contributory negligence. The plaintiff's evidence showed that the plaintiff as an intending passenger boarded the defendant's train at Woodlawn Junction, a suburb of the city of Birmingham, for return passage to her home in Columbus, Ga., on an excursion or round-trip ticket which she had purchased and paid for from the defendant railroad company at said Columbus, Ga., and on which she had been carried from

Columbus to Birmingham a few days previously; that she boarded the train in good faith, believing that she had the right to do so, and to be transported back to her home in Columbus on said ticket, which she tendered to the conductor, but which he refused to accept as fare for transportation because the same had not been "validated" as provided for in the ticket contract, and required the plaintiff to leave the train. The plaintiff testified: That she did not know of the required "validation" of the ticket until so informed by the conductor when she tendered it to him, and that, when she purchased it, she was not required by the selling agent to sign her name. The evidence of the plaintiff further showed that she was 57 years old at the time of the alleged injury, and was infirm; that the time she was required to leave the train was in the early morning before good daylight, the car she was leaving being lighted up, the morning foggy and very cold, the ground frozen. She carried a heavy suit case, and the conductor saw her when she was in the act of quitting the car, but offered no assistance. She left the car from the rear platform, and the distance from the steps of the platform to the ground was between three and four feet. That at the time she could not tell the distance to the ground from the step; it being too dark for her to see the ground. That, when the conductor told her she would have to get off, she asked him if she must get off at that place, and he replied, "Yes; right here." These were facts relevant and competent in evidence to go to the jury under the issues, and were properly admitted by the court.

While the defendant was under no legal duty to carry the plaintiff as a passenger on the return ticket without the same having been "validated" as provided in the contract, and had the right to eject her upon refusal to pay fare, yet in ejecting her the defendant was bound to consider her safety, and not to eject her at a dangerous place. In Hutchinson on Carriers, § 1084, it is said: "And in general it may be said that while the carrier may not be required to pay regard to the mere convenience of the passenger, when he has forfeited his right to be carried by his conduct or refusal to comply with his regulations, he cannot eject him in such manner as to endanger his safety, as by ejecting him while the train is in motion, *or in a dangerous place* (italics ours), without making himself liable for the consequences." And in section 1083 (same author) it is said: "Regard must be had for the age, sex, and condition of the passenger, and the surrounding circumstances, such as the state of the weather, the time of the day, the condition of the country. * * * The question of the suitableness of the time and place is therefore ordinarily one for the jury." In the case of *Louisville & Nashville Railroad Company v. Johnson, Adm'x*, 108 Ala. 62, 66, 19 South. 51, 53 (31 L. R. A. 372), this court, speaking through Haralson, J., said: "It is opposed to authority and reason and the common instincts of humanity to allow, because the passenger is intoxicated, whether to a greater or less degree, and misbehaves in a manner authorizing the conductor to expel him from the train, that such expulsion may be made without the exercise of due care for the safety of the passenger, having reference to the time, place and surroundings."

So it appears upon reason and authority that the defendant, in the exercise of its right in the expulsion of the plaintiff from its train, was bound to act with due care for her safety; and, in the determination of this question, the elements of time, place, condition of the weather, the age and sex of the party are to be taken into consideration by the jury. The carrier is bound to take notice of the character of the place at which he exercises his right of ejecting or expelling a passenger from his train.

And whether or not it is a dangerous place becomes a question of fact for the determination of the jury under all the attendant circumstances.

There was no error in overruling defendant's objections to questions put to the witness Moncrief on cross-examination. It does not appear from the record that the purpose of the questions was to lay any predicate for impeachment of the witness.—*Floyd v. State*, 82 Ala. 21, 2 South. 683.

The latitude of a cross-examination for the purpose of testing the memory, sincerity, etc., of the witness, is largely within the discretion of the trial court, and may and often does relate to immaterial matters without the issues of the case.—*Southern Railway Co. v. Brantley*, 132 Ala. 657, 32 South. 300; *Sloss-Sheffield Steel & Iron Co. v. House*, 157 Ala. 663, 47 South. 573; *Noblin v. State*, 100 Ala. 14, 14 South. 767; *Tobias & Co. v. Triest & Co.*, 103 Ala. 670, 15 South. 914.

There was no error in refusing to allow the witness Moncrief, on the objection of the plaintiff, to give his opinion as an expert as to whether the place was a reasonably safe place for the plaintiff to leave the train. This was no matter for expert testimony, and, as well stated by the trial court, it was for the witness to state the facts as to the nature of the place, and for the jury to determine whether it was reasonably safe.

The plaintiff in leaving the train at the place where she was required by the conductor to leave under the circumstances had a right to assume that it was a safe place for her to get off, and in getting off with her suit case in her hand could not be said, as a matter of law, to have been guilty of negligence; and the question was one properly left to the jury and the general affirmative charges requested by the defendant along this line under the pleas of contributory negligence were properly refused.

Assuming that the plaintiff boarded the train in good faith and honestly believing that she would be carried on her return trip ticket back to Columbus, Ga., to all intents and purposes as to her safety in being put off of the train, there existed the relation of passenger and carrier, and the defendant was under the same duty of rendering needful assistance in discharging the plaintiff from the train as if she had been a passenger. Written charges 20, 21, and 22, requested by the defendant, were therefore properly refused.

Charge 26, if not otherwise faulty, was properly refused as being argumentative.

Charge 27 was invasive of the province of the jury and was properly refused.

Charge 28, refused to the defendant, has been frequently condemned by this court. The court is not required to tell the jury that there is no evidence of a particular fact.

Charge 12 was not only misleading in tendency, but was otherwise inherently bad.

The duty rested on the defendant's conductor to know of the perils of the place where he required the plaintiff to leave the train.

Charges 14, 16, 17, and 19, refused to the defendant, are each and all of them in their statement of the law opposed to the views we entertain, and as herein above expressed, and no error was committed in their refusal.

Charge 24 assumes that the long step down from the steps of the car to the ground was obvious, while the plaintiff testified that she could not see the ground as she was descending the steps of the car, and the charge was therefore bad, besides being misleading in other respects.

We fail to find any reversible error in the record, and the judgment is affirmed.

Affirmed.

SIMPSON, McCLELLAN, and MAYFIELD, JJ., concur.

Birmingham Railway, Light & Power Co. *v.* Fisher.

Injury to Passenger.

(Decided June 15, 1911. 55 South. 995.)

1. *Carriers; Passengers; Negligence; Complaint.*—Counts charging simple negligence of a common carrier to the injury of a passenger on one of its cars, which alleged that the defendant was a common carrier of passengers, that plaintiff was a passenger and that it so negligently conducted itself in and about her carriage thereon that at a certain time and place plaintiff was thrown or caused to fall from said car, are sufficient.

2. *Same; Proximate Cause.*—It is enough that the facts averred in an action for injury to a passenger lead with requisite certainty to the conclusion that the injury proximately resulted from the negligence charged.

3. *Same; Wantonness.*—A count for wanton injury which alleges that the servant or agent of defendant in control or charge of its cars while acting within the line and scope of his authority as such, wantonly or intentionally caused plaintiff to be injured, is not subject to demurrer for uncertainty or indefiniteness.

4. *Same; Proximate Cause; Instructions.*—In an action for injury to a passenger the hypotheses in instruction must include the condition that the negligence or wrong charged in the complaint afforded the proximate cause of the injury, as a basis of recovery.

5. *Same; Wantonness; Evidence.*—The evidence in this case held sufficient to go to the jury, on the question of willfulness or wantonness of the injury to a passenger while alighting from an electric car, with the consequent right of imposition of punitive damages.

6. *Evidence; Expert; Hypothetical Question.*—It is a party's right to ask an expert's opinion on the state of the evidence tending to support his theory of the subject of the inquiry for expert opinion.

7. *Contributory Negligence; Necessity of Pleading.*—Where contributory negligence is not pleaded the defendant is not entitled to have instructions on that issue.

8. *Same; Wantonness.*—Contributory negligence will not defeat a recovery for wanton or willful wrong.

APPEAL from Jefferson Circuit Court.

Heard before Hon. A. O. LANE.

Action by Mrs. Ora M. Fisher against the Birmingham Railway, Light & Power Company for damages for injury to her while a passenger. Judgment for plaintiff, and defendant appeals. Affirmed.

The complaint was as follows: Count 1: "Plaintiff claims of defendant $10,000 as damage, for that heretofore, to wit, on the 18th day of November, 1909, defendant was a common carrier of passengers by means of a car operated by electricity upon a railway known as the 'East Lake Line,' in Jefferson county, Alabama; that on said day plaintiff was defendant's passenger on said car, and the defendant so negligently conducted itself in or about carrying plaintiff as defendant's passenger on such car that while plaintiff was defendant's passenger on said car, and said car was at a point on said line, to wit, at or near Forty-seventh street, plaintiff was struck by an object, to wit, a gate on said car, and was thrown or caused to fall, and was cut, bruised, shocked and otherwise injured in her person. (Here follows the catalogue of her injuries.)" Count 2: "The plaintiff claims of defendant $10,000 damages, for that, heretofore, on, to wit, the 18th day of November, 1909, defendant was a common carrier of passengers by means of a car operated by electricity upon a railway known as the 'East Lake Line,' in Jefferson county, Alabama; that on said day, while plaintiff was defendant's passenger on said car, defendant's servant or agent in charge or control of said car, acting within the line and scope of his authority as such, wantonly or intentionally caused plaintiff to be injured in her person while on said car, and while said car was at a point on said line, to wit, at or near Forty-seventh street, and to suffer the injuries and damage set out in the first count of the complaint." Count 3: "Plaintiff claims of defendant $10,000 as damages, for that heretofore, to wit, on the 18th day of November, 1909, defendant was a common carrier of passengers by means of a car operated by electricity upon a railway known as the 'East Lake Line,' in Jefferson county, Alabama; that on said day plaintiff was defendant's passenger on said car, and the defendant so negligently conducted itself in or about carrying plaintiff as defendant's passenger on said car that, while plaintiff was defendant's passenger on said car and said car was at a point on said line, to wit, at or near Forty-seventh street, plaintiff was thrown or caused to fall, and suffered the injuries and damage set out in the first count of the complaint, wherefore she sues."

The demurrers are that the counts are vague, uncertain, and indefinite; that it does not appear with sufficient certainy what duty the defendant owed the plaintiff; it does not appear how the duty was violated, or that any duty was violated; said counts are repugnant and inconsistent; the facts averred do not constitute actual negligence; the negligence averred is merely the conclusion of the pleader, and it does not appear that the negligence complained of was the proximate cause of the injury.

The following is the question propounded to Dr. Talley: "If the lady hadn't had that pain before, and on or about the 18th of November, 1909, that is, prior to the time you saw her, she had been struck in the face with a car gate and knocked backward, and then, being out on the platform of the car, the car was started and knocked or threw her against the car, and she was dazed from that, and she wasn't off the car, or got off the car, and in a little while went to a house near by and was put to bed, and that day went home and remained in bed for some time, and at the time she was hurt, or from the time she was hurt, continued to suffer that pain in her spine, and had not suffered it before, what, in your judgment, would be the cause of·that pain and that condition of the spine?'"

TILLMAN, BRADLEY & MORROW, and CHARLES E. RICE, for appellant. The court erred in overruling appellant's demurrer to the first count.—*W. Ry. v. Mutch*, 97 Ala. 196; *B. R. L. & P. Co. v. Moore*, 163 Ala. 44; *B. R. L & P. Co. v. Jones*, 146 Ala. 277; *Hudgins v. So. Ry.*. 148 Ala. 154; 1 Cooley on Torts, 99. The court erred in permitting the hypothetical question to Dr. Talley.—*B. R. L. & P. Co. v. Butler*, 135 Ala. 388; 113 Ill. App. 188; 72 Pac. 590. The court erred in overruling demurrer to the second count of the complaint.—*M. & C. R. R. Co. v. Martin*, 117 Ala. 382; *L. & N. v. Mitchell*, 134 Ala. 266; *L. & N. v. Orr*, 121 Ala. 489. The court erred in overruling demurrer to the third count.—Authorities, supra. The court erred in refusing charge 4 to the appellant.— *Watkins v. B. R. L. & P. Co.* 120 Ala. 146. Counsel discuss other charges given and refused, but without further citation of authority.

BOWMAN, HARSH & BEDDOW, for appellee. The first count was sufficient.—2 Chitty, 596; 1 Cyc. 572. There was no error in permitting the hypothetical question.—*Parrish v. The State*, 139 Ala. 43; *B. R. & E. Co. v. Ellard*, 135 Ala. 443. The second count sufficiently avers wantonness.—*C. of G. v. Foshee*, 125 Ala. 226; *Haley v. K. C. M. & B.*,

113 Ala. 651; *L. & N. v. Orr*, 121 Ala. 489; *Russell v. Huntsville R. L. & P. Co.* 137 Ala. 628. The evidence was sufficient to support the averment of wantonness.—*So. Ry. v. Bush*, 122 Ala. 471; *Same v. Shelton*, 136 Ala. 192. Counsel discuss charges given and refused but without further citation of authority.

McCLELLAN, J.—Action for damages for personal injuries by passenger against the carrier.

The first and third counts, charging simple negligence to the injury of plaintiff, were not subject to demurrer. —*L. & N. R. R. Co. v. Perkins*, 152 Ala. 133, 44 South. 602.

In instructions to the jury it is essential that the hypotheses to a recovery include the condition that the negligence or wrong charged in the complaint afforded the proximate cause of the injury complained of.—*B. R. L. & P. Co. v. Moore*, 163 Ala. 44, 50 South. 115; *B. R. L. & P. Co.. v. Jones*, 146 Ala. 277, 41 South. 146.

In pleading a count is sufficient in that respect if the facts averred lead, with requisite certainty, to the conclusion that the injury suffered proximately resulted from the negligence charged.

The second count was not subject to the demurrer.

The court did not err in overruling the objection to the hypothetical question put to the expert witness, Dr. Tally. The grounds of objection to the question were that it did not sufficiently hypothesize the facts in evidence, that it invaded the jury's province, and that it sought a conclusion. It was the examiner's right to seek the expert's opinion upon the state of the evidence tending to support his theory of the subject of the inquiry for expert opinion.—*L. & N. R. R. Co. v. Banks*, 132 Ala. 471, 31 South. 573; *B. R. L. & P. Co. v. Ellard*, 135 Ala. 433, 33 South. 276.

There was testimony upon which, if credited, the jury might have rested a finding justifying the imposition of punitive damages. It appeared from some of the evidence that the plaintiff was injured as the result of the closing of two entrance gates, blocking, when closed, the passage from the platform, over the step, to the ground. These gates were operated by means of a lever. To open them the lever was pulled; and to close them the lever was pushed back. The mechanism was designed to be operated by the motorman from his position on the car. It did not appear from the testimony that the closing (if so) of the gates on this occasion was otherwise caused than by the means and by the servant indicated. There was testimony tending to show that the motorman was in his place at the time. The motorman testified, on the cross, that from his place he "could see a passenger in the act of getting off" the car; that the cars "are all arranged so the motorman can look back through the car and then look into the mirror and see what is going on along the gate side of the car, and at the place for passengers to get off."

If, as some of the testimony tended to show, the gates were closed while plaintiff was in the act of alighting from the step flush with the outer edge of which the lower lines of the. gates were constructed, it was open to the jury to find from the testimony that the motorman operated the lever, and that he could have seen and did see the plaintiff then so situated with reference to the gates as that, if they were then closed, the plaintiff would be struck by one or both of them. And, if these conclusions were entertained by the jury, it was then further open to them to find that the act of closing the gates, under those circumstances, was so colored as to bring the event within the aggravated wrong charged in count 2 of the complaint. Upon the indicated theory of concurrent fact and knowledge, the ruling stated conforms with those made in *B. R. L. & P. Co. v. Jung,* 161 Ala. 461, 49 South. 434; *Sou. Ry. Co. v. Bush.* 122 Ala. 471, 26 South. 168, and *R. & D. R. R. Co. v. Vance,* 93 Ala. 144, 9 South. 574, 30 Am. St. Rep. 41, among others. Accordingly, the affirmative charge, upon count 2, and charge 6, instructing against the awarding of punitive damages, were properly refused to defendant.

No plea of contributory negligence appears in the transcript. For that reason charge 4 was well refused to defendant. Furthermore, that defense, if interposed, would not have sufficed to defeat a recovery under some of the evidence on the count (2) charging wanton or intentional wrong.

The evidence required the submission of the determination of the issues of fact under the pleading to the jury. Hence the several affirmative charges requested by the defendant were correctly refused.

No error appearing, the judgment is affirmed.

Affirmed.

SIMPSON, ANDERSON, and MAYFIELD, JJ., concur.

Alabama City G. & A. Ry. Co. *v.* Cox.

Injury to Passenger.

(Decided June 17, 1911. 55 South. 909.)

1. *Carriers; Breach of Contract; Passengers.*—Where the action was for injury received by a passenger while attempting to walk back to the station after being carried beyond it, it was immaterial whether the carrier's conductor knew that the passenger did not know of a safe route from the point where she alighted, back to her station, or that the trainmen had reason to believe that the passenger would encounter danger.

[Alabama City G. & A. Ry. Co. v. Cox.]

2. *Same; Complaint; Sufficiency.*—In an action by a passenger for injuries received while returning to a station beyond which he had been negligently carried, the complaint need not negative the fact that there was an open, obvious and safe way which the passenger could have traveled back to the station, since such facts were available in defense.

3. *Same; Carrying Beyond Destination; Liability.*—Where it was undisputed that a carrier stopped its train beyond a station, and that a passenger destined for that station alighted at night to walk back to that station, that she was aged and feeble, and was injured when attempting to walk back to the station, but there was a conflict in the evidence as to whether the train stopped at the station for the reception and discharge of passengers, the question of the liability of the carrier was one for the jury.

4. *Same; Complaint.*—A complaint for injuries to a passenger carried beyond her destination and required to alight and walk back to the station need not allege 'hat her eyesight was defective, or that she could not see at night, or that her affliction was apparent to the conductor, in order to state a cause of action.

5. *Same.*—The fact that a passenger carried beyond her station pursued a dangerous way back to the station, when a safe way was obvious and open to her selection was available only in support of the defense of contributory negligence, and need not have been negatived by the complaint.

6. *Same; Continuance of Relation.*—The relation of passenger and carrier continues to exist until the passenger has had reasonable time and opportunity to alight from a train and leave the carrier's premises in the ordinary way.

7. *Same; Defenses.*—In the absence of any allegation in the complaint as to defective eyesight, a defendant believing that the injuries were caused from the defective eysight of the plaintiff must by special plea allege such facts in order to make them available as a defense.

8. *Charge of Court; Requisites.*—Instructions must refer to and be hypothesized upon the evidence in the case.

9. *Same; Construction.*—Where a charge as a whole correctly states the law, it will be held sufficient although isolated portions thereof may be erroneous.

APPEAL from Gadsden City Court.

Heard before Hon. JOHN H. DISQUE.

Action by Mary E. Cox against Alabama City, Gadsden & Attalla Railway Company. From a judgment for plaintiff, defendant appeals. Affirmed.

The complaint consisted of four counts, and, as amended, count 1 states the relation between the parties to have been that of passenger and carrier, the pay-

ment of fare, the information to the conductor in charge
of the car that the plaintiff desired to alight at Car
Works station, and the negligent failure of the servants
or agents of the defendant in charge of the car to stop
said car at said station, which was a regular and convenient place for passengers to alight, and which was
located on the public highway, coupled with the further
allegation that the servants or agents in charge of the
car negligently allowed said car to pass by and beyond
said station 40 yards or more before stopping said car.
Then follows the catalogue of her injuries, which are
alleged to be permanent. It is also averred that the only
apparent way to plaintiff or open way for her to return
to said station from the point where she was put off was
along defendant's line of railway. This was well known
to the conductor, or by the exercise of ordinary diligence
should have been known to him; but the existence
of the railroad crossing on said line of railway, and the
existence of the trestle or culvert between the point
where plaintiff was put off and the station of her destination, rendered said way dangerous to be traveled by
plaintiff at the time and under the circumstances stated.
The second count was charged out. The third count alleges the plaintiff's injuries to have resulted proximately
from the negligence of the conductor in charge of the
car upon which she was a passenger, in that at the time
he caused plaintiff to alight from said car he knew, or
by the exercise of ordinary diligence ought to have
known, that plaintiff would probably return to the Car
Works station by walking along defendant's railway
track, and also knew of the existence of said railway
crossing, and said trestle or culvert, and also knew, or
by the exercise of reasonable diligence could have
known, that the existence of such crossing or culvert
or trestle rendered it dangerous to plaintiff to walk

along said railroad track to said Car Works station, without the knowledge of existence of such switch and culvert or trestle, and also knew, or by the exercise of ordinary diligence should have known, that the existence of the conditions above mentioned were unknown to plaintiff, and negligently failed to notify or warn plaintiff of the existence of said railroad crossing, and of the existence of said switch, or trestle, or culvert. The fourth count avers the negligent carrying of plaintiff beyond her destination, and the negligent failure to stop at the station, with the further averment that the route which she took to travel back to such station was the one which a reasonably prudent person would have taken under the circumstances surrounding plaintiff at the time. The demurrers raise the point discussed in the opinion.

The charges referred to in the opinion are as follows: (5) "If the injuries resulting to plaintiff were proximately caused by the defective eyesight of plaintiff, she cannot recover." (6) "If the defect of eyesight of plaintiff was an intervening sufficient cause of her injury, she is not entitled to recover." (7) "The court charges the jury that the plaintiff in her complaint does charge that her injuries were caused by her defective eyesight, not that the defective condition of her eyesight contributed to her injuries. If the jury are satisfied from the evidence that plaintiff's injuries were proximately caused by the defective eyesight, she cannot recover." (8) "If the plaintiff's injuries would likely not have occurred, had it not been for the defective condition of plaintiff's eyesight, she cannot recover." (9) "If the jury are reasonably satisfied from the evidence that plaintiff's injury would not have occurred, had it not been for the defective condition of her eyesight, she cannot recover."

HOOD & MURPHREE, for appellant. The complaint was subject to demurrers interposed.—*Sellers' case*, 93 Ala. 9; *Quick's case*, 126 Ala. 564; *Dancy's case*, 97 Ala. 338; *Morgan's case*, 49 South. 865. The court erred in its oral charge to the jury, and in refusing the charges requested by appellant.—Authorities, supra.

GOODHUE & BLACKWOOD, for appellee. No brief reached the reporter.

MAYFIELD, J.—The appellee, a woman about 60 or 65 years of age, sued appellant, a common carrier of passengers.

Each count of the complaint upon which the trial was had, as last amended, alleged the relation of passenger and common carrier between plaintiff and defendant, and therefrom a duty on the part of the latter to carry plaintiff as a passenger, in accordance with a contract alleged, from the city of Gadsden to a station upon its line known as Car Works station; and then alleged a breach of that duty, in that the carrier failed to stop its car at the station of the plaintiff's destination, but carried her by and beyond it some 40 yards or more, and there put her off; that the plaintiff, in attempting to find her way back to the station, fell over a switch of defendant's railway, and thereby injured herself; and that later, while still on her way back to the station, along the defendant's railway track, she stepped into an open culvert or trestle, thereby severely injuring herself. Each count contains the usual and appropriate averments as to the injuries and damages suffered by the plaintiff; and each alleges that such injuries and damages were the proximate result of the negligence of the defendant's agents or servants in charge of the car, in failing to put her off at her station, and carrying her such a distance beyond it in the night time. Each count of the complaint, as last amended, stated a good cause of action, and was not subject to any grounds of demurrer assigned as error.

It was not necessary that the complaint should allege that the defendant's conductor was cognizant that the plaintifff did not know of a safe route from the point where she alighted back to the station; nor that the defendant's servants or agents had reason to believe that the plaintiff would encounter danger at the place and time, and in the manner, alleged. It was the duty of the defendant to put the plaintiff off at her station, and not some 40 yards beyond it.

It was not necessary for the complaint to negative the fact that there was an open, obvious, and safe way, which the plaintiff could have traveled, from the point where she was put off, back to the station. If this were so, it would be proper matter for a plea, and not for the complaint to negative.

The complaint averred the advanced age and feeble conditions of the plaintiff, and that it was in the nighttime that she was carried some 40 yards past her station; this being an actionable breach of duty on the part of the defendant toward the plaintiff. If the defendant's servants or agents in charge or control of the car on this occasion had actual knowledge of the plaintiff's infirmities, and of the danger which she would probably incur in consequence of the breach, such fact would be proper to go to the amount of the damages recoverable; but it is not necessary to the recovery of any damages, and is therefore not necessary to the statement of a good cause of action.

"Carriers must be equally careful not to pass beyond the alighting platform or station, and thus to require or make it necessary for the passenger to alight without returning to it. * * * And where the passen-

ger is required, either expressly or impliedly, to leave the car without assistance, and to find his way unaided back to the station, during which time he received injury, the carrier is liable. This is held to be true, even though the passenger is carried upon a freight train. Much less does the carrier discharge his duty where he puts the passenger off away from the depot, at night, in a strange place, and requires him thence to return to the place at which he should have been discharged."
—2 Hutchinson on Carriers, § 1126.

"As a general rule, it may be said that the relation of carrier and passenger does not cease with the arrival of the train at the passenger's destination, but continues until the passenger has had a reasonable time and opportunity to safely alight from the train at the place provided by the carrier for the discharge of passengers, and to leave the carrier's premises in the customary manner."—*Ib.*, § 1016.

"Where a passenger signaled a street car conductor to put her off at a given stopping place, and the conductor understood the signal, but failed to put her off at the proper station, held to be culpable negligence, and that if the plaintiff, while attempting to cross the track to go to her home, fell and suffered injury on account of being put off at the wrong place, the carrier would be liable."—*Melton v. Railway Co.,* 153 Ala. 95, 45 South. 151, 16 L. R. A. (N. S.) 467.

"Passengers are entitled to be carried to their destination, and carriers have no right to put them off the train before reaching it."—*L. & N. R. R. Co. v. Quinn,* 146 Ala. 330, 39 South. 756.

"It is the duty of the conductor of a common carrier to take up the tickets within a reasonable time after leaving a station, and when he takes up the ticket to a flag station, it is notice to him that the passenger desires to get off at such station."—*L. & N. R. R. Co. v. Seale,* 160 Ala. 584, 49 South. 323.

"It is the duty of common carriers to stop their trains at their stations long enough to allow passengers a reasonable time in which to alight. What is a sufficient time is usually a question for the jury."—*Dilburn v. L. & N. R. R. Co.,* 156 Ala. 28, 47 South. 210.

"It is the duty of common carriers, such as street car companies, to exercise the highest degree of care in stopping their cars for passengers to alight, and in providing a reasonably safe place for them to alight."—*Mobile Light Co. v. Walsh,* 146 Ala. 295, 40 South. 560.

"Common carriers are liable in damages to passengers who are carried beyond their destination without fault on the part of the passenger, whether resulting from the negligence of the carrier or a breach of his contract."—*North Ala. Co. v. Daniel,* 158 Ala. 414, 48 South. 50.

Whether the car stopped at the station on this occasion for the reception or discharge of passengers was a disputed question, and the defendant was not entitled to the affirmative charge on the theory that the car was stopped at the plaintiff's destination. The evidence is without dispute that it did stop beyond the station (though the exact distance is in dispute), that the plaintiff was put off the car beyond her station, at night, that she was aged and feeble, and that she was injured in the manner alleged, while attempting to find her way back to the station.

It was not necessary that the complaint should allege that the appellee's eyesight was defective, or that she could not see at night, nor for the complaint to allege, nor the evidence to show, that this affliction was apparent to the conductor, in order to state a cause of action. As before stated, such allegations or proof might be proper or necessary as to punitive damages, and therefore go to the amount of the recovery, but not to the absolute right of recovery, as is insisted by the appellant in this case.

If the plaintiff pursued a dangerous way back to the station, when a safe path was obvious and open to her selection, this would be matter proper for a plea of contributory negligence, and it was not necessary for the plaintiff to negative it in her pleadings, nor was she required to prove such negative matter, in order to entitle her to recover.

The trial court, among other things, charged the jury that: "Passengers who take passage on a street car remain passengers until they get to their destination, and this relation of passenger and common carrier would exist between the passenger and the defendant until she got back to her place of destination." Again the court charged that: "The relation of passenger and common carrier would exist between the passenger and the defendant until she got back to her place of destination." If there can be said to be any erroneous or misleading tendencies in these excerpts from the charge of the court, they were cured or relieved of such infirmities when considered in connection with the charge of the court as a whole.

The instructions of the court must, of course, be referred to the evidence of the particular case on trial; and when those under consideration are so referred we feel confident that there was no error, nor injury to the defendant, either in the charge of the court as a whole, or in those parts to which it reserved exceptions.

Of course, the relation of passenger and carrier continues to exist only until the passenger has had reasonable time and opportunity to alight from the train, and to leave the carrier's premises in the customary manner. Whether the passenger failed to depart within a reasonable time, or whether she left the train or the carrier's premises by an unusual route, and in a careless or negligent manner, was a question for the jury. There is nothing in the charge of the court in this case contrary to the rules stated by Mr. Hutchinson and Mr. Elliott, and recognized by the courts, as to when such relation ceases.

We are unable to find any possible theory upon which the defendant was entitled to the affirmative charge. There was no error in the refusal to give any of the defendant's requested charges assigned as error in this case. Most of these charges (5, 6, 7, 8, and 9) were requested upon the theory that it was the duty of the court to charge the jury that, if the plaintiff's injuries were proximately caused by her defective eyesight, she was not entitled to recover; and the refusal to give them is here insisted on as error. We cannot agree with counsel for appellant that it was the duty of the court to give these instructions, for this would be tantamount to its instructing the jury that if the plaintiff's eyesight was defective she could not recover in this case, because she had failed to allege such defect in her complaint.

If the defendant conceived that the injury complained of was the result of, or was proximately caused by, the defective eyesight of the plaintiff, and not by the negligence of its agents or servants, as alleged in the complaint, it should have set up such matter by a special plea, and thereby made it an issuable fact. It is conceded by counsel for defendant that it was not one of the issues on trial, because there was no allegation in the complaint as to such defective sight, nor was there any plea averring that the injuries suffered by the plaintiff were in consequence of such defective sight. The charges were therefore abstract and misleading. As before stated, there was ample evidence to support the verdict of the jury, and the mere fact that some of the evidence tended to show that the plaintiff's eyesight was defective was not sufficient to take from the jury the question whether or not the plaintiff had proved any count of her complaint.

While the plaintiff probably could have based a count upon the negligence of the defendant in putting her off the car in the manner described, and because of her defective eyesight, which was known to the defendant's agents or servants in charge of the car, if such fact was known, it was not necessary for her to do so. She had other counts which were sufficient, and evidence ample to support them, believed by the jury. The defendant had no right to require that she should seek recovery on such count. As before stated, if the defendant conceived that plaintiff's injuries were the result of her defective eyesight, which was unknown to its agents or servants in charge of the car, and was therefore not the result of the negligence of the defendant, it should have pleaded such matter as a special defense.

Finding no error, the judgment of the trial court must be affirmed.

Affirmed.

SIMPSON, McCLELLAN, and SAYRE, JJ., concur.

Scales v. Central Iron & Coal Co.

Injury to Servant.

(Decided April 13, 1911.　Rehearing denied May 5, 1911.
55 South. 821.)

1. *Pleading; Filing; Time; Tuscaloosa County Court.*—Acts 1896-7, p. 267, requires plea to be filed within thirty days after service of complaint, and authorizes default on motion at any time thereafter, and in the absence of a motion for judgment by default it is not error to refuse to strike pleas filed after the thirty day period.

2. *Evidence; Opinions.*—Questions asked a witness as to the cause of the reduction of plaintiff's wages were properly excluded as calling for an opinion.

3. *Master and Servant; Injury; Jury Question.*—The evidence in this case examined and held to require a submission to the jury of whether or not plaintiff's foreman was guilty of negligence, causing the injury complained of.

(Simpson and Sayre, JJ., dissent.)

APPEAL from Tuscaloosa County Court.

Heard before Hon. H. B. FOSTER.

Action by Willis A. Scales against the Central Iron & Coal Company, for damages for injuries alleged to have been received while in its employment. Judgment for the defendant and plaintiff appeals. Reversed and remanded.

BROWNE & WARD, for appellant. The court erred in overruling appellant's motion to strike the pleas filed more than thirty days after service.—Acts 1896-7, p. 267. The court erred in overruling demurrers to plea 3. —*Meriwether v. Sayre M. & M. Co.*, 49 South. 916; *So. Ry. Co. v. Guyton*, 25 South. 38. The court erred in giving the general charge for the appellee.—*B. So. Ry. v. Fox*, 52 South. 889, and authorities supra. An employe does not assume risks incident to the failure of his superior to guard against dangers, which may be guarded against by the exercise of ordinary care.—*T. C. I. & R. R. Co. v. King*, 50 South. 75; *S. L. & S. F. Ry. Co. v. Brantly*, 53 South. 308. It was a question for the jury whether the foreman was negligent to plaintiff's damage.—*Bessemer L. & I. Co. v. Campbell*, 25 South. 793; *Western S. C. & F. Co. v. Hammond*, 40 South. 280, and authorities supra.

JONES & PENICK, for appellee. There was no evidence to sustain the 1st, 2nd, 3rd, 4th and 6th counts, and the 5th count was not sufficiently made out.—*M. & O. v.* against the appellee, for personal injuries receibed by plaintiff assumed the risk.—1 Lebatt 611-614.

SIMPSON, J.—This is an action by the appellant eleventh section of said act provides that defendants the plaintiff while working as a carpenter on the furnace plant of defendant.

The first assignment of error insisted on, is to the action of the court in refusing to strike defendant's pleas 3, 4, 5, and 6, the contention being that said pleas were not filed within the time prescribed by the special act under which said Tuscaloosa county law and equity court was established.—Acts 1896-97, p. 262. The eleventh section of said act provides that defendants shall appear and demur or plead to the complaint within 30 days after service, and authorizes judgment by default, on motion of plaintiff, at any time thereafter. The complaint was filed February 14, 1910, and served February 16, 1910, demurrer filed May 20, 1910, and said pleas were filed June 6 and 7, 1910. In the meantime no motion was made for a judgment by default. Said section of said act prescribes terms upon which pleas may be filed after judgment by default, but makes no special requirements as to terms on filing pleadings after the 30 days and before default claimed. There was no error in refusing to strike said pleas.

There was no error in sustaining the objection to the questions as to the cause of the reduction of plaintiff's wages, as the questions called for the opinion of the witness, and should have asked for facts, leaving it to the jury to determine why the wages were reduced.

The plaintiff, as a carpenter, was working under the orders of Mack Powell, to whose orders he was bound to conform, and did conform. The dust box is cylindrical in shape, from 10 to 18 feet in diameter, and 20 feet or more in length, large enough for men to walk inside. The dust was transmitted from the furnace above, down into said dust box, through large pipelike passageways called "down comers," which are large enough for a man to pass through. For the purpose of relining said dust box, the carpenters had erected a scaffold therein, upon which scaffold were placed sections of ovalshaped lagging which supported the brick that were used in lining said dust box, until sufficiently dried for said lagging to be removed. No light came into said dust box except such as shone through two explosion doors in the top thereof, one being at each end of said dust box, and each large enough for a man to crawl through. There were wires for transmitting electricity, hanging through the explosion doors, upon which were placed electric lights, but there were no bulbs or electric lamps in the sockets, though there had been the day before.

While the plaintiff was in the performance of his general duties, he and his squad were ordered by said Powell to go into said dust box and tear out the scaffolding or lagging, there then being one or more electric lights furnishing sufficient light to work in said dust box. On the next morning, when plaintiff went into said dust box to continue said work, he discovered that there was no electric lamp or bulb therein, and he came out and reported the fact to said Powell, stating that he did not like to go in and work in the dark while the brick masons were working above, in the "down comer," for fear that something might fall on him; and said Powell ordered him to go back to work, stating that they could not wait for the electrician to put lights in. Plaintiff, in obedience to orders, then went back, and when he had passed one piece of lumber through the bootleg below, a piece of lumber, with an eight or ten penny nail protruding from the end thereof, fell from some point above and struck plaintiff on the head, causing the injury complained of. Plaintiff could not see said plank, nor how to protect himself therefrom, nor where it came from.

[Scales v. Central Iron & Coal Co.]

It will be observed that the only negligence complained of is the failure to renew the electric bulb.
There is no evidence tending to show that if the bulb
had been there, the plaintiff could have seen into the
regions above him, so as to discover the falling plank
in time to avoid it; no causal connection is shown between the absence of the light, and the falling of the
plank, and there is no evidence tending to show whether the falling of the plank was the result of the negligence of any one; and there is no allegation or proof as
to who was responsible for the falling of the plank.
For aught that appears, it may have resulted from the
negligence of the plaintiff and his co-workers, in constructing the scaffold. In fact, the explosion doors being closed, there was no place for the plank to fall
from, except the platform that had been erected by
plaintiff and his co-employes.

There was no error in the action of the court in sustaining the motion to exclude the evidence of the plaintiff, and giving the general charge in favor of the defendant. This being the case, it is unnecessary to notice exceptions to rulings on the pleadings.

The judgment of the court is affirmed.

Affirmed.

McCLELLAN, MAYFIELD, and SOMERVILLE, JJ., concur.

On Rehearing.

SIMPSON, J.—The majority of the court, consisting
of ANDERSON, McCLELLAN, MAYFIELD, and SOMERVILLE,
JJ., hold that the evidence was sufficient to leave it to
the jury to say whether or not the injury resulted from
the negligence of Mack Powell. The writer's views,
concurred in by SAYRE, J., are as follows:

It is claimed on application for rehearing that the
failure to have the light renewed was not the only neg-

ligence complained of, and the court's attention is invited to the fifth count of the complaint. It is manifest that, under that count the burden was on the plaintiff to show by the evidence that it was negligent in
Powell to order plaintiff to go into the dust box to
work, and to show a causal connection between such
negligence and the injury.—*Creola Lumber Co. v. Mills*,
149 Ala. 474, 485, 42 South. 1019. "Where the evidence is equally consistent with either view, with the
existence or non-existence of negligence, it is not competent for the judge to leave the matter to the jury.
The party who affirms negligence has failed to establish it. This is a rule which ought never to be lost sight
of."—1 Bailey's Personal Injuries, p. 560, § 1660. The
burden is on the plaintiff to show, by the evidence, the
causal connection between the negligence and the injury. A mere conjecture cannot be submitted to the
jury, without evidence.—1 Bailey's Personal Injuries,
p. 563, §§ 1672, 1675; p. 565, § 1682; p. 566, § 1688; p.
568, § 1694.

There is not a particle of evidence tending to show
that the order was negligent, unless because the light
was out; that was the reason given by the plaintiff
when he objected to work, and that is the only reason
suggested in the plaintiff's brief either on the original
hearing or on this rehearing. There is no evidence as
to where or how the "down comer" enters the dust box,
whether into the top, where the explosion doors were,
or into the side. There is no evidence that any one was
in the "down comers," or that there was any scaffold
therein; the only evidence about any scaffold being the
testimony of plaintiff that the carpenters had erected
"a scaffold" in the dust box.

Said fifth count alleges that said Powell "did negligently order the plaintiff to work in the place and in
the manner, in which he was then engaged," etc.; and

so far from there being any evidence that Powell ordered plaintiff to work in the manner which he did, the plaintiff testified that Powell was not anywhere near where the work was being done, and "that the only orders that Powell gave were to go in there and tear out the scaffolding or lagging, and that he gave no orders or directions as to the manner of doing the work, and was not where he could see and did not see the work as it progressed, or the particular manner in which it was being done," and yet in the face of this plain statement by the plaintiff himself, counsel would have us declare that said Powell did direct the manner in which the work should be done, because he told him to go there and work when there was no light there. "Manner" in this sentence means only the mode or method in which the thing is done, and cannot refer to the condition of the place in which the work is done. There is not only no proof that the said Powell directed the manner in which the work should be done, but there is none as to the manner in which it was done, further than as stated by the plaintiff—"when he and Charlie Merckle had passed one piece of lumber through the boot-leg to Lehman Merckle down on the ground, and when he had been in said dust box not more than fifteen minutes a piece of lumber * * * fell from some point above." It does not appear what position the plaintiff was occupying, but from the facts that there is no evidence of any, but the one scaffold in the dust box, and that plaintiff was passing the pieces of lumber through the bootleg, down to a man on the ground, the presumption is strong that he was below said scaffold, and that he was there to remove, and that if there was any negligence about it, it was that of plaintiff himself, or of Merckle, who was working with him; in which case, of course, he could not recover.

In regard to the exclusion of the evidence on the part of the plaintiff, whether we follow the cases which hold that this is a proper proceeding, when the plaintiff has failed to make out a prima facie case, or adopt the suggestion in one of our cases that if it be a case in which the general charge could be properly given it is error without injury, it matters not, the result being the same. The general charge was given for the defendant in this case, and it was proper, whether the evidence was in or out. In regard to this, it may be further said that as the bill of exceptions does not state that it contains all the evidence, and there is no conflict in the evidence therein contained, the court cannot be placed in error for giving the general charge.

This court has frequently held that where the general charge is properly given, or where the party is entitled to the general charge, it is not necessary to consider other matters.

The rehearing is granted; and the judgment of the court is reversed and the cause remanded.

MAYFIELD, J.—I concur in granting this application for a rehearing, and in reversing the judgment of the trial court, upon the ground that there was sufficient evidence to carry the case to the jury upon one of the counts; but I am of the opinion that the case should be reversed upon an entirely different ground.

The court, on defendant's motion and over the objection of plaintiff, excluded all of the plaintiff's evidence from consideration by the jury. This was undoubtedly error. No trial court can refuse to admit, or can exclude, over the objection of a party, such evidence as is shown by this record, without committing error. The error may be cured by subsequently admitting the evidence; or if the error be without possible injury to the party complaining, it is not, therefore, error to reverse the judgment or revise the erroneous ruling. But unless one of these things, or something else is shown, to cure the error or render it harmless, it is error which must work a reversal.

I am aware that such a practice has in recent years grown up in this state, and is often resorted to by defendants in the trial of civil cases, and is practiced by many of the ablest and most eminent counsel in the state, and that it is allowed by many of the most learned and experienced trial judges, and that it has been allowed by this court in a number of cases; but it has never been approved further than by the failure to prohibit it, and has been one or more times criticised and adversely.

The practice has sometimes been said by this court not to be error, and at other times, to be error without injury. When it was said not to be error, of course, the court meant, not *reversible* error in that particular case. It is of course error, and necessarily so, technically speaking.

The rule is firmly settled in this state that, error being shown, injury is presumed. Appellate courts will indulge all reasonable intendments and presumptions to save the trial court from error; but they never make any such intendments or presumptions as to injury. On the other hand the presumption is the other way as to injury. An appellant never has to show injury in order to obtain a reversal; if he shows error, injury is presumed, unless the contrary is made to appear clearly and affirmatively. In other words, on appeal, the burden is on the appellant as to error, but on the appellee as to injury. To illustrate these two rules, let them be applied to the facts of this case as shown on the appeal by the transcript:

Suppose the trial court had declined to exclude the evidence, but had given the affirmative charge for the defendant. We could not reverse this case though the evidence in the record did tend to prove the issue; because, in order for the appellate court to say there was error, it would have to know all the evidence, and this record does not show or purport to show all, and the court would presume that evidence omitted would justify the charge. But if the trial court excluded evidence which was material, relevant, and competent and tended to prove the issue, this was error, whether it was all or a part only—whether one word or a book. This was all appellant was required to show; he was not required to show that this was all the evidence, or that he was injured thereby; and if he shows error the appellate court will presume there was injury.

The burden is on the appellee to show that the error was harmless, and if he does not discharge this burden the case must be reversed. This burden is not discharged in this case. It does not appear that it was all the evidence, nor otherwise that it was harmless. But I do not mean to say that it would not be reversible error if it was shown that it was all the evidence, and it did not make out a prima facie case for plaintiff. If competent and relevant, and tending to prove any issue on trial, it cannot be excluded over the objection of either party without the commission of reversible error. It is reversible error because the statutes of this state have provided the modes by which the court, instead of the jury, may test the sufficiency of the plaintiff's evidence to support the verdict, and these modes established by statute are exclusive of other modes which deprive the parties of advantages secured by the statutory mode. Either party has the right to have it tested by these modes, and no other can be resorted to unless by consent.

Courts certainly have no more power or authority to establish, sanction, or allow a practice or procedure which would deprive a person of his rights or property without due process of law, than the Legislature has, to enact a statute to that end. The Constitution inhbits judges and courts in this matter, as much as it does the Legislature.

At an early date, to wit, June, 1822, it was decided by this court, that the trial court, unless so directed by statute, could not order a nonsuit. In that case it was said: "If the evidence shows a claim irrelevant to the form of action, or to the issue, it is competent for the court to so instruct the jury; but if the plaintiff appears, and refuses to submit to the nonsuit, and insists that the jury shall render a verdict, the court has no power to direct a nonsuit, and cannot enforce its opinion, except by instructing the jury, and awarding a new trial."—*Smith v. Seaton*, Minor, 75. This language of the court was quoted and reaffirmed in the case of *Hunt v. Stewart*, 7 Ala. 528. In that case it was said: "It is clear from what is already said that he (plaintiff) failed to make out his case, and the court would have been authorized to instruct the jury to find against him, and the jury could not without a disregard or misapprehension of duty, refuse to do so. This being the case, the plaintiff is not prejudiced, and if the point was res. integra, we might be inclined to consider the nonsuit as a mere irregularity which did not avail on error; but it was held by our predecessors at a very early date that it was not allowable for a court, unless directed by statute, to order the plaintiff to be nonsuited. * * * The plaintiff insists upon a verdict whenever he puts his case before a jury, and does not consent to a withdrawal. Upon the authority of the case last cited, the judgment is reversed and the cause remanded." These cases have been subsequently followed, and never departed from, and the statutes, which the courts then held did not allow it, remain to this day, and have been

often readopted and amended, not to the end of allowing such a practice, but of further preventing it. Consequently, it is too late now to overrule such statutes
and depart from that practice.

The practice of excluding all the plaintiff's evidence,
or all of that of both parties, is nothing more nor less
than the court's declining to submit it to the jury with
instructions; and this, the statutes of this state do not
authorize, while the decisions of this court have held
that the trial court could not so decline, in the absence
of statutory authorization. On the other hand, it is the
purpose and effect of the statute to expressly declare
that the plaintiff has, in such case, the absolute right
to insist upon a verdict under such conditions, when
he puts his case to the jury, and that he does not consent to a withdrawal of his evidence; and the court cannot compel him to withdraw it, though it be authorized
to instruct the jury to find against him on it, and to set
aside the verdict if they fail to obey. It is futile to say
that the practice of excluding all the evidence, and then
charging the jury that if they believe the evidence they
must find for the defendant, is not a nonsuit. This is
nothing short of an attempt to avoid the statutes as to
nonsuits, and to make the judgment a bar to another
suit, which would not have that effect if a nonsuit was
entered. To exclude a plaintiff's evidence when he insists that it is sufficient to go to the jury on, as tending
to prove the issue made, is nothing more nor less than
compelling the plaintiff to take a nonsuit.

It is a farcical comedy to allow or compel parties to
go to the jury after the evidence is all excluded. There
is nothing for the jury to consider, nothing for them to
believe or not believe; the only thing to do is to enter
up a judgment for the defendant; but it is a judgment
of nonsuit, or nol pros., and not a judgment final based
on the verdict of the jury (the jury have nothing to

base a verdict upon), so as to preclude or bar another suit. In order to have this effect, the case must be submitted to the jury upon the evidence offered, even though the court is authorized to direct a verdict; there being nothing worthy of the consideration of the jury. And this is the exact purpose and effect of our statutes, as declared by our courts; while the practice complained of is a clear evasion of these statutes, and is depriving the plaintiff of his rights conferred by the statute.

Of course it is not error for the court to give the affirmative charge for the defendant after the evidence is excluded, the burden of proof being upon the plaintiff. It is really nonsense to request or give such instructions to the jury. If the plaintiff has anything to complain of in this practice, it is the action of the court in excluding his evidence; and this is nothing more nor less than the court's directing, if not compelling, him to take a nonsuit, which is exactly what the statutes are intended to prevent the trial court from doing, and which this court has said it could not do without committing error, though, under the same state of facts, it might direct a verdict.

In the case of *Leavitt v. Dawson*, 4 Ala. 335, the court, in speaking of compulsory nonsuit, said: "It is not important to consider whether the term 'nonsuit' is the most proper to designate this mode of action by the court, because the effect to the plaintiffs is the same as a judgment of nol pros., which is the technical judgment in all cases where the plaintiff refuses to proceed further with his suit." And in that case it was held error to enter a nonsuit, and that the plaintiff could not have been presumed to have consented to a nonsuit.

A plaintiff may, of course, at any time, voluntarily nonsuit, and then bring another action, provided he pay the cost of the first suit; but he can have this ruling reviewed on appeal only by conforming to the requirements of the statute.—*Kemp v. Coxe*, 14 Ala. 614.

A nonsuit, even upon the merits of a case, is not necessarily a bar to another action for the same cause, except in a few cases, as stated in Co. Lit. 139a. This is the difference between a nonsuit and a retraxit; the latter is a bar, but the former is not. In England the practice was that if the judge ordered a nonsuit, and the plaintiff brought another suit, the trial court would stay the proceedings upon the second action until the cost of the first was paid, the second action being deemed vexatious; yet, the party could not be deprived of his second action if he submitted to the condition of paying the costs which accrued upon the first suit. This is the uniform practice in most of the states.—*Bridge v. Summer*, 1 Pick. (Mass.) 371.

We have thus far shown the rights of which the plaintiff is deprived, and will now show the rights conferred upon the defendant by this practice, which are in addition to those conferred upon him by statute, or other law, and without subjecting him to any of the penalties which he would incur by pursuing the remedy given him by statute, when he desires to test the sufficiency of the plaintiff's evidence to support a judgment.

Our statutes have from an early period provided two methods by which a defendant could have this question determined by the court, instead of having the effect of the evidence determined by the jury. The first is a demurrer to the evidence; and the other, by requesting the court to charge the jury that they find for the defendant, or, that they cannot find for the plaintiff. In each of these methods the defendant is required by the law to take the chance of a judgment being entered against him. If he merely requests the court to exclude the evidence, he takes no risk—cannot possibly incur any penalty. If the court grants his motion, then, as a matter of course, the court must give the charge for him, as it would be error to refuse, when the burden of proof was on the plaintiffff, and there was no evidence. If the court should refuse his motion to exclude the evidence, he would not be injured at all, as he had no right to make such a motion; and would have no ground of exception, much less cause, for reversal. This principle was announced very clearly by the Supreme Court of Massachusetts, through its great justice, Shaw, to the effect that if a judge before whom an action is on trial is of the opinion that the plaintiff is not, upon the whole evidence, entitled to recover, he may recommend a nonsuit on that ground. If he does so, and the nonsuit takes place, the plaintiff may allege exceptions; but if the judge is of the opinion that there is evidence to be considered by the jury, and declines to order a nonsuit, this decision is no ground for exceptions by defendant.

The statute has adopted the remedy of demurring to the evidence but not that of involuntary nonsuit. This gives him the right to have the evidence made of record by the court, and by admitting every inference or conclusion which the jury can legally deduce therefrom. He thereby devolves upon the court, instead of on the jury, the duty of determining the issue of fact between the parties, as well as of law. This was the effect of the demurrer to the evidence at common law, and our statute has copied the words announcing the effect, purpose and object of demurrer to the evidence.—See section 5343 of the Code. But in order to do this—that is, to place the duty upon the court to determine this issue —he must take the chance of the court's entering a judgment against him, as well as one against the plaintiff. He therefore clearly avoids and evades this statute when he is allowed to have the plaintiff's evidence excluded and thereby obtains an involuntary nonsuit.

The other remedy given him by the statute consists
of those Code provisions as to charges or instructions to
the jury. Our Code contains regulations as to this matter, prohibiting trial courts, ex mero motu, from charging upon the effect of the evidence, and only authorizing the courts so to do when requested in writing by the
parties; the statute giving either party the right so to
do; that is to say, our statute (section 5362) provides
that the court shall not charge upon the effect of the
testimony unless requested so to do by one of the parties. If so requested, the statutes require the charge to
be in writing. The statutes allow both parties to request the affirmative charge upon the whole evidence in
any given case; and such charge is inappropriate in any
case except upon consideration of all the evidence. If
the practice of excluding all the evidence is allowed,, it
would be worse than folly for the plaintiffff to request
such a charge when the burden of proof is upon him;
while, on the other hand, it is eminently proper and unquestionably without error for the court to direct a verdict for the defendant in such case. So the defendant,
by this process, wholly deprives the plaintiff of the
right, or any advantage to accrue therefrom.

To sum it all up in a few words, the practice of excluding the plaintiff's evidence is an unauthorized and
unwarranted one, the effect of which is to avoid and
evade the statutes provided for such cases. It deprives
the plaintiff of the rights conferred upon him by statute, and confers upon the defendant rights which are
prohibited by statute. It therefore follows that such
practice ought not to be sanctioned or allowed by the
courts of this state. I do not doubt that such practice
is allowable in those states in which involuntary nonsuit is allowed, because that is what excluding the
plaintiff's evidence amounts to. The two are one and
the same thing in practice and in legal effect; but, as

we have shown above, the practice of involuntary nonsuit has never been allowed in this state. The statutes
provide for nonsuits when made necessary by adverse
rulings, but the result obtained thereby is quite different from this complained of.

The state of Missouri has a system of pleading and
practice very similar to that of Alabama, and the Supreme Court of that state nipped this practice in the
bud when it was first attempted there, in the following
language: "There is no law in this state authorizing
the court, at the close of the plaintiff's case, to strike
out his testimony on the ground that the same is insufficient to make out a case for the plaintiff."—*McFarland v. Bellows*, 49 Mo. 311.

The Supreme Court of West Virginia, in speaking of
the practice which had been allowed to prevail in that
state, said: "Looking to the manner in which this practice has been abused in some of the circuit courts of this
state, I cannot refrain from expressing the regret that
when it first made its appearance here, it was not met
with the declaration which was made by the Supreme
Court of Missouri."—*Carrico v. W. Va., C. & P. R. Co..*,
35 W. Va. 395, 14 S. E. 14. That court, in the same
case, said that it had been unable to find any case in the
reports of the mother state, Virginia, which would be
authority for the practice in West Virginia, and that
the court was constrained to believe that the practice
was an importation from other states, which had been
ingrafted upon its procedure in a manner not entirely
in accordance with the spirit of its former decisions.
This is certainly true in this state, and, it may be added,
it is in direct conflict with the early decisions and contrary to express Code provisions which have prevailed
in this state for many years. But the West Virginia
court proceeds to show that, although the practice prevails in that state, it is limited to cases, first, where all

the evidence of the plaintiff is incompetent; second, where there was an entire and fatal variance between the allegations and the proof; and, third, in those cases where the plaintiff's evidence did not tend in any degree to prove his case.

I believe it will be found upon an examination that the practice has never been allowed to prevail to any great extent except in the states in which an involuntary nonsuit was allowed when the plaintiff had failed to prove his case, because it would be a non sequitur to say that the right to compel a nonsuit does not exist, and yet allow the court to exclude all the plaintiff's evidence when he insisted upon the right to go to the jury upon that question.

As I have before stated, I do not believe that the courts of this state have the power to authorize, sanction, or give effect to any such practice, because the Legislature had provided a procedure for such cases, and the litigants have a right to have that procedure complied with, and it is the duty of the courts to enforce it.

It may be said, and it is possibly true, that when the court excludes the plaintiff's evidence on the defendant's motion, the plaintiff might then take a nonsuit, with a bill of exceptions, because the ruling is adverse to him; but the answer to that is that the law does not require him to do this; and because the defendant and the court have resorted to an unwarranted practice, they cannot escape their error, nor be excused therefrom, because the plaintiff did not resort to some other remedy. The law gives him the option in that instance, and not to the court or the defendant.

As I have pointed out before, though he may not have made out his case, yet, if he thought he had, he had a right to submit that question to the jury unless the defendant demurred to the evidence, or requested the af-

firmative charge and the court gave it; and the defendant and the court could not deprive him of his option
in determining whether he should take a nonsuit or submit the question to the jury, if a jury case, and, if not,
to the court, in the mode and manner provided by law.
The defendant and the court have no power to deprive
him of these rights which the statutes have conferred
upon him, and escape upon the doctrine of "error without injury;" nor should they be heard to say to him:
"You should have taken a nonsuit, and not allowed
judgment final to be rendered against you."

If the defendant desires to submit the sufficiency of
the evidence to the court instead of to the jury, the statutes have pointed out to him, how he shall do it, and
have given him the option of two remedies; one, by demurring to the evidence; and the other, by requested
charges or instructions from the court. The court has
no power to allow him to select some other mode, and
thereby escape the burdens which the statutes impose
upon him in the event he decides to have the court, instead of the jury, pass upon the sufficiency of the plaintiff's evidence.

McCLELLAN, J.—I concur in the conclusions of my
Brother MAYFIELD, first, that the exclusion, on motion,
of *all* of a plaintiff's evidence is error, and presumptively injurious; but that the latter may be and is refuted, and *reversible* error averted, if the entire evidence so excluded did not make out a prima facie case
for the plaintiff; and, second, that the practice of excluding, on motion, the entire evidence of the plaintiff,
on the asserted ground of its insufficiency to sustain,
prima facie, the plaintiff's case, is fundamentally wrong
and ought not to be longer sanctioned. The movant, in
such case, should be put to his right to demur to the evidence, or relegated to his other right to test the question by special written charge.

Sloss-Sheffield Steel & Iron Co. v. Milbra.

Damage for Death of Servant.

(Decided June 27, 1911. 55 South. 890.)

1. *Pleading; Duplicity.*—A plea, called a plea in abatement, which sets up facts, which, if true, would be good in bar as a plea of ne unques administrator, and in abatement as a plea of another action pending, is bad for duplicity.

2. *Same; Dilatory Pleas.*—At common law, pleas in abatement were not favored.

3. *Same; Demurrer; Grounds.*—In pleas in bar at the common law, defects in form were treated as defects in substance, and all defects in such pleas, except for duplicity, were reached by a general demurrer.

4. *Same; Distinction Between Abatement and Bar.*—Under the present Code, pleas in bar and in abatement stand upon the same footing as to form while the main distinction at common law between the two pleas was that the plea in abatement must not only point out the plaintiff's error, but must show how the error should be corrected; in other words, must give the plaintiff a better writ.

5. *Same; Another Action Pending; Sufficiency.*—Where the action was by an administrator for damages for the death of his intestate, and the defendant pleaded in abatement that previously the administrator of this same intestate instituted suit in the circuit court of the same county, a court having jurisdiction of the subject matter and parties of this suit, against this defendant upon the identical cause of action stated in the suit filed in this cause, in which suit defendant had impleaded, which said suit was still pending in this county undisposed of, was good on demurrer under section 5330, Code 1907.

6. *Same; Abatement; Form and Requisite.*—A plea in abatement must set out facts which will show that the first action operates to abate the second; but the plea need not ask that the summons be quashed or the suit abated, although that should be the effect of sustaining the pleas; nor need the pleas recite or set out the summons or complaint in either action, but it is necessary, however, to allege that the first suit was pending when the plea was filed.

7. *Appeal and Error; Harmless Error; Pleading.*—Where a demurrer to a good plea in abatement is sustained, and another plea, called a plea in abatement, but which in effect, is both a plea in abatement, and a plea in bar, was overruled, the sustaining of the demurrer to the first plea in abatement is prejudicial error, since to sustain the second plea, the defendant would not only have to prove his plea in abatement, but also his plea in bar, and the proof which would support the verdict upon the first plea would not have supported one under the second.

8. *Abatement and Revivor; Another Action Pending.*—The pen-dency of a prior suit in a court of competent jurisdiction between the same parties will abate a later suit because the latter is deemed unnecessary and vexatious; but the plea is not available unless the judgment which would be rendered in the prior action would be conclusive between the parties and operate as a bar to the same. .

9. *Charge of Court; Explanatory Charges.*—Charges explanatory of charges given for the adversary party should not be refused.

10. *Same; Invading Province of Jury.*—Where the action was for damages for negligence causing the death of plaintiff's intestate, a charge asserting that if the negligence of a third person was the sole proximate cause of the death of plaintiff's intestate, plaintiff could not recover; but if defendant is guilty of negligence which proximately helped to cause the death of intestate, then the negli-gence, if any, of such third person, even though it also helped to cause death, would be no answer to the negligence of defendant, states a correct proposition of law, applicable to and illustrated by the facts of the particular case, as it does not request or even sug-gest a finding for the plaintiff on the facts hypothesized, or on any other facts.

APPEAL from Birmingham City Court.

Heard before Hon. CHARLES A. SENN.

Action by Levi Milbra, as administrator, against the Sloss-Sheffield Steel & Iron Company. Judgment for plaintiff, and defendant appeals. Reversed and re-manded.

The pleadings noted in the opinion sufficiently ap-pear therefrom. Charge 2, given for the plaintiff, is as follows: "While, if the negligence of John Moore was the sole proximate cause of the death of Edward Milbra, plaintiff could not recover, yet if the jury are reasonably satisfied from the evidence that the defend-ant was guilty of negligence which proximately helped to cause the death of Edward Milbra, then the negli-gence, if any, of John Moore, even though it also helped to cause the death, would be no answer to the said negligence of the defendant, if any."

TILLMAN, BRADLEY & MORROW, and L. C. LEAD-BEATER, for appellant. The court erred in sustaining demurrer to defendant's plea in abatement.—Section 2490, Code 1907; *Foster v. Napier*, 73 Ala. 596; *Watson*

v. Jones, 20 L. Ed. 666; *Elliott v. Gwinn*, 98 N. W. 625;
Richardson v. Opelt, 82 N. W. 377; 48 N. E. 352; 1 Cyc.
33; *Martin v. Ellerbe*, 70 Ala. 326; *Orman v. Lane*, 130
Ala. 305. The court erred in his charge given for the
plaintiff.—*Bullard v. A. G. S.*, 167 Ala. 618; *Garth v.
N. Ala. T. Co.*, 148 Ala. 103. The court erred in over-
ruling defendant's motion for a new trial.—*Florence C.
& I. Co. v. Fields*, 104 Ala. 480; *E. T. V. & G. Co.. v.
Bayliss*, 75 Ala. 466.

BOWMAN, HARSH & BEDDOW, for appellee. Pleas
in abatement are not favored, and are construed most
strongly against the pleader.—4 Mayf. 499. The plea
does not sufficiently allege who was the administrator
bringing the prior suit.—*Hooper v. Scarbrough*, 57 Ala.
513; *McDowell v. Jones*, 58 Ala. 25; *Hickey v. Stallworth*, 143 Ala. 539. It was necessary that the plea
show that the former cause of action was pending at
the time the plea was filed.—*Coldale B. & T. Co. v.
Southern C. Co.*, 110 Ala. 613. There was no error in
giving charge 2 for the plaintiff, as the charge was
the mere statement of a correct proposition of law
without direction to find for the plaintiff on the facts
hypothesized. There was no error in declining to grant
motion for a new trial.—*Jackson v. The State*, 34
South. 188; *Brown v. Johnson*, 135 Ala. 613.

MAYFIELD, J.—This action is by Levi Milbra, as
personal representative, to recover damages for the
wrongful death of his intestate, Edward Milbra.

The complaint joins counts under the employer's liability act (Code 1907, § 3910) with counts under the
homicide act (Code 1907, § 2486). The complaint was
filed on the 15th day of June, 1909, and on the 23d day
of June, eight days thereafter, the defendant filed the
following plea in abatement of the action, which was
sworn to: "Now comes the defendant in the above-en-

titled cause, in its own proper person, and pleads in abatement to the suit filed in said cause that the plaintiff ought not to have and maintain this suit,'for that, heretofore, to wit, on the 8th day of May, 1909, the administrator of this identical intestate, appointed by the probate court of Jefferson county, Alabama, instituted suit in the circuit court of Jefferson county, Alabama, which said court had jurisdiction of the parties and subject-matter of this suit, said suit being No. 8,108 in the circuit court of Jefferson county, against this identical defendant, upon the identical cause of action stated in the suit filed in this cause, which said suit is still pending in the said circuit court of Jefferson county, undisposed of; for that, long prior to the institution of the above-styled cause, this identical defendant impleaded in the said suit No. 8,108 in said circuit court in the identical cause of action heretofore instituted in said circuit court on the 8th day of May, 1909, as heretofore stated. Wherefore, the defendant prays judgment of this honorable court whether the plaintiff herein ought to further maintain this suit." No further pleadings were interposed nor action by the court taken until February 14, 1910, when separate and special demurrers were interposed to this plea in abatement, and were on the same date overruled.

The defendant on the same date filed a demurrer to the complaint, and pleas 1, 2, 3, and 5. Of these pleas, plea 1 was the general issue; plea 2 was contributory negligence; plea 3 was a plea of ne unques administrator; and plea 5 (as called on its face), a plea in abatement; but, in fact, law, and effect, it is a double plea— in bar and in abatement—in that it sets up facts which, if true, would be good in bar as a plea of ne unques administrator, and in abatement as a plea of another action pending. On the same day these pleas were filed, the court overruled demurrers to the third and fifth, and sustained demurrers to the second, and the trial was had on the first, third, and fifth pleas, resulting in verdict and judgment for the plaintiff. From such judgment, this appeal is prosecuted.

It therefore sufficiently appears that the court sustained a demurrer to the plea in abatement set out above, which was filed June 23, 1909, and it expressly appears that the court overruled a demurrer to plea 5, which is called a plea in abatement, but is, in effect, a plea both in bar and abatement. In this the trial court was in error in both instances. The plea set out above —and to which the demurrer was sustained—was a good plea in abatement, while plea 5 was bad, in that it joined matter, both in bar and in abatement; but the latter ruling is only material on this appeal on the question as to whether the sustaining of the demurrer to the other plea was error, without injury. We cannot say that such was without injury. In order to sustain the fifth plea, defendant would not only have to prove his plea in abatement, but also to prove his plea in bar, that is, a plea of ne unques administrator. Proof which would have supported a verdict under the second would not have supported one under the fifth.

We do not know upon what theory the trial court held this plea in abatement insufficient. It seems to conform to all the requisites of such pleas. It is true that at common law pleas in abatement were not favored. Defects in form, as to such, were treated as defects in substance as to pleas in bar; and all defects in such pleas, except for duplicity, were then reached by a general demurrer. The English statute of 4 Anne, c. 16, § 1, requiring special demurrers as to various causes, had no application to pleas in abatement. But by our statute of 1807 (Clay's Digest, p. 321) it became necessary to demur specially as to any defect of form in writs, complaints, pleas, or other pleadings. However, by the act of 1824 (Clay's Digest, p. 334), special demurrers, for all purposes, were abolished for all purposes, the statute providing that "no demurrer shall have any other effect than that of a general demurrer;" but this last act was held not to extend to pleas in abatement.—*Casey v. Cleveland*, 7 Port. 445; *Humphrey v. Whitten*, 17 Ala. 30. But the Code of 1852 instituted a new system of pleading and practice in this state. Section 2236 of that Code (section 5330, Code of 1907) provided that pleas must consist of a sufficient statement of the facts relied on in bar or *abatement* of the suit, and no objection can be taken thereto, if the facts are so stated that a material issue can be taken thereto.

Since the Code of 1852, it has been ruled by this court that pleas in bar and abatement stand upon the same footing.—*Hall v. Brazelton*, 46 Ala. 359; *Lang v. Waters*, 47 Ala. 624; *Mohr v. Chaffe*, 75 Ala. 387. Many decisions of this court may be found cited in Mayfield's Digest, vol. 4, p. 499, and in note to section 5330 of the Code, under the different statutes which have governed in this state, and when the statutes change the law, of course, the decisions must of necessity change. One of the main distinctions between pleas in abatement and pleas in bar is that the former must not only point out the plaintiff's error, but must show how the error can and should be corrected; in other words, it must give the plaintiff a better writ.—1 Chit. Pl. (16th Ed.) 362.

It was said by this court (speaking by BRICKELL, C. J.), in the case of *Foster v. Napier*, 73 Ala. 603: "The principle is well settled that the pendency of a prior suit for the same thing, or, as is generally said, for the same cause of action, in a court of competent jurisdiction, between the same parties, will abate a later suit; because the latter is deemed unnecessary and vexatious. * * * The reason of the principle is well expressed

in the familiar maxim, 'Nemo debet bis vexari, si con-
stet curiæ quod sit, pro una et eadam causa.' The doctrine is thus stated in 1 Bac. Ab. 28, M.: "The law ab-
hors multiplicity of actions, and therefore, whenever it
appears on record that the plaintiff has sued out two
writs against the same defendant, for the same thing,
the second writ shall abate; for if it were allowed that
a man should be twice arrested, or twice attached by
his goods for the same thing, by the same reason he
might suffer in infinitum; and it is not necessary that
both should be pending at the time of the defendant's
pleading in abatement; for if there was a writ in being
at the time of the suing out of the second, it is plain
that the second was vexatious and ill ab initio.' It is
the pendency of two suits for the same cause—their
existence simul et semel—the law deems vexatious and
discountenances. However meritorious may be the
cause of action, it must not be employed for the purpose of oppression; and when a defendant is twice impleaded by the same plaintiff, for the same thing, the
oppression and vexation is not matter of fact; it is a
conclusion of law, and is not dependent upon an inquiry into the actual circumstances of the two cases.
* * * The plea of pendency of a prior action for the
same cause, between the same parties, stands upon like
principles, and is supported by like evidence, as a plea
of a former recovery. The two pleas have not the same,
but a like, office; the difference is that the one is interposed because of the pendency of the first action, the
other after its termination; the one is in abatement of
the second suit, the other in bar, to defeat it absolutely.
The plea is not, therefore, available, unless the judgment which could be rendered in the prior action would
be conclusive between the parties, and operate as a bar
to the second.—*Rood v. Eslava*, 17 Ala. 430; *Newell v.
Newton*, 10 Pick. [Mass.] 470."

Tested by these rules, under our statutory system of pleading and practice, the plea was sufficient. If the facts stated in that plea were true, there can be no doubt that the causes of action in the suits were the same, and that the pendency of either one should abate the other, and that judgment and satisfaction in the one case would be·a bar to recovery in the other.

We cannot agree with counsel for appellee that this plea was so "confused and misleading as to be almost unintelligible." It contained such a succinct statement of the necessary facts to abate the suit brought that a material issue could and should have been taken thereon.—Code, § 5330.

It was not necessary that the plea should state the name of the personal representative who brought the other suit, or show that it was the same person who brought this action. It showed that both suits were for the same cause of action, viz., the wrongful death of this plaintiff's intestate; and that the former action was brought,·by the personal representative of such intestate, on the same cause of action on which this plaintiff, as such administrator, had brought this suit. If the facts stated in that plea are true, it is certain to all intents that this defendant was being prosecuted in two suits, in two state courts having concurrent jurisdiction, for one and the same cause of action. This is what the law does not allow and what the plea intended to prevent; and, if the facts stated therein were true, it would have been prevented but for the error of the court in sustaining the demurrer thereto. If the facts stated in this plea are true, this last action brought was both unnecessary and vexatious. It is for this reason that the pendency of the first is ground for abating the second. It is the purpose of such pleas to invoke an inquiry into the facts, and to thus determine whether the second is unnecessary and vexatious.—*State v. Dougherty*, 45 Mo. 294; *Gamsby v. Ray*, 52 N. H. 513,

The plea, to be good, must, of course, set out facts which will show that the first action operates to abate the second.—*Miller v. Rigney,* 16 Ind. 327. The plea need not ask that the summons be quashed or the suit abated, though that should be the effect of sustaining the plea.—*Dawley v. Brown,* 9 Hun (N. Y.) 461. Nor need the plea recite or set out the summons or complaint in either action.—*Lee v. Hefley,* 21 Ind. 98. The plea not only alleged that the first suit was pending when the second was brought, but also alleged that it was pending when the plea was filed; and it was therefore sufficient, under the rule declared on the application for a rehearing in the case of *Coaldale Brick Co. v. Sou. Const. Co.,* 110 Ala. 605, 613, 19 South. 45, which decision changed the rule in this state as to the necessity of alleging that the first suit was pending when the plea was filed.

There was no error in the giving of charge 2, at the request of the plaintiff. It appears that this charge was probably explantory of other charges given at the request of defendant, and for this purpose, if for no other, it was proper and free from error. It is not open to the objection urged against it that it authorized or requested a verdict upon proof of facts not alleged, or of facts outside of the issues upon which the case was tried. The charge did not request or suggest a finding for the plaintiff on the facts hypothesized, or upon any other facts. It merely stated a correct proposition of law which was applicable to, and illustrated by, the facts of the particular case. There was neither harm nor error in giving the charge.

As the case must be reversed, it is unnecessary to pass upon the question going to the denial of the motion for a new trial.

Reversed and remanded.

SIMPSON, ANDERSON, SAYRE, and SOMERVILLE, JJ., concur.

[Pratt Consolidated Coal Company v. Davidson.]

Pratt Consolidated Coal Company v. Davidson.

Damages for Death of Employe.

(Decided June 1, 1911. Rehearing denied June 27, 1911.
55 South. 886.)

1. *Master and Servant; Injury to Servant; Duty of Superintendence.*—The duty of a fire boss of a mine to examine the condition of the mine when gas is known to exist therein, before men are permitted to enter for work, is a duty of superintendence within subdivision 2 of section 3910, Code 1907, notwithstanding the provisions of section 1031, Code 1907.

2. *Master and Servant; Assumption of Risk.*—In the absence of a special contract based on a sufficient consideration an employe in a mine does not assume the risk of the owner or operator's failure to observe the provision of section 1016, Code 1907.

3. *Same.*—In the absence of a special contract based on a sufficient consideration, an employe does not assume the risk of negligence in superintendence under subdivision 2, section 3910, Code 1907.

4. *Same; Contributory Negligence.*—An employe in a mine may be guilty of contributory negligence in going into a place where he knows gas to exist in dangerous quantities, or where he has been specially warned not to go, though the owner or operator had not complied with the requirements of section 1016 and 1031, Code 1907.

5. *Same; Obligation to the Master; Statutory Regulation.*—An operator of a mine cannot evade responsibility for a failure to comply with the requirements of section 1016 and 1031, Code 1907, by setting up general rules for the conduct of the business as a substitute for the precautions prescribed by the statute, and he may not by such regulation impose on any employe the duty of ascertaining whether the law has been complied with.

6. *Depositions; Responsiveness of Answer; Admissibility.*—Where the answers of a witness to interrogatories were responsive to the issues as made up by the court's approval, and were not otherwise objectionable, it was error to strike portions of the depositions containing the answers on the grounds that the answers were not responsive to the interrogatories.

7. *Charge of Court; Conformity to Issues.*—Where the court had erroneously overruled a demurrer to a plea which there was evidence to support, it was error to refuse to instruct that if the facts alleged in the plea were found to be true, the verdict should be for the defendant, as it is not proper to change the issues as developed by the pleading by giving or refusing instructions.

8. *Appeal and Error; Harmless Error; Instructions.*—Since this court cannot know on appeal what the evidence would have been if

the issues had been differently shaped, or that the defendant might not have amended his insufficient pleas so as to have presented a meritorious defense, if the demurrers thereto had been sustained, errors in charges which depart from the theory observed in passing on the demurrers were prejudicial, notwithstanding plaintiff made out a prima facie case by proof without conflict, and the facts as stated by the bill of exceptions seem to preclude any special defense.

APPEAL from Birmingham City Court.

Heard before Hon. C. W. FERGUSON.

Action by J. J. Davidson, as administrator, against the Pratt Consolidated Coal Company, for damages for causing the death of his intestate, an employe. Judgment for plaintiff and defendant appeals. Reversed and remanded.

LAMKIN & WATTS, and BANKHEAD & BANKHEAD, for appellant. The court erred in striking portions of defendant's answers to plaintiff's interrogatories.—*Carwile v. Frankklin*, 51 South. 396. The court erred in refusing to instruct the jury as requested by the defendant.—*Williams v. Thacker*, 40 L. R. A. 812. An employe may assume the risk growing out of the violation of a statutory duty.—*Republic I. & S. Co. v. Thomas*, 99 C. C. A. 523; *Bir. R. & E. Co. v. Allen*, 99 Ala. 356; Dresser 603-4; 26 Cyc. 1090-91, and authorities there cited . The court is firmly committed to the doctrine of volenti non fit injuria, and consequently, the court erred in its oral charge.—*Woodward I. Co. v. Cook*, 124 Ala. 553; *Tutwiler C. & C. Co. v. Farington*, 144 Ala. 157; *Whitmore v. Ala. C. & C. Co.*, 51 South. 397. A mine foreman is a fellow servant of a miner.—4 Mayf. 153. Charges 16, 17, 20, 21 and 25 should have been given.—*Sloss-S. S. & I. Co. v. Knowles*, 129 Ala. 400; *Alterac v. West P. C. Co.*, 161 Ala. 435. Charges 19, 24 and 27 should have been given.—*Landsell v. Northern Ala. R. R. Co.*, 138 Ala. 548. The risk of injury from noxious gases is assumed.—4 Thomp. sec. 4701, 4644.

[Pratt Consolidated Coal Company v. Davidson.]

W. H. SMITH, for appellee. The appellee had a good cause of action under sections 1031, and 1016, Code 1907.—*Sloss-Sheffield Steel & I. Co. v. Sharpe*, 161 Ala. 432; *Foley v. Pioneer M. & M. Co.*, 144 Ala. 178. The appellee was entitled to the affirmative charge, and hence, the court did not err in the charges given or refused.

SAYRE, J.—Plaintiff's intestate, who was a miner, lost his life by an explosion of gas in the defendant company's mine where he was mining coal.· The case went to the jury on counts 3, 4, and 5, the general issue, and various pleas of contributory negligence and assumption of risk.

Section 1031 of the Code of 1907 requires that, "when gas is known to exist, the owner, agent, or operator of any coal mine shall employ a competent fire boss, whose duties it shall be to examine every place in the mine before the men are permitted to enter for work. Said fire boss shall be at some convenient place each day to inform every man as to the state and condition of his working place before entering. Said work shall be carefully examined every morning with a safety lamp by the fire boss before the workmen are allowed to enter therein." Subsection 2 of the employer's liability act (section 3910 of the Code) makes the employer liable for injury to his employe "when the injury is caused by reason of the negligence of any person in the service or employment of the master or employer, who has any superintendence intrusted to him, whilst in the exercise of such superintendence."

Count 4, after alleging conditions which put into operation the statute requiring the appointment of a fire boss and prescribing his duties, alleges a breach of the duty imposed, and that it caused the death of plaintiff's intestate. The duty of a fire boss—discharged in

this case by a person called "mine foreman"—is a duty
of superintendence, within or without section 1031 of
the Code. The count, as for any objection taken to it,
was well framed under the second subdivision of the
employer's liability act.

When answering interrogatories propounded to it
under the statute, defendant's superintendent answering for it, defendant deposed: "As gas had been discovered in only a certain part of the mine far removed
from the entrance, and for this reason, no warning or
sign was given or placed at the entrance to the mine.
The warning signals were placed nearer the locality
where gas had been discovered." And further: "As
before explained, the warnings were given or placed
further down in the mine and near the locality in said
mine where gas had been discovered." Those parts of
the depositions which have been quoted were, on motion
of the plaintiff, stricken, on the ground that they were
not responsive to the interrogatories. To the defenses
set up in the special pleas, the substance of which will
sufficiently appear later on, those parts of the deposition stricken by the court were relevant and material,
as the appellant concedes. Such being the case, according to both the earliest and the most recent decisions of this court, from which we have no disposition to
depart again,, there was error in striking the quoted
parts of the deposition on the ground that they were not
responsive to the interrogatories propounded. They
were responsive to the issues, as they had been made
up with the court's approval, and, not being otherwise
objectionable, the defendant was entitled to whatever
weight they might have had with the jury.—*Carwile v.
Franklin*, 164 Ala. 543, 51 South. 396, and cases there
cited. It is said, however, that this error was not prejudicial to the defendant. If the case had been tried on
any true line, and without other error, we think a

proper application of the doctrine of error without injury in respect to this particular ruling might be worked out on one or more considerations. But there was other error which makes a reversal necessary.

The complaint upon which the case was tried proceeded upon two theories: One, that defendant had not complied with the requirements of section 1016 of the Code, for that it had failed to provide and maintain ample means of ventilation for the circulation of air through all the working places in its mine to an extent that would dilute, carry off, and render harmless noxious gases generated in the mine; and the other, that there had been negligence on the part of defendant's superintendent or fire boss in the performance of the duties of superintendence committed to him as required by section 1031 of the Code. To hold, in the absence of a special contract on sufficient consideration, that plaintiff's intestate, at the time of entering defendant's service or by afterwards remaining in that service, assumed the risk of defendant's default in the observance of the statute, or of negligence in superintendence under the employer's liability act, would emasculate those statutes by defeating their clear purpose; nor could the defendant evade responsibility for its failure to observe the statute by setting up different general rules and regulations for the conduct of its business which it may have considered a sufficient substitute for the precautions enjoined by the statute; nor could it by such means impose upon plaintiff's intestate and other employes in similar cases the duty of ascertaining whether it had complied with the law. Plaintiff's intestate may, however, have been guilty of contributory negligence in going into a place where he knew gas existed at the time in dangerous quantity, or where he had been specially warned not to go.—*Woodward Iron Co. v. Andrews*, 114 Ala. 243, 21 South. 440; *A. G. S. R.*

R. Co. v. Brooks, 135 Ala. 401, 33 South. 181; *Ala. Steel & Wire Co. v. Wrenn,* 136 Ala. 475, 34 South. 970; *K. C. M. & B. R. R. Co. v. Thornhill,* 141 Ala. 228, 37 South. 412; *Moss v. Moseley,* 148 Ala. 178, 41 South. 1012; *Briggs v. Tenn. Co.,* 163 Ala. 237, 50 South. 1025; *L. & N. R. R. Co. v. Wynn,* 166 Ala. 413, 51 South. 976; *St. L. & San F. R. R. Co. v. Brantley,* 168 Ala. 579, 53 South. 305; *L. & N. R. R. Co. v. Sharp,* 171 Ala. 212, 55 South. 139. The case of *Birmingham Ry. & Electric Co. v. Allen,* 99 Ala. 359, 13 South. 8, 20 L. R. A. 457, cited by appellant to the proposition that employes who have knowledge of unsafe conditions assume the additional risk thereof if they continue in the service after the lapse of a reasonable time in which to remedy or remove such conditions, and others to the same effect which might be cited, are cases in which the injury to the employe was caused by some defect in the condition of the ways, works, machinery, or plant connected with or used in the master's business. The doctrine of even those cases was, shortly before plaintiff's intestate suffered his injury, greatly modified by the addition to section 3910 of the following proviso: "That in no event shall it be contributory negligence or an assumption of the risk on the part of a servant to remain in the employment of the master or employer after knowledge of the defect or negligence causing the injury, unless he be a servant whose duty it is to remedy the defect or who committed the negligent act causing the injury complained of."

In this case the facts were that two or three months before the catastrophe in question gas had been discovered in the heading of defendant's mine most remote from the entrance, the heading in which plaintiff's intestate worked. Defendant then employed a fire boss, but it does not appear that section 1031 of the Code was in other respects complied with. At least, it is undisputed that neither the fire boss, nor the mine foreman, who sometimes undertook his duties, informed plaintiff's intestate on the day of his injury as to the state and condition of his working place. In fact, defendant, considering that there was gas in the most remote heading of its mine and not elsewhere, as a substitute for the statutory precaution, had caused a signal board to be erected near the entrance to the heading, which board was intended to display a daily statement in respect to the safety of the heading; and had adopted a rule that its employes should not go into that heading on any day unless the signal board showed a statement, dated as of the current day, that the heading was safe. However, the defendant continued to work that heading. Indeed, it seems that the mine was being developed in that direction, and that work was more constant there than at any other point in the mine. In various pleas, which had the court's approval, the defendant had pleaded plaintiff's intestate's knowledge of the facts stated above, that the signal board on the morning of the accident failed to show that the heading was safe, and that under these conditions plaintiff's intestate went into the heading where there was gas which exploded and caused his death. It was nowhere alleged, however, that plaintiff's intestate knew of the presence of gas in the heading in which he was working at the time he went into it. These facts were diversely pleaded as contributory negligence and assumption of risk. In ruling upon demurrers to these pleas, the court failed to observe the principles of law which have been stated. This seemed to give the defendant the advantage of insufficient pleas. But when the court came to give the law of the case in charge to the jury, in both the general oral charge and in special instructions given at the plaintiff's request, as well as in the refusal of special instructions requested by the defendant, it de-

parted from that theory which it had observed in passing upon the demurrers to pleas, and stated the law
more in accord with the principles which ought to have
controlled the disposition of the case.. For example,
there was evidence to sustain the averments of plea A,
demurrer to which had been overruled, but the court
refused to the defendant a charge which directed a verdict for the defendant in the event the jury were reasonably satisfied by the evidence of facts hypothesized
in the language of the plea. To these instructions and
these refusals to instruct the defendant duly excepted.
Under the circumstances the court's rulings in the matter of the instructions were erroneous, however nearly
in accord with the law of the case they would have been
if the issues had been so shaped as to ascertain the
rights of the parties on correct principles. The defendant was entitled to have its liability ascertained and declared upon some consistent theory which it might have
reviewed. Nor can the doctrine of harmless error save
a reversal. True, the plaintiff made out his prima facie
case by proof without conflict. And on the facts as they
are stated in the bill of exceptions no special defense
seems open to the defendant. But we cannot assume
to know what the evidence would have been if issues
had been differently shaped, nor that the defendant, if
demurrers to its defective pleas had been sustained,
might not have amended so as to present a meritorious
defense. Instructions must be pertinent to the issues
formed between the parties. "A court has no right, by
instructions to the jury, to change the issues, or miti-
gate the requirements of its pleadings."—*Moffatt v.
Conklin*, 35 Mo. 453. We are come, therefore, to the
conclusion that the judgment must be reversed.

Reversed and remanded.

DOWDELL, C. J., and ANDERSON and SOMERVILLE, JJ.,
concur.

Louisville & Nashville R. R. Co. v. Holland.

Damage for Death of Person on Track.

(Decided May 11, 1911.   Rehearing denied June 27, 1911.
55 South. 1001.)

1. *Railroads; Person on Track; Pleading; Construction.*—Where the action was against a railroad company for the death of a person on track a count alleging that the decedent, while asleep upon the track, was struck by a locomotive, and that defendant's engineer, though aware of the peril of decedent, negligently failed to use all proper means to prevent injuring him, was not objectionable as confusing the common law and statutory liability, as it avers no employment at the time of being injured, and hence, there can be no basis for an appeal to the Employers' Liability Act, although the terms used would be apt had the count been drawn under such statute.

2. *Same; Jury Question.*—Where the evidence will support a finding that the defendant's engineer saw decedent lying dangerously near the track while far enough away to have stopped the train, and that he ran over decedent, the jury might find that the engineer's act was wanton, as that must be largely a matter of inference from facts proven; hence, without invading the jury's province, the trial court could not have determined whether the conduct of the engineer was willful or wanton.

3. *Same; Care Required.*—The efforts of an engineer to avoid injury after discovering a person in peril that will exculpate the railroad must be the efforts that a prudent and skillful man in his station would have made, and hence, the fact that the engineer did everything in his power to prevent the injury was not sufficient.

4. *Trial; Province of Court and Jury.*—Where there is evidence tending to support the issues, the question becomes one for the jury.

5. *Appeal and Error; Harmless Error; Evidence.*—It being the rule that the erroneous exclusion of evidence is cured by the later admission of such evidence, the exclusion of an answer of a witness was not prejudicial where, upon interrogatories propounded by plaintiff under the statute, the witness testified to the excluded facts, and the depositions were introduced.

6. *Same; Objections Below; Requested Instructions.*—One not satisfied with an oral charge, because omitting certain elements, should request a special charge covering this feature before he is entitled to complain.

7. *Same; Waiver of Error.*—The submission on brief without insistence on a certain assignment is a waiver of such assignment under Supreme Court Rule 10.

8. *Same.*—Where the appellant has waived the error in a certain assignment by a submission on brief without an insistence on it, he

cannot at a later date retract the waiver and in a supplementary brief insist upon the assignment.

9. *Same; Estoppel to Allege Error.*—Where one count proceeded on the theory that the deceased was a stranger to the railroad company, and the defendant requested and obtained a charge that deceased was a trespasser, and that the railroad owed him no duty, except in good faith to make an effort to avoid injuring him after discovering his peril, the defendant could not urge on appeal that there was a variance in that the proof showed that the relation of master and servant existed.

10. *Same; Harmless Error; Instructions.*—Where part of the oral charge might have misled the jury to the belief that the mortality tables were conclusive upon the question of life expectancy, a further instruction that they were not compelled to look to these tables, but might do so in determining the probable expectancy, cured the error.

11. *Evidence; Judicial Notice; General Panics.*—The courts take judicial notice of general panics or financial disturbances, such as the one of 1907.

12. *Same.*—The court will not take judicial notice that the prevalence of a panic reduced the earnings of the persons engaged during the year next preceding this, and hence, it was error for the plaintiff's counsel to make such a statement in argument, in the absence of proof of that fact.

13. *Trial; Argument of Counsel; Necessity of Objection.*—Where the objection was not specifically directed to the erroneous part of the argument, part of which was proper, it was not error to overrule a general objection.

14. *Jury; Competency; Relationship; Affinity.*—Affinity is the relation existing between a husband and the blood relations of the wife, or between the wife and the blood relations of the husband, but one spouse is not related to the affinities of the other spouse, and hence, a juror related by affinity to plaintiff's wife is not related to plaintiff.

15. *New Trial; Misconduct of Juror.*—The fact that a juror during an intermission in the trial went into a room adjoining the court room and greeted a near relation of the decedent, was not grounds for a new trial, where it did not appear that the cause on trial was the subject of the conversation, the action being for the wrongful death of the decedent.

16. *Charge of Court; Prominence to Particular Facts.*—Charges that the jury had the right to infer that the personal expenses of plaintiff's intestate were greater than $19.50 per month, and that in connection with the other evidence on the amount of the decedent's earnings, which were devoted to his personal expenses, the jury might look to the testimony of intestate's wife on the former trial, that it took about half his earnings to support himself, not only gave undue importance to isolated portions of the evidence, but were argumentative as well.

17. *Same; Meeting Argument.*—It is always proper to refuse charges requested for the purpose of meeting argument of opposing counsel.

18. *Same; Covered by Those Given.*—It is not error to refuse charges already coverd in substance by those given.

19. *Same; Ignoring Issues.*—In an action against a railroad for wrongful death based both on wanton negligence and the simple negligence of the engineer after discovering the peril of plaintiff's intestate, a charge which omits in hypothesis liability for the simple negligence was properly refused.

20. *Same; Weight of Evidence.*—In an action against a railroad for the wrongful death of a person on the track in which there was evidence that the use of sand was a supplementary aid to the quick stopping of the train, charges to the jury that the failure to use sand would not be negligence, unless its use would have prevented the injury, were invasive of the province of the jury, and hence, erroneous.

21. *Same; Assuming Facts.*—The evidence in this case examined and it is held that the engineers' evidence as to the position of intestate's head did not conflict with plaintiff's evidence on that subject, and that a charge was not erroneous in assuming as a matter of fact that plaintiff's head was upon the rail.

22. *Evidence; Documentary; Mortality Tables.*—Mortality tables are not conclusive on the issue of life expectancy in an action for wrongful death.

APPEAL from Limestone Circuit Court.

Heard before Hon. D. W. SPEAKE.

Action by W. T. Holland, as administrator, against the Louisville & Nashville Railroad Company, for damages for death of his intestate. Judgment for plaintiff, and defendant appeals. Affirmed.

Count D is as follows: "The plaintiff, W. T. Holland, as administrator of the estate of Ranzy L. Holland, deceased, claims of the defendant, the Louisville & Nashville Railroad Company, a corporation, the sum of $25,000, for this: That, whereas, said defendant was, is now, and had been theretofore on, to wit, the 6th day of March, 1908, engaged in the business of operating a railroad in and through the town of Athens, county of Limestone, state of Alabama, for the transportation of persons and freight for hire; that on said day, to wit, the 6th day of March, 1908, plaintiff's intestate was in said town of Athens, Alabama; that plaintiff's said intestate fell asleep on or close to the railway track of defendant, and while thus asleep on or close to the railway track of defendant was struck by an engine or locomotive on the railway track of said

defendant, and was so injured therefrom that, as a
proximate consequence thereof, he died. And plaintiff
avers that one of defendant's engineers, T. J. Douglass,
who had charge or control of said locomotive or engine
operated then and there on said railway track of defendant, and to which engine or locomotive cars were
attached, after discovering that plaintiff's intestate was
thus in a perilous position, and that plaintiff's said intestate was totally unconscious of said peril, the said
engineer who thus saw the perilous position of plaintiff's intestate and the unconsciousness of his peril by
plaintiff's said intestate in time to avoid injuring him
by the proper use of appliances at his command, list-
lessly, inadvertently, or negligently failed to resort to
the proper use of all preventive means at his hands in
the conservation of the safety of plaintiff's said intestate, all to the great damage of plaintiff as aforesaid."

The demurrers raise the proposition that the complaint shows that plaintiff's intestate was guilty of
contributory negligence, and nothing more than simple
negligence is charged therein, and because count D is
inconsistent, in that a part thereof is based upon the
common-law liability and a part under the employer's
liability act, and because said count is indefinite and
uncertain in this: That it fails to show whether it is
grounded on the common-law liability or the statutory
liability of an employer.

The following charges were refused the defendant:
(5) "Unless the jury believe from the evidence that
after the actual discovery by the engineer that the deceased would not leave the track, and the conduct of
the engineer was such as to show a reckless disregard
for the life of Ranzy L. Holland, they must find for the
defendant." (7) "If the jury believe from the evidence
that the engineer, as soon as he discovered that the deceased would not leave the track in time to escape the

injury, applied the brakes and emergency, and sounded the alarm signal, and if they further believe that the use of sand would not have prevented the injury, and that the engineer did all he could to stop the engine, they must find for the defendant." (8) "If the jury believe from the evidence that the engineer, after discovering that the deceased would not leave the track in time to escape the danger, immediately did all in his power to stop the engine, then they must find a verdict for the defendant." (G) "The failure to use sand by the engineer would not amount to negligence, creating liability in this case, unless you believe the use of the same would have prevented the injury." (P) "I charge you, gentlemen of the jury, that the use of the sand by the engineer could not, according to the evidence in this case, have operated to bring the train to a stop before it struck plaintiff's intestate." (Q) "I charge you, gentlemen of the jury, that under the uncontradicted evidence in this case the use of sand in connection with the other means adopted for bringing the train to a stop would not have operated to stop the train in time to avoid striking plaintiff's intestate." (8) "I charge you that in connection with all of the other evidence in this case bearing upon the question of the amount of the earnings of plaintiff's intestate, which were devoted to his personal expenses, you may look to the testimony of Mrs. Holland on the former trial that his earnings would not average more than $55 per month, and that it took about half of that amount for the support of plaintiff's intestate." (T) "I charge you in connection with all of the other evidence in this case bearing upon the question of the amount of the earnings of plaintiff's intestate, which were devoted to his personal expenses, you may look to the testimony of Mrs. Holland, the widow of plaintiff's intestate, on the former trial of this cause, and which former testimony she admitted upon this trial having given at that time, that the earnings of her said husband would not average more than $55 per month, and that it took about half of that for his support." (X) "You have the right to infer from the evidence in this case that the personal expenses of plaintiff were greater than $19.50 per month."

SANDERS & THACH, for appellant.   The court erred in overruling demurrer to count D.—4 Enc. P. & P. 619; 5 *Ib.* 303 and 334; *Dusenberry's Case,* 94 Ala. 413. The court erred in excluding that portion of Douglass's testimony objected to by plaintiff.—*L. & N. v. Holland,* 164 Ala. 73.   The court erred in its oral charge to the jury as to the mortality tables and the life expectancy. —*Mary L. C. & R. Co. v. Sanders,* 97 Ala. 171; *Davis' Case,* 99 Ala. 593; *R. & D. R. R. Co. v. Hissong,* 97 Ala. 187.   The court erred in refusing the written charges asked by the defendant to the effect that the verdict of the jury should be for the defendant if the engineer in charge of the engine used all of its appliances to avoid injuring plaintiff's intestate after discovering his peril. —*L. & N. R. R. Co. v. Brown,* 121 Ala. 227; *N. C. & St. L. v. Harris,* 37 South. 794; s. c. 44 South. 962; *L. & N. v. Holland, supra; Duncan v. S. L. & S. F.,* 44 South. 418; *Haley's Case,* 113 Ala. 648; *Glass' Case,* 94 Ala. 581.   The courts judicially know or notice such things as are or should be generally known in their respective jurisdiction.—17 A. & E. Enc. of Law, 895, but the rule is limited to matters of a general and public nature. Hence, the court was in error in his ruling on the argument of counsel.   The juror William E. Rowe was incompetent because of the relationship to plaintiff's wife. —*Kirby v. The State,* 89 Ala. 63; *Kelly v. Kelly,* 56 Am. Dec. 288; *State v. Wall,* 79 Am. St. Rep. 195.   This disqualification was not known by defendant until after trial.—*Sowell v. Bank of Brewton,* 119 Ala. 92; 29 Cyc.

769. The affirmative charge as to count D of the complaint should have been given.—*Choate v. A. G. S. R. R. Co.*, 54 South. 507.

W. R. WALKER, for appellee. On the question of judicial notice and argument of counsel, the following cases are cited.—*T. & C. R. R. Co. v. Stanford*, 112 Ala. 80; *Andrews v. Frierson*, 144 Ala. 470; 92 C. C. A. 357; 105 U. S. 45; 4 Wig. secs. 2566, 2580. The court properly denied the motion for a new trial, as the juror was not related by affinity to the wife of intestate, but merely to the wife's affinity.—*Kirby's Case*, 89 Ala. 63; 1 Coke on Littleton, 157; 24 Cyc. 274; Bishop on Marriage, sec. 744; 84 Ga. 145; 10 Lea. 1; 2 Snead 184. Counsel discuss other assignments of error, but insist that they were without merit for the reason that the questions involved were for the jury, and that they were fairly submitted to the jury and by them adversely decided to appellant.

McCLELLAN, J.—A report of the former appeal of this cause may be found in 164 Ala. 73, 51 South. 365, 137 Am. St. Rep. 25.

After remandment, the plaintiff withdrew all of the counts theretofore in the pleading, and amended the complaint by adding counts A, B, C, and D. Count A was later withdrawn, and this action took out of the case the issues made by special pleas 2 to 7, inclusive, to that count only, leaving the general traverse of counts B, C, and D, as presenting the issues finally submitted to the jury. These counts (B, C, and D) proceed on the theory of misconduct or omission after discovery of intestate's peril; the first ascribing willfulness or wantonness to the servant in charge of the locomotive, in inflicting the fatal injury, and the last two imputing simple negligence to that servant in respect of his conduct after discovery of intestate's peril.

The only error assigned and argued in brief, as upon rulings on the pleading, complains against the over-ruling of the demurrer to count D. The point of criticism of the count is that it confuses, in averments, common-law and statutory liability. The objection is not well founded. The count avers no relationship of employment, existing at the time of injury, between intestate and defendant, and without such an averment, at least as a *necessary* inference from facts alleged, the essential basis for an appeal to the provisions of the employer's liability statute is wanting. There being no averment of relationship in employment, the count must be taken as undertaking to charge a breach of the common-law duty toward one, of whose peril defendant's servant had become aware. That terms aptly descriptive of the character of the negligence imputed and of the *means* of the injury, had the count been drawn under the liability statute, were employed in this count cannot control the construction of the count. It is the gravamen of the whole count, and not to the abstract meaning of descriptive terms employed, nor to their association, upon occasion, with statutory or other rights and remedies, that controls the nature and character of the cause of action declared on. . The count is not uncertain or duplex in the particular upon which it is assailed.

The distance from intestate at which the engineer first discovered him in a position, dejected or recumbent, dangerously near or upon the track, was a controverted issue under the evidence, as was also the inquiry whether the engineer so omitted his duty, after becoming aware of intestate's peril, as to bring his conduct within the definitions approved by this court of wanton or willful misconduct resulting in injury. Whether the consciousness essential to render conduct or omission willful or wanton, as the cause of injury, was present upon the occasion must have been, as generally and of necessity, a matter of inference from pertinent facts and circumstances proven. In this case it was open to be found, from the tendencies of the evidence, that the engineer saw the intestate on or dangerously near the track ahead, and so, in a recumbent posture, indicative of obliviousness to the impending danger from the on-coming train; that the point at which the engineer be-came so aware was beyond that from which, as related to intestate, the locomotive and train could have been stopped by the employment, promptly and in order, of the means provided and known to skillful men in his station; that these appliances were not so employed, since (evidently speaking) the train was not stopped within the distance some of the evidence tended to show it could have been brought to a stop; that to sand the track, through appliances afforded, is a supplemen-tary aid to, if it does not itself facilitate, a quicker stop of a moving train; and that the sand was not used in this instance. Whether the engineer omitted or de-layed doing his duty, and, if so, with a conscious disre-gard of the consequences of his omission or delay, in view of the peril in which he knew intestate was, could not have been pronounced by the court below without invading the jury's province. It is true he testified that all was done promptly and in order that could have been done to avert the injury; yet from other evidence it was reasonably open to be found that, though he knew of intestate's peril and saw his prostrate, appar-ently unconscious, posture in dangerous proximity to the track ahead, he delayed to avail, as he should not have done, of the appliances at hand to avoid the injury, even, according to some of the evidence, to a point almost upon that at which intestate was; whereas, it appeared from some of the evidence that, had proper prudence been employed within a reasonable time after the engineer was aware of intestate's plight, preventive measures would have averted the injury.

In such state of reasonably possible finding of fact, it cannot be held that there was no reasonable warrant for the jury to conclude that the injury was willfully or wantonly inflicted.—*A. G. S. R. R. Co. v. Hamilton*, 135 Ala. 343, 33 South. 157. Whether these bases of extreme culpability of the engineer ought to have been found, from the whole evidence, by the jury were inquiries the court could not determine. There was evidence, as stated, leading to such a finding. Upon review of the trial on the motion for a new trial, the trial court resolved the issues of willfulness, wantonness, and simple negligence, vel non, in favor of the verdict. We are not convinced that that conclusion is so plainly erroneous as to justify its reversal.—*Cobb v. Malone*, 92 Ala. 630, 9 South. 738; *Hamilton's Case, supra.*

This question was propounded by counsel for defendant to the witness Cartwright: : "State whether or not the train stopped quickly after you heard the short, sharp distress signal?" The response was: "I think it stopped about as quick as it could have been stopped." The court sustained the motion of plaintiff's counsel to exclude the question and the answer thereto. The error, if such it was, was entirely cured when the witness, on subsequent examination, stated, "and, as stated before, after the distress signals were first sounded, the train appeared to have stopped about as quick as it could have slowed up."

On redirect examination by counsel for defendant, the witness Douglass was examined as follows: "Q.

State to the jury whether or not the road crossing at the third crossing (just north of which intestate was killed) south of the depot in Athens, the street crossing there, is not elevated somewhat above the track just north of it? A. Yes, sir; that ground is considerably lower. Q. Where? A. Just north of that crossing, where the street crossing comes up over it; that is what prevented me from seeing the man." On motion of plaintiff's counsel, no grounds being shown by the bill, the court excluded the expression, "that is what prevented me from seeing the man." If it be assumed (for the occasion) that this ruling was error, it was harmless, since the same matter, in substance and effect, was admitted in evidence at the instance of both plaintiff and defendant. In the answer of the witness Douglass, to interrogatories propounded by plaintiff to defendant under the statute, this appears: "At a point a few feet south of where Holland was lying when he was struck, there is a street crossing somewhat elevated above the point where Holland was lying at the time he was truck, and this elevation was the only obstruction between Holland and the engineer." In the further examination of Douglass he said: "* * * That the crossing rising above it was what prevented him from seeing him further off; * * * that the elevation of the dirt road as traveled at the third crossing above the ground just north of that crossing obscured the object which was lying there from his vision until he got to within the distance which he had testified to," etc.

In the course of the oral charge to the jury, at different times, the court used this language, to which exceptions were separately reserved: "(a) You take into consideration the distance above the rail that his head was;" and "(b) You take into consideration all the facts and circumstances, * * *. the height of Holland's head above the rail." The back of the skull of intestate was crushed. This wound appears to have been the cause of his death. The engineer testified that the heel of the pilot struck intestate's person; "that from his (engineer's) position he could not see what portion of his head or face was towards him, but that the back of his head was resting on his arm, which was between the ties: * * * that the object did not move until the heel of the pilot struck it."

Three witnesses for the plaintiff testified that intestate's head, just before he was struck, was above the rail. Unless the testimony of the witness Douglass, which we have quoted in part, instituted a conflict with the plaintiff's witnesses referred to, the relative location of the intestate's head, in respect to elevation above the rail, was not a matter of dispute. As counsel for appellant insist, the relative posture of intestate, as the train approached, was a vital factor in the determination of the engineer's culpability. The elevation (if so) of intestate's head above the lateral line of the rail, on the east side of the track, had the immediate tendency to show that the engineer, steadily looking ahead as he testified he was doing, discovered intestate's peril at a greater distance south of intestate than he (engineer) admitted. On his examination in chief, Douglass testified: "That he did not see anything unusual on the track on ringing the bell. but when he got up 125 or 150 feet he saw a man lying out east and north, with his head resting on his arm, and was at the end of the tie or on the rail, and that it was between the ties."

After cautious review of Douglass's testimony, we do not find that he anywhere undertook to fix the location of intestate's head as respected the level of the rail, unless we except where, as we have quoted above, he used the phrase, *"or on the rail."* Whether this phrase had reference to the head, the arm, or the body (proper) of the intestate is very doubtful. The other feature of his quoted testimony, where he said "that the back of his head was resting on his arm, *which* was between the ties," does not tend to show the relative (to the rail) elevation of intestate's head; *"which"* had reference, it appears to *"arm."* There having been, as we view it, no conflict as respected the relative (to the rail) elevation of the intestate's head, the court did not err to defendant's prejudice in assuming, as a matter of fact, that which was, without dispute, proven on the trial.

Two other parts of the oral charge are complained of in assignments 7 and 8. Mortality tables are not conclusive upon the issue of life expectancy. If the original statement of the court in respect to such tables was calculated to impress the jury that they were bound by the table, the idea was fully eradicated by the explanatory statement, made by the court to the jury, wherein it was said: "I do not mean that you are compelled to look to these (mortality tables) but you may look to these in determining the probable expectancy of Holland." The criticism of the other excerpt from the oral charge is that the court prejudicially emphasized the expectancy of intestate, at the time of his death, as being 36 years. Construing the whole of this feature (the ascertainment of the amount of the compensatory damages, if plaintiff was entitled to recover) of the oral charge, it appears that the court was attempting to more fully inform the jury, in the premises, by means of illustration. The reiteration of the expectancy shown by the mortality table introduced in evidence was doubtless unnecessary, even to the illustration. But the explanation by the court before quoted removed any impression that the expectancy shown by the mortality table was binding on the jury. If the defendant was not content with the oral charge, because omissive of the elements bearing on life expectancy, stated in *Mary Lee Coal & Railroad Company v. Chambliss*, 97 Ala. 171, 11 South. 897, special charges on that subject should have been requested.

Charge 1, refused to defendant, was covered in substance by those given for defendant—charges 4, 6, and 16. Charge 3, refused to defendant, was a substantial duplicate of that given for defendant—charge 4, among others. Charge 5, refused to defendant, was incomplete; besides it tended to mislead and confuse the jury by omitting, in hypothesis, the right to a recovery by plaintiff as upon the theory of simple negligence, after discovery of intestate's peril. Charge 7, refused to defendant, was faulty, unless interpreted as being in substance and effect the same as given, for defendant, charges 4, 6, and 16.

However, the refusal of charges 7 and 8 was justified by reason of the fact that in each the hypothesis in part was that the engineer did all in *his* power to stop the engine; whereas, in any event it was the standard of duty, if negligence was to be avoided, that the engineer's preventive effort be such as was known to prudent and skillful men, in his station, in use of the means at hand to avert the impending injury.—*L. & N. R. R. Co. v. Young*, 153 Ala. 232, 236-237, 45 South. 238, 16 L. R. A. (N. S.) 301.

Charge G, refused to defendant, invaded the province of the jury and ignored the tendency of the evidence to the effect that the use of sand was a supplementary aid to, if it did not itself facilitate, the quicker stopping of a moving train. If the omission to use sand contributed to the failure to stop the train before the injury was inflicted, and if the use of sand was one of the means known to skillful men in the station Douglass occupied to stop trains, under the conditions shown by the evi-

dence in this instance, and if the appliances to enable
the use of sand were afforded on this locomotive, and if
there was time—opportunity—to avail of its use, then
it would have been error to give charge G, whereby the
failure indicated was predicated for culpability upon
the condition that its use would have prevented the injury. This charge, as well as those lettered P and Q,
to similar effect, was well refused.

This charge was refused to defendant: "(K) I charge
you that you cannot take judicial knowledge of the fact
that R. L. Holland earned less the last year of his life
than he had theretofore." The recitals of the bill, in
respect of this charge, are these: "The last preceding
charge was requested to meet the argument of counsel
for plaintiff before the jury. Counsel for plaintiff in
his argument to the jury stated that the court and the
jury would take judicial knowledge of the fact that for
many months prior to the death of plaintiff's intestate
a panic had been on, and that they would take judicial
knowledge of the fact that plaintiff's intestate had
earned less on account of said panic than he had prior
thereto. Counsel for defendant objected to this statement of counsel for plaintiff, and moved the court to
exclude the statement from the jury. The court declined to sustain the objection to the argument of
counsel for plaintiff, and overruled the motion of the
defendant to exclude the argument from the consideration of the jury. The defendant duly and legally excepted to this action of the court."

Charge K was correctly refused. As appears from
the bill, it "was requested to meet the argument of
counsel for plaintiff before the jury." It is the settled
rule in this court that it is not error to refuse such
charges.—*B. R. L. & P. Co. v. Morris*, 163 Ala. 190, 209,
50 South. 198; *Hill v. State*, 161 Ala. 67, 69, 50 South.
41; *Birmingham Water Co. v. Copeland*, 161 Ala. 310,

312, 50 South. 57; *Thomas' Case,* 150 Ala. 31, 44, 43
South. 371; *Moss v. Mosely,* 148 Ala. 168, 187, 41 South.
1012; *Mitchell's Case,* 129 Ala. 25, 30 South. 348; *White
v. State,* 133 Ala. 123, 127, 32 South. 139; *Ridgell v.
State,* 1 Ala. App. 94, 55 South. 327; *B. R. L. &
P. Co. v. Chastain,* 158 Ala. 421, 428, 429, 48
South. 85, among others. The cases of *Etheridge
v. State,* 124 Ala. 106, 27 South. 320, *Haynes
v. McRea,* 101 Ala. 318, 13 South. 270, and perhaps others of earlier pronouncement, seem to invite, if
not affirm, a conclusion opposed to the later and now
established rule before stated, and must therefore be
taken as disapproved. Nor do we think the ruling in
respect of the objection to and exclusion of the argument of counsel in the particular indicated error, and
so for the reasons to be stated.

The statement of counsel that court and jury would
take judicial knowledge that a condition of panic prevailed "for many months prior to the death of plaintiff's intestate" on March 6, 1908, was not objectionable. Courts will take judicial notice of what is generally known within the limits of their jurisdiction; of
facts, without evidence thereof, presumably known to
everybody; of facts which everybody does know.—*Gordon et al. v. Tweedy,* 74 Ala. 232, 237, 49 Am. Rep. 813;
Wall v. State, 78 Ala. 417, 418; and other cases cited
in Mayfield's Digest, vol. 3, p. 437.

Consistent with the general rule stated, this court, in
Clifton Iron Co. v. Dye, 87 Ala. 468, 471, 6 South. 192,
decided in 1888, took judicial knowledge "of the fact
that in the development of the mineral interests of this
state, recently made, very large sums of money have
been invested." This view was approvingly quoted in
Drake v. Lady Ensley Co., 102 Ala. 501, 506, 14 South.
749, 24 L. R. A. 64, 48 Am. St. Rep. 77. Such recognition of the fact as the quoted case made necesarily com-

prehended an assumed knowledge, unaided by evidence, of industrial activity in the mineral region of this state. The result cannot be different when reference is had, as here, to a condition of "panic" in our country. The press teemed with news of its prevalence during the winter of 1907-08, as well as with evidences of its effect upon enterprises and industrial activity. Many large and small banks of deposit throughout the country issued "clearing house certificates," and these were used, accepted, as tokens of the value their faces purported to assure. Withal, the fact of financial and industrial depression throughout the country, during the period indicated, was universally known. So we think the part of the argument just considered was not without justification.—*Ashley v. Martin*, 50 Ala. 537.

The latter feature of the argument, viz., that judicial knowledge would be taken that the effect of the "panic" was to reduce the earnings of intestate, below what they had been prior to the panic, was the statement of a material fact without any support in the evidence and without the pale of judicial knowledge. Had this phase of the argument been objected to and the objection overruled, error would have resulted. But the objection and motion, here pressed for appellant, included, without separation, the phase of the argument which, as we have ruled, was unobjectionable. Having embraced in the one objection and motion matter unobjectionable with matter that would have been objectionable, the trial court will not be put in error for its action in overruling such objection and motion.

Special charges S, T, and X, were well refused. S and T were argumentative, as well as possessing the vice of singling out and giving undue importance to a feature or features of the evidence. Charge X was subject to the latter criticism of charges S and T.

William Rowe served as a juror on the trial His wife was Edna Lewis. She was the daughter of Eula

Lewis. Eula Lewis was a daughter of George Hughey. George Hughey was a son of Isaac Hughey (common ancestor). And plaintiff's (W. T. Holland's) wife was a daughter of Isaac Hughey. Juror Rowe, appellant insists, was related within a prohibitive degre of affinity to plaintiff through plaintiff's wife. It is argued that Rowe was related by affinity in the fourth degree to plaintiff, because plaintiff's wife was so related by affinity to Rowe.

"Affinity" is the relation, the product of marriage, between the husband and the consanguinei of the wife, or between the wife and the consanguinei of the husband. —*Kirby's Case,* 89 Ala. 63, 8 South. 110; *Danzey's Case,* 126 Ala. 15, 28 South. 697; *Lowman v. State,* 161 Ala. 47, 50 South. 43. The husband is not related to the affines of the wife.—2 Steph. Com. 285; *Lowman v. State, supra.* The juror's wife was related by affinity to the plaintiff, since she (Edna Rowe) was the greatniece of plaintiff's wife; and the juror was related by affinity to plaintiff's wife, by the same strain as connected plaintiff with the juror's wife. But since the affines of the wife are not related to the husband, and vice versa, the plaintiff and the juror were not related by affinity.

One of the grounds of motion for new trial was rested on the alleged bias or prejudice of the juror Rowe in favor of the beneficiaries of the recovery in this action. The basis for this insistence seems to be that Rowe, during an intermission in the trial, went into a room adjoining the court-room, wherein the father, father-in-law, widow, and children, of the intestate were, and greeted and talked to them. The bill recites: "It was admitted by counsel for the parties that defendant's counsel saw juror W. E. Rowe go into the room and converse with said parties mentioned in the evidence, * * * and such occurrence was told to the judge the follow-

ing morning on the bench; such occurrence not being
known to counsel for plaintiff." It does not appear
that the cause on trial was the subject, directly or indirectly, of the conversation stated. While the described action of this juror did not evince the very nicest sensibility for the proprieties, that all possible suspicion of his impartiality might be avoided, it was not
such action as amounted to misconduct or that tended,
without more (not here present), to prove bias or prejudice in favor of plaintiff or of the beneficiaries of the
recovery under the statute.—*Montgomery Traction Co.
v. Knabe*, 158 Ala. 458, 48 South. 501.

Every assignment of error insisted on in brief on
submission has been considered and treated in the opinion. We find no error therein, so the judgment must
be arffimed.

Affirmed.

DOWDELL, C. J., and SIMPSON and SOMERVILLE, JJ.,
concur.

On Rehearing.

This appeal was submitted May 18, 1910. Assignment of error No. 20 complained of the action of the
court in refusing to defendant (appellant) charge D.
This was the affirmative charge for defendant as to
count D of the complaint. In the brief filed for appellant upon the original submission, there was, as is conceded for appellant, no insistence whatever upon assignment No. 20. In April, 1911, appellant's counsel
filed what is denominated as "Additional Brief for Appellant." It consisted of the statement that "the general charge as to count D of the complaint should have
been given," and closed with the citation, in support of
the statement, of *Choate v. A. G. S. R. R. Co.*, 170 Ala.
590, 54 South. 507-509. A copy thereof was served

upon counsel for appellee, according to the certificate, on April 5, 1911. The opinion was delivered on May 11, 1911. In its closing lines, this statement appears: "Every assignment of error insisted on in brief *on submission* (italics supplied) has been considered and treated in the opinion." Necessarily the restriction of the consideration of the assignments of error to those only insisted upon in brief *on submission* excluded the belated argument expressed in the "Additional Brief for Appellant." The question whether the belated insistence could be noticed was thoroughly considered by the court in consultation, and determined against appellant, as the quoted statement indicates. On rehearing, counsel for appellant again press the proposition and insist that the *additional brief* was within rule 13 of Supreme Court practice, and that its contention should be considered and given effect.

It is too well settled to now admit of doubt that the failure of an applicant to insist, in this court, upon errors assigned on the record is a *waiver* and abandonment thereof.—*M. & C. R. R. Co. v. Martin*, 131 Ala. 269, 280, 30 South. 827; *Beyer v. Fields*, 134 Ala. 236, 238, 32 South. 742; *Pickering v. Townsend*, 118 Ala. 351, 357, 23 South. 703; *Western Railway Co. v. Arnett*, 137 Ala. 414, 425, 34 South. 997; *North Ala. Railway Co. v. Counts*, 166 Ala. 550, 51 South. 938; among others. See, also, 4 Enc. L. & P. pp. 605, 606. The *submission* on brief, without insistence upon assignment 20, was, hence, a waiver and abandonment of that assignment.—Rule 10, Supreme Court Practice (Civil Code 1907, p. 1508). Pending the period between the *submission* and the presentation of the *additional brief*, many months afterwards, obviously the waiver was effective. So, under our practice, the real question is, Could the appellant retract, long after *submission*, the waiver thus deliberately made by the filing of an *addi-*

tional brief, as was here done? Rule 13 of Supreme
Court practice has no reference to the retraction of the
waiver wrought by the failure to insist upon an assignment of error. The *additional brief* thereby contemplated must, as far as appellant is concerned, be in support of errors already urged upon submission.

The time for appellant's election of the errors assigned upon which he will rely and insist (rule 10, S.
C. Pr.) is when the appeal is submitted. If he does not
do so, he has abandoned—waived—the error assigned.
If then he must have elected, with waiver as to those
errors not then urged, there can be, in the nature of
things, no other stage of the proceeding in this court
where he may retract the legal effect of his former inaction with respect to errors assigned. His submission
of the appeal upon a brief wholly silent as to one or
more of the errors assigned commits the appeal to the
court just as if the waived or abandoned errors had not
been assigned. The assignment of errors being in the
nature of a complaint in pleading by appellant, his
abandonment or waiver of one or more assignments is
not different, in principle, from like action by a plaintiff at nisi prius, with reference to counts in his declaration after the submission of the case to the trier
thereof. As a matter of orderly procedure alone in this
court, any other practice in this regard would be confusing and retarding. If an appellant might, months
after submission and before the decision was delivered,
press errors not insisted on at the submission, it would
be required that appellee have a reasonable opportunity
in which to reply to the insistence upon theretofore
abandoned errors; and hence the consideration of the
appeal by the court suspended during this period. Indeed it might, and, if the practice were allowed, doubtless would often, occur that the questions urged *on the
submission* had been decided and the opinion of the

court prepared to be delivered when the new insistence was presented by *additional brief,* whereupon the court would be required, after reasonable opportunity afforded appellee to reply to appellant's additional brief, to restore the appeal to a status of consideration; whereas, it had been fully decided upon the questions urged at the submission. It is evident that the practice this appellant's contention would lead to would permit the assignment of numerous errors and the submission upon an insistence as to one only of them, and a periodic presentation of arguments in support of theretofore unurged assignments. An artful appellant, who desired delay, might thus be invited to effect his purpose. The following decisions, noted on brief for appellee, of other jurisdictions, with others cited in them, support our conclusion in this regard:—*Gates v. B. & O. Ry. Co.,* 154 Ind. 338, 56 N. E. 722; *Sligh v. Shelton R. Co.,* 20 Wash. 16, 54 Pac. 764; *Foster v. East Jordan Lumber Co.,* 141 Mich. 316, 104 N. W. 617; *State v. Omaha Nat. Bank,* 59 Neb. 483, 81 N. W. 322.

But had appellant included in his brief on submission an insistence on assignment 20, as upon the authority of *Choate v. A. G. S. R. R. Co., supra,* it would not have availed. At the request of the defendant (appellant) the court gave charge 2, as follows: "I charge you, gentlemen of the jury, that Ranzy L. Holland was a trespasser, and the defendant owed him no duty, except to, in good faith, make an effort to avoid injuring him after actually discovering his peril."

The theory upon which appellant would apply the ruling in *Choate v. A. G. S. R. R. Co., supra,* was that Holland was alleged in count D to have been, when stricken, a stranger (and he was, if a trespasser) in respect of relation in employment to the appellant; whereas, the evidence showed that the relation of master and servant existed, and negligence by Holland, in the performance of a duty while in that relation.—*Helton v. Ala. Mid. R. 'R. Co.*, 97 Ala. 284, 12 South. 276. As is evident, the quoted charge given at appellant's insistence and request advised the jury in immediate opposition to the theory of variance taken and applied in *Choate v. A. G. S. R. R. Co.*, *supra*. Having induced the court to so instruct the jury, the appellant cannot, in this court, complain of the refusal of an instruction that, to have been properly given, must have assumed a status immediately opposed to that pronounced in the instruction (2) that was given at appellant's request. —*Clarke v. Dunn*, 161 Ala. 633, 639, 50 South. 93, and authorities therein cited; *Shelton's Case*, 73 Ala. 5; *Leonard's Case*, 66 Ala. 461.

The application for rehearing is denied.

DOWDELL, C. J., and ANDERSON, MAYFIELD, SAYRE, and SOMERVILLE, JJ., concur.

Southern Railway Company *v.* Smith.

Damage for Death of Person on Track.

(Decided June 6, 1911.   55 South. 913.)

1. *Railroads; Persons on Track; Trespasser; Children.*—Where a child six years old was a trespasser on a railroad track, and was killed by a train, the railroad company and its servants owed it no more duty than it owed other trespassers under similar conditions, considering the fact of its age and condition, and that it was apparently asleep on the track at the time of the injury.

2. *Same; Pleading.*—Where the action was for damages for the death of a child on a railroad track, it was not necessary that the counts should allege that the child was on the particular track on which the train was, and that there was but one track.

3. *Same; Evidence.*—Where the action was for causing the death of a child on the track, evidence that the track at the point of the injury was constantly used by the public as a footway, though not admissible to show any right that the decedent had to be on the track, or to show that he was not a trespasser, was admissible on the question of wanton negligence, in connection with the evidence

that those in charge of the train knew of such use of the track by the public.

4. *Same; Jury Question.*—The evidence in this case examined and held insufficient to warrant the submission of the question of wantonness to the jury.

5. *Pleading; Objection; Aider by Proof.*—In an action for causing the death of a child on the track, a demurrer to a count because it did not show that the injury occurred in this state was properly overruled where it appeared that the cause had once been tried and all the evidence showed that the injury did occur in this state.

6. *Appeal and Error; Reversal; New Pleading; Dilatory Plea.*—Where an action for causing the death of a child on a railroad track had been once tried, and on appeal the judgment was reversed, it was within the discretion of the trial court on the second trial to refuse to permit the defendant to file a dilatory plea setting up that the plaintiff was not the administrator at the time the plea was offered.

7. *Same; Decision; Effect in Lower Court.*—Where it was held on a former appeal that the question as to the duty to keep a lookout at the place of the injury was for the jury, it was proper on a subsequent trial to refuse instructions asserting that neither the speed of the train nor the failure to keep a lookout were evidence of negligence, and that the trainmen owed no duty to the deceased to keep a lookout.

8. *Charg of Court; Argumentative.*—Where the action was for damages for causing the death of a child, brought under the homicide act, a charge asserting that the damages recoverable are not intended to compensate the parents for the death of the child, but should be such sum as would be sufficient to punish the act done, and if defendant's engineer ran the engine against the deceased through mere negligence or error of judgment, plaintiff ought not to recover as much as if it had been wantonly or intentionally done, was argumentative and properly refused.

9. *Same.*—Charges asserting that the jury will consider that men and women may be operated on by their sympathies, one way or the other, that the sympathies of the people come out strongly in favor of the weaker party, or the female sex, or the poor man, but the jurors have no right to act on any prejudice or sympathy of that kind, but are to try to do exact justice between the parties as though they were two individuals standing on perfect equality in all respects, that the case should be considered by the jury as between two persons of equal standing, and that the fact that one of the parties is a corporation should not affect their minds in any way, are argumentative and properly refused.

10. *Same; Excluding Issues.*—Where the evidence presented a question of subsequent negligence, a charge asserting that under the undisputd evidence plaintiff's decedent was unlawfully on the track, and the defendant owed him no duty except not to injure him wantonly, negligently or intentionally, was properly refused as excluding the issue of such subsequent negligence.

11. *Same; Weight and Sufficiency of Evidence.*—The trial courts are under no duty to charge juries that there is no evidence of a given fact.

12. *Same; Confused Instructions.*—Charges which are confused and uncertain in meaning may be refused without error.

APPEAL from Jackson Circuit Court.

Heard before Hon. W. W. HARALSON.

Action by A. J. Smith, as administrator, against the Southern Railway Company. From a judgment for plaintiff, defendant appeals. Reversed and remanded.

The rulings on the pleadings sufficiently appear from the opinion of the court, as do the facts in the case.

The following charges were refused to the defendant: (10) "The damages recoverable in this case, if any, are not intended in any way to compensate the parents of deceased for the death of their son, but would be such sum as in your judgment would be sufficient to punish the act done; and if you believe from the evidence that the engineer ran the engine against deceased through mere negligence or error of judgment, plaintiff ought not to recover as much as if the engineer had wantonly or intentionally run his train against deceased." (12) "You will consider that men and women may be operated on by their sympathies one way or another. The sympathies of people come out very strongly sometimes in favor of the weaker party, or the female sex, or the poor man; but the jurors have no right to act upon any prejudice or any sympathy of that kind. You are to try to do exact justice between the parties, just as though they were two individuals standing upon perfect equality in all respects. Their rights are the same, and your duties to each party are the same, and they are not to be evaded." (18) "The court instructs the jury that this case should be considered by the jury as between two persons of equal standing in a community. The fact that one of the parties is a corporation should not affect your minds in any way; but the right of each party should and must be determined upon the evidence introduced in the case, and the instructions given to the jury, which are the law to guide you in your deliberations." (21) "Neither the speed of the train nor the failure to keep a lookout are evidence of negligence in this case. I charge you that from the evidence in this case the child was a trespasser, and the fact, if it be a fact, that people were accustomed to pass along the track at said place in large numbers would not make Robert Smith any the less a trespasser." (31) "The trainmen owed deceased no duty to keep a lookout. Any negligence of the trainmen sufficient to permit of a recovery in this case must have occurred after the child's presence on the track was discovered by them." (25) "Under the undisputed evidence in this case the deceased was unlawfully on the track, and the defendant owed him no duty, except not to injure him wantonly, recklessly, or intentionally." (33) "There is no evidence in this case which would authorize the jury to presume that the engineer was reckless of human life, and acted in a way that is in disregard of the duties imposed upon him as the engineer of the train." Charge 34, in the record, is the general affirmative charge for the defendant. (36) "No recovery can be had in this case for any negligence of the engineer in failing to discover the child on the track, or for a failure to discover him sooner than he did, if you find from the evidence that he did discover him before the engine struck him, under the fourth count."

LAWRENCE E. BROWN, for appellant. Counsel discuss the demurrers to the complaint, but without citation of authority. The court erred in not permitting defendant to file plea C.—Sec. 5331, Code 1907; *Espalla v. Richards*, 94 Ala. 163; *L. & N. v. Trammel*, 93 Ala. 353; *Wilson v. Brothwell*, 50 Ala. 378; *Sadler v. Fisher*, 3 Ala. 202. The court erred in permitting proof as to the frequency of the use of the track as a pass way.—

Glass v. M. & C. Ry. Co., 94 Ala. 581. Written charge 10 should have been given.—Sec. 2486, Code 1907; *Sullivan's Case,* 59 Ala. 272. Charges 12 and 18 were proper.—71 Mich. 61; 102 Mo. 110. Charges 21 and 25 should have been given.—*So. Ry. v. Stewart,* 51 South. 325; *So. Ry. v. Forrester,* 158 Ala. 477; *A. G. S. .v. Fulton,* 144 Ala. 332; *A. G. S. v. Lynn,* 103 Ala. 139. Charge 26 should have been given.—*B. R. L. & P. Co. v. Jones,* 153 Ala. 157. Written charge A should have been given, as the evidence was not sufficient to submit to the jury the question of wantonness.—*So. Ry. Co. v. Stewart,* 51 South. 325. Counsel discuss other written charges refused, but without citation of authority, but insist that on the authority of *So. Ry. v. Drake,* 51 South. 996, that the evidence did not establish negligence after the discovery of peril.

VIRGIL BOULDIN, for appellee. The evidence warranted the finding of wanton injury after discovery of peril. —*Forrester's Case,* 158 Ala. 477; *Bush's Case,* 122 Ala. 470; *Burgess' Case,* 114 Ala. 587. It also warranted a finding of wantonness because of imputed notice of danger at that point.—*Fox's Case,* 52 South. 889; *Hyde's Case,* 51 South. 368; *Wallace's Case,* 51 South. 371. The evidence certainly warranted a finding of negligence after such discovery of peril.—*So. Ry. Co. v. Smith,* 163 Ala. 174. Charge 21 was properly refused. —*N. C. & St. L. v. Harris,* 142 Ala. 253; *So. Ry. v. Smith, supra; Talley's Case,* 102 Ala. 21. It was within the discretion of the court to decline to permit the dilatory plea offered.—*Davis Co. v. Cannon,* 129 Ala. 301; *Reid L. Co. v. Lewis,* 94 Ala. 626. Written charge 10 was properly refused.—Sec. 2486, Code 1907; *Bush's Case, supra.* Counsel discuss other charges refused, but without citation of authority.

MAYFIELD, J.—The action is under the homicide statute (Code 1907, § 2485) for the wrongful death of a child six years old. The child was killed by being run over by a passenger train on appellant's railroad. The injury occurred about 1 o'clock in the afternoon, and at a point about a quarter of a mile from a station, on appellant's road, in the little town or village of Larkinsville.

　The parents of the child lived within a few yards of the railroad track, very near the place at which the child was killed. The child and its older brother were at the home of their parents at the time of the injury. The older one was in the house, attending to some domestic duties, while intestate was playing out of doors. The older child had observed the younger on the track a few minutes (estimated at eight) before the accident. The mother had gone to the depot, which was about a quarter of a mile from her home and the scene of the accident. No one seems to have seen the child that was killed from the time its brother saw it, about eight minutes before the accident, to the time it was discovered by the engineer in charge of the locomotive that struck it—just a few seconds before the injury.

　The engineer was the only person shown to have witnessed the accident. His evidence was that he saw the child lying on the track, near the middle, with one foot across one of the rails, and apparently asleep; that he first discovered it when within 80, 90, or 100 yards of it, when the train was running about 25 miles per hour. He testified that as soon as he discovered the presence of the child on the track he shut off steam and applied the emergency brakes, and that this was all he could do; that he brought the train to a stop in about "four car lengths and the engine and tender;" that this would be about 20 yards to the car, and that the engine and tender are equally as long; that the cars were all about the same length, except the ladies' car, which was about 70 feet in length. The engine and train had just left Larkinsville.

One Mrs. Downs testified that she lived about 100 yards from the place of the accident; that she went to the scene of the accident as soon as the train stopped; that she asked the engineer what he killed Mr. Albert Smith's little boy for, and he said he saw the child, but kept thinking it would get off the track, until it was too late to stop the engine, and that he said the child must have been asleep. The engineer denied having made this statement to this witness.

Another witness for plaintiff, who was a passenger on the train, testified that the engineer told him, on the occasion of the injury, that when he (the engineer) first saw something on the track he thought it was a piece of paper but that when he discovered that it was a child it was too late to stop the train; that the train had gotten under good headway. The plaintiff testified that he had been on engines in motion, and that he could see as well as when on the ground.

There was evidence that the railroad track at the place of the injury was frequently and much used by the public, and that this fact was known to the engineer and other agents in charge of the train. To the introduction of this evidence the defendant reserved many exceptions.

It was ruled by this court (and we think correctly), on the former appeal, that the unfortunate child was a trespasser upon the track of the defendant when it was killed, and therefore that the defendant and its servants owed it only the duty they owed other trespassers under similar conditions, considering the facts of its age and condition, and that it was apparently asleep on the track at the time of the injury. The law on this subject (the killing of an infant while a trespasser on a

railroad track) has been often declared by this court.—
G. P. R. R. Co. v. Blanton, 84 Ala. 154, 4 South. 621; *A.
G. S. R. R. Co. v. Moorer,* 116 Ala. 642, 22 South. 900;
H. A. & B. R R. Co. v Robbins, 124 Ala. 113,, 27 South.
422, 82 Am. St. Rep. 153; *G. & A. U. Ry. Co.. v.. Julian,*
133 Ala. 371, 32 South. 135.

Moorer's Case, supra, reviews the authorities on the
subject, and adopts the rule stated by Mr. Elliott, in his
work on Railroads (section 125), as the correct one. In
the above case this court said: " 'In actions for injuries to children, as in other cases, there can be no recovery, unless defendant has been guilty of a breach of duty. * * * There is a sharp conflict among the authorities, however, as to what the duty of a railroad
company is to children who come upon its premises as
trespassers or mere licensees. We believe the true rule
to be that, although the age of the child may be important in determining the question of contributory negligence, or the duty of the company after discovering
him, the company is, in general, no more bound to keep
its premises safe for children who are trespassers or
bare licensees, not invited or enticed by it, than it is to
keep them safe for adults.' This rule, of course, does
not apply to children, or to any other person, at a place
where they have a right to be, as for instance in a public highway, where it crosses the track, in which case
they are not to be treated as trespassers."

The court properly overruled defendant's demurrer to
count 2. The only reason urged to show error is that
this count did not show that the injury occurred in the
state of Alabama. This cause has been tried once before; and all the evidence, including that of defendant,
showed that the injury, and only injury, complained of
did occur in Alabama. The trial court and the parties
all knew the particular injury relied upon, and knew
that the injury did occur in this state. The want of

jurisdiction did not affirmatively appear on the face of
the count, so as to subject it to demurrer for such want;
nor was there any necessity to make it more certain as
to where the injury occurred. This all the parties and
the court knew when this demurrer was passed upon

It was likewise not necessary for count 4 to allege
that the child was on the particular track upon which
the train was, and that there was but one track. If
there were more than one track at this point, and the
child was upon a different track, this was a subject for
a special plea; it was not necessary for the complainant
to negative that there were more tracks than one at this
point.

The court very properly declined to allow the defendant to file the dilatory plea that plaintiff was not the
administrator at the time such plea was offered. The
case had been tried once, and appealed to this court and
reversed, and it was the second trial before the plea was
offered. It came too late for the defendant to be entitled, as matter of right, to file it; and it is not made to
appear that the trial court abused its discretion in declining to allow it to be filed.

The trial court properly allowed evidence tending to
show that the track of the defendant railroad company
at the point of the injury was constantly used by the
public as a path or footway. In other words, under the
issues in this case of wanton and subsequent negligence, it was permissible to show that the track of defendant at the point of the injury was a way over which
the public were wont to go frequently and in great numbers, and that this fact was known to the servants or
agents of defendant in charge of the train on the fatal
occasion. Such evidence was not admissible for the
purpose of showing that decedent had a right to be on
the track—that he was not a trespasser; but it was admissible on the question of wanton negligence, in con-

nection with evidence that those in charge of the train had knowledge of such use of the track by the public.

In *Fox's Case*, 167 Ala. 281, 52 South. 890, this court spoke on this subject as follows: "It is true that it is said in *Glass' Case*, 94 Ala. 586, 10 South. 215, that evidence of such custom or habit is not admissible; but what the writer evidently meant was that such evidence was not admissible for the purpose of showing that a person on the track, under such conditions, was a trespasser nevertheless. That is evident from the quotation which immediately precedes it, and from what the writer says immediately thereafter, in the same opinion. Such evidence is not admissible for the purpose of showing that the person on the track is not a trespasser, for he is, notwithstanding the custom or habit, still a trespasser, but it is competent and admissible, in connection with other evidence, to show wanton negligence or willful injury on the part of the engineer or persons in control of the train while passing such point."

Charges 10, 12, and 18, if not otherwise objectionable, were argumentative, and for that reason were properly refused.

As was ruled in this case on the former appeal, it was a question for the jury as to the duty to keep a lookout at the place of the injury; and for this reason charge 21 and 31 were properly refused.

Charge 25 was not correct when applied to the evidence in this case. The question of subsequent negligence was one for the jury, and this charge took that question from the jury.

Trial courts, as has been often ruled by this court, are under no duty to charge juries that there is no evidence of a given fact. For this reason, if for no other, charge 33 was properly refused.

Charge 36 is confused and uncertain in its meaning, and for this reason, if for no other, was properly refused.

[Southern Railway Company v. Smith.]

The evidence in this case has been carefully examined, and we have reached the conclusion that it did not warrant the submission of the question of wantonness to the jury. The court instructed the jury, at defendant's request, that there could be no recovery as for willful injury; and we are of opinion that the court erred in refusing the affirmative charge to the defendant as to the second count, which declared on wanton conduct. There was no evidence of a willful or intentional injury, nor was there any evidence of such wanton conduct as would be the equivalent of willful or intentional injury. The only culpability shown was that of simple negligence alone. While some of the conditions were shown which often attend wantonness, such as that the injury occurred at a point on the defendant's track which was frequently used by the public, and this fact of use was known to the servants or agents of defendant in charge or control of the train, yet there was no evidence of any act or omission, on the part of these servants, which could be said to be wantonness.

The train was not being run at a rapid rate of speed, but only at the usual speed of 25 miles per hour. It was not shown that there was a willful or negligent failure to keep a lookout for persons on the track; but, on the contrary, it was affirmatively shown that such a lookout was being kept, and that the unfortunate child was discovered to be on the track when the engine was within 80, 90, or 100 yards of it, and that the engineer used all the means within his power, after discovery of the peril, to stop the train, though his efforts proved unavailing. While there was evidence tending to show that he did not use such means at the very moment he discovered the presence of the child, or an object, on the track, yet this evidence showed that he did so as soon as he was aware that it was a child, and that it was not going to move, or could not move or get off the track.

Adverting to the testimony of the woman, to the effect that the engineer told her (at the time of the accident) that he kept thinking the child would get off the track, and that it must have been asleep, and to that of the witness who said the engineer told him that when he first saw the object on the track he thought it was a piece of paper, while this evidence may have tended to show negligence on the part of the engineer in not using all the preventive means at hand or known to skillful engineers, and that he did not use these methods as soon as he might or should have used them, or to show that a skillful and competent engineer could and would have prevented the accident by discovering the child and recognizing its peril sooner, or that a skillful and competent engineer, or even the one in question, could have prevented the injury after the discovery of the peril, by using other and different methods of preventing the injury, such as blowing the whistle, ringing the bell, or reversing the engine, yet a failure to do these things, as made clear by all the evidence, disputed and undisputed, shows or tends to show nothing more than simple and subsequent negligence.

As has been often said by this court, a mere error of judgment as to the result of doing an act, or of failing to act, having no evil purpose or intent, nor consciousness of probable injury, may constitute simple negligence, but cannot rise to the degree of wanton negligence or willful wrong. Under all the evidence in this case, and under the law as often iterated by this court, the plaintiff was not entitled to recover under the second count of the complaint, which declared on wanton negligence.—See *Bowers' Case,* 110 Ala. 328, 20 South. 345; *Lee's Case,* 92 Ala. 272, 9 South. 230; *Webb's Case,* 97 Ala. 308, 12 South. 374; *Anchors' Case,* 114 Ala. 501, 22 South. 279, 62 Am. St. Rep. 116; *Moorer's Case,* 116 Ala. 645, 22 South. 900.

[Darby v. City of Union Springs.]

While there was no direct or positive evidence of subsequent negligence after discovery of the peril, there was such evidence of fact, and such conflict of evidence, as to authorize the jury to infer the existence of such negligence; and for this reason the trial court properly declined to give the affirmative charge for the defendant as to the count declaring on subsequent negligence after discovery of peril.

For the error pointed out, the judgment must be reversed, and the cause remanded.

Reversed and remanded.

DOWDELL, C. J., and SIMPSON, ANDERSON, SAYRE, and SOMERVILLE, JJ., concur.

Darby *v.* City of Union Springs.

Damages for Death at Municipal Plant.

(Decided Feb. 2, 1911. Rehearing denied June 27, 1911.
55 South. 889.)

1. *Evidence; Judicial Notice Special Acts.*—The courts take judicial notice of public acts, local as to territory, creating municipal corporations or amending their charters, and that a particular municipality was created by several local acts which impliedly, if not expressly, authorized it to own and operate electric lighting plants.

2. *Municipal Corporation; Acts in Private Capacity; Maintaining Electric Light Plant.*—Under Local Acts, 1892-3, p. 231, and Local Acts 1894-5, p. 938, the town of Union Springs was authorized to own and operate an electric lighting plant so as to render it liable for the negligence of its servants or agents, by reason of which an uninsulated guy wire was permitted to become heavily charged with electricity resulting in the death of the child who came in contact therewith.

APPEAL from Bullock Circuit Court.

Heard before Hon. A. A. EVANS.

Action by Ida L. Darby as administratrix, against the City of Union Springs for damages for the death of her minor child, caused by coming in contact with a heavily charged electric wire. Judgment for the defendant and plaintiff appeals. Reversed and remanded.

ERNEST L. BLUE, for appellant. The municipal Code act did not go into effect until September, 1908.—45 South. 638. Under the authority of its several charters the city of Union Springs had authority to own, maintain and operate an electric lighting plant, and this authority rendered it liable for the negligence of its servants and agents which results in injury to others.—24 Ala. 112; 60 Ala. 486; 111 Ala. 337; 112 Ala. 105; 113 Ala. 365; 132 Ala.. 546; 11 L. R. A. (N. S.) 449; 7 L. R. A. (N. S.) 294; 15 Cyc. 466; 14 L. R .A. (N. S.) 268; 101 Am. St. Rep. 825; 146 U. S. 258; 200 U. S. 22; 28 Cyc. 615; Acts 1903, p. 59. The complaint sufficiently alleged constructive notice or knowledge of the defective condition of the wire.—86 Am. St. Rep. 732; 49 *Ib.*, 477; 85 *Ib.*, 735; 43 *Ib.*, 30; 100 *Ib.*, 505; 2 N. J. L. 451. .

RAY RUSHTON, L. M. MOSELY, J. D. NORMAN, and WILLIAM M. WILLIAMS, for appellee. *The assignments of error by appellant are too general, and do not conform to Rule 1 of the Supreme Court Practice. For that reason the judgment should be affirmed.—Williams v. Coosa Mfg. Co.,* 138 Ala. . 73; *Glover v. Lyons,* 57 Ala. 3 5; *Alexander v. Rhea,* 50 Ala. 403. *The demurrers based on the theory of ultra vires were properly sustained.* It is well settled that neither the officers, nor servants nor agents of a municipal corporation can incur any liability, on the part of the city, either in contract or tort, when the act complained of is not authorized by the corporation's charter.—*Posey v. Town of North Birmingham,* 154 Ala. 511, and cases cited; *Albany v. Conniff,* 2 N. Y. 165; *Borland v. City of New York,* 1 Sandf. (N. Y.) 27; *Morrison v. City of Lawrence,* 98 Mass. 219. And it is also well settled that the

charters of municipal corporations are to be strictly
construed, and any reasonable doubt concerning the existence of power is resolved by the courts against the
corporation, and the power is denied.—*City of Eufaula
v. McNabb*, 67 Ala. 588, 589; *Birmingham, &c, v. Birmingham Ry.*, 79 Ala. 465, 471; *Posey v. Town of North
Birmingham*, 154 Ala. 511, 515, and cases therein cited.
It might here be noted that neither of the Acts, above
referred to, purports to be an amendment to the charter
of Union Springs.   Courts take judicial knowledge of
the charter of a municipal corporation (*City Council
of Montgomery v. Wright*, 72 Ala. 411, and cases there
cited).   This failure to embody in the Acts the *direct*
and *expressed* authority to "erect and maintain," and
to so frame these Acts as to be amendments to the charter, are quite significant, and lead only to the conclusion that the intention to grant to the city the right to
operate a plant was not only absent from the minds of
the legislators who passed the bill, but also that
there was no such intention. *The demurrers based
on the theory that the failure of the city to keep
the wires in a safe condition was the breach of a
governmental and not a ministerial duty, and that there
was no law authorizing a private action against the city,
or requiring the city to keep the wires in repair or safe
condition, were properly sustained.*   The duties enjoined upon it by law are enjoined upon it as a part of
government, and not otherwise.   They are, therefore,
public in nature,—duties to the State,—and not to private persons.—*Campbell v. City Council*, 53 Ala.. 528;
City Council of Montgomery v. Gilmer, 33 Ala.. 116,
131; *Borland v. City of New York*, 1 Sandf. (N. Y.) 27.
The gist of each count of the complaint in the case at
bar, is the breach of the city's duty to the general public in failing to keep the wires repaired and in safe condition.   The charter of Union Springs (Laws 1869-70.

p. 276) does not, and we have been unable to find any
law that does, require the city to keep the wires in repair. In the absence of any law requiring the city to
repair these wires, or a law authorizing an action by a
private individual against the city for such failure, we
submit, the duty, if any at all, was merely that of police
regulation, or a governmental function, the breach of
which fastened no liability on the city.—See extensive
note and numerous cases cited and digested, 13 L. R. A.
(N. S.) 1219. And the appellant can receive no comfort from Code, Section 2486, for a suit is permissible
under that section only when the intestate could have
maintained an action for the same act or omission had
he lived.—*S. & N. R. R. Co. v. Sullivan,* 59 Ala. 272,
281; *Sharman, Admr. v. Jefferson County,* 125 Ala. 384.
*The demurrers based on the theory that the averments
of the complaint failed to allege that the city had
knowledge of the alleged unsafe condition of the wires
or that this condition had existed a sufficient length of
time under such circumstances that the city could be
said in law to have constructive knowledge thereof,
were properly sustained.—Town of Cullman v. Mc-
Mims,* 109 Ala. 614; *City Council v. Wright,* 72 Ala.
411; *Davis v. Alexander City,* 137 Ala. 206, 209. *The
demurrers based on the theory that plaintiff's intestate
at the time he was injured was not using the street for
ordinary purposes of travel, and was at that time engaged in childish play therein, were properly sustained.*
It has been many times decided, in different jurisdictions, when an injury happens to a child by reason of
a defect in or an unsafe condition of a public street,
and the child was at the time using the street for play,
that the child loses his rights as a traveler or passer by
or along the street, and the city whose duty it was to
keep the street in a safe condition, is not liable.—*Tighe
v. City of Lowell,* 119 Mass. 472; *Blodgett v. City of*

Boston, 8 Allen, 237; *Gaughan v. City of Philadelphia,*
119 Pa. St. 503, 507; *Bridge Co. v. Jackson,* 114 Pa. St.
321, 327; *Stinson v. Gardiner,* 42 Me. 228; *Lyons v.
Brookline,* 119 Mass. 491.

MAYFIELD, J.—This action is brought, under the
homicide statute, against the appellee, a municipal corporation.

The deceased was plaintiff's minor child, nine years
of age.

The complaint was evidently modeled after forms
often approved by this court as sufficient in all respects, except as to certain alleged defects pointed out
by the demurrer, to be hereafter noticed specifically.

The complaint in short, among other things, alleged
that the defendant municipal corporation, on and before the date of the alleged wrongful death of plaintiff's intestate, "owned and was engaged in operating
an electric light plant, and lines of electric wires," and
that it also attached an uninsulated guy wire to its
electric poles used in this business, so as to be dangerous to the public, and allowed the same to remain in
this dangerous condition; and that plaintiff's intestate,
a boy nine years of age, came in contact with said wire,
which, owing to the defendant's negligence, had become
heavily charged with electricity, and was thereby
wrongfully killed.

The city demurred to the complaint on the grounds:
First, because the court judicially knows that the defendant had no legislative authority for operating an
electric light plant and lines of electric light wires;
second, because the defendant's charter did not authorize it to so operate such plant and wires; third, because
the court judicially knows that there is no statute making it the duty of said municipality to keep such wires
in good condition. There were various other grounds

alleged; but they need not be considered, as they were without merit, or were overruled by the trial court.

From the judgment sustaining the demurrer (or demurrers, as they seem to have been treated), the plaintiff, under the statute for such cases provided, took a nonsuit with a bill of exceptions, in order to review such adverse rulings of the trial court. In this ruling upon the demurrer we are of the opinion that the trial court was in error. The ruling of the trial court was probably based upon a former decision of this court, in the case of *Posey v. North Birmingham,* 154 Ala. 511, 45 South. 663, 15 L. R. A. (N. S.) 711. However, that case is clearly distinguishable from this. While they are identical in many—nearly all—respects, they are different in one; and it was with sole reference to this one that the decision in that case was based. That decision concludes as follows: "Our conclusion is that the defendant municipality had not the power under the general statute, which contained all of its charter powers, to engage in the operation of an electric lighting plant. It follows that the act complained of was ultra vires the corporation, and the resulting injury fixed upon it no liability."

In this case we do not judicially know that defendant corporation was incorporated under the general statutes, or that such statute contained all its charter powers, and therefore conclude that it had no power to engage in the operation of an electric plant.

On the other hand, we take judicial notice of such public acts, though local as to territory, such acts creating municipal corporations or amending their charters, and we know that the defendant corporation's charter was created under several local acts of the Legislature, which impliedly, if not expressly, authorized it to own and operate electric light plants.

The charter powers of the defendant, prior to the new Municipal Code, are to be found in the various lo-

cal acts of the Legislature passed since the 1st day of
March, 1870, at which time a new charter was established by such act (Acts 1869-70, p. 276 et seq.), which
act or charter has been many times amended by other
local acts. Save the local acts of 1892-93 (page 231)
and 1894-95 (page 938), all these amendatory acts are
unnecessary to .be here mentioned. But these specified
acts authorize the city to erect and maintain an electric light plant. This, we think, implies the authority
to own and operate such plant, in such manner as to
render it liable for the negligence of its servants or
agents when engaged in the line and scope of their authority, as is alleged in this complaint. In fact, this
much was expressly decided in *Posey's Case, supra,* in
which the court, speaking through DOWDELL, J. (now
Chief Justice), said: "It seems to be settled as authority, where a municipal corporation, acting within its
charter powers, maintains and operates an electric
lighting plant, the corporation may be held for the negligence of its servants or agents as any other person.—
Fisher v. Newbern, 140 N. C. 506, 53 S. E. 342, 5 L.. R.
A. (N. S.) 541, 111 Am. St. Rep. 857; *Owensboro v.
Knox,* 116 Ky. 451, 76 S. W. 191; *Emory v. Philadelphia,* 208 Pa. 492, 57 Atl. 977; *Herron v. Pittsburg,* 204
Pa. 509, 54 Atl. 311, 93 Am. St. Rep. 798; *Twist v.
Rochester,* 165 N. Y. 619, 59 N. E. 1131; *Emporian v.
Burns,* 67 Kan. 523, 73 Pa. 94. See, also, note to *Her-
bert v. Lake Charles Ice Co.,* 100 Am. St. Rep. 535."

It follows, therefore, that the court erred in sustaining the demurrer to the complaint.

The writer, however, does not desire to commit himself to the conclusions reached in the *Posey Case. supra,*
upon which that case was affirmed, thus sustaining demurrers to a complaint like the complaint in this case,
save as to the authority or power of the two corporations. While, as before stated, it is not in conflict with

the decision in this case, but is authority for it, yet, as it was relied upon by the trial court, and is cited and twice quoted in this case, the writer does not desire to be understood as agreeing to the conclusion in that case in so far as it held that the town of North Birmingham, organized as it was, under the general laws of the state, had no authority to own or operate an electric light plant. He thinks that municipal corporations have the inherent power to light their streets and public buildings. This power is essential to their declared objects and purposes; and, having this power and authority, it is a matter of discretion and expediency as to how they will light them—whether by pine knots, candles, lamps, natural or artificial gas, gasoline, acetylene, or electricity.

Reversed and remanded. All the Justices concur in the conclusion.

MEMORANDA

CASES DECIDED DURING THE PERIOD EMBRACED IN THIS
VOLUME, WHICH ARE ORDERED NOT TO BE
REPORTED IN FULL.

ALABAMA COAL & COKE CO. V. EMPIRE LAND CO.
(Decided May 18, 1911.)

APPEAL from Walker Law and Equity Court.

Heard before Hon. T. L. SOWELL.

W. H. SMITH, for appellant. W. C. DAVIS, and BROONS & STOUTZ, for appellee.

ANDERSON, J.—Affirmed on the authority of *Alabama Coal & Coke Co. v. Gulf Coal & Coke Co.*, 165 Ala. 304; 51 South. 570.

DOWDELL, C. J., SAYRE and SOMERVILLE, JJ., concur.

ALLEN V. ENSLEN, ET AL.
(Decided May 11, 1911.)

APPEAL from Jefferson Chancery Court.

Heard before Hon. A. H. BENNERS.

SAM WILL JOHN, for appellant. GEORGE HUDDLE-STON, for appellee.

McCLELLAN, C. J.—Affirmed on the authority of *Enslen, et al. v. Allen*, 160 Ala. 529, 49 South. 430.

DOWDELL, C. J., SIMPSON and MAYFIELD, JJ., concur.

ANNISTON LIME & STONE CO. V. CITY OF ANNISTON.
(Decided May 30, 1911.)

APPEAL from City Court of Anniston.

Heard before Hon. THOS. W. COLEMAN, JR.

No counsel marked for either party.

Per curiam. Appeal dismissed.

BANK OF MOBILE V. ROBERTSON BANKING COMPANY.
(Decided Feb. 7, 1911.)

APPEAL from Marengo Law and Equity Court.

Heard before Hon.W. H. HERBERT.

ERWIN & MCALEER, for appellant. No counsel marked for appellee.

Per curiam. Appeal dismissed on motion of appellant.

BLEDSOE, ET AL. V. LOGAN.
(Decided June 16, 1911.)

APPEAL from Bibb Chancery Court.

Heard before Hon. A. H. BENNERS.

No counsel marked for either party.

Per curiam. Affirmed on certificate.

BOONE V. LOUISVILLE & NASHVILLE R. R. CO.
(Decided May 9, 1911.)

APPEAL from Talladega Circuit Court.

Heard before Hon. JOHN PELHAM.

BOWMAN, HARSH & BEDDOW, for appellant. KNOX, ACKER, DIXON & SIMS, for appellee.

Per curiam. Dismissed by agreement.

BRENNEN V. ELLIS, ET AL.
(Decided Jan. 29, 1911. Rehearing denied April 27, 1911.)

APPEAL from Birmingham City Court.

Heard before Hon. C. C. NESMITH.

NATHAN L. MILLER, and N. A. GRAHAM, for appellant. TILLMAN, BRADLEY & MORROW, for appellee.

MAYFIELD, J.—Reversed and rendered on the authority of *McCann v. Ellis*, 172 Ala. 60; 55 South. 303.

DOWDELL, C. J., SIMPSON, and MCCLELLAN, JJ., concur.

BURTON, ET AL. V. PIERCE.
(Decided Jan. 12, 1911.)

APPEAL from Birmingham City Court.

Heard before Hon. J. J. RAY.

J. S. KENNEDY, for appellant.　W. K. TERRY, for appellee.

Per curiam.　Affirmed on certificate.

DICKENSON V. THE STATE.
(Decided Feb. 2, 1911.)

APPEAL from Walker Law and Equity Court.

Heard before Hon. T. L. SOWELL.

LEITH & GUNN, for appellant.　ROBERT C. BRICKELL, Attorney General, for the State.

Per curiam.　Dismissed by agreement.

EX PARTE JOHNSON.
(Decided Dec. 19, 1910.)

Original petition in the Supreme Court.

C. E. O. TIMMERMAN, for petitioner.　ALEXANDER M. GARBER, Attorney General, for the State.

Per curiam.　Petition denied.

EX PARTE JONES.
(Decided Feb. 2, 1911.)

Original petition in the Supreme Court.

RIDDLE, ELLIS, RIDDLE & PRUET, for petitioner.　E. S. LYMAN, pro se.

Per curiam.　Rule nisi denied.

GOODWATER MANUFACTURING CO. V. HARDY-TYNES MFG. CO.
(Decided Jan. 19, 1911.)

APPEAL from Coosa Circuit Court.

Heard before Hon. S. L. BREWER.

No counsel marked for appellant.　JOHN A. DARDEN, for appellee.

Per curiam.　Affirmed on certificate.

HEARD V. THE STATE.
(Decided June 15, 1911.)

APPEAL from Anniston City Court.

Heard before Hon. THOS. W. COLEMAN, JR.

Knox, Acker, Dixon & Blackmon, for appellant.
R. C. Brickell, Attorney General, for the State.

McClellan, J.—Affirmed.

Simpson, Anderson and Mayfield, JJ., concur.

KIRKPATRICK V. THE STATE.
(Decided June 16, 1911.)

Appeal from Anniston City Court.

Heard before Hon. Thomas. W. Coleman.

Niel P. Sterne, for appellant. Robert C. Brickell, Attorney General, for the State.

Anderson, J.—Affirmed.

Simpson, McClellan and Mayfield, JJ., concur.

LIGE V. THE STATE.
(Decided June 6, 1911.)

Appeal from Gadsden City Court.

Heard before Hon. James A. Bilbro.

No counsel marked for appellant. Robert C. Brickell, Attorney General, for the State.

Sayre. J.—Affirmed, all the justices concurring.

McCORMACK & CO· V. KINNEY.
(Decided June 29, 1911.)

Appeal from Cullman Circuit Court.

Heard before Hon. D. W. Speake.

Gaston & Pettus. for appellant. J. B. Brown, for appellee.

Sayre. J.—Reversed and remanded on the authority of *Oliver r. Kinney, infra;* 56 South. 203.

Simpson. Anderson and Somerville, JJ., concur.

MARTIN V. CHATTAHOOCHEE VALLEY RAILROAD CO.
(Decided Nov. 22, 1910. Rehearing denied Feb. 1, 1911.)

Appeal from Lee Law and Equity Court.

Heard before Hon. A. E. Barnett.

Barnes & Denson. for appellant. N. D. Denson, for appellee.

Per curiam. Settled and appeal dismissed.

PROVIDENCE OIL & GAS CO. V. GARBER.
(Decided Dec. 14, 1910.)

APPEAL from Jefferson Chancery Court.

Heard before Hon. A. H. BENNERS.

J. L. DAVIDSON, and SMITH & SMITH, for appellant. FRANK S. WHITE & SONS, for appellee.

Per curiam. Dismissed on motion of appellant.

RITTENBERRY, ET AL. V. BEDDOW.
(Decided Dec. 8, 1910.)

APPEAL from Birmingham City Court.

Heard before Hon. CHARLES H. SENN.

J. S. KENNEDY, and ARTHUR L. BROWN, for appellant. C. P. BEDDOW, pro se.

Per curiam. Affirmed on certificate.

RIVENAC CONSTRUCTION CO. V. KINNEY.
(Decided June 29, 1911.)

APPEAL from Cullman Circuit Court.

Heard before Hon. D. W. SPEAKE.

GASTON & PETTUS, for appellant. J. B. BROWN, for appellee.

SAYRE, J.—Reversed and remanded on the authority of *Oliver v. Kinney, infra;* 56 South. 203.

SIMPSON, ANDERSON and SOMERVILLE, JJ., concur.

SPANGLER V. ODOM, ET AL.
(Decided Jan. 12, 1911.)

APPEAL from Lawrence Chancery Court.

Heard before Hon. W. H. SIMPSON.

ALMON & ANDREWS, for appellant.. KIRK, CARMICHAEL & RATHER, for appellee.

Per curiam. Appeal dismissed on motion of appellant.

STATE V. PATTERSON.
(Decided Feb. 2, 1911.)

APPEAL from order of W. W. WHITESIDE, Chancellor.

ROBERT C. BRICKELL, Attorney General, for the State.
WHATLEY & CORNELIUS, for appellee..

McCLELLAN, J.—Dismissed because the question is moot.

TAVELL, EX PARTE.
(Decided June 16, 1911.)

Original petition in Supreme Court.

A. LATADY, for petitioner. A. LEO OBERDORFER,, for appellee.

Per curiam. Prohibition denied.

THOMAS V. GLOVER.
(Decided Feb. 2, 1911.)

APPEAL from Marshall Circuit Court.

Heard before Hon. W. W. HARALSON.

No counsel marked for either party.

Per curiam. Affirmed on certificate.

TWITTY V. THE STATE.
(Decided April 20, 1912.)

APPEAL from Jefferson Criminal Court.

Heard before Hon. S. L. WEAVER.

No counsel marked for either party.

Per curiam. Abated by death of appellant.

VANN V. E. E. FORBES PIANO CO.
(Decided Dec. 1, 1910.)

APPEAL from Birmingham City Court.

Heard before Hon. CHARLES A. SENN.

No counsel marked for appellant. CARMICHAEL & WINN, for appellee.

Per curiam. Affirmed on certificate.

WALKER V. THE STATE.
(Decided April 13, 1911.)

APPEAL from Mobile City Court.

Heard before Hon. O. J. SEMMES.

No counsel marked for appellant. ROBERT C. BRICK-ELL, Attorney General, for the State.

McCLELLAN, J.—No errors of record. Affirmed.

SIMPSON, MAYFIELD and SOMERVILLE, JJ., concur.

WINTER-LOEB GROCERY CO. V. RHEA.
(Decided May 9, 1911.)

APPEAL from Montgomery City Court.

Heard before Hon. WILLIAM H. THOMAS.

No counsel marked for either party.

Per curiam. Dismissed on motion of appellant.

CRANE V. THE STATE.
(Decided May 16, 1911.)

APPEAL from Jefferson Criminal Court.

Heard before Hon. S. L. WEAVER.

No counsel marked for appellant. ROBERT C. BRICK-ELL, Attorney General, for the State.

SAYRE, J.—Reversed and remanded on the authority of *Harris v. The State*, 172 Ala. 413; 55 South. 609.

MILLER, TREASURER, V. PAYNE..
(Decided Jan. 30, 1911.)

APPEAL from Birmingham City Court.

Heard before Hon. C. C. NESMITH.

J. D. PAYNE was appointed by the judges of the city court of Birmingham to act as bailiff of said court, and the county treasurer having refused to pay his monthly salary, he applied for and obtained a mandamus requiring him to pay such salary. The case of *Miller v. Griffith*, was brought by Griffith as the appointee of the sheriff, and not of the judges.

NATHAN L. MILLER,. and NEEDHAM A. GRAHAM, for appellant. No counsel marked for appellee.

SIMPSON, J.—Affirmed on authority of *Miller v. Griffith*, 171 Ala. 337, 54 South. 650.

DOWDELL, C. J., McCLELLAN and MAYFIELD, J., concurring.

INGRAM V. THE STATE.
(Decided Jan. 19, 1911.)

APPEAL from Clay County Court.

Heard before Hon. E. J. GARRISON.

WHATLEY & CORNELIUS, for .appellant. ALEXANDER M. GARBER, Attorney General, for the State.

SOMERVILLE, J.—As to the organization of the grand jury, the questions presented were decided adversely to the appellant in *Patterson v. The State*, 171 Ala. 2; 54 South. 696. The predicate for the admission of dying declarations was sufficient.—*McEwen v. The State*, 152 Ala. 38; 44 South. 619. Affirmed.

DOWDELL, C. J., ANDERSON and SAYRE, JJ., concur.

STATE EX REL. CITY OF TUSCALOOSA V. COURT OF COUNTY COMMISSIONERS OF TUSCALOOSA COUNTY.
(Decided July 6, 1911.)

APPEAL from Tuscaloosa County Court.

Heard before Hon. H. B. FOSTER.

SOMERVILLE & CLARKSON, for appellant. OLIVER, VERNER & RICE, for appellee.

DOWDELL, C. J.—Affirmed on the authority of *Board of Revenue of Jefferson County,, State ex rel. City of Birmingham*, 172 Ala. 138, 54 South. 757.

ANDERSON, MCCLELLAN, MAYFIELD. SAYRE and EVANS, JJ., concur.

SUBJECT INDEX.

ABATEMENT AND REVIVOR.

See Pleading, § 4.

Abatement and Revivor; Another Action Pending.—The pendency of a prior suit in a court of competent jurisdiction between the same parties will abate a later suit because the latter is deemed unnecessary and vexatious; but the plea is not available unless the judgment which would be rendered in the prior action would be conclusive between the parties and operate as a bar to the same.—*Sloss-S. S. & I. Co. v. Milbra*, 658.

ACTIONS.

1. Same Person in Both Relations.

Actions; Same Person as Plaintiff and Defendant; Sale of Infant's Land.—An administrator could not as next friend of his infant ward prosecute a suit chiefly against himself both as administrator and as his guardian for the sale of lands of an estate.—*Swope v. Swope*, 157.

ACTS CITED OR CONSTRUED.

General.

1900-1, p. 2099. Sullivan v. Central L. Co., 426.
1907- p. 425. Touart v. State ex rel. Callaghan, 453.
1907 (S. S.) p. 179. Dowling v. City of Troy, 468.
1909- p. 70. Com. Ct. Pike County v. City of Troy, 442.
1909- p. 304. Com. Ct. Pike County v. City of Troy, 442.
1909- p. 304. Oberhaus v. State ex rel. McNamara, 483.
1911- p. 449. Dowling v. City of Troy, 468.

Local.

1871-2, p. 109. Oberhaus v. State ex rel. McNamara, 483.
1888-9, p. 210. Oberhaus v. State ex rel. McNamara, 483.
1892-3, p. 231. Darby City of Union Springs, 709.
1894-5, p. 938. Darby v. City of Union Springs. 709.
1896-7, p. 267. Scales v. Central I. & C. Co., 639.

ADVERSE POSSESSION.

See Ejectment; Deeds.

Adverse Possession; Agreed Line; Occupancy.—Where coterminus owners of land agreed on a dividing line, and followed up the agreement by the joint construction of a division fence, and afterwards occupied to the fence, their possession was adverse, and having continued for twenty years, conferred title to the line.—*Davis, et al. v. Grant*, 4.

Adverse Possession; Effect; Evidence of Title.—Actual possession of land for about fifty years under color of title extending proximately to the boundary line of the land of an adjacent owner, and exclusive user of an alley over the land for over thirty years is of itself evidence of title to the alley.—*Barker v. Mobile Elec. Co.*, 28.

Adverse Possessions; Instructions; Burden of Proof.—The burden being upon the plaintiff to make out a prima facie right to recover, a charge asserting that the burden was upon the defendant to prove his plea of adverse possession, is properly refused as misleading, where it is a question for the jury as to whether the prima facie right to recover has been made out.—*Hardy v. Randall*, 516.

Same; Claim or Color.—A deed void for uncertainty or indefiniteness in description cannot operate as color of title; but a deed

ADVERSE POSSESSION—*Continued.*

may serve as color of title although it does not so describe the land as from it alone the land may be identified, if the description can be made so.—*Ib.*, 516.

Adverse Possession; Actual Possession; Occupation of Part.— As a rule, occupancy of a part of land entered upon in good faith under color of title extends to the boundaries described in the color of title, though a part of the land is not actually occupied; but this rule does not apply where the conveyance is of two distinct tracts, to only one of which the grantee has the legal title, and actual occupancy. However, each governmental subdivision or quartersection does not of itself constitute a distinct tract within the exception. —*Marietta Fert. Co. v. Blair*, 524.

Same.—Adverse possession of the whole of a tract, within the boundaries described by the color of title, by actual occupancy of a part thereof, is, in legal contemplation, actual and not constructive possession, and may be restricted as to the part not actually occupied by the actual occupancy of another.—*Ib.*, 524.

Same—In gaining by adverse possession title to the whole of tract, by the actual occupancy of a part thereof, the relative proportion of the whole contiguous tract to the part actually occupied is immaterial, and title to an entire half section was gained by the adverse occupation, and actual cultivation of fifteen or twenty acres thereof under color of title to the whole tract.—*Ib.*, 524.

AFFINES.

See Jury.

AMENDMENTS.

See Equity, § 1; Appeal and Error, § 4a; Pleading, § 1.

ANCIENT DOCUMENTS.

See Evidence, § 1.

APPEAL AND ERROR.

1. Findings.

Appeal and Error, Findings; Injunction.—Conclusions for or against dissolving an injunction made on a motion for dissolution must, under the statutes, be treated on appeal as any other finding of fact at equity.—*Nelson, et al. v. Hammond*, 14.

Same; Findings; Conclusiveness.—Where motion was made to dissolve an injunction and the complainant and his son were improperly permitted to testify orally and have their testimony reduced to writing, although irregular, this court will review the findings upon such testimony, the affidavits and sworn bill and answer, and the findings will not be annulled unless so insufficiently supported that a verdict thereon will be set aside, and this notwithstanding the chancellor's findings of the facts should have no weight upon a review thereof. *Ib.*, 14.

2. Record.

(a) Conclusiveness.

Same; Record; Conclusiveness.—An assertion in brief of counsel cannot be taken to supplement or contradict the record.—*Nelson, et al. v. Hammond.* 14.

Appeal and Error; Conclusiveness of Record; Bill of Exceptions.—Where a judge changes a bill of exceptions, whether properly or not, and without action to establish a proper one, the one so signed, is made a part of the record. it will be considered by this court, as the proper one, and cannot be changed or corrected by resorting to extraneous matters.—*Hughes v. Albertville Merc. Co.*, 559.

Appeal and Error; Record; Conclusiveness; Impeachment; Fraud.—While a record imports verity, it may be attacked for fraud; hence, although the affidavit and bond required to be made

APPEAL AND ERROR—*Continued.*

in attachment proceedings appeared upon the fact of the record on appeal, the defendant could show that they were in the record illegally by fraud.—*Oliver v. Kinney,* 593.

(b) Questions Presented.

Appeal and Error; Questions Presented; Record.—Where the record showed that pleas 1 and 2 were not refiled to the substituted bill as last amended but that pleas 3 and 4 were filed to such bill, and the decree recites that the cause was then submitted for decree upon the sufficiency of the plea, it did not affirmatively appear that the cause was set down for hearing on pleas 1 and 2 to the bill as amended.—*Cartwright v. West,* 198.

Appeal and Error; Review; Questions Presented.—Where it affirmatively appears from the record that all of the testimony of witnesses on their several examinations is not set out, any difference in their testimony on different examinations cannot be considered on appeal with reference to their credibility.—*Hall & Farley v. Ala. T. & I. Co.,* 398.

3. Objection in Lower Court.

Appeal and Error; Objections Below; Parties.—If not taken advantage of by plea, demurrer or answer, an objection that a bill is defective because of want of proper parties, is waived, but if the cause cannot be properly disposed of on its merits, without the presence of the absent parties, the objection may be made at the hearing, or on error, or may be taken by the court ex mero motu. However, the question of a person, not made a party, being a necessary party cannot be considered on appeal from a decree sustaining demurrers to the bill, where want of proper parties is not one of the grounds of demurrer.—*Singo, et al. v. Brainard,* 64.

Appeal and Error; Objection Below; Necessity.—An appellate court will not pass upon a ground of demurrer not presented in the lower court although argued in brief on appeal.—*Ellis v. Vandegrift,* 142.

Same; Objections Below; Requested Instructions.—One not satisfied with an oral charge, because omitting certain elements, should request a special charge covering this feature before he is entitled to complain.—*L. & N. R. R. Co. v. Holland,* 675.

4. Harmless Error.

(a) Amendment.

Appeal and Error; Harmless Error; Amendment to Prayer.—Where the relief given by the decree against the respondent in default was authorized by the facts and the general prayer contained in the bill error cannot be predicated on the allowance of an amendment which was only the addition of a special prayer, without notice.—*Rosenau v. Powell,* 123.

(b) Pleadings.

Appeal and Error; Harmless Error; Pleading.—Where a demurrer to a good plea in abatement is sustained, and another plea, called a plea in abatement, but which in effect, is both a plea in abatement, and a plea in bar, was overruled, the sustaining of the demurrer to the first plea in abatement is prejudicial error, since to sustain the second plea, the defendant would not only have to prove his plea in abatement, but also his plea in bar, and the proof which would support the verdict upon the first plea would not have supported one under the second.—*Sloss.-S. S. & I. Co. v. Milbra,* 658.

(c) Instructions.

Appeal and Error; Harmless Error; Instructions.—Since this court cannot know on appeal what the evidence would have been if the issues had been differently shaped, or that the defendant might not have amended his insufficient pleas so as to have presented a

APPEAL AND ERROR—*Continued.*

meritorious defense, if the demurrers thereto had been sustained, errors in charges which depart from the theory observed in passing on the demurrers were prejudicial, notwithstanding plaintiff made out a prima facie case by proof without conflict, and the facts as stated by the bill of exceptions seem to preclude any special defense.—*Pratt Cons. C. Co. v. Davidson,* 667.

Same; Harmless Error; Instructions.—Where part of the oral charge might have misled the jury to the belief that the mortality tables were conclusive upon the question of life expectancy, a further instruction that they were not compelled to look to these tables, but might do so in determining the probable expectancy, cured the error.—*L. & N. R. R. Co. v. Holland,* 675.

(d) Evidence.

Appeal and Error; Harmless Error; Evidence.—It being the rule that the erroneous exclusion of evidence is cured by the later admission of such evidence, the exclusion of an answer of a witness was not prejudicial where, upon interrogatories propounded by plaintiff under the statute, the witness testified to the excluded facts, and the depositions were introduced.—*L. & N. R. R. Co. v. Holland,* 675.

5. Assignments of and Waiver.

Appeal and Error; Assignment; Joint.—Where error is jointly assigned injury must be shown to all parties joining in the assignment to sustain it.—*Cook, et al. v. Atkins,* 363.

Same; Waiver of Error.—The submission on brief without insistence on a certain assignment is a waiver of such assignment under Supreme Court Rule 10.—*L. & N. R. R. Co. v. Holland,* 675.

Same.—Where the appellant has waived the error in a certain assignment by a submission on brief without an insistence on it, he cannot at a later date retract the waiver and in a supplementary brief insist upon the assignment.—*Ib.,* 675.

Same; Estoppel to Allege Error.—Where one count proceeded on the theory that the deceased was a stranger to the railroad company, and the defendant requested and obtained a charge that deceased was a trespasser, and that the railroad owed him no duty, except in good faith to make an effort to avoid injuring him after discovering his peril, the defendant could not urge on appeal that there was a variance in that the proof showed that the relation of master and servant existed.—*Ib.,* 675.

6. Review.

(a) Discretion.

Appeal and Error; Review; Discretion.—The discretion of the trial court in excluding drawings offered by counsel in argument without formal offer as evidence with the statement that it was not a map but merely an illustrated drawing based upon the evidence in the case, will not be disturbed except upon abuse shown. —*Hardy v. Randall,* 516.

(b) Matters Reviewable.

Same; Review; Grounds; Specifications.—Where matter was admitted in evidence under the rulings of the trial court, and was not palpably inadmissible, its admission will not be reviewed where no specific objections were taken.—*Hardy v. Randall,* 516.

7. Reversal and Effect.

Appeal and Error; Reversal; New Pleading; Dilatory Plea.— Where an action for causing the death of a child on a railroad track had been once tried, and on appeal the judgment was reversed, it was within the discretion of the trial court on the second trial to refuse to permit the defendant to file a dilatory plea set-

APPEAL AND ERROR—*Continued.*

ting up that the plaintiff was not the administrator at the time the plea was offered.—*So. Ry. Co. v. Smith*, 697.

8. Decision.

Same; Decision; Effect in Lower Court.—Where it was held on a former appeal that the question as to the duty to keep a lookout at the place of the injury was for the jury, it was proper on a subsequent trial to refuse instructions asserting that neither the speed of the train nor the failure to keep a lookout were evidence of negligence, and that the trainmen owed no duty to the deceased to keep a lookout.—*So. Ry. Co. v. Smith*, 697.

APPEARANCE.

Appearance; Jurisdiction of Person; Special Appearance.—An appearance made for a special purpose does not give the court jurisdiction over the defendant's person further than the determining of the question presented to it for the determination on such appearance.—*Oliver v. Kinney*, 593.

ASSIGNMENTS—BENEFIT CREDITORS.

Assignments; Benefit of Creditor; What Constitutes.—Under section 4295, Code 1907, the word "creditor" is used in its broad and general sense, and includes a surety who has not paid the debt; hence a conveyance by the debtor of substantially all of his property to the surety in consideration that the surety would pay the debt was a general assignment for the benefit of all the creditors.—*Smith v. Young*, 190.

Assignments; Benefit of Creditors; Constructive Assignment.—Section 4295, Code 1907, makes an assignment thereunder a general one for the benefit of all creditors regardless of the character of their debts or securities, and hence, where a debtor had had a thousand dollars exempted to him in a bankruptcy proceeding, and had paid it out to certain creditors holding waive notes against him, a creditor of the same class could not require or maintain a bill against the debtor and the preferred creditors to declare said payment a general assignment for the benefit of a class, the remedy being to declare it a general assignment for the benefit of all creditors. —*J. Loeb Gro. Co. v. Brickman & Co.*, 316.

Same; Lien; Effect.—Where a transfer or assignment of property is declared to be a general one for the benefit of all creditors, under the provisions of section 4295, Code 1907, it does not destroy or affect any existing lien which any creditor or class of creditors had upon the property at the time of its assignment.—*Ib.*, 316.

Same; Liens; Waiver of Exemptions.—Where creditors held notes in which the debtor waived his exemptions to personal property, the mere fact that they could have subjected such property to the payment of their debts under execution, and that such property could not be so subjected by other creditors, gives them no lien upon the property assigned or any greater rights than other creditors.—*Ib.*, 316.

ASSUMPSIT.

Assumpsit; Action; Grounds; Counts.—Where the contract has been fully executed by the plaintiff, and nothing remains to be done by the defendant except to pay the amount stipulated, an assumpsit on the common counts is proper, although the claim arose out of a special contract.—*Jos. Joseph & Bros. Co. v. Hoffman, et al.*, 568.

ASSUMPTION OF RISK.

See Master and Servant, § 1c.

ATTACHMENT.

See Judgment, § 7.

Attachment; Purpose.—The whole purpose of an attachment is to fix a lien upon specific property before the determination of

ATTACHMENT—*Continued.*

the main suit; the attachment resting on its own facts, and not on the facts of the main action.—*Oliver v. Kinney*, 593.

Same; Affidavit; Failure to Make; Cure.—The affidavit required by the statute in attachment proceedings is the foundation of the proceedings, and an abatement of the writ for want of affidavit, destroys the lien, although the defendant executed a forthcoming bond and bond to discharge the garnishment in order to regain possession of the property taken from him by the void process, the execution of such bond not having the effect of validating the attachment.—*Ib.*, 593.

Same; Abatement; Grounds; Validity.—Notwithstanding section 2964, Code 1907, provides that an attachment issued without affidavit and bond may be abated on defendant's motion, the lien could be destroyed for other reasons as by showing there had been no lawful levy.—*Ib.*, 593.

Same; Time of Filing Plea.—So long as it is open to defendant to file the pleas in abatement prescribed by section 2964, Code 1907, he may also file other pleas having the effect of destroying the writ, provided that he has not already pleaded or otherwise challenged the validity of the lien, in which case, the cause stands for trial upon the day set by the clerk pursuant to section 5348, Code 1907, and cannot be called before that day except by consent.—*Ib.*, 593.

Same; Judgment; Time of Entry.—Under section 2964, Code 1907, an attachment judgment nil dicit was premature when taken before the expiration of the third day of the return term.—*Ib.*, 593.

ATTORNEY AND CLIENT.

Attorney and Client; Duties and Liabilities to Client.—So long as the relation of attorney and client exists, the attorney is a trustee for his client in and about the cause or the subject thereof, and any trade that he makes or benefit that he may derive resulting from the litigation, or a sale of the subject thereof, will inure to the benefit of the client.—*Singo v. Brainard*, 64.

Attorney and Client; Fiduciary Relations; Effect.—While transactions between an attorney and client should be strictly scrutinized, and the attorney should give to the client the benefit of all the information he has regarding the value of property purchased by him from the client, yet such purchases are voidable only upon timely application.—*Dawson v. Copeland*, 267.

BANKS AND BANKING.

Banks and Banking; Deposits; Right to Set-off.—Unless the claim of the bank is certain, definite and liquidated, or capable of liquidation by calculation without the aid of the jury to determine the amount, such claim cannot be set off as against the depositor, and his deposit.—*Tallapoosa Co. Bank v. Wynn*, 272.

BANKRUPTCY.

Bankruptcy; Capacity of Trustee; Fraudulent Conveyance.—While ordinarily the trustee in bankruptcy is a representative of both the bankrupt and the creditors, yet when he files a bill to set aside a fraudulent conveyance made by the bankrupt, he represents the creditors alone.—*Cartwright v. West*, 198.

Same; Action by Trustee; Limitations.—Where a trustee in bankruptcy files a bill to set aside certain conveyances of the bankrupt as being fraudulent, the respondents are entitled to set up by way of plea, that certain creditors named in the bill had not filed their claims within the time allowed, and hence were barred by limitation, as creditors entitled to participate in distribution of the estate.—*Ib.*, 198.

Bankruptcy; Forthcoming Bond; Action; Pleading.—In an action against a surety on a forth coming bond, of an alleged bankrupt, pleas alleging that after the bankruptcy adjudication, a writ

BANKRUPTCY—*Continued.*

of error was duly sued out to review the same, but which failed to show whether or not, or when the decree was finally confirmed, or whether the writ was still pending and undetermined, or whether it had been dismissed, were insufficient either as pleas in abatement or in bar, under the bankruptcy statute.—*Moore Bros. v. Cowan,* 536.

Same; Jurisdiction; Adjudication.—The Federal Court has exclusive jurisdiction to adjudge a person a bankrupt, and to appoint a receiver, and such appointment and adjudication, cannot be collaterally attacked in a suit on the forthcoming bond, executed by the bankrupt.—*Ib.,* 536.

Same; Forthcoming Bond; Estoppel.—A defendant who is surety or a principal in a forthcoming bond in bankruptcy executed to two persons named therein as receivers in the above cause, are estopped from questioning the validity of the receiver's appointment. --*Ib.,* 536.

Same; Defenses.—Where a certain bankrupt was so adjudged in involuntary proceedings against him and executed a forthcoming bond, for the purpose of retaining his assets, and then sued out a writ of error to review the adjudication, it was no defense to a subsequent action on the bond that after its execution, the property was taken from the alleged bankrupts pursuant to a voluntary bankrupt proceeding instituted by him, it not being denied that the voluntary proceedings were instituted for the bankrupt's benefit, and it not being shown that the assets were returned to and accepted by the person to whom they were surrendered as receiver in the bankruptcy proceeding.—*Ib.,* 536.

BILLS AND NOTES.

1. Interest on.

Bills and Notes; Interest; Payment.—Where the payor of the note which was deposited with a stranger as custodian pending litigation, had the right to pay off the note and stop interest at the time he paid it to the custodian, and would have paid it into court had not the custodian accepted payment, by accepting the payment the custodian did not prejudice the rights of the litigant entitled to the proceeds of the note so as to be chargeable with interest beyond the time the note was paid.—*Rutledge v. Cramton.* 306.

BILLS OF EXCEPTIONS.

1. Presentation and Signing.

Bill of Exceptions; Presentation; Time; Motion to Strike.—Where the bill of exceptions is not presented to the trial judge within ninety days, from the date of the judgment. a motion to strike such bill must prevail, under section 3019, Code 1907.—*Smith v. Smith,* 547.

2. Establishment.

Bill of Exceptions; Establishment; Grounds; Signature of Judge.—Although under section 3021, Code 1907, a judge is not at default for a failure or refusal to sign the bill of exceptions, so as to enable the aggrieved party to establish the bill, until a correct bill is tendered, yet when a correct bill is tendered the judge, it is his duty to sign it as presented, and his signing it, after improperly changing it, is not a signing of the bill, but is in effect, a failure or refusal which will enable the aggrieved party to establish it under the statute, although it was signed after being changed. —*Hughes v. Albertville Merc. Co.,* 559.

BILLS OF PARTICULARS.

Appeal and Error; Objection; Bill of Particulars.—To be available on appeal. an objection to a bill of particulars as being too indefinite, should be taken at the beginning of the trial.—*Jos. Joseph & Bros. Co. v. Hoffman, et al.,* 568.

BOUNDARIES.

Boundaries; Monuments; Courses and Distances.—Where by giving monuments a controlling influence, absurd consequences would ensue, and where it is obvious that courses and distances furnish the most certain guide to the location and quantity of the land, courses and distances must be followed, and the rule that in the description of the boundaries of land conveyed, monuments, whether natural or artificial, dominate courses and distances, does not apply.—*Barker v. Mobile Elec. Co.*, 28.

Same; Evidence.—Evidence examined and held to show that the alley was located on the lands of another who held exclusive possession thereof as his own, and that the adjacent owner had no rights therein.—*Ib.*, 28.

Same; Distances; Courses.—A deed conveying a lot on the side of an alley, describing the lot by depth so as to take in a part of the alley, but further describing it as extending to a point on the alley, and thence along the boundary line of the alley, does not convey any part of the alley.—*Ib.*, 28.

CANCELLATION OF INSTRUMENTS.

Cancellation of Instrument; Equity Jurisdiction; Legal Remedy—A court of equity has jurisdiction to cancel a fraudulent contract at the instance of the injured party, notwithstanding he may sue at law upon the covenants of warrant therein, or for deceit.—*So. St. F. & C. Co. v. Whatley*, 101.

Cancellation of Instruments; Conveyance to Attorney; Laches.—A client is not entitled to cancellation of a conveyance to his attorney where the client did not act promptly but awaited the termination of the litigation affecting the property, even if such conveyance was obtained without a disclosure by the attorney of his information.—*Dawson v. Copeland*, 267.

Cancellation of Instrument; Bill; Incidental Relief.—The bill examined and under its allegations, it is held that, though the money was procured at a different time from the execution of the deed, the money having been secured after intestate's death, yet sufficient connection was shown between the two wrongs so as to authorize relief as to the money if a cause of action for cancellation of the deeds was established.—*Robinson v. Griffin*, 372.

CARRIERS.

1. Of Passengers.

(a) Complaint.

Carrier; Passenger; Complaint.—In an action for injury to a passenger, a complaint which alleges that the conductor negligently required the passenger to leave the train at a place highly dangerous for her to do so, on his refusal to accept her ticket, and which sets forth the facts as to danger of the place for an old and infirm person to disembark, states a cause of action as against the demurrer interposed.—*C. of Ga. Ry. Co. v. Bagley*, 611.

Carriers; Passengers; Negligence; Complaint.—Counts charging simple negligence of a common carrier to the injury of a passenger on one of its cars, which alleged that the defendant was a common carrier of passengers, that plaintiff was a passenger and that it so negligently conducted itself in and about her carriage thereon that at a certain time and place plaintiff was thrown or caused to fall from said car, are sufficient.—*B'ham. Ry. L. & P. Co. v. Fisher*, 623.

Same; Proximate Cause.—It is enough that the facts averred in an action for injury to a passenger lead with requisite certainty to the conclusion that the injury proximately resulted from the negligence charged.—*Ib.*, 623.

Same; Wantonness.—A count for wanton injury which alleges that the servant or agent of defendant in control or charge of its cars while acting within the line and scope of his authority as such,

CARRIERS—*Continued.*

wantonly or intentionally caused plaintiff to be injured, is not subject to demurrer for uncertainty or indefiniteness.—*Ib.*, 623.

Same; Complaint; Sufficiency.—In an action by a passenger for injuries received while returning to a station beyond which he had been negligently carried, the complaint need not negative the fact that there was an open, obvious and safe way which the passenger could have traveled back to the station, since such facts were available in defense.—*A. C. G. & A. Ry. Co. v. Cox*, 629.

Same; Complaint.—A complaint for injuries to a passenger carried beyond her destination and required to alight and walk back to the station need not allege 'hat her eyesight was defective, or that she could not see at night, or that her affliction was apparent to the conductor. in order to state a cause of action.—*Ib.*, 629.

Same.—The fact that a passenger carried beyond her station pursued a dangerous way back to the station, when a safe way was obvious and open to her selection was available only in support of the defense of contributory negligence, and need not have been negatived by the complaint.—*Ib.*, 629.

(b) Issues and Evidence.

Same; Issues; Evidence.—Where the action was for injury to a passenger who was required to disembark because her ticket was defective, and because she refused to pay fare, and the issues were the negligence of the carrier in requiring her to disembark at a dangerous place, and the plaintiff's contributory negligence, evidence that the passenger was old and infirm, that she was required to leave the train in the early morning before good daylight, that she carried a suitcase, that the conductor saw her but offered no assistance, that she left the car from the rear platform, and that the distance from the steps of the platform to the ground was from three to four feet, was competent under the issues.—*C. of Ga. Ry. Co. v. Bagcy*, 611.

(c) Ejection of.

Same; Right to Eject Passenger.—A carrier issuing a round trip ticket which needs to be validated to be good on the return trip need not carry a passenger on such ticket when the same has not been validated, and where such passenger refuses to pay fare, the passenger may be ejected.—*C. of G. Ry. Co. v. Bagley*, 611.

Same.—In ejecting a .passenger, which the carrier was authorized to do, the carrier must consider the safety of the passenger and not eject the passenger at a dangerous pace.—*Ib.*, 611.

Same.—Under the evidence in this case, it was a question for the jury as to whether in the justifiable ejection of the passenger, such passenger was ejected at a dangerous place resulting in injuries.—*Ib.*, 611.

Same.—Whether an aged, female passenger was guilty of contributory negligence, in disembarking at a place designated by the carrier's agent, was under the facts in this case, a question for the jury.—*Ib.*, 611.

Same.—Where a passenger believed in good faith that a ticket was good, and was required to leave the train because of a failure to present a good ticket or pay fare, such passenger could assume that the place selected by the conductor for her to alight with her baggage. was a safe pace.—*Ib.*, 611.

(d) Relation, Existence and Termination.

Same; Existence of Relations; Obligation of Carrier.—A person who boards a train in good faith believing that her ticket was good is a passenger, and the carrier owes her a duty as such when requiring her to disembark.—*C. of Ga. Ry. Co. v. Bagley*, 611.

Same.—A conductor who requires a passenger to disembark from the train because of the insufficiency of her ticket, and her re-

CARRIERS—*Continued.*

fusal to pay the fare is required to know the perils of the place where he requires the passenger to disembark.—*Ib.*, 611.

. *Same; Misleading Instructions.*—Where the action was for injury to a passenger who was required to disembark because of the insufficiency of her ticket, and her refusal to pay fare, a charge asserting that if the jury were not reasonably satisfied that the conductor knew of the passenger's infirmity, and the peril attending her leaving the train at the time and place required, the carrier was not liable for injuries sustained in alighting, was misleading and properly refused.—*Ib.*, 611.

Same; Continuance of Relation.—The relation of passenger and carrier continues to exist until the passenger has had reasonable time and opportunity to alight from a train and leave the carrier's premises in the ordinary way.—*A. C. G. & A. Ry. Co. v. Cox.* 629.

Same; Defenses.—In the absence of any allegation in the complaint as to defective eyesight, a defendant believing that the injuries were caused from the defective eysight of the plaintiff must by special plea allege such facts in order to make them available as a defense.—*Ib.*, 629.

(e) Proximate Cause.

Same; Proximate Cause; Instructions.—In an action for injury to a passenger the hypotheses in instruction must include the condition that the negligence or wrong charged in the complaint afforded the proximate cause of the injury, as a basis of recovery.—*B'ham Ry. L. & P. Co. v. Fisher,* 623.

(f) Wantonness.

Same; Wantonness; Evidence.—The evidence in this case held sufficient to go to the jury, on the question of willfulness or wantonness of the injury to a passenger while alighting from an electric car, with the consequent right of imposition of punitive damages.—*B'ham. Ry. L. & P. Co. v. Fisher,* 623.

(g) Carrying Beyond Destination.

Carriers; Breach of Contract; Passengers.—Where the action was for injury received by a passenger while attempting to walk back to the station after being carried beyond it, it was immaterial whether the carrier's conductor knew that the passenger did not know of a safe route from the point where she alighted, back to her station, or that the trainmen had reason to believe that the passenger would encounter danger.—*A. C. G. & A. Ry. Co. v. Cox,* 629.

Same; Carrying Beyond Destination; Liability.—Where it was undisputed that a carrier stopped its train beyond a station, and that a passenger destined for that station alighted at night to walk back to that station, that she was aged and feeble, and was injured when attempting to walk back to the station, but there was a conflict in the evidence as to whether the train stopped at the station for the reception and discharge of passengers, the question of the liability of the carrier was one for the jury.—*Ib.*, 629.

CHARGE OF COURT.

1. Undue Prominence to Particular Evidence.

Charge of Court; Undue Prominence.—Where the burden of carrying some of the issues was upon the plaintiff in ejectment, a requested instruction that the burden was upon the defendant to prove his plea of adverse possession is properly refused, as the effect would be to improperly contract the issue to that one upon which it was predicated.—*Hardy v. Randall,* 516.

Charge of Court; Prominence to Particular Facts.—Charges that the jury had the right to infer that the personal expenses of plaintiff's intestate were greater than $19.50 per month, and that in connection with the other evidence on the amount of the decedent's

CHARGE OF COURT—*Continued.*

earnings, which were devoted to his personal expenses, the jury might look to the testimony of intestate's wife on the former trial, that it took about half his earnings to support himself, not only gave undue importance to isolated portions of the evidence, but were argumentative as well.—*L. & N. R. R. Co. v. Holland,* 675.

1½. Explanatory.

Charge of Court; Explanatory Charges.—Charges explanatory of charges given for the adversary party should not be refused.—*Sloss-S. S. & I. Co. v. Milbra,* 658.

2. Argumentative.

Charge of Court; Argumentative Instructions.—A charge asserting that the jury cannot find that a person is old and infirm because fifty-six or fifty-seven years old, is properly refused as argumentative.—*C. of Ga. Ry. Co. v. Bagley,* 611.

Charg of Court; Argumentative.—Where the action was for damages for causing the death of a child, brought under the homicide act, a charge asserting that the damages recoverable are not intended to compensate the parents for the death of the child, but should be such sum as would be sufficient to punish the act done, and if defendant's engineer ran the engine against the deceased through mere negligence or error of judgment, plaintiff ought not to recover as much as if it had been wantonly or intentionally done, was argumentative and properly refused.—*So. Ry. Co. v. Smith,* 697.

Same.—Charges asserting that the jury will consider that men and women may be operated on by their sympathies, one way or the other, that the sympathies of the people come out strongly in favor of the weaker party, or the female sex, or the poor man, but the jurors have no right to act on any prejudice or sympathy of that kind, but are to try to do exact justice between the parties as though they were two individuals standing on perfect equality in all respects, that the case should be considered by the jury as between two persons of equal standing, and that the fact that one of the parties is a corporation should not affect their minds in any way, are argumentative and properly refused.—*Ib.,* 697.

2½. Meeting Argument.

Same; Meeting Argument.—It is always proper to refuse charges requested for the purpose of meeting argument of opposing counsel.—*L. & N. R. R. Co. v. Holland,* 675.

3. Invading Province of Jury.

Same; Invading Province of Jury.—A charge asserting that if the jury believe the evidence they cannot find a particular fact, and one asserting that there is no evidence of a particular fact, may be properly refused as invading the province of the jury.—*C. of Ga. Ry. Co. v. Bagley,* 611.

Same; Invading Province of Jury.—Where the action was for damages for negligence causing the death of plaintiff's intestate, a charge asserting that if the negligence of a third person was the sole proximate cause of the death of plaintiff's intestate, plaintiff could not recover; but if defendant is guilty of negligence which proximately helped to cause the death of intestate, then the negligence, if any, of such third person, even though it also helped to cause death, would be no answer to the negligence of defendant, states a correct proposition of law, applicable to and illustrated by the facts of the particular case, as it does not request or even suggest a finding for the plaintiff on the facts hypothesized, or on any other facts.—*Sloss-S. S. & I. Co. v. Milbra,* 658.

CHARGE OF COURT—*Continued.*

4. Conformity to Issues and Evidence.

Same; Conformity to Evidence.—A charge predicated upon facts contrary to the evidence may be properly refused.—*C. of Ga. Ry. Co. v. Bagley,* 611.

Charge of Court; Conformity to Issues.—Where the court had erroneously overruled a demurrer to a plea which there was evidence to support, it was error to refuse to instruct that if the facts alleged in the plea were found to be true, the verdict should be for the defendant, as it is not proper to change the issues as developed by the pleading by giving or refusing instructions.—*Pratt Cons. C. Co. v. Davidson,* 667.

Same; Ignoring Issues.—In an action against a railroad for wrongful death based both on wanton negligence and the simple negligence of the engineer after discovering the peril of plaintiff's intestate, a charge which omits in hypothesis liability for the simple negligence was properly refused.—*L. & N. R. R. Co. v. Holland,* 675.

Same; Excluding Issues.—Where the evidence presented a question of subsequent negligence, a charge asserting that under the undisputed evidence plaintiff's decedent was unlawfully on the track, and the defendant owed him no duty except not to injure him wantonly, negligently or intentionally, was properly refused as excluding the issue of such subsequent negligence.—*So. Ry. Co. v. Smith,* 697.

5. Requisites and Construction.

Charge of Court; Requisites.—Instructions must refer to and be hypothesized upon the evidence in the case.—*A. C. G. & A. Ry. Co. v. Cox,* 629.

Same; Construction.—Where a charge as a whole correctly states the law, it will be held sufficient although isolated portions thereof may be erroneous.—*Ib.,* 629.

6. Covered by Those Given.

Same; Covered by Those Given.—It is not error to refuse charges already covered in substance by those given.—*L. & N. R. R. Co. v. Holland,* 675.

7. Weight of Evidence.

Same; Weight of Evidence.—In an action against a railroad for the wrongful death of a person on the track in which there was evidence that the use of sand was a supplementary aid to the quick stopping of the train, charges to the jury that the failure to use sand would not be negligence, unless its use would have prevented the injury, were invasive of the province of the jury, and hence, erroneous.—*L. & N. R. R. Co. v. Holland,* 675.

Same; Weight and Sufficiency of Evidence.—The trial courts are under no duty to charge juries that there is no evidence of a given fact.—*So. Ry. Co. v. Smith,* 697.

8. Assuming Facts.

Same; Assuming Facts.—The evidence in this case examined and it is held that the engineers' evidence as to the position of intestate's head did not conflict with plaintiff's evidence on that subject, and that a charge was not erroneous in assuming as a matter of fact that plaintiff's head was upon the rail.—*L. & N. R. R. Co. v. Holland,* 675.

9. Confusing.

Same; Confused Instructions.—Charges which are confused and uncertain in meaning may be refused without error.—*So. Ry. Co. v. Smith,* 697.

CHARITIES.

Charities; Religious Doctrine; Judicial Determination.—Where property is devoted to the teaching of some specific form of religious

CHARITIES.—*Continued.*

doctrine by the express terms of the deed or will, the courts, as in all cases, of special trust, will take jurisdiction to see that the property is not diverted from the special purpose for which it has been conveyed.—*Harris v. Cosby, et al.*, 81.

CHURCH.

See Religious Societies; Charities.

CODE SECTIONS CITED OR CONSTRUED.

COLLATERAL ATTACK.

See Judgments, § 2; Insane Persons.

COMITY.

See Courts, § 2.

CONSTITUTIONAL LAW.

See Statutes.

1. Interpretation.

Constitutional Law; Contemporaneous Interpretation.—**Where** a constitutional provision has been interpreted by judicial decision and has been re-enacted, it will be presumed that it was re-enacted with the interpretation put upon it by such decisions.—*Stocks v. City of Gadsden*, 321.

CONSTITUTION CITED OR CONSTRUED.

1901.
Section.
45. Dowling v. Cly of Troy, 468.
48. Oberhaus v. State ex rel. McNamara, 483.
115. Oberhaus v. State ex rel. McNamara, 483.
116. Oberhaus v. State ex rel. McNamara, 483.
173. Touart v. State ex rel. Callaghan, 454.
175. Touart v. State ex rel. Callaghan, 454.
205. Winkles v. Powell, 46.
206. Winkles v. Powell, 46.
215. Com. Ct. Pike County v. City of Troy, 442.
224. Goodson v. Dean, 301.
235. Stocks v. City of Gadedsn, 321.
243. Horton v. So. Ry. Co., 231.

1875.
Art. 4, Section 23. Winkles v. Powell, 46.

CONTEMPTS.

Contempt; Depositaries; Acts Constituting.—The custodian of a note in litigation who received payment thereof according to its tenure before the litigation was finally terminated, was not guilty of a contempt or breach of duty by seeking to review final decree which directed him to turn over the note itself in order to obtain judicial confirmance of his receipt of payment, there having been no final accounting of the money received by him until thereafter.—*Rutledge v. Cramton, 306.*

CONTRIBUTORY NEGLIGENCE.

See Negligence; Master and Servant, § 1d.

CORPORATIONS.

1. Stockholders, Rights and Liabilities.

Corporation; Stockholders; Suit on Behalf of Corporation.—While a corporation is primarily entitled to sue to redress corporate wrongs, stockholders may sue for that purpose, where the corporation refuses to act. or where the litigation would be in the control of the wrong doers.—*Ellis v. Vandegrift, 142.*

Same; Conditions Precedent.—A stockholder suing on behalf of a corporation to redress corporate wrongs need not make a demand or request of the corporate authorities to act where such a demand or request will be refused.—*Ib., 142.*

Same.—The facts made by the bill stated and examined and held to authorize suit by the minority stockholders on behalf of the corporation to redress corporate wrongs without demand or request of the corporate authorities to do so; also held that as against the appealing respondent the cause of action against him did not depend upon the dissolution of the corporation, and hence that he could not complain of any defects in the cause of action for the dissolution of the corporation.—*Ib., 142.*

Corporations; Sale of Assets; Power; Rights of Stockholders.—In the absence of fraud, breach of duty or bad faith, minority stockholders were not entitled to avoid or invalidate a sale made by the majority stockholders of all the lands and minerals which constituted all the property of the corporation, on the ground that the corporation was thereby denuded, where it appeared that the corporation was authorized to rent or purchase mineral lands and to sell and lease the same.—*Mabin v. Gulf C. & C. Co., 259.*

Same; Sale of Property; Effect; Franchise.—A sale of all of a corporation's property does not necessarily terminate the corporation nor operate as a transfer of such corporate powers or franchises as it had.—*Ib., 259.*

CORPORATIONS—*Continued.*

Corporations; Dissolution; Minority Stockholders.—In a suit by minority stockholders to dissolve the corporation on the ground of an abandonment by the sockholders, the court must determine the right of the parties on the facts existing at the time of the filing of the bill, and the fact that since that time, efforts had been made to put the corporation on a better footing as to the conditions of its property, and as to the formality and regularity of the meetings of the stockholders, and the fact that the time fixed by statute for the life of the corporation has expired since the filing of the bill, cannot be considered.—*Sullivan v. Central L. Co.*, 426.

Same.—In the absence of evidence of the insolvency of the corporation or bad faith in its management, the court will not order a sale of the property at the suit of the minority stockholders for the dissolution of the corporation.—*Ib.*, 426.

Same; Abandonment by Stockholders; Meetings Outside the State.—Although the meeting of the stockholders of a domestic corporation are irregular, or illegal because of the absence of any statute authorizing such meeting, still they show that the stockholders retained an interest in the corporation, and are attempting to exercise its powers, hence, minority stockholders suing for a dissolution of the corporation on the ground of abandonment by the stockholders cannot relie thereon to show such abandonment.—*Ib.*, 426.

Same; Office in State; Agent in State; Object.—The purpose of the statute in requiring corporations to keep its principal officer or agent in the state, is to aid the state in the supervision and control of the corporation, and has no regard to the financial interests of the corporation, and a failure to comply with this requirement may or may not evidence a purpose to abandon corporate functions, and hence, the mere fact that a corporation for a time failed to observe the statute, did not show an abandonment, where all the time it had agents in the state for the management of its property.—*Ib.*, 426.

Same; Management of Business; Remedy of Minority Stockholder.—Where the question of corporate management is one of discretion, or of doubtful event in the undertaking in which the corporation is engaged, minority stockholders cannot resort to equity, their remedy being to sell their stock.—*Ib.*, 426.

2. Unpaid Stock Subscriptions and Manner of Reaching.

Corporations; Creditor's Action; Remedy; Fraud.—Upon return of execution nulla bona, a bill in equity may be maintained by a judgment creditor of an insolvent corporation to reach amounts alleged to be due the corporation from its original stockholders on unpaid stock subscriptions, and fraud in the transfer or withholding the assets from the creditors is not necessary to equity jurisdiction. —*Hall v Farley & Ala. T. & I. Co.*, 398.

Same; Creditor's Action; Adequate Legal Remedy.—The jurisdiction of a court of equity to subject the indebtedness of the stockholders on their unpaid stock subscription to the payment of judgments against an insolvent corporation after execution returned nulla bona, is founded upon the inadequacy of the legal remedy, and not on fraud vel non, and the inadequacy of the legal remedy is the better test of equity jurisdiction in such cases.—*Ib.*, 398.

Same; Stockholder's Liability; Fraud.—Where a corporation purchases shares of its own capital stock in an attempt to discharge the liability of its original stockholders on unpaid subscriptions by the use of assets of the corporation, there is a fraud on the creditors.—*Ib.*, 398.

3. Transfer of Stock and Incidents.

Same; Effect of Transfer; Bona Fide.—Where a subscriber to the capital stock of the corporation, while the corporation was solvent, and while a balance was due on his subscription, transferred his stock in good faith to other stockholders who were solvent, and who, as part of the considerations for said transfer, as-

CORPORATIONS—*Continued.*

sumed the liability to the corporation for the balance due, and with full knowledge of all the facts the corporation accepted the purchasers in the place of the original subscribers as the owners of said stock, and agreed to look to them for the balance due, such original subscribers were discharged from any liability for a fraud upon a subsequent creditor resulting from transactions between the corporation, and the purchasers of his stock, since a subsequent creditor cannot complain of the disposition of the property by a corporation unless such disposition was made with the intent to hinder, delay or defraud subsequent creditors, and actually had that effect.—*Hall & Farley v. Ala. T. & I. Co.*, 398.

Same; Burden of Proof.—Where subscribers to the capital stock of a corporation have transferred their stock in good faith to purchasers who have been accepted by the corporation, a subsequent creditor of the corporation who seeks to enforce the former's liability to the corporation on the grounds of fraud in the transfer has the burden of proof.—*Ib.*, 398.

Same; Effect of Transfer.—Where the purchaser of stock agrees expressly to assume all the transferor's liability thereon, and when such agreement is acceded to by the corporation on making the transfer, the rule that a stockholder, on a bona fide transfer of his stock, is only discharged from liability as to future calls for payment on stock, and not from liability for amounts due upon previous calls, has no application.—*Ib.*, 398.

Same; Transfer of Shares; Registration.—Section 1262, must be construed with sections 1263 and 1265, Code 1907, and is for the protection of creditors of and purchasers from the stockholders, and not for creditors of the corporation; hence a failure to register a bona fide transfer will not render the transfer void as to creditors of the corporation so as to entitle them to sue the transferor to recover on unpaid subscriptions on the stock.—*Ib.*, 398.

Same; Officers; Representation; Ratification.—Where a corporation, without express authorization at a regular meeting, leaves the entire management of its affairs to its president, and the president assents to a transfer of stock by the subscribers to the capital stock, on which a balance is unpaid, and accepts the purchases instead of the subscribers, as owners of the stock, and liable for the unpaid balance, such acts, when ratified, become the acts of the corporation as they were such acts as could have been regularly authorized.—*Ib.*, 398.

4. Powers.

Same; Powers; Purchase of Own Stock.—Unless so authorized, a corporation may not buy its own capital stock.—*Hall & Farley v. Ala. T. & I. Co.*, 398.

5. Officers and Duties.

Same; Officers; Nature of Office.—So far as the creditors of the corporation are concerned, the directors of the corporation have the right to leave to the president the entire management and discretion as to the transfer of stock of a subscriber, on which a balance is unpaid, and as to accepting the purchaser as owner of the stock and liable for any unpaid balance, as the officers of the corporation are trustees for the stockholders and not for the creditors.—*Hall & Farley v. Ala. T. & I. Co.*, 398.

6. Shares and Property in.

Same; Capital Stock; Nature of Property in Shares.—Stock in a corporation is only evidence of the right of the holder or owner to share in the proceeds of the corporation's property, and a share of stock only represents an aliquot part of the corporation's property, or the right to share in the proceeds to that extent when distributed according to law and equity.—*Hall & Farley v. Ala. T. I. Co.*, 398.

COSTS.

See Partition.

1. On Appeal.

Costs; Appeal; Records; Agreement as to Contents; Presumptions.—Construing section 2848, and rules of practice 27 and 28, it is to be presumed that the appellant might have had an agreement for an abridgement of the record, and in the absence of such an agreement, the court will not strike out any part of the record so as to deny the register his costs.—*Stocks v. City of Gadsden*, 321.

2. In Criminal Cases.

Costs; Criminal Prosecution; Sentence.—Acts 1907, p. 179, in so far as it relates to costs on conviction of crime, being unconstitutional, in sentencing for costs, the rate should be 75 cents per day as provided by section 7635, Code 1907.—*Dowling v. City of Troy*, 468.

COUNTIES.

1. Indebtedness of.

Counties; Limitation of Indebtedness; Time of Incurring Debt.—Under section 224, Constitution 1901, and section 158, Code 1907, it is held that the inhibition is against the indebtedness and not against the preliminary steps to ascertain the wishes of the voters, and hence, the validity of the bond issue would depend on the condition of the county indebtedness when the bonds were issued, and not at the date of the election.—*Goodson v. Dean*, 301.

Same; Bond Issue; Illegal Act.—A tax payer cannot maintain a suit to enjoin the county judge and the county commissioners from issuing bonds for which authority had been voted, on the ground that the issue of the bond would create an unconstitutional indebtedness, since such officers are charged with ascertaining first, whether the authority has been granted for the proposed issue, and second, whether the issue will create an unconstitutional indebtedness, before authorizing an issuance of the bonds, and it will not be presumed that they will issue them illegally.—*Ib.*, 301.

Same; Issuance.—Section 168, Code 1907, must be construed in connection with section 224, Constitution 1901, and does not authorize or require the issuance of bonds, although voted for if the issue would be in contravention of the constitution limiting a county's indebtedness to $3\frac{1}{2}$ per cent of the assessed value of its property.—*Ib.*, 301.

Same; Commissioner's Court; Order; Effect.—An order of the commissioner's court directing an election to determine whether certain bonds of the county should be issued, was complete when passed and was not defective because the probate judge did not record the order until after the court had adjourned.—*Ib.*, 301.

2. Officers of.

Counties; Officers; Removal.—Under Section 175, Constitution 1901, a county officer who has been elected or appointed to fill a fixed term cannot be removed from office during that term except by impeachment for cause enumerated in Section 173, Constitution 1901, in which proceeding he has the right of jury trial and appeal.—*Touart v. State ex rel. Callaghan*, 453.

Same; County Officer.—A county tax commissioner is a county officer who may be removed under Section 175, Constitution 1901, by impeachment for cause specified in Section 173, Constitution 1901, but the section is not limited to county offices created or even mentioned in the Constitution, nor is it limited to those county officers who are elected by the people or the legislature, but extends as well as to those who are appointed. The provisions are for the protection of county officers from removal, except as authorized, during the term for which they were appointed or elected, and was not intended to apply to those county officers, the terms of whose incumbency is fixed or determined by the appointing power.—*Ib.*, 453.

COUNTIES—*Continued.*

Same; Removal.—Construing Acts 1907, p. 425, and section 2238, Code 1907, it is held that the respondent was appointed for a term to be at the will of the governor, or appointing power, and that under section 2238, his removal by the governor with or without cause terminated his right to the office.—*Ib.*, 453.

COURSES AND DISTANCES.

See Boundaries.

COURTS.

1. Jurisdiction.

Courts; Jurisdiction; Shown by Record.—The existence of jurisdictional facts in respect to judicial acts of courts exercising special and limited jurisdiction is not to be inferred from the mere exercise of that jurisdiction but must affirmatively appear from the record.—*Martin v. Martin*, 106.

Courts; Priority of Jurisdiction; Settlement of Estate.—As Probate and Chancery courts have concurrent jurisdiction of the settlement of an estate, the court first acquiring jurisdiction should be allowed to continue unless some special reason arises for equitable interference.—*Swope, et al. v. Swope, et al.*, 157.

Courts; Jurisdiction; Quo Warranto.—Construing Acts 1871-2, p. 109, and sections 3259, 3206, and 5455, Code 1907, it is held that the city court of Mobile had jurisdiction to grant a writ of quo warranto to determine title to the office of jury commissioner of Mobile County—*Oberhaus v. State, ex rel. McNamara*, 483.

2. Comity.

Court; Comity; Stay of Proceedings; Different States.—Where a court of another state on an action brought therein is advised that the courts of this state in their jurisdiction has been first invoked by the parties, that court may, on the grounds of comity, stay its jurisdiction, but before judgment in the courts of this state, such action on the part of the court of another state is a matter of grace and not the observance of a legal duty.—*Jos. Joseph & Bros. Co. v. Hoffman*, 568.

COURT RULES.

10. Sup. Ct. L. & N. R. R. Co. v. Holland, 675.
15. Chan. Pr. Woodward v. The State, 7.
27. Chan. Pr. Stocks v. City of Gadsden, 321.
28. Chan. Pr. Stocks v. City of Gadsden, 321.
44. Chan. Pr. Rosenau v. Powell, 123.

DEEDS.

Deeds; Property Conveyed; Description.—Where the evidence showed that the entire length of the square was 242 feet, that complainants held under deed describing their lot as 82 feet deep from the street on which it fronted, and bounded on the rear by the land claimed by defendant under deeds describing the depth of his lot as 157 feet from the opposite street, complainants did not show title to an alley way which lay 82 feet from the street on which his lot fronted.—*Barker v. Mobile Elec. Co.*, 28.

Deeds; Validity; Undue Influence.—Where the action was to cancel a deed to respondent by complainant's intestate, the burden of proof shifted to the respondent after proof by complainant of confidential relations existing between intestate and respondent.—*Robinson v. Griffin*, 372.

Same; Fraud and Undue Influence; Sufficiency of Evidence.—The evidence in this case stated and examined and held not to show undue influence or fraud in procuring the deed.—*Ib.*, 372.

DEEDS—*Continued.*

. *Deeds; Taking Effect; Death of Grantor.*—Notwithstanding the common law rule that an estate in remainder could be supported only by a prior freehold, an estate in land may be created to take effect in possession on the death of a grantor, with a reservation to the grantor of the intervening use and possession.—*Farr v. Perkins*, 500.

Same; Remainders; Precedent Estate.—Where a husband conveyed lands to his wife for life with all the privileges and appurtenances, and at her death to descend to the youngest son in fee, and in the event of the youngest son's death before he became of age, and in the event of his death without issue, then to the second youngest son, and so on to the next oldest child, and in the event of the death of all the sons without heirs surviving, then the remander after the life estate to his daughter Catharine, and her heirs forever, tne deed created in the wife an equitable separate estate, the legal title during her life, and the life of the husband vesting in the husband as trustee for the wife, and operating as a complete divestiture of the grantor's estate, and creating a prior particular freehold sufficient to support the remainder in the youngest son.— *Ib.*, 500.

Same;Construction; Base Fee.—Under the deed above set forth, on the falling in of the widow's life estate, there was vested in the youngest son an estate in fee, which, however, was a base or qualified fee, since it was subject to be defeated by his death before arriving at the age of maturity without lawful issue.—*Ib.*, 500.

Same; Words of Limitation or Purchase.—The above deed examined and held, that since the youngest son was never married, but survived his two older brothers, the oldest of which left children surviving nim, tne deed did not indicate an intent on the part of the grantor to engraft contingent remainder to possible grand children or to the conditional limitation to his several sons, nor to make such possible grandchildren joint purchasers with their respective fathers, but that the explanatory clause appended to the grant to each son was intended to restrict the descent in each case to the next youngest son "then alive," the varying phases referred to heirs or lawful heirs, or children, being understood as words of limitation intended only to convey a contingent bass fee to the son, and not as words of purchase to the grandchildren, so as to vest title to the entire property in the surviving children of the oldest son, on the death of the youngest son without issue.—*Ib.*, 500.

Same; Conditional Limitation; Construction.—Since it was possible under the deed, as actually happened, that none of the successive contingent grantees would be alive and satisfy the conditions in the deed, either there was left in the grantor a quasi reversion, the possibility of ultimate interests not limited over by the deed, or else by reason of the impossibility of the conditional limitations taking effect, a condition which arose during the lifetime of the youngest son by the death of his two older brothers, one of whom left children, wnich defeated the limitation to the daughter, so that the terminable fee in the youngest son became a fee simple, although he died after his two brothers, but without issue.—*Ib.*, 500.

Same; Life Estate; Limitations Over; Validity.—Where a grantor conveyed property to his wife with remainder to their youngest son in fee except that if he should die before maturity without issue, then to the next youngest son, and so on to each son, and then to the daughter, were valid conditional limitations. *Ib.* 500.

DEPOSITARIES.

See Contempts.

Depositary; Duties.—A custodian of a note pending litigation is not bound to earn protfis in the way of interest upon the amount paid him on the note beyond that called for by the note.—*Rutledge v. Cramton*, 306.

DEPOSITIONS.

Depositions; Examination without Order; Waiver.—By cross examining the witnesses without objection, the adversary party waived the fact that the witnesses were examined after their depositions had been taken without an order of court first obtained.—*Hall & Farley v. Ala. T. & I. Co.*, 398.

Same; Suppression.—Whether depositions should be suppressed, because taken without special order is discretionary with the trial judge according as he thinks the right of the parties would be best subserved.—*Ib.*, 398.

Depositions; Responsiveness of Answer; Admissibility.—Where the answers of a witness to interrogatories were responsive to the issues as made up by the court's approval, and were not otherwise objectionable, it was error to strike portions of the depositions containing the answers on the grounds that the answers were not responsive to the interrogatories.—*Pratt Cons. C. Co. v. Davidson*, 667.

DESCENT AND DISTRIBUTION.

Descent and Distribution; Obligation of Heirs.—Where real estate descended to heirs incumbered by a mortgage, and was partitioned among them subject to the mortgage the debt could not be said to be the personal obligation of the heirs and they were under no duty to pay.—*Caldwell v. Caldwell*, 216.

DISCOVERIES.

Discovery; Statutory Provisions.—The remedy given by Section 3135, Code 1907, is cumulative to the right of discovery previously existing and implies a right to exhibit such interrogatories and have them answered, although the bill waives answer under oath.—*Rosenau v. Powell*, 123.

Same; Filing.—Under section 3136, Code 1907, where a complainant places his interrogatories to the respondent in the official custody of the register he does not lose his right to have them answered although such officer does not indorse the same as his duty requires.—*Ib.*, 123.

Same; Order Fixing Time to Answer.—Under section 3136, Code 1907, it is enough that a formal order in writing fixing the time for answer was made, and a copy of same served on respondent, though the order was not placed on the minute book of the court.—*Ib.*, 123.

Same; Failure to Answer; Decree.—On failure to answer interrogatories within the time fixed, the provisions of section 3135, Code 1907, became operative, and under it a decree granting relief to complainant means such a decree as may be proper in the then condition of the cause, and hence authorizes a decree pro confesso, if that is the only proper decree in the case at the time of the default.—*Ib.*, 123.

DISMISSAL AND NONSUIT.

Dismissal and Non-Suit; Agreement of Parties.—Where an order was made on the agreement of the parties as recited in said agreement that the cause be dismissed if the plaintiff failed to give security for costs according to the agreement, the defendant was entitled to a dismissal of the cause upon an ascertainment by the court that there had been a non-compliance with the agreement.—*Smith v. Smith*, 547.

DIVORCE.

See Husband and Wife.

Divorce; Special Legislation; Granting Divorce.—A special act granting a divorce was unconstitutional under section 23, Article 4, Constitution 1871.—*Winkles v. Powell*, 46.

Same; Grounds; Abandonment.—The refusal of the wife to accompany the husband to the domicile selected by him is an abandonment, and if continued for the statutory period is grounds for divorce.—*Ib.*, 46.

Divorce; Equity; Jurisdiction.—The power to grant a divorce a vinculo is not within the general jurisdiction of courts of equity; their jurisdiction to grant divorces is purely statutory and although a court of general jurisdiction, yet when exercising a special authority in derogation of the common law, it is quoad hoc an inferior or limited court.—*Martin v. Martin*, 106.

Same; Decree; Jurisdictional Facts; Residence of Parties.—Section 3802 Code 1907, established bona fide residence in this State for one year next before the filing of the bill as a jurisdictional prerequisite to a valid decree of divorce against a respondent who is a non-resident;, and this must be shown by the record in order for the decree to withstand a collateral attack.—*Ib.*, 106.

Same.—The allegations of the bill for divorce stated and examined and held insufficient as jurisdictional averment of residence within the provisions of section 3802 Code 1907 to protect the decree entered thereon against collateral attack, and declaring the decree void.—*Ib.*, 106.

Same; Jurisdiction; Residence; Pleading.—It is not necessary that a pleading in an action for divorce adopt the exact terms of the statute as to the jurisdictional fact of residence; it is sufficient if the averments convey the same idea in equivalent terms.—*Ib.*, 106.

Divorce; Temporary Alimony.—The provisions of section 3803, Code 1907, do not require the allowance of temporary alimony if the husband has already provided for such support.—*Bulke v. Bulke*, 138.

Same; Attorney's Fee.—The allowance for attorney's fees in a divorce suit, in the absence of the statutory provisions, is governed by the general principles of law as to the propriety of such allowance, which depends upon the good faith of the proceedings, the probability of success, etc.—*Ib.*, 138.

Same; Bill; Condoning Derelictions.—Where the cross-bill of the husband in answer to the wife's suit for a divorce alleges that subsequent to the wife's dereliction, he received her back into his home and supported her, it is not subject to demurrer, though not alleging that he lived with her as his wife so as to condone her former dereliction.—*Ib.*, 138.

EASEMENTS.

Easement; Injunction; Right of Complainant.—One seeking an injunction to protect a right of way over an alley must establish his right thereto, and cannot rely on the weakness of the title of the adversary party.—*Barker v. Mobile Elec. Co.*, 28.

Same; Establishment; Rights Acquired.—Where a way established as of legal right divides the property of two owners, the presumption is that each has contributed the land for the way in equal parts, and a conveyance of an abutting ownership carries a fee to the center of the way; where the way has been laid out entirely on the land on one side of the property line, a subsequent grant by the owner must be deemed to convey the fee in the whole way.—*Ib.*, 28.

Same; Right of Way; Adverse User.—Where one has no title to the soil in a way which he uses as common with the owner, his user is presumptively permissive, and so remains until knowledge of the claim as of right is brought home to the owner, and to establish an easement by adverse user, the user must have been adverse and continuous for a period of time which will pass title to the land by adverse possession.—*Ib.*, 28.

Same; Evidence.—The fact that a tenant of one claiming an easement in a right of way by adverse user had complained that on one occasion, that poles had been piled on the right of way obstructing it, and that the agent of the owner removed the same, was not evidence of an assertion of right to use the way sufficient to ripen into title by adverse user.—*Ib.*, 28.

EJECTMENT.

See Deeds. Adverse Possession.

Ejectment; Defenses.—Where defendant in ejectment was in possession under certain tenants in common, every defense available to them was equally available to the defenadnt.—*Farr v. Perkins*, 500.

Same—A tenant in common cannot maintain ejectment against a co-tenant in possession unless there has been an ouster of the plaintiff by the defendant before suit brought, or something equivalent thereto.—*Ib.*, 500.

Same.—Where one tenant in common sues another in ejectment, the burden is on the plaintiff who asserts an ouster to overcome by proof the presumption of possession for the common benefit of all.—*Ib.*, 500.

Same; Ouster; Repudiation.—A defendant's co-tenant's repudiation of the existence of the relation of tenant in common is sufficient evidence of previous ouster to excuse demand by plaintiff to be let into possession before suit brought.—*Ib.*, 500.

Same; Evidence.—Formal demand by one co-tenant to be let into possession or enjoyment of his right as a co-tenant, and a refusal is clear evidence of ouster autnorizing the bringing of ejectment.—*Ib.*, 500.

Ejectment; Evidence; Deeds.—Where the action is ejectment and the defense adverse possession, and there is testimony tending to show a long possession of lands described by deeds offered, such deeds are properly received in evidence as color of title.—*Hardy v. Randall*, 576.

ELECTIONS.

See Quo Warranto; Mandamus.

Elections; Polling Places; Validity.—The action of the council of a town in selecting a polling place after the mayor had given notice of the holding of the election at another place did not invalidate the election held at the place fixed by the council.—*Mizell v. State ex rel. Gresham*, 434.

Same; Selection; Contest.—Where the qualified electors of a town had an opportunity to vote at an election, and a majority voted at the polling place fixed by the council of the town, and the minority cast their ballots at an unauthorized place, and the inspectors of the election were eligible to hold that office, the election was not void, but was subject to contest within section 1168, Code 1907.—*Ib.*, 434.

Same; Election Officers; Selection.—While the law contemplates that inspectors of an election of a town shall be selected at the time the election was ordered, yet, the changing them at a subsequent date does not invalidate the election, and upon discovering that the inspectors appointed are unfit, the council of the town may appoint others, notwithstanding the provision of section 1164, Code 1907.—*Ib.*, 434.

Election; Contest; Registration List.—While section 6806, Code 1907, makes it a misdemeanor to make a copy of the poll list, of any election, said section does no abrogate, but must be construed with section 458, which requires the probate judge to deliver to any party to an election contest a certified copy of such list.—*Sartain v. Shepcrd*, 474.

Same.—The changes made in the election law from the Code of 1896, did not repeal section 458, and that statute by necessary implication gives the probate judge the right of access to such lists though they be in the custody of another officer.—*Ib.*, 474.

Same.—Construing sections 415, 417, 420, 425 and 458, Code 1907, it is held that by necessary implication, the first poll list prepared by the election inspectors should be transmitted to the judge of probate who shall be the legal custodian of said lists.—*Ib.*, 474.

EMINENT DOMAIN.

Eminent Domain; Compensation; Closing Streets; Abutting Owners.—Although the bill alleges that the property abutted on the street, but failed to allege that it abutted on the part vacated, and the description of the boundaries and the diagram made an exhibit to the bill, showed that the complainant's lots did not abut on the portion vacated, it was not sufficiently shown that the plaintiff was an abutting owner and entitled to damages against the city for closing the street and permitting the railway to acquire it.—*Albes v. So. Ry. Co.*, 279.

Eminent Domain; Necessity of Payment; Entry on Making Payment or Deposit in Court.—Under section 235, Constitution 1901, the rights of an owner who files a bill to enjoin a street grade improvement-until he shall be compensated for the injury to his abutting property, are protected by an order of reference to ascertain full indemnity to the owner and costs, and a deposit with the register of the amount so ascertained, to abide the results of the suit.—*Stocks v. City of Gadsden*, 321.

EQUITY.

For Equitable Actions, see appropriate title.

1. Bill and Incidents.

Equity; Pleading; Bill; Construction.—A bill will be sustained if the facts alleged, whether well or poorly pleaded, show a case for equitable relief, as a bill will be given every reasonable intendment, except adding facts not set forth therein.—*Woodward v. The State*, 7.

Same; Bill; Dismissal.—Although section 3121, Code 1907, puts the respondent to a general demurrer, instead of motion to dismiss for want of equity, that right, in cases of injunction, is preserved by § 4526, Code 1907.—*Ib.*, 7.

Equity; Bill; Amendment.—Under section 2837 Code 1907, a decree sustaining or overruling a demurrer to a bill for want of equity is an interlocutory decree, and where the supreme court renders a decree reversing a decree overruling such a demurrer, and remanding the cause, this was an interlocutory decree, and could not become final until the bill was formally dismissed by the trial court, and hence the provisions of section 3126 Code 1907, are applicable. The rule that in passing on a general demurrer to a bill amendable defects should be considered as made relates only to facts set out defectively, and not to facts not set out in the bill.—*Singo v. Brainard*, 64.

Equity; Pleading; Bill.—Where the bill is by a shareholder in a corporation to dissolve the corporation and seeks relief against the alleged fraudulent conduct of the directors and officers, and seeks the disallowance of the claim assigned by the directors or officers to a respondent, with the alternate prayer that if such claim be found valid, it should be paid out of the assets of the corporation, then such respondent is not concerned with those phases of the bill relating to the dissolution of the corporation, and the fraud of the directors, unless the entire equity of the bill depends on the solution of those questions.—*Ellis v. Vandegrift*, 142.

Same; Bill; Multifariousness.—A party not prejudiced thereby cannot object to a bill on account of multifariousness.—*Ib.*, 142.

Same; Bills; Multifariousness.—Where the bill was by the minority stockholders seeking to dissolve a corporation and to relieve it from the effect of fraudulent acts of its directors and majority stockholders and also to have relief against a claim held by a respondent, alleged to have been created by the directors and assigned to him that he might file a petition in bankruptcy against the corporation, and also seeking reimbursement of the sums expended by the minority stockholders in resisting the bankruptcy petition, it was not multifariousness with respect to the respondent holding the alleged fraudulent claim, either because he was not

EQUITY.—*Continued.*

interested in winding up the corporation, or that the necessary parties are different in the different phases of the bill, or that it sought reimbursement for the sums expended in resisting the petition in bankruptcy, as such relief was not sought against the respondent, but against others.—*Ib.*, 142.

Same.—As it is not necessary that all the parties to a bill should have an interest in all the matters in controversy, it being sufficient that each respondent has an interest in some of the matters involved, and if they are connected with the others, a bill is not multifarious as to a respondent because he has no connection with a large part of the record, or that the same defense is not applicable to the different aspects, or that no common relief is sought as against him.—*Ib.*, 142.

Equity; Bill; Multifariousness.—Under section 3095, Code 1907, a bill to have an assignment of substantially all a debtor's property to his surety in consideration that the surety would pay the debt, declared a general assignment for the benefit of all the creditors, or an alternative that it be declared fraudulent as to such creditors, was not multifariousness.—*Smith v. Young,* 190.

Equity; Bill; Amendment; Footnote.—Amendments to a bill made by interlineations in red ink do not require an additional footnote pointing out the particular statements or interrogatories which the complainants desire the respondents to answer.—*Johnson v. Gartman,* 290.

Equity; Bill; Numbering.—Although rule of practice No. 8, requires bills of equity to be numbered, the fact that the paragraphs were lettered instead of being numbered was not objectionable where the purpose of the rule was effectuated by the course pursued.—*Grubbs v. Hawes,* 382.

2. Demurrer.

Equity; Demurrer; Amendment to; Right to File.—After a demurrer is overruled, and the time for an appeal from such decree has passed, the defendant cannot file a so-called amended demurrer, which raises no other objection than those determined by the former demurrer.—*Turner v. Durr, et al.,* 72.

Same; Effect.—A decree overruling a demurrer to a bill, though interlocutory, tests and determines the sufficiency of the bill as to the grounds of demurrer interposed.—*Ib.,* 72.

Same; Demurrer; Sufficiency.—Where the bill has equity independent of the defect set up in the demurrer, a demurrer addressed to the whole bill should be overruled.—*So. St. F. & C. I. Co. v. Whatley,* 101.

Same; Demurrer; Office.—The purpose of a demurrer in equity is to accelerate the decision of the complainant's right upon the confessed averments of his pleading, and a demurrant cannot obect to imperfections in the bill not related to the cause of action asserted against him.—*Ellis v. Vandegrift,* 142.

Same; Pleading; Adoption of Demurrer.—Where a respondent by most general terms adopts the grounds of demurrer of another respondent such adoption does not entitle him to rely upon the waiver of the bar of the statute of limitation which was set up in the demurrer adopted.—*Ib.,* 142.

Equity; Pleading; Demurrer.—The allegations of a bill must be accepted as true on demurrer.—*City of Birmingham v. Coffman,* 213.

Same; General Demurrer.—If the bill contains any equity, a general demurrer is properly overruled.—*Ib.,* 213.

Equity; Demurrer; Good in Part.—Where a demurrer went to the bill as a whole, it was properly overruled, though a part of the relief demanded was obtainable in a court of law, and could only be granted in equity as incidental to purely equitable relief, also prayed for.—*Robinson v. Griffin,* 372.

EQUITY—*Continued.*

3. Parties Necessary and Proper.

Parties; Transferee of Notes.—Where the bill to rescind a contract for the purchase of stock and for the surrender and cancellation of the notes given therefor, on the grounds of fraud inducing the purchase, avers that on discovery of the fraud, and before the certificates of stock was received, complainant offered to rescind the contract and the respondent declined, and also refused to deliver him his notes, and that the notes were discounted and the proceeds placed to the credit of the defendant, the bill shows equity and can be maintained, whether the holder be a bona fide holder or not, and whether the bank discounting the note be joined as a party respondent or not.—*So. St. F. & C. I. Co. v. Whatley,* 101.

3½. Submission—Trial.

Equity; Trial; Submission.—Where a suit was submitted for a decree on Oct. 29th, 1907, under an agreement allowing ninety days to take testimony, and the case was continued from time to time, and amendments, demurrers, etc., were filed, and submissions and decrees on demurrer, and other proceedings had indicating that the parties were treating the case as if the submissions had been set aside, the respondent even examining a witness whose depositions were filed Feb. 6, 1908, the court did not err in entering a decree on Nov. 18, 1909, setting aside the former submission, and declaring that the order had effect from the adjournment of the April term, 1909, admitting the testimony regularly taken in the meantime, although the respondent objected to the issuance of a commission to take testimony on Nov. 2, 1909, since the original submission had in fact ceased to be effective.—*Johnson v. Gartman,* 290.

4. Remedy at Law.

Equity; Remedy at Law; Adequacy.—The test of equity jurisdiction, where there is a concurrent remedy at law is whether the remedy is adequate and will not subject the party to vexatious litigation.—*So. St. F. & C. I. Co. v. Whatley,* 101.

5. Jurisdiction.

Same; Jurisdiction; Disposal of Entire Matter.—Where the jurisdiction of the court of equity has been properly invoked it will dispose of all the questions involved in the controversy and a respondent cannot object that some of these questions could have been adjudicated in an action at law.—*Ellis v. Vandegrift,* 142.

Equity; Jurisdiction; Multiplicity of Suits.—To give equity jurisdiction on the ground of preventing a multiplicity of suits, a community of interest in the subject matter of the several actions is necessary; community of interest in the question at law and facts involved in the several actions not being enough.—*Roanoke Guano Co. v. Saunders,* 347.

6. Pleadings.

Equity; Pleading; Verification.—Where pleas are received without verification the lack of verification is not a ground for holding them insufficient.—*Cartwright v. West,* 198.

Same; Sufficiency.—A respondent in equity cannot be denied the benefit of his defense of the statutory bar by limitation set up by way of special plea based on facts averred therein, by complainant's amendment of his bill alleging a state of facts contrary to those averred in the pleas.—*Ib.,* 198.

Same; Plea to Part of Bill.—In chancery practice a plea may be filed to a part of a bill.—*Ib.,* 198.

ESTATES.

See Courts, § 1; Executors and Administrators.

ESTOPPEL.

See Landlord and Tenant; Judgment; Bankruptcy.

Estoppel; By Deed; Person Estopped.—Recitals in a deed as to the boundaries of the land thereby conveyed are not binding on strangers to the deed.—*Barker v. Mobile Elec. Co.*, 28.

Same.—Where the owner of the entire frontage on a street conveyed a certain amount of frontage to a grantee, and subsequently conveyed to a third person a further frontage, the first grantee and those claiming under him, were not estopped, by the subsequent deed, from relying on the boundaries described in the earlier deed, especially where the deed to the third person described the land conveyed as bounded by the land of the grantee.—*Ib.*, 28.

EVIDENCE.

1. Ancient Documents.

Evidence; Ancient Documents.—A copy of the map of the city, prepared about fifty years ago by one employed by the city to lay out a map thereof, is an ancient document, and when coming from the proper custody is competent to show boundary lines of property owners.—*Barker v. Mobile Elec. Co.*, 28.

1½. Documentary.

Evidence; Documentary; Mortality Tables.—Mortality tables are not conclusive on the issue of life expectancy in an action for wrongful death.—*L. & N. R. R. Co. v. Holland*, 675.

2. Judicial Notice.

Evidence; Judicial Notice Special Acts.—The courts take judicial notice of public acts, local as to territory, creating municipal corporations or amending their charters, and that a particular municipality was created by several local acts which impliedly, if not expressly, authorized it to own and operate electric lighting plants.—*Darby v. City of Union Springs*, 709.

Evidence; Judicial Notice; Public Records.—The issuance of a commission to a public officer by the Governor is a public act of public record of which the courts must take judicial notice.—*Casey v. Bryce.* 129.

Same.—The courts take judicial notice of the declared results of a general election and of the fact that one has been declared elected to the office of sheriff of a county and has received the Governor's commission.—*Ib.*, 129.

Same; Conclusiveness.—The courts take judicial notice of matters of public record and the facts disclosed by such records are conclusive.—*Ib.*, 129.

Evidence; Judicial Notice; Appointment in Terms of Officers.—Courts take judicial notice of the commissioned officers of the state and of the terms for which they hold and the extent of their authority.—*Touart v. State ex rel. Callaghan*, 453.

Same; Signatures.—Courts will take judicial notice of the genuineness of the signature of the commissioned officers of the state.—*Ib.*, 453.

Evidence; Judicial Notice.—The courts will take judicial notice that the governor installed in 1907, was installed on January 15, and that his successor was inaugurated and installed on Monday, January 16, 1911, at 2:15 P. M.—*Oberhaus v. State ex rel. McNamara*, 483.

Evidence; Judicial Notice; General Panics.—The courts take judicial notice of general panics or financial disturbances, such as the one of 1907.—*L. & N. R. R. Co. v. Holland*, 675.

Same.—The court will not take judicial notice that the prevalence of a panic reduced the earnings of the persons engaged during the year next preceding this, and hence, it was error for the plaintiff's counsel to make such a statement in argument, in the absence of proof of that fact.—*Ib.*, 675.

EXECUTORS AND ADMINISTRATORS—*Continued.*

a bill to have land of the estate sold for distribution.—*Swope v. Swope*, 157.

Executors and Administrators; Sale of Land; Nature of Proceeding.—Proceedings for the sale of lands in the probate court are in rem.—*Johnson v. Gartman*, 290.

3. Property Subject; Bequests.

Executors and Administrators; Wills; Claims; Claimant.—The personal property of the testator is the fund primarily for the discharge of debts and legacies, and they are not chargeable upon the land, unless the intention to so charge them is manifested by the express word, or by fair implication from the will, read in the light of the environments of the testator and his estate.—*Pitts v. Campbell*, 604.

FIXTURES.

See Mortgages.

Fixtures; Questions.—It is a mixed question of law and fact whether a chattel has become a part of the realty.—*Grubbs v. Hawes*, 383.

Same; Intention of Parties.—The intention with which a chattel is attached to the realty is of great importance in determining whether it had become a fixture.—*Ib.*, 383.

Same; Mortgagor and Mortgagee; Foreclosure.—A mortgagor of a lot and building in which machinery was erected after the execution of the mortgage was not prejudiced by permitting the mortgagee to pay off the balance due upon the machinery which had become a fixture so as to permit the building and machinery to be sold as a whole on foreclosure, since the machinery could be treated as between the mortgagor and mortgagee as a fixture, although as between the mortgagor and the original seller. it was a chattel.—*Ib.*, 383.

Same; Pleading.—The bill examined and held to sufficiently allege that the machinery was a part of the realty so as to be covered by the mortgagee.—*Ib.*, 383.

FRAUDULENT CONVEYANCES.

Fraudulent Conveyance; Creditor; Surety as Creditor.—A surety is a creditor within the provisions of section 4295, Code 1907, from the inception of his contingent liability, and after he has paid the debt he may maintain a creditor's bill against his principal and other creditors to set aside a conveyance as fraudulent, made while the liability was contingent, or to have such conveyances declared a general assignment.—*Smith v. Young*, 190.

Fraudulent Conveyance; Preference.—At the common law, a debtor had a right to prefer one or more of his creditors even to the entire exclusion of others.—*J. Loeb Gro. Co. v. Brickman & Co.*, 316.

FRAUDS, STATUTE OF.

1. Land.

Frauds, Statute of; Contracts for Sale of Land; Description.—Where the option to purchase definitely described the lands, except as to its western boundary, and that was to be determined by a line run on a level with the crest of the contemplated dam across a river. which dam was to be erected by the purchaser who could fix the crest of the dam in advance of its actual construction, and the purchaser within the period of the option, fixed the crest of the proposed dam, and located the western boundary line by survey, and ascertained the number of acres included within the boundary so fixed, the exercise of the option and a designation of the land rendered the contract valid under the statute of frauds.—*Wilkins v. Hardaway*, 57.

GARNISHMENT.

See Judgments.

Garnishment; Persons Subject; Plaintiff.—The rule is not recognized in this state that permits the plaintiff to make himself a garnishee in his own action.—*Jos. Joseph & Bros. Co. v. Hoffman, et al.,* 568.

Same; Nature of Remedy; Proceeding in Rem.—A garnishment proceeding in a court of another state where a plaintiff may make himself a garnishee of his indebtedness to a non-resident defendant not personally served with process, and not appearing to defend, is a proceeding in rem.—*Ib.,* 568.

Same; Foreign Judgment; Constitutional Provision.—Where a court of another state has jurisdiction and ascertains that a plaintiff, who has made himself the garnishee of his indebtedness to a non-resident defendant not personally served with process, nor appearing therein, is himself found indected to the defendant in an ascertained sum, and that sum is reduced by the amount of the garnished indebtedness, thereby discharging any indebtedness from or liability of the plaintiff there to the defendant to the extent only of the sum condemned, this court is bound to observe and give effect to the judgment only so far as it is a judgment in rem. under the full faith and credit clause of the Constitution of the United States. —*Ib.,* 568.

GIFTS.

See Wills.

GOVERNOR.

1. Term.

Time; Governor; Term of Office.—Construing sections 115, 116 and 48, Constitution 1901, it is held that the legislature may count the votes on any day within seven days of their meeting, and that the governor's term expired at midnight on the first Monday after the second Tuesday in January, after the election of his successor, and that the incoming governor's term begins on the beginning of the third Tuesday in January after his election, notwithstanding the provision of section 1461 and 1570, Code 1907, and that the governor and other officers, are entitled to salary from the day on which they are inducted into office.—*Oberhaus v. State ex rel. McNamara,* 483.

GUARDIAN.

See Infants; Insane Persons; Substitution of Records.

HIGHWAYS.

1. Improvement.

Highways; Taxation; Apportionment.—The special road tax collected under authority of section 215, Constitution 1901, cannot be apportioned among various parts of the county, and hence, acts 1909, pp. 205 and 304, are inoperative as to special taxes so collected.— *Com. Court Pike Co. v. City of Troy,* 442.

HOMESTEAD.

Homestead; Right of Wife.—The wife has no estate in the husband's homestead, he having the legal title. Her only right is that of joint occupancy with him, and the right to veto his alienation of it under the statute.—*Winkles v. Powell,* 46.

Same; Abandonment; Right of Husband.—Under Section 4190 Code 1907, a husband may be entitled without his wife's consent to abandon the homestead, but he cannot, by abandoning both the homestead and the family, deprive them of their right to hold the homestead so long as they use it as such.—*Ib.,* 46.

Same; Ratification by Wife.—Where the husband conveyed the homestead by deed without the wife joining therein, or consenting thereto, a subsequent approval of the deed by the wife did not validate the deed.—*Ib.,* 46.

HUSBAND AND WIFE.

See Homestead.

1. Maintenance.

Husband and Wife; Maintenance; Action Reviewed.—Where the petitioner, the wife, filed a petition for separate maintenance and had a decree awarding her a certain amount monthly as alimony, and she thereafter filed a bill in the city court for divorce and alimony, the order of the chancellor, denying without prejudice her petition filed, pending the divorce suit, setting up that the husband was five months in arrears in the payments of such allowance, and seeking an order to compel the payment, will not be disturbed on appeal; especially where from all that appears on the record, temporary alimony covering a part of such five months may have been allowed in the divorce suit filed in the city court, it being inequitable for petitioner to receive alimony from both sources at the same time.—*Clisby v. Clisby*, 22.

Husband and Wife; Domicile; Husband's Right to Select.—If the wife's health or safety is not imperiled thereby the husband has the right to select and designate the family domicile.—*Winkles v. Powell*, 46.

Husband and Wife; Support; Contract; Abrogation.—Even if a husband not only received his wife back into his home, but lived with her as his wife, thereby condoning the wife's dereliction, this would not necessarily abrogate the contract by which she had received a definite amount from him in lieu of all obligations of support.—*Bulke v. Bulke*, 138

INFANTS.

Infants; Next Friend; Removal.—While any one can act as next friend for an infant in bringing a suit, and while it requires no authority from the court to bring such suit, the court may and should revoke the authority of the next friend when it appears that he is not a proper party to prosecute the suit.—*Swope v. Swope*, 157.

Same; Party.—While a next friend is not technically speaking a party to a suit, he is a party in the contemplation of the statutes, and the practice of courts as to the conduct of the suit.—*Ib.*, 157.

INJUNCTION.

See Intoxicating Liquors; Appeal and Error, § 1.

Injunction; Dissolution.—Section 4535 Code 1907, abrogated the former rule and now the court may consider the affidavit of the parties as well as the sworn bill and the answer on the motion to dissolve the injunction.—*Nelson, et al. v. Hammond*, 14.

Same; Affidavit.—The reduction of plaintiff's testimony to writing after his oral examination before the chancellor on a motion to dissolve the injunction was not an affidavit within the meaning of section 4535 Code 1907, and should not be substituted for the affidavit required unless waived by the opposite party.—*Ib.*, 14.

Injunction; Right; Equity.—A bill without equity will not support an injunction of any character under any circumstances.—*McHann v. McMurray*, 182.

Same; Application; Bill; Intendments.—Where an application for an injunction is presented under section 4528, the complainant is the actor, and his bill, when attacked for want of equity, cannot be aided by presumption that amendable defects have been cured, as is the case on a motion to dissolve an injunction already granted for want of equity in the bill.—*Ib.*, 182.

Same; Threatened Injury.—The allegations examined and held to contain no facts from which it could be reasonably inferred that the threatened injury was likely to happen and that the application was devoid of equity as such application sought relief merely from a prospective nuisance, concerning which the injury was contingent. —*Ib.*, 182.

INJUNCTION—*Continued.*

Injunction; Proceedings at Law.—A bank is not entitled to an injunction restraining the maintenance of a suit by the depositor's administrator against it to recover the deposit, where there was no claim that the depositor's estate was insolvent, or not amply able to answer any claim that might be established against it by the bank, nor that the bank had applied the amount of the deposit or any part of it to any debt or demand owing by the depositor or his estate to the bank.—*Tallapoosa Co. Bank v. Wynn*, 272.

Same; Dissolution in Vacation.—Where a final decree granting a perpetual injunction was reversed on appeal, and the cause remanded, the cause in the trial court stood in the same situation as though there had never been any final decree, and the respondent was entitled to move to vacate the injunction on ten days' notice in vacation under section 4526, Code 1907.—*Ib.*, 272.

Injunction; Restraining Action.—In a bill by one maintaining a guano factory, sulphuric fumes from which injure the lands owned separately, to enjoin their separate actions for damages, and have the damages assessed and determined in one suit is not given equity by the additional prayer that if the factory be found to be a nuisance, it be abated; for, while those injured could have maintained a joint bill to abate the nuisance, they could not have recovered damages therein, and they and not the wrong doer, have the right to elect whether they will maintain such a suit or separately sue for damages.—*Roanoke Guano Co. v. Saunders*, 347.

INSANE PERSONS.

Insane Persons; Guardian; Appointment; Collateral Attack.—The fact that the jury which pronounced a person insane was composed of ten instead of twelve persons, was an irregularity merely, which would not make the appointment of the guardian void, it not being necessary that the records of the probate court show such facts; hence, that question cannot be raised on collateral attack by a stranger to the proceedings, so as to question the authority of the guardian to maintain a bill for patition. Such questions should be raised by appeal or in direct proceedings.—*Powell v. Union B. & T. Co.*, 332.

INTEREST.

See Bills and Notes.

INTOXICATING LIQUORS.

Intoxicating Liquors; Injunction; Bill; Verification.—Where a bill was filed by the solicitor under Acts 1909, p. 70, and set forth the solicitor had probable cause for believing, and did believe on information, that the defendant, etc., and the bill was verified by a citizen, who recited upon oath that he, the affiant, was informed and had probable cause for believing, and did believe, that the statements in the bill were true, the verification was insufficient under section 20 of said Act. as it was an affirmation merely of the affiant's belief that the solicitor believed that the facts stated existed.—*Woodward v. The State*, 7.

Same.—Construing section 20 of the Fuller Bill, and Rule 15 Chancery Practice. it is held that where a bill filed by the solicitor to abate a liquor nuisance was verified by a citizen. it must appear that the officer was unwilling to make affidavit, and the citizens authority for making the affidavit should be disclosed by the affidavit. —*Ib.*, 7.

Same; Injunction; Facts to be Stated.—Where the solicitor filed a bill for injunction to abate a liquor nuisance, and alleged that he was informed. and had probable cause for believing. and did believe, that the defendant had in his possession, or operated a room or place of business wherein he kept for sale and sold prohibited liquors. that he had within the past twelve months offered and sold quantities of

INTOXICATING LIQUORS—*Continued.*

such liquors, and allowed some of it to be drunk on the premises creating and maintaining a common liquor nuisance in violation of law, and that the accused was not a druggist, and did not keep a drugstore at his place of business, and that his place of business was not exclusively used as a dwelling house, the bill averred no facts, and was therefore insufficient, and could not be supported by the rule that a bill will be given every reasonable intendment.—*Ib.,* 7.

Injunction; Motion to Discharge; Motion to Dissolve.—A motion to dissolve an injunction lies only where there is a want of equity in the bill, or where there has been a full and complete denial of its equities by the answer; a motion to discharge lies for irregularities in the bill, or for irregularities in the order granting the injunction. —*Ib.,* 7.

Same; Waiver of Defect.—Section 4526 Code 1907, authorizes a motion to discharge and to dissolve to be made and to be heard at the same time without prejudice, and hence a motion to dissolve is not a waiver of a right to move to discharge.—*Ib.,* 7.

Same; Discharge; Defect of Verification.—The defect in verification of a bill is an irregularity, and it should be attacked by a motion to discharge the injunction, but the motion should not be granted until opportunity is given to supply the defective affidavit.—*Ib.,* 7.

JUDGMENT.

See Attachment: Appearance; Garnishment

1. Res Judicata.

Judgment; Res Adjudicata; When Available.—Unless pleaded, a former adjudication is not available.—*Winkles v. Powell,* 46.

Judgment; Estoppel of.—Since there should be an end to litigation the doctrine of estoppel by judgment is not disfavored.—*Hall & Farley v. Ala. T. & I. Co.,* 398.

Same; Pleading.—Where a creditor sought to reach sums alleged to be due to an insolvent corporation on their unpaid stock subscription, a plea in estoppel or defense, by such stockholders, that a former judgment was rendered in a suit by such creditor against respondents as garnishees of the same indebtedness or chose in action in favor of the respondent, after its answer was contested and after a trial and determination of the case on its merits, is sufficient as to its averments.—*Ib.,* 398.

Same; Burden of Proof.—The burden is upon the respondent to prove a special plea of res judicata as alleged.—*Ib.,* 398.

1½. Parties; Landlords.

Judgment; Against Landlord; Parties.—Since the object of sections 3840, and 3844, is either to bind the landlord by the judgment, or to permit him as of right to effectually defend the suit in his own proper person, and since a judgment for possession in fact operates only on the tenant in possession, the intervention of a false landlord in such action could not give plaintiff a right either to a joint judgment against both the landlord and the tenant, or against the landlord separately, in case the tenant's possession was rightful.—*Farr v. Perkins,* 500.

2. Collateral Attack.

Judgment; Collateral Attack; Presumption.—On collateral attack of a judgment or decree there is no presumption of the existence of jurisdictional facts, but every reasonable intendent will be made in favor of the validity thereof, as a matter of construction only; and where the pleading is reasonably susceptible of a construction presenting the essential jurisdictional facts, without supplying omitted essential averments, that construction will be adopted, but pleading must be understood as it is reasonable to in-

JUDGMENT—*Continued.*

fer that the party who made it and the judge who acted upon it understood it, and not as they were bound to understand it.—*Martin v. Martin,* 106.

Same; Laches.—Where it appears from the face of the record that a judgment or decree is wholly void, delay or inaction by the party whose rights will be affected thereby, will not invest the judgment or decree with any force as against a collateral attack, it being a nullity under all circumstances.—*Ib.,* 106.

Judgment; Collateral Attack; Probate Court.—Where the jurisdiction of the probate court had attached and it had proceeded to exercise that jurisdiction, irregularities in the subsequent proceedings will not subject the decree rendered to collateral attack; this rule being extended to a failure to make interested persons parties or to notify necessary parties.—*Powell v. Union B. & T. Co.,* 332.

3. Conclusiveness and Matters Concluded.

Same; Conclusiveness; Requisites as Estoppel.—The judgment of a court of concurrent jurisdiction directly upon the point is a plea in bar, or is evidence conclusive, between the same parties upon the same matter directly in question in another court, but in the absence of any one of these ingredients, the defense fails.—*Hall & Farley v. Ala. T. & I. Co.,* 398.

Matters Concluded.—A judgment is conclusive between the same parties when rendered on a verdict on the merits not only as to the facts actually litigated and decided, but as to all the facts necessarily involved in the issue; and although a particular matter is not necessarily involved in the issue, yet if the issue is broad enough to cover it, and it actually arose and was determined, it may then be connected with the record by evidence aliunde.—*Ib.,* 398.

Same; Present Case.—Held by an equally divided court in a subsequent proceeding in equity that the judgment therein was res judicata of complainant's right to recover in that proceeding.—*Ib.,* 398.

Same; Conclusiveness.—The rule that the first judgment rendered controls, whether the action in which it is reached be instituted before the other or not, applies where the first judgment is rendered in another state.—*Jos. Joseph & Bros. Co. v. Hoffman, et al.,* 568.

Same; Matters Concluded.—Where an action for damages for a breach of contract is brought in another state, and the plaintiff garnishees his own debt due to a non-resident defendant, who had not been served with process, and who does not appear, and takes a judgment in personam for an amount reduced by the amount of the indebtedness condemned, a finding by that court of a breach of the contract is not conclusive on the issue of breach vel non of the contract declared on.—*Ib.,* 568.

4. Process to Sustain.

Judgment; Process to Sustain; Personal Judgment; Garnishment.—A court of another state which has jurisdiction to subject the indebtedness of the plaintiff there to the defendant to the satisfaction of the plaintiff's demand, on plaintiff's garnishment of himself, in his own action against the defendant, has no jurisdiction to render a personal judgment over against a non resident defendant, not personally served in the garnishment proceedings, and not appearing therein, and any such judgment is a nullity; the rule in such cases being to ascertain the amount of the plaintiff's demand, and then render judgment only condemning the property or indebtedness of the defendant to the satisfaction of the ascertained demand.—*Jos. Joseph & Bros. Co. v. Hoffman, et al.,* 568.

5. Foreign.

Same; Foreign Judgment; Fraud or Misconduct.—Where an action by a seller against a non resident buyer is instituted in this

JUDGMENT—*Continued.*

state before an action brought by the buyer against the seller was begun in another state, where it went to final judgment there, before the judgment in the action here was rendered, and there is no evidence of fraud in the proceedings in the other state, the mere fact that the buyer knew that complaint had been filed against him in this state, does not show fraud or misconduct in obtaining a judgment in such other state.—*Jos. Joseph & Bros. Co. v. Hoffman, et al.*, 568.

6. Discharge and Set Off.

Same; Discharge; Set Off.—Where, in an action in this state, a plaintiff is shown to be entitled to a judgment for $2,517, for goods sold, and the defendant shows a right to recover $1,174, the amount of an indebtedness of plaintiff to defendant which was condemned in garnishment proceedings against the plaintiff as a defendant in another state, the judgment here should be reduced by setting off the indebtedness condemned by the foreign judgment, and hence, a judgment against a garnished fund of $2,000 in this state is excessive and erroneous.—*Jos. Joseph & Bros. Co. v. Hoffman,* 568.

7. Attachment.

Judgment; Attachment; Nature; Personal Judgment.—Where the defendant is not personally served and does not appear generally, the court cannot render a personal judgment, but may only bind the property in an attachment proceeding, as such proceedings are in the nature of proceedings in rem; but a defendant becomes liable as on personal service where he executes a forthcoming bond or bond for the discharge of the garnishment in a suit begun by attachment, and thereafter the proceedings become a personal action, and proceeds as if the attachment was sued out in aid of a pending suit, except as provided by the statute, so as to authorize a personal judgment.—*Oliver v. Kinney,* 593.

Same; Record; Construction; Appearance.—Notwithstanding the judgment in an attachment case recites defendant's appearance, that recital should be construed with the other parts of the record on that question.—*Ib.,* 593.

JUDICIAL NOTICE.

See Evidence, § 2.

JURISDICTION.

See Equity; Courts.

JURY.

1. Competency.

Jury; Competency; Relationship; Affinity.—Affinity is the relation existing between a husband and the blood relations of the wife, or between the wife and the blood relations of the husband, but one spouse is not related to the affinities of the other spouse, and hence, a juror related by affinity to plaintiff's wife is not related to plaintiff.—*L. & N. R. R. Co. v. Holland,* 675.

JURY COMMISSIONERS.

Same; Jury Commissioners; Term.—Under Acts 1909, p. 305, the jury commissioners appointed by the governor did not include any part, as to term of office, of the first Monday after the second Tuesday in January, 1911, and that since the term of the then governor did include that day, there was a vacancy in the office of jury commissioner which the then governor had power to fill by appointment.—*Oberhaus v. State ex rel. McNamara,* 483.

LACHES.

See Tenants in Common; Lis Pendens; Judgments.

LANDLORD AND TENANT.

1. Estoppel.

Landlord and Tenant; Estoppel of Tenant.—The fact that one owning the soil of an alley and the exclusive right to use the same accepted a lease from the adjacent owner describing the alley as a joint alley used by the parties jointly, did not estop him from asserting his superior right and title.—*Barker v. Mobile Elec. Co.*, 28.

Landlord and Tenant; Estoppel; Title; Dealings With.—The fact that while in ignorance and in distress at her husband's illness, one of the complainants agreed to pay and did pay rent to a grantee of respondent, who had notice of the transaction between defendant and complainant, and of complainant's interest and equities in the land conveyed, does not estop complainants from seeking a cancellation of their deed to defendant, and to have the deed declared a mortgage.—*Irwin v. Coleman*, 175.

2. Status of One in Default.

Landlord and Tenant; Vendor and Purchaser; Default.—Where a purchaser is let into possession under an executory contract, a default in the payment of the purchase money, though it destroys his right as a purchaser does not make him a tenant of the vendor.—*Bush v. Fuller*, 511.

Same; Tendency at Sufferance.—Where a purchaser of land was let into possession under an executory agreement, and made default, but remained in possession, he became a tenant by sufferance by operation of law, and was not entitled to notice to quit.—*Ib.*, 511.

Same; Ejectment; Notice to Quit.—Ejectment being a possessory action, the plaintiff must not only show title but right of possession at the commencement of the suit, and hence, ejectment cannot be maintained against a tenant at will, who has not been given ten days notice to quit as required by law.—*Ib.*, 511.

Same; Tenancy at Will.—While a mistaken notion on the part of landlord that the tenant was a tenant at will, could not have the effect of changing a tenancy by sufferance to one at will, yet a notice by the landlord to the tenant wherein he recited that the tenancy was one at will, justifies an inference that the holding is in fact a tenancy at will.—*Ib.*, 511.

Same; Notice to Quit.—Where a landlord serves notice on a tenant at sufferance demanding possession in ten days, such notice by necessary implication extended defendant's possession until the expiration of ten days, and nothing short of a demand could make the possession unlawful before the expiration of that time so as to authorize ejectment.—*Ib.*, 511.

LIFE ESTATE.

See Deeds.

Life Estate; Character of Possession; Life Tenant.—The possession of the widow as a life tenant of lands belonging to her husband is not adverse to the heirs of the husband.—*Winkles v. Powell*, 46.

LIMITATION OF ACTIONS.

See Bankruptcy; Vendor and Purchaser.

Limitation of Action; Pleading; Necessity.—As a bar to an action limitations must be pleaded, else it is waived.—*Cartwright v. West*, 198.

Same.—Although under section 3115, Code 1907, the bar of the statute of limitation may be asserted as a defense by answer, yet that does not deprive a respondent of setting it up by special plea. —*Ib.*, 198.

Limitation of Action; Suspension of Statute; Payment.—If an heir of the vendee acted as agent for the other heirs in making payment of interest on the purchase money note, his payment operated to toll the statute as to all of them.—*Cook v. Atkins*, 363.

LIMITATIONS OF ACTIONS—*Continued.*

Same; Payment of Interest.—As analagous to the rule in case of a mortgage lien where heirs of a vendee who inherited the land subject to a purchase money lien paid interest on the purchase money notes before an action to establish the lien was barred, they acknowledged the debt as a lien, and the lien was continued by such payment for twenty years thereafter. Section 4850, Code 1907.)—*Ib.,* 363.

LIS PENDENS.

Lis Pendens; Proceedings in Probate Court.—The doctrine of lis pendens applies as fully to the proceedings in the probate court in which land is disposed of and the title and interest of the parties must be determined, as to proceedings affecting the land in other courts.—*Johnson v. Gartman,* 290.

Same; Purchaser Pending Probate Proceedings.—The decedent purchased and occupied as a homestead the lots in controversy, but later removed to other lands in the country on which he lived till his death. His wife refused to go to the country but continued to reside on the land in controversy and after the husband's death the wife remarried. She obtained a deed to the lot from her deceased husband's vendor, and in proceedings by the husband's administrator to sell the lots for the payment of debts and for distribution claimed that she had paid the purchase money and had acquired title by purchase from the vendor, and that if her husband had acquired any interest in the land they were his homestead. But the probate court found that the lands occupied by decedent in the country were his homestead, and that he had the equitable title to the lots in controversy, and that it was subject to sale. Pending these proceedings in the probate court the widow conveyed the lots to J. Held, that J. was a pendente lite purchaser and was concluded by the determination of the probate court under the doctrine of lis pendens, and therefore, acquired by his purchase only the widow's dower interest.—*Ib.,* 290.

Same; Enforcement of Decree; Laches.—Where a probate decree for the sale of lands for the payment of debts was rendered August 2, 1909, pending the proceedings leading thereto, decedent's widow had conveyed the lots to J. on March 30, 1905, and a decree for sale of the lots for division was filed May 10, 1905, the complainant alleging that the property was advertised to be sold under the decree Sept. 19, 1904, and that no bidders could be obtained because the widow appeared on that day ,and gave notice that she claimed the property, the complainants were not barred by laches under the rule that a party claiming the benefit of lis pendens must prosecute his actions to final judgment without such unreasonable delay as would amount to abandonment of the action and terminate the lis pendens.—*Ib.,* 290.

MANDAMUS.

Mandamus; Eelection; Contest; Poll List; Duty of Sheriff.— Although the sheriff had custody of the poll list, he is not required to furnish a copy thereof except on the requisition of the judge of probate (section 458, Code 1907,) and as section 6806, Code 1907, makes it a misdemeanor for anyone to furnish such a list, the sheriff cannot be compelled by mandamus to furnish a poll list for one contesting an election.—*Sartain v. Gray,* 472.

MASTER AND SERVANT.
1. Injury to Servant.
   (a) Evidence.

Master and Servant; Injury; Jury Question.—The evidence in this case examined and held to require a submission to the jury of whether or not plaintiff's foreman was guilty of negligence, causing the injury complained of.—*Scales v. Central I. & C. Co.,* 639.

MASTER AND SERVANT—*Continued.*

(b) Duty of Superintendence.

Master and Servant; Injury to Servant; Duty of Superintendence.—The duty of a fire boss of a mine to examine the condition of the mine when gas is known to exist therein, before men are permitted to enter for work, is a duty of superintendence within subdivision 2 of section 3910, Code 1907, notwithstanding the provisions of section 1031, Code 1907.—*Pratt Cons. C. Co. v. Davidson,* 667.

(c) Assumption of Risk.

Master and Servant; Assumption of Risk.—In the absence of a special contract based on a sufficient consideration an employe in a mine does not assume the risk of the owner or operator's failure to observe the provision of section 1016. Code 1907.—*Pratt Cons. C. Co. v. Davidson,* 667.

Same.—In the absence of a special contract based on a sufficient consideration, an employe does not assume the risk of negligence in superintendence under subdivision 2, section 3910, Code 1907.—*Ib.,* 667.

(d) Contributory Negligence.

Same; Contributory Negligence.—An employe in a mine may be guilty of contributory negligence in going into a place where he knows gas to exist in dangerous quantities, or where he has been specially warned not to go, though the owner or operator had not complied with the requirements of section 1016 and 1031, Code 1907. —*Pratt Cons. C. & I. Co. v. Davidson,* 667.

(e) Duty of Master—Mining.

Same; Obligation to the Master; Statutory Regulation.—An operator of a mine cannot evade responsibility for a failure to comply with the requirements of section 1016 and 1031, Code 1907, by setting up general rules for the conduct of the business as a substitute for the precautions prescribed by the statute, and he may not by such regulation impose on any employe the duty of ascertaining whether the law has been complied with.—*Pratt Cons. C. Co. v. Davidson,* 667.

MONUMENTS.

See Boundaries.

MORTGAGES.

See Tenants in Common; Fixtures.

1. Deed as.

Mortgages; Deed as Mortgage; Character of Transaction.— Where the relation of debtor and creditor exists at the time of the execution of a deed absolute on its face, or where the transaction commences in a negotiation for the loan of money, or where there is a great disparity in the value of the property conveyed and the consideration paid, or where there is a debt continuing for the payment of which the grantor is liable, the transaction is regarded as a mortgage rather than a conditional sale unless the purchaser overcomes these facts by clear and convincing proof.—*Irwin v. Coleman,* 175.

Same.—As between a conditional deed and a mortgage, in case of doubt, the court will always lean toward the mortgage.—*Ib.,* 175.

Same; Fraud.—Where the complainants, ignorant people, applied to the repondent for a loan and executed an agreement that in consideration of the loan and the interest to be charged thereon they had sold certain property to defendant, which agreement contained stipulations as to interest and payment, and a stipulation by the defendant to reconvey the land to complainant upon payment of the loan, and complainants executed notes to the defendant, and ignorantly signed a paper represented as a copy of their agreement,

MORTGAGES—*Continued*.

but which was in fact a deed conveying the property to the defendant, complainant was entitled to have the deed cancelled and declared to be a mortgage.—*Ib.*, 175.

Same; Existence of Debt.—Where the complainants, on execution of a deed to respondent procured respondents to assume their indebtedness to a loan association, the existence of a debt on the part of the respondent to be secured by the conveyance, is to be considered in determining whether the conveyance was a deed or mortgage.—*Ib.*, 175.

2. Foreclosure.

Mortgages; Foreclosure; Right of Mortgagee to Purchase.—Where a mortgagee forecloses a mortgage upon real estate, which had been partitioned among the joint owners, subject to the lien of the mortgage, the mortgagee may purchase at such a sale and acquire title subject only to the right of redemption.—*Caldwell v. Caldwell*, 216.

MULTIFARIOUSNESS.

See Equity, § 1.

MULTIPLICITY OF SUITS.

See Equity, § 5.

MUNICIPAL CORPORATIONS.

See Quieting Title; Elections.

1. Power of Courts over.

Municipal Corporations; Duty Not Enjoined by Law; Power of Courts.—Unless the duty is enjoined by a charter or other statutory law the courts will not compel a municipality to perform such duty. —*Horton v. So. Ry. Co.*, 231.

2. Streets.

Municipal Corporations; Streets; Change of Grade.—It is the duty and the right of the municipal corporation to make its streets safe and convenient by establishing grades or changing grades already established.—*Stocks v. City of Gadsden*, 321.

Same; Improvements; Discretion; Review.—Where the bill alleged that the grading proposed would not add to the safety or convenience of the street, but would cause the street to be four or five feet lower than the grade of complainant's property, and would render ingress and egress difficult, and the sworn answer did not take issue as to the difficulty of ingress or egress but averred that the grade would not lower the street more than one or one and one-half feet for a short distance and that the cost of making the property conveniently accessible would be small and that the grading would enhance its value it is held that even if the court had power to control the discretion of the city in a case where a great abuse was shown no construction of the answer in this case would require such a review.—*Ib.*, 321.

3. Acts in Private Capacity.

Municipal Corporation; Acts in Private Capacity; Maintaining Electric Light Plant.—Under Local Acts, 1892-3. p. 231, and Local Acts 1894-5, p. 938, the town of Union Springs was authorized to own and operate an electric lighting plant so as to render it liable for the negligence of its servants or agents, by reason of which an uninsulated guy wire was permitted to become heavily charged with electricity resulting in the death of the child who came in contact therewith.—*Darby v. City of U. S.*, 709.

NEGLIGENCE.

1. Contributory Negligence.

(a) Necessity of Pleading.

Contributory Negligence; Necessity of Pleading.—Where contributory negligence is not pleaded the defendant is not entitled to have instructions on that issue.—*Birmingham Ry. L. & P. Co. v. Fisher*, 623.

(b) Wantonness.

Same; Wantonness.—Contributory negligence will not defeat a recovery for wanton or willful wrong.—*Birmingham Ry. L. & P. Co. v. Fisher*, 623.

NEW TRIAL.

New Trial; Misconduct of Juror.—The fact that a juror during an intermission in the trial went into a room adjoining the court room and greeted a near relation of the decedent, was not grounds for a new trial, where it did not appear that the cause on trial was the subject of the conversation, the action being for the wrongful death of the decedent.—*L. & N. R. R. Co. v. Holland*, 675.

NEXT FRIEND.

See Infants.

NUISANCE.

Nuisances; Public; Special Injury.—Where the value of property abutting on a street is lessened by the dumping of slag in the street, whereby the owner of the property is compelled to take a more round about way in travelling from his property to the business section of the city, such property owner sustains a special damage, and may file bill to abate the nuisance; and in determining the question the court will not compare the injury to the complainant by the maintenance of the nuisance with the inconvenience and expense accruing to the respondent in having to remove the slag elsewhere.—*Sloss-S. S. & I. Co. v. McLaughlin*, 76.

Same; Abatement; Adequate Remedy at Law.—One suffering special damages on account of the maintenance of a public nuisance is not deprived of his right to have the same abated by bill because he has a right of action at law for damages resulting from the maintenance of such nuisance.—*Ib.*, 76.

Nuisance; Public Nuisance; Relief by Private Individual.—To entitle private individuals to an injunction against the construction of buildings, or the operation of agencies performing duties to the public generally, or to a considerable part thereof, such individuals must allege that the construction or alteration complained of will be a nuisance in fact, and that they will suffer some substantial injury different in kind and degree from that suffered by the public generally.—*Horton v. So. Ry Co*, 231.

OFFICERS

See Counties.

1. Title and Right to Office.

Officers; Title to Office; Certificate of Election.—A commission from the Governor based on a certificate of election, confers prima facie title to the office, and entitles one duly qualified holding such commission to enter on the discharge of the office; hence his title under such conditions is conclusive until determined on statutory contest, and no inquiry as to his title to the office will be entertained in any collateral proceedings.—*Casey v. Bryce*, 129.

Same; Right of Outgoing Officer; Injunction.—An officer whose term of office is about to expire cannot bring a bill in equity to prevent one who has received a certificate of election and a commission from the Governor to occupy said office, from taking possession

OFFICERS—*Continued.*

of said office pending a contest brought by his opponents to determine his right thereto.—*Ib.*, 129.

Same; Bill; Sufficiency.—An outgoing officer may not sue for an injunction to restrain a candidate who has a certificate of election and a commission from the Governor, from taking the office to which his commission entitles him, and an allegation in a bill by an outgoing officer that a third person, who was a candidate for the office, has instituted a contest of the election of such commissioned officer, according to the statutes, shows that such candidate has been declared elected to the office and is entitled to a commission from the Governor, and in the absence of a contrary allegation it will be presumed that a commission has been issued in due course. —*Ib.*, 129.

Same; Right of Incumbent; Injunctive Relief.—Equity will protect by injunction the incumbent of a public office against the intrusion of an adverse claimant out of possession and whose title has not been established; but to obtain such relief the complainant must show a continuing prima facie right to occupy the office, or show prima facie that there is no other person authorized by law to hold the office.—*Ib.*, 129.

Officers; Appointment; Expiration of Term.—Where an officer's term would expire one day before the expiration of the term of office of the existing governor. the governor was authorized to fill the vacancy by appointment before the officer's term had, in fact, expired.—*Oberhaus v. State ex rel. McNamara*, 483.

2. Creation, Abolition and Removal.

Officers; Creation and Abolition.—The legislature may abolish any office that it can create, and the abolition of such office terminates the right of the incumbent to exercise the rights and duties thereof.—*Touart v. State ex rel. Callaghan*, 453.

Same; Removal; Term Fixed by Appointing Power.—Where the appointing power is given the right to fix the term during which a officer is to hold office, the officer's right to his office terminates at the end of the will of the appointing power, by which he may be removed at pleasure unless the act authorizing his appointment provides otherwise.—*Ib.*, 453.

Same; Special Provisions; Right to Notice and Hearing.—Where a statute provides for the removal of an officer for cause, it contemplates notice of the charge and a judicial hearing of some character to determine whether cause for removal exists, and whether such officer can be removed. but a removal under section 2238, Code 1907, requires neither a notice nor a hearing.—*Ib.*, 453.

Same; Issuance of Commission to a Successor.—Where the approval of the governor is required for the removal of a officer, his commission issued to another appointing him to that office is an approval of the removal.—*Ib.*, 453.

Same; Tenure; Evidence—In a quo warranto proceeding to be admitted to an office of which another retains possession under claim of right. it is not necessary for the relator to introduce any other proof of his right to the office than his commission from the proper authority to that effect. (Section 5462, Code 1907.)—*Ib.*, 453.

Officers; Tenure; Removal.—The power to appoint an officer carries with it as an incident, the right to remove such officer, in the absence of constitutional or statutory restraint.—*Ib.*, 453.

OVERRULED CASES.

So. Steel Co. v. Hopkins, 157 Ala. 175, by Roanoke Guano Co. v. Saunders, 348.

Lawrence v. Alabama State Land Company, 144 Ala. 524, by Marietta Fert. Co. v. Blair, 524.

Etheridge v. The State, 124 Ala. 106, and Haynes v. McRae, 101 Ala. 318, by L. & N. R. R. Co. v. Holland, 675.

PARTIES.

See Equity, § 3.

PARTITION.

Partition; Apportionment of Costs; Discretion.—The apportionment of the costs among the several heirs in a partition proceeding rests in the sound discretion of the chancellor, and will not be disturbed on appeal.—*Winkles v. Powell,* 46.

Partition; Distribution; Adverse Claim.—The provisions of section 3176, Code 1907, have no application to a sale for distribution as authorized by section 3178.—*Johnson v. Gartman,* 290.

Partition; Pleading; Sufficiency.—A bill for partition of land which describes the land, states the interest of each party and alleges that it could not be equitably divided between them, and prays for a division, states a case for relief by sale for division.—*Foley v. Brock,* 336.

Same; Incumbent Property.—Where six tenants in common owned land over which a railroad right of way passed, and the railroad company had not acquired the rights of two of the tenants, the land should be sold, which was not encumbered by the right of way, and the proceeds distributed, and the two tenants whose interest was not acquired by the railroad should be left to obtain such relief as they could against the railroad.—*Ib.,* 336.

PAYMENT.

Payment; Pleas; Burden of Proof.—Where the action is by an administrator on account for attorney's services, and the plea is payment, it will not be presumed from the mere evidence of the rendition of the service that the services were not paid for when rendered, the plaintiff being required, in order to establish a prima facie case, to prove not only the rendition of the service, but that they were not paid for when rendered, and this is true, notwithstanding the burden of proof of a plea of payment was on the defendant.—*Pollak v. Winter,* 550.

PERPETUITIES.

Perpetuities; Will; Heirs.—A will devising the income from certain real estate to testators' daughter during her life, and on her death one-half of the income to go to her issue, if any, and the balance to testator's surviving heirs, was not objectionable as creating a perpetuity; the word "heirs" being used in the sense of children, and the devise of the income, not being limited, carrying the property itself.—*Guesnard v. Guesnard,* 250.

Perpetuities; Limitation Over to Children.—Under section 3417, Code 1907, a deed to a wife for life with remainder to the youngest son in fee except in case he died before maturity without issue, and in case none of them died leaving lawful issue, then to the grantor's daughter and her heirs, was not a limitation violative of the rule against perpetuities.—*Farr v. Perkins,* 500.

PLEADINGS.

(1) Amendment—Departure.

Pleading; Amendment; Departure.—Where both bills relate to the same subject matter, or transactions between the same parties, an amended bill is not a departure from the original bill, under section 3095, Code 1907.—*Irwin v. Coleman,* 175.

2. Demurrer—Construction.

Pleading; Demurrer; Construction.—On demurrer, the allegations of the pleading are taken most strongly against the pleader.—*Grubbs v. Hawes,* 383.

Same; Demurrer; Grounds.—In pleas in bar at the common law, defects in form were treated as defects in substance, and all defects in such pleas, except for duplicity, were reached by a general demurrer.—*Sloss-S. S. & I. Co. v. Milbra,* 658.

PLEADING—*Continued.*

3. Matters Not Appearing.

Pleading; Demurrer; Matters Not Appearing on the Face.—Independent facts not appearing on the face of the pleading are not grounds for demurrer.—*Sartain v. Shepherd,* 474.

4. Abatement.

Pleading; Abatement; Verification.—Under section 5332, Code 1907. a plea alleging the suing out of a writ of error to review the action of the court in adjudging defendants' bankrupt, was demurrable when not verified.—*Moore Bros. v. Cowan,* 536:

Same; Distinction Between Abatement and Bar.—Under the present Code, pleas in bar and in abatement stand upon the same footing as to form while the main distinction at common law between the two pleas was that the plea in abatement must not only point out the plaintiff's error, but must show how the error should be corrected; in other words, must give the plaintiff a better writ.—*Sloss-S. S. & I. Co. v. Milbra,* 658.

Same; Another Action Pending; Sufficiency.—Where the action was by an administrator for damages for the death of his intestate, and the defendant pleaded in abatement that previously the administrator of this same intestate instituted suit in the circuit court of the same county, a court having jurisdiction of the subject matter and parties of this suit, against this defendant upon the identical cause of action stated in the suit filed in this cause, in which suit defendant had impleaded, which said suit was still pending in this county undisposed of, was good on demurrer under section 5330, Code 1907.—*Ib.,* 658.

Same; Abatement; Form and Requisite.—A plea in abatement must set out facts which will show that the first action operates to abate the second; but the plea need not ask that the summons be quashed or the suit abated, although that should be the effect of sustaining the pleas; nor need the pleas recite or set out the summons or complaint in either action, but it is necessary, however, to allege that the first suit was pending when the plea was filed.—*Ib.,* 658.

Same; Dilatory Pleas.—At common law, pleas in abatement were not favored.—*Ib.,* 658.

5. Special Pleas—General Issue.

Same; Special Plea; General Issue.—Where matters set up in a special plea are available under the general issue, or are tantamount to a plea of the general issue, and the general issue is pleaded, it is not error to reversal to sustain demurrers to such plea.—*Moore Bros. v. Cowan,* 536.

6. Time of Filing.

Pleading; Filing; Time; Tuscaloosa County Court.—Acts 1896-7, p. 267, requires plea to be filed within thirty days after service of complaint, and authorizes default on motion at any time thereafter, and in the absence of a motion for judgment by default it is not error to refuse to strike pleas filed after the thirty day period.—*Scales v. Central I. & C. Co.,* 639.

7. Duplicity.

Pleading; Duplicity.—A plea, called a plea in abatement, which sets up facts, which, if true, would be good in bar as a plea of ne unques administrator, and in abatement as a plea of another action pending, is bad for duplicity.—*Sloss-S. S. & I. Co v Milbra,* 658.

8. Aider by Proof.

Pleading; Objection; Aider by Proof.—In an action for causing the death of a child on the track, a demurrer to a count be-

PLEADING—*Continued.*

cause it did not show that the injury occurred in this state was properly overruled where it appeared that the cause had once been tried and all the evidence showed that the injury did occur in this state.—*So. Ry. Co. v. Smith,* 697.

POLL LISTS.

See Mandamus; Elections.

PRINCIPAL AND AGENT.

Principal and Agent; Acts of Agent; Effect as to Principal.— The mere fact that an agent of one claiming to be the sole owner of a right of way had joined in a petition to the board of public works of a city, requesting that one-half of the cost of paving the street in front of the way should be taxed against the owner, did not estop the owner from insisting on his exclusive ownership of the way, especially where the agent was unacquainted with the status of the title at the time, and the adjacent owner claiming an interest in the way, did not suffer any change of condition by reason of said petition.—*Barker v. Mobile Elec. Co.,* 28.

PRINCIPAL AND SURETY.

Principal and Surety; Right of Surety; Accrual of Action.—A surety cannot maintain an action against his principal on a liability created by his suretyship until he has paid part or all of the debt, the right of action not accruing until such payment.—*Smith v. Young,* 190.

PUBLIC LANDS.

Public Lands; Homestead; Resulting Trusts.—No trust results in favor of a married woman in public land homesteaded by her husband merely because she furnished the money to purchase a prior entryman's relinquishment.—*Carroll v. Draughon,* 327.

Same; Patent; Effect.—A patent to public land presumptively vests the legal title in the parties to whom it was issued.—*Ib.,* 327.

Same.—A patent to public lands is prima facie evidence of a compliance with all preliminary requirements to its issuance.—*Ib.,* 327.

Same; Homestead; Title of Entryman.—Under the United States statute, title cannot inure to the benefit of or in trust for any one but the entryman.—*Ib.,* 327

QUIETING TITLE.

Quieting Title; Right of Action; Cloud on Title.—Where the bill was not only to enjoin an action of ejectment, but also to require entry of satisfaction for payment of purchase money for the property in question, and to declare invalid a conveyance made during complainant's possession under a conditional deed, and to remove the conveyance as a cloud upon title, the test as to whether there is an adequate remedy at law is whether the holder of the property, in an action of ejectment brought by the adverse party founded on his deed, would be required to offer evidence to defeat a recovery. If such proof would be necessary, the cloud exists. —*Rankin v. Dean, et al.,* 60.

Same; Right of Action; Remedy at Law.—Purchasers of land holding under a conditional deed, which they cannot set up in a court of law till the payment of the purchase money, have no adequate remedy at law which would defeat a bill to enjoin an action of ejectment brought against them by a subsequent grantee of their vendor, and to declare invalid such subsequent conveyance and to remove it as a cloud on the title.—*Ib.,* 60.

Quieting Title; Evidence.—The evidence in this case stated and held to establish title to the land in the respondent.—*Birmingham Sec. Co. v. So. Univ.,* 116.

QUIETING TITLE—*Continued.*

Quieting Title; Action; Requisites.—Under the statutes authorizing a bill to quiet title a complainant is not required to show title. or such adverse possession as would ripen into title, but to show peaceable possession.—*Newell v. Manly,* 206.

Same; Possession; Character.—In a bill to quiet title, where the land involved was a continuous tract of but eighty acres, and plaintiff's possession was shown to have covered at least five acres, and at one time thirteen or fourteen acres, and was accompanied by actual ownership, the possession was not so slight as to deprive him of the benefit of his title.—*Ib.,* 206.

Quieting Title; Grounds; Illegal Assessment.—An ordinance framed for the improvement of streets, which is void on its face for want of the requisite formalities, and which seeks to create a lien on property for the improvement done under such ordinance creates such a cloud on the title as will support a bill to remove same.—*City of Birmingham v. Coffman,* 213.

QUO WARRANTO.

Quo Warranto.—The validity of a municipal election authorized by section 1068 and 1164, and ordered by those in authority, cannot be determined on quo warranto, but the election may be contested under the provisions of section 1168, Code 1907, although the court may determine on quo warranto the validity of an election not authorized by a valid law, or an election in territory not included in the law, or an election ordered by those having no color of authority. (Section 5464, Code 1907.)—*Mizell v. State ex rel. Gresham,* 434.

. *Quo Warranto; Relief; Judgment.*—Under section 5462, Code 1907, the judgement in a quo warranto proceeding may be rendered adjudging the relator entitled to the office as against the person continuing in occupancy, under a former appointment, where the relator appointed to office is found to be entitled thereto.—*Touart v. State ex rel. Callaghan,* 453.

RAILROADS.

1. Location of Station.

Railroads; Location of Station; Legislative Powers.—If such requirement is not so unreasonable as to amount to confiscation of property, or destruction of the business of the carrier, the legislature may require the railroads to establish depots at particular points.—*Horton v. So. Ry. Co.,* 231.

Same.—The legislature may confer on the railroad commission power to determine the location of depots and make the conclusion of the commission final, or permit its action to be reviewed by the courts.—*Ib.,* 231.

Same; Judicial Power.—The courts may compel a carrier to perform the duties imposed upon it by law and may restrain acts in excess of the power granted.—*Ib.,* 231.

Same; Regulation; Statutory Power.—The matter of locating depots is legislative and within the power of the railroad commission to determine, under section 243, Constitution 1901, and sections 5651, et seq. Code 1907, and hence, the court of chancery will not entertain jurisdiction of a bill by a private individual against a carrier to restrain it from moving its passenger depot from one location to another.—*Ib.,* 231.

Same.—One seeking to enjoin a railroad from removing its depot from one location to another in the city, on the ground that the carrier owes a duty to the public and to the complainants to continue to maintain the depot at its present site, has the burden to

RAILROADS—*Continued.*

show both in allegation and in proof some special injury different in kind and degree from that sustained by the general public.—*Ib.,* 231.

Same; Injunction; Evidence.—The evidence in this case examined and held not sufficient to show such irreparable injury to complainant as to warrant a temporary injunction, complainant's right not having been established by law, and the railroad commission having declined to interfere after a full hearing.—*Ib.,* 231.

2. Persons on Track.

Railroads; Person on Track; Pleading; Construction.—Where the action was against a railroad company for the death of a person on track a count alleging that the decedent, while asleep upon the track, was struck by a locomotive, and that defendant's engineer, though aware of the peril of decedent, negligently failed to use all proper means to prevent injuring him, was not objectionable as confusing the common law and statutory liability, as it avers no employment at the time of being injured, and hence, there can be no basis for an appeal to the Employers' Liability Act, although the terms used would be apt had the count been drawn under such statute.—*L. & N. R. R. Co. v. Holland,* 675.

Same; Jury Question.—Where the evidence will support a finding that the defendant's engineer saw decedent lying dangerously near the track while far enough away to have stopped the train, and that he ran over decedent, the jury might find that the engineer's act was wanton, as that must be largely a matter of inference from facts proven; hence, without invading the jury's province, the trial court could not have determined whether the conduct of the engineer was willful or wanton.—*Ib.,* 675.

Same; Care Required.—The efforts of an engineer to avoid injury after discovering a person in peril that will exculpate the railroad must be the efforts that a prudent and skillful man in his station would have made, and hence, the fact that the engineer did everything in his power to prevent the injury was not sufficient.—*Ib.,* 675.

Railroads; Persons on Track; Trespasser; Children.—Where a child six years old was a trespasser on a railroad track, and was killed by a train, the railroad company and its servants owed it no more duty than it owed other trespassers under similar conditions, considering the fact of its age and condition, and that it was apparently asleep on the track at the time of the injury.—*So. Ry. Co. v. Smith,* 697.

Same; Pleading.—Where the action was for damages for the death of a child on a railroad track, it was not necessary that the counts should allege that the child was on the particular track on which the train was, and that there was but one track.—*Ib.,* 697.

Same; Evidence.—Where the action was for causing the death of a child on the track, evidence that the track at the point of the injury was constantly used by the public as a footway, though not admissible to show any right that the decedent had to be on the track, or to show that he was not a trespasser, was admissible on the question of wanton negligence, in connection with the evidence that those in charge of the train knew of such use of the track by the public.—*Ib.,* 697.

Same; Jury Question.—The evidence in this case examined and held insufficient to warrant the submission of the question of wantonness to the jury.—*Ib.,* 697.

RECORDS.

See Substitution of Records.

RELIGIOUS SOCIETY.

Religious Societies; Presbyterian Church; General Assembly; Authority; Constitution.—Under the constitution of the Cumberland Presbyterian Church, with the consent of the majority of the Presbyteries, the General Assembly of said church could abolish itself and create another supreme judicial legislative body, and hence had constitutional power to carry out a desire to unite the Cumberland Presbyterian Church with the Presbyterian Church of the United States of America, and to so modify the church creed and government as to make such union possible.—*Harris, et al. v. Cosby, et al.*, 81.

Same; Church Government; Right of Majority.—Where property is held by a religious congregation which, by virtue of its organization, is strictly independent of other ecclesiastical associations, and, so far as church government is concerned, owes no fealty to higher authority, and its principles of government is that the majority rule, then the majority of the members are entitled to control the property.—*Ib.*, 81.

Same; Church; Courts; Decisions; Conclusiveness.—Where an ecclesiastical body or congregation holding property is but a subordinate member of some general church organization in which there are superior ecclesiastical tribunals with a general and ultimate power of control in some supreme judiciary over the whole membership, the determination of questions of ecclesiastical rule, discipline or faith, by the highest of such judiciatories, will be regarded as binding on the civil courts.—*Ib.*, 81.

Same; Church Adjudicatories; Jurisdiction; Union with Other Churches.—Under the constitution of the Cumberland Presbyterian Church the general assembly, with the consent of the Presbyteries, had full power to conduct proceedings for union with the Presbyterian Church of America, such general assembly being the highest judicatory in that church, and it also had power to determine that the proceedings to carry out the desired union had been legally and constitutionally conducted, and that the union had been effectuated, notwithstanding the constitution of the church, since it must be regarded as a grant rather than a limitation of power.—*Ib.*, 81.

Same; Civil Rights; Doctrine.—Where a civil right depends upon an ecclesiastical matter, its determination is for the civil, and not for the ecclesiastical courts though the civil court try only the civil rights, taking the ecclesiastical decisions out of which the right arises as it finds it.—*Ib.*, 81.

REMAINDERS.

See Deeds.

RES ADJUDICATA.

See Judgment, § 1.

RESTITUTION.

Restitution; Appeal; Reversion.—One who pays money or is dispossessed under a judgment afterwards reversed on appeal, is entitled to restitution as a general thing.—*Carroll v. Draughon*, 338.

Same; Enforcement.—The right to restitution, upon reversal of the judgment under which money was paid, or possession taken, may be enforced by provision in the judgment on appeal, or by motion in the trial court.—*Ib.*, 338.

Same; Restitution.—Where it appears that it was finally determined in another suit that a person had no interest in the land, such person was not entitled to restitution of land of which he was dispossed, under a sale in partition, although the decree was reversed and the suit dismissed on appeal.—*Ib.*, 338.

SET-OFF AND COUNTERCLAIM.

See Banks and Banking.

SPECIFIC PERFORMANCE.

Specific Performance; Persons Liable.—A grantee of land with knowledge of an existing contract giving a third person an option to purchase, occupies the same position as to such third person as the grantor, and may be compelled to specifically perform just as the grantor could, had he not parted with the legal title.—*Forney v. City of Birmingham,* 1.

Same; Remedy at Law.—The fact that the holder of an option contract for the purchase of land has a remedy against his vendor for breach of the contract because he has conveyed the property to another who had knowledge of the existence of the option, does not take away from the holder of the option his equitable remedy to compel specific performance of the contract.—*Ib.,* 1.

Same; Option Contract; Validity; Enforcement.—The fact that the holder of an option contract for the purchase of real estate was an alderman of the city, which subsequently purchased the property from the original vendor with knowledge of the option contract, does not destroy the right of the holder of the option contract to compel specific performance, the holder not having acquired his rights through any transaction with the city.—*Ib.,* 1.

Specific Performance; Bill; Sufficiency.—Where the bill alleges a contract for the sale and purchase of land, payment of part of the purchase price by the complainant and his taking possession and that respondent is attempting to or has contracted to sell 80 acres of said land to another, and that such other has entered and cut timber to plaintiff's damage; that complainant has offered to pay defendant the balance due, which defendant had refused to accept, that the purchaser of the 80 acres had notice of complainant's equity, and praying for specific performance, and an accounting for timber cut, and general relief, as well as for injunction to restrain defendant from disposing of said 80 acres, it was not demurrable for want of equity, even if the agreement alleged was not reduced to writing, since the bill alleges a sufficient compliance with the statute of fraud by alleging part payment and the putting of complainant in possession, and any unnecessary allegation as to the subordinate relief sought could not have the effect to nullify the equity of the bill.—*Nelson, et al. v. Hammond,* 14.

STATUTES.

See Constitutional Law.

1. Title.

Statutes; Title; Sufficiency.—The title of Act 1907, (S. S.) p. 179, is not sufficient to authorize the inclusion in the act of a provision requiring the court in imposing a sentence for cost to determine the time required to work out the cost at 40 cents per day, and hence, that provision of the act is violative of section 45, Constitution 1901.—*Dowling v. City of Troy,* 468.

SUBSTITUTION OF RECORDS.

Guardian and Ward; Substitution of Records; Parties.—Since a petition under section 5741, Code 1907, relates to the evidence of title to the land under a sale made by the guardian, and not to the proceeds, as to which the guardian was accountable, the personal representative of the guardian was not a necessary party.—*Arnett v. Birmingham C. & I. Co.,* 532.

Records; Establishment of Title After Loss; Right of Action.—Under section 5741, Code 1907, an action for substitution of probate records and of a guardian sale of land may be maintained by an owner who was not a party to the original proceeding where such records are material evidence of a link in petitioner's chain of title.—*Ib.,* 532.

Same; Evidence.—The evidence in this case examined and held sufficient to authorize an order of substitution of the lost records.—*Ib.,* 532.

SURETY.

See Principal and Surety.

TAXATION.

See Highways.

Taxation; Assessment; Injunction; Equity Jurisdiction.—A bill is without equity that seeks to restrain the collection of a tax levied on the increased assessment made by the State Tax Commission, which alleges that the increase was illegal for want of notice, and charging that if the complainant was forced to pay the difference he would be without any remedy to force the refunding thereof, and further alleging that the acts creating the Alabama Tax Commission, in so far as they authorize an increase of valuation without notice to the tax payer, were unconstitutional.—*Oates v. Whitehead,* 209.

TENANTS IN COMMON.

Tenancy in Common; Right of Co-Tenants; Acquisition of Outstanding Title.—The facts in this case stated and examined and held not to show such fraud in the acquisition of the title of the mortgagee by one of the co-tenants as to entitle the other co-tenant to relief by being permitted to come in and redeem their part of the property.—*Caldwell v. Caldwell,* 216.

Same; Confidential Relation.—Where a co-tenant verbally agreed with his co-tenant that he would purchase all the property under the mortgage foreclosure sale and give each of his co-tenants time to redeem, and in pursuance of the said agreement said other co-tenant did not bid at the sale, a confidential relation existed between all the co-tenants, which precluded the one acquiring title to the entire land under a deed from the mortgagee who purchased at his foreclosure sale, and authorizing and empowering the other co-tenants to demand within a reasonable time that the purchase should inure to their benefit on their contributing their proportion. *Ib.*, 216.

Same; Laches.—Where heirs who inherited land incumbered by a mortgage, agreed with one of the heirs that he should purchase the land at the foreclosure sale and give the others time to redeem, and the purchasing heir acquired the entire title for himself, a delay by the others of five years before demanding that the purchaser should permit the purchase to inure to their benefit was not such laches as would deprive them of their right. However, they could not dispossess bona fide purchasers of the heir acquiring title, but could only compel such purchasing heir to account for the proceeds.—*Ib.*, 216.

Same; Rights of Co-Tenant.—Where real estate was incumbered by a mortgage executed by the owner before his death and his heirs after his death, partitioned the property subject to the mortgage so that each owned and occupied a distinct part; they were tenants in common as to the mortgage.—*Caldwell v. Caldwell,* 216.

Tenancy in Common; Termination; Foreclosure of Mortgage.—The foreclosure of a mortgage on property owned by tenants in common, or a failure to redeem before the expiration of the period allowed, vested the title in the purchaser and terminated the tenancy in common and all the rights of persons claiming as co-tenants. —*Coleman v. Coleman,* 282.

TRIAL.

1. Argument of Counsel.

Trial; Argument of Counsel; Maps and Exhibits.—Whether or not counsel shall be permitted against objection to explain the facts in controversy by reference in argument to a drawing which has not been proven to be correct nor admitted in evidence, is within the discretion of the court.—*Hardy v. Randall,* 516.

Trial; Argument of Counsel; Necessity of Objection.—Where the objection was not specifically directed to the erroneous part of the argument, part of which was proper, it was not error to overrule a general objection.—*L. & N. R. R. Co. v. Holland*, 675.

2. Province of Court and Jury.

Trial; Province of Court and Jury.—Where there is evidence tending to support the issues, the question becomes one for the jury. —*L. & N. R. R. Co. v. Holland*, 675.

TRUSTS.

Trusts; Resulting. Trusts.—The fact that a tenant in common in possession promised to pay certain debts and advanced money to the common source of title, for which such tenant was given a second mortgage on the land, and out of such advances the first mortgage was to be satisfied, and the first mortgage was foreclosed, and after the time to redeem had expired, the mortgagee having purchased at the sale, conveyed to the promising tenant, the lands so purchased, who then mortgaged the land to secure his own debt, was not sufficient to raise a resulting or constructive trust in the land.—*Coleman v. Coleman*, 282.

Same; Creation; Persons in Possession; Recognition of Trust Character.—Where a trust is regularly fixed on land, the fact that the person in possession recognizes the trust character thereof is important in determining the question of laches, but is not effective to fix a trust on the land where none previously existed.—*Ib.*, 282.

Same; Oral Agreement.—An oral agreement by a tenant in common in possession to advance money to pay a mortgage on the common property and other debts of a common source of title is not sufficient to create a trust on the land.—(Sections 3412 and 4289, Code 1907.—*Ib.*, 282.

Trusts; Resulting Trusts; Innocent Purchasers.—Even if a wife could enforce a resulting trust in lands acquired by her husband with money furnished by her, as against him and his heirs, she cannot as against bona fide purchasers for value.—*Carroll v. Draughon*, 327.

Same; Establishment; Resulting.—The occupancy of the land jointly with her children, heirs of decedent, without claiming a resulting trust, though having furnished money for the acquisition of the land, does not charge purchasers from the heirs with notice of the widow's equity.—*Ib.*, 327.

VENDOR AND PURCHASER.

Vendor and Purchaser; Contract; Option; Effect.—An option to purchase land is unilateral and only becomes effective and binding upon the purchaser exercising the right of option.—*Wilkins v. Hardaway.* 57.

Vendor and Purchaser; Lien; Waiver.—The receipt of payments of interest by a vendor on a purchase money note from an heir of the vendee would not be the acceptance of an independent security from such heir so as to waive the vendor's lien.—*Cook, et al. v. Atkins*, 363.

Same; Suit to Establish; Decree.—The fact that the bill so vaguely described a small part of the land that a decree with respect thereto could not be made, would not prevent the granting of relief since the final decree could provide for the rights of the parties with respect thereto.—*Ib.*, 363.

Same; Right to Lien.—In the absence of satisfactory evidence of a purpose to exclude it equity raises a vendor's lien by implication, and the formal acknowledgment in the deed of the receipt of the consideration for the conveyance would not prevent the grantor from claiming the existence of a vendor's lien if the price was not in fact paid.—*Ib.*, 363.

VENDOR AND PURCHASER—*Continued.*

Same; Action to Establish; Burden of Proof.—In the enforcement of a vendor's lien, where the purchase price has not been paid, the burden rests on the resisting vendee to show that a lien was intentionally waived or relinquished by the parties; the lien attaching if doubtful.—*Ib.*, 363.

Same; Collateral Security.—The recital in a purchase money note that it was given to secure the purchase price evidenced the intention of the parties to retain a vendor's lien.—*Ib.*, 363.

Same.—An agreement by the vendee that if he could not pay the principal he would pay the interest, and deliver up the land to the lawful holder of the purchase money notes, was not a collateral security in such sense as to waive the vendor's lien, being a mere option of discharging the principal of the debt by reconveying the land.—*Ib.*, 363.

Same; Limitation.—An action to enforce a vendor's lien against the personal representative of the vendee was barred where brought forty years after the accrual of the lien and the death of the vendee. —*Ib.*, 363.

WANTONNESS.
See Carriers, § 3; Contributory Negligence.

WILLS.
1. Construction.

Wills; Construction; Per Capita or Per Stirpes; "Between;" "Heirs."—The will considered and held that the word "heirs" as used in the will meant children, and that the devisees under such clause took per capita and not per stirpes; the word "between" not being used in its technical sense as a reference to two only, but as applying to a division among many.—*Guesnard v. Guesnard*, 250.

Wills; Construction.—Where the performance of a condition subsequent in a will has become impossible, without any fault of the devisee, the condition will not be regarded as broken, in law and there will be no defeasance.—*Pitts v. Campbell*, 604.

Same.—Where a testator left his wife his farm during her natural lifetime subject to certain limitations, with remainder over to all his nieces in equal parts, and succeeding item of the will provided that certain legacies to two of his nieces should be paid in cash out of his estate, whether real or personal, except the land left to his wife during her natural life, and the will further provided, that it was the intention of the testator to give to the two nieces named a certain amount more than to his other nieces, it constituted a special devise of the farm properties, and such property was not chargeable with such legacies.—*Ib.*, 604.

Same; Gifts.—A clear gift under a will is not to be cut down by anything which does not with reasonable certainty indicate an intention to cut it down.—*Ib.*, 604.

WITNESS.
1. Examination and Cross.

Witnesses, Examination; Cross.—Where a question is not confusing or unintelligible, though somewhat lengthy, and has reference to what counsel supposed the witness had testied to in a certain particular, it is within the scope of a proper cross examination.—*Hardy v. Randall*, 516.

Witnesses; Cross Examination; Discretion.—The latitude of cross examination to test the memory and sincerity of a witness rests largely within the discretion of the trial court.—*C. of Ga. Ry. Co. v. Bagley*, 611.

WORDS AND PHRASES.
Words and Phrases; Constructive Possession.—Constructive possession is used to denote, sometimes, that legal fiction which extends actual possession of a part of a tract of land to the whole